INTELLIGENT
TUTORING
SYSTEMS

Lessons Learned

INTELLIGENT
TUTORING
SYSTEMS

Lessons Learned

Edited by

Joseph Psotka
Army Research Institute

L. Dan Massey
BBN Laboratories

Sharon A. Mutter
Catholic University

Advisory Editor

John Seely Brown
Vice President of Advanced Research Center at Xerox Palo Alto

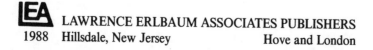 LAWRENCE ERLBAUM ASSOCIATES PUBLISHERS
1988   Hillsdale, New Jersey   Hove and London

Lawrence Erlbaum Associates, Inc., Publishers
365 Broadway
Hillsdale, New Jersey 07642

Library of Congress Cataloging-in-Publication Data

Intelligent tutoring systems : lessons learned / edited by Joseph Psotka, L. Dan Massey,
   Sharon A. Mutter.
        p.   cm.
   Bibliography: p.
   Includes indexes.
   ISBN 0-8058-0023-9.   ISBN 0-8058-0192-8 (pbk.)
      1. Military education—United States—Automation—Congresses.   2. Intelligent
tutoring systems—United States—Congresses.   I. Psotka, Joseph.   II. Massey, L.
Daniel (Leonard Daniel)   III. Mutter, Sharon A.
U408.3.I58 1988
355'.007'073—dc19   87-22686
                                                                                      CIP

Printed in the United States of America
10 9 8 7 6 5 4 3 2 1

Contents

2

Cognitive Task Analysis as a Basis for Tutor Development: Articulating Abstract Knowledge Representations — 35

Barbara Means and Sherrie P. Gott

3

The Development of Troubleshooting Expertise in Radar Mechanics — 59

Yvette J. Tenney and Laura C. Kurland

4

What Mental Model Should Be Taught: Choosing Instructional Content for Complex Engineered Systems — 85

David E. Kieras

SECTION II   Intelligent Instructional Design   **113**
Joseph Psotka, L. Dan Massey, Sharon A. Mutter

5

Issues in Developing an Intelligent Tutor for a Real-World Domain: Training in Radar Mechanics   119
Laura C. Kurland and Yvette J. Tenney

6

The Problem Space of Instructional Design   **181**
Peter L. Pirolli and James G. Greeno

7

The Instructional-Design Environment   **203**
Daniel M. Russell, Thomas P. Moran, Daniel S. Jordan

8

Instructional Planners: Lessons Learned   229
Stuart A. Macmillan, David Emme, Melissa Berkowitz

9

Using and Evaluating Differential Modeling in Intelligent Tutoring and Apprentice Learning Systems   257
David C. Wilkins, William J. Clancey, Bruce G. Buchanan

SECTION **III**   **Knowledge Representation**   279
Joseph Psotka, L. Dan Massey, Sharon A. Mutter

10

Teaching Real-Time Tactical Thinking   285
Frank Ritter and Wallace Feurzeig

11

Intelligent Computer Aids for Fault Diagnosis
Training of Expert Operators
of Large Dynamic Systems   303
T. Govindaraj

12

IDE: The Interpreter   323
Daniel M. Russell

13

Intelligent Tutoring Systems for Electronic Troubleshooting   351

John R. Frederiksen, Barbara Y. White, Allan Collins, Gary Eggan

14

A Training System for System Maintenance   369

L. Dan Massey, Jos de Bruin, Bruce Roberts

Joseph Psotka, L. Dan Massey, Sharon A. Mutter

15

Bridge: Tutoring the Programming Process   409

Jeffrey G. Bonar and Robert Cunningham

16

Understanding Reflective Problem Solving   435
Wallace Feurzeig and Frank Ritter

17

The Next Wave of Problems in ITS: Confronting the "User Issues" of Interface Design and System Evaluation   451
Douglas Frye, David C. Littman, Elliot Soloway

18

The Intelligent Maintenance Training System 479
Douglas M. Towne and Allen Munro

Contributors

Melissa Berkowitz, PhD   *FMC Corporation, Central Engineering Laboratories, 1185 Coleman Avenue, Box 580, Santa Clara, CA 95052*

Jeff Bonar, PhD   *Learning Research and Development Center, University of Pittsburgh, 3939 O'Hara Street, Pittsburgh, PA 15260*

John S. Brown, PhD   *XEROX Palo Alto Research Center, 3333 Coyote Road, Palo Alto, CA 94304*

Bruce Buchanan, PhD   *Department of Computer Science, Stanford University, Stanford, CA 94306*

William J. Clancey, PhD   *Department of Computer Science, Stanford University, Stanford, CA 94306*

Allan M. Collins, PhD   *BBN Laboratories Incorporated, 10 Moulton Street, Cambridge, MA 02238*

Robert Cunningham   *Learning Research and Development Center, University of Pittsburgh, 3939 O'Hara Street, Pittsburgh, PA 15260*

Jos de Bruin   *Cartesian products bv, Wilhelmina Gasthuis Plein 316, 1054 SG Amsterdam, The Netherlands*

Gary Eggan   *Learning Research and Development Center, University of Pittsburgh, 3939 O'Hara Street, Pittsburgh, PA 15260*

David Emme   *Amdahl Corporation, M/S 158, P.O. Box 3470, Sunnyvale, CA 94088-3470*

Wallace Feurzeig   *Department of Educational Technology, BBN Laboratories Incorporated, 10 Moulton Street, Cambridge, MA 02238*

John R. Frederiksen, PhD   *BBN Laboratories Incorporated, 10 Moulton Street, Cambridge, MA 02238*

Douglas Frye, PhD   *Department of Computer Science, Yale University, P.O. Box 2158 Yale Station, New Haven, CT 06520-2158*

Sherrie Gott, PhD   *AFHRL/MODJ, Brooks AFB, TX 78235*

T. Govindaraj, PhD   *Georgia Institute of Technology, School of Industrial Systems Engineering, Atlanta, GA 30332-0205*

James G. Greeno, PhD   *Institute for Research on Learning, 3333 Coyote Hill Rd., Palo Alto, CA 94304*

William B. Johnson   *Senior Scientist, Search Technology, Inc., 5550a Peachtree Pkwy #500, Norcross, GA 30092*

Daniel Jordan   *XEROX Palo Alto Research Center, 3333 Coyote Road, Palo Alto, CA 94304*

David Kieras, PhD   *Technical Communications Program, TIDAL Building, 2360 Bonisteel Blvd., University of Michigan, Ann Arbor, MI 48109*

Laura C. Kurland   *BBN Laboratories Incorporated, 10 Moulton Street, Cambridge, MA 02238*

David Littman   *Department of Computer Science, Yale University, P.O. Box 2158 Yale Station, New Haven, CT 06520-2158*

Stuart Macmillan, PhD   *Sun Microsystems, 2300 Geng Road, Annex 4-33, Palo Alto, CA 94043*

L. Dan Massey, Jr., PhD   *BBN Laboratories Incorporated, 10 Moulton St., Cambridge, MA 02238*

Barbara Means, PhD   *HumRRO, 1100 South Washington Street, Alexandria, VA 22314*

Mark Miller, PhD   *COMPUTER-THOUGHT Corporation, 840 Ave. F, Suite 104, Plano, TX 75075*

Tom Moran, PhD   *Xerox PARC, 3333 Coyote Hill Rd., Palo Alto, CA 94304*

Allen Munro, PhD   *Behavioral Technology Laboratories, 1845 Elena Avenue, Fourth Floor, Redondo Beach, CA 90277*

Sharon A. Mutter, PhD   *Human Performance Laboratory, The Catholic University of America, Washington, DC 20064*

Peter Pirolli, PhD   *University of California, Berkeley, Assistant Professor, Education Department, Berkeley CA 94720*

Joseph Psotka, PhD   *Army Research Institute for the Behavioral and Social Sciences, ATTN: PERI-ICC, 5001 Eisenhower Avenue, Alexandria, VA 2333-5600*

Frank E. Ritter   *BBN Laboratories Incorporated, 10 Moulton Street, Cambridge, MA 02238*

Bruce Roberts   *BBN Laboratories Incorporated, 10 Moulton Street, Cambridge, MA 02238*

Kenneth Rose   *HQ Tradoc, Fort Monroe, VA 23651-5000.*

Daniel Russell, PhD   *Xerox PARC, 3333 Coyote Hill Road, Palo Alto, CA 94304*

Elliot Soloway, PhD   *Department of Computer Science, Yale University, P.O. Box 2158, New Haven, CT 06520*

Yvette Tenney, PhD   *BBN Laboratories Incorporated, 10 Moulton Street, Cambridge, MA 02238*

Douglas Towne, PhD   *Behavioral Technology Labs, 1845 S. Elena Avenue, Redondo Beach, CA 90277*

Barbara Y. White, PhD   *BBN Laboratories Incorporated, 10 Moulton Street, Cambridge, MA 02238*

David C. Wilkins, PhD   *Department of Computer Science, University of Illinois, 1304 West Springfield Road, Urbana, IL 61801*

Preface

In October of 1986 the small village of Smugglers Notch in Vermont became for three days the Intelligent Tutoring center of the world. Gathered there for a review of ongoing research in artificial intelligence applications to training and instruction were many of the world's leading authorities and participants in the development of really practical Intelligent Tutoring Systems (ITS). For a brief time we considered ourselves the Vermont Intelligent Tutoring Association (VITA), an acronym that seemed appropriate from two perspectives: one, the purpose of the workshop in the context of a curriculum vitae— the "lessons learned" from life and experience; and the other, the abor vita—the tree of life showing the pedigree of the many exciting ideas in the field of ITS. Perhaps a third, more subdued current also energized the acronym VITA; the notion that intelligent systems for training and instruction were truly coming to life.

We met to share the many lessons learned: our experiences, knowledge, and insights from many diverse, large and small research efforts. The editors were embarking on an undertaking funded by the U.S. Army to produce an ITS (MACH-III) for training maintenance techniques on a HAWK radar system. Aspects of this project are described in several of the chapters in this volume. We hoped that a compilation of several prominent research efforts and, in particular, the lessons that other researchers guiding those efforts learned from their experiences would in turn guide the design and development of the MACH-III project.

Our expectations were overwhelmed by the experience. Several large projects were well underway and their findings and analyses did not merely meet the requirements for this particular workshop, but went a long way toward defining the state of the field. The field was in fact tremendously active and productive. It had not been described thoroughly since Sleeman and Brown's (1982) landmark effort that arose from a special issue of the *International Journal of Man–Machine Studies,* Volume 11 (1979). The time appeared ripe for a volume to update the state of research applications of ITS, and the participants at the VITA meeting provided the right information to do just that.

As we prepared for the workshop, we learned that the U.S. Air Force intended to sponsor a related activity, a workshop to help them plan their research program in ITS for the next several years. Their planning took a structural turn: What is the state of knowledge and research about each of the top-level modular components of an ITS: the expert, the student, the environment, the instructor, and the interface? In contrast, our planning had a more functional orientation toward the development of ITS: How does one acquire the knowledge? What are the relevant principles of instructional design? How does one select the best form of knowledge representation? What is the most appropriate ITS architecture? and, above all, What lessons have we learned to guide the process?

It became clear that these were two very complementary efforts, and it is with great satisfaction that we see these two workshops recorded as complementary volumes on Intelligent Tutoring Systems in the same series.

The chapters in this volume tend to be more practically oriented than those in Richardson and Polson (1988). It is our hope that they will help guide others in the development of ITS for all the broad range of instructional activities this new technology is so ably suited to support. Although many of the chapters deal with maintenance, troubleshooting, and computer programming, it is evident that they carry implications for any teaching domain. We provide a comprehensive index, a name index, and definitions of some complex terminology in the hope of making this material more accessible to trainers and instructors with no special experience with Artificial Intelligence tools and techniques. It is our conclusion that many of these techniques are now readily available and the lessons learned are clear enough that a curriculum can be drawn up to instruct others in the development of these systems. We hope that this volume will encourage a fuller exploration and exploitation of this knowledge.

We would be ungrateful if we did not include a special thanks to all the contributors, whose stimulating work and discussion and unstinting assistance helped make the preparation of this volume a thorough pleasure. Section Prefaces have largely been taken from videotapes of the lively discussion that originally took place at the VITA meeting. Nothing can capture the excitement that comes from such congenial and well-informed interaction, but we hope that some of its spirit remains alive in this volume.

We are also grateful to Julia Hough of Lawrence Erlbaum Associates for her help and encouragement in bringing this volume to print; to Dexter Fletcher, Wayne Gray, Bob Lawler, and Merryanna Swartz, for advice and criticism; and to Zita Simutis for her reassuring guidance.

Joseph Psotka
Sharon A. Mutter
Alexandria, Virginia

L. Dan Massey
Cambridge, Massachusets

Foreword

Lt. Col. Kenneth H. Rose
Headquarters,
United States Army Training and Doctrine Command

The Conference on which this book was based was funded by the Army, whose two basic expectations of intelligent training systems are to meet training needs in current contexts and to open the door to new and better ways of training in the future. We have considerable resources invested in a massive training system that serves hundreds of thousands of students each year. Our training managers have extensive experience with this system; they know what works well for the organization. Intelligent training systems should provide opportunities to improve this system through modification and augmentation. Of course, the current system will not last forever. Ongoing research in learning will provide additional illumination of the education process that may suggest alteration of fundamental Army training concepts and procedures. Intelligent training systems should make it feasible to train soldiers in ways we do not deem possible today.

Current Army training is heavily oriented toward traditional institutional instruction—a classroom, a teacher, and a group of students. This is extremely expensive in terms of instructors, support staff, physical plant, materials, travel expenses, and student time. The technical world that we live in demands more continuous training in order to keep up, suggesting that future training will be more of a life-long process than a periodic, incremental process.

In the long term, we expect intelligent training systems to address both knowledge acquisition and skill refinement. Means and Gott (chapter 2) describe some new techniques for knowledge acquisition by novices, to include the use of "war stories" and pitting experts against each other in order to analyze their problem-solving techniques. Skill refinement is another, yet closely related, matter. Though we believe that the best way to learn to drive a tank is to get in one and drive it, we do not ignore the cognitive component of such skills. The things that good drivers do can be passed along to student drivers before they even see a tank. Overall, we look to intelligent training systems to improve soldier performance, whether that performance is principally cognitive or psychomotor.

Finally, but perhaps most important, intelligent training systems must provide some explicit benefit. We are not interested in applying new technology just because it is new technology. Benefits must be clear. They must be expressed in terms of effectiveness, material covered, time, and costs. Of course, a sure winner would be a system that offers more training that is more effective in less time for less cost. Any combination of these benefits is of possible interest, depending on the situation. Reduced training time might be significant in one situation, but trivial in another. For some degree of improvement to be beneficial, it must be useful in our environment. Because evaluation is so situational, it is very difficult. Explicit tests as described by Frye, Littman, and Soloway (chapter 17) are essential, but not sufficient. The answer is never easy when the question is, "Yes, we can, but should we?" It is heartening to note that most of the systems described in this text are directed toward real-world interactions and not hybrid applications in academic communities.

In one sentence the Army expects intelligent training systems to improve our ability to train soldiers today and in the future. That should come as no great revelation—that is what everyone expects. But, there is an important difference. Training soldiers is more difficult and serious than training plumbers or TV repairmen. To do so efficiently is a matter of public trust; to do so effectively is a matter of national well being. We do the best we can with what we have. Always, we would like to improve. The substantial lessons learned from the research described here lend support to cautious optimism that intelligent instructional tools will be available to do just that.

Introduction

Joseph Psotka
Army Research Institute
L. Dan Massey
BBN Laboratories
Sharon A. Mutter
Catholic University

The revolutionary potential of computers for instructional use was evident from the first years of common computer usage (Uttal, 1962; Bork, 1981). Yet, the vision of what is possible, even from the most visionary, has grown rapidly and constantly. The many examples of work in progress in this volume provide a vivid demonstration of the vitality of the field. Research is being conducted at a rapid pace with real life implementations that are even now greatly extending the limits of our understanding of this technology. The work described here represents the best and in most cases the first implementations of many diverse theoretical frameworks that have emerged from leading academic and industrial research environments. It demonstrates a recent and vigorous flourishing of the technology. Quite suddenly, the work grown in research hothouses (e.g., Anderson, 1983; Anderson, Boyle, & Reiser, 1985; Brown & Burton, 1986; Brown, Moran, & Williams, 1982; Collins & Stevens, 1981; Clancey, 1986)[1] over the past decade is finding its way, with great demand, into many pragmatic venues.

One firm conclusion that is already evident from this current research and development effort is that although advances in the field are dramatic and far-reaching, our vision still far exceeds our grasp. Thus, while the work described in this volume demonstrates the impressive power and potential of ITS (Intelligent Tutoring System) technology, it also points out the current limitations of our

---

[1]Complete references are located in the Editors' Reference section on page 528.

understanding and practice, and underscores the topics where research is truly needed to flesh out and substantiate the reaches of our vision. The valuable lessons learned from this experience are only now beginning to rise up into a general consensus; but they will undoubtedly reshape once again our vision of what is possible in the next decade.

AI, CAI, AND COGNITIVE SCIENCE

Computer-based instruction (CBI), using an immense panoply of techniques ranging from simple text presentation to exciting and imaginative simulations and interactive microworlds, is becoming quite commonplace in homes, schools, and the workplace. The technology of CBI has been driven by rapid advances in the cognitive sciences and Artificial Intelligence (AI) and by dramatic increases in the underlying power of computers. Similarly, the convergence of these three phenomenally productive fields is having an explosive effect on the growth and implementation of ITS technology. It is clear that a sea change in these three fields underlies the vigor of the research and development reported in this volume.

Despite broad advances in these fields, ITSs are now and will continue to be enormously complicated. Working ITSs will demand all the power anyone can conceivably provide; they will continue to grow as quickly as the underlying computational machinery will allow. Within this volume the many examples of how to create various components of an ITS already tax the power of very sophisticated LISP workstations, even though none of these working ITSs makes use of all the techniques possible, nor do any of them implement even one of the major techniques (e.g., knowledge representation of a device, student modeling, or natural language interaction) to its fullest extent. Clearly, any one of these techniques implemented fully would bring a mainframe to its knees. Yet these techniques and more are necessary if the more complicated aspects of thinking skills (Nickerson, Perkins, & Smith, 1985) are to be brought under instructional control.

KNOWLEDGE REPRESENTATION AND ITS
LEVELS OF KNOWLEDGE

There are many levels to knowledge. At the highest level, concepts have little detail, are very general, and enclose a broad variety of instances. More specific concepts at lower levels encompass and categorize only a subset of these instances. This partial ordering of coverage has been used to define hierarchies (Reitman & Rueter, 1980) where less general concepts are linked to the more general concepts that partly enclose them. For example, the concepts of "robin" and "canary" can be seen as instances or specializations of the more general concept of "bird," so they would be linked to "bird" in a concept hierarchy. Further down the hierarchy, the attributes (or predicates) "red" and "yellow" would be linked to "robin" and "canary," respectively. Inheritance within these hierarchies can be used to avoid reduplicating the links and nodes. For instance, a particular canary, "Tweetie," could be placed as a node linked below "canary," but it would not need to be linked directly to "yellow" if it inherited "yellow" from "canary" by default.

Although inheritance hierarchies provide considerable savings in the representation of knowledge, recent attempts to characterize this knowledge symbolically, using inheritance, have proven just how difficult it is to create the proper structures (predicates and arguments; nodes and links, cf. Amsler, 1980). The main problem is complexity. As knowledge is decomposed, additional details become evident and necessary. As the grain becomes finer and more revealing, the concomitant increase in complexity can become literally overwhelming for both man and machine.

It would be convenient to have a zoom mechanism that allowed one to traverse multiple levels of knowledge easily. It would even be better to make these levels consistent with each other, but often we are forced to accept reductionist positions that are fundamentally inconsistent. Within the field of electricity, for instance, it is very difficult to coordinate an understanding based on everyday experience with wires and resistors with an understanding of the quantum mechanical electromagnetic effect of electrons. Haertel (1987) is beginning to work out an ICAI curriculum that allows one to move fluidly among multiple levels of knowledge with something approaching consistent effects. However, simulations and qualitative models that consistently map onto these levels can be very difficult to create when basic inconsistencies remain. Even when a consistent hierarchical decomposition of knowledge can be constructed, the fundamental problem remains of deciding how to order these levels in the instructional sequence, how much detail to introduce, and what diagnostic criteria to use for teaching each level.

Representing Knowledge in ITS

A fundamental reason for the extraordinary complexity of ITS is the interrelatedness of knowledge (Schvaneveldt, Durso, & Dearholt, 1985). Facts and procedures are not isolated objects. Instead, they are integrated into a context, a situation, or a mental model (Carey, 1986). Any piece of knowledge can be and, for most people is connected to many other pieces. We may understand an event by relying on a recognition process involving comparison of the event with an existing compendium of individual cases (Barsalou, in press), or else we may analyze the situation in terms of a metaphor or causal model (Forbus & Gentner, 1986). For instance, the metaphorical relationship between a radar and a radio set is abstract and tenuous. It is undoubtedly useful for instructional purposes to build on such distantly related knowledge elements in the same way that knowledge of the solar system is useful as a causal model for understanding Rutherford's views of the atom.

The interrelatedness of knowledge places heavy demands on current knowledge representation and storage techniques. Fundamentally, there appear to be two specific ways of representing knowledge on computers—rules and qualitative models—and one very general way—text. Using any of these representational techniques, the very large amount to be stored for any significant understanding to be modeled (on the order of 10E9 units, Landauer, 1986), demands the development of unique indexing and hypertext systems in combination with large memory systems such as CD-ROMs and VLSI. The rapid increases in computer size and speed that have constantly occurred since the first machines were developed in the late 1940s suggest a trend toward continued doubling every two to three years. Whether this trend will continue long enough to enable all the sophistications of ITS components to be fully developed remains to be seen. Parallel processing systems with multiple processors suggest that it will indeed be possible: There are other dimensions to use for increased complexity. Knowledge-based systems such as ITS for broad domains will use up all this power for their sophisticated interactions, student models, and elaborate linkages and control structures.

Knowledge and instruction. As we learn more about how to create effective instruction, the structure of ITS will begin to display more of the strengths and features of a good, personalized teacher. Analyzing the strengths of good teaching can provide a framework for structuring ITS (Collins & Stevens, 1981). Much more needs to be done, however, to uncover the knowledge and strategies good teachers use, and formalize them as computer data structures and algorithms. One very promising approach for obtaining this information is based on the analysis of apprenticeship teaching systems within a naturalistic setting. This technique uses two-person problem-solving situations involving an expert and a novice, and is capable of eliciting both expert and novice knowledge structures and sensible teaching strategies that can be used in the development of ITSs.

It is fairly clear that ITSs cannot replace human instructors in the foreseeable future. Instead, ITSs provide ways of augmenting and extending the power of teachers. ITSs can serve as instructional amplifiers that let teachers personalize instruction more than they now are able to. Not only can ITSs provide some of the lower levels of tutorial interaction, they can motivate students by enriching environments and creating new microworlds for instruction. ITSs can reify the invisible and abstract and bring into the classroom the powerful commonsense reasoning that people so fluidly use in their everyday interaction with objects in the world (Lawler & Yazdani, 1987).

Intelligent Tutoring Systems' Spinoffs for CAI

The results and analyses of the procedures and conceptual structures used for creating ITS are also fostering dramatic improvements in the construction of less sophisticated CAI (Pliske & Psotka, 1986). Using the technology of semantic networks and object-oriented graphics, very powerful training systems can be created on smaller, more commonplace personal computers (e.g., Woolf, Blegen, Jansen, & Verloop, 1986). As the power of these computers increases, this trend will see a continuous merging between traditional CAI and ICAI, as both become more effective.

Nowhere is the progress toward effective use of ITS technology for training as widespread and evident as in the military (Halff, Hollan, & Hutchins, 1986). In part this is because there is an urgent need for effective performance. This is combined with rapid turnover of personnel who must be trained to use highly complex and unique equipment. And, in large measure, it is occurring because computers are rapidly becoming cheaper and more powerful, and technical competence in using the technology for instruction is rapidly improving. Because of the diverse knowledge and skills used throughout the military, these applications have a broad relevance for ITS. They provide generic possibilities. The technology developed in military settings has immediate potential, not just for the military, but for schools, universities, industrial training, and home education.

Structure of ITS

It is remarkable how clearly the structural components of modern ITSs were foreseen in the early work of the pioneers in intelligent tutoring. The best and most thorough review of the history of ITSs is provided in Sleeman and Brown (1982). Brief summaries of the early work are also available in Barr and Feigenbaum (1982), and a more recent and very thorough description is given by Wenger (1987). Although many of the outstanding characteristics of ITSs have changed profoundly over the years, many of the research goals, at the top level, have remained unchanged. The advances of the past decade follow a clear route laid out by the early work in this area. The chapters in this volume do not depart from this path.

Although many remarkable advances have been made, we have yet acquired only the roughest understanding of ITS capabilities and how to use these new tools and environments. The potential is enormous. Throughout this volume, many different architectural components are described and used in unique combinations and often with unique structures. In spite of the terrific variety, a general framework is emerging, instantiated in various ways. Each ITS is built out of several qualitative models (Clancey, 1986). Some describe components of the instructional strategy domain, such as objectives, plans, and teaching approach. Others describe the domain knowledge, the instructional sequence, and the interface approaches. Still other models capture the history of interactions and index a student model that helps to constrain the instructional approach. Others determine the interface: direct manipulation visuals or hypertext written materials, for instance. Each of these models supports the general flow of ITS instruction and learning. This framework is suitable for ITSs that primarily deal with either declarative knowledge or interactive simulations. The role of each of these models is gradually becoming better understood, and their structure within the ITS framework is becoming clearer.

ITS and Efficiency

This volume provides some concrete evidence for exactly how quickly the technology of Intelligent Tutoring Systems is gaining competence, and what situations it is best suited to serve. The advances in technology reported in this book represent a snapshot of ongoing work and the culmination of massive efforts funded by the military, research foundations, government agencies, and universities. Yet the expenditure is a small fraction of the cost of the activities these ITSs are intended to improve. Military spending on explicit training and education totals roughly $20 billion a year (Fletcher & Psotka, 1986). Industrial training costs more than twice that amount. Both of these amounts are dwarfed by the total school bill from kindergarten through graduate school: about $250 billion per year. Anything that reduces individual instruction costs per student or trainee can pay for itself very quickly. Computer technology has exactly this prospect by individualizing instruction and speeding it up with one-on-one tutoring (Bloom, 1984). In addition, it has the potential to make instruction more interesting and motivating. As an amplifier and extender of instructional environments, ICAI can stimulate exploration, foster higher order problem-solving skills, provide insight and self-awareness, recreate apprenticeship learning opportunities, and generally remove learners from stuffy abstract situations into more interesting real-world environments. These pragmatic consequences of ITS are demonstrated throughout this volume.

STRUCTURE OF THE BOOK

We have structured the book to parallel the sequence of issues that are generally addressed in developing the complex architecture of an ITS. In the Introduction, we overview these concerns and provide historical perspective on the more recent work. It remains remarkable to see how clearly the early work mapped out the framework for current research, in spite of the impoverished early computational environments. The early work provides a prologue to the issues addressed by more recent work with more powerful computational environments and more embracing knowledge representation languages like LOOPS, KREME, and Notecards.

The book is divided into four roughly equal sections dealing with knowledge acquisition, intelligent instructional design, knowledge representation, and intelligent tutoring architectures. Each section has its own preface, in which we summarize the section, draw salient relations to the other sections, and highlight lessons learned.

Knowledge and Acquisition

The first section deals with the difficult problem of knowledge acquisition. To reify the knowledge and skills that need to be taught, this knowledge must first be formalized. The goal of all instruction is to provide an environment in which students can learn the concepts and procedures their teachers and other experts possess. To make it possible for a computer to do the teaching, each concept and procedure must first be thoroughly analyzed and explicitly described. Tacit and deep understanding must be brought to the surface in the form of open, even of manipulable, knowledge structures.

There are divergent opinions about how to structure this knowledge clearly. Some researchers favor an approach from purely formal perspectives, such as engineering and design principles, and scientific laws. Others propose that knowledge be organized in ITSs to parallel the organizations that working experts, SMEs, (subject matter experts) in the field use, and that novices need to acquire. D. Kieras offers (in chapter 4) some very potent heuristics for combining formal analyses with information extracted from task analyses and information available in Technical Manuals. Usually this information is heavily laden with engineering principles and knowledge. The approaches in this section generally adopt the latter view, that is, that experts possess a fragmented, chaotic organization of things that has considerable pragmatic value in dealing with problems in the domains of their expertise. Instead of an ordered set of scientific principles, everyday experts apparently use an assortment of heuristics and makeshift concepts. Analyzing this knowledge and how it develops creates an instructional curriculum better focused on the tasks, concepts, and terminology of real-world jobs. It should also make the knowledge easier to learn, because it views the knowledge from a base of prerequisites that are commonly shared—the things the expert learned are most likely the things the novice will have to learn as well. Moreover, heuristics for combining information extracted from task analyses and information available in technical manuals can greatly reduce the amount of knowledge that must be acquired by the novices. However, it may be more difficult to code and represent this knowledge in machines, just because it is not fully consistent and because it is highly constrained, having references and links to extensive networks of knowledge.

As ITSs have increased their power, they have moved from academic prototypes with very limited capabilities (usually addressing only one component of an ITS's architecture) to systems that have had to engage in tasks that have not been formally analyzed. The source of information and expertise for these ITSs usually resides with experts unschooled in structuring their knowledge in the precise form demanded by computer technology. Yet, these experts may often be the users of the ITS and the people who really decide whether or not the system is effective. Johnson (chapter 1) introduces these concerns and analyzes their history and importance. As a result of this history, a variety of techniques are documented in this section for extracting information from these subject matter experts.

Means and Gott (chapter 2) provide an extremely thorough analysis of replicable, formal procedures to gather knowledge from experts, even if the knowledge extractor (usually a psychologist) is not particularly familiar or competent in the particular domain. Their technique yields a curriculum as part of its product by analyzing significant problems and situations in the experts' environment. Tenney and Kurland (chapter 3) continue this detailed analysis with another study of electronic maintenance experts. Again they expose details of the procedure and provide an exquisite dimensional analysis of the course of developing expertise in a domain so complex that even 10 years of daily learning does not result in mastery.

Kieras (chapter 4) uses technical documentation as an alternative source of information for constructing intelligent simulations. However, he constrains the design with principles derived from an explicit analysis of the task and the information needed to perform that task. He makes the important point that verdicality of the simulation design is overridden by issues like functional and procedural understanding when the simulation is part of an ITS. But his central concern is with an analysis of how the mental models for carrying out a task constrain the shape, complexity, and level of approximation of the simulation incorporated into the instruction.

Intelligent Instructional Design

The knowledge extracted from experts and formalized for instruction can be used effectively only if it is incorporated into sound instructional designs. Kurland and Tenney (chapter 5) bridge the gap between the analysis of an SME's knowledge and the integration of that knowledge into an extensive curriculum for an ITS on electronic maintenance.

Other analyses of several aspects of intelligent instructional design in this second section encompass the range of academic instruction, the activities of good teachers, instructional planning, and the design of ITSs.

Pirolli and Greeno (chapter 6) provide the first intensive analysis of the impact of ITS technologies on our understanding of instructional design. Although there are many commonalities with instructional design issues stemming from the last decades of the CBI tradition, they suggest that ITSs offer some dramatically new insights. In particular, ITSs have forced a closer connection between instruction and theories of learning. Moreover, ITSs have created ways to make cognitive skills as perspicuous and accessible to coaching as motor skills were in the past.

Many of these new issues are encapsulated in the Intelligent Design Environment (IDE) described by Russell, Moran, and Jordan (chapter 7). This environment supports and facilitates the extensive linkages and recycling of revisions that characterize good instructional planning. It also facilitates the decomposition of instructional plans into goals, methods, and principles that shape and support good instructional design. The system is useful for deciding on the proper grain size of instructional components and creating a declarative hierarchy that accurately describes the knowledge extracted from experts or formal design documents. This is particularly useful when one is organizing very complex fields of knowledge that go beyond simple linear or hierarchical structures of procedural components (VanLehn, in press).

Macmillan, Emme, and Berkowitz (chapter 8) extend this analysis by describing the functionalities of an on-line, interactive intelligent planner. As more ITSs are being implemented, their primitive instructional-planning capabilities are being enlarged to include more sophisticated machine-planning activity. Their Self-Improving Instructional Planner (SIIP) is based on a BLACKBOARD architecture that covers many planning components at various levels of abstraction. They provide an instructive description of generic instructional sequences.

Wilkins, Clancey, and Buchanan (chapter 9) end the section with a cautionary reminder that the best of plans can go astray because of uncertainties in the structure of knowledge. Their paper proposes a framework for analyzing the knowledge structure of an expert system and finding differences between it and either a student or SME. Their important conclusion is that knowledge represented declaratively makes the task of adding and improving that knowledge considerably easier. This leads directly into the next section on knowledge representation.

Knowledge Representation

Once knowledge is formalized and instruction is designed and planned, it is necessary to implement an appropriate representation for the knowledge. The third section deals explicitly with knowledge representations by providing several prototype working systems that act as models for generic techniques of teaching real-time tactical thinking (Ritter & Feurzeig), qualitative approximation (Govindaraj), mental modeling and qualitative models (Frederiksen, White, Collins, & Eggan), declarative hypertext structures (Russell, Moran & Jordan), and explanation-based hierarchical simulations using an object-oriented approach (de Bruin, Massey, & Roberts).

Ritter and Feurzeig (chapter 10) analyze the use of knowledge in a dynamically changing environment in which decision-making skills need to be critiqued swiftly but tersely as the action unfolds.

They propose, for expert demonstrations, a goal-based rule hierarchy that becomes selectively active as the situation changes. This keeps the number of rules low and the action, realistic. For interactive critiques of student performance while in the environment they use a restricted number at active daemons. More complicated aspects of the scenario must be deferred until later debriefings. During the later debriefing, there is time for extended explanations, rerunning the simulation at critical points, and additional instruction. This provides a flexible environment for real-time training of rich, dynamic tactical skills.

For more complex situations, but more leisurely tasks, Govindaraj (chapter 11) provides an engineering model of relatively straightforward mechanical systems that can be modeled with appropriate precision using difference equations. The approximation preserves natural hierarchies within the system and provides a convenient accommodation of both case-based symptom–cause relationships and reasoning from first principles. Frederiksen, White, Collins, and Eggan (chapter 13) offer a description of the benefits of further constraining the verdicality of simulations by graduating them to approximate the growth of learners' knowledge. They propose that novices can learn general knowledge of devices, general troubleshooting strategies, and general self-monitoring skills if they are given qualitative models of the systems and these models are used to present graduated problems systematically. They describe their techniques for creating many tutoring systems to be used by the Air Force for teaching troubleshooting procedures on complex manual test-station simulators. Their focus is on generalizable skills that can transfer from one set of equipment to another.

As a counterpart to the development of detailed simulations, Russell (chapter 12) emphasizes the power of control structures that manipulate the presentation of clearly organized, hierarchical text, as well as simulations. He describes the IDE interpreter, a set of functions that map down complex declarative hierarchies to decide on what instructional strategies to use, what quizzes to provide, and how to present simulations and textual information. The IDE interpreter is also unique in that it can create instruction automatically from the structure of the knowledge itself. Once the knowledge is organized into hierarchical units, it can be presented under the control of expressly selected instructional strategies.

Finally, the MACH-III project (de Bruin, Massey, & Roberts, chapter 14) creates simulations at different levels of complexity and detail constrained by a particular instructional purpose. The qualitative simulation designs are constrained by the goal of generating satisfying explanations from elaborately informal qualitative models of devices. Using object-oriented environments to describe battery-replaceable units (BRUs) and abstract components, such as feedback loops and information flow, modeling has proceeded with sufficient fidelity to support the principled production of commonsense explanations of circuit operation and troubleshooting procedures.

Although three of these are working ITSs in every sense of the word, the presentations here offer somewhat cleaner and clearer implementations of these architectural perspectives than the more complex and eclectic systems in the next section.

Intelligent Tutoring Architectures

The fourth section provides alternative perspectives on how these versions of knowledge representation technologies and instructional design models can be combined into architectures for working, complex ITSs.

Bonar and Cunningham (chapter 16) provide an elegant set of techniques for tutoring PASCAL programming by beginning with the natural language plans that students bring with them to the programming situation. Programming then becomes a type of abstract problem solving connected to the real world. An extraordinary iconic programming language even makes the programs look more like physical devices with input–output ports, modular structures, and a hierarchical organization that one might mistake for a radar set. The emphasis of this dramatic design is on the human interface—not just to make it friendly and usable, but to begin answering the challenge of making programming as natural and effortless as talking. In fact, programming from this perspective might not be seen as programming at all, but more like problem solving in a dynamic environment.

Feurzeig and Ritter (chapter 15) offer insights into interactive student modeling by enriching the ITSs understanding of the student with a monitor that requests the reasons for a student's action. As Towne and Munro (chapter 18) point out, automatic student modeling is still inadequate to capture the complexities of student interactions with the ITS. One incorrect diagnosis by the ITS can undermine all future interactions. Feurzeig and Ritter suggest a simple expedient that is often effective: Ask the students to explain and help in their own diagnoses. The requested diagnostic menu information is obtained by selection or pointing at system components. The approach can yield extensive insights into goals, plans, and the status of requisite knowledge and can substantially reduce the computational penalties of extensive inferencing. Again, the emphasis is on a human interface structure that can let the user provide complex information to the machine in a fairly easy and flexible fashion.

Frye, Littman, and Soloway (chapter 17) give some preliminary analyses of many more general human interface issues and the problems of evaluating working ITSs. In spite of many years of designing human interfaces, simple mistakes that could be avoided are often made. Although the principles of interface design appear to be well understood, there are in fact many pitfalls that can easily be overlooked. As well, the authors point out that the evaluation of the effectiveness of ITS is still something of a stepchild of the discipline. In the past, evaluating the effectiveness of CAI has relied on comparisons of numbers of correct answers to problems by students who do, and do not, use CAI. These coarse measures of competence do not provide good indications of the effect of the computer on the process of problem solving. In their chapter, Frye, Littman, and Soloway show how cognitive science can provide a basis for assessing the impact of ITS on the processes students use to solve problems.

Towne and Munro (chapter 18) conclude the section with a description of the most fully developed implementation of a tutor in this volume. Their ITS is for troubleshooting the Navy's helicopter Bladefold system. The centerpiece of their work is a unique human interface to models of physical devises through visual displays. It contains excellent descriptions of tools for creating this simulation system that displays an accurate working model of a complex device and its functionalities directly in visual form. Troubleshooting and fault diagnosis proceed directly from the visually represented components. The completed system provides an excellent overview of the many design decisions, compromises for computational efficiency, and streamlining for effective instruction that have to be made judiciously for a fully working system in all its dramatic complexity. Towne and Munro comment extensively on all the major topics in this volume. Their chapter can be read as a summary of the many issues and opportunities facing developers of ITS.

Mark Miller provided a wonderfully informative talk at VITA, but his paper was not completed in time to become a chapter in this volume. A brief summary is provided in the editors' preface to this final section. He gave a unique and informative perspective of five years of developing an ITS, his many pitfalls and triumphs. The lessons learned are complex and qualified by many cautions, but the overall optimism about this technology is clearly conveyed.

CONCLUSION

The volume is perhaps best read in this simple sequential order that parallels a relatively common sequence for developing ITS. However, it is already abundantly evident that constructing ITS is not a simple linear, cumulative process. As in any complicated design effort, many restarts and revisions are required, and the exploratory intermediate products have enormous potency for improving final versions.

Constructing an ITS is also an architectural adventure and an exploration of new territory. The act of putting familiar pieces together with novel, untried components in one working system is an act of discovery and experiment, of unusual complexity. In the same sense, each of these chapters cannot focus on any one component to the exclusion of others. Because of the broad spread of interactions, each chapter must deal with many issues from widely discrepant perspectives. The result is a set of somewhat contradictory and uncertain, conflicting interpretations of specific points, but a broad-brush agreement on the fundamental approach to creating ITSs for many uses.

It is this building consensus on fundamental issues that marks the growing maturity of ITS technologies. These lessons learned are cumulative and point to an emergence of instructional technique from the cloak of personal intuition into the open workplace of engineering and scientific method. Yet it is virtually certain that when we look back 10 years from now, our assessment of current activities will look hopelessly foolish and nearsighted. It appears to be our destiny to be undermined by rapid technological change that makes the impossible obvious, and the hard-won efficiencies so craftily wrought, unnecessary. In this work, there is the shape of things to come, if only we could recognize it.

Knowledge Acquisition

Joseph Psotka
Army Research Institute
L. Dan Massey
BBN Laboratories
Sharon A. Mutter
Catholic University

As ITSs become more practical and effective, their applications are moving from well-understood and structured academic domains to fuzzier, informal everyday situations. At the same time they are beginning to deal with ever more complex topics and broader areas of world knowledge. Techniques (such as mathematical modeling and hierarchical decomposition) that are well suited to simpler topics founder on the complexity of these new domains. The difficulty is particularly severe when it comes to knowledge acquisition. The tools provided by AI and cognitive science are stretched to their limits.

Knowledge acquisition for the purpose of creating an ITS is a somewhat different problem from knowledge acquisition for general expert systems. It is not only important to get a decomposition of knowledge into rules, models, and simulations that work; it is also important to create a meaningful curriculum of instruction . Acquiring the knowledge is subject to the well-known knowledge-acquisition bottleneck; and creating meaningful instruction is subject to its own difficulties. Trade-offs between these two goals are often mandatory.

How to acquire and formalize knowledge on topics in everyday environments without the help of formal academic descriptions and organizations of those topics is poorly understood and the subject of considerable controversy. This section introduces that controversy by providing a fairly unified view that knowledge should be acquired from real-world experts: so-called subject matter experts (SMEs). As an introduction to this section then, we would like to delineate some strengths and limitations to this approach.

The overall consensus of the chapters in this section is that SMEs not only provide a fast, efficient route into the knowledge base, but the very same techniques used to acquire this knowledge can be used to create a curriculum of instruction. Thus the two goals are unified. All these chapters provide convincing arguments for the importance of involving the SMEs early in the construction of an ITS so that they will have vested interests in employing it and making it succeed. They also emphasize the need to construct knowledge in a form that students and trainees need for acquiring the relevant skills. Often, the knowledge extracted from an SME has a face validity that motivates both learner and instructor (Johnson, chapter 1). When this knowledge acquisition is combined with a detailed task analysis, increased efficiency of knowledge representation is expected, as well as more cogent instruction.

Two-Person Debugging Game

Means and Gott (chapter 2) and Tenney and Kurland (chapter 3) provide a thoroughly enlightening description of a technology for acquiring knowledge from SMEs. The technique of problem-centered knowledge decomposition they describe clearly has its roots in the two-person debugging game used by Brown, Burton and deKleer (1982). (See also Brown & Burton, 1986.)[1] In these new adaptations the game centers around three people: two experts (or an expert and a novice) and the knowledge engineer. One of the experts creates and inserts salient problems for the other expert or novice to troubleshoot under supervision while the knowledge-acquisition expert monitors the situation. There are two powerful benefits: The knowledge engineers can see which problems are more important, and problem spaces that may be very large because of the combinatorics of possible steps are usually reduced to a few hundred steps.

Tenney and Kurland (chapter 3) uncover a clear pattern in the growth of mental models for a complex radar system. Novices generally view the radar in terms of electrical power distribution, physical characteristics (looks), and linear circuits with some branching. In contrast, for each of these perspectives experts have an alternative model: information flow, functional dynamics (works), and loops within loops within loops. These more sophisticated versions of the radar underlie superior troubleshooting techniques based on runnable, causal models.

All researchers with experience with this methodology confirm

---

[1] Complete references are located in the Editors' Reference section on page 56.

that technicians love playing these debugging games with each other, and that novices find them compelling learning vehicles. The connections between this knowledge-acquisition method and reciprocal teaching (Palincsar & Brown, 1984) are obvious and suggest that games designed in this way may provide superior forms of instruction.

The significant benefit that these procedures have for resolving the knowledge-acquisition bottleneck is that they make it possible for relatively novice knowledge engineers to describe a complex domain adequately. Generally, the problem of decomposing knowledge in complex domains demands too much domain expertise for psychologists and others to begin to structure the knowledge properly for instructional purposes, so they need the help of local experts, SMEs, just to get started. The SMEs not only restructure the domain so that salient knowledge and heuristics for troubleshooting are immediately emphasized but they manage also to restrict the exponential combinatorics of troubleshooting alternatives to manageable proportions.

Narratives and Instructional Design

There is a fundamental connection between the two-person debugging games and the "war stories" that Orr (1986) found to be frameworks for communicating particular troubleshooting skills to other technicians. Experts without a scientific or engineering understanding of a device still have an enormously versatile bag of tricks and heuristics for using the limited understanding they have. They construct narratives that transmit the essential contexts and skills of troubleshooting to other experts or to novices. Often they select unusual and interesting faults.

It seems worthwhile to point out that the expert who inserts the faults in the game apparently uses similar narrative skills to structure the two-person debugging game. This can provide very useful knowledge for instructional design. Drawing on an understanding of how others might troubleshoot, the SME may select faults that are particularly informative and instructional, not merely hard to troubleshoot. In other words, an SME may use the understanding of a novice's misconceptions to select particularly meaningful and instructive faults. An instructional designer should find it informative to watch these interactions. For the designer the explanations that occur or hints that are given are informative about the overarching framework a troubleshooter is using and how to communicate (instruct) this scaffolding. A curriculum may be more or less directly extracted from the interactions observed. As a result, major components of the curriculum can be made clear by analyzing these narratives and the interaction of experts and novices in the debugging games.

The Case for Formal Knowledge

Against these very clear benefits of acquiring knowledge from experts, one can line up impressive arguments that knowledge structures for ITS need to be taken from design documents and other fundamental engineering and scientific principles. The fundamental issue is that SMEs may well have only a limited understanding of the functioning of a real-life device. Tenney and Kurland (chapter 3) find that even after 10 years of learning opportunities with a complex system like the HAWK radar, there is still much an expert can learn of its operation and construction.

SMEs may be fundamentally mistaken about the operation of a system, and any hierarchical decomposition of the system or any troubleshooting tasks built into a simulation may fail to work properly. The issue is brought out very clearly by Kieras (chapter 4) and by Towne and Munro (chapter 18). In fact, Towne and Munro demonstrate precisely this possibility when they point out that the system as described to them (from design documents!) failed to work when they modeled it—they had to make logical changes. Kieras also based his analysis of a mental model on a device-and-task decomposition extracted from a Technical Manual (TM). The task analysis resulted in a restriction on the knowledge components necessary for the model to a much smaller number than those provided by the TM.

The papers generally agree that it is very difficult to coordinate heuristic, everyday knowledge with formalized knowledge as it is generally taught in schools and universities. Chapter 14 by de Bruin, Massey, and Roberts focuses on techniques for bridging this gulf between formal and everyday knowledge. Their main insight is that everyday knowledge has a narrow perspective on formal knowledge, using only some of it. Everyday knowledge draws a great deal of support from the common objects within the local environment. Thus the mental models of the journeyman (built out of everyday experiences) gloss over the complexities of a scientist's view by using an appropriate (but ultimately misleading) metaphor.

Heuristics for Knowledge Acquisition

Kieras (chapter 4) raises a clear set of heuristics that designers of ITS for training complex devices ought to use. Because most of the later systems in this book are for just that purpose, it is intriguing to analyze how they select appropriate mental models for instruction. Most of these heuristics deal with how to choose the mental model: relevance of model functions to task goals, accessibility of device components to direct manipulation by the user, and critical procedures, as they relate to how-it-works knowledge. By and large, these heuristics appear to be parsimonious expressions of the actual strategies used in the ITS described in later chapters.

Frederiksen, White, Collins, and Eggan (chapter 13) expressly agree with these heuristics, and focus on the problem-solving skills they raise.

SUMMARY

The knowledge-acquisition bottleneck remains a real problem for developers who wish to use TMs and design documents. Like the use of two-person debugging games, the use of Kieras' heuristics for creating an appropriate mental model of a device may serve to open the knowledge-acquisition bottleneck. Realistically, however, the problem of getting accurate design information from formal engineering and scientific sources may be just as difficult as getting information from SMEs. Although the device or artifact is directly inspectable, and reverse engineering is possible, it takes an enormous expertise to construct a plausible, workable abstraction of the device in order to create a working simulation or explanation system. So, except in unusual circumstances (i.e., where one has an exceptional design expert or an outstanding SME) the best pragmatic course of action would appear to be to use all sources of knowledge to integrate troubleshooting, design, and technical manual information in the most robust way possible.

Developing Expert System Knowledge Bases in Technical Training Environments[1]

William B. Johnson
Search Technology, Inc.
Atlanta, Georgia

INTRODUCTION

There is "nothing as practical as good theory." This statement from Kurt Lewin, the field theorist of the 1930s, holds true today in regard to Intelligent Tutoring Systems (ITSs). However, well-founded theoretical principles (i.e., "good theory") and a state-of-the-art technology do not, in themselves, guarantee that ITSs will be successfully integrated into training environments. Numerous people-oriented and organizational issues are also important factors that affect whether innovations like ITSs result in successful applications. Foremost among these issues is the manner in which subject matter experts are to be involved in the development of knowledge bases for ITSs. This chapter focuses on this issue and suggests methods that maximize contributions to the development, implementation, and evaluation of ITSs.

Developing knowledge bases relies on solid theoretical principles, good system development planning, and good tools. However, the development also relies on individual personalities, group dynamics, and organizational politics. A harmonious relationship among all of

---

[1]This chapter is complemented by Johnson, W. B. (in press). Pragmatic considerations in development and implementation of intelligent tutoring systems. In M. Polson and R. J. Richardson (Eds.), *Foundations of intelligent tutoring systems*, Hillsdale, NJ: Lawrence Erlbaum Associates, Inc. This chapter was prepared for the ARI Workshop on Intelligent Tutoring Systems and Smart Training Technology, October 1986.

the above is necessary to accomplish knowledge-base development and training-system implementation and evaluation. A multitude of potential difficulties is avoided when there is an open and continuous two-way flow of ideas and information among all the participants involved in developing ITSs.

The discussion presented in this chapter is based on over a decade of experience in the development, implementation, and evaluation of computer-based training systems in areas such as automotive and aviation mechanics, communication/electronics, and nuclear safety systems (Johnson, 1987). These efforts involved extensive interactions with curriculum developers, instructors, students, and managers in the Army, Navy, electric utility industry, and postsecondary technical training environments. The work has included basic research on human problem solving (Hunt & Rouse, 1981; Johnson, 1981) as well as training applications in operational environments (Johnson & Fath, 1984; Maddox, Johnson, & Frey, 1986). Throughout this research, particular emphasis has been placed on operational constraints and restrictions that occur outside the laboratory in the applied world. This basic research has direct applicability to the topic of developing knowledge bases and is described in the following section.

STUDYING HUMAN PROBLEM SOLVING

In 1976, William Rouse began a project for NASA that focused on understanding human problem-solving skills during troubleshooting. He developed a context-free problem-solving paradigm called Troubleshooting by the Application of Structural Knowledge (TASK). Figure 1.1 is an example of a TASK problem. In 1978, the Army Research Institute for the Behavioral and Social Sciences began to sponsor the work with an emphasis on training for problem solving, specifically troubleshooting in technical environments. This research led to the formulation and testing of numerous hypotheses about how humans gather information and make decisions in problem-solving tasks (Rouse & Hunt, 1984). Three of these hypotheses are relevant to designing ITSs:

1. Computer-based job aids affect subsequent performance only when the user understands what the aid is doing.
2. Problem solvers do not make effective use of information about system components that have not failed.
3. Complex feedback or job aids may do more harm than good for novice problem solvers.

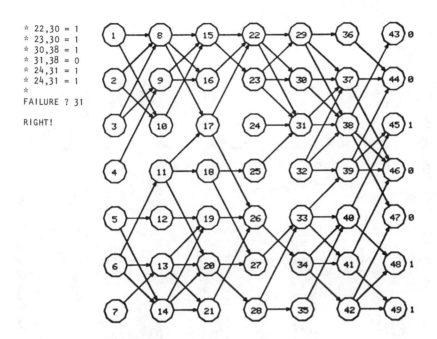

```
*  22,30 = 1
*  23,30 = 1
*  30,38 = 1
*  31,38 = 0
*  24,31 = 1
*  24,31 = 1
*
FAILURE ? 31

RIGHT!
```

FIGURE 1.1 An example of a TASK problem.

Rouse's early experiments provided insights about how humans approach problem solving and the kind of feedback that may be of value. The work was concerned with quality and quantity of feedback (Rouse, Rouse, & Pellegrino, 1980) and also with the nature of the learner receiving that feedback. The research also made it clear that problem solving is not context-free; thus, research on diagnostic training must have a contextual focus.

Ruston Hunt and I joined Rouse in 1978 to study problem solving and troubleshooting in the domain of aviation mechanics using context-free and context-specific simulation-based training. This work centered on a context-specific simulation called Framework for Aiding the Understanding of Logical Troubleshooting (FAULT). FAULT was somewhat like TASK, but provided system-specific content via functional flow diagrams (see Figure 1.2). The goal of this research was to determine whether Rouse's context-free findings would hold true in an applied setting. Transfer-of-training experiments in the aircraft mechanics domain were conducted to investigate the effects of various types of computer-based aiding and feedback.

Intelligent versions of FAULT were developed for those experiments. The "intelligence" was based on an information-theoretic model of problem solving to provide feedback, advice, and explanation

1. CONTROL, STARTING, COMBUSTION AIR, AND FUEL TO CYLINDERS

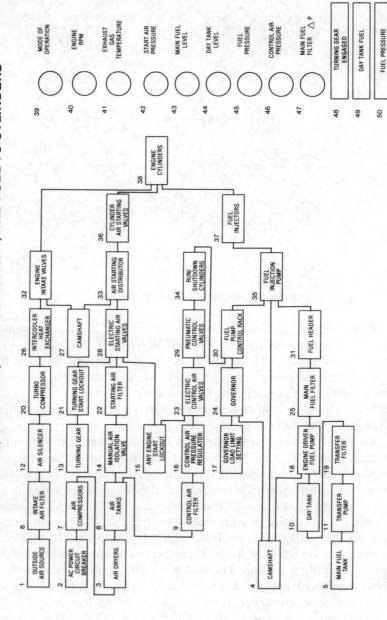

FIGURE 1.2 An example of a FAULT functional flow diagram.

(Hunt & Rouse, 1981). The model was used to encourage experiment participants to maximize the amount of information gain for each diagnostic action. The transfer-of-training evaluations showed that the intelligent training with FAULT had a significant effect on posttraining performance in computer-based simulations as well as on problem solving in real systems (Johnson, 1981, 1987).

This research moved from the laboratory to industry and the military in the early 1980s, and the emphasis switched from a study of how humans solve problems to the development of new technical systems using the original TASK and FAULT concepts. As the research evolved from basic to applied, attention was given to such delivery aspects as user interfaces, embedded instructions, improved graphics, and friendlier feedback.

By 1985, there were a number of FAULT systems being used for day-to-day technical training (see Table 1.1). A research vehicle (i.e., FAULT simulation) that had been developed, with a sensitivity toward operational constraints, continued to prosper in the applied world. Moreover, the lessons learned from this work, particularly with respect to knowledge-base development, are contributing to the development efforts such as the Navy's Intelligent Maintenance Training System project at the University of Southern California (Towne & Monroe, chap. 18, this volume) and an Air Force Human Resource Laboratory project called "Microcomputer Intelligence for Technical Training" (Johnson, Norton, Duncan, & Hunt, 1988).

FAULT and Expert Systems

Current Artificial Intelligence (AI) wisdom suggests that, in general, the inference engine in an expert system should be limited to very simple reasoning processes. The complex relationships inherent in the domain of interest should reside in the knowledge base. Expert systems built in this fashion have the advantage of being modular and infinitely expandable. This is a necessity in domains such as medicine and mineral prospecting where more knowledge is continually being uncovered and existing knowledge seldom becomes obsolete. The disadvantage is that a knowledge base may become very large and unmanageable even for a very modest technical domain.

Like most expert systems, FAULT consists of two parts: an inference engine and a knowledge base. The approach taken by the developers of FAULT was to create an inference engine tailored only to the task of technical training and fault diagnosis. By doing this, it was possible to create a robust simulation with a modest knowledge base. As new systems are developed and old ones become obsolete,

TABLE 1.1
FAULT Systems in Use in 1985.

Applicatons	Approximate Number of FAULT Systems	Years
Ship mechanical and environmental control systems	15	Since 1980
U.S. Army electronics	7	Since 1982
Nuclear plant auxiliary generator	3	Since 1985

the costs associated with creating new knowledge bases are kept within reason. The disadvantage of this approach is the difficulty of customizing a knowledge base to represent system-specific peculiarities.

For most expert systems, the inference engine is more likely to be a smaller part of the program than the knowledge base, which is composed of many rules. Thus, each new expert system requires substantial new effort on the part of the knowledge engineers and team of subject matter experts. Although an expert system is considerably more difficult to develop than a FAULT system, it has the advantage of more context-specific advice in the form of if–then rules. What is needed is a combination of these two technologies (see Figure 1.3). The FAULT-like inference engine could permit relative ease of knowledge base development; the expert system-like rule-based system can include varying amounts of more robust descriptions of the functional relationships within the system. The result would be powerful intelligent tutoring developed with a reasonable level of effort.

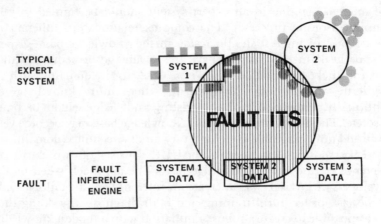

FIGURE 1.3 Comparison of FAULT system with typical expert systems.

TASK/FAULT Lessons Learned

The FAULT simulation was developed as an experimental tool, but it is flourishing in operational settings as well. As recently suggested by Dallman (1986), new research in ITSs should not ignore the efforts of prior research, development, implementation, and evaluation of computer-assisted instruction and intelligent computer-assisted instruction. The following are the characteristics of FAULT that promoted initial and continued user (i.e., subject matter expert and instructor) acceptance:

> Subject matter experts aided in simulation design, as well as data base development.
>
> Simulation developers became knowledgeable of technical subject matter.
>
> Data base capitalized on existing written documentation.
>
> Data base was easy to modify.
>
> Simulation software underwent extensive formative and summative evaluation.
>
> Project used affordable off-the-shelf computer hardware.
>
> On-line instructions were provided.
>
> Understandable intelligent feedback and aiding were provided for the student.

Perhaps the most important lesson learned is to embody the knowledge of subject matter experts in intelligent training systems. In the case of FAULT developments in the military, subject matter experts were U.S. Army enlisted personnel or civilian instructors. For the private sector, the experts were system operators, engineers, and technical training instructors. In many cases, the technical expert cannot initially relate to the complexity of the project, the organized knowledge base requirements, the capability of the hardware, or how the finished training systems may behave. As a result, the answers to questions and/or the information provided may be incomplete or ambiguous. Therefore, the knowledge engineer or researcher responsible for data collection must foster enthusiastic participation from the technical expert. If the technical expert is alienated, the quality of the knowledge base, and perhaps the entire project, will be jeopardized.

The knowledge engineer or educational technologist developing FAULT systems must become familiar with the technical system. This requires a large initial time investment to learn the technical system, but experience has shown this practice to be cost effective. On complex equipment systems, it is not possible to convert the knowledge engineer to a subject matter expert. However, the knowledge engineer must understand the systems well enough to discuss the equipment and training with the subject matter expert. Some developers of computer-based instruction claim it is easier to convert a subject matter expert to an educational technologist than vice versa. Of course, such a conversion is a function of equipment complexity and is most likely to result in either a mediocre subject matter expert or a novice educational technologist.

The knowledge engineer can build equipment-specific expertise via technical training on the equipment for which the knowledge base will be developed. In addition to developing equipment-specific expertise, the knowledge engineer may elect to attend technical schools to better understand the current training and to experience learning from the perspective of the student. Attending these schools permits the knowledge engineer to learn how the training organization works and to identify personnel most likely to provide assistance for knowledge base development.

An assumption has been made that intelligent training system development will always occur on existing equipment. On new prime weapon systems, there may be little or no human expertise and certainly no existing technical school. In this situation, the knowledge must be derived from design and manufacturing data. Additional information can be extrapolated from similar equipment systems. Development of ITSs for new equipment will require an environment that can be easily modified and can adapt and mature as the prime system is transitioned to actual field use.

KNOWLEDGE BASE DEVELOPMENT IN ITS

The Instructor/Subject Matter Expert as a Knowledge Base Developer.

Development of expert systems requires significant input from potential users. These users are subject matter experts such as physicians, geologists, mechanics, engineers, equipment operators, or electronic technicians. Instructional personnel represent the interests of the users. Therefore, the development of ITSs requires major input from the instructors who provide expertise in the subject matter and, often, in pedagogy. Technical instructors are often the ideal subject matter experts for knowledge-base development because technical instructors are people-oriented, combine technical and instructional expertise, understand instructional systems development, understand technical pedagogy, translate technical material for instruction, and are interested in instructional technology.

The following discussion of technical instructors is based on experience with the U.S. Army, the U.S. Navy, and the American nuclear power industry. It is not meant to suggest that all instructional staff can or should help to develop ITSs.

Generally speaking, technical instructors have many advantages over pure technical experts with respect to the development of ITSs. First, instructional personnel are usually interested in working with people. They have good communication skills and relate to the ideas of others. Second, in most cases instructors have served in an operational role previous to the instructor assignment, thus combining various levels of technical as well as instructional expertise. Field experience is not always a prerequisite for instructors, but such experience is particularly helpful for subject matter experts who are knowledge base developers. However, instructors without the extensive field experience usually know who to call to obtain information they do not have. Third, instructors are likely to understand the instructional systems development process. This is particularly true for military instructors and is becoming prevalent in the private sector as well. With a working familiarity of the development process, instructors are better able to identify the knowledge, skills, and attitudes the training system should develop in the student. Fourth, instructors can relate to those aspects of the content that are most difficult to learn and, therefore, most difficult to teach. Fifth, instructors usually have the ability to translate pure technical information, such as schematics, diagrams, and laboratory statistical reports, into data that students can relate to and understand. This ability is critical to supporting the development of ITSs. Finally, in most cases, instructors today are interested in instructional technology and are willing to join in the training innovation. Such involvement usually permits the instructor to share in the attention that inevitably is given to new high technology projects. Furthermore, it permits the instructor to develop new knowledge and skills for career enhancement.

The characteristics of technical instructors described above show that they often have a great deal of input to offer. This input should not be limited to technical content expertise. The knowledge engineer must not only inquire about the subject matter expert's subject knowledge, but also what the expert thinks an instructional knowledge base should include. Instructors should have input to the design and evaluation of graphic displays and the kind of information the student will receive while using the displays. The instructor should also have input regarding the feedback the student receives throughout the interaction with the ITS.

Some Successful Guidelines for Knowledge Base Development

Feigenbaum and McCorduck (1983) described methods that a knowledge engineer uses to ensure the cooperation of experts. They also offer a set of guidelines pertaining to knowledge engineering. However, others emphasize that there is a good deal of variability in knowledge engineering methods (Reitman, Weischedel, Boff, Jones, & Martino, 1985). I suggest that the psychology and politics of eliciting technical information from instructors/subject matter experts is an art, but that some general guidelines have been successful.

The first guideline is to foster quality communication between the knowledge engineer and the subject matter expert. In order to facilitate communication between subject matter experts and ITS developers, mockups of displays, written scenarios of student–tutoring system exchanges, and other means to cross the bridge from the conceptual to the practical can be used. Tools for rapid prototyping will aid in these communications (see Russell, chap. 12, this volume). This continuing communication provides ongoing formative evaluation. Formative evaluation serves to ensure that the system is meeting design expectations throughout the development process. ITSs cannot wait until completion to undergo review. If that happens the familiar line "that will be too expensive to change now" is likely to emerge as a standard response.

The second guideline involves the nature of the technical information that the knowledge engineer elicits from the subject matter expert. Information needs should be structured in the same format as the existing information. Even though this has proven to be a difficult goal, it prevents the need to redraw schematics and associated technical drawings. If drawings and the format of information must be radically modified, subject matter experts will be forced to alter their internal models of the technical system. Such restructuring may not necessarily be incorrect, nevertheless, it is a potential problem area.

The third guideline involves treating subject matter experts as active team members. Knowledge engineers and software engineers must review and implement the subject matter experts' ideas and suggestions. When the ideas cannot be implemented, subject matter experts are entitled to a reasonable explanation of why the ideas cannot be done. Such discussions will also permit subject matter experts to better understand the hardware and software capabilities of the ITSs.

Understanding these capabilities inevitably will promote increasingly enlightened input from subject matter experts.

The fourth guideline is to design the system so subject matter experts can easily modify the knowledge base as needed. The system should provide adequate on-line or off-line documentation to facilitate modification.

Finally instructors should be involved in the evaluation of ITSs as the systems are integrated into the training environment. Such an evaluation helps to identify unanticipated student user difficulties. The most sophisticated evaluations also assess the extent to which the training system prepares the student for posttraining job performance.

Building Tools for ITS Development

If ITSs are to thrive in technical training environments, the instructors will have to take a leadership role in development and implementation. In order for this to happen, the tools must be developed to permit subject matter experts to create a knowledge base without the presence of knowledge engineers or AI computer experts. The development of such tools was one of the goals of the STEAMER project (Hollan, Hutchins, & Weitzman, 1984) and is also a primary goal of the U.S. Navy's Intelligent Maintenance Training System (Towne, 1987).

If an ITS is written in LISP, PROLOG, or another AI language, the complexity of this effort far surpasses the work required to use an ITS development system. A development system, or authoring system, permits the subject matter experts to build an ITS without the use of programming skills. However, with such an authoring system, developers are limited to the ITS design constraints imposed by the authoring system developers. More important, complete ITS development packages are not available. The best compromise at this time is an "open" system that would provide authoring tools and also permit the combined use of an AI programming language as needed by the user (see Russell, chaps. 7 and 12).

The development and field use of authoring tools should be a high priority for the ITS research and development community. An authoring system for ITSs could be used by content experts and instructors, first working with AI researchers, then by themselves. Practical applications for these tools will permit researchers to identify problems and new development needs. These field tests will permit authoring systems to mature in conjunction with the evolution of ITS science.

SUMMARY

This chapter began with the statement that good theory and new technology will not ensure that ITSs will find acceptance and effective use in technical training. The effective use of personnel and organization must also be considered to ensure development and implementation of ITSs. For any technology to succeed, there must be a harmonious combination of solid basic research, technology, and people.

The technical instructor/subject matter expert understands the operation of technical equipment, expert rules for system operation and maintenance, and the instructional needs of students. In addition, the instructor has the ability to affect the organization by creating an organizational attitude that will lead to the acceptance or rejection of ITSs. Constructive involvement of technical instructors in the development of these systems will ensure that positive momentum is created to help ITSs gain early and continued acceptance in technical training environments.

REFERENCES

Dallman, B. (1986). Intelligent tutorial systems research. *Proceedings of the Air Force Conference on Technology in Training and Education* (pp. I-30–I-60). Montgomery, AL: Air University, U.S. Air Force Academy.

Feigenbaum, E. A., & McCorduck, P. (1983). *The fifth generation: Artificial intelligence and Japan's computer challenge to the world*. Reading, MA: Addison-Wesley.

Hollan, J. D., Hutchins, E. L., & Weitzman, L. (1984). STEAMER: An interactive inspectable simulation-based training system. *The AI Magazine, 5*(2), 15–27.

Hunt, R. M., & Rouse, W. B. (1981). Problem solving skills of maintenance trainees in diagnosing faults in simulated powerplants. *Human Factors, 23*(3), 317–328.

Johnson, W. B. (1981). Computer simulations for fault diagnosis training: An empirical study of learning from simulation to live system performance. Doctoral dissertation, University of Illinois. *Dissertation Abstracts International, 41*(11), 4625-A.

Johnson, W. B. (1981). Computer simulations for fault diagnosis training: An empirical study of learning simulation to live system performance. *Dissertation Abstracts International, 41*(11), 4625–A.

Johnson, W. B. (1987). Development and evaluation of simulation-oriented computer-based instruction for diagnostic training. In W. B. Rouse (Ed.), *Advances in man–machine systems research* Vol. 3, pp. 99–127. Greenwich, CT: JAI Press.

Johnson, W. B., & Fath, J. L. (1984). *Implementation of a mixed-fidelity approach to maintenance training* (TR-661). Alexandria, VA: U.S. Army Research Institute for the Behavioral and Social Sciences.

Johnson, W. B., Norton, J. E., Duncan, P. C., & Hunt, R. M. (1988). *Development and demonstration of microcomputer intelligence for technical training (MITT): Phase I final report*. Norcross, GA: Search Technology, Inc.

Maddox, M. E., Johnson, W. B., & Frey, P. R. (1986). *Diagnostic training for nuclear power plant personnel. Vol. 2: Implementation and evaluation* (EPRI NP-3829). Palo Alto, CA: Electric Power Research Institute.

Reitman, W., Weischedel, R. M., Boff, K. R., Jones, M. E., & Martino, J. P. (1985). Automated information management technology *(AIM-TECH): Considerations for a technology investment strategy* (Rep. No. AFAMRL-TR-85-042). Wright-Patterson Air Force Base, OH: Air Force Armstrong Aerospace Medical Research Laboratory.

Rouse, W. B., & Hunt, R. M. (1984). Human problem solving in fault diagnosis tasks. In W. B. Rouse (ed.), *Advances in man–machine systems research* (Vol. 1, pp. 195–222). Greenwich, CT: JAI Press.

Rouse, W. B., Rouse, S. H., & Pellegrino, S. J. (1980) A rule-based model of human problem solving performance in fault diagnosis tasks. *IEEE Transactions on Systems, Man, and Cybernetics, SMC-10*(7), 366–376.

Towne, Douglas M. (1987). The generalized maintenance trainer: Evolution and revolution. In W. B. Rouse (Ed.), *Advances in man–machine systems research* (Vol. 3, pp. 1–63). Greenwich, CT: JAI Press.

Cognitive Task Analysis as a Basis for Tutor Development: Articulating Abstract Knowledge Representations

Barbara Means
Human Resources Research Organization
Sherrie P. Gott
Air Force Human Resources Laboratory

Much of what constitutes domain-specific problem-solving expertise has never been articulated. It resides in the heads of tutors, getting there through experience, abstracted but not necessarily accessible in an articulatable form. Since a computer-based coach has limited opportunities to learn experientially, at least in the foreseeable future, its designers must make this knowledge explicit.
—Sleeman & Brown, 1982, p. 9.

INTRODUCTION

Expert-novice studies have consistently implicated domain-specific problem solving skills—or strong, precisely tuned solution methods— as the hallmark of expertise (Chi, Glaser, & Rees, 1982; Feltovich, 1981; Glaser et al., 1985; Lesgold, Feltovich, Glaser, & Wang, 1981; Newell, 1980). Domain-specific methods thus represent important instructional goals for intelligent learning environments, which foster proceduralized knowledge through extensive, coached practice on a carefully selected set of problems.

The most powerful aspect of expertise and, at the same time, the hardest aspect to capture is what Sleeman and Brown (1982) called its "abstracted" character. The abstracted memory stores used by experts as they represent and solve novel problems are at the core of the expert knowledge that must be represented by designers of intelligent tutoring systems. At the same time, the expert is often unaware of the abstract principles, constructed out of experience, that guide his or her problem solving. In this paper, we report methods and some interim results for a large-scale study concerned with explicating the nature of expertise in dozens of technical domains. Even though the distal goal of our cognitive task analysis is the abstract characterization of domain knowledge, we have found that we need to make contact with specific domain problems, both in order to obtain access to experts' tacit, abstract representations and to identify the detailed domain-specific facts and operations needed for teaching.

This Air Force-sponsored project has been concerned mainly with understanding expertise in various domains involving maintenance of complex electronic systems. These systems can be faulted in thousands or even millions of ways. The expert technician's actions in coping with these problems cannot be reduced to a small set of algorithms. The good troubleshooter has a tool kit containing a variety of strategies and measurement techniques (Brown, Burton, & deKleer, 1981). He or she will select one strategy or another and explore one part of the system or another depending upon his or her interpretation of the system symptomatology. The knowledge representing this relationship between symptom patterns and particular problem characterizations, or what Feltovich (1981) has called "the partitions good diagnosticians use" is very hard to capture. Given the context of a specific problem, experts can readily specify what they would do in that particular case. They are much less able to provide explicit rules defining the classes of situations in which a given problem representation, strategy, or piece of system knowledge will be evoked. Our method for cognitive task analysis employs particular problems, within which we can observe the expert's selection of strategies and use of knowledge. We then seek to work with domain experts to induce the range of applicability for various problem categories and troubleshooting strategies.

Our goals in this paper are (a) to describe briefly the problem of technical competence in the Air Force that has spawned this research, with an accompanying overview of the overall research program that has been formulated in response to the problem, and (b) to present and illustrate the knowledge engineering methods being used to generate both specific and abstracted characterizations of technical expertise.

NEED FOR ANALYSES
OF EXPERT TROUBLESHOOTERS

Military technicians maintaining complex, sophisticated equipment systems typically have less experience than their civilian counterparts—

at any one time, about 25% of them are relatively new to the job (Nawrocki, 1981). Not surprisingly, maintenance problems are common. The Navy estimates, for example, that 60% to 80% of the circuit boards removed from shipboard equipment and sent to depot for repair have nothing wrong with them (Atkinson & Hiatt, 1985). A review of field maintenance studies (cited in Christiansen & Howard, 1981) concluded that 50% to 70% of the failures in electronic equipment are caused by human technicians. Unnecessary replacements and the additional failures that are removal-induced contribute heavily toward the 25% to 30% of the military budget that is devoted to maintenance (Nawrocki, 1981).

The military response to the increasing complexity of avionic and communications systems has been to push for automated maintenance: If machines maintain themselves, we do not have to worry very much about the type of training provided to the humans who carry out manual actions dictated by these machines. This line of reasoning has been presented for at least the last two generations of electronic equipment, but time and again actual experience has fallen considerably short of the ideal of error-free self-diagnosis. The built-in test equipment in the Improved Hawk missile, for example, was supposed to be able to accurately diagnose the location of 90% of equipment faults. The actual diagnostic hit rate has been just 60% (Atkinson & Hiatt, 1985). Moreover, automated test equipment itself requires maintenance and, in fact, often presents the most difficult-to-diagnose faults (Glaser et al., 1985; Nawrocki, 1981).

At the same time, current training does not provide the kind of practice that enables technicians to cope with the nonroutine faults that are not detected by built-in tests. Formal training emphasizes general electronics principles taught in declarative form on the one hand and equipment-specific rote procedures on the other. In many cases, there is little or no opportunity in the schoolhouse to actually troubleshoot faulty equipment of the type one will have to maintain. Neither is there extensive practice on nonroutine problems out in the field. In the workplace, emphasis is placed on keeping the system in operation. When those difficult faults occur that are not detected by built-in tests, the new technician has very little equipment-specific conceptual knowledge on which to rely. When routine diagnostic tests fail to isolate a fault, the problem is likely to be referred to more-experienced employees, often civilians. Hence, new technicians receive relatively few experiences in solving a difficult problem from start to finish.

Such concerns prompted the Air Force to sponsor a program of research to identify the core knowledge, strategies, and procedural skills underlying competent performance in the most demanding Air Force enlisted positions. Over 100 jobs, principally in electronics and communication systems maintenance fields, were identified as targets for concern. The ultimate goal of this 7-year effort is the development of training that will supplement the current job-specific technical training program and produce measurable gains in performance on these jobs.

Intelligent tutoring systems will constitute an important tool for achieving this goal. An intelligent tutor, which can generate an appropriate set of system problems, has the potential for vastly increasing the amount of problem solving practice a technician receives within a given time period. Moreover, there is no danger to the individual or to the equipment. Operations are not hindered, and the time-consuming but intellectually unchallenging process of manually connecting and disconnecting major components can be simulated in a matter of seconds. Within this compressed time frame, the relationship between actions and results becomes more obvious, with consequent benefits for learning (Vidulich, Yeh, & Schneider, 1983). In addition, the equipment system itself can be presented in an abstracted, simplified representation that highlights functional relationships. Considering the relative rarity of each particular fault within modern electronic systems, it is not at all unrealistic to think about providing the equivalent of 5 years of problem-solving experience in just 50 hours with an automated tutor.

Because our cognitive task analysis will be feeding the development of such tutors, we are focusing upon realistic troubleshooting problems that are appropriate not only as criteria (the aspects of job performance we are trying to enhance) but also as contexts for diagnosis and training. Discussions with members of our research team who are responsible for tutor development (Alan Lesgold of the Learning Research and Development Center and Allan Collins, John Frederiksen, and Barbara White of Bolt Beranek and Newman) clarified the objectives of our cognitive task analysis. To support their work, our analyses need to address five issues:

1. *Tasks constituting the target performance for the job.* What tasks represent the major hard portions of this job? What specific problems (i.e., faults) are related to these tasks? What are hard, medium, and easy problems related to these tasks like, and what makes them differ in terms of difficulty?

2. *Skills involved in performing the target tasks.* How are the problems solved when troubleshooting is performed well? What procedural skills and what system knowledge are involved?

3. *Heuristics and mental models used by experts.* Are there general strategies employed by experts across different types of problems? What are the

nature and content of problem-solving plans used by experts? What mental models guide expert problem-solving, and in what manner?

4. *Difficulties novices encounter.* What do novices do when given these problems? What knowledge, skills, and strategies do they lack? Do they show consistent misconceptions? Are novices able to employ procedures (e.g., writing program code or using test equipment) in a variety of circumstances?

5. *Where to concentrate teaching.* Which of the skills, knowledge, and strategies employed by experts are generally acquired through technical training? Where are the trouble spots that are either missed by current instruction or resistant to instruction?

PREVIEW OF THE APPROACH

To anticipate the following approach, we note that it is based upon having domain experts solve problems while thinking aloud. The analysis of each step in their problem solution provides the core data for the task analysis. The approach reflects our belief that if troubleshooting difficult problems is the performance we are trying to enhance, we need to study that performance explicitly rather than look for other tasks or tests that are correlates of troubleshooting proficiency. The wisdom of this approach was suggested by earlier Air Force-sponsored work (Glaser et al., 1985), which found no difference between more- and less-expert troubleshooters on component skills such as basic electronics knowledge and use of test equipment when these skills were tested in isolation, but did find important differences in these skills when they had to be executed as part of the complex task of troubleshooting.

Accepting the argument that we need to stick close to the phenomenon we want to influence, with all its complexity, one might still wonder why we do not merely ask domain experts what someone needs to know to troubleshoot problems encountered in his or her job. Our concern is that asking this question without supplying a more specific context (e.g., "What skills do you need to do troubleshooting in this job?") is likely to elicit a "laundry list" of skills, presented uncritically. Many of them will be good candidates for instruction, but such lists tend to be influenced by the expert's recollection of what he or she was taught or of impressive things that top troubleshooters can do. In some cases, the relevance of a skill for troubleshooting a particular system will be negligible.

More troubling than such cases of overinclusion is the likelihood that domain experts will not report important aspects of knowledge organization and strategy selection. As Sleeman and Brown (1982) pointed out, much of experts' knowledge is tacit. They may never have reflected upon how they organize what they know about the way a system works. They are likely to report *what* they do, but skip over much of the pattern recognition, planning, and weighing of alternative strategies that precede execution of a sequence of actions. Experts have a variety of ways of thinking about a system (e.g., different device models covering different system functions or different levels of detail) and a tool kit of alternative strategies and procedures. Novices need to acquire not only the device models and strategies of the good troubleshooter, but also the ability to quickly assess a particular model or strategy that is useful in a given situation. If experts are unaware of their implicit rules governing model or strategy selection, they cannot teach those rules in any direct way to their apprentices. This is the same kind of missing link Greeno (1977) found among geometry instructors, and it has been argued that instruction generally has been weak in terms of explication of the conditions of applicability for trained procedures (Simon, 1980). It would seem that the specification of these conditions is particularly important and particularly difficult with the kind of complex, ill-structured problems encountered in system troubleshooting.

In summary, our experience parallels that of Glaser et al. (1985) in suggesting that we cannot get a complete account of the core skills and knowledge needed for troubleshooting merely by asking domain experts to list them. We believe that experts are more likely to be able to explicate these skills in the context of solving specific problems. With a particular problem to talk about, experts can be prompted to describe what they would do and why. The analyst then has a window on the skills and knowledge expert troubleshooters employ when reasoning about realistic problems. By analyzing expert performance across many problems, we can attack the issue of conditions of applicability. A useful by-product of this approach is the development of realistic system problems, which can later be used in developing tutoring and diagnostic instruments.

DEVELOPMENT OF TROUBLESHOOTING PROBLEMS

Having decided to base our cognitive task analysis upon experts' reports of the mental and physical steps they would take in solving realistic troubleshooting problems, we then faced some thorny practical issues. To obtain problem-solving protocols, we had to have problems. To make the problems meaningful and realistic, we would have to know a great deal about the equipment system and the failure rates of various components. This is no small feat given that we are talking about dozens of equipment systems that often occupy as much as 100 cubic feet of space, that may contain hundreds of circuit cards, and that may be specified in 50 or 60 volumes of schematics and block diagrams. Further, we could not give experts our problems using the actual equipment systems because these systems are too expensive and in too much operational demand to permit faulting them for research purposes. Thus, we would have to administer troubleshooting problems verbally. Further, we knew that in describing how they would troubleshoot a given problem, experts would, of course, say that they would take certain measurements or run diagnostic programs. We had to be prepared to tell them what the results of those actions would be. Thus, developing and administering problems to experts requires a great deal of knowledge about the particular equipment system involved. Given the number of jobs to be studied in this project and the complexity of each equipment system, it was not feasible for researchers to acquire this kind of expertise about each and every system.

Our approach to this situation entails using domain experts not only as subjects but also as research collaborators. Simply put, we have experts develop problems and give them to each other to solve. In outline, our data-collection method includes five major activities.

1. Specification and categorization of types of troubleshooting problems
2. Generation of representative problems
3. Anticipation of alternative solution paths
4. Expert problem solving
5. Novice problem solving

The first issue we must address, once a job has been selected for study, is specification of the tasks or problems that constitute the hard parts of the job. For the jobs we have studied thus far, these have been troubleshooting tasks where routine diagnostic procedures do not specify the location of the fault. Even given this limitation in the target domain, for a complex system, thousands of specific problems of this type are possible. We could not hope to analyze all of them, yet our training goal is to improve performance on any set of faults within the system, not merely a handful of particular problems.

Accordingly, we put considerable effort into defining and categorizing the domain of difficult troubleshooting problems for each job. We begin by asking domain experts to generate the universe of fault types that are job bottlenecks—that is, the types of faults that elicit wasteful actions on the part of technicians, even after 2 or 3 years of on-the-job experience. A fault type would be something like "loose ground on an interface test adaptor." Although fairly specific in nature, these fault types ignore trivial distinctions, such as which pin on a logic chip in an address circuit is faulty. Multiple experts develop candidate sets of fault types, which subsequently are consolidated, removing any redundancies. Experts are then asked to classify fault types into increasingly general categories of faults that require similar skills and concepts to troubleshoot. (For example, problems involving synchronization between clock pulses and data.) The resulting fault categories represent the troubleshooting requirements of the job.

For each problem category, a domain expert takes responsibility for developing a representative problem that is appropriate for use as a diagnostic tool and as a context for training. The expert works with a researcher, discussing the skills and knowledge required for solving problems in that category and the problem features that are associated with greater skill requirements. For example, troubleshooting for some system components is done at the unit level: If some power supplies are identified as bad, the technician is supposed to swap the entire power supply. Other components are maintained at the circuit-card or chip level: If the technician identifies one of these other power supplies as faulty, he or she is supposed to identify the part within the power supply that is bad and replace that. The latter, "deeper" level of troubleshooting would require reading circuit schematics rather than just block diagrams of the system and is more likely to require use of external test equipment. In developing a power supply problem, the domain expert and the researcher are likely to choose to place the fault in a component for which the deeper level of troubleshooting is required. By doing so, they can require the problem solver to use a broader array of skills. Similarly, the amount of troubleshooting required—the amount of circuit tracing required and the number of measurements to be taken and interpreted—can be manipulated by strategically locating the fault. For instance, with a stationary system, a general troubleshooting rule is to assume that wiring or cables are good until everything else in the circuit has been eliminated as the locus of the fault. By placing the fault in a cable or in the connection between a cable and some major component, we can make problem solvers test out everything they think is involved in the system function with which the problem is concerned (e.g., computer-controlled generation and measurement of test signals). This provides the fullest view of the problem solver's understanding of what is involved in this system function.

Once the domain expert has come up with a particular problem to represent the problem category in terms of its skill requirements, the researcher asks him or her to describe what the fault's symptom would be and a scenario under which one might encounter that symptom. He or she is asked also to draw out a representation of the parts of the system relevant to the problem. Such an abstracted device topology for an example problem is shown in Figure 2.1. This problem involves power coming into the main computer (called the CCDP) of an automated test station (used to test "black boxes" coming off aircraft). The figure shows relevant functional connections, in this case, those components supplying power to the computer. Other types of connections, which are not relevant to this type of malfunction (data, signal, clock), are not shown. As in the example, these representations will typically incorporate different levels of detail for different parts of the system. Blocks representing major components are sufficient for parts of the system that are eliminated early on (in this example, the components labeled PDP and Aux A). Internal circuit cards or components on cards are typically needed for the major component within which a fault is located (here, the I/O). Test points and connections may be specified as well.

After sketching out this problem representation, the expert is asked to describe how he or she would troubleshoot the fault. Starting with the specified symptom, the researcher seeks to identify each step in the expert's troubleshooting. Steps are defined with enough detail that a first-term technician given the sequence of steps could execute them. In addition to the steps themselves, we seek to uncover: (a) the plan guiding a series of actions, (b) the hypothesis or goal motivating each individual action, (c) the consequence of each action (e.g., the measurement obtained, or the fault flag obtained from a diagnostic

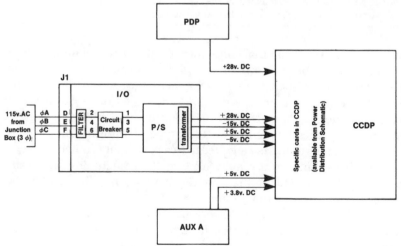

FIGURE 2.1 Expert problem representation.

TABLE 2.1
Think-Aloud Probes for Troubleshooting Problems

Identifying Cognitive Precursors for Actions

At this point, what things do you think it might be?
Why would you think that?
Why would you do that first (next)?
What would that tell you?

Explicating Actions

What are you going to do first (next)?
How would you do that?
How would you know that (to) . . . ?

Determining Consequences

What would the result of that measurement be?
What would the diagnostic program say?
What would happen when you did that?

Identifying Conslusions Drawn from Feedback

What would that tell you?
What would you think after getting that result?
Would that change your picture of what is involved?
What would that mean to you?

Explicating Alternative Solution Paths

At this point, what else might someone try?
Would a less-experienced troubleshooter do what you did (at this point)?
Why would someone do that rather than what you did?

program), and (d) what that consequence tells the troubleshooter (how it modifies or confirms his or her plan or hypothesis). These four elements serve to structure the researcher's probes and the resulting record of expert responses. Table 2.1 shows a set of probes designed to get at these issues. (It should be noted that Table 2.1 contains alternative probes for getting at each type of information and that these probes may be further adapted to fit a particular problem context.) Our probe techniques are more akin to the content-directed probes used by Clancey (1985) than to the general, nondirective probes employed by Ericsson and Simon (1984).

As part of this process of working up a problem, the researcher also has the expert identify the technical documentation he or she would use and the system feedback that would be obtained from measurements, diagnostic programs, or other actions taken. Some of the consequences of actions require some labor to compute; by having the problem developer figure them out in advance, later problem-solving sessions are facilitated.

As the expert describes how he or she would troubleshoot the problem, the researcher sketches out a "solution path" or flowchartlike notation of the steps in solution. For each step, the researcher records the associated plan, hypothesis, consequence, and interpretation. After the expert has described how to troubleshoot the problem, the researcher then takes him or her back through the solution path, node by node, asking the expert to anticipate alternative actions that other troubleshooters might take. For example, in the problem for which an expert generated Figure 2.1, another troubleshooter might initially explore circuit cards within the main computer itself rather than investigate external sources of power to the computer. Identification of these alternative solution paths and computation of the results of the measurements and diagnostic tests contained within them are of both theoretical and practical importance. The problem will be given to other expert and less-than-expert technicians who may or may not approach it in the same manner as the expert who developed the problem. Because troubleshooters require feedback (e.g., results from voltage checks) to proceed, it is useful to anticipate alternative problem-solving approaches and associated system outcomes. From a conceptual standpoint, the identification of alternative actions provides a useful context for asking the expert why he or she chose a particular action rather than the alternative. The experts' justifications for their actions and strategies provide insights into the abstract categories of conditions associated with the use of particular troubleshooting strategies and ways of thinking about the system.

These alternative paths, added to the original path, constitute the first pass at an "effective problem space" for the problem. Figure 2.2 shows the effective problem space for our sample problem.

In an earlier study designed to test the feasibility of cognitive task analysis for Air Force jobs, Glaser et al. (1985) noted that whereas the full problem space (cf. Newell & Simon, 1972) for problems of the complexity of those encountered in these jobs would be enormous, the number of different actions that a technician might reasonably take at any decision point in the problem space is actually quite limited. Thus, they were able to work with domain experts to develop problems and graph out effective problem spaces with fewer than 100 nodes. We have borrowed their strategy and the term "effective problem space" to denote the fact that we are laying out the approaches that someone is likely to consider, rather than all possible paths through the problem space.

Given the number of jobs to be studied under the current project,

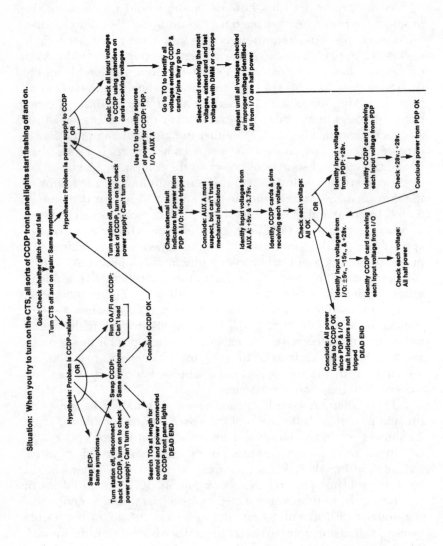

Situation: When you try to turn on the CTS, all sorts of CCDP front panel lights start flashing off and on.

Goal: Check whether glitch or hard fail

Turn CTS off and on again: Same symptoms

Hypothesis: Problem is CCDP-related

Swap ECP:
Same symptoms

Turn station off, disconnect
back of CCDP, turn on to check
power supply: Can't turn on

Search TOs at length for
control and power connected
to CCDP front panel lights
DEAD END

Swap CCDP:
Same symptoms

Run OA/FI on CCDP:
Can't load

Conclude CCDP OK

Hypothesis: Problem is power supply to CCDP

Turn station off, disconnect
back of CCDP, turn on to check
power supply: Can't turn on

Use TO to identify sources
of power for CCDP: PDP,
I/O, AUX A

Check external fault
indicators for power from
PDP & I/O: None tripped

Conclude: AUX A most
suspect, but can't trust
mechanical indicators

Identify input voltages from
AUX A: +5v, & +3.75v.

Identify CCDP cards & pins
receiving each voltage

Check each voltage:
All OK

Conclude: All power
inputs to CCDP OK
since PDP & I/O
fault indicators not
tripped
DEAD END

Identify input voltages from
I/O: ±5v,, −15v,, & +28v.

Identify CCDP card receiving
each input voltage from I/O

Check each voltage:
All half power

Goal: Check all input voltages
to CCDP using extenders on
cards receiving voltages

Go to TO to identify all
voltages entering CCDP &
cards/pins they go to

Select card receiving the most
voltages, extend card and test
voltages with DMM or o-scope

Repeat until all voltages checked
or improper voltage identified:
All from I/O are half power

Identify input voltages
from PDP: ±28v.

Identify CCDP card receiving
each input voltage from PDP

Check +28v,; −28v.

Conclude power from PDP OK

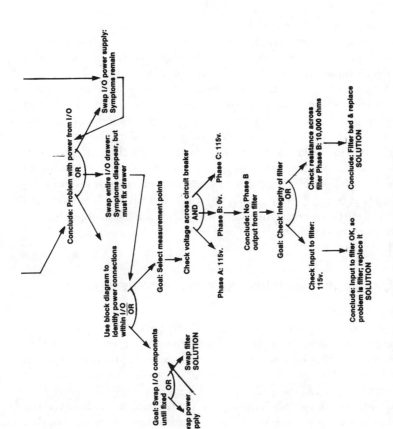

FIGURE 2.2 Effective problem space graph.

one of our major advances has been the discovery that the researcher, working with a domain expert, can map out a rough version of the effective problem space on site in a matter of a few hours. The problem space gets elaborated as solutions are collected from additional technicians, and it may be refined after protocol analysis. But major savings in research time and cost are experienced because a problem can be developed on one day and administered to subjects on subsequent days without an intervening period for transcription and problem-space development in the research laboratory.

The sessions with problem developers have proven quite useful, even beyond their utility in developing a problem space and anticipating consequences of actions that later problem solvers will want to take. In the course of developing a problem, the expert will discuss the consequences of placing the fault at different places in the system. This gives the researcher and later test and training developers information needed for developing variants of the original problem that require a larger or smaller set of skills. Problem variants are also useful in preventing tutor users from memorizing solutions to a small set of problems.

PROBLEM-SOLVING SESSIONS: THE TWO-EXPERT METHOD

Equipped with the draft effective problem space, the researcher and the expert who developed the problem can then give it to another expert to solve. This second expert is given a description of the situation (the initial problem symptom) and is asked to think aloud as he or she describes how to deal with these symptoms in the shop.

Again, the researcher employs a set of probes to discover the hypothesis or plan underlying each action and the interpretation that the problem solver draws from the consequences of his or her actions. The problem solver is also urged to sketch the problem as he or she sees it at different points in the course of solving it. The researcher asks the problem solver to sketch the relevant portion of the system (or to revise an earlier drawing) every time the problem solver's focus (a) moves to a part of the system not included in the previous representation or (b) changes in level of detail (e.g., chip vs. circuit-card level). Having the domain expert sketch out this problem representation proves very useful to the researcher on a pragmatic level, that is, as an aid to understanding the sequence of hypotheses the problem solver entertains in describing how he or she would troubleshoot to narrow down the range of possible fault locations. The model also has theoretical importance in helping us to understand the linkages between classes of symptom features and associated solution methods. Finally, the expert's mental model itself provides a potential target for instruction.

The expert who developed the problem provides feedback. When the problem solver says that he or she would take a measurement, run a diagnostic test, swap a circuit card, or perform some other action on the system, the problem generator tells him or her what the consequence of that action would be (e.g., zero volts, fails test 21237, or fault symptoms persist). In the course of problem solving, the solver is allowed to use any technical documentation he or she desires, just as in the shop. The researcher records each troubleshooting action, along with the associated plan, hypothesis, system feedback, and interpretation. Sessions are audio recorded to permit later transcription and analysis, all technical documentation used during problem solving is noted, and any sketches or notes produced by the subject are retained.

After the problem solver has identified the fault, the researcher reviews the record of the problem solver's solution with him or her to verify its accuracy. The researcher then takes the domain expert back through the problem space, asking him or her to anticipate alternative actions that less-experienced troubleshooters might take. When alternative actions are identified, the experts are asked to reflect upon the strategy or knowledge, which they themselves have used, that steers them away from the novice path. In this way, we try to obtain domain experts' insights into the skills and knowledge they use at each step in problem solving. (It should be noted, however, that experts provide more complete specifications of the alternatives other experts will consider than those that novices will entertain. Our less-than-expert problem solvers have often surprised the experts, as described below.)

The social structure of these sessions deserves some comment; we believe it contributes significantly to the efficacy of our method. Problem-solving sessions involve two domain experts, who know each other well, and one psychologist. The domain experts switch roles back and forth; each gets to solve problems and to pose problems. The domain experts feel very much at ease in this situation. They outnumber the research staff; they know much more than the researcher about the topic at hand; they feel like (and are) participants in the research process rather than objects of an evaluation. In addition, the two experts often stimulate each other to provide a more domain-rich description than the researcher could elicit on his or her own: They know enough to ask tough questions and to know when important details of a procedure are being glossed over. There is an intellectual excitement that attends real problem solving, and the structure of these sessions appears able to capture it.

LESS-THAN-EXPERT PROBLEM SOLUTIONS

After having domain experts trade problems, we also administer selected problems to less-experienced technicians. These sessions are run in the same manner as those with expert problem solvers, except that less-experienced technicians are not asked to anticipate how other people might approach the same problem or to reflect upon the skills and knowledge they have used.

Problem-solving sessions with less-experienced technicians are not as predictable as those with expert problem solvers. Inexperienced troubleshooters take more unanticipated actions and are more likely to go down dead-end paths. They may continue to look for a fault within the complicated circuitry of a component even though a previous action or some other aspect of system behavior rules out that component as the fault location. The presence of a domain expert as a research collaborator is especially vital when such unanticipated actions are taken, because the consequences of those actions must be generated extemporaneously.

We have developed a strategy for dealing with dead-end path situations, errors, and incomplete knowledge that reflects our primary goal of finding out as much as we can about what the problem solver does and does not know. We let the problem solver pursue an incorrect path for some time until we are confident that it really is a dead end and he or she will not make any self-corrections. Instead of terminating the session at that point, we then supply hints to get the problem solver back on the right path and see where he or she can go from there. This part of the session could be described as "clinical" (in a Piagetian sense). The hints we provide are tailored to the researcher's understanding of the nature of the problem solver's difficulty. Some hints entail only a minimal amount of information; they are basically working memory aids in that we simply review the actions the problem solver has already taken. For a problem solver who has forgotten that he or she had already tested some component and found it good, such a review often gets him or her back on a viable path. But other problem solvers pursue dead ends because they do not know what else to do. Alternatively, they may know that they want to do something, such as take a particular measurement, but not know how to execute the action. A third common deficiency is simply not knowing all the parts of the system that are involved in the problem. Different types of hints address each of these apparent deficits. We supply the piece of information or procedure that appears to be lacking and observe how the problem solver carries on from there. In a sense, the provision of such hints can help confirm the cognitive analysis. If the researcher has correctly diagnosed the locus of the problem solver's difficulty and the solver has all the other "pieces" needed, provision of the missing (or faulty) knowledge component should enable the problem solver to proceed. Moreover, this kind of assisted problem solving nicely foreshadows the coaching that will be embodied in the intelligent tutor.

A SAMPLE ANALYSIS

In applying our method of cognitive task analysis to four jobs, one of the most striking differences between expert and novice solutions we have observed has been the way experts use their functional understanding of the equipment system to construct—and constrain— their problem space. This finding parallels findings by Chi, Glaser, and Rees (1982) and Hinsley, Hayes, and Simon (1977) in other domains. Experts think of an electronics system in terms of functions. Each of the systems must have a *control* function, usually emanating from a central computer. *Power* must be applied to the system in order for it to operate. Control will be executed by data which must be *generated* and *routed* appropriately to other components. Most of the systems we have looked at have included analog *signals* as well. Signals are generated or received as input from outside the system; they are conditioned, routed, and *measured* or presented to users (e.g., on visual displays). The generation and measurement of signals depends upon *timing*. Various physical parts of the system—particular components or circuits—are involved in different functions. Experts capitalize on this feature of the system: When the set of symptoms implicates a problem with a particular function, they consider the circuitry and components relevant to that function in their problem representation. In the problem depicted in Figure 2.1, for example, the expert interprets the symptoms as indicative of a problem with one of the power inputs to the central computer. Hence, power input connections are included in the problem representation, but it does not include the myriad other connections such as control data going out or measurement results coming back in. This greatly constrains the search space for the problem, reduces memory load, and makes systematic troubleshooting of a complex system feasible.

A brief description of one of the solutions obtained from an expert and a less-than-expert troubleshooter given the problem depicted in Figures 2.1 and 2.2 can be used to illustrate how our method exposes the details of expert–novice differences and the missing knowledge and strategies on which novices might be tutored.

When an expert considered the problem symptoms (all the lights on the central computer front panel flashing on and off randomly), the first hypothesis he chose to pursue was that there was some kind of problem with power coming into the computer. He knew that there must be some power present, because lights came on, but such a massive, random malfunctioning strongly suggests a problem with power, rather than, for example, a problem with signal measurement. Thinking only about power connections to the central computer, the expert eliminated a wealth of possibilities from consideration. It is just this wealth of possibilities that confused one of the less-than-expert technicians given this problem—he did not associate the problem symptoms with any particular function of the system. Instead, he started looking for any kind of connection to the front panel lights (the physical location of the symptom). Because there are many kinds of connections, and many front panel lights, he was quickly enmeshed in more detail than he could handle.

> S: [while leafing through a volume of schematics] What I'm trying to do . . . I can't recall right offhand what controls the front panel, what tells those lights . . . what supplies . . . I'm trying to go there because I know it's what I want to look at. That's where the lights are at. I want to get a good idea of what it's doing and where it's getting—say, like—its power supply, or its ground, or its control from.

Unlike the expert, this subject did not initially approach the problem at a macrolevel, reasoning about system functions and connections between major components within the system. Rather, he started looking at all sorts of schematics. However, he was not sure whether he was looking for control or power, or whether he was tracing in the right direction, and hence whether the schematic/tracing effort would bear any fruit. This activity consumed quite a bit of time— 45 minutes—at the end of which the subject said he still had no idea what was causing the problem. At this point the subject was given a prearranged hint (external power fault indicators for the relevant component trip) designed to make the problem easier. The hint did lead him to narrow his further search to power connections. Even so, this less-than-expert subject differed from the expert who constructed the problem in that he never developed a comprehensive picture of the power inputs to the computer. The sketch he provided when asked to draw out the problem is shown in Figure 2.3. Comparing his drawing to the complete representation in Figure 2.1 shows that this subject displayed incomplete knowledge at both the macro- and the microlevels. His sketch is missing one of the three major components supplying power to the computer. Of seven specific input

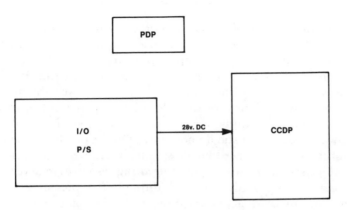

FIGURE 2.3 Less-than-expert problem representation.

voltages—any one of which could be missing or insufficient—he showed only one. He did at some point test one input voltage from the third power source, so he knew more than he put in his drawing, but both his sketch and his actions (i.e., he tested only three of the input voltages) reflect a failure to obtain anything like a technically complete problem representation. He did not have the system knowledge—or the ability to use available system documentation— to ascertain when his representation of power distribution was complete.

This problem also brought to light a basic troubleshooting skill exploited by the expert but not by the less-than-expert technician. To check power, one must leave the system on. Trying to take measurements at major component connections (i.e., at the back of the central computer) with the system on is both awkward and somewhat dangerous. The expert, however, knows how to find a complete listing of the pins and cards inside the computer to which each input voltage will be routed. By putting specific circuit cards on extenders, he can safely and efficiently check each voltage. The less-than-expert subject, on the other hand, got to the point where he wanted to check a power input to the computer but did not know how to do it.

> *S:* I can't disconnect the CCDP . . . my power. . . . So if I were to turn on and disconnect . . . I'd like to look at [power from] the Aux A, but I'm trying to figure out a way where I can look at it with power on in the situation.

Even a hint from the experimenter ("Is there some way you can find out which cards get power from the Aux A? Check the input to certain cards?") fails to elicit the preferred procedure. Two other technicians at intermediate levels of expertise worked with this problem and similarly failed to use the expert approach. In this way, our method identifies skills that we would propose tutoring.

Administration of problems to novice and intermediate-level problem solvers is useful in a number of ways. Because the tutoring systems will be developed for these less-than-expert troubleshooters, it is important that training developers have a good picture of what such troubleshooters do and do not know. On the one hand, we must take into account the fact that most tutor users will not be totally naive subjects; there is little point in devoting resources to developing skills that are uniformly acquired through the present technical training that precedes a job assignment. At the same time, if less-than-expert troubleshooters have consistent misconceptions or strategic weaknesses, such as focusing on the physical rather than the functional structure of the system, these weaknesses should be considered when developing the tutor curriculum. Protocols from novices are also helpful in identifying the skills, knowledge, and strategies that produce expert performance: Novice problem solving provides a background against which the figure of expert solution methods is seen more clearly.

ABSTRACTING EXPERT KNOWLEDGE

One of the more striking differences between expert and novice approaches to the problem used in our example involved the initial representation of the problem. Whereas the novice "categorized" the problem in terms of the physical location of the symptoms (the central computer) and tried to deal with all of the functions occurring there, the expert thought about the problem in terms of a particular functional area—power inputs—and that decision provided a structure for his troubleshooting. Thus, given the particular symptoms used in this problem, we know that a really good troubleshooter is likely to entertain a power-related hypothesis first. Although this piece of information about expert performance will be useful when we are designing tutoring or assessment measures (this problem could be used for either), we also want to identify the more abstract version of the expert's rule, the principle upon which his choice of an initial hypothesis is based. This is another aspect of our cognitive task analysis. We try to discover these rules by asking experts directly ("Why did you think about power to the computer first?"). In this case, the expert told us that the alternative set of hypotheses involved something inside the central computer, such as a bad clocking board or CPU, and that these alternatives would have required much more difficult troubleshooting. Further, he knew that the central computer for this particular system is pretty reliable, so power supply to the computer was the preferred first hypothesis—it had both a higher likelihood of payoff and was easier to test. We then pressed the expert further to try to ascertain the range of situations in which power-related hypotheses would be considered first. Here, the expert pointed out that you are unable to do anything with the system and that the symptoms (all the front panel lights going on and off sporadically) are both widespread and seemingly random. According to this expert, when you get massive, "weird" symptoms rather than a single, hard fail, power is the first thing to check.

Having obtained a first pass at a general rule for when to entertain power-related hypotheses, we can then "test" the rule against our observations of other experts solving other problems. (We have, in fact, obtained similar characterizations of when to check power first from experts in other jobs.) In this way, such rules can be further refined. In addition, this more abstract characterization is applicable across different equipment systems (i.e., different job domains).

Generality of application is extremely important for our purposes. First, the abstract characterizations derived from an analysis of one job domain greatly facilitate our analysis of new domains. They focus the protocol collector's attention on important issues ("What would you think about first in this situation? Why did you consider power-related things first on this problem but not on this other one?"). The abstract characterizations of expert knowledge in the domains we have studied already thus serve as templates for identifying the same skills and strategies in the context of new problems encountered in studying other jobs. Second, we are seeking to identify generalizable skills that apply across job domains. The derivation of commonalities across domains can bring power and economy to the large instructional system that will be based upon this work. Such power is needed not only to make the intelligent tutoring development economically feasible, but also to provide learners with the general principles and abstract problem schemas (cf. Holyoak, 1984) that they can continue to use when their system is replaced by a new one or they are reassigned to another job.

Although we want to facilitate the development of the abstract, generalizable knowledge that characterizes expertise, we still believe that we will be most effective in doing so if we use specific problem contexts that are appropriate for the learner's particular job. We will want to teach many of the same principles to troubleshooters in dozens of different jobs (e.g., when to consider power hypotheses first, or the split-half strategy), but we would use different problems, appropriate to the system maintained by the particular troubleshooter.

Thus, our approach to cognitive task analysis embraces both context-specific and abstracted representations of expert knowledge.

ACKNOWLEDGMENTS

The work described in this paper was supported by Air Force Contract No. F33615-84-C-0058. The views, opinions, and findings contained in this report are those of the authors and should not be construed as an official Department of the Air Force position, policy, or decision, unless so designated by other official documentation.

Many members of our research team contributed to the development of these methods. In particular, we want to note the important roles played by Chris Roth of HumRRO, Gary Eggan of the Air Force Engineering Technical Service (now at LRDC), and Allan Collins of BBN. In addition, these methods build upon the concept of the "effective" problem space and the verbal troubleshooting tasks developed by Glaser et al. (1985).

REFERENCES

Atkinson, R., & Hiatt, F. (1985, August 18). Nation's high-tech weaponry requires high-priced repairs. *The Washington Post*, pp. 1, 8.

Brown, J. S., Burton, R. R. & deKleer, J. (1981). Pedagogical, natural language and knowledge-engineering techniques in SOPHIE I, II, and III. In D. Sleeman & J. S. Brown (Eds.), *Intelligent tutoring systems* (pp. 227–280). London: Academic Press.

Chi, M. T. H., Glaser, R., & Rees, E. (1982). Expertise in problem solving. In R. Sternberg (Ed.), *Advances in the psychology of human intelligence* (Vol. 1, pp. 7–75). Hillsdale, NJ: Lawrence Erlbaum Associates.

Christiansen, J. M., & Howard, J. M. (1981). Field experience in maintenance. In J. Rasmussen & W. B. Rouse (Eds.), *Human detection and diagnosis of system failures* (pp. 111–133). New York: Plenum Press.

Clancey, W. J. (1985). *Acquiring, representing, and evaluating a competence model of diagnostic strategy.* (Rep. No. STAN-CS-1067.) Stanford, CA: Department of Computer Science, Stanford University.

Ericsson, K. A., & Simon, H. A. (1984) *Protocol analysis: Verbal reports as data.* Cambridge, MA: MIT Press.

Feltovich, P. J. (1981). *Knowledge-based components of expertise in medical diagnosis* (Rep. PDS-2). Pittsburgh, Learning Research and Development Center, University of Pittsburgh.

Glaser, R., Lesgold, A., Lajoie, S., Eastman, R., Greenberg, L., Logan, D., Magone, M., Weiner, A., Wolf, R., & Yengo, L. (1985). *Cognitive task analysis to enhance technical skills training and assessment.* (Final Report to the Air Force Human Resources Laboratory on Contract No. F41689-83-C-0029.) Pittsburgh: Learning Research and Development Center, University of Pittsburgh.

Greeno, J. G. (1977). Process of understanding in problem solving. In N. J. Castellan, D. B. Pisoni, & G. R. Potts (Eds.), *Cognitive theory*, (Vol. 2, pp. 43–83). Hillsdale, NJ: Lawrence Erlbaum Associates.

Hinsley, D. A., Hayes, J. R., & Simon, H. A. (1977). From words to equations: Meaning and representation in algebra word problems. In M. A. Just & P. A. Carpenter (Eds.), *Cognitive processes in comprehension,* (pp. 89–106). Hillsdale, NJ: Lawrence Erlbaum Associates.

Holyoak, K. J. (1984). Mental models in problem solving. In J. R. Anderson & S. M. Kosslyn (Eds.), *Tutorials in learning and memory* (pp. 193–218). San Francisco: Freeman.

Lesgold, A. M., Feltovich, P. J., Glaser, R., & Wang, Y. (1981). *The acquisition of perceptual diagnostic skill in radiology* (Rep. PDS-1). Pittsburgh: Learning Research and Development Center, University of Pittsburgh.

Nawrocki, L. H. (1981). Computer-based maintenance training in the military. In J. Rasmussen & W. B. Rouse (Eds.), *Human detection and diagnosis of system failures* (pp. 605–620). New York: Plenum Press.

Newell, A. (1980). One final word. In D. T. Tuma & F. Reif (Eds.), *Problem solving and education: Issues in teaching and research* (pp. 175–189). Hillsdale, NJ: Lawrence Erlbaum Associates.

Newell, A., & Simon, H. A. (1972). *Human problem solving.* Englewood Cliffs, NJ: Prentice-Hall.

Simon, H. A. (1980). Problem solving and education. In D. T. Tuma & F. Reif (Eds.), *Problem solving and education: Issues in teaching and research* (pp. 81–96). Hillsdale, NJ: Lawrence Erlbaum Associates.

Sleeman, D., & Brown, J. S. (1982). Introduction: Intelligent tutoring systems. In D. Sleeman & J. S. Brown (Eds.), *Intelligent tutoring systems* (pp. 1–11). London: Academic Press.

Vidulich, M., Yeh, Y., & Schneider, W. (1983). Time components for air intercept control skills. In *Proceedings of the Human Factors Society 27th Annual Meeting* (pp. 161–164). Santa Monica, CA: Human Factors Society.

The Development of Troubleshooting Expertise in Radar Mechanics

Yvette J. Tenney
Laura C. Kurland
Bolt Beranek & Newman Labs, Inc.

INTRODUCTION

In this chapter, some preliminary studies are described concerning the cognitive skills of radar mechanics. The purpose of this investigation was to facilitate the designing of an intelligent tutoring system to teach maintenance and repair of the HIPIR radar of the HAWK Air Defense System, under contract to the Army Research Institute, Training Research Lab. The design of the system is described in two companion chapters in this volume (see Kurland & Tenney for instructional issues; de Bruin, Massey, & Roberts for implementation questions).

In order to find out how troubleshooting expertise develops, we asked three mechanics, who differed in years of experience, to describe how the radar works (Study 1). The interviews were analyzed in terms of the mechanics' mental models of the radar. Subsequently, we videotaped the same mechanics each solving two problems on the radar while "thinking aloud" (Study 2). These observations were analyzed in terms of problem-solving skills. We also had an opportunity to observe the subject matter expert who had helped us with the testing solve five planted problems (Study 3). On the basis of this work, we have formulated some working hypotheses about the nature of cognitive change in the development of radar expertise. These findings have shaped our ideas about the role of a tutor in maintenance training.

Background

Our approach to the study of the development of expertise stems from recent work in cognitive science on mental models (Gentner & Stevens,

1983). The term *mental model* refers to an understanding of a system that includes knowledge of the possible states of each component as well as the temporal and causal links between components. Mental models are abstract in the sense that some aspects of the system are invariably lumped together or ignored. Mental models are concrete in the sense of being imaginable and "runnable." A mental model can serve as a tool for problem solving by allowing the thinker to mentally "run" the model to observe the effects that a change in one part of the system has on the other parts. An adequate model can support the inferences that are needed to generate hypotheses about possible faults in the system and to make decisions about possible courses of action.

The most direct evidence for the role of mental models in troubleshooting comes from an extensive study of avionics technicians (Gitomer, 1984; Glaser et al., 1985). Individuals who were rated as high and low in on-the-job problem solving, but had received similar training, were administered a series of experimental tasks to determine what cognitive factors contributed to the group differences. One of the significant findings to emerge from this research was that the skilled group knew more about the overall functioning of the system, as well as about specific procedures. The two groups did not differ in knowledge that was not directly related to the job. These results suggest that the successful problem solvers had acquired an understanding of the system, or mental model, that was optimal for their particular task.

A second line of evidence for the power of a model as a thinking tool comes from research on instructions. Kieras and Bovair (1984) have shown that providing students with information about the structure and functioning of a technical system prior to their receiving instruction in how to use that system produced faster and more error-free learning. Furthermore, the ability to localize faults in the system was similarly enhanced by providing a model. Using a similar procedure, Smith and Spoehr (1985) showed that having a model facilitated (a) memory of the components, (b) comprehension of instructional steps, (c) accurate execution of the steps, and (d) reasoning about a new procedure. Thus, the psychological literature provides support for the position that mental models are potentially powerful tools for reasoning about complex systems.

STUDY 1: MENTAL MODELS OF THE RADAR AS A FUNCTION OF EXPERIENCE

The purpose of this study was to see how the mechanics' views, or mental models, of the radar changed as they acquired experience.

Method

Subjects. Subjects were three members of the equipment maintenance staff at the U.S. Army Air Defense Artillery School at Fort Bliss, Texas. They had 1, 5, and 10 years of experience on the job, respectively.

Procedure. Each subject was asked to explain how the radar works in an interview that lasted from 2 to 4 hours. In the first part of the interview, subjects were instructed to make any diagrams that they thought would be helpful. In the second part, they were specifically asked to draw functional block diagrams of the radar, using boxes and arrows.

Results and Discussion

The drawings of the radar produced by the subjects during the interview were analyzed in terms of the following categories:

1. *Depiction of physical features (e.g., panels, meters, lights).* This variable was of interest because studies of novice–expert differences in physics (Larkin, 1983) have shown that novices classify problems in terms of surface similarity, (e.g., problems involving inclined planes), whereas experts classify on the basis of the underlying physical principle (e.g., conservation of energy). Thus surface features seem to be more salient to the novice.

2. *Depiction of current or voltage.* This variable was of interest because the power distribution system of the radar is the first topic to be discussed in the classroom and is the source of many faults in laboratory troubleshooting exercises. Also, students are required to complete a course in basic electricity before enrolling in the program. Thus, there is considerable emphasis on electricity in the course of training.

3. *Depiction of information flow (one-way).* This variable was of particular interest in light of recent work by Gitomer (1984) and Glaser et al. (1985) that suggests that the training that mechanics receive may not be adequate to ensure the kind of understanding of the system that is necessary for effective problem solving. In order to fix a radar system, for example, the mechanic must understand the flow of information as well as the flow of electricity. An example of the flow of information between two components is when a mechanical gear moves a certain amount, causing an electro-mechanical device to turn and generate voltage proportional to the degree of the turn. The flow of information in a radar system, in other words, may involve different kinds of energy (e.g., electrical, mechanical, and RF). An examination of the drawings of a radar system produced by avionics mechanics showed that novices

overgeneralized the power distribution links and underrepresented the informational links between subsystems (Gitomer, 1984).

4. *Depiction of information flow (in loops).* The notion of a feedback loop is essential in understanding the flow of information in a radar system. A loop is a higher order structure consisting of several components that act together to instantaneously perform one function. The function of the loop cannot be derived in a serial, causal manner. It is not the case that one component affects the next in domino fashion around the loop. Students first encounter the notion of a loop in studying electricity. In an electrical circuit, current is the same in all portions of the circuit. Because students reason serially, rather than in terms of a loop, they have difficulty understanding why current in the portion of the circuit after the resistor is not less than current in the portion before the resistor (Haertel, 1982). Because students have difficulty understanding feedback loops in the more familiar domain of electricity, we suspected they would have difficulty with feedback loops involving other kinds of energy (e.g., RF noise cancellation, antenna tracking).

An analysis of the drawings in terms of these factors showed that subjects depicted the radar quite differently, depending upon their level of experience. The differences that were observed suggested three trends:

1. Novices focus on the physical aspects of the radar; experts on functional aspects.
2. Novices focus on the distribution of power; experts on the flow of information.
3. Experts are more likely to think of the system in terms of a number of feedback loops.

These conclusions were based on evidence of drawings by the 1st-year, 5th-year, and 10-year mechanics.

Drawings by 1st-year mechanic. Although all subjects had been exposed to functional block diagrams of the radar in school, the 1st-year mechanic was baffled by the experimenter's request to "give an overview of how the radar works." After asking her to be more specific about what she wanted, the 1st-year mechanic thought for a moment and said, "Well, then we'll divide down by cabinets." As shown in the example (see Figure 3.1), he drew the cabinetry of the radar in intricate detail, emphasizing the physical aspects of the radar. Figure 3.1 shows the four panels of the transmitter cabinet, complete with buttons, lights, and meters. The arrows point to inside views of the cabinets, with the front panels removed. An emphasis on sensory aspects was also apparent in his verbal descriptions: "A red light comes

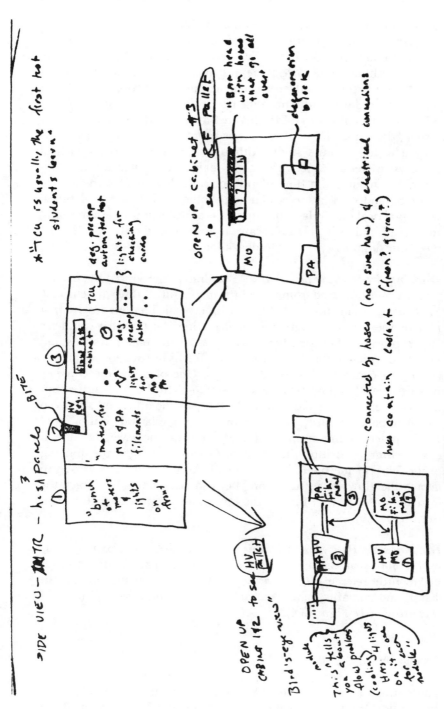

FIGURE 3.1 Drawing made by 1st-year mechanic.

on, and you hear a click, and your dial is all messed up."

When he was specifically asked to make a functional diagram, in the second part of the interview, the 1st-year mechanic drew a series of boxes. Although he correctly represented most of the major systems (see Figure 3.2), the only consistent connection between the boxes that he showed was a link from the power distribution system to every other system. Gitomer (1984) obtained a similar drawing of a radar system, depicting links to the power source, from an inexperienced subject in his avionics study. Although this is not wrong—each of these systems requires electrical power—it ignores what is unique about the radar, namely the flow of information that enables the system to locate and track a target. The only other link that was depicted was a practical one. When the antenna is aimed below a certain point, the elevation dial in the TIC ceases to function. Finally, the 1st-year mechanic did not depict any feedback loops.

Drawings by 5th-year mechanic.   The drawing produced by the 5th-year mechanic differed from that of the novice on all three dimensions. First, he spontaneously produced a functional diagram in the first part of the interview, rather than depicting the physical cabinetry (see Figure 3.3). He used boxes to represent the major systems and arrows to represent the flow of information. His use of two-way arrows suggests a concern with feedback loops. One of these, the two-way link between signal processor and the servo-control unit, is important because it enables the radar to track a target. The other link, between a control panel and the system it monitors, is a relatively minor loop. It has practical importance for the mechanic, however, because it enables him to position the antenna. In terms of stages, the drawing of the 5th-year mechanic is transitional. Although he uses arrows to depict the flow of information, he also uses them to depict the distribution of power, that is, the low voltage inputs to each system (see Figure 3.3).

Drawings by 10th-year mechanic.   By contrast, the drawing made by the 10th-year mechanic is more advanced in terms of stages. It makes little reference to power, depicts the flow of information in detail, and contains many feedback loops, as indicated by the two-way arrows (see Figure 3.4).

Conclusion

The results of this pilot study suggest that novices focus on power distribution and the physical layout of the radar, whereas experts have

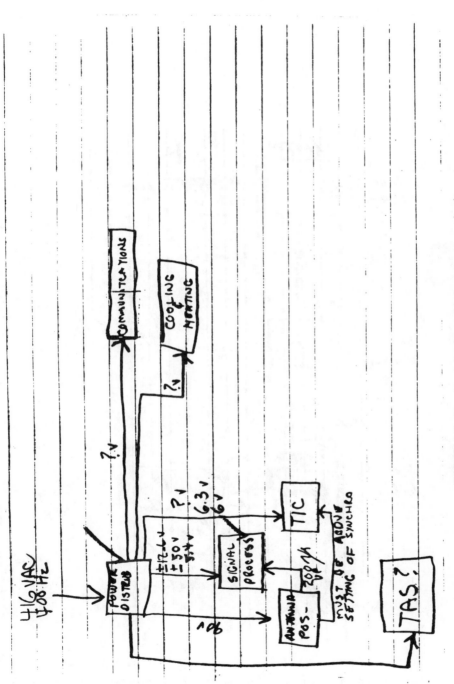

FIGURE 3.2 Functional diagram made by 1st-year mechanic.

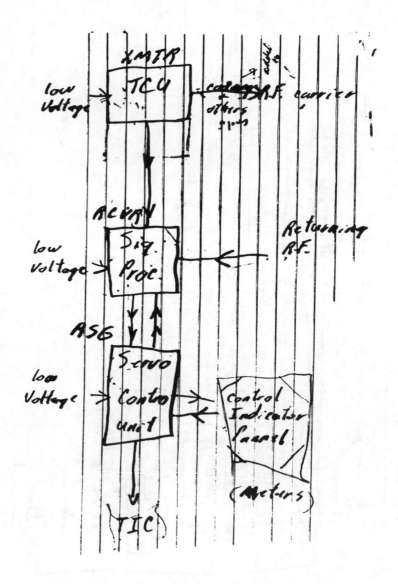

FIGURE 3.3 Functional diagram made by 5th-year mechanic.

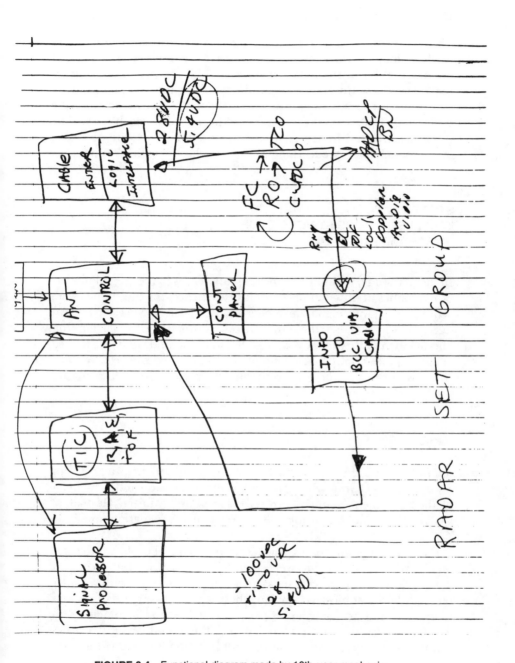

FIGURE 3.4 Functional diagram made by 10th-year mechanic.

a better functional understanding of the flow of information, including feedback loops. Evidently, it is difficult for the novice to think about the functioning of the radar when faced with the physical reality of the radar. These findings have implications for the design of a tutor. An important aspect of training is to help the student to map the functional aspects of the radar onto the physical machinery. The problems involved in achieving this instructional goal are discussed in another chapter (see Kurland & Tenney, chapter 5, this volume).

STUDIES 2 AND 3:
TROUBLESHOOTING STRATEGIES OF
NOVICE AND EXPERT MECHANICS

In the first study, we found interesting differences in the mental models of mechanics at different levels. With experience, the mechanics were acquiring a more elaborate model of the radar. However, the real question was whether these differences in functional understanding affected their ability to fix the radar. So, in the second study, we looked at the troubleshooting behavior of the same three subjects. A third study was carried out to investigate the performance of a master mechanic.

Method

Subjects. The three subjects from Study 1 served in Study 2. For Study 3, a mechanic who was a platform instructor and a member of the equipment maintenance staff, served as a subject. He had 13 years of experience on the job and was reputed to be a master mechanic.

Procedure. In both studies, subjects were given real problems to solve on the radar. The problems were created by having someone disconnect a wire, remove a part, or exchange a functioning part with a faulty one, while the subject was out of the room. The subject's task was to find the fault using any appropriate procedures and documentation. Available documentation included the Daily and Weekly Checks (routine maintenance procedures), Fault Isolation Procedures (detailed troubleshooting procedures), and Schematics (detailed wiring diagrams).

At the beginning of each problem, the subject was directed to a particular place in the Daily and Weekly Checks and told to begin looking for the fault. The Checks consist of a small number of routine tests that are designed to reveal gross symptoms of malfunction. The particular starting point was chosen to lead subjects to the discovery of the first symptom quickly.

Once the initial symptom was discovered, the subject had several options. He or she could turn to the section of the Fault Isolation Procedures (FIP) that corresponded to the given symptom, continue to carry out the Daily and Weekly Checks, consult the wiring Schematics, or try to work without any documentation. The most efficient strategy is to turn to the prescribed section of the Fault Isolation Procedures as soon as one of the tests in the Daily and Weekly Checks fails. The Fault Isolation Procedures contain a series of contingent tests designed to rule out fault possibilities systematically. A mechanic who chooses to continue with the Checks rather than turn directly to the Fault Isolation Procedures may obtain useful information, since there is some overlap between the two documents, but is likely to carry out unnecessary steps.

In study 2, the master mechanic created two problems for subjects to solve on the radar and supervised the sessions. In study 3, the master mechanic solved five problems that were created for him by the 5th- and 10th-year mechanics. The problems were chosen to be representative of those encountered on the job and average in difficulty.

Results and Discussion

In analyzing the results of the troubleshooting studies we had to contend with the fact that they were carried out in a naturalistic setting. Even though use of the actual radar to study problem solving simplifies our task in some respects (see chapter 2 by Means & Gott), it can create unexpected difficulties. First, unintentional faults may appear in addition to the fault that was planted, complicating the original problem. Second, the mentor who plants the problem does not always remain a silent collaborator. He may feel obligated to offer advice to the subject, especially in the case of an inexperienced mechanic. As a result, in analyzing the data, we had to tease apart the effect of tutoring from the developmental differences we were trying to observe. The opportunity to analyze what the human tutor was doing, however, proved to be invaluable in planning and designing a computer tutor.

Number of steps. The troubleshooting protocols were analyzed in a number of ways. The first variable was the number of steps to solution. (Steps taken in pursuit of unplanned faults were not counted.) A step was defined as any test that the mechanic carried out. There were a number of different kinds of tests that the mechanics could make. They could run the built-in tests. They could read meters. Sometimes switches had to be set before reading the meter, sometimes an adjustment had to be made to see if the meter reading could be brought within a certain tolerance, and sometimes the meter was simply read. In any case, the whole operation of reading the meter counted as one step. Another step consisted of tracing wires in the circuit. Circuit tracing was accomplished either by removing wires and testing the resistance to see if there was an open, or by leaving the circuit intact and testing voltages. For ease of coding, testing a particular circuit counted as one step, regardless of the number of readings.

As shown in Table 3.1, the expert took 7.2 steps to solve problems that could be solved in an average of 5.8 steps, according to the Fault Isolation Procedures. The 5th- and 10th-year mechanics, on the other hand, required 19.0 and 17.5 steps, respectively, to solve problems that could have been completed in an average of 10 steps. So the expert was clearly more efficient. The 1st-year novice, surprisingly, solved the problems with record efficiency (i.e., in 8.5 steps vs. a recommended 10 steps). This result was misleading, however, because further analyses showed that the novice was receiving a disproportionate amount of help from the mentor. The relevant data will be presented in a subsequent section.

Proximity to recommended fault isolation procedures. In order to see how closely the mechanics were following the procedures recommended by the troubleshooting manual, all the steps called for in the detailed Fault Isolation Procedures were listed and checked off against the steps actually carried out by the mechanic. A note was made as to whether the step was carried out directly (by actually referring to the manual) or indirectly (without actually referring to the manual).

As shown in Table 3.1, the expert carried out a total of 72.4% of the steps recommended by the manual. In other words, his procedures corresponded fairly closely to the recommended procedures, although close examination revealed that he modified some of the procedures and often changed their order. The 10th- and 5th-year mechanics carried out increasingly fewer of the recommended steps (65.0% and 55.0% respectively). The novice, once again, resembled the expert in carrying out a high proportion (80.0%) of the procedures recommended by the manual.

Although the novice appeared to be similar to the expert in carrying out a high proportion of the recommended steps, an important difference emerged when direct versus indirect matches were considered. As seen in Table 3.1, almost all of the novice's matches were direct

TABLE 3.1
Novice–Expert Differences in Problem Solving

Years of Expertise (N = 1)	Number of Steps	Number of Steps in FIP	Percent of FIP Steps Matched	Number of Direct Matches	Number of Indirect Matches	Number of Extra Steps	Number of Mentor Comments: Number of Steps
Average of Five Problems							
13	7.2	5.8	72.4	1.4	2.8	3.0	1:4
Average of Two Problems							
10	17.5	10.0	65.0	0.5	6.0	11.0	1:4
5	19.0	10.0	55.0	3.5	2.0	13.5	1:4
1	8.5	10.0	80.0	7.0	1.0	0.5	2:1

(7.0 out of 8.0), whereas a majority of the expert's matches were indirect (2.8 out of 4.2). These results suggest a difference in strategy. The novice was able to reproduce few of the recommended procedures without the aid of the manual. The expert, on the other hand, was able to reproduce an average of 1.2 steps per problem from memory (i.e., without any aids), 0.8 steps by studying the wiring schematics, and 0.8 steps by carrying out steps in the Daily and Weekly Check manual that overlapped the recommended Fault Isolation Procedures.

The 5th and 10th-year mechanics, though similar to each other in some respects, also differed on this dimension. As can be seen in Table 3.1, almost all of the 10th-year mechanic's matches were indirect (6.0 out of 6.5), whereas a majority of the 5th-year mechanic's were direct (3.5 out of 5.5). The 10th-year mechanic, like the expert, achieved a high proportion of indirect matches by remembering the procedures (an average of 3.0 steps per problem), by deriving the recommended procedures from an examination of the wiring schematics (1.0 step per problem), and by carrying out steps in the Daily and Weekly Maintenance Procedures that overlap the Fault Isolation Procedures (2.0 steps per problem). The 5th-year mechanic, like the 1st-year novice, had a higher proportion of direct than indirect matches, suggesting less ability to generate the recommended procedures without the manual.

Extra steps.   Finally, a count was made of the number of steps that the mechanics carried out that were not part of the Fault Isolation Procedures. Some of the extra steps came from following the Daily and Weekly Check Procedures in the general maintenance manual beyond the recommended point. These additional checks were coded as extra steps, unless they happened to coincide with steps in the Fault Isolation Procedures. A second way in which subjects reduced their efficiency was by repeating steps within the Fault Isolation Procedures. This duplication came about when subjects consulted the manual sporadically rather than following it closely. Subjects also carried out extra steps that involved using their senses to see, hear, and feel if the radar was running properly. For example, they would look at the brushes in the motors, listen for noise, and feel for vibrations. As shown in Table 3.1, the expert did a few extra steps, whereas the 10th- and 5th-year mechanics did many extra steps, presumably because they were working without the manual. The novice, on the other hand, who had few resources outside of the manual, had virtually no extra steps.

Help from mentor. An analysis of mentor comments confirmed the suspicion that the novice was getting a lot of help. The last column of Table 3.1 shows the ratio of mentor comments to steps carried out. All subjects, except for the novice, received minimal advice (one comment for every four steps they carried out). The novice, on the other hand, received two comments for every step that he took.

The picture that emerges from these pilot data is that the novice reads through the manual of Fault Isolation Procedures and waits for the mentor to help him interpret the instructions. The 5th- or 10th-year mechanic solves problems on his own with little help from the manual or from the mentor. But he ends up doing some extra steps in the process. The expert solves a problem in fewer steps by sticking more closely to the recommended procedures. Unlike the novice, he is able to derive many of the steps on his own and can alter them for his own convenience.

Novice-expert differences in solution antecedents. These impressions received further support from an analysis of solution antecedents. The purpose of this analysis was to see what single event immediately preceded discovery of the fault. A number of different categories were observed. In some cases, a comment from the mentor preceded the discovery. In other cases, the mechanic discovered the fault directly after consulting the Fault Isolation Manual or the schematics. Finally, in other cases, no external aid was apparent. The mechanic simply uncovered the fault.

The results were compatible with the two trends observed earlier. In particular, there was a growing ability, as experience increased, to generate procedures without benefit of the manual, and finally, at the expert level, a tendency to use the documentation to reduce unnecessary steps. As shown in Table 3.2, the tendency to find the solution without consulting external aids increased from 0%, to 50%, to 100% of the problems for the 1st-, 5th-, and 10th-year mechanics, respectively. The proportion for the expert was back down to 20%. The superficial resemblance between the expert and novice, however, disappeared when the other categories were considered. As shown in Table 3.2, the expert was the only subject to consult the wiring schematics just before finding the fault (40% of problems). When the interviewer asked him, in one case, why he had turned to the schematics, he replied, "Just to make sure of what I have already looked at in the FIP—that I know where I'm at on the schematics, for one thing—to relate the two together, mostly." The ability to relate information from the two sources gave the expert an advantage in dealing with situations, to be discussed later, in which "blind" following of the steps in the Fault Isolation Procedures would not work. The 1st-year novice, by contrast, was the only subject to receive critical help from the mentor. On one-half of his problems (1 out of 2), help from the mentor, rather than the manual, led directly to the problem solution.

Spontaneous tutoring.   Although we had not expected the expert to play a role in the testing session, the spontaneous advice that he gave the subjects when they were having difficulty enabled us to observe a human tutor in action. His comments could be classified into four categories (see Table 3.3), as follows:

1. *Procedures.* The most frequent help in this category involved pointing out where a specific part, such as a particular pin, was physically located on the radar, where to look in the schematics for a particular circuit, and the correct settings for switches, particularly safety switches.

TABLE 3.2
Novice–Expert Differences in Solution Antecedent

Years of Expertise (N = 1)	*Proportion of Problems of Five Problems*			
	Mentor Hint	Fault Isolation Manual	Schematics	No External Aids
13	0.0	0.4	0.4	0.2
	Proportion of Problems of Two Problems			
10	0.0	0.0	0.0	1.0
5	0.0	0.5	0.0	0.5
1	0.5	0.5	0.0	0.0

TABLE 3.3
Categories of Expert Advice

---

1. *Procedures*
   Location on radar
   Location on schematics
   Correct procedure

2. *General Hints*
   Results of time-consuming procedures
   Ignore unplanned faults
   Use Fault Isolation Manual

3. *Reasoning*
   Why step unnecessary
   Hypotheses to consider
   Conclusions to draw

4. *Other*
   General support
   Physical assistance
   Results of procedure not attainable on school radar

---

2. *General hints.* One type of hint was telling the subject the results of time-consuming procedures. For example, one of the steps in the manual called for checking the resistance in the wires between 24 sets of pins. The mentor, however, said, "OK, you've checked them and they are fine." Another type of hint had to do with unplanned faults. When a symptom appeared that should not have been there, the mentor would say, "OK, you can ignore that problem," again saving the mechanic time. Finally, the mentor sometimes hinted that the mechanic refer to a section of the manual, knowing that it would lead directly to the fault. This kind of hint was unnecessary in the case of the novice, who used the manual all the time, but was helpful for some of the other mechanics who tried to solve problems on their own. These suggestions were categorized as general hints because they did not involve any explanations about how the radar works.

3. *Reasoning.* This category consisted of suggestions from the tutor that involved reasoning about the radar. The first type consisted of telling the mechanic why a step he proposed to carry out was unnecessary. For example, in one of the problems, in which the antenna would not move in the azimuth direction, the student decided to test the 416 volt input to the antenna positioning system. The tutor explained that this test was unnecessary. The fact that there was movement in the elevation direction meant that the input voltage had to be present. The tutor also pointed out hypotheses to consider. In other words, he explained why certain faults were possible, given

the dynamics of the radar system. Finally, he sometimes explained how a conclusion could be reached. He would tell the mechanic to stop collecting data and consider the implications of what he already knew.

4. *Miscellaneous.* The fourth category of mentor feedback consisted of general support, physical assistance, and the results of procedures that appear in the Fault Isolation Procedures but cannot be carried out on the school radar.

Once these categories of mentor advice were defined, it was possible to see how the advice given to subjects changed with their level of expertise. The first problem, involving a disconnected cable in an amplifier that is used in noise reduction, showed clear developmental trends, as expected (see Table 3.4). Procedural help, general hints, and other support all increased as the level of expertise decreased. Reasoning was not given at any level because this problem did not involve any complicated deductions.

The results for the second problem, involving a missing brush in the motor tachometer that moves the antenna in the azimuth direction, were surprising (see Table 3.4). The 1st-year mechanic again received a lot of help, whereas the 5th-year received considerably less. However, the 10th-year mechanic, contrary to expectation, received a lot of help in the categories of general hints and reasoning. We suspected that this need for intervention was related to the fact that

TABLE 3.4
Type of Advice Received

Problem: Disconnected Afrf Amplifier Cable				
Years Expertise (N = 1)	Hints	Reasoning	Procedures	Other
10	0	0	0	0
5	3	0	3	0
1	6	0	4	4
Problem: Missing Brush in Motor Tachometer				
Years of Expertise (N = 1)	Hints	Reasoning	Procedures	Other
10	5	6	0	0
5	0	0	3	2
1	1	10	10	8

TABLE 3.5
Troubleshooting Slips

Number of Errors per Problem

Years of Expertise (N = 1)	Circuit Measurement Errors		Test Errors		Errors in Use of Manual		Total
	Afrf Prob.	Brush Prob.	Afrf Prob.	Brush Prob.	Afrf Prob.	Brush Prob.	
10	0	0	0	1 (hand-wheel)	0	1 (FIP Section)	2
5	0	0	1 (button)	1 (card #)	0	0	2
1	0	1 (90 volt)	0	0	0	0	1

he made several mistakes. So we decided to look at slips, or unintended behaviors (see Table 3.5).

Troubleshooting slips. The slips were analyzed in terms of three categories: circuit measurement errors (i.e., measuring at the wrong pin), test errors, (i.e., forgetting to set a switch), and errors in the use of the manual (e.g., turning to the wrong section). As shown in Table 3.5, the 10th-year mechanic made two mistakes, both on the brush problem on which he received so much help. One of his mistakes was a test error—he forgot to turn the handwheel when measuring the voltage. As a result, he got an unexpected voltage reading of zero. (When the handwheel is turned, there is a position error signal that gives a voltage reading that is proportional to the degree of the turning.) As a result of this unanticipated reading, he erroneously concluded that there was a problem with the handwheel and spent a lot of unnecessary effort tracing that portion of the circuit.

His second mistake on the brush problem involved use of the manual. According to the manual, he was supposed to check whether the antenna problem occurred in remote only, local only, or in both local and remote modes. Because it is not possible to check the remote mode on the school radar, he should have asked the mentor for this information. Instead, he assumed that the problem was in the local mode only, which was not true, and branched to the wrong section of the manual. Once there, he conducted a test that revealed what, in fact, was an unintended fault in the radar, and was led on a lengthy tangent.

TABLE 3.6
Immediate vs. Delayed Correction of Slips

Total Number of Corrected Errors of Two Problems

Years of Expertise (N = 1)	Correction of Circuit Measurement Errors		Correction of Test Errors		Correction of Errors in Use of Manual		Av.
	Immed.	*Del.*	*Immed.*	*Del.*	*Immed.*	*Del.*	*Av.*
10	0	0	0	1 (S)[a]	0	1 (T)[a]	1.0
5	0	0	2 (S, T)[a]	0	0	0	1.0
1	1 (T)[a]	0	0	0	0	0	0.5

Total Number of Corrected Errors of Five Problems

Years of Expertise (N = 1)	*Immed.*	*Del.*	*Immed.*	*Del.*	*Immed.*	*Del.*	*Av.*
13	2 (S, S)[a]	0	0	0	0	1 (T)[a]	0.6

[a]S = Self-corrected; T = Tutor-corrected.

Immediate and delayed correction. Although the error analysis provided some insight into why the 10th-year mechanic required so much help, it was not completely satisfactory, because others had made mistakes, too. The 5th-year mechanic made two test errors. He forgot to hold down a button, and he confused two cards. The 1st-year mechanic mismeasured a 90 volt circuit. However, we suspected that the tutor may have bailed out the less-experienced mechanics sooner.

To check on this possibility, we divided mistakes into those that were corrected immediately, either by the mentor or by the mechanic himself, and those that were not corrected until after a delay. As shown in the first half of Table 3.6, in which data from the two problems have been combined, our suspicions were confirmed. The 1st- and 5th-year mechanics received immediate correction from the tutor, if they did not correct their mistakes themselves, whereas the 10th-year mechanic was left to bear the consequences of his own errors. Although he eventually detected the handwheel error himself, he did not discover that he was in the wrong section of the manual until the expert finally directed him to the correct place. So, the fact that the 10th-year mechanic required a strong dose of intervention can be explained by the fact that he made errors that were not immediately corrected.

To see if the 10th-year mechanic was atypical in his propensity to make mistakes, we looked at the protocol of the expert. As shown at the bottom of Table 3.6, the expert made mistakes, too. He made two circuit-measurement errors that he corrected immediately. He also went to the wrong section of the manual. Evidently this is easy to do. In this case, there were two fans that were described in different sections of the manual. Although he was working on the right fan (i.e., the one that was not running), he turned to the section of the manual for the wrong fan and consequently was referred to the wrong schematic diagram. The diagrams of the two fans looked very similar, so he did not suspect anything until he began to get unexpected voltage readings. Just as he was pondering the unlikely possibility that a whole host of wires had been disconnected, the 5th-year mechanic, who had planted the problem, told him that he was looking at the wrong documentation. Evidently mistakes in using the manual are a big problem in troubleshooting. They are easy to make and difficult to correct without outside help.

Conclusion

Our findings suggest three stages of troubleshooting expertise. The novice follows the Fault Isolation Manual literally, but needs lots of help with reasoning and procedures, as well as general hints. Left alone with the manual, he would not be able to solve many problems. The intermediate has a repertoire of procedures that he knows well and likes to use. He does not like to use the manual. He ends up solving problems on his own, but not efficiently. Finally, the expert follows the Fault Isolation Manual, but in a flexible order. He knows how to adapt the procedures so they will be more convenient. He solves problems confidently and efficiently. We also discovered that mistakes in troubleshooting are universal. Some mistakes are more detrimental than others. It is particularly hard to recover from a choice of the wrong section of the manual.

GENERAL DISCUSSION

Goals of Tutoring

How, then, can we design instruction that will enable novices to become more like experts? Our plans for instruction are discussed in another chapter (see Kurland & Tenney, chapter 5, this volume). What we would like to design is a computer tutor that carries out the most important functions that we observed in our human tutor. If we consider the kinds of feedback that the human tutor provided (see Table 3.3), in light of the requirement of our subjects, the first category, "Procedures," is of medium priority, the second, "General Hints," is of high priority, the third "Reasoning," is of even higher priority, and the fourth, which includes encouragement and physical assistance, is not a priority. Not surprisingly, the ease of implementing the top three priorities is inversely related to their importance.

Procedures.   Help with procedures is of medium importance because it is needed only in the initial stages of learning. We found that the 1st-year mechanic required information about how to carry out particular tests, whereas the 5th- and 10th-year mechanics did not. This kind of training can be provided by a simulation of the system that includes replicas of the instruments needed to carry out the tests called for in the Fault Isolation Procedures.

Hints.   The category of general hints, as we have seen, was important in helping subjects solve the problems within a reasonable amount of time. In particular, hints were needed to get students back to the correct section of the manual when they made procedural or other errors that caused them to end up in the wrong section of the manual. (Most of the steps in the manual are contingent on the outcome of previous steps, so a mismeasurement can cause the mechanic to "branch and get lost.") Though not easy to implement, troubleshooting knowledge of this type is crucial for any training system. Fortunately, there will be no need for hints about the results of time-consuming procedures and unplanned faults, because the simulation will provide rapid information and will not be subject to spurious faults.

Dynamic reasoning.   Finally, the category of reasoning, we believe, is of the highest priority, though it will be the hardest to implement. We have seen that novices know less than experts about the functioning of the radar. As a result, they need to be exposed to the kind of reasoning that the expert goes through in deciding what faults are possible, what fault possibilities have been eliminated, and when all but one possibility has been ruled out. Although this kind of information underlies the steps described in the Fault Isolation Procedures, it is not apparent to the reader. For example, when the FIP instructs the mechanic to branch to a particular section, it, in effect, eliminates certain faults from further consideration. However, it does not tell the reader which faults have been eliminated. So, unless the mechanic understands the system quite well, he may not be able to infer the purpose of the particular test he has conducted.

The opaqueness of the Fault Isolation Procedures would not be a problem if "blind" following of the instructions were possible. However, considerable judgment is called for in the use of the FIP. Some of the steps are repetitive, time-consuming, cumbersome, or require unavailable parts. Furthermore, there are occasional faults in the manual, the test instruments are not always reliable, and more important, as we have seen, even the most advanced mechanic is likely to make mistakes. Studies of repair manuals in other domains suggest that these kinds of problems result in the nonuse of manuals among a sizable proportion of mechanics (Kern, 1985). As a result, we believe that troubleshooting skill depends upon the ability to reason about a complex system, which in turn depends on an adequate mental model.

A SCENARIO

The real virtue of a computer training system is that it can be used to teach the kind of dynamic model that is needed for troubleshooting. Such a model allows the mechanic to infer the rationale behind the steps in the manual and generate alternative procedures on his own. The job of building an intelligent tutor that can help the mechanic reason about the system in the course of troubleshooting is an ambitious one. Consider, for example, this interchange that occurred in Study 2 between the expert and the 1st-year mechanic. The novice mechanic had conducted a number of tests, but did not realize that he had gathered enough information to come to a conclusion. The expert, serving as mentor, helped the student to reason backward from the symptoms observed to the underlying fault.

The radar fault, in this problem, was a broken azimuth motor tachometer (i.e., temporarily broken by removing a brush). The initial symptom was a failure of the antenna to move in the azimuth direction.

1. *Expert:* Make a determination as to what is wrong. Is the voltage present to the motor tach?
2. *Novice:* Sure is!
3. *Expert:* Is the motor tach working?
4. *Novice:* It should be, if we get the voltage there.
5. *Expert:* Is the antenna moving?
6. *Novice:* No.

7. *Expert:* Is the motor tach working?

8. *Novice:* Well, no, it's not.

9. *Expert:* What is corrective action? The motor tach is connected by gears directly to the antenna.

10. *Novice:* Azimuth drive gear train?

11. *Expert:* It's good. The one component you're looking at. If you were on site, or you were here by yourself, what would you do at this point in time?

12. *Novice:* Your azimuth control current, that's good, right? Replace that motor tach.

13. *Expert:* Exactly.

14. *Novice:* You've got your voltage, you've got your current. They're both working, we checked it. There's nothing wrong after it. It's got to be your tach.

In this example, the expert points out that sufficient data have been gathered to identify the fault and tells the novice to consider the results of the latest test he has conducted (i.e., the voltage input to the motor tachometer) (1).

On the basis of this response (2), he asks the novice to draw a conclusion about the intactness of the motor tachometer (3). This leading question uncovers a misconception on the part of the novice. He reasons incorrectly that if the motor tachometer has sufficient voltage, it must be working (4). This misconception is an interesting one, because it relates to the tendency discussed earlier of novices to focus on power distribution rather than on the flow of information.

The expert then calls the novice's attention to the functional aspects of the radar by asking him about the movement of the antenna, which is one of the main functions of the motor tachometer (5). When the novice admits that this function is not being carried out (6), he asks him to draw an implication about the motor tachometer (7).

At this point, the novice is confronted with a contradiction and presumably realizes his mistake (8). According to voltage considerations, the motor tachometer is working. According to functional considerations, the tachometer is not working. The expert does not try to resolve the contradiction, but tries to lead the novice to the conclusion; if the tachometer is not working, then replace it (9).

However, he misleads the novice temporarily by giving him information about the physical connection between the motor tachometer and the antenna, via the gear train (9). This information would have been helpful if it had been presented in line (7). Here it is misleading and causes the novice to look for additional symptoms in the gear train (10).

After getting the novice back on track, the expert tells him he has all the information he needs to come to a conclusion (11). The novice draws the correct conclusion (12), to the satisfaction of the expert (13), and spontaneously reviews the lesson he has learned: If the voltage is good, but the function is not being carried out, and everything prior to and subsequent to that point is working, then the part must be faulty (14).

Conclusion

This sample dialogue suggests two important points concerning intelligent tutoring systems for radar troubleshooting. First, to be truly useful, an expert system will have to do more than teach procedures. If it is going to free the instructor, it will need to teach the user to reason about the flow of power and information. Otherwise, it will bear little resemblance to a skilled human tutor.

Second, this example points out the close ties between a trainee's mental model of the radar system and troubleshooting performance. The claim is that misconceptions are likely to lead to obstacles in troubleshooting. Although there has been little research in this area, it seems clear from this example that the emphasis on power that we observed in the mental model of the novice caused him to overlook the possibility that a particular part was broken. To use an analogy, it is as if a student, faced with a burnt-out bulb in a simple circuit (White & Frederiksen, 1985), had tested the feed and the ground portions of the circuit and had concluded that the bulb was working, without ever checking to see if it was lit!

Returning to the dialogue between expert and novice, it is clear that the expert had good Socratic teaching methods, like those typically observed in experienced tutors (Collins, Warnock, & Passafiume, 1975), in addition to a functional model of the radar that was well adapted to the task of troubleshooting. A computer system that demonstrates such skill will deserve to be called an intelligent maintenance trainer.

REFERENCES

Collins, A., Warnock, E. H., & Passafiume, J. J. (1975). Analysis and synthesis of tutorial dialogues. In G. H. Bower (Ed.) *Advances in learning and motivation, 9,* New York: Academic Press.

Gentner, D., & Stevens, A. L., Eds. (1983). *Mental models.* Hillsdale, NJ: Lawrence Erlbaum Associates.

Gitomer, D. H. (1984). *A cognitive analysis of a complex troubleshooting task.* Unpublished doctoral dissertation, University of Pittsburgh, Pittsburgh, PA.

Glaser, R., Lesgold, A., Lajoie, S., Eastman, R., Greenberg, L., Logan, D., Magone, M., Weiner, A., Wolf, R., & Yengo, L. (1985). *Cognitive task analysis to enhance technical skills training and assessment.* Final report of project on Feasibility of Cognitive Information Processing Models for Basic Skills Assessment and Enhancement, prepared for the Air Force Human Resources Laboratory, University of Pittsburgh, Learning Research and Development Center.

Haertel, H. (1982). The electric circuit as a system: A new approach. *European Journal of Science Education, 4,* 45–55.

Kieras, D. E., & Bovair, S. (1984). The role of a mental model in learning to operate a device. *Cognitive Science, 8,* 255–273.

Kern, R. P. (1985). Modeling users and their use of technical manuals. In T. M. Duffy & R. Waller (Eds.) *Designing usable texts,* (pp. 341–375.). New York: Academic Press.

Larkin, J. H. (1983). The role of problem representation in physics. In D. Gentner & A. L. Stevens (Eds.), *Mental models.* Hillsdale, NJ: Lawrence Erlbaum Associates.

Smith, E. E., & Spoehr, K. T. (1985). *Basic processes and individual differences in understanding and using instructions.* (Final Report No. 3029). Cambridge, MA: Bolt Beranek & Newman Labs.

White, B. Y., & Frederiksen, J. R. (1985). QUEST: Qualitative understanding of electrical system troubleshooting. *ACM SIGART Newsletter, 93,* 34–37.

What Mental Model Should Be Taught: Choosing Instructional Content for Complex Engineered Systems

David E. Kieras
University of Michigan

INTRODUCTION

The choice of content for any instructional system is a critical question. The quality of delivery of instruction is clearly of little import unless the right content is taught. For a complex engineered system such as a radar set, a computer, or an airplane, this choice of content can be particularly important, because such systems are often extremely complex and can be viewed at many levels of detail. In an organization such as the military, people often interact with the same piece of equipment at many different levels of analysis. One person may need to know a lot about the system, whereas another needs to know very little; in addition, different users may have to know different kinds of information, as well as different levels of detail. Thus the choice of content involves choosing the appropriate mental model for the equipment.

Because intelligent tutoring systems are computer-based systems, they must be fully specified. The developers of intelligent tutoring systems are therefore in a position to choose the content of training more systematically and more efficiently than the developers of traditional training. But it is also very clear that if the choice of content is not right, then an intelligent tutoring system is simply a more expensive, difficult, and clumsy way to deliver bad instruction than traditional methods. Thus the ultimate success of intelligent tutoring systems will involve combining the technical advances in developing such systems with similar advances in the choice of the content of instruction.

MENTAL MODELS OF ENGINEERED SYSTEMS

Knowledge of Equipment

People can have a very rich set of kinds of knowledge about a particular piece of equipment. Table 4.1, based on studies reported in Kieras (1982), lists some of the types of knowledge that appeared when expert and novice subjects were asked to describe actual pieces of equipment ranging from devices as simple and familiar as alarm clocks to those as complicated and unfamiliar as pieces of electronic laboratory equipment. Clearly, there are both a large amount and many types of knowledge that people can have about specific pieces of equipment. A full expert will have considerable knowledge built up from long-term experience. But for tasks such as maintaining or troubleshooting, some of this knowledge is probably vital, but other knowledge might be unimportant. The questions is: What do people need to know?

As suggested by Table 4.1, most knowledge about devices seems to be related to using the device, as opposed to how-it-works knowledge about the internal structure and operation of the device. For example, Kieras (1982) observed that when asked to freely describe a device, experts would provide considerable detail on the procedures for using a piece of equipment, but often they did not consider it necessary to provide any details about how the device worked, although it was clear that they could do so.

It is, in fact, debatable whether people need to have how-it-works knowledge for equipment. There are conflicting intuitions and practices throughout the technological world. For example, most training materials for computer-based products such as word processors follow the "task-oriented" philosophy of simply telling the user how to get tasks done, rather than providing the user with "theoretical" knowledge of how the system works. In marked contrast, pilot training in the military seems to be based on a philosophy that the more the pilot knows about the airplane, the better.

Electronics maintenance seems to be somewhere in between these extremes, with the optimal knowledge depending on the level of analysis of the equipment required by the troubleshooting task. This discrete component level of knowledge, in which the person interacts with the device at the level of the individual component resistors, capacitors, transistors, and so forth, is close to the "learn-everything" level, but not quite. That is, much of the circuitry of real electronic equipment is there to meet certain design constraints, many of which are not relevant even to a sophisticated troubleshooter. Diagnosing and correcting failures in the circuitry usually does not require knowing the design considerations behind the circuit configuration,

TABLE 4.1
Kinds of Knowledge People Have About Devices

Label or name of the device
Function or purpose (what goals can be accomplished)
Controls and indicators
Inputs, outputs, and connections
Power source and requirements
External layout and appearance
Internal layout and appearance
External behavior (input–output function)
How to operate the device to accomplish goals
Procedures for troubleshooting and maintenance
Internal structure and mechanisms (how it works)

but only the identification of components that are not working correctly.

One simple example of the independence of design constraints and troubleshooting appears in Figure 4.1. This configuration of components often appears in circuitry involving certain types of transistors. Some of the components (R1, R2, R4, and C2) are there to ensure that the transistor is operating at the proper voltages and currents. Selecting the right values for the resistors is an important step in the design of the circuit, because incorrect choices could easily result in the circuit performing improperly or even being prone to catastrophic failure of the transistor. However, almost all failures in such circuits can be identified and corrected without knowledge of the design considerations dictating the circuit configuration or the specific component values. From the expert troubleshooter's point of view, this is simply a standard configuration of components, and some of the components, such as the resistors, are quite unlikely to fail, whereas others, such as the transistor, are more likely to fail. These failures can be localized by making voltage readings, which can then be compared to the normative readings provided by prior knowledge, the equipment documentation, or by simple forms of qualitative reasoning. For example, if R1 is shorted, the voltage at point B will be too high, point C too low, and the transistor may be hot to the touch and damaged. Thus, even at the most detailed level of troubleshooting, it is not necessary to know everything about how the system works. The choice of which how-it-works knowledge people need to know is basically a choice of which knowledge is most suitable for supporting activities such as troubleshooting.

Content of Mental Models for Devices

The term *mental model* has been used in a variety of ways in recent

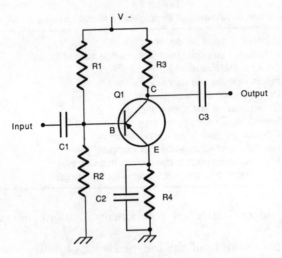

FIGURE 4.1 A common circuit configuration dictated by design requirements but which can usually be diagnosed in the absence of design knowledge.

years. In the context of equipment, a mental model contains two forms of knowledge: the how-it-works knowledge of how the equipment itself works, that is, its internal structure and mechanisms, and the knowledge of how to *use* this how-it-works knowledge to perform a task. These two together make up a "runnable" mental model.

How-it-works knowledge. The knowledge of how a device works is a hierarchy, in which each level corresponds to a level of analysis of the equipment itself. For example, one can understand a radar set at the level of the overall function of the device, in which the radar set is a "black box," or one can successively unpack this knowledge into a finer level of analysis where the radar set consists of a set of black boxes, each of which performs a subfunction. Finer levels can be defined, with the lowest normal level of analysis being at the circuit component level, such as the individual resistors, transistors, or integrated circuits. Logically, of course, the level of analysis can be extended down to subatomic physics, but this is not normally done in the context of electronic systems. Nevertheless, some treatment at this level of basic atomic structure is often included in the technical training for electronics maintenance personnel.

At each level of analysis, the how-it-works knowledge consists of information about the components of the system at that level, the component behavior in terms of the input–output functions, and the system topology at that level. For example, at the discrete component level, the topology for a radar set is similar to the usual schematic diagram that includes resistors and transistors. At the level of the major functional components, however, the system topology will typically consist only of the major signal flow paths. Finally, at each level of analysis, there is knowledge of the system principles that are appropriate for that level. For example, at the level of a functional block diagram of the radar set, the system principles will include concepts such as signal flow, in which a signal can be the output of one box and the input of another, but a separate path is required if the second box is supposed to signal the first box. In contrast, at the level of discrete components, the principles concern concepts such as voltage and current.

As an example, Figure 4.2 is a "block diagram" from a military radar technical manual that shows the overall functional components in the radar system. The same document includes intermediate block diagrams such as Figure 4.3. Figure 4.4 shows a fragment of the schematic diagram at the discrete component level. Because this particular radar set uses analog vacuum tube technology, there are only about three levels of description. There is not the intermediate level of analysis that we associate with digital circuitry, in which the equipment is made up of a large number of units, each of which is very adequately specified by its input–output function; in digital circuitry it is rarely necessary to consider the circuitry inside of a logic chip.

Strategic knowledge. The second portion of the knowledge in a mental model for a device is the knowledge of how to use the how-it-works knowledge. Basically, this consists of procedural knowledge for various strategies that allow the person to perform tasks such as inferring or predicting the internal state or behavior of the system. Other strategies are for inferring the procedures for operating the device, identifying causes of malfunctions, and compensating for malfunctions (as was shown in Kieras & Bovair, 1984). These inference strategies should be contrasted with the operating or troubleshooting procedures that are sometimes explicitly taught. Inference strategies make use of system principles to enable the person to infer information that was not explicitly stated. In addition, devices are generally made up of a relatively small number of components, whose behavior in combination can be derived from relatively few principles. Thus, within a given class of device and level of analysis, such strategies and much of the underlying knowledge should be generic, applicable to any device in the class. In the domain of electronic systems, these inference strategies are usually not made explicit in training materials. The trainee seems to be left to pick them up from examples in the training materials or during apprenticeship.

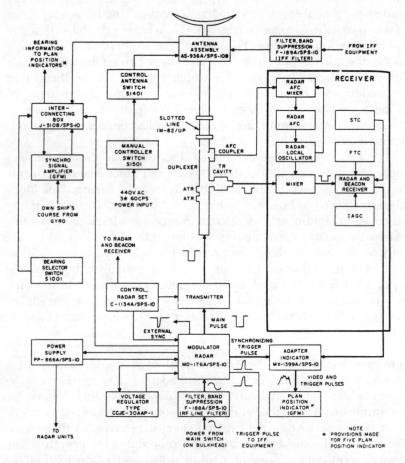

FIGURE 4.2 The "Functional Block Diagram" from the Technical Manual for a military radar set (AN/SPS-10).

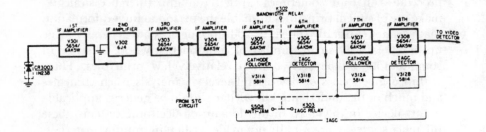

FIGURE 4.3 The block diagram from the Technical Manual of part of one of the blocks shown in Figure 4.2.

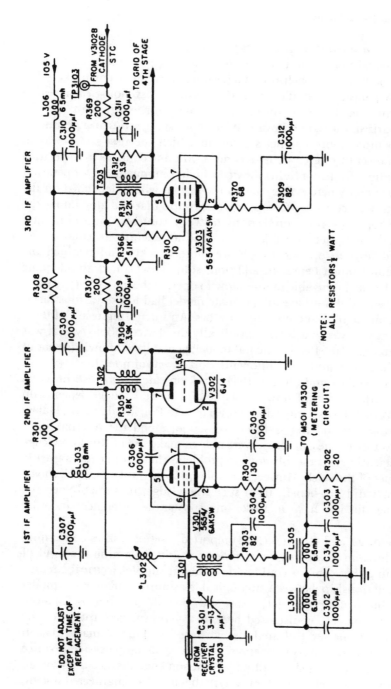

FIGURE 4.4 The component-level schematic diagram from the Technical Manual of the first three blocks in Figure 4.3.

Value of Mental Models

When is a mental model useful? Given the above characterization of a mental model for a device, the following question arises: Under what conditions is it helpful for a person to have such a mental model? Some examples of studies from the cognitive psychological research literature on the role of mental models for equipment can be summarized. Kieras and Bovair (1984) conducted a series of experiments on a simple control panel system, in which the user's task was to route power through a series of components and controls to a specified destination. Indicator lights showed which components were operating properly and where power was in the system which depended on the settings and controls. Compared to groups that did not know the device topology (the connections between controls, indicators, and internal components), subjects who had an adequate mental model learned how to operate the device more quickly and retained the procedures much better. In addition, subjects who had an adequate mental model were able to infer how to operate the device very readily. Those who did not have an adequate model had to use various forms of systematic trial-and-error approaches. An interesting result of these experiments was that it was specifically the device topology that was important for an effective mental model; generalized knowledge about how the system and its components worked was of no value.

The Halasz and Moran (1983) work on calculators also provides a good illustration of how the value of a mental model depends on the task that the user must do. Using a reverse-Polish calculator, Halasz and Moran found that subjects who understood the internal stack architecture of the calculator were able to make use of this knowledge in efficiently devising solutions to problems that could benefit greatly from use of the stack. However, simpler problems that could be solved routinely did not benefit from such knowledge, presumably because the user did not have to make any substantial inferences in order to solve them.

Gentner and Gentner (1983) reported a set of studies concerning how different analogies for electricity would determine the kind of reasoning that subjects could perform about simple electrical circuits. The relationship between analogical reasoning and mental model reasoning is not completely clear, and so could use some discussion. A mental model, as discussed here, is a veridical description of the system at some level of analysis, whereas no claim is made that an analogy system is a correct representation of the target system. Notice that in domains such as physical phenomena, the accuracy of an analogy may be debatable; however, in the case of an engineered system, there does exist a veridical understanding in the technical field itself about how the system actually works. Thus, explanations based on this understanding are not analogies but are correct descriptions.

Despite these differences, the significance of the Gentner and Gentner studies is that the reasoning people could perform about electrical circuits depended on the kind of inferences that the specific analogy enabled. If one thinks of an analogy as being a kind of mental model, then these studies show that the kind of information in the mental model will be related to the kind of inferences one can draw about the target system.

These results can be summarized in the following way: First, a mental model will help a user interact with a piece of equipment only if knowing the mental model allows the user to infer the exact procedures for operating (or troubleshooting) the device. Note that the criterion is being able to infer the *exact* procedures, not just vague ideas about the procedures. Second, a mental model will help for a piece of equipment only if it is an advantage in the task environment to be able to infer the procedures. One example of such an advantage is that being able to infer procedures facilitates learning by providing an additional encoding or elaboration of the procedure that later assists recall (Kieras & Bovair, 1984). In addition, being able to infer procedures could be an advantage if the task requires operating the equipment in situations that were not explicitly trained or recognizing inefficient procedures and improving them. (Halasz & Moran, 1983; Kieras & Bovair, 1984.)

When is a mental model not useful? In the maintenance situation, a large amount of the how-it-works knowledge of the system is probably irrelevant. The question is: How could one tell what knowledge is irrelevant?

The above description of when mental model knowledge is important yields some criteria for when how-it-works knowledge is not needed: (a) If the procedures are easy to learn by rote, then the mnemonic assist provided by being able to infer the procedures is of little value; (b) the device is so simple that the user does not need to make inference based on knowledge of how the device works; (c) a mental model is of little value if it is too difficult or complicated for the user to acquire and use; and (d) mental model is useless if it fails to support the inferences that the user needs to make, or alternatively, supports inferences that the user does not need to make.

For some devices, either very limited mental models seem to be adequate, or how-it-works knowledge is simply not necessary. Such devices seem to be those that represent a good match between the user's task and the user interface.

Perhaps the best example that does not require how-it-works knowledge is the ordinary telephone system. Telephone systems are very complex, but they are also quite reliable, and the user interface is physically and logically simple. Thus, the telephone is easy to learn how to use, and almost everyone knows how to use it, even young children. But almost nobody knows how the switching system itself works. Some people know the general principle of the telephone, such as sound waves being converted into electrical signals which are converted back to sound waves, but this principle has few implications for how to use the telephone, and almost none for how to dial it (e.g., why do you have to take the handset off the hook before dialing?).

The technology of telephone systems has undergone essentially a full century of evolution; automatic dial systems were in existence at the turn of the century. This, together with the fact that in the United States the telephone was developed as a universally available device, has resulted in an evolution of the user interface to the point where it is nearly as optimal as it can be within the limits of technology. The only way it could be substantially improved upon is if we did not have to associate numbers with people: Suppose we could simply pick up the telephone and speak the name of the person we wanted to call instead of dialing a code number (such devices are beginning to appear).

Consider certain aspects of the procedure of using a telephone, such as why one has to dial "1" before the area code to place a long-distance call, as opposed to dialing it after the number. This question can only be answered correctly by reference to the actual switching system mechanisms and by knowledge of why the available technology makes it important to dial the "access code" first. But, in practice, remembering to dial the access code first puts such a low burden on the user's rote learning ability that it does not seem to be necessary to provide an explanation. Thus, the standard telephone book provides detail on the procedures to be executed to place different kinds of long-distance calls, but contains absolutely no information on the principles of the switching system that might justify or rationalize these procedures.

Thus, the telephone system is an example of a situation in which the fit of the device to the user's task, and the technological means to simplify the user's task, are at a point where little or no how-it-works knowledge is required. In a real sense, the technology used in the device and the design of the device in this example are mature. If substantial how-it-works knowledge seems to be required for successful operation of the device in the specified task environment, either the technology is not mature or there is a defect in the design.

HOW TO CHOOSE A MENTAL MODEL

The basic idea proposed here for how a good mental model for an engineered system can be chosen is that both the choice of concepts and the optimum level of detail in the mental model depends on what kind of inferences the task requires. Clearly, choosing a mental model requires a fairly detailed analysis of the task. In such an analysis several questions need to be answered. What procedures does the trainee need to be able to do? Which will be trained directly? Can the trained procedures be learned easily by rote, or do they need the mnemonic assist provided by a mental model? Is it possible and practical for the user to acquire and apply the mental model? Is it necessary, possible, and desirable to have the user infer some of the procedures, instead of executing them by rote?

Once these questions have been answered, then the problem is how to pick the desirable content for a mental model out of the vast quantity of information that could be conveyed about an engineered system. It is important to realize that traditionally constructed documentation and training materials can be seriously wrong in this choice. Thus, there is a need for a relatively formal, as opposed to the traditionally intuitive, analysis of the task and the instructional content.

Analysis Approaches

Cognitive modeling. One approach to choosing mental model material has been described elsewhere (Kieras, in press). This is to construct an explicit cognitive simulation model of how the user would do the task. This model can then be used to specify the content to be conveyed to the trainee. More specifically, cognitive simulation modeling techniques can be used to define explicitly the declarative and procedural knowledge involved in acquiring and using the mental model in the specific task domain. One would start with the documentation for the engineered system, expert knowledge of the domain, whatever psychological theory and data are available and relevant, and a rational analysis of the task. By rational analysis of the task is meant analysis from the point of view of what the *logical* requirements are for conducting the task, as opposed to a *psychological* analysis of what skilled users seem to know or to do. The model is then constructed and modified until it can perform the task using the appropriate mix of inferences and specified procedures, using knowledge and processes that it is plausible that humans could acquire.

The content of the simulation model then defines the declarative knowledge (facts about the system) and the procedural knowledge (strategies and procedures) that should be taught.

The basic problem with this approach is that constructing such a simulation model for a complex task and a complex piece of equipment can be a major undertaking and so may not be at all practical. But if the proposed intelligent tutoring system will contain an explicit representation of the to-be-taught mental model reasoning, then constructing the cognitive simulation model is essentially the construction of this representation. Because much of the knowledge is generic, the results could be used for many pieces of equipment. A possible example of such an approach is the QUEST electronic troubleshooting tutoring system (see Frederiksen, White, Collins, & Eggan, this volume).

Heuristic selection.   The cognitive modeling approach is perhaps the most scientifically interesting from the viewpoint of both cognitive psychology and artificial intelligence, because it involves the characterization and construction of a system for doing reasoning. However, it is difficult to overstate the amount of work involved. There are other possible approaches in which the task analysis is used in combination with *selection heuristics* to choose the content for a mental model.

In a heuristic-based approach, sources such as the system documentation together with expert domain knowledge and a rational task analysis would be used to define implicitly the pool of all possible things the user could know about how the system works, what kinds of inferences the user needs to perform and what procedures the user has to be able to execute. Once this implicit pool is defined, some heuristics would be applied to select the subset of the mental model knowledge that is relevant to the user's task, as specified by the task analysis. This is the mental model content that should be taught. The key concept is that the selection heuristics are simple enough to be applied on a large scale. In the following section several selection heuristics are described as "recipes" to be followed.

Some Possible Heuristics

Relevance to task goals.   Define the hierarchy of how-it-works explanations in terms of increasingly deeper levels of analysis, as just discussed. The overall operation of the system is at the top, and the most detailed level of hardware and software functioning is at the bottom. Similarly, define a hierarchy of the user's task knowledge, with the most general goals at the top, and individual control actions (such as pushing a particular button) at the bottom of the hierarchy. Such a structure is similar to the GOMS model goal hierarchy discussed in Card, Moran, and Newell (1983).

Then, for each goal in the user's goal hierarchy, find a match with a subtree in the explanation hierarchy that provides an explanation for why the user needs to be able to accomplish that goal in terms of how the device works. Select just the portions and levels of the explanation hierarchy that can be so matched to the user's goals. This is the how-it-works knowledge that is relevant to the user's task. Portions of the hierarchy that are not included, or levels of detail that are not included, are not relevant to the user's task. (See Kieras & Polson, 1985, for other discussion.)

Accessibility to user.   Consider the hierarchical decomposition of the device structure and mechanisms, in conjunction with the "operators" (in the GOMS model sense) that the user can apply, to either affect the device or to collect information about its state (basically defined by the controls and displays). What parts of the system are accessible to the user through those operators? Select just the levels of detail and portions of the system in which the smallest components can be observed or operated on by the user. Lower-level components or inaccessible components are not task-relevant, because the user cannot interact with them. Consult an expert to determine whether something important has been left out, such as information that is not provided by the device displays but is provided by some other source (e.g., tactile sensing of vibrations).

Critical procedures and inference strategies.   Identify the procedures that are especially important for the user to be able to perform accurately and which contain apparently arbitrary content. These are the procedures that might benefit from the user being able to infer them. Select the how-it-works knowledge that seems to be related to these procedures or provides an explanation or justification for the arbitrary features.

Select all of the inference strategies that the user would have to be able to apply in order to perform the task. Such strategies are essential to good performance, but for skills such as troubleshooting, they are rarely explicitly taught in traditional training. Analyze each such strategy and select the how-it-works knowledge that is required by each strategy. This selection may require detailed analysis, because the aspects of the system that must be known in order to support such inferences are not usually obvious from existing documentation or training materials.

Examples of Heuristic Selection

Example domain.   Some examples of how these heuristics would apply to selecting mental model content are presented below. The systems used for these examples are some of the electrical and mechanical subsystems of the T38 supersonic trainer aircraft. Although a jet fighter aircraft may seem overly ambitious to use for examples, there are in fact some features of the pilot's task, and the nature of the airplane, that make some of these analyses very simple to carry out.

First of all, notice that the pilot's task with regard to the electrical and mechanical subsystems of the plane is actually relatively simple. The pilot is basically only an operator of these systems; the pilot does not fix them, nor does he or she have to build them. What the pilot does have to do is to operate the airplane in a highly reliable and accurate manner, because it can easily be damaged by improper operation, and also to diagnose malfunctioning systems in the aircraft and compensate for them when possible. In order to carry out these tasks, the pilot has a simple set of available operators. Basically, the pilot can observe the various instruments provided in the cockpit, sense other information, such as vibrations and other aspects of the "feel" of the airplane, and can influence these systems by manipulating the available controls. In the case of many of the electrical and mechanical subsystems, these controls are limited in number and in the effects they have.

As just mentioned, pilot training typically seems to be based on the concept that the pilot should know quite a bit about the how-it-works of the airplane. This is reflected in the typical pilot's document that accompanies a military airplane, which in this case is the *T38 Flight Manual*. This document assumes that the pilot already knows flying and piloting skills and so is intended to provide information about the specific systems and procedures for this particular airplane. Because I am not a fighter pilot, the systems I have chosen for these examples are not specific to airplanes or flying, but rather are electrical and mechanical systems whose operation does not depend in any fundamental way on the fact that they appear in an airplane.

It should be acknowledged that there may be many good reasons why pilots are required to learn what they do about the systems in the airplane. It is not my goal here to criticize pilot training philosophy. The analysis here is intended only to illustrate an analysis of the mental model content of the Flight Manual. As the examples will show, in some cases the Flight Manual fails to include information that the pilot needs, or fails to present it clearly. In other cases, far more information is presented than the pilot needs. I have not had the opportunity to present these analyses to a domain expert to discover if they are flawed. Thus these analyses represent what might be termed a logical analysis based on the T38 Flight Manual document, in conjunction with general expertise on technical systems. But there may be aspects of these systems that are not reflected in the Flight Manual that may radically change the outcome of these analyses. Thus any conclusions about whether pilots know what they should know may be wrong, because they are based only on a reading of the Flight Manual, not on the overall content of pilot training.

Relevance to task goals. This heuristic calls for comparing the user's task goal structure with the explanation hierarchy of how the system works and choosing just those portions of how-it-works knowledge that can be matched as explanations to the user's task goals. The example here concerns the *airframe-mounted gearbox* and the electrical generating system. In this case, the manual provides key information to support the inference and explanation of certain emergency procedures. Thus this is an example of where the document succeeded in supplying important mental model information.

Table 4.2 is an excerpt from the manual that describes the airframe-mounted gearbox. Each engine drives a gearbox that turns a hydraulic pump and an AC electrical generator. The frequency of the AC power produced by an AC generator depends on the speed of rotation of the generator. The gearbox has been equipped with an automatic transmission to keep the rotational speed of the generator relatively constant, even though the engine RPM varies over a relatively wide range. Notice from Table 4.2 that the manual goes on to describe the actual resulting frequency range of the AC power. Consider that there is much more information that could be supplied in this context, such as why it is important that the AC power be kept in a relatively narrow frequency range (this has to do with the efficiencies of inductors such as power transformers). One might thus wonder how much of the information in Table 4.2 is actually important.

One of the emergency procedures for operating the airplane states that if you lose AC electrical power from one of your generators, you should try either speeding up or slowing down the corresponding engine in order to restore generator power. In the absence of the how-it-works explanation, it is hard to understand why the RPM would have an all-or-none effect on whether the generator is working. But this emergency procedure can be explained by the fact that if one of the gears in the gearbox has failed, it is possible to restore generator power by putting the engine into the RPM range that will engage the other gear. Table 4.3 is the excerpt from the Flight Manual that gives this procedure. Notice that the procedure is expressed directly

TABLE 4.2
Flight Manual Excerpt, Gearbox Description

AIRFRAME-MOUNTED GEARBOX

An airframe-mounted gearbox (figure 1–1) for each engine operates a hydraulic pump and an AC generator. A shift mechanism keeps AC generator output between 320 and 480 cycles per second. Gearbox shift occurs in the 65% to 70% RPM range.

in terms of the gearbox and the shift-range information provided in the how-it-works description in Table 4.2. However, notice that of the two specific quantitative details provided about the gearbox, only the engine RPM shift point is necessary to support this procedure; the actual frequency range for the AC generator output does not seem to be important.

In terms of the heuristic, this analysis is illustrated in Figure 4.5. On the left side of the figure is a sketch of the explanation hierarchy for this portion of the aircraft. The AC power source is made up of the engine, a gearbox, and an AC generator. The gearbox in turn includes a shift mechanism. The explanation of the shift mechanism involves the RPM shift range and the generator output frequency range. The explanation of the generator output frequency range involves the efficiencies of the aircraft power supplies and electric motors, which in turn involve the fact that inductors are involved, and so forth. On the right-hand side of the diagram is shown a sketch of the user's goal structure, in which the top-level goal for this task is to restore AC power. This involves accomplishing the subgoals of operating on the engine and changing the engine RPM in the manner specified, namely, if it is high, make it low, and vice versa. Each of these levels in the user's goal hierarchy can be related to a portion of the explanation hierarchy as shown by the double-headed arrows connecting the two trees. The goal of restoring AC power can be matched up with the AC power source, the goal of operating the engine can be matched with the explanation that the engine is part of the power source,

TABLE 4.3
Emergency Procedure from the T38 Flight Manual

GEARBOX FAILURE — AIRFRAME-MOUNTED

If Gearbox Fails Completely:
 1. Throttle (affected engine)—OFF, if excessive vibration exists.

If Gearbox Fails to Shift:
 1. Engine RPM—Return to range where generator operation can be maintained.
 2. Generator Switch—RESET then ON, if necessary.
 3. Engine RPM—Leave in range of successful generator operation until on final approach; then use as necessary to complete landing.

and the goal of changing the RPM can be matched with the explanation that a shift mechanism is involved. The goals of making the RPM low or high can be matched with the explanation of the RPM at which the shift occurs. Notice that nowhere in the user's goal structure appears a goal of keeping the generator speed constant, or a goal of ensuring that the power supplies work efficiently. If such goals were present, they would match with the explanation of why it is necessary to keep the RPM constant. Thus, the explanation tree for the system can be *pruned* based on the user's goal structure, to select the portions and level of detail of the how-it-works knowledge that is relevant to the user's task. This selected portion is shown in Figure 4.5.

Accessibility to user. This heuristic is based on determining the potential ways the user can interact with the system components. The example concerns the subsystems of the jet engines in the T38. This is a case in which apparently more information has been provided than is actually necessary to operate the aircraft. Figure 4.6 is the diagram in the Flight Manual showing some of the engine subsystems, mainly the fuel system. Controlling the fuel supplied to the engine regulates the engine RPM and thrust. When the throttle is put into the maximum thrust region, the engine afterburner is also supplied

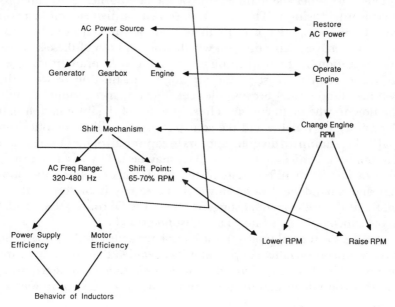

FIGURE 4.5 An example of the task-goal heuristic showing the selected relevant how-it-works information.

with fuel. There are additional control operations that are performed automatically. These include adjusting the air inlet vanes and the engine exhaust nozzle diameter. The diagram in Figure 4.6 shows how these subsystems are related to each other; there is a main fuel system control box that provides the automatic control functions. The diagram also shows additional details, such as the fact that the main engine fuel line is used as a heat sink for the engine oil cooling system.

Based on the diagram, it appears that the pilot's only control input into this system is the throttle position. Everything else shown in the diagram (e.g., the exhaust nozzle) is automatically regulated. The only output to the user *shown in* the diagram is the fuel flow rate. There are other outputs not shown in the diagram, such as the engine RPM and the exhaust gas temperature, which are important in ensuring that the engine is operating properly. Note that the fuel flow rate meter shows the rate of flow of fuel only to the main portion of the engine, not the afterburner.

The heuristic of whether the user has access to the subcomponents of the system suggests that the pilot needs to know very much less about the engine system than the diagram shows. The actual required knowledge is shown in the simplified diagram in Figure 4.7. From the pilot's point of view, the engine control system consists of a throttle that instructs a fuel control subsystem to provide fuel in the appropriate amounts to either the main engine or the afterburner as required by the throttle position. The engine is shown as divided into a main and afterburner section because there are clear differences in how the airplane behaves, depending on whether one or both of these sections is in operation, so this distinction is observable to the pilot. In addition, it is important to preserve the topological distinction between the two fuel supply lines because the fuel flow rate meter monitors only the flow for the main engine. Thus, in terms of the information that the pilot has available and the control operations that the pilot can make, this simplified diagram appears to capture all of the task-relevant information. Notice that this analysis may be wildly incorrect; there may in fact be manifestations of the subsystems of which the pilot can and should be aware. However, my analysis of the available information in the manual suggests otherwise. Of course, the manual may be incomplete, or I may have misunderstood it.

Thus the mental model of the engine presented to the pilot could have been considerably simpler and less detailed than the one in the manual. This heuristic simplifies the device topology by aggregating together subsystems that the user cannot directly observe or influence.

Critical procedures and inference strategies. The last example uses heuristics based on the idea of identifying procedures that would be

ENGINE FUEL CONTROL SYSTEM

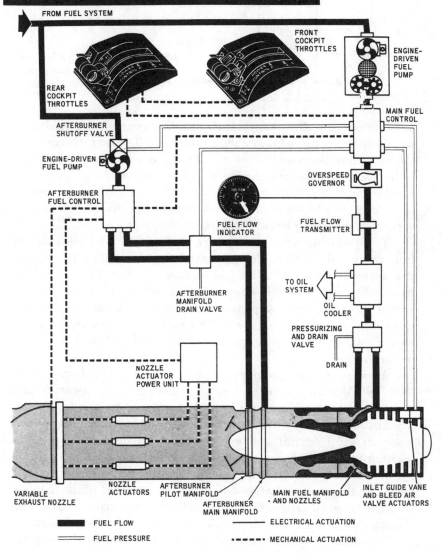

FIGURE 4.6   The T38 Flight Manual diagram for the engine fuel control system.

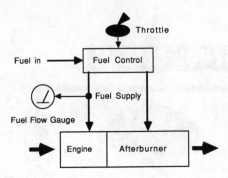

FIGURE 4.7 A simplified diagram of the engine fuel system containing only user-accessible components.

difficult to learn, due to apparently arbitrary content, and analyzing what would be required to be able to infer them. The example concerns the procedures for starting the aircraft engines and how they relate to the electrical system and some auxiliary mechanical systems. The conclusion of this fairly elaborate analysis is that the information provided in the Flight Manual is incomplete and that some of it also appears at the wrong levels of analysis.

The procedures are summarized in Table 4.4 and are excerpts from the actual manual. There are certain aspects of these procedures that appear arbitrary: Why are you supposed to start the right engine first? When *must* the right engine be first? When can the left engine be first? What are the consequences if the right engine cannot be started first? Why is it necessary to wait 30 seconds before starting the left engine, and why does this appear to apply only when the plane is on the ground?

Answering these questions involved a fairly detailed analysis of the Flight Manual to collect information from a variety of paragraphs scattered about the document. The key insights are the following: The airplane is not symetrical; there are some arbitrary design decisions made in the electrical and engine starting systems; and there is apparently "poor" design involved, in that a simplified mechanical system was used which has the consequence of complicating the pilot's task. The diagrams and related information provided in the manual simply were not detailed enough to convey the required mental model information, but the same diagrams had excessive detail elsewhere.

A sample of the relevant information from the Flight Manual is provided in Table 4.5 and in Figure 4.8. Table 4.5 shows an excerpt from the flight manual that discusses the *starting air diverter valve* and also makes reference to a *static inverter,* which is also referred to in several other places throughout the manual.

The air diverter valve is a critical part of the engine starting system. What is not known to most of us, but is known to the pilot, is that the engine is started by blowing air into it, causing the engine to spin, or "windmill." The compressed air is supplied by a little truck

TABLE 4.4
Engine Starting Procedures from the T38 Flight Manual

STARTING ENGINES
RIGHT ENGINE.

Start the right engine first, using the following procedure:
1. Signal for air supply.
2. Engine Start Button—Push Momentarily.
3. Throttle—Advance to IDLE at 14% minimum RPM.

LEFT ENGINE.
1. Left Engine—Start Same As Right Engine.

CAUTION

Do not push left engine start button until a minimum of 30 seconds has elapsed after right engine start button has been pushed. The left engine start cycle will be shortened and may result in a hot start due to loss of external air to the engine.

2. Signal ground crew to disconnect external power and/or air supply.
3. Battery switch—Check ON.

RESTART DURING FLIGHT.

. . .

4. Battery Switch—Check ON.

. . .

5. Engine Start Button—Push Momentarily.
6. Throttle (windmilling engine)—Advance to slightly above IDLE, then retard to IDLE.

NOTE

- Leave throttle at IDLE for 30 seconds before aborting a start.
- If dual engine flameout occurs, right engine should be attempted first, because right engine instruments will operate normally as soon as engine start button is pushed.

ALTERNATE AIRSTART.

The alternate airstart is primarily designed for use at low altitude when thrust requirements are critical. An airstart may be accomplished by advancing the throttle to MAX range. This energizes normal and afterburner ignition for approximately 30 seconds (if throttle remains in MAX range). If the engine does not start after 30 seconds, additional starts may be attempted by retarding the throttle out of MAX range to reset the circuit and again advancing the throttle into MAX range to reactivate the ignition cycle. After engine starts, the throttle may be left in MAX range if afterburner operation is desired.

If alternate airstart is required, proceed as follows:
1. THROTTLE(S)—MAX.

WARNING

- If throttle is already in MAX, recycle throttle MIL to MAX.
- With dual engine failure, battery switch must be at ON to provide ignition.

on the ground. The diverter valve routes the air to either one engine or the other.

The static inverter is a device that converts the 28 volt DC power supplied by the aircraft battery to the 400 Hz 115 volt AC power required by a variety of systems in the aircraft, including the starting ignition devices for the engines. The engine generators normally supply this power. The static inverter apparently exists to enable the emergency procedures shown in Table 4.4, in which both engines flame out while the plane is flying and only the battery power will be available for restarting the engines.

The remarkable thing is that the static inverter is not shown in the overall electrical system diagram (Figure 4.8); it is merely listed as if it were any other power-consuming device. The diagram also does not show that the output of the static inverter is fed to a subset of the AC power distribution system that includes only some of the aircraft devices and not others.

The omission of these key pieces of information is not a result of a general decision to omit detail in the diagram. The diagram shows what is in the relay contactor box (shown at the top of the diagram), which automatically shunts power between generators and different electrical distribution systems in the event of the failure of one of the generators. The detail inside this box is in fact a description of the internal structure of a conventional electromagnetic relay, a rather low-level description.

By carefully analyzing the manual content, and making some guesses, I was able to construct Figure 4.9, which shows a more complete picture of the engine starting system, and makes the key relationships more explicit. This figure shows both the starting air diverter valve referred to in Table 4.5, and also the subset of the electrical system that is concerned with starting the engines. Apparently, the static inverter powers a subset of the AC power distribution bus, which I've titled the "emergency" AC bus. The static inverter is turned on by activating the starting system for either engine. When either of the starting buttons is pressed, or the throttle is advanced to the appropriate place, a timing device is activated. This timing device turns on the static inverter and also turns on the igniter for the engine.

In addition, the timer circuit operates an actuator motor for the air diverter valve. The actuator motor is apparently a device that has properties similar to an ordinary solenoid in that it can be pulled against as well as pull. Thus, when the right engine starting button is pressed, the right engine valve actuator is energized, which sets the valve to the position where the starting air is passed to the right engine. The timer runs for 30 seconds and then shuts off, deenergizing

TABLE 4.5
Excerpt from T38 Flight Manual, Engine Starting System

ENGINE START AND IGNITION SYSTEM

Engine starts require compressor motoring (low pressure air supply), DC power to energize the ignition holding relay, and AC power for ignitor firing. Two engine-start pushbuttons (Figures 1-9, 1-10) are located in the left subpanel of each cockpit. For ground starts only, a diverter valve is automatically positioned to direct air to the selected engine. If the left start button is pressed before the right engine 30-second cycle is completed, the diverter valve will move to the neutral position and will remain at neutral until the right engine 30-second start cycle is completed. The valve will then divert air to the left engine, but only for the time that is remaining on the left engine start cycle, which started when the left engine start button was pushed. The resulting air supply loss may cause an overtemperature condition. Moving the throttles to MAX range energizes the main and afterburner igniters for 30 seconds. The throttles must be retarded to MIL and returned to MAX range to recycle the starting timer. With the throttles at MAX range, the igniters may be energized for longer than 30 seconds by pushing and holding the engine start buttons. AC power from a battery-operated static inverter (Figure 1-15) may be used for ground start (one engine) or air starts (either engine). For battery start, the right engine should be started first, as the static inverter supplies AC power for the right engine instruments during the start cycle.

---

the actuator motor. If the left engine starting button is pressed while the right starting timer is still on, the left engine igniter will be turned on, but the diverter valve actuator motor for the left engine will be energized and will apparently pull against the right engine valve actuator motor, pulling the valve to the neutral position. As a result, neither engine will be getting the full flow of starting air, and various malfunctions will occur.

The diverter valve arrangement is an example of possibly poor design. The two starting systems are not interlocked in any way, making it possible for the pilot to put the starting system into an inappropriate state in which neither engine is being started properly. But regardless of the design quality, this how-it-works knowledge explains why it is necessary to wait 30 seconds before starting the left engine, and why this applies only on the ground: Only on the ground is starting air being supplied through the valve. In the air, the flow of air through the engine air inlets spins the engines for starting, and so it is possible to start both engines simultaneously.

However, the air start procedure in Table 4.4 recommends that the right engine be started first in the case of a dual flameout. This is important because, as shown in Figure 4.9, only the instruments for the right engine are attached to the emergency AC bus; the left engine instruments require the normal AC power. Thus, if one wants to be able to use engine instruments to monitor the start, it is necessary to start the right engine first, because only in this case will the static inverter supply power to the engine instruments. Once the right engine is running, then full AC power will be available (by virtue of the contactor relay in Figure 4.8) and the left engine start can then be monitored.

Now that this how-it-works knowledge is explicit, we see that the left engine could definitely be started first if the right could not be, and it is only the need for the engine instruments that dictate

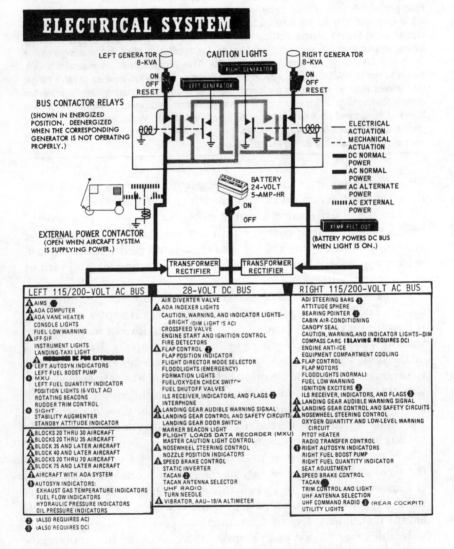

FIGURE 4.8 The T38 Flight Manual diagram of the aircraft electrical system.

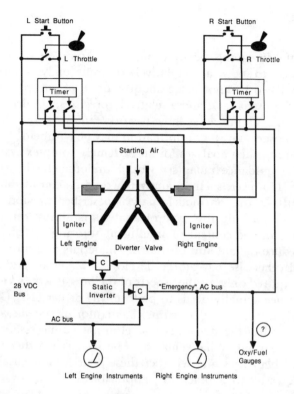

FIGURE 4.9 A more useful presentation of the electrical and mechanical systems associated with engine-starting procedures.

that the right be started first in the air. But based on the available information, there appears to be no reason in terms of the structure of the airplane why the right engine should be started first on the ground, because according to Figure 4.8, full AC power is available. Perhaps it is simply a good practice to habitually start the right engine first.

From this fairly extended example, it is clear that certain key justifications for the procedures for operating the airplane were not well supported by the mental model information in the manual. In some cases the information was not very clearly presented, as with the diverter valve, and could have been better presented by more explicit textual description and diagrams. In other cases, key information, such as the existence of the "emergency" AC bus and its relation to the other instruments and systems aboard the airplane, had been entirely suppressed. And finally, we see that some information that was presented, such as the internal details of the relay contactor box in Figure 4.8, was quite unnecessary, and was presented in extreme detail.

CONCLUSION

Although the foregoing examples may be incomplete or inaccurate, they do appear to show that a relatively rigorous analysis can be made of the how-it-works knowledge about a piece of equipment in the context of the user's task, and a relatively precise set of decisions can then be made about what how-it-works information should be presented to users and what information may be withheld.

Performing such analyses for an extremely complex system such as a missile guidance radar set would undoubtedly be very time consuming. However, such an analysis would be considerably easier than the full simulation model analysis described previously. More important, performing this type of analysis is almost certain to be cost effective in the context of intelligent tutoring systems because it would reduce the amount of tutoring materials and training tasks that would otherwise have to be developed. Materials and training would be required only for the aspects of the how-it-works knowledge that the trainee actually needs to perform his or her task. Given the current difficulty of constructing intelligent tutoring systems, any effort that will simplify the materials and eliminate unnecessary content is bound to pay off. What remains to be seen is whether there are other useful heuristics and whether these heuristics are usable on a large enough scale to be practically applicable.

ACKNOWLEDGMENT

Work on this chapter was supported in part by the Office of Naval Research, Personnel and Training Research Programs, Contract No. N00014-85-K-0138, NR 667-543.

REFERENCES

Card, S., Moran, T., & Newell, A. (1983). *The psychology of human–computer interaction.* Hillsdale, NJ: Lawrence Erlbaum Associates.

Gentner, D., & Gentner, D. R. (1983). Flowing waters or teaming crowds: Mental models of electricity. In D. Gentner & A. L. Stevens (Eds.), *Mental models* (pp. 99–130). Hillsdale, NJ: Lawrence Erlbaum Associates.

Halasz, F. G. & Moran, T. P. (1983). Mental models and problem solving in using a calculator. In *Proceedings of CHI'83 human factors in computing systems.* New York: Association for Computing Machinery.

Kieras, D. E. (1982). *What people know about electronic devices: A descriptive study* (Tech. Rep. No. 12), Ann Arbor, MI: University of Michigan.

Kieras, D. E. (in press). The role of cognitive simulation models in the development of advanced training and testing systems. In Frederiksen, N., Glaser, R., Lesgold, A., and Shafto, M. (Eds.), *Diagnostic monitoring of skill and knowledge acquisition.* Hillsdale, NJ: Lawrence Erlbaum Associates.

Kieras, D. E., & Bovair, S. (1984). The role of a mental model in learning to operate a device. *Cognitive Science, 8,* 255–273.

Kieras, D. E., & Polson, P. G. (1985). An approach to the formal analysis of user complexity. *International Journal of Man-Machine Studies, 22,* 365–394.

Intelligent
Instructional Design

Joseph Psotka
Army Research Institute
L. Dan Massey
BBN Laboratories
Sharon A. Mutter
Catholic University

The next important step in providing good and effective instruction after the knowledge has been clearly organized and thoroughly understood is to decide how best to teach it—the instructional design step. The design of intelligent tutoring systems must deal with constraints that are very much like those involved with human tutoring. The existing analyses of human tutoring provide essential components of this design. Collins and Stevens (1981) provided a foundation for research in this area. The knowledge that good teachers have about the goals and best techniques for instruction is still largely untapped. The complexities of analyzing even the simplest of teaching strategies and interactions with trainees have left conventional analytic techniques relatively uninformative and unproductive. However, ITSs force the rationalization of processes that are largely abstract and intuitive. The strength of ITS is that the design is then an open, inspectable system that can be critiqued by a community of experts and users. The analyses of good teaching practices and techniques as implemented on the computer tutor are subject to revision and improvement in ways inapplicable to the practices of human tutors.

The process of rationalizing instructional design forces other changes in perspectives and concerns. Above all, it pressures designers into taking a new perspective on human expertise. The careful analyses of SME knowledge and skills described in the section on Knowledge Acquisition are necessary grist for the instructional design process. They have energized a concern with the situational support that real-world training provides. Collins, Brown, and Newman (1987) offered a recent review of these concerns about situated learning in the form of a new pedagogy they call *cognitive apprenticeship*. Finally, a particular strength ITS brings to instructional design is a concern for learning and the fundamental cognitive science research on learning theories and machine learning.

As the authors in this section point out, there are several common components of instructional design. Merrill (1987) described the issues that good designers have followed in producing CAI during the past decade:

1. Selecting the goals
2. Selecting the strategies
3. Managing the sequence of interaction
4. Managing the learning

   For an ITS, these steps have somewhat different meaning and must be augmented as part of a continuing, interactive cycle.

Recent research on cognitive science and AI has raised additional issues and cognate components. The goals of instruction have become concerned with the content: strategic knowledge as well as procedural skills and concepts. The strategies of instruction must consider the methods that support learning: modeling, coaching, reflection, and exploratory environments for learning by doing; and sequencing instruction must be based on a decomposition of knowledge that specifies depth and breadth. Finally, managing the learning activities has to take into account the motivating effects of games, cooperation, and competition.

Goals

The goals of instruction need to broaden to include the new capabilities ITSs make possible, particularly for learning by simulated doing. The extensive work on acquiring and organizing knowledge from SMEs highlights the differences between formal knowledge as it is taught in schools and expert knowledge as it is practiced in everyday situations (Kurland & Tenney, chapter 5). The conceptual understanding expert troubleshooters have is thoroughly integrated with their problem-solving knowledge. The relations they perceive between structure, function, and specific scientific-domain perspectives operate fluently over a broad range of devices; for example, electrical, mechanical, magnetic. The SMEs go easily from design knowledge (e.g., electrical constraints or mechanical linkages) to troubleshooting. Their knowledge is not brittle because it is supported thoroughly by the environment and local context, and because it has been learned incrementally through a process of learning by doing. The studies reported in this volume provide the basis for incorporating teaching the semantics of procedures (Brown, Moran, & Williams, 1982) into regular classroom instruction.

Learning by doing generates flexible conceptual models, as opposed to the brittle theories generated by rote learning, because of the role of causal models in the learning process. Reactive environments do not teach these causal models in a rote fashion. Instead, the causal mental models can be simulated symbolically in complex computational environments and used to create seed crystals for knowledge restructuring in trainees. These seed crystals can then grow the structures that support the development of appropriate goals in the learning process.

Sequences

ITSs offer the potential of creating interactive, reactive environments and taking advantage of people's obvious ability to build on existing mental structures and add new declarative appendices to them with very little effort. Simply presenting a good clear story (theory/explanation/set of facts, etc.) is often sufficient evidence for dramatic knowledge restructuring, and forcing someone through the overhead of a complicated reactive environment is redundant and unnecessary. Where text and didactic explanations are insufficient, complex supporting structures, including simulations, can be introduced to make abstractions real and tenable.

The key component of an ITS that allows this capitalization on individualizing learning is an interactive instructional planner (Macmillan, Emme, & Berkowitz, chapter 8). Only by taking into account the diverse experiences of individual students can learning be accelerated and optimized. Only if a detailed history of student knowledge is used to design the sequence of instruction can knowledge be presented in the most favorable and learnable way. Instructional planners must make best use of the experiential knowledge of each student.

How does one get formal knowledge and experiential knowledge to connect? DiSessa (1982) points out convincingly that the observer will often fail to see what his or her theories do not predict. How can the invisible be made visible? Only with foreknowledge of the potential misconceptions and errors in thought that students bring to any situation. Formal knowledge must be differentiated sufficiently to contact individual experiences, and experiential knowledge must be accreted and abstracted sufficiently to contact general formal models. Hypothesis formation and problem solving would seem to force differentiation of mental model structures, but it is not clear where the pressures for inductive abstraction come from, if it is not from mediating experts and coaches. The potential strength of ITS designs is to provide this mediation flexibly.

SMEs are able to use "prototypical experiences" or "cliches" in their troubleshooting analyses. These cliches bear the burden of demonstrating ideal causal sequences and act as compendia or summaries of experience that make a good causal story. Orr (1986) argued that there is an ecological pattern to stories that helps communicate important system models. Bransford (1987, p. 1082) suggested that these stories help keep ideas and concepts alive and growing by evoking them in a useful social context in the way apprenticeship learning naturally and historically has evolved (Lave, Murtaugh, & de la Rocha, 1984). ITSs offer the opportunity of bringing this kind of situated apprenticeship learning into the classroom.

Methods

The complexity of instruction has never before been appreciated as clearly as now. The advent of computer technology has permitted the symbolic instantiation of teaching practices. The complex activities that go on effortlessly in classrooms or as part of on-the-job training cannot be understood without all the support this technology offers. It is particularly true that the connnections between scientific, causal understanding, design knowledge, encapsulated experience, and instruction are not well formed.

There are growing paradigms that provide patterns of understanding these connections between teaching and experience: reciprocal teaching, collaborative learning, situated learning, mediated learning, all focus on the powerful support that the environment and helpful experts (coaches, tutors, and good teachers) can provide in helping to restructure knowledge. Human tutors can in fact be seen as the dominant component of the current teaching and learning environment, and the growth of AI-based tutors will accentuate the importance of the nonhuman environment in shaping and fostering learning. Their help depends to a large extent on their ability to understand a novice's current state of knowledge and how it is expressed in performance. Tutors can provide the support that fosters knowledge growth by insisting on that help when it is needed and then fading away as the student acquires competence.

Significantly, the role of cognitive science and AI tools and environments has been largely to reify the abstract connectivity of conceptual structures to make them amenable to public inspection. Nowhere is this phenomenon clearer than in the ability of ICAI computer programs to manifest and actually run the mental skills of solving problems through procedural nets of functions (VanLehn, in press). Work on reifying declarative conceptual structures is proceeding apace and can in some sense be seen as the special focus of the IDE supportive environment (Russell, Moran, & Jordan, chapter 7; Russell, chapter 12; see also Lenat, Prakash, & Shepherd, 1986). The growth of these understanding perspectives has emboldened a vision of profoundly influencing mental skills of thinking and problem solving in much the same way as athletic and music coaches have influenced the growth of performance skills (Pirolli & Greeno, chapter 6). As ITSs adapt to increasing the ecological validity (Scribner, 1984) of their instruction, their designers will need to learn how concepts are acquired in an apprenticeship and social context.

Explanations

In earlier ITSs, such as SOPHIE II, the articulate expert was a set of pre-canned and handcrafted schemata stored at nodes of an augmented decision tree. The tree supported explanations within clearly determined contexts and histories, so misconceptions and support could be made explicit and cogent. Intelligent design for current ITSs tries to make these explanations interactive by generating them (Wilkins, Clancey, & Buchanan, chapter 9). Although declarative knowledge structures make it particularly appropriate to model students, diagnose their conceptual structures, and offer explanations, their ability to test the troubleshooting skills of trainees is somewhat limited. This is particularly the strength of active simulations. Simulations promote vigorous interaction and permit the use of scaffolding procedures such as those provided by reciprocal teaching (Palincsar & Brown, 1984). This scaffolding approach appears to acknowledge the fundamental difficulty with reactive environments: Students are apt to hop about from topic to topic without consistent guidance. Their peripatetic activity, it seems, stems from incomplete, and fragmented, causal theories about the domain. Using a consistent qualitative model in the simulation creates an orderly sequence of instruction that builds knowledge continuously.

Learning

Farr (1986) made a series of recommendations for improving long-term retention of knowledge and skills. Many of these are relevant for the design of ITSs. He emphasized the need to consider the ecological support every situation provides for tasks: This is particularly salient for troubleshooting tasks where the structure of the device itself will support problem solving. Support is in many modes; terminological and structural. For instance, within the real world the connectivity of any device is readily inspectable. Salient cues such as smells and sounds are ambient. And the visual form of the device is self-evident. All these supports provide a scaffolding for performance of the task and act as powerful retrieval cues for the troubleshooting process. They need to be incorporated judiciously into a simulation for learning.

Second, Farr suggested that during the training task analysis, a designer should rate each task component for its memorability and complexity. Given this rating it would be possible to selectively provide training beyond criterion to insulate these skills from decay with disuse (Hagman & Rose, 1983). For this, we need to develop an understanding that is sufficiently precise to predict the course of forgetting over time for all types of tasks as a function of the cognitive demands of the learning task, the conditions of learning, and the nature of an individual's learning ability. Also, it presupposes a task decomposition into meaningful units, and this is not easy. Generally, when tasks are extracted from their natural situations, they lose much of their meaning, and a significant part of their motivating force.

One of the most influential components of learning is the motivation of the learner. In general the interactive environments and tutoring systems that are the products of the efforts described in this volume are highly compelling and motivating. In part they follow the advice given by researchers (e.g., Malone, 1981) to design systems that are intrinsically motivating. But in the main they induce a spirit of cooperation and benign competition by designing a system that gives trainees the personally supportive and rewarding help of a good coach and teacher.

Issues in Developing an Intelligent Tutor for a Real-World Domain: Training in Radar Mechanics

Laura C. Kurland
Yvette J. Tenney
Bolt Beranek and Newman Labs, Inc.

INTRODUCTION

This chapter discusses instructional issues relevant to the design and implementation of the HAWK MACH-III intelligent maintenance tutor. The goal for the HAWK MACH-III system, currently in the early stages of implementation, is to teach novice radar mechanics to maintain and troubleshoot a complex electronic system, the AN/MPQ-57 HIPIR radar of the HAWK Air Defense Missile System.

This chapter accompanies two other chapters in this volume. A project introduction and design review may be found in the chapter 14 by deBruin, Massey, and Roberts, and chapter 3 by Tenney and Kurland describes the results of several cognitive studies of radar mechanics with varying levels of expertise.

Training Context

The training site for this work is the U.S. Army Air Defense Artillery School (USAADASCH) at Fort Bliss in El Paso, Texas. After an introductory course on basic electronics, novice radar mechanics (called 24 Charlies or 24 C's) begin instruction on the High Power HAWK radar. Their instruction takes place in two different settings: classroom lectures ("conferences") and hands-on exercises ("practicals") with the actual radar unit. In the classroom, students are lectured on the theory of the radar, using functional block diagrams, and are taught how to trace signals, using the wiring schematics. Approximately 15 students attend the classroom lectures. In the practical exercises, students are first given a brief review of the functional theory ("practical" theory). Then a particular fault is inserted in the radar and they are coached through the relevant documentation (the daily and weekly check procedures, the wiring schematics, and the fault isolation procedures) until the fault is discovered and fixed. The number of students in the practical exercises ranges between five and eight.

Tests are given in both training contexts. Classroom tests consist of written short-answer and multiple-choice items. Practical exams consist of two timed parts: One part of the test requires the student to locate parts and name their function. For the second part, students must do three things: (a) perform the daily and weekly checks (and adjustments) correctly, (b) use the checks to both identify fault symptoms and to jump to the correct set of fault isolation procedures, and (c) locate and troubleshoot the planted fault via the procedures and the wiring schematics. Students are also scored on equipment use and safety.

The Radar Mechanic's Job

The radar maintenance mechanic's job is to ensure that the radar performs certain functions. The HIPIR (High-Powered Illuminator Radar), like any radar, uses radio waves (the signal) to detect targets and determine their range and direction. (*Radar* stands for radio automatic detection and ranging.) The mechanic needs to ensure that the transmitter not only produces a signal strong enough to travel to and from the target, but that the signal is clean and correctly modulated (shaped in a particular frequency pattern).

Another major function that the mechanic must be concerned with is how the radar processes the received signal. Because the target's range and rate of approach can be calculated from the differences between the transmitted and received signals, a mechanic must make sure that the stronger noise from the transmitter and surrounding area does not overwhelm the weaker received signal.

Third, a mechanic must also ensure that the radar calculates a target's anticipated flight from the received signal so that the antenna accurately moves with the (i.e., *tracks*) the target, rather than lags behind it. If a jamming signal is present, the mechanic needs to make sure that the radar can detect its presence and continue to track the target correctly.

To properly maintain the radar so that it performs these functions accurately, the mechanic needs to understand how the radar works and how to perform highly complex, and often dangerous, procedures.

Problem Areas for Novices

To find out in what areas novices have difficulty, we interviewed several mechanics of varying experience to determine their mental model of how the radar works. We then observed these mechanics troubleshooting the radar. (The results of these studies are reported in chapter 3 by Tenney & Kurland.) Following the troubleshooting observations, we asked the instructor (an expert) and an intermediate mechanic what made troubleshooting difficult for them. Their comments were vastly different, as described below.

The intermediate mechanic (5 years of experience) described what was hard for him and for mechanics more junior than he:

> You have to trace circuits in the schematics.
>
> You have not worked on the circuit much.
>
> You have to go through many steps.
>
> The FIP [Fault Isolation Procedures] is not adequate enough for the problem.

In contrast, the troubleshooting expert (13 years of experience) mentioned two things that made troubleshooting difficult for him:

> When test indications are ambiguous, you have to spend a long time on the wrong path.
>
> When the schematics are not detailed enough to show the actual wiring.

What is striking about these comments is what is and is not mentioned. The less-experienced mechanic expressed difficulty in extracting and understanding the relevant information from the detailed documentation. He was concerned with the number of steps to follow, because each step could lead to a possible mistake or difficulty. In contrast, the expert was comfortable with the documentation and had trouble only when he believed the documentation lacked enough detail. The expert did not mention the number of steps (and, indeed, from observing him troubleshoot, was not at all disturbed by the length of the procedures). His comment about pursuing the wrong path suggests that he was tackling the problem in an organized manner, rather than merely following an arbitrary set of instructions.

Problems other than documentation are also indicated from these comments. The less-experienced mechanic's second comment, "You have not worked on a circuit much," closely relates to a comment made by a mechanic with one year of work experience who said that he could not describe any of the components in a particular location because he "hadn't replaced them yet." These comments indicate that a novice mechanic's functional understanding of how the system works is strongly tied to his or her actual work with the components, rather than what was learned from the documentation or in school.

These comments by the mechanics, the preliminary mental models' interviews and our troubleshooting observations (plus the struggles of those project members who are not engineers) indicate that the difficulties novices experience fall into five areas:

1. *Information Overload:* The information in the documentation that is critical for troubleshooting is either too difficult for a novice to extract or is simply not available.

2. *Lack of a Hierarchical Organization:* Novices do not have a hierarchically organized, cognitive framework that is suitable for troubleshooting. An appropriate framework is needed to store and recall relevant functional and procedural knowledge.

3. *Inadequate Mental Model:* Novices lack a functional understanding of how the radar works, and thus do not troubleshoot logically. A well-elaborated mental model helps reduce the cognitive overload by reducing the need for recalling dozens of fixed procedures or searching through the manuals for them.

4. *Inadequate System Understanding:* Novices' inadequate mental models of the radar are partially attributable to missing underlying system concepts. Novices need to have models of the radar's devices and how these devices are designed to work together for certain radar functions.

5. *Lack of Strategies:* Aside from the lack of an appropriate mental model, novices lack a functional understanding of the FIP and its implicit strategies. Novices need to develop robust, flexible troubleshooting strategies that are based on a functional understanding of both the system and the procedures in order to cope with unexpected occurrences while troubleshooting and to recover from any errors they may have made.

These issues are discussed within the context of specific problem areas. The first part of this chapter describes the differences between novice and expert radar mechanics, with special attention paid to novices' difficulties with the documentation and inadequacies in their understanding of the radar system. The second part describes how the HAWK intelligent maintenance tutor can help novices to learn how to maintain and troubleshoot the radar.

COGNITIVE TASK ANALYSIS

The cognitive task analysis begins with documentation problems that appear to hinder novice mechanics from efficiently and accurately learning to maintain and troubleshoot the radar. These problems pertain to three areas: (a) the organization of the schematics and curriculum by functional blocks, (b) the actual wiring schematics, and (c) the FIP.

Functional Block Organization

The HIPIR is a very complex system that contains thousands of electrical, mechanical, and RF (microwave) components. To document it fully, a hierarchical organization is required. The current curriculum is organized around the hierarchy provided in the schematics.

Functional Block Description.

In the schematics, the radar is broken down by "functional blocks." The highest level, as shown in Figure 5.1, depicts the most important signals flowing between the major subsystems (the large blocks) in the radar. As can be seen, the simplest view that the student sees is still quite complex—there are many signals. Four of the large blocks, the functional subsystems, pertain to discrete physical entities: the transmitter, receiver, signal processor, and the target intercept computer. The other subsystems are physically distributed throughout the radar.

Most of these functional blocks can be broken down into the units that compose them. For example, the functional block called the "receiving system" can be broken down into three functional blocks: the signal circuits, the feedthrough nulling (noise–cancellation) circuits, and the local oscillator. Figure 5.2 shows our simplification of the receiver's three functional blocks and the major signals that flow between them. In Figure 5.3, the three functional blocks have been "exploded" to show the functional units that compose them. This is the official documentation's top-level view of the receiver block.

The breakdown of this functional organization seems very logical and hierarchically organized. The narrative section of the schematics (and the program of instruction) follows this same hierarchical functional organization. Two questions immediately come to mind: Why are novices having difficulty retaining this hierarchically organized information and using it while troubleshooting? Is this the

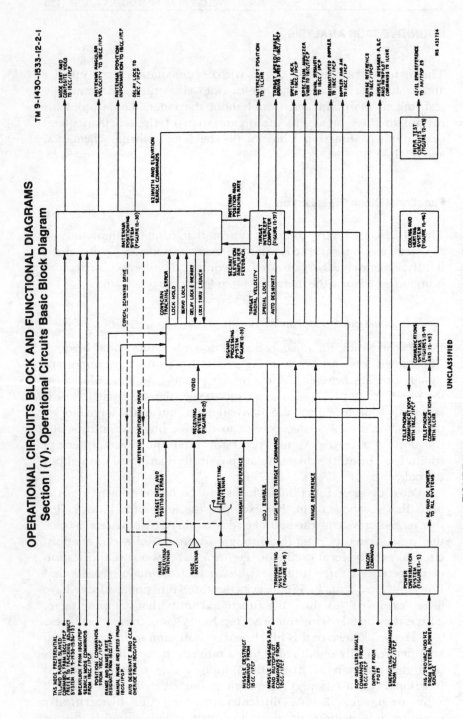

OPERATIONAL CIRCUITS BLOCK AND FUNCTIONAL DIAGRAMS
Section I (V). Operational Circuits Basic Block Diagram

TM 9-1430-1533-12-2-1

UNCLASSIFIED

FIGURE 5.1 High-level overview: Functional block diagram.

Simplified Receiver

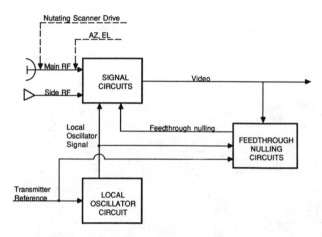

FIGURE 5.2 Functional block diagram of the receiving system.

hierarchy used by experts, and if not, what sort of hierarchy (presuming there is one) is most useful for troubleshooting?

Physical-Functional Mismatch

Having described the documentation's organization, we shall now look at the problems novices have attaining the hierarchy of the functional information in a real-world context, the radar itself. Figure 5.4 shows the physical representation of the receiver. The local oscillator, a single physical object as well as a functional block, is easily located in the bottom right corner of the receiver housing. However, the signal circuits and the feedthrough nulling circuits are nowhere to be seen. Where are they? If one looks at the bottom left corner of the receiver housing, there is a physical entity called the "receiver assembly," which consists of two boxes: The top box is called the frequency converter and the bottom box is the receiver IF [sometimes called receiver A-1]. The signal circuits and the feedthrough nulling circuits are physically distributed *between* the frequency converter box and the receiver IF box. The physical distribution of these functional units is hand drawn over the detailed view of the receiving system functional block diagram in Figure 5.5. This physical distribution is not explicitly shown in the documentation.

It seems that even if a novice mechanic fully comprehends the functional information presented in the classroom lecture and has stored this information in a hierarchy exactly like the schematic's functional organization, he or she will still be faced with the strikingly

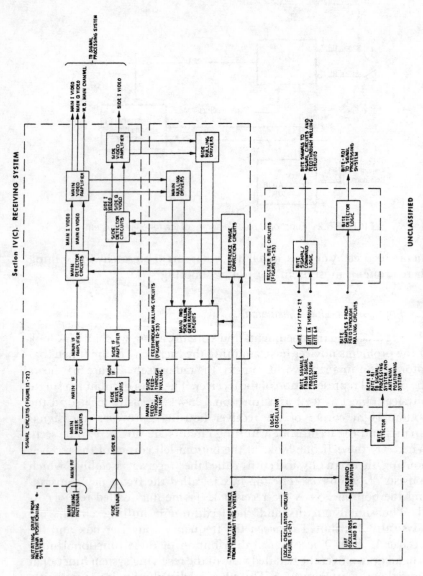

FIGURE 5.3 More detailed receiver functional block diagram.

UNCLASSIFIED

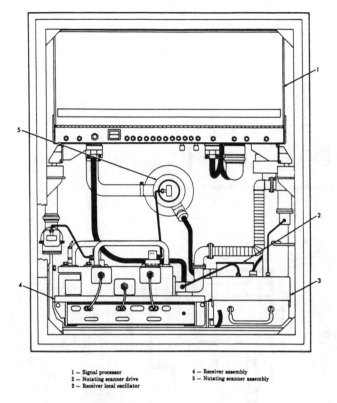

1 — Signal processor   4 — Receiver assembly
2 — Nutating scanner drive   5 — Nutating scanner assembly
3 — Receiver local oscillator

FIGURE 5.4 Physical view of receiver.

different physical organization of the radar. The physical organization is important, because the mechanic has to know where the component is located and whether that component is measurable or replaceable. Thus the mechanic has the difficult task of relating the knowledge that is organized by the functional block hierarchy to the physical organization of the radar (and vice versa). Resolving the mismatch between the differing functional and physical organizations is important, because the likelihood of a functional entity coinciding with the physical entity (such as with the local oscillator), is fairly small.

A Different Functional Hierarchy

When we asked the expert troubleshooter to explain the receiver's function and some troubleshooting problems involving the receiver, he provided several representations, one of which is shown in Figure 5.6. This drawing neatly summarizes the feedthrough nulling (FTN) function by showing three entities:

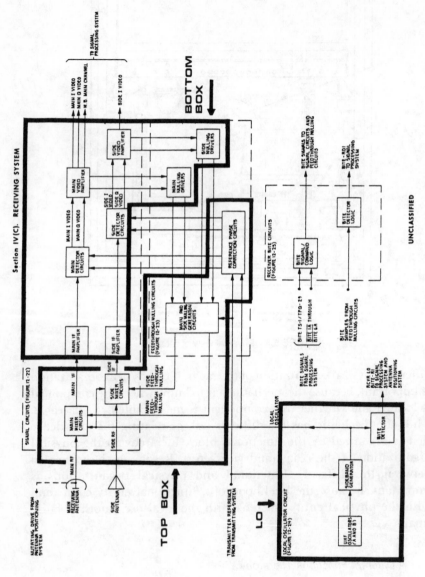

FIGURE 5.5 Physical distribution of functional units in the receiver.

1. Major physical components (the frequency converter box and the receiver A-1 (IF) box).[1]

2. The adjustable or replaceable parts (mixer crystals [CR 3-6], wires [W2, W4, W5], phase adjust knob, and the FTN fail lamp).

3. The flow and relationship of important signals (f_t, range, doppler, IF, coding, RF reference, Main Q, Main I, Side Q, Side I, and FTN. Also note the inverse relationship of the signals at the bottom left).

Note that this summary diagram of the FTN process does not show any of the detailed functional blocks of the receiving system, except for measurable or replaceable parts. It also shows the frequency converter and the receiver assembly A-1 boxes as separate physical entities, even though they are replaced as one unit. This is because a mechanic can test and replace the wires that carry four signals (the main and side I and Q signals) flowing between the two boxes. There are no boxes labeled "signal circuits" and "feedthrough nulling circuits." Instead, there is a box labeled "FTN (noise cancellation)." This label refers to the *function* that cancels feedthrough noise, rather than to the specific functional block called the "feedthrough nulling circuits." The function encompasses both the signal circuits and feedthrough nulling circuits functional blocks.

There are several pieces of evidence indicating that this is not just a nomenclature difference, but a difference between how experts organize their radar troubleshooting knowledge and how the documentation organizes the radar.

Figure 5.7 was drawn by the same expert during another interview and is a summary of the same FTN function previously shown in Figure 5.6. Figure 5.7 shows the antennas and the signal flow through the entire receiver, which has been broken down into two parts— the receiver front end and the FTN circuits ("FTN ckts"). Below the label "FTN ckts" is a box that represents the entire receiver assembly. Emerging from it is a signal with an arrow that loops around and intersects with the signal going into the "FTN ckts" box. The arrow symbol on the signal represents a dynamically tuned functional feedback loop, the FTN cancellation loop.

Both of the expert's diagrams show the FTN cancellation feedback loop, rather than the functional blocks for the signal circuits and feedthrough nulling circuits. The loop encompasses both circuit types, the physical components, and the signals flowing into and out of the components. Everything encompassed by the FTN loop is

---

[1]His drawing shows these boxes twice, because he was explaining how the RF REF path and the Main RF path go through these two boxes and link up.

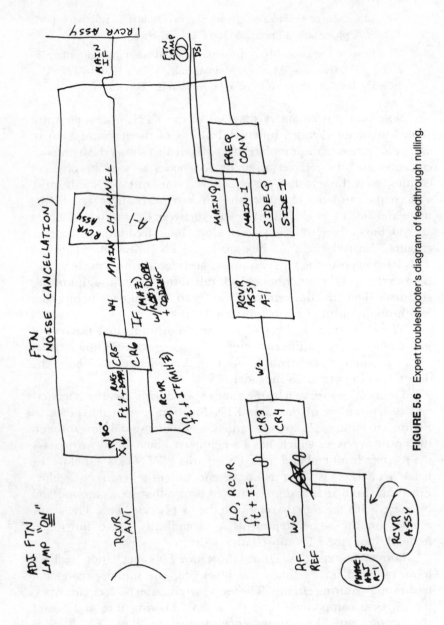

FIGURE 5.6 Expert troubleshooter's diagram of feedthrough nulling.

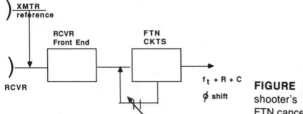

FIGURE 5.7 Expert trouble-shooter's summary diagram of FTN cancellation.

represented by the label, "FTN ckts." In other words, the feedthrough nulling loop is an important functional organizer for the expert troubleshooter, not merely a specific functional block. The loop appears to be an important concept for troubleshooting, because there are many loops in the radar. From our interviews, an understanding of loops distinguishes experts from novices. The loop concept is also a significant concept in the design of radars and other complex systems. In "System Concepts and Knowledge Organization," loops are discussed in considerable detail.

More support for this viewpoint comes from a cued-recall experiment we conducted, which "failed" because it did not fully discriminate between the expert and novice mechanics. For each subsystem of the radar, boxes were labeled with the documentation's functional block names on a sheet of paper. A list of signals relevant to that subsystem was provided on the side of the paper. A sample is shown in Figure 5.8. The subjects were to show the signals that went into, came from, or went between the boxes. During the untimed test, subjects were not given access to their documents. These sheets were given to a group of six maintenance mechanics and two instructors; their radar experience ranged from recent graduates to 30 years of experience. Although the two instructors (13 and 30 years experience) performed somewhat better than the other mechanics (possibly because the instructors were very familiar with the documentation's view of the radar), performance was generally very poor, even for the more experienced mechanics. Because the data from the mental models interviews indicated that these two instructors understood the flow of signals very well, it seems that the functional block labels used in the test were not a suitable measure of a mechanic's functional knowledge for two possible reasons: (a) mechanics think of signal flow emanating from one physical component to another (e.g., from the frequency converter to receiver IF) instead of from one functional block to another (e.g., from the signal circuits to FTN circuits), and/or (b) some of the functional block labels have come to mean something else that is more generalized.

Looking closely at the hierarchical organization of the documentation, the functional block is a radar engineer's classification of the circuit types contained within a subsystem. In other words,

Simplified Receiver

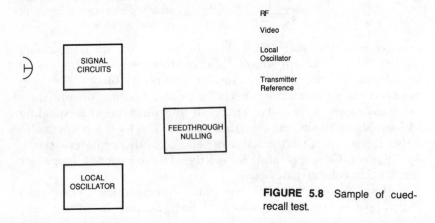

FEEDTHROUGH NULLING

SIGNAL CIRCUITS

LOCAL OSCILLATOR

RF

Video

Local Oscillator

Transmitter Reference

FIGURE 5.8 Sample of cued-recall test.

it is a taxonomic organization, rather than a functional organization designed for troubleshooting. This taxonomic view does not really help a mechanic to troubleshoot, because it does not indicate which physical parts (measurable or replaceable) are involved, nor does it show the causal flow of signal information through the physical system. This information is vital for troubleshooting. Thus, the data from our interviews seem to indicate that even though experts certainly understand the documentation's functional (taxonomic) hierarchy this does not appear to be the same hierarchy in which they store their troubleshooting knowledge and therefore is not recalled easily. This does not mean that they do not have any functional hierarchy, rather, their hierarchy appears to be organized by higher order functions (e.g., "cancels noise") and contains the knowledge of which physical components perform these functions, what information and power signals they require and produce, and how that information flows through the system and is relevant to the system's operation.

Novices have difficulty with the documentation's functional block diagrams because the documentation does not explicitly show the physical organization or the causal flow of signals through the system. Thus, the physical-functional mismatch makes the functional information difficult to comprehend and retain.

The instructional implications of this different hierarchy and the issues surrounding physical organization and signal flow, particularly loops, are discussed in a forthcoming section after other documentation problems are described.

Schematics

Tracing signals through the schematics is an extremely complex task for a number of reasons: The schematics are full of abstract symbols that are, in essence, another language a mechanic must learn to "read." Second, the schematics are organized by a radar engineer's taxonomy, that is, the functional blocks cut across physical units, instead of being organized for troubleshooting, which requires knowing what functions are performed by specific physical components. Finally, it is difficult to extract the causal flow of signals from the schematics, partly because the schematics are organized by the functional blocks and partly because of the overwhelming detail. These problems are discussed in this section.

Reading Schematics

As in the case of learning to read text, students must not only learn to decode the symbols into meaningful terms (such as matching the symbol to a part or identifying a specific signal), they must also come to comprehend what those terms mean in the system's operation. It is not surprising that novice mechanics "read" much slower than more experienced mechanics, because of problems with decoding the schematic symbols. In Figure 5.9, a sample page from the schematics is shown.

Decoding the symbology of the schematics is very difficult for a number of reasons, one being the density and complexity of the symbology on the page. Each symbol represents a specific device on the radar. One aspect of matching symbols to parts pertains to the categorical labels and location of parts. In both the schematics and fault isolation procedures, the radar parts have cryptic alphanumeric labels (such as jacks [J], plugs [P], wires [W], and assemblies [A], which contain many parts). For example, item A3A2W1 is not the same as item A2A3W1. A3 in the first item is an assembly that contains A2W1 and is at the same level as A2 in the second item, which is an assembly that contains A3W1.

Another complication is that parts are not always labeled consistently in the documentation or on the actual physical radar component, making the part identification process harder. Sometimes, the whole code label is listed (A3A2W1), other times it is listed as W1, leaving the reader uncertain about whether he or she is referring to the correct W1 or not.

The less experienced mechanics that we have observed generally do not know where these alphanumerically referenced items are located, because they do not really understand the alphanumeric categorization

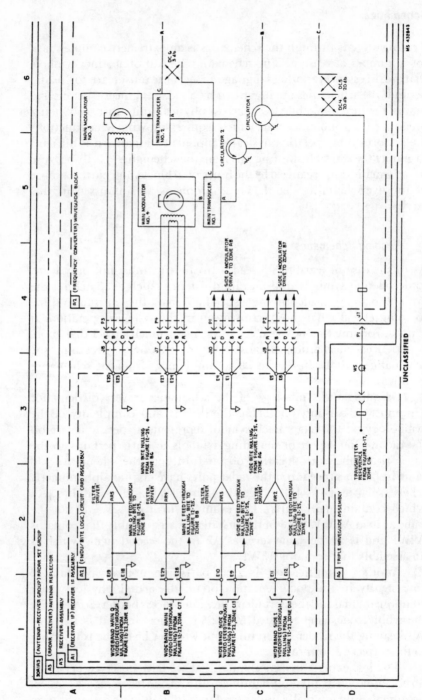

FIGURE 5.9 Sample page of schematic.

system. Mechanics prefer to use the parts' names for those parts that do have names (usually component devices, such as *isomodulator*) or a physically descriptive term commonly used in the mechanic "culture," such as *rear tower*. Wires, jacks, and plugs generally do not have names, only alphanumeric labels. Thus, novice mechanics usually have to cope with several different terms for the same device component and an ambiguous alphanumeric categorization system for nondevice components. It is important to know which part to measure or replace, because an error can consume vast amounts of time and get the mechanic helplessly lost in the Fault Isolation Procedures.

From our troubleshooting observations of mechanics with different levels of experience, schematic decoding, like reading text, generally appears to steadily increase in speed with experience and familiarity with a circuit. In fact, some experienced mechanics have mentioned that they only refer to the schematics for specific details, such as particular pin numbers, for testing voltages. We have observed that experienced mechanics who are "familiar with a circuit" utilize the schematics as a means of refreshing their memory or filling in details. They appear to have a general framework or knowledge of that particular problem space, which includes the physical components and their location on the radar, and signal flow between those components. This relevant background knowledge enables them to read the schematics more easily, just as background knowledge helps in reading comprehension. Because experts know more about the system, they are better able to make sense of the schematics. The novices, who have the most to gain from external documentation, benefit from it the least.

Thus, like reading comprehension skills, signal tracing is really several skills, decoding symbols and matching them to physical components; and connecting those components through signal flow. Novice problems with finding signal flow in the schematics are discussed in the following section.

Organization Problems and Signal Flow

When following troubleshooting procedures, a mechanic must be able to quickly find the relevant signals or components on the radar from the schematics, but this is difficult to do for several reasons: First, the functional block organization obscures any sense of continuity; second, the schematics contain so many details that the mechanic has difficulty extracting important information and relating it to the physical reality of the radar; and finally, the schematics do not provide critical functional information, such as signal relationships or the direction of signal flow.

Functional block problems. In the case of the receiver, one of the simplest subsystems, each functional box (e.g., the local oscillator, the signal circuits, and the feedthrough nulling circuits) shown previously in the detailed functional block diagram in Figure 5.3, has been expanded even further to show the complex wiring details. For example, Figure 5.9 is just one of three schematic pages for the signal circuit functional block. Thus, one functional block's set[2] of schematic drawings can spread across as many as 14 pages of spaghettilike drawings. Because each page of the wiring schematics is visually organized into four rows (A–D) and eight columns, one functional block may contain a total of 100 or so columns.

Each schematic page is like a small window; the novice can only see a tiny portion of the circuit at a time. This obscures signal flow. Signals coming from or going into another part of the circuit or another subsystem "pop" in or out of the page. (They appear as a line ending in a dot with a label indicating the row and column of a set of functional block diagrams.) To see the "full picture" of a circuit, mechanics must constantly flip the pages back and forth to trace a signal from its origin to its destination—and simultaneously keep track of whatever troubleshooting objective they had, too. If any one wire is shorted, all the wires carrying that signal—which may be in every area of the radar—will be affected, and the mechanic will have to track down every wire carrying that signal through the schematics. For the novice, tracing signals through the schematics is, in some sense, a massive distraction task.

A related difficulty to signal tracing pertains to the problem of nomenclature. Oftentimes when signals go into different subsystems, the name of the signal changes, because its purpose in that subsystem also changes. Without an explicitly designated reference to these nomenclature changes, a cognitive gap can occur. When hundreds of signals disappear or appear into or out of thin air, the functional organization of knowledge can be seriously impaired.

Relationship to physical layout. When troubleshooting, mechanics are also hindered by the schematics' lack of spatial relationship to the physical layout of the radar. The novice constantly has to face the difficult task of trying to bridge the gap between the 4-row × 8-column paper representation and 3-dimensional equipment. In the schematics, components are shown in a highly abstract manner,

---

[2]Each set of schematic pages for a functional block is confusingly called a "Figure."

irrespective of functional importance, size, location, or shape. In other words, all parts are shown at the same level of detail. As the expert troubleshooter/instructor put it, " . . . in the book, it looks nice and straight, and then you open the door, and it's just a glob of green"

For example, in Figure 5.9, the triple waveguide assembly (a large hoselike apparatus) is the same size as a minute, inaccessible amplifier inside a circuit card and a 4-inch coaxial cable. Similarly, components that appear to be directly connected on paper may actually be a considerable distance apart. The novice mechanic needs to know where components are located, whether they are accessible or measurable, and what signals the components process or create. Some components and connections are hidden in deep recesses and may be seen only if the radar is completely dismantled or by a cross-sectional view of the radar. Unnecessary time expenditures could be avoided if the schematics explicitly indicated where components are located and whether they are accessible.

Similarly, a novice mechanic runs into difficulty if he or she wants to know what a neighboring physical component does. If a neighboring component is categorized under a different taxonomic function, the mechanic will literally have to search through each page of the schematics for other functional blocks to find how that component is involved. Furthermore, some components perform more than one function, and thus will appear in more than one functional block. Because it is difficult to determine what component signals come from and go to, physical proximity of components can be easily confused with function, an occurrence that has been observed with novice mechanics.

Signals. A third reason that mechanics are hindered from troubleshooting by the schematics pertains to missing or inexplicit functional signal information. This includes signal relationships, various types of signal inputs for devices, and the causal flow of signals through the system.

Because the schematics do not explicitly show the relationship of signals, the likelihood that a novice could derive signal relationships alone without any instructional support is very low. Indeed, because the function of many parts in the radar involve complex physics and engineering theory, even radar engineers and experienced mechanics must struggle to comprehend what the system is really doing. An example of an important signal relationship that is never explicitly shown in the schematics can be seen in the bottom left corner of the expert's diagram (figure 5.6). The two wave signals ($\curvearrowright$ $\curvearrowleft$) that are shown with an inverse relationship (180° out of phase) are a critical part of the feedthrough nulling process in the receiver. An understanding of how signals relate to one another is important for troubleshooting, because that knowledge can help reduce the problem space.

Another item missing from the schematics that would help reduce the problem space is an indication of causal flow in the schematics. The causal flow of signals occurs when certain input signals cause a component to produce a certain type of signal, which in turn, causes another component to react a certain way, and so on. For example, the sample schematic, Figure 5.9, does not explicitly show the general flow of information going from left to right. The arrowheads in the diagram symbolize specific types of connections, not signal flow. This particular schematics represents only a small piece of the expert's diagram. At the intersection of rows A–D and column 1, the four feedthrough nulling signals[3] are shown "popping in" from the signal circuit functional block's set of schematics, located several pages away. Thus, because of the functional block organization and the lack of causal flow, it is nearly impossible for a novice to attain a mental representation like the expert's drawing, Figure 5.6.

The causal flow of signals entails understanding the concept of information and distinguishing that from power. From our observations and from those in the Pittsburgh HumMRO study on Air Force mechanics (Gitomer, 1984, Glaser, et al., 1985), novice mechanics tend to think in terms of electrical power, rather than in terms of information, as experts do. Reasons as to why novices have this tendency follow.

First of all, novices may not understand the functional difference between power and information signals. A student mechanic needs to know that a *power* input signal simply *enables* (energizes) a device component to operate. In contrast, an *information* signal *controls* either how the device operates (as in the range of motor speeds) or how the device processes incoming information and produces a signal. Thus, the information signal controls the quality of the signal produced, that is, whether it is a noisy, absent, or invalid signal.

Furthermore, a power signal[4] is either present or absent. However, an information signal may appear in any one of several "energy" forms: electrical, mechanical, or RF. The information is carried by the *pattern* of the energy form. The following are examples of energy patterns that represent information: electrical—a varying voltage from 0 to 115 VAC; RF—the modulations imposed on the returning RF

---

[3]Main I and Q, side I and Q.

[4]In the radar, power is generally an electrical signal, except in the transmitter, where the RF carrier signal is produced.

signal; and mechanical—the amount or rate at which an antenna turns.

Second, because the causal flow of signals is not shown in the schematics, problems and misconceptions can arise, particularly when mechanical devices and RF devices are involved. Signal tracing is not merely a matter of flipping through schematics pages looking for electrical signals. Mechanical or electromechanical devices, such as gears or synchros, provided mechanical information signals. Although the mechanical connection is shown in the schematics, student mechanics do not understand that when a mechanical device turns, it produces a signal (mechanical information) that is part of a *signal path* (such as a loop).

Moreover, mechanical devices often perform multiple functions, which often means they participate in several signal paths. This is not readily apparent from the schematics, because there are no arrows indicating that the mechanical connection is part of a particular signal path. Without any indication of causal direction or information flow, the involvement of mechanical devices is often overlooked or misconstrued, particularly when they are involved in loops.

Third, novice mechanics also appear unaware that many radar components (and components in other complex electronic systems), may not only require more than one input, but may require more than one power and information input signal to operate. Because the functional block organization of the schematics can often obscure a device's inputs and because multiple-input devices are not commonly found in daily life, it may be difficult for novices to think in terms other than a single power input.

Distinguishing power from information signals becomes important when a component simultaneously needs *both* power and information signals to operate. For example, a three-input device may produce a signal only when it has two power signals (e.g., 5 and 10 VDC) to energize its circuits and one information signal (e.g., a mechanical signal indicating how fast something is turning) to control its operation. If any of three input signals is absent, the device does not operate and no signal is produced. However, if the power signals are present, and the information signal is present, but poor in quality (e.g., the mechanical signal is barely there), the device could work and produce some kind of signal, however bad a signal (noisy, wrong value, etc.) it may be.

Thus, novices are faced with many difficulties when they wish to trace signals through the schematics. They must learn to decode the symbology, decipher obscure alphanumeric labels, and match them to the radar's physical components. Additionally, the organization of the schematics and its highly detailed representation often obscures or does not explicitly show the causal flow of signals through the system's components or the important signal relationships. Novices who cannot find the information in the schematics will have an incomplete picture of the problem space, that is, the physical components and the signals that flow between these components, as well as the functions they perform.

Fault Isolation Procedures

As with the schematics, it is difficult to relate the Fault Isolation Procedures to the physical layout of the radar. Sometimes there is a physical description of where to look for the relevant component or signal; more often it is categorically labeled with an alphanumeric code, for example, A3A2W1 or A2A3W1.

As previously described, the code labels on the radar parts do not lend themselves to immediate identification; neither are these labels consistently applied. Thus, it is possible to have two W1s in the same physical location, such as the receiver, even though each wire is technically classified as belonging to two separate assemblies. If the FIP simply asks the mechanic to measure pins (A,E) and (C,H) on W1, the potential for error is quite high.

Another problem is that the FIP is designed for a single mechanic to troubleshoot a fault. Thus, although there may be easier, more direct ways to troubleshoot the radar with assistance, the FIP cannot assume this situation. For example, the easiest way to test a particular signal may be to see if a voltage is generated when a handwheel is turned, but if the handwheel is on another side of the radar from where the signal can be measured, this is not a viable procedure for one mechanic to perform alone. As a result, procedures are often more complicated and less efficient than if two mechanics were present.

A third problem is that there are no diagrams shown in the FIP to relate the component parts to their inputs and outputs. It is difficult to understand whether the signal carries power or information signals or both. This information can sometimes be gleaned from the schematics, once all the components' inputs and outputs have been located, or from the mechanic's functional knowledge, but obtaining this information is very difficult to do, as explained in the previous section on the schematics.

The FIP is not designed to locate every possible fault[5], but to reduce the search to a replaceable unit, not the specific faulted component contained by the replaceable unit. Even though this does

---

[5]Otherwise, it would be several magnitudes larger than it already is. (It is quite cumbersome as it stands.)

not appear to a be problem at first glance, it can prevent the mechanic from acquiring a functional understanding of how the system works. Because the mechanic never gets to test inaccessible components within a replaceable unit, he or she may not understand why that unit behaves as it does.

For example, recall that the whole receiver assembly contains the frequency converter box and the receiver IF box. Neither box is separately replaceable, nor can it be opened up. However, there are connections going into, out of, and between the two boxes, that allow measurements to be taken. The FIP directs the mechanic to selectively measure some or all of these inputs and outputs, depending on the symptoms. If an amplifier within the receiver IF (A-1) assembly box were faulted, the whole receiver assembly would have to be replaced, because this would be the smallest battery-replaceable unit. In this case, the mechanic would be unable to determine what specific item was faulted inside the receiver IF assembly box, because he or she would be unable to open it up to measure anything inside it; the mechanic could only measure the inputs going into and outputs coming out of the receiver IF unit. Because the components within are inaccessible, novices may not develop an understanding of how these components affect the system's operation.

Finally, the FIP's strategies are implicit, not explicit; the actual strategies are the *pattern of branching,* which may not be the most time efficient or logical. The mechanic implements the FIP's strategies by branching from one procedure's steps to another procedure's steps, depending on the test results obtained during those steps. Thus if, during the course of testing a component for certain signals, a mechanic finds that one of the component's signals is missing or has the incorrect voltages, the mechanic branches to another set of procedures. The idea is to systematically test certain areas of the circuit that may contain a fault. If an area does not have a fault, the FIP may refer the mechanic back to the original procedure, or it may refer the mechanic to still another procedural branch to test another area.

Difficulties arise from this implicit branching structure. Redundant test steps are a frequent problem, because the current set of procedures cannot assume the mechanic has arrived at that point without performing certain prerequisite tests, that is, several different branches may eventually lead to one particular procedural branch. For efficiency reasons, a mechanic has to selectively discard certain steps, which may lead to errors, because he or she may omit a critical test. Ambiguity in the FIP's branching instructions is a serious problem for mechanics. After each branch point, the procedures say to "go [return] to entry status", leaving the mechanic wondering whether to return to the last procedure or any of the previous branches that he or she may have taken. Inaccuracies in the manual or a single testing error can exacerbate this situation by sending the mechanic down an endless series of procedural branches or into an infinite loop. Some mechanics have called this frustrating experience "branch and get lost," and for this reason many use the FIP only as a last resort.

The implicit nature of the FIP (the branching pattern) does not provide the mechanic with any sense of why or where testing is done, or what has been ruled out. The FIP does not explain the functional importance of the signal that is being tested, that is, the function of the signal in terms of system operation. To comprehend what the FIP is testing, the mechanic must already have a mental model of the system's circuitry and integrate this model with the FIP's procedures. A mechanic who does not have a suitably complex mental model of how the system's circuits are supposed to operate has no choice but to try to solve the problem in a rote fashion, either by following the FIP or by trying whatever worked before, both of which novices have been observed doing for the radar and in other situations. Thus, to effectively utilize the FIP, novices need to have a functional understanding of how the system works, or a mental model. This issue will be discussed in the next section.

Mental Models and Strategic Reasoning

An appropriate mental model is expected to enhance problem solving in a troubleshooting context for several reasons. First, the model can serve to reduce the memory load. Mechanics who have acquired a mental model do not have to remember dozens of fixed procedures; neither do they have to expend effort in searching through a manual. Many specific procedures can be generated from a suitably complex mental model. Second, a model provides flexibility. A mechanic with an appropriate mental model can deal with unfamiliar situations not covered by fixed procedures, such as a test error.

Work on cognitive change suggests that the novice's understanding of a physical system progresses with experience through a series of increasingly specific models. Miyake (1986) recorded subjects who were attempting to understand how a sewing machine produces a stitch. An analysis of the dialogues showed that subjects understood the functioning of the system at different levels. At the simplest level they understood that a stitch was needed and that two threads interact. More specific was the understanding that the bottom thread goes through the loop of the upper thread and that the bobbin is involved. The precise functioning of the bobbin constituted the deepest level of understanding. In progressing through these levels subjects oscillated between feeling that they understood the device and feeling that there was more to be explained.

Characteristics of Advanced Mental Models

From our interviews and troubleshooting observations (see chapter 3 by Tenney & Kurland, this volume) and from research on avionics technicians (Gitomer, 1984; Glaser et al., 1985), it is clear that experienced mechanics, in contrast to novices, have a better functional understanding of the system and of the troubleshooting procedures.

Having an accurate mental model of the system entails knowing what functional circuits constitute the system. "Being familiar" with each functional circuit appears to include the following types of knowledge:

1. *Devices.* Device knowledge includes knowing that physical devices are involved in the circuit and where the devices are located on the radar and in the schematics. It also includes having a model of each device: knowing what signal inputs (both power and information signals) it requires, how it operates, what signal outputs it produces, and what overall function it performs.

2. *Signals.* Signal knowledge includes discriminating between power and information signals, knowing the directional flow of information signals between devices, and understanding the relationship of those signals to one another.

3. *Functions.* Functional knowledge includes knowing the function of each functional circuit and its composite subfunctional areas, that is, what component groupings perform these subfunctions. It also includes knowing how each functional circuit "fits into" a subsystem or across subsystems.

4. *System Concepts.* System understanding extends from knowing how each functional circuit affects each subsystem's operation, and how this, in turn, affects the overall system's operation. This system understanding entails a qualitative understanding of how the system's circuitry is designed to work and any underlying concepts needed to grasp this qualitative model, such as loops. (This is discussed in the following subsection.)

Radar mechanics who are "familiar with a circuit" demonstrate a qualitative understanding of that circuit when they are troubleshooting. There are several indications that they have a suitably complex model: They can generate their own procedures indirectly, that is, from memory. They can also quickly rule out large portions of the circuit that appear to be functioning correctly by observing (visually, tactually, and aurally) what components appear to work. They consult the detailed schematics to make specific voltage measurements only after they have ruled out areas. In other words, the schematics are a reference for specific details such as pin numbers. This pattern is consistent with observations about electrical engineers, as described by deKleer (1985): "An engineer does not perform a qualitative analysis unless he first understands the circuit at a qualitative level (p. 275)." In other words, mechanics who are familiar with a circuit know what functions the circuit performs and can reduce the problem space by deducing, from their model and from the radar's behavior (the symptoms), the presence of the proper signals in certain functional areas. Thus, a signal's voltage appears to be a secondary troubleshooting concern that becomes important only after the impaired functional area has been isolated.

In contrast, novices appear overly focused on measuring voltages. They tended to persevere unnecessarily in remeasuring "good" connections within a circuit, rather than ruling out a functional area and focusing on an impaired area based on the results of their measurements. When the novice mechanics were stuck measuring an area, we observed that the mentor asked leading questions to get them going again, such as: "What does that measurement tell you about that circuit?" [Novice: "It's good."] "Right. So where haven't you measured yet?" [Novice names another possibility from memory or from the FIP's list of possible faults.]

Mental Models and Troubleshooting Performance

The results of our studies (see chapter 3 by Tenney and Kurland, this volume) showed a strong correlation between the complexity of a mechanic's mental model and actual troubleshooting performance. To troubleshoot accurately and efficiently, the data suggest that mechanics require a very complex and detailed model of the system. To develop this, mechanics appear to need a deep functional understanding of the procedures and general troubleshooting principles.

First of all, there is evidence that the complexity of a mechanic's mental model strongly affects his or her ability to troubleshoot flexibly. In our interviews about how the radar worked, the expert's and the 10-year mechanic's models were much more complex and accurate than the 5- and 1-year mechanics' models, because the complex models emphasized information flow and many more loops and functions. Although the expert, 10- and 5-year mechanics could generate procedures, indicating the presence of qualitative models, the troubleshooting data suggest that both the expert's and the 10-year mechanic's more complex models allowed them to generate more steps from memory than could the 5- and 1-year mechanics.

The troubleshooting data also suggest that troubleshooting efficiency and accuracy and the ability to recover quickly from errors are strongly affected by the mechanic's depth of procedural understanding and also by whether those procedures are organized under general troubleshooting principles. The depth of procedural understanding is different from how well the procedures can be recalled. Mechanics may have performed certain procedures so often that performance is automatic, but this does not ensure that they understand the global purpose of that particular step.

Evidence for this point of view comes from our data. The expert's performance, unlike those of the novice or intermediate mechanic, indicated a deep procedural understanding. He knew when it was appropriate to apply certain procedures—he not only generated more procedural steps from memory, he also generated the fewest extra steps. Furthermore, he quickly detected and recovered from errors. This indicated that he understood what the test procedures' results implied as to what was possible and what was ruled out. Finally, the expert also seemed to have organized those procedures into some general troubleshooting principles, as shown in the example below.

> (The expert turns on the radar. While he waits for it to attain the "radiate" state, he quickly does a few checks. Below, he starts to read two built-in monitors, the MO [Master Oscillator] meter and the PA [Power Amplifier] meter, both of which measure forward RF power. A minute or so has gone by.)
>
> *Subject:* OK, check forward RF power, in PA, I have none [no signal]. In MO, I have forward RF. So it looks like I have a problem in monitoring forward RF power. Now there's a reason to believe that the radar is up in radiate. Find out here in just a minute. . . . I'll give it about a minute here to see if this cavity will lock up [He waits a minute, then checks the meter again.]
>
> *Experimenter:* So what do you think the problems are so far?
>
> *S:* Well, right now, I don't have any PA forward RF power. When I go to the MO, I do. It tells me that the MO is generating RF power. The PA is either not getting it [the power], or it's not amplifying it, or I'm just not monitoring it

Within minutes, the expert has isolated the symptom and come up with three specific hypotheses as to what the fault could be, the correct one being a monitoring problem. Three troubleshooting principles are evident in his hypotheses. If a component does not appear to be working, then (a) a (power or information) signal to the component could be missing, (b) the component could be defective,

(c) the device monitoring the component could be faulty. Throughout this and the troubleshooting sessions, the expert pursued only those particular procedures that pertained to a specific hypothesis. Because he knew the procedures well enough and had clear expectations for what was considered "normal" result, he quickly detected when procedural results seemed contrary to his expectations and checked for errors. The expert clearly understood the purpose and function of each procedural step and knew when it was appropriate to apply or ignore them. In other words, he appeared to have them organized under general troubleshooting principles.

The role of a functional understanding of the procedures and troubleshooting principles in the development of a sufficiently complex model for troubleshooting is suggested by the troubleshooting data. Even though the 10-year mechanic, like the expert, had a model that was conceptually complex enough to include loops and information and enabled him to generate many steps from memory, he performed like the 5-year mechanic. They both performed extra procedural steps and made more errors from which they did not recover quickly. They were strongly reluctant to use the FIP because they did not want to "branch and get lost." This, plus the fact that the two mechanics did not seem to know when it was appropriate to apply particular procedures, suggests that their models did not include a functional understanding of the FIP.

The data suggest that an understanding of the procedures is necessary to further refine and develop the mechanic's model of the system beyond the ability to just generate procedures. In other words, a sufficiently complex model includes not only an understanding of what the procedures are testing and how they rule things out, but also an organization of the procedures under general troubleshooting principles, so the mechanic will know when to apply the procedure. With this sufficiently complex model, a mechanic's performance is more efficient and accurate, because he or she can concentrate only on those areas (and the procedures pertaining to them) that have not been ruled out. A complex model also helps promote faster error recovery, because the mechanic is aware of test results that contradict other test results.

Hurdles in Developing a Mental Model and a Repertoire of Troubleshooting Skills

Novices are hindered from constructing an accurate mental model and developing a repertoire of procedural strategies for several reasons. First, the information in the documentation is either too general or too specific to help the novice develop a functional understanding of the system. Second, novices have difficulty developing generalizable skills or knowledge from their troubleshooting experiences. Third, novices lack essential, underlying concepts about how the system operates.

First of all, to develop a suitable model, novices need a functional hierarchy relevant to troubleshooting that explicitly shows functional circuits (the relevant problem space) and their composite subfunctions, including (a) the physical layout and signal inputs for the device in the circuit, (b) the flow of information through the functional circuit, and (c) important signal relationships.

Second, novices have difficulty developing generalizable knowledge or skills (such as a suitable model or a repertoire of troubleshooting skills), through troubleshooting practice, because they are not systematically exposed to realistic faults and because they do not get sufficient troubleshooting practice at school or on the job. At school, student mechanics practice troubleshooting faults that are easily inserted and do not damage the school's radars. Although these concerns are certainly reasonable, these problems do not adequately reflect the types of faults students will face in the field. In addition, because troubleshooting ordinarily takes a long time, students do not get sufficient practice troubleshooting problems. Practice is left for on-the-job training, which usually starts several months after the mechanic has completed school.

On the job, novice mechanics must wait for the faults to occur in the field. Because the priority is to have the radar operational as quickly as possible, novice mechanics often learn "swaptronics," where they remove and replace items (which may or may not be relevant to the circuit), rather than using the documentation, which is a frustrating, time-consuming, and error-prone experience. One novice mechanic with one year of work experience described his troubleshooting approach:

> *Novice Mechanic:* Usually you'll replace things that you think might be bad. You first go with your experience and what you think it might be, and if that fixes it, that's good, because you didn't have to rely on the book [the FIP]. If you can't fix it, that's when you go get this stuff [the documentation] or get someone who's got a lot more experience. . . . He'll say, "Well, did you check this, did you replace that?" and if you said no, then you just go there.

This novice's approach, in which he either tries to replace whatever worked last time or rotely follows suggestions from more senior mechanics (whose functional understanding may vary in accuracy), is rather typical. Some experienced mechanics who were interviewed expressed the view that "every radar is different," that is, each radar is prone to a particular set of faults, and that their troubleshooting ability was determined by their "experience" or exposure to certain problems. One expert succinctly described the problem with this comment:

> *Expert:* It's hard to cope . . . The cause is not always the same . . . They'll [the radars] do it at different times [in] different ways . . .It's not a doctrinal procedure . . . It's a thought process that is learned, but is not described.

Thus, a mechanic's abilities appear to depend upon his situation-driven, haphazard exposure to a variety of radar faults, and upon the quality of the teaching apprenticeship with his supervisor. From this type of troubleshooting situation, novices have difficulty developing any generalizable skills or knowledges that are necessary for functional troubleshooting. Instead, serious misconceptions about how the radar works may arise.

Another problem hindering novices from developing generalizable skills is that it is difficult to develop a functional understanding of the individual procedures, because the documentation does not explicitly describe the procedure's purpose nor what it rules out. Without this procedural understanding, it is not surprising that novices and intermediate mechanics do not understand the strategies behind the FIP's implicit branching. Furthermore, without a basic functional understanding of the procedures, novices cannot derive any troubleshooting principles, much less organize those procedures under those principles, and when troubleshooting apply them efficiently and accurately.

Finally, the third hurdle novices face in forming a proper model and logical reasoning skills is that the documentation does not provide underlying system concepts that are critical for a functional understanding of how the system is designed to work, neither does the documentation organize this knowledge in a cognitive framework suitable for troubleshooting. These concepts and their organization are described in the following section.

System Concepts and Knowledge Organization

To develop an accurate mental model of the radar, a mechanic must understand certain underlying concepts about how the radar actually works. That is, mechanics need to understand, on a qualitative level, how radar is designed to perform certain functions, before they can diagnose it in a faulty state. This section will describe four important areas: (a) how two concepts, information and loops, are tied to system understanding and troubleshooting expertise; (b) how the design of the system is relevant to system understanding; (c) novices' difficulties with attaining system understanding; and (d) why loops are important for the radar technician.

Information and Loops

From our mental models data (see Tenney & Kurland, chapter 3, this volume), we have observed several developmental changes in mechanics' understanding of how the radar works: The novice focused on power signals, organized his knowledge by the physical cabinetry, and appeared unaware of both the information and the loop concepts. In contrast, experts mentioned information frequently, and downplayed power. From the previous discussion on "Functional Block Diagrams," supporting evidence was given for the case that expert radar mechanics have a different functional organization for troubleshooting than the documentation's functional block hierarchy. Their knowledge appears to be organized around higher order functions implemented by the causal flow of information through the system.

One salient characteristic of the expert's mental model involved the concept of functional feedback loops. As previously shown in the expert's drawing of the receiver (Figure 5.6), the feedthrough nulling feedback loop serves an important function, which is feedthrough (unwanted transmitter noise) cancellation. Discussions with other expert mechanics and one expert radar engineer have confirmed that the loops are indeed important and critical for developing a functional understanding of how the radar works.

Because neither the information signals nor loops are explicitly indicated in the documentation, and because recently graduated mechanics appear unaware of the loop and information concepts, questions arise: When do these concepts appear, and in what order? What situations make these concepts most salient? Why are these concepts difficult to understand? Though these questions cannot be answered definitively, we can examine the midpoint of our developmental trend, the 5-year mechanic, for clues.

The first appearance of the loop concept occurred with the 5-year intermediate mechanic, who drew a major loop between two subsystems and a minor loop between a subsystem and a monitoring panel. This mechanic was coincidentally given a troubleshooting problem that involved the major loop. While troubleshooting this problem, he mentioned the concept of "information," which he did not do during his interview about how the radar works. An excerpt of the troubleshooting transcript is given below—the experimenter is asking the subject what he sees on the schematic page that he has selected:

1. *Experimenter:* So which way is the signal going? This way or that way?
2. *Subject:* No, it's going this way. See, this is what actually moves the antenna in azimuth.
3. *E:* The mechanical part?
4. *S:* Well, it turns the voltage into mechanical—
5. *E:* And so it's coming this way?
6. *S:* Mmm hmm.
7. *E:* And does it come out this way, too, or —
8. *S:* Okay. This would give you your azimuth tracking rate. In other words, it would feed electrical information back down to your TIC circuits.

In the transcript above, the mechanic specifically mentioned electrical information signal (line 8). He referred (in line 4) to the transformation of an electrical signal into a mechanical signal, that is, he understood that information flows through the system along a signal path, which, in this particular case, is a functional feedback loop.

Thus, from this example, there appears to be a relationship in the development between the flow of information concept and the loop concept. We shall discuss these implications once we have discussed some aspects of the radar's circuitry and how they pertain to the information and loop concepts.

Complex System Circuit Types

The radar actually contains two functional systems: the system that monitors how well the radar is working, and the system that dynamically produces the desired effect (e.g., tracking the target) in spite of changing external conditions that affect the system. (These systems, usually called "automatic feedback control system," will be called "effector systems" for brevity in this discussion.)

The monitoring portion of the radar contains built-in test equipment (BITE). These are circuits that test the functionality of the other circuits, the overall system, and three subsystems: the transmitter, the receiver-signal processor, and the antenna positioning system. Many newer systems contain these automated test circuits. Sometimes, as in the case of Air Force/HUMMRO project, the automated test circuits become a separate entity altogether (see Means & Gott, chapter 2, this volume).[6] Most of the radar's BITE circuits are contained within sets of circuit cards. These BITE circuits monitor the system and subsystems by collecting "data" by tapping into various electrical signal circuits and measuring the signals traveling through those connections. When a faulty (i.e., a missing, invalid, noisy, or mistimed) signal is detected by comparison to some reference signal, a visual indication is given, usually in the form of a fault indicator light.

The radar can be classified primarily as an effector system, because the vast majority of its circuits are involved in producing a specific effect or a change. These effects depend upon feedback loops. Although feedback loops occur at the level of resistors and amplifiers (the "micro-level"), large complex systems like the radar characteristically contain many "macro-level" feedback loops, where groups of component devices (such as generators, gears, or motor tachometers) are involved in a variety of "energy" changes within and across subsystems. These macro-level feedback loops often contain many micro-level feedback loops, which are not apparent to maintenance personnel, because the micro loops occur within circuit cards. Moreover, the loops often intersect or overlap with other macroloops in the system.

A specified effect or change may be a mechanical change (movement or position)[7] or a change in another "energy" form (electrical or microwave). For example, a mechanical change is positioning the antenna, and a microwave change is shaping (modulating) the transmitted RF beam to a particular frequency or amplitude. Other types of specified changes are speed (speed control systems control the speed of turbines or engines), temperature, flow, pressure (flow and pressure control systems control air or fluids), or torque (Raven, 1961).

Whatever media the effector system involves, certain basic concepts apply to all feedback systems. The fundamental difference between, say, monitoring systems and effector systems is that monitoring is a relatively static process, because it essentially "reports" signal status. In contrast, a feedback control (effector) system is designed to *dynamically adjust* its output to produce a specific effect or change despite external disturbances impinging on the system.

For an effector system to produce a dynamically controlled effect,

---

[6]The Air Force test station's tests are programmable, unlike the radar's BITE, which has a preset test agenda that is activated with a "TEST" pushbutton.

[7]These systems are often called servo-mechanical systems, but the radar is much more than a servo-mechanism, because it also involves the technology of RF generation and detection.

it depends on "macro-level" feedback loops. The key idea of a feedback loop is that the components involved in each feedback loop must be capable of both creating the signals that initiate the effect and controlling the creating of the affecting signals. In this way, *the signal controls its own acquisition.*

At a more technical level, the relationship between the input and the output is completely determined by how the feedback signal is generated. This entails producing an error signal by measuring the output and comparing that with a reference input. The error signal is used to actuate the control elements, that is, the error signal drives the elements in the feedback loop to change the output so as to minimize the difference between the output and the reference signal (Bender, 1962).

A control systems engineer has quite a variety of component options when designing an automatic feedback control system— options that directly affect the radar technician. Although some system types are more suitable for certain operations than others, many applications can be accomplished by mechanical, electrical, hydraulic, or pneumatic systems, or by a combination. To get a good fit between the desired features of the system and the characteristics of a component, designers have to know the basic laws and equations that characterize that component's operation (Raven, 1961). The mathematical relationships of control systems are generally represented by a diagram of the type shown in Figure 5.2, where a specific functional relationship is portrayed by the signal or information flow (arrows) and certain functional blocks that are independent of one another. For engineers, this functional representation (with arrows) generally portrays the mathematical relationships more clearly than abstract formulas alone, particularly when the representation shows the functional relationships between system variables.

These engineering concerns become relevant to the technician, because as discussed previously, expert mechanics emphasized that it is important to know the relevant physical components and their functional relationships, particularly if that function involves a loop.

Because each component that helps create the final output signal can be represented mathematically, analogous comparisons may be made across different types of systems. When engineers design a system, these analogous comparisons between systems are useful, because the engineers must balance various factors, such as accuracy, speed, efficiency, ruggedness, cost, weight, and so on. An analogous comparison can be made when the differential equation of operation for one system has the same form as another; terms that correspond between the two systems are called analogous quantities. For example, a series mechanical system and a series electrical system are analogous (force-voltage analogy). For a force-current analogy, series mechanical elements may replace parallel electrical, as may parallel mechanical elements with series electrical elements. In a torque-force analogy, series translational mechanical elements can be replaced by series rotational elements (Raven, 1961).

Thus, there are many ways for an engineer to design a system to bring about a particular effect. Because those particular components and their arrangement specify the performance of each feedback loop, it is important to provide a novice technician with the high-level information about what function the designer intended to accomplish with each feedback control loop in the system, what components compose each loop, and how they contribute to the loop's performance.

Why Are Loops Difficult to Learn?

In this section, we shall consider why loops seem so difficult to learn. The 5-year mechanic, who did very well in a self-paced learning program, seemed to know about only one major loop in the radar, although there are many other essential ones, which, we have been assured by instructors, are described in the curriculum. In the following section, I shall describe possible reasons why mechanics have difficulty understanding the radar system's loops.

One important reason why novices appear unaware of loops is that the documentation does not explicitly show or describe them. Because a loop may include a variety of components (e.g., electrical, mechanical, RF), and because the direction of signal flow is not shown, the specific configuration of a loop in the schematics is not obvious. Often, one must have a cross-sectional view of the system to locate a loop, because it cuts across several subsystems. In the radar and other effector (control) systems, many functional feedback loops are often intertwined, making them more difficult to find. In fact, one very experienced radar instructor-mechanic (30 years) said, "There are feedback loops you wouldn't believe in this radar—wheels within wheels within wheels within wheels."

Second, the concept of a functional feedback loop is a difficult one to grasp. To understand loops, one must first understand the information signal concept. Also, loops rarely occur in one's everyday experience, so there are very few concrete examples on which one can base this concept. Moreover, loops have certain characteristics, which, in turn, entail specific troubleshooting methods. These issues are elaborated below.

To understand how loops work involves distinguishing power from information signals. The signals dynamically produced and controlled within the loop are information signals. Because many of the device components within the loop require both power and an information signal to operate, a mechanic must already know the difference between information and power signals to understand how a loop works. Thus, the concept of an information signal appears to be an enabling concept for the loop concept.

Because loops rarely occur in one's everyday experience, there are very few concrete examples on which one can base this concept. The functional feedback loop comes from a field of control systems theory. The essential concept of a loop is that it acts as one entity, that is, it performs a *single function*, even though it may be composed of many parts. However, just knowing what components are contained within the loop will not predict its function; one must know the *specific arrangement* (configuration) of the parts in the loop. The specific arrangement controls the flow of information around the loop: Part of the loop creates a signal, and the other part controls the creation of the signal. However, this does not tell the full story of a loop's function; its function is actually more than a sequential series of component actions, it is a "gestalt." If any one part of a loop is faulted, the whole loop is faulted, not just the part.

A concrete analogy of a functional loop is the bicycle chain. The function of the bicycle chain is to turn the wheel. When one chain link is pushed with the pedal, the whole chain is pushed and the wheel turns; similarly, when one link is broken, the whole link is broken and the wheel does not move. Although the loop does not move like the bicycle chain, this analogy gives one a sense of how a fault propagates through the loop, affecting all the components and signals within it.

Finally, because of the interrelated nature of the loop's components, troubleshooting a loop requires special troubleshooting methods, because the loop is actually a special type of circuit. Loops can be divided into two parts: the forward and the backward portions. The forward part is involved in the creation of the signal, whereas the backward portion is involved in controlling the signal (usually feedback). One simplified method that would troubleshoot a majority of faulty loops involves the following principled approach: If one of the components within the forward portion is faulted, then the signal is not created, that is, the signal is absent. If one of the components within the backward portion of the loop is faulted, then a signal is produced, but poorly. A poorly produced signal may be noisy or invalid, but something is still coming out. Having isolated the fault to the forward or backward portion of the loop, one can then troubleshoot that portion by iteratively halving the faulty portion to see which half contains the fault until a faulty component or wire is located.

In a situation where there are two overlapping loops (i.e., they share a common component group), a mechanic must ascertain whether one or both loops are actually faulty, because a fault in one loop will propagate through both loops. In this case, iterative versions of the above "divide-and-conquer" strategy can be applied, focusing on the areas (components) where the two loops merge and diverge. An example of two overlapping loops, the azimuth position error loop (darkened) and the tracking rate loop (on the right), for the antenna positioning system is shown in Figure 5.10. The forward and backward portions for just the azimuth position error loop are shown at the top.

Why Are Loops Important?

From our data on the mechanics' mental models and from the discussion in "Functional Blocks," loops appear important for organizing an expert mechanic's general understanding and his or her troubleshooting knowledge. We shall examine reasons for why this is so.

The work by Chi, Glaser, and Rees (1981) on novice and expert physics problem solvers makes a case for why loops are important for troubleshooting. Chi, Glaser, and Rees attributed the novices' problem primarily to inadequate knowledge bases; that is, experts and novices organized their knowledge differently. Although novices had elaborate and detailed knowledge, it appeared organized by superficial physical characteristics and did not contain the knowledge needed to generate potential solution methods. In contrast, the experts' knowledge not only appeared to be organized by principle, it contained procedures to generate solutions and the *conditions* for applying those procedures.

Novice radar mechanics, like novice physics problem solvers, organize their radar knowledge by superficial physical characteristics, the cabinetry. Similarly, when faced with an unknown fault, they do not seem to have the knowledge to generate a solution, particularly if the FIP does not have accurate procedures or if they make an error and branch to the wrong step.

In contrast, once expert mechanics have ascertained which function is impaired, they can generate solution methods rapidly and flexibly. The loop appears to be a very useful concept for troubleshooting for several reasons. Because a loop has a function, for example, "removes RF noise from returning RF signal," the troubleshooter can organize the knowledge pertaining to the loop under that function. Furthermore, a loop is cognitively economical in that one can store away factual knowledge about the multitude

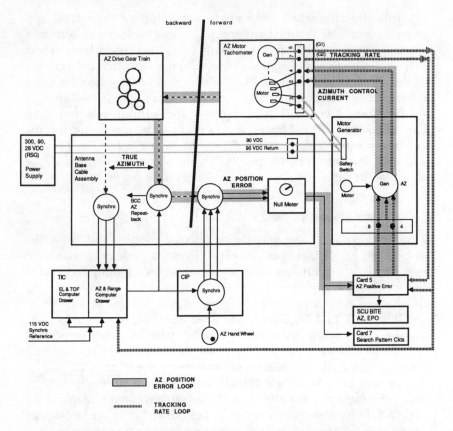

backward   forward

AZ Drive Gear Train

AZ Motor
Tachometer   Gen

(G1)
(G2) TRACKING RATE

Motor

AZIMUTH CONTROL
CURRENT

300, 90,
28 VDC
(RSG)

Power
Supply

Antenna
Base
Cable
Assembly

TRUE
AZIMUTH

90 VDC
90 VDC Return

Motor
Generator

Safety
Switch

BCC
AZ
Repeat-
back

Synchro

Synchro

Synchro

AZ POSITION
ERROR

Synchro

Null Meter

Motor

Gen   AZ

6   4

TIC

EL & TOF
Computer
Drawer

AZ & Range
Computer
Drawer

CIP

Synchro

Card 5
AZ Positive Error

SCU BITE
AZ, EPO

115 VDC
Synchro
Reference

AZ Hand Wheel

Card 7
Search Pattern Ckts

AZ POSITION
ERROR LOOP

TRACKING
RATE LOOP

FIGURE 5.10   Functional feedback looks for positioning the antenna.

of relevant components and signals that are involved in the loop, for example, signals coming into the components within the loop, the causal flow of information through the loop, the relationship of the signals, and the output signal produced by the loop. Moreover, there are two basic conditions in which a loop may be faulted: forward and backward. This conditional knowledge includes how the information flow in the loop could be disrupted. Finally, the procedures for troubleshooting depend on the faulty conditions, that is, the fault path.

In short, the loop, an important concept for understanding the radar system, meets the conditions for a higher-level organizer. For expert troubleshooters, as shown in Figure 5.6, loops are a known concept. From our interviews, we have seen evidence that loops are continually used in expert descriptions of how the radar works. Indeed, one cannot understand how the radar works without this concept, because loops perform many functions. Moreover, because the majority of the radar's loops are involved in noise reduction, particularly in the receiver and the transmitter, and, as one expert estimated, approximately 50% of the radar problems involve noise reduction within the system, loops are critical for troubleshooting. Thus the instructional importance of understanding how loops work cannot be ignored.

ADDRESSING INSTRUCTIONAL NEEDS WITH AN ITS

Instructional Needs

In light of novices' difficulties in gaining an understanding of the system, the primary instructional issue is how to organize and present the knowledge novices need to learn in order to troubleshoot. Although the problems associated with the documentation are critical problems, it is beyond the scope of this project to redesign the manuals. Indeed, as research has shown (Kern, 1985), technical manuals often do not meet the needs of users. Mechanics' ability to effectively use a manual depends upon their prior knowledge, that is, they need an accurate functional understanding of the system to understand what the documentation is asking them to do. Ideally, manuals should address the novice mechanic's point of view, but because the occurrence of the perfect manual is unlikely, an instructional program should prepare students to live with imperfect manuals and provide them with the knowledge they need to use them. The cognitive research literature, reviewed below, suggests what a mechanic needs to know, and how that knowledge should be organized and presented.

Cognitive Research

Generally speaking, what a student needs to know is how to find problems, when and how to apply certain skills, and how to exploit properties of the current situation (Collins, Brown, & Newman, in press). Similarly, the physics problem-solving literature (Chi, Glaser, and Rees, 1981) indicates that experts can solve problems rapidly and accurately, because their knowledge, hierarchically organized by basic principles, contains declaratively (factual) knowledge, conditions for applying that knowledge, and procedures for attaining solutions under those conditions.

The cognitive research literature suggests guidelines on how to organize the domain to facilitate learning and recall. Tulving and Thomson (1973) showed that a hierarchical organization at the time of encoding facilitates recall. Additionally, Kintsch (1978), Meyer, Brandt, and Bluth (1980), and Eylon and Reif (1984) have found that higher level or more meaningful information is recalled better than lower level information. Studies on knowledge structures and advance organizers (Ausubel, 1968; Eylon & Reif, 1984; Novak, 1977; & Thro, 1978), have shown that advance organizers facilitate learning new knowledge and cause students' knowledge structures to more closely resemble those of instructors and the course materials.

Not only should a knowledge structure be hierarchically organized, but it should also contain an explicit description of the relations (links) between the levels. A study by Eylon and Reif (1984) made two recommendations:

1. The higher levels of hierarchical information should contain information which is used most frequently or which facilitates retrieval of other related information
2. The knowledge unit should contain information that is small enough to be processed, but large enough to make the task of relating the various knowledge units a manageable one by keeping the number of units down.

With a system as complex as the radar, a hierarchical organization is certainly critical to facilitate learning and retrieval of that knowledge. However, there are many ways to hierarchically organize information. Because the type of hierarchy affects the recall performance (Eylon & Reif, 1984), the hierarchical organization should be adapted to reflect the nature of the task, which, in this case, is to troubleshoot effectively.

Organizing Radar Knowledge

As shown by our data, expert radar mechanics organize their knowledge by functions, as do experts in other technical domains (Egan & Schwartz, 1979; Gitomer, 1984; Glaser et al., 1985). Within the expert radar mechanics' functional organization are the components that perform specific functions, and these functions appear to be linked together by the flow of information signals through the system's components.

As discussed previously, loops appear to be an important high-level organizer that facilitates the recall of troubleshooting knowledge. As designed by systems control engineers, loops perform specific functions, and this allows them to fit neatly into an expert troubleshooter's functional knowledge organization. They provide a cognitively economical framework in which to store knowledge about which components are involved, the contribution of those components to the loop's operation (and automatic control), the conditions under which the loop can be faulted, and procedural principles by which one can troubleshoot the loop. Indeed, because the loop is essentially a functional gestalt, one cannot break the loop down into smaller, independent functional entities and still comprehend its function in total.

In contrast, the novice radar mechanic does not appear to have a hierarchically and functionally organized knowledge structure, or underlying concepts such as information or loops. Even with instructional aids to explicitly depict and explain qualitative ideas and underlying concepts, many of the radar's functions are still too complex for novices to absorb all at once.

To address this problem, our intelligent tutoring system focuses on five areas:

1. Show the problem space at various levels of detail for each functional area.
2. Provide troubleshooting practice on problems that increase in difficulty.
3. Provide a range of procedural help.
4. Provide supports to make strategies explicit.
5. Provide general and specific explanations about the purpose, location, and behaviors of devices, signals, and circuits.

These five areas are described in the following sections.

Show the Problem Space

One approach to bridging the gap between the documentation and the physical reality of the radar is to visually present "views" that both summarize the relevant circuit and "chunk" it in ways relevant to troubleshooting. These two aspects are described below.

Summarizing the Circuit

One instructional aid to help the novice radar mechanic construct a simple, but accurate model for the radar is for the system to present, for each functional area, a simplified "summary" diagram on which the novice can practice simple troubleshooting problems. In the simulation of the radar these summary diagrams will provide functional and physical mappings among the schematics, the FIP, and the radar, because they will show the functional flow of information in a physical context. As the novice successfully troubleshoots faults in the simple diagrams, more detailed views can be made available for viewing and troubleshooting practice. Thus, while practicing troubleshooting problems in the simulation, the student mechanic will be able to select the view with the desired level of detail.

Research has shown that diagrams are useful in solving physics dynamics problems (Larkin & Simon, 1985). Larkin and Simon attribute two roles to the diagrams: (a) they serve as an external augmentation to working memory, easing the burden that schematics impose, and (b) they also make apparent relationships that are not obvious or are difficult to describe in a verbal, propositional form, for example, changes in state over time, dependency relationships, or signal relationships.

In our system, the information contained within the summary diagrams will provide conceptual support, temporary models, and higher level organizers (such as feedback loops) for incoming knowledge (Glaser, 1985), and thereby remove many of the early hurdles that novices have for constructing an accurate mental model of the system. For example, some physical-functional mappings, such as signal relationships that are produced by the system, are nearly impossible to extract from the schematics without supporting high-level concepts derived from the fields of theoretical physics, systems control theory, and electrical engineering. Mappings such as signal relationships are prerequisite for understanding how the system functions, and thus are critical for troubleshooting. Novice mechanics clearly need help constructing these mappings, which the summary diagrams could provide in a simple and qualitative manner.

For each functional area, these summary diagrams should explicitly:

1. Show the relevant component devices and their connections (e.g., jacks, plugs, wires) in the circuit that perform a function and their relationship to the physical layout.

2. Show the causal flow of information through the circuit (If two functional circuits overlap, each circuit and the information signal they share should be shown.)

3. Show the flow of power to component devices, and distinguish that from information signals.

4. Show important signal relationships, for example, 180° out of phase.

5. Make the troubleshooting strategy more explicit by indicating which components are replaceable or measurable by the FIP, and, if a particular sequence of steps is required, make apparent why that order is important.

6. Visually group components within the circuit by functions and by circuit type.

With these summary diagrams, the radar mechanic can practice troubleshooting a circuit with the FIP. The diagrams will show the functional circuit—what key component devices are involved, their inputs and outputs, and how they are physically arranged. Showing the physical arrangement of the components in the circuit, especially the measurable and replaceable parts referenced by the FIP, will help build a mental bridge among the schematics, the FIP, and the radar, saving the novice mechanic considerable effort, and, one hopes, facilitate transfer.

Evidence from our own study as well as others (Gitomer 1984; Glaser et al., 1985) have shown that novices often do not have a model of the device, that is, they do not know all of its inputs. They also do not understand the distinction between power and information signals. It is important for the student to understand this distinction, because a component device often requires both types (and perhaps several of each). The summary diagrams can explicitly show (through color coding, labeling, etc.) whether the signal is supplying power or information, what components that signal comes from and goes to, and how that signal can interrupt both the device's as well as the circuit's operation.

The simulation's diagrams will also explicitly show the causal flow of this information (with directional graphics), because faulty information can propagate throughout the system. Showing how information signals propagate through the system will help the novice to logically isolate a faulty device. This visual representation of the circuit will also help the novice to relate the function of the information to the purpose of the FIP steps, by showing what signal is being measured.

Chunking the Circuit by Function

Because the radar is so complex, it is important to hierarchically organize its many components. As we have described, experts organize their knowledge of the radar by function, that is, they group those component devices that are involved in performing a particular function. These groups are tied together through the causal flow of information through the system. These functional groups serve as higher level organizers.

For each subsystem's simple, high-level summary diagram, the components pertaining to a functional unit will be highlighted, providing novices with a functional organization of the radar that is immediately useful for troubleshooting. Any signal product(s) emerging from that unit will also be explicitly indicated, because these signals tie the functional units together.

An example of grouping the components involved in a particular function is shown in Figure 5.11. For example, if a symptom pertains to "removing the noise," they can focus on the functional group of components that pertain to removing noise. This reasoning rules out other functions not relevant to the impaired function and thus narrows the problem space into more manageable portions. Also, because a component device can be involved in more than one function, it is important to know which functions are tied together by that component.

As the novice learns to identify which portions of the circuit pertain to certain functions, these "chunks" of the simplified circuit can be further decomposed (dynamically with the simulation) into smaller, more detailed functions until the most detailed view is shown. If the novice becomes confused with the detailed view, he or she can request that the ITS help by regrouping the components back into their larger functional groups. For example, this could be accomplished with the ITS by highlighting and explaining which components pertain to a particular function. Another possibility may be to present a menu of functions in that circuit; selection of the function will result in a list of those components involved in that function.

Chunking by Circuit Type

In the radar, there are three patterns of device connections: chains, branches, and loops. These circuit connections do not refer to standard electrical circuits, rather, they describe high-level patterns of connections between information-processing devices, that is, the causal flow of information. An important difference to keep in mind in the following discussion is that information does not return to the source, that is, these information patterns do not have return paths, as electrical circuit paths do. However, these information circuit patterns may encompass electrical circuits and their returns, but this is a lower level procedural issue, which will be suppressed in high-level summary diagrams that show how the circuit functions.

Although chains involve straight connections (wires), which may divide into various signals, the signals do not recombine to form a new information signal. (That is, the signal flows "away" from the starting point.) Branches occur when an information signal splits into two signals; the two signals are separately processed (changed) and then are recombined to produce a new signal. Functional feedback

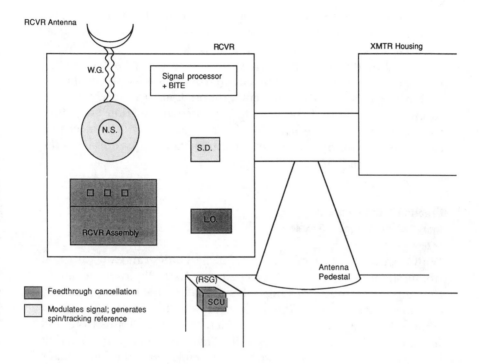

FIGURE 5.11 Chunking the circuit.

loops perform a particular function that depends upon the specific arrangement of the components within the loop.

Chunking the circuit into circuit types is a means of explicitly helping the novice to select a troubleshooting strategy. For each circuit type, there is a principled troubleshooting approach that can be applied in a general way. For a chain that forks into two or more chains, the faulty side of the chain can be isolated by measuring from the beginning (at the "fork") to the endpoint. The strategy for troubleshooting that faulty chain is to recursively "halve" each faulty section until the faulted wiring or component is located. With branch and loop circuits (assuming a correct input signal), the strategy is to systematically "break" the circuit into portions that act like chain circuits. For the branch circuit, a fault can lie within the splitting or recombining component, or within either of the two branches; for the loop, the fault can lie within either the forward or backward part of the loop, or within the splitting or recombining components. Once the fault has been isolated to a certain segment of the branch or loop, the chain method of troubleshooting can be applied to the relevant segment.

Complex effector systems often have a combination of these three circuit types involved in a major functional area, like the receiver. To troubleshoot a fault, a mechanic must know what functions are performed by the entire area, what component groups are associated with each function, and what circuit combinations are contained within the functional component groups. Once the mechanic has surmised that the fault pertains to a particular function and, thus, what portion of the entire circuit is probably faulted, the mechanic can apply the appropriate troubleshooting strategy appropriate to the circuit type(s) in that portion of the circuit.

Practice Troubleshooting
Increasingly Difficult Problems

With the tutoring system, novice radar mechanics can gain sufficient troubleshooting practice on faults that systematically cover the radar's functions. The restricted range of practical problems, as previously described, has been a serious impediment for learning how to troubleshoot the radar. Practice facilitates the acquisition and integration of problem-solving skills (Schneider, 1985). The amount of practice required to reach mastery depends upon the individual's learning style and speed of acquisition. Expertise, characterized by rapid problem solving, is a product of extended practice. A significant amount of practice is required for a skill to be employed automatically (Anderson, 1985; Glaser et al., 1985), that is, without conscious thought.

As previously described, there is a large gap between the hierarchical "functional block" organization of the documentation and the physical organization of the radar. The diagrams presented in the simulation will help bridge this physical-functional gap by providing a context for problem solving.

By providing problems that emphasize information flow and require functional reasoning, we anticipate that student mechanics will internalize the model represented by these diagrams. With the simulation, students can easily highlight or suppress certain aspects of the diagrams. Problem difficulty can easily be increased by "exploding" an aspect of the simplified view for a particular functional area into a more detailed view, thus requiring the student to understand more about that portion of the circuit. It is important for the mechanic to have internalized the model presented in these diagrams, because the mechanic will only have the official documentation when he or she leaves school. (We cannot assume that these diagrams will become official documentation.)

In some sense, progressing from simple to more detailed diagrams mimics the current instructional process. We have observed that when an instructor in the practical "hands-on" classes introduces a particular area, he or she first draws a simple representation (which shows the flow of information and power signals through the physical pieces of the radar) and explains it. Following this high-level introduction, he or she then points out the relevant sections in the detailed wiring schematics. The students are then "walked through" the various procedural checks of the FIP. Later, a fault is inserted and the students measure and/or replace components or wires to find the fault, using the documentation. Individual students eventually are given problems to troubleshoot while their peers stand nearby.

In the simulation, students can solve problems using the diagram that represents the physical context for a specific functional area, such as the receiver. These problems, selectively organized by levels of difficulty, will require the students to use a principled approach, including: what functions are involved in the relevant area, what function is impaired, what functions specific procedures test and rule out, what current types are involved, what portions of the circuit individual procedures test, and how the procedures handle the various types of circuits.

From our interviews and observations, factors that appear to affect the difficulty of a problem seem to fall into five areas: (a) signal type, (b) the number of functions within and between subsystems, (c) circuit type, (d) the number of possible parts to measure or replace, and (e) the number of procedural steps required to get results. These five factors vary according to their conceptual difficulty, the amount of detail required (in both a procedural and knowledge sense), and in the size of the problem space. These five factors, not necessarily orthogonal to one another, appear to have an effect on troubleshooting strategy and implementation. These five factors are described below.

Signal Type

One way to vary problem difficulty is with signal type. Novice mechanics first need to understand that a complex system like radar has both power and information signals, and that these two signal types differ in their function. Second, novices also need to understand the three types of information signals: electrical, mechanical and RF (microwave).

In terms of problem complexity, problems that pertain only to power signals will most likely be the easiest, because novices appear to think only in terms of power. Problems that require an understanding of how power and information signals differ will probably be more difficult for novices to comprehend. Within this power-information group, difficulty will vary with the type of information involved. As previously discussed in the subsection "Signals," novice mechanics need to understand the functional difference between power and information signals: a *power* input signal simply *enables* (energizes) a device component to operate, and an *information* signal (as carried by the pattern of an electrical, mechanical, or RF signal) *controls* how the device works.

Distinguishing power from information is important to make explicit in the summary diagrams for two reasons: First, the majority of component devices in the radar often requires more than one of each signal type as input to operate. Novice mechanics may be unaware that many device components need both input types because of the difficulty in finding a device's inputs in the schematics and/or because the procedures place such an emphasis on measuring voltages. Because electrical information signals usually have measurable voltages like electrical power signals, and because the procedures do not explicitly say that a particular signal is an information signal, novices can easily confuse electrical power with electrical information signals.

Second, distinguishing power from information is important, because the concept of information flow is essential for understanding how functional feedback loops work. Although information "flows" around the loop, controlling the involved devices, many of those devices require at least one power input. By showing these two signals types as device inputs in the simulation's diagrams, and by providing problems where students will have to decide whether it is a power signal or a type of information signal, the power-information concept will, one hopes, be made explicitly clear. Once they understand, students will have ample opportunity to review this concept, because there are many devices that require electrical power, but are controlled by electrical information signals.

Whether the concept of mechanical information is acquired earlier or later than the concept of electrical information is unclear. As discussed earlier, the 5-year mechanic seemed to understand the concept of electrical information and its transformation into mechanical information. This troubleshooting problem involved the only major feedback loop that he described in his model of the radar. The translation of mechanical information into electrical information may be a more elusive concept. This is not to say that novices do not understand that a mechanical device (such as a gear) moves. They do. They also understand that a synchro, an electromechanical device which they study quite early, generates an electrical signal when it is turned (such as when the handwheel is rotated). However, novices do not seem to understand that the turning of the device itself is a mechanical information signal, which is part of a signal path (or paths, because the device may participate in more than one functional circuit). The specific signal generated depends on how far the device turned. That is, they need to know that when a mechanical part turns, the mechanical signal directionally flows to the next part, whereupon a specific action occurs that depends on how far and/or how fast the mechanical part turned. For example, in Fig. 5.10, the mechanical signal generated by the azimuth motor tachometer is split between two signal paths—it turns the antenna gears, which are part of the position error loop. It also turns a low-voltage generator (mechanically attached to the motor tachometer), which is part of the tracking rate loop.

The most difficult information signal to understand is the RF (microwave) energy. Although created from extremely high levels of electrical voltage, RF signals have qualitatively different, more complex properties than simple electrical signals. In this radar, RF is characterized by two orthogonal dimensions, frequency and phase, whereas simple electrical signals in the radar are characterized by one dimension, amplitude. RF is essentially "invisible" to a mechanic and can be only measured with specialized, built-in equipment, because it is very dangerous. According to one radar instructor, RF takes about 10 years for a mechanic to understand. Aside from its elusive and qualitatively complex nature, RF is also generally involved in many intertwined functional loops, making it even more difficult to comprehend. This is particularly true for the transmitter, where eight major, highly intertwined, complex functional feedback loops are involved in producing, refining, and monitoring the RF signal that is sent out.

Thus, novice radar mechanics must learn to distinguish between power and information signals and to discern the type of information signal involved (electrical, mechanical, or RF), before they can understand how many devices operate and how functional feedback loops work.

Number of Functions Performed

Another way to vary problem difficulty is to vary the number of functions shown in a summary diagram for a particular functional circuit within a subsystem. Within a subsystem (for example, the receiver), there are a multitude of functions being performed by groups of components, many of which can be hierarchically subsumed under a few high-level functions. The portion of the circuit pertaining to these major functions can be visually "cordoned off" in a summary diagram that has a physical orientation, as shown in Figure 5.12.

Once students have solved problems based on an understanding of these major functional groupings, problem difficulty can be gradually increased by recursively breaking down each larger functional grouping into its smaller, composite functions, but within the physical layout, that is, showing components and spatial relations. Thus, even though the summary diagram "explodes" to show a more detailed view of the relevant circuitry and signals, the novice can still see both the physical and the functional units. For example in Figure 5.13, a more detailed view of the receiver's circuitry is shown within the physical context of the receiver assembly's two constitutent components: the frequency converter and the receiver IF assembly. The most difficult level would show the most detailed view of the circuitry and signal flow. Thus the more detailed the view of the subsystem, the more the student will have to understand, analyze, and test.

Problem complexity can also be increased by expanding the problem over two or more subsystems' functional circuit(s). In the radar, signals frequently flow between subsystems and change their

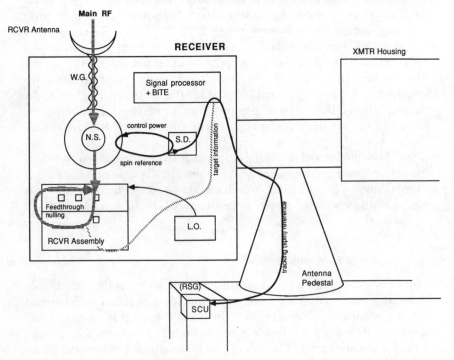

FIGURE 5.12 Functional block.

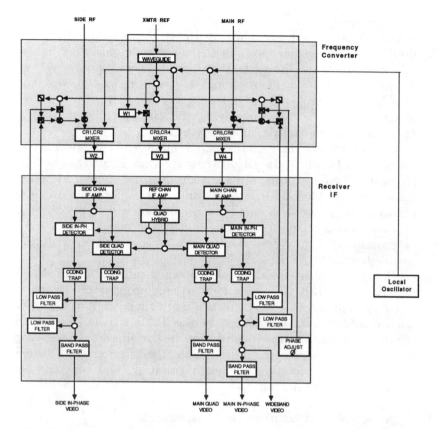

FIGURE 5.13 Functional breakdown of a receiver assembly within a physical context.

names along the way. Because signal flow within a subsystem is often not explicitly indicated in the documentation, it is even more difficult for the novice to trace signals flowing from one subsystem to another and to comprehend how those signals affect the other subsystem. Once students have individually mastered two subsystems, they can be given problems involving functions in both subsystems. This, in effect, increases the problem space, making the problem more difficult.

Circuit Type

The type of circuit, that is, the pattern of information-processing, affects the complexity of troubleshooting strategies, and thus is a way to vary problem difficulty. As already described, the three information circuit configurations (chains, branches, and loops) involve explicit high-level or qualitative troubleshooting strategies. To troubleshoot these three circuit types, the student must understand the concepts and troubleshooting strategies inherent in their structure. Both branches and loops are more difficult to understand and to troubleshoot. When they appear in a circuit, they should be highlighted as a unit and a specific strategy on how to troubleshoot that type of circuit (branch or loop) should be recommended. Loops and branches can be broken down in such a way that they become groups of chain circuits, thus simplifying the circuit. This should be graphically supported by a tutoring system.

Within each of these categories, the number of components and the physical length of the circuit (how far away it stretches or how physically distributed it is) can add additional complexity. Although the addition of physical length or number of components does not change the basic troubleshooting strategy inherent in the type of circuit, the number of procedural steps generally does increase. Keeping track of procedural details and results adds a cognitive load during troubleshooting.

Loops also have an additional complexity variable, because loops may be intertwined. Because a loop has the property of essentially acting "instantaneously" to perform a single function, it follows that intertwined loops act simultaneously as well. Thus, if one intertwined loop is faulty, the other intertwined loops are also affected. The ensuing troubleshooting strategies must isolate the affected loop before applying the basic loop troubleshooting strategy. This is potentially the most complex situation.

Number of Possible Measurable-Replaceable Parts

For each subsystem or functional area, problems can range in complexity by varying the number of possible measurements or replacements within that area, thus increasing the number of procedural steps that are involved. Because there are an overwhelming number of possible measurable/replaceable parts in the radar, initially "chunking" a functional area into its major composite functions within a physical context would simplify matters for novice mechanics by reducing the number of possible parts, yet would still allow them to practice troubleshooting on a functional basis. This high-level chunking has the effect of reducing the problem space. As the student grasps the high-level functional concepts and procedures, more detailed views of the circuitry can be presented, providing the student mechanic with a larger, more realistic problem space to troubleshoot, that is, a greater number of parts to measure or replace.

Vary Number of Procedural Steps for Results

The last way in which problem difficulty can be manipulated is by varying the number of procedural steps required to get results; it is also a way to emphasize and develop logical reasoning skills. Performing a series of voltage measurements to get a result is, in some sense, a time-consuming distraction task that could be saved for a more advanced stage.

Initially, the rank beginner needs to know only that a power or information signal is "good," "bad," or "absent;" the result of this "functional test" mimics interactions we have observed between an instructor and a student mechanic in an effort to save time. With a "functional test," stronger and more explicit emphasis can be placed on deciding what the signal's status means in terms of the system's function and what should be done next. For example, a student could request a simplified test through a menu, such as "Measurement Test" or "Replacement Test," then select the intended object for measurement or replacement with a mouse. The ITS could immediately return a simplified test result ("Result: Good" or "Result: Bad"), still leaving the novice with the problem: "So what does this mean and what do I do next?"

Explicit reasoning supports in the form of questions and possible alternatives or conclusions could be provided via dialogue boxes and a menu. By explicitly querying the student as to what the results imply, reasoning and decision-making skills can be enhanced.

As students become more proficient at making decisions based on "good" or "bad" test results, the level of detailed knowledge required for performing the test and for interpreting the test results can be increased. For example, students may have to be more specific about the test. Thus, instead of selecting "Measurement Test," they would have to indicate the type of test measurement, for example, "Test for Open" or "Test for Short." Similarly, students would have to further interpret test results. A simple interpretation may pertain to deciding what to do based on various "bad" result types, such as noisy, absent, or invalid signals. Later, a more knowledgeable interpretation of test results would be required when the test result is quantitative, for example, "Result: < 10 VDC." The student would have to know whether the test result's value was within the range of normal indications or whether it meant the signal was noisy, absent, or invalid.

Provide a Range of Procedural Help

In addition to showing the problem space and providing problems that vary in difficulty in the five ways discussed, another way for the intelligent tutoring system to help the student learn to troubleshoot is to provide a range of procedural help. Though procedural help is not a top-priority item, it can facilitate the troubleshooting process. As was observed between the expert and other mechanics during the troubleshooting problems, the expert not only provided the mechanics with the results of procedural tests, he also provided them with other procedural supports, including the following:

1. The physical location of a particular component (if its location is totally unknown).
2. Where to measure or replace (if a certain segment of a cable or a portion of an assembly is specified in the procedures).
3. The correct setting of a switch.
4. The correct step sequence (if a certain order is required, such as disconnecting a cable prior to measuring or replacing).
5. Incorrect use of the documentation (e.g., wrong page of the schematics, branching to the wrong procedure).

The tutoring system can address these behaviors, with the possible exception of the last item. The radar contains an extraordinary number of components with long, complex names, which can overwhelm students. The ITS can help them locate the desired part and which particular segment or portion of the part is currently relevant. For example, a signal may be carried within five cable segments, two of which are end-to-end cable segments of one wire, named W3. The remaining three segments may be branches of the cable. The student needs to know where each of those segments are (they may have a wide physical distribution), and which end is currently relevant for measurement. Furthermore, some cable segments are replaceable, whereas for other cables, all segments and branches are replaced as a unit.

In the case of switch settings, failure to test in the appropriate mode may result in measuring the wrong signal, because a switch or relay may route the relevant signal along a different circuit path. Performing the correct step sequence may be particularly important at certain times. Because many signals travel through a cable (cables contain many wires within them), disconnecting a cable may prevent another signal that is required for the relevant component's operation, such as power, thus preventing an accurate measurement of that component's status.

Thus the tutoring system can, like an expert instructor, provide mechanics with a range of procedural supports that help them implement the troubleshooting steps correctly and quickly.

Provide Supports to Make Reasoning Strategies Explicit

The fourth area in which the ITS can help is in making reasoning strategies explicit, and probably the area that the ITS can contribute to the most. Because visual representations are the modus operandi of an ITS, it can make the current implicit reasoning process explicit and concrete. It is important for the novice mechanic to see and understand what the FIP accomplishes—what portion of the circuit and what signals are being tested, why a certain sequence of steps matters, and what is being ruled out.

The supports not only need to make the reasoning process explicit—both the novice's and the expert's reasoning—they need to make the process easier for the novice. If, for example, the system's behavior does not meet the novice mechanic's expectations of how it should work, he or she needs to learn to logically hypothesize (predict) about the source of the discrepancy and generate an efficient way to check that hypothesis, based on the novice's model of how the circuit that performs the impaired function should work. As the trouble-shooting process continues, the mechanic has to keep track of which alternatives have been tried and their results and which alternatives have not been tested—a sizable cognitive burden for the novice mechanic.

The tutoring system should also demonstrate how an expert would troubleshoot the problem, providing an "inside look" into not only what possibilities the expert pursued, but, also, what alternatives were ruled out. The expert model has two purposes: (a) to initially demonstrate how that type of problem can be solved and what issues need to be considered and (b) to provide a standard to which novices can compare their performances. Thus, the tutoring system's supports should not only make strategies explicit, but also should help lighten the student's cognitive load. These supports and others are described below.

Predicting and articulating hypotheses. The ITS needs to explicitly show (e.g., via a menu) what functions in a particular subsystem could be impaired (e.g., "Doesn't remove feedthrough noise"). For each functional fault, the student could request that the system show the components that perform the function (e.g., Feedthrough Nulling Loop), and thus may be potentially faulty. The student would have to specify which component within the group that he or she would like to test.

These menus can provide a way to monitor students' thinking processes, by requiring them to "articulate" (select) the most likely fault hypothesis (a specific impaired function) and to select what component to test for a fault. By requiring students to select a hypothesis and to specify a component within the portion of the circuit that performs the hypothetically impaired function, students can acquire and practice functional reasoning skills. This also provides a way to guide the student away from vague or incorrect fault hypotheses or from associating components with the wrong function.

Alerting student to inconsistencies. If a student's testing (measurement or replacement) action does not coincide with the selected fault hypothesis, the ITS should alert the student of this inconsistency, and allow the student to change his or her hypothesis or to select a component within the relevant component group for that function.

Reducing search space. By providing a visual means of showing those portions of the circuit that are functioning correctly and thus have been ruled out, students can be prevented from getting stuck and retesting components within those portions. By providing this "crossing out" facility, the student can be guided into thinking in terms of reducing the search space of possible faults, and consequently, also see with a single glance what areas remain for testing.

Providing action and plan history. A window that shows what hypotheses have been considered, what tests were performed, and their results will also help students to both systematically reduce the search space and to consider alternative hypotheses. Students will also have a visual trace of their reasoning process and can use this to compare their approach to the expert model in terms of efficiency and of logical reasoning accuracy.

Providing hints. Students who are "stuck" should not lose the opportunity to practice their reasoning skills by getting a full solution every time they run into difficulty. By providing a facility that gives increasingly more specific hints in logical reasoning, the ITS perhaps can give students the appropriate level of help.

Modeling expert's solution path and reasoning. Modeling an expert's solution not only can show what steps are performed, but it can also provide an opportunity to articulate critical metacognitive reasoning and problem-solving skills that are so often implicit during troubleshooting. For example, the solution could make explicit the types of questions (conditions) experts ask themselves and give reasons for performing those procedural actions, such as

1. What function(s) appear to be impaired? [First, consider the portion of the circuit that performs the function that is earliest in the flow of information through that subsystem.]

2. Does the functional circuit have a "good" input information signal? [If not, something prior to this is not working.]

3. Does the functional circuit produce a "good" output information signal? [If it does, something after this is not working. If it does not produce good output and it has good information input, then the functional circuit is not working.]

4. Use "divide-and-conquer" strategy specific to the type of information circuit (chain, branch, loop), measuring components (or connections) at strategic dividing points.

5. Does the component have a "good" input information signal and produce a "good" output signal? [Same conclusions as for functional circuit above.]

6. Does the component have power? [If not, first check the cables bringing power to the component, then the power supply.]

7. Is the component broken? [All power and information signals are present going into the component, and "bad" signals or no signals are coming out, so replace the component.]

8. Is the BITE monitoring correctly, that is, is it working? [If the BITE test does not run, does it have the power or have the lights themselves faulted? If the BITE test runs, but fails, does it have the right information?]

Thus, by providing supports that make strategies, that is, the reasoning process, explicit and that also lighten the cognitive burden of problem solving, that is, records hypotheses, tests, and results, an ITS can help the novice radar mechanic to develop an accurate mental model and to develop and practice the skills needed for functional troubleshooting.

Provide Explanations

The final area in which the ITS can help the student is by providing verbal explanations to accompany the physical-functional diagrams of graduated detail in their dynamic (simulated) and static modes. Explanations fall into five areas: function, topology, modularity, simulation, behaviors, and general.

Function

Function explanations pertain primarily to devices. Loops are also included here, because loops actually act like devices at a high level, that is, they require input signals, produce output, and perform a function. The types of questions a novice may ask about device functions may be:

1. What is it for? The system would provide a simple statement about the purpose or goal of the device or loop.
2. What does it do? This would describe the input signals a device needs to function, and the signals that are produced (output). This would also include a high-level description of the device's behavior, including its role in a larger context (e.g., the role of the frequency converter within the receiver block within the receiver).
3. How does it do it? This would provide a detailed explanation of how the device performs its function – that is, the process.

Topology

Topology explanations mainly pertain to location. Because novices have difficulty matching up the physical organization of the radar to the schematic wiring diagrams, this feature should help them locate items more easily and to understand the flow of information and power signals. The questions novice mechanics can ask include:

1. Where does the signal come from? This would describe, at a local level, what device(s) produced the signal as output.
2. Where does the signal go? This would describe what device(s) receive(s) the signal as input.
3. Where is the device? In addition to explaining where the device is, the system can provide the options of showing the actual device and its context.

Modularity

Modularity explanations provide higher level information than the function and topology categories above. Modularity explanations describe how devices and signals are grouped into their larger modules and correspond to the views that show how the circuit is "chunked" into its composite functions and circuit types, as previously described.

Simulation Behavior

Simulation behavior explanations essentially tell the student what he or she is seeing on the screen, what the simulation is doing at that moment. For example, "The signal coming from the receiver is valid."

This feature allows students to selectively "break" a component and see how it affects the rest of the circuit's components and signals, as well as the rest of the system.

The reverse situation, in which the student requests a particular effect (such as a noisy signal) to find out what possible causes could produce that effect, is much more reflective of the troubleshooting situation. This will require the system to trace backward and say what faults could possibly cause that effect. Even though the system can easily generate a list of every possible component prior to producing that signal, getting the system to produce a succinct description that reflects functional reasoning will be harder to implement. However, a novice mechanic will find the latter much easier and much more meaningful, and that feature should be implemented in the tutoring system if at all possible.

General Explanations

General explanations pertain to device taxonomy. This taxonomy is based on classes of devices that, at a very high level of understanding, essentially perform the same function. One class of devices is involved in transforming a signal from one "energy" form to another. In the case of a synchro, a mechanical signal is transformed into an electrical signal. Another class of devices is involved in signal refinement. Although the receiver (which takes an RF signal and derives an electrical signal from) performs the reverse of the transmitter (which has electrical power and generates an RF signal), both subsystems remove unwanted noise through loops to obtain a refined signal product.

Another type of taxomic explanation pertains to the classification of troubleshooting procedures, that is, very high-level strategies from which mechanics can come to understand and generate their own fault isolation procedures. These explanations pertain to the metacognitive reasoning and problem-solving skills modeled when the expert solves the problem, as already described.

The metacognitive reasoning processes a mechanic needs will help him or her to knowledgeably select (and monitor):

1. A strategy to determine which functions are impaired in a subsystem and to monitor the results of that strategy.
2. The perspective to focus on the impaired function that either comes first in the flow of information through that subsystem, or if the impaired function involves a loop, focuses on the loop and uses a strategy appropriate to loop circuits.
3. Which "divide-and-conquer" strategy helps isolate the portion of the

functional circuit that is faulted, where the strategy depends on the type of circuit.

4. The strategy to select particular procedures that will determine whether a device appears broken because its input signals (power and/or information) are missing or invalid, because the device itself is broken, or because it is not being monitored correctly.

Thus, by providing explanations that describe the function of devices, the location of signals and devices, the simulation's behaviors, and a high-level taxonomy for devices and procedures, student mechanics can develop a complex, functional understanding of how the radar works and learn to flexibly and efficiently troubleshoot faults in the radar.

CONCLUSION

The HAWK intelligent tutoring system, as it is implemented, has two related focuses for training novice radar mechanics: One focus is to help novices develop increasingly more complex models of the radar. A second focus (as novices' models become more refined) is to help them develop a correspondingly richer and flexible repertoire of strategic troubleshooting skills based on a functional understanding of the procedures.

To help students develop increasingly refined models and to reduce the information overload produced by the detailed schematics, the ITS will provide summary views varying in detail and emphasis for each functional circuit. Realistic faults will be inserted in those views to expose students to a systematic selection of faults and to provide sufficient troubleshooting practice. Because these views will vary in their level of detail, so, too, will the problems vary in their difficulty level. These problems will be designed to help students acquire a functional understanding of each functional circuit, and its composite subfunctions, and underlying system concepts, such as the signal types, information circuit types, device models, and loops.

By providing problems, explanations, and strategic supports that explicitly portray how certain conditions impair functions and by modeling how to locate the faults, the ITS can enable students to find problems and to know when and how to apply their skills in a given situation. The tutoring system's strategic supports will provide students the means to select and test relevant hypotheses for a particular functional area. Through the expert, high-level troubleshooting strategies and metacognitive reasoning, skills can be made explicit by showing students how to rule out areas and locate the fault through strategic applications of test procedures and the interpretation of test results. With guided problem-solving practice and with the expert model to compare their performance to, students can develop a repertoire of troubleshooting strategies.

As the tutoring system is developed, instructors will be asked to help refine the views, explanations, and supports. The system will be continually evaluated for its effects on students' models and their problem solving with the system. With this iterative evaluation, we hope to attain the final goal of successfully transferring the knowledge and skills that students have learned with the tutor to actual troubleshooting on the radar.

ACKNOWLEDGMENT

Support for this project comes from the Training Research Laboratory of the Army Research Institute for Behavioral and Social Sciences under contract MDA903-85-C-0425.

REFERENCES

Anderson, J. R. (1985). The development of expertise. In J. R. Anderson (Ed.). *Cognitive psychology and its implications* (pp. 232–260). New York: W. H. Freeman.

Ausubel, D. P. (1968). *Educational psychology: A cognitive view.* New York: Holt, Rinehart & Winston.

Bender, W. G. (1962). *The language of system structure-graphical models.* In A. D. Hall, *A methodology for systems engineering* (pp. 341–378). Princeton: D. Van Nostrand.

Collins, A. M., Brown, J. S., & Newman (in press). The new apprenticeship: Teaching students the craft of reading, writing, and mathematics. In L. B. Resnick (Ed.), *Cognition and instruction: Issues and agenda.* Hillsdale, NJ: Lawrence Erlbaum Associates.

Chi, M. T. H., Glaser, R., & Rees, E. (1981). *Expertise in problem solving.* Learning Research and Development Center, University of Pittsburgh (Tech. Rep. No. 5).

deKleer, J. (1985). How circuits work. In D. G. Bobrow (Ed.), *Qualitative reasoning about physical systems.* Cambridge, MA: MIT Press.

Egan, D. E., & Schwartz, B. J. (1979). Chunking in recall of symbolic drawings. *Memory and Cognition, 7,* 149–158.

Eylon, B., & Reif, F. (1984). Effects of knowledge organization on task performance. *Cognition and Instruction, 1,* 5–44.

Gentner, D., & Stevens, A. L. (1983). *Mental models.* Hillsdale, NJ: Lawrence Erlbaum Associates.

Gitomer, D. H. (1984). *A cognitive analysis of a complex troubleshooting task.* Unpublished doctoral dissertation. Learning Research and Development Center, University of Pittsburgh.

Glaser, R. (1985). *Thoughts on expertise.* Technical Report No. 8, Learning Research and Development Center, University of Pittsburgh.

Glaser, R., Lesgold, A., Lajoie, S., Eastman, R., Greenberg, L., Logan, D., Magone, M., Weiner, A., Wolf, R., & Yengo, L. (1985). *Cognitive task analysis to enhance technical skills training and assessment.* Final report of project on Feasibility of Cognitive Information Processing Models for Basic Skills Assessment and Enhancement, prepared for the Air Force Human Resources Laboratory, Learning Research and Development Center, University of Pittsburgh.

Kern, R. P. (1985). Modeling users and their use of technical manuals. In T. M. Duffy and R. Waller (Eds.), *Designing usable texts* (pp. 341-375). New York: Academic Press.

Kintsch, W. (1978). On comprehending stories. In M. A. Just & P. A. Carpenter (Eds.), *Cognitive processes in comprehension: Carnegie-Mellon symposium.* Halstead Press.

Larkin, J. H. & Simon, H. A. (1985). *Why a picture is worth ten thousand words.* Center for Information Processing Report No 454. Carnegie-Mellon University, Pittsburgh, PA.

Meyer, B. J. F., Brandt, D. M., & Bluth, G. J. (1980) Use of top-level structure in text: Key for reading comprehension of ninth grade students. *Reading Research Quarterly, 16,* 72-103.

Miyake, N. (1986). Constructive interaction. *Cognitive Science, 10,* 151-177.

Novak, J. D. (1977). *A theory of education.* Ithaca: Cornell University Press.

Raven, F. H. (1961). *Automatic control engineering.* New York: McGraw-Hill.

Schneider, W. (1985). Training high-performance skills: Fallacies and guidelines. *Human Factors, 27,* 285-300.

Thro, M. P. (1978). Relationships between associative and content structure of physics concepts. *Journal of Educational Psychology, 70,* 971-978.

Tulving, E., & Thomson, D. M. (1973). Encoding specificity and retrieval processes in episodic memory. *Psychology Review, 80,* 352-373.

6

The Problem Space
of Instructional Design

Peter L. Pirolli
James G. Greeno
University of California, Berkeley

INTRODUCTION

We propose a framework for analysis and study of the design of
instruction. One objective is to contribute to the formulation of general
principles in the field of intelligent tutoring systems that will facilitate
systematic and cumulative progress in research. Another objective is
to understand relations between work on instructional design
conducted by researchers in intelligent tutoring systems, instructional-
design scientists (e.g., Gagné & Briggs, 1979; Reigeluth, 1983a), and
computer-assisted instruction (e.g., Bork, 1981; Heines, 1984; Suppes,
1981).

This framework considers instructional design as a problem-
solving task, centered on a characterization of decisions and methods
in what we call the *instructional-design problem space*. Instructional
designs are artifacts of instructional design processes. General features
of designed systems were discussed by Simon (1969), using classical
problem-solving terms (e.g., Newell & Simon, 1972). An instructional
design, like other designs, involves selecting among alternative means
to achieve certain ends. These ends are instructional goals that we
wish to achieve under specified constraints of the instructional
situation. These general terms have also been used in discussions of
instructional design (e.g., Landa, 1983; Reigeluth, 1983b). If we
consider the task of instructional design as a problem-solving process,
we are led to formulate the task environment of instructional design
using concepts that have been useful in analyses of other problem-

solving tasks. In particular, it is important to characterize the problem space of instructional design.

In general, the problem space of a task characterizes the alternatives that a problem solver has available and the various states that can be produced during problem solving by the decisions that the problem solver makes in choosing among alternatives. As instructional scientists have recognized, the design of instruction involves alternatives and decisions at several levels or subspaces.

We have found it useful to distinguish nine subspaces, involving different levels and aspects of instruction, shown in Figure 6.1. The levels involve global issues, issues of intermediate generality, and local details. These levels correspond approximately to issues in designing courses, designing lessons, and designing specific presentations and activities.

The issues at each level involve (a) goals and constraints, (b) technological resources, and (c) theoretical resources. These three classes of issues are interrelated: technological resources provide the means for achieving goals and satisfying constraints; and theoretical resources provide reasons and explanations for decisions that are made in selecting from alternative goals and methods.

We consider the contribution of theories to design as a set of resources, not as a set of prescriptions, as they often are considered by others. To be sure, theoretical principles can have prescriptive force, as they do when they specify conditions that are required to achieve certain results. Another function of theory, however, is to provide analyses that identify and clarify alternative forms in which learning and instruction can be designed. Then the theoretical resource expands the space of possibilities in which the designer works, and principles link these possibilities to the decisions that the designer is able to make.

The reasons and explanations for instructional decisions, drawn from theoretical resources, can be included in a document along with instructional materials, and the Instructional Design Environment, described by Russell, Moran, and Jordan (chapter 7, this volume), is intended to facilitate construction of instructional designs that enable other designers or instructors to understand the design principles that provide reasons and explanations for the instructional materials.

A problem-solving framework for instructional design allows consideration and integration of the products of design, instructional materials, and the processes of designing instruction. This chapter is concerned mainly with characteristics of instructional materials and activities, but we also consider the framework potentially useful as a basis for empirical research about problem-solving processes and knowledge involved in the task of designing instruction.

		Goals and Constraints	Technological Resources	Theoretical Resources
	Global	Forms and Content of Learning	Learning Environments	Principles of Epistemology
Levels of Design Issues	Intermediate	Lessons and Activities	Content Topics, Tasks, Cognitive Models, Diagnostic Systems, Systems of Representation	Methods of Task Analysis, Structure of Subject-Matter Disciplines
	Local	Presentations and Specific Tasks	Texts, Lectures, Conversation, Graphics Design, Human-Computer Interface	Principles of Component Display, Theory of Communication

FIGURE 6.1   Components of the instructional-design problem space.

THE PROBLEM SPACE

This section features the main components of our characterization of the problem space for instructional design, organized according to levels of generality of the issues.

Global-Level Design Issues

A general set of decisions is made, deliberately or by default, to determine the main content of instruction and the general goals that instruction will attempt to achieve.

Global goals and constraints. In most discussions of instructional design, the goals of instruction are to transmit knowledge of concepts, principles, and specific skills to students. There are important alternatives to these essentially didactic goals of instruction and learning. These include enhancing abilities for formulating questions and arguments in a domain, modifying attitudes and beliefs about the domain, sharpening general reasoning skills, and metacognitive capabilities.

Goals of subject matter content are often considered as "given" for the process of instructional design, based on judgments of experts in the subject matter domain. Choices must be made, however, and these reflect judgments about the value of various aspects of knowledge in the domain—for example, is it more important for students to know a broad set of facts and principles of a domain or to acquire a deeper understanding of a few topics? Recent research on misconceptions has emphasized that students may complete instruction that presents a set of concepts, but still understand the domain in terms of different concepts that they had before the instruction. Alternative ways to organize subject matter concepts should be considered in planning instruction in a domain to make its structure more likely to result in acquisition of integrated understanding by students, including a correct set of intuitions and connections between their informal and formal knowledge.

Choices of subject matter content also are influenced by constraints based on the capabilities of students to understand and learn, as well as relations of the material to other instruction that has preceded or will follow the material that is being designed.

Global technological resources.   Until recently, theories of instructional design assumed that instruction would be presented to groups of students, largely in the form of lectures, demonstrations, and texts, or in a limited form of tutorial instruction in which the tutor guides a student through an organized body of concepts and information. Early forms of computer-assisted instruction presented information and exercises in a domain in the form of simple branching programs. These technologies of presenting instruction are appropriate for the goal of assisting students in acquiring the content of a subject matter domain, but are probably less effective for broader cognitive goals of instruction, such as helping them to form questions and make judgments in a domain, to acquire general reasoning skills, and to integrate new concepts with existing informal knowledge and understanding.

Alternative environments for instruction have included laboratories in which students perform experiments or otherwise gain practical experience, group discussions in which students pose questions as well as give answers, and peer teaching situations in which more knowledgeable students share the responsibility for instruction. More recently, computational systems have been developed in which students can engage in dialogues about physical systems (e.g., Bork, 1981).

Recent research has provided three further kinds of instructional environments. One class of environment involves an exploratory microworld, where students can manipulate objects in a computational system that is designed to embody a set of theoretical principles. Examples of exploratory instruction include Dugdale's (1982) game,

Green Globs, for algebra, in which students write expressions for functions so their graphs pass through sets of points that are displayed; diSessa's (1982) system, Dynaturtle, in which objects move according to Newtonian principles; and Uarushalmy and Houde's (1986) Geometric Supposer, in which students explore conjectures about objects and properties in Euclidean geometry.

Another kind of environment involves a sort of apprenticeship, in which a teacher first models behaviors that he or she wants students to emulate and then coaches students as they work to acquire the skill. Examples include Palincsar's and Brown's (1984) method of reciprocal teaching, in which students observe and then carry out activities of asking questions, summarizing, and other metacognitive activities involved in successful comprehension, and Schoenfeld's (1985) method of teaching problem solving in mathematics, in which the teacher demonstrates and encourages active monitoring of the progress that students are making on problems, rather than focusing entirely on the final solutions that are achieved.

A third kind of learning environment emphasizes collaboration, either among students or between the teacher and students on intellectual goals that they share. Examples include Fawcett's (1938) course in geometry, in which the students and teacher worked together on developing the definitions and axioms of formal reasoning, both in geometry and in other reasoning domains, and Lampert's (in press) method of conversational teaching in which she and her students work together on the task of making sense of elementary mathematical notation and procedures.

Global theoretical resources. Theoretical resources provide reasons and explanations for choices that are made in the design of instruction. The theories that apply to global features of instruction are in the domain of epistemology, involving general analyses of knowledge, including forms of knowledge and values of knowledge in different settings.

Theoretical resources for global features of instruction include empirically based theories that identify alternative forms of knowledge and learning and their general characteristics. For example, recent theories of qualitative physics (e.g., deKleer & Brown, 1984; Forbus, 1984) provide hypotheses about reasoning about causal relations that is different from use of formulas. Studies of conceptual growth, such as that of Carey (1985), provide understanding of ways in which knowledge in a domain can involve changes in theoretical principles that are used in interpreting a broad range of phenomena. Studies of reasoning in practical settings, such as those of Lave, Murtaugh, and de la Roch (1984) show characteristics of knowledge used in situations in which problems are structured by social environments rather than by the organization of academic disciplines.

Epistemological principles also are involved in important dimensions of individual difference. Metacognitive beliefs about the nature of knowing and learning differ significantly among individuals, varying from belief that one's learning involves receiving truth from authorities to belief that knowledge is construed through an active personal and interpersonal process (Belenky, Clinchy, Goldberger, & Tarule, 1986). Individuals differ in what it means to know a subject, varying from a criterion of being able to solve text problems correctly to grasping the relations among concepts (diSessa, 1985; Schoenfeld, 1985).

Philosophical analyses of knowledge also provide important resources for choosing and justifying general goals of instruction. An example is Kitcher's (1984) study of mathematical knowledge. Kitcher focused on a concept of knowing a *mathematical practice*, which includes mathematical language, established results, accepted questions, accepted reasonings, metamathematical views, and the goals of mathematical study. Values of alternative kinds of knowledge are also important, as Posner and Rudnitsky (1986) noted.

Intermediate-Level Design Issues

An instructional designer constructs a set of lessons and activities arranged in a sequence, possibly contingent on student progress. Choice of these units and their sequential arrangement is a major subject of many discussions of instructional design (e.g., Gagné & Briggs, 1979; Gropper, 1983; Landa, 1983; Mager, 1962; Posner & Rudnitsky, 1986; Reigeluth & Stein, 1983; Scandura, 1983).

Intermediate goals and constraints. Choosing the subgoals of a lesson is analogous to choosing the components of a device that one wants to build, or deciding about the parts of an essay that one wants to write. The parts of a lesson involve knowledge of components of subject matter and components of a cognitive skill. A coherent and progressive sequence of presentations and activities is constructed that will result in knowledge and cognitive capability that the instruction is intended to provide. If the instruction is interactive, as in tutorial instruction, the designer constructs a set of instructional activities and a set of rules that will determine the sequence that occurs in the instructional situation. In instruction that is provided by human teachers, the instructional plan usually does not specify rules for proceeding through the lesson, but the teacher's knowledge includes a rich set of routines and situated skill that determines the sequence of activities in the instructional context (cf. Leinhardt & Greeno, 1986).

Constraints on the subgoals and sequence of instruction are provided by relations among the units of knowledge, including necessary or facilitating prerequisites for learning new material or acquiring new components of skill.

Intermediate technological resources. The main resources for constructing lessons are known components of subject matter knowledge and classes of problems and questions that students are asked to solve and answer. In many cases of instructional design, these resources are obtained from subject matter experts. Subject matter experts also can provide information about relations between tasks, guiding arrangements of instructional sequences and tests for progress that are used in branching CAI programs.

Instruction that uses games, exploratory environments, and collaborative work requires resources in the form of activities that are given or suggested to students. The activities provide goals for the student's exploration of the environment or the collaborative work that the students engage in together or with the teacher.

A broader range of resources is also becoming available through developments in cognitive research and artificial intelligence. These resources include cognitive models of successful performance of instructional tasks. These models can suggest tasks that focus on aspects of performance that are usually not instructed explicitly, such as the information required to understand word problems or the valid transformations of arithmetic expressions that preserve value (Greeno et al., 1986). Such models can also be used as expert problem solvers in tutorial systems to provide correct solutions that are compared with solutions provided by students. Examples include the Geometry Tutor and the LISP tutor, developed by Anderson and his associates (Anderson, Boyle, & Yost, 1985; Pirolli, 1986; Reiser, Anderson, & Farrell, 1985), which provide detailed feedback using a scheme called *model tracing* in which each step of a student's performance is compared with the performance of the model. Models of successful performance also are used in tutorial systems for teaching proof skills in logic (Suppes, 1981) and for teaching programming in PASCAL (Bonar & Cunningham, chapter 16, this volume). These tutorial systems use the models to provide guidance and feedback to the students at the level of their goals and plans, as well as at the level of specific steps in solving problems.

More sophisticated resources have been developed in research on intelligent tutoring systems. For example, systems such as BUGGY (Brown & Burton, 1978) are based on analyses of a space of possible procedures for performing the task, including correct performance as well as variations that produce systematic incorrect performance. Coaching systems such as WEST (Burton & Brown, 1982) diagnose student strategies and provide hints and suggestions at the level of strategic performance.

Resources for designing lessons also include systems of representation that are used to display information to students. Traditionally, systems of representation have included demonstrations of laboratory phenomena, pieces of equipment or models of systems that the teacher is discussing, and concrete materials such as place-value blocks for displaying abstract relations in concrete form, in addition to the standard presentation media of texts and diagrams.

Recent additions to the armamentarium of representation systems include computer displays that simulate systems that students can interact with, and that provide graphical displays of data taken from real or simulated experiments. Additional systems of representation have been developed to display information explicitly to students that is usually implicit, embedded in the process of understanding or reasoning about problems. Examples of these include graphical displays of the steps taken in solving problems in algebra (Brown, 1983) and in geometry (Anderson, Boyle, & Yost, 1985). Additional examples include graphical displays of semantic relations in texts of word problems (Greeno et al., 1986).

Intermediate theoretical resources.   The theoretical resources relevant to designing lessons include principles for analyzing the structure of subject matter domains and requirements of instructional tasks for the purposes of learning and instruction. The methods of behavioral task analysis provide the theoretical basis of much of the designed instruction that has been developed in the past 20 years.

An alternative set of principles involves the structure of concepts and principles in the subject matter domain, rather than in behaviors that students have to perform. Efforts to redesign the school mathematics and science curricula according to principles of subject matter structure were pursued energetically in the 1950s and 1960s, with important innovative materials produced by groups such as the School Mathematics Study Group and the Project Physics Group. Recent discussions of course organization, such as Reigeluth's and Stein's (1983) elaboration theory, have developed ideas about relations between topics according to a scheme involving degrees of generality of material, defined differently for different kinds of content.

Recent research has provided enhanced resources for analysis of cognitive requirements of instructional tasks. Cognitive models of knowledge structures and cognitive processes used in solving problems and answering questions have provided explicit hypotheses about requirements of successful performance that are usually tacit, and these hypotheses have been used as the basis for instruction directed at specific sources of difficulty in performance. Advances have also been made in developing models of the process of learning specific skills, and these provide guidance in the design of rules for feedback to students. In addition, important advances have been made recently in understanding misconceptions about theoretical concepts and principles, especially in physics. Efforts can be made now to develop new principles of organization for the content of subject matter domains in ways that are more coherent with student's intuitive understanding and with natural progression of conceptual growth.

Local-Level Design Issues

When instruction occurs, information is presented in specific texts and vocal presentations, conversations, diagrams, and specific tasks and questions.

Detailed goals and constraints. The instructional designer or developer constructs these specific presentations and activities, including such details as the size of print and arrangement of material in text or screen displays, and the amount of time that will be spent on specific problems or demonstrations. Relevant considerations include clarity of presentation, ease of reading type, consistency of layout, and other concerns that influence the ease of understanding and interaction with information systems.

Technological resources for presentations. Resources for designing specific presentations and activities are provided in the fields of graphics design and human–computer interaction (e.g., Norman & Draper, 1986), including discussions that are specifically oriented toward instructional materials (e.g., Heines, 1984). Recent discussions by Newell and Card (1985) and Pirolli (1986) have pointed out how intelligent tutoring systems offer significant opportunities for research in human–computer interaction by providing tools for gathering and modeling data on the communication of knowledge in the computational medium.

Theoretical resources for presentations. Principles of design for specific instructional transactions have been discussed in instructional science, notably by Merrill (1983) in his component display theory. This theory is based on a particular analysis of types of subject matter contents and types of presentation, and concerns prescriptive statements that relate subject matter categories to optimal presentation forms. Component display theory presents an analysis of subject matter categorized by types of content and types of performance. Types of content are facts, concepts, procedures, and principles. Types of performance include remembering an instance or abstraction, using an abstraction, and finding an abstraction. Merrill (1983) also presented an analysis of *presentation forms*, which break down into primary and secondary presentation forms. Primary presentation forms are expository or inquisitory and concern either generalities (e.g., the definition of a concept) or instances (e.g., an example of the concept). These are the main methods of instruction. Secondary presentation forms are mainly elaborations of the primary forms and are used to facilitate the student's processing of primary presentations or to maintain interest. Component display theory concerns which primary and secondary presentation forms are best suited for each type of content and performance. Although the theory was developed largely with a style of instruction involving expositions and inquisitions in mind, Merrill (in press) has recently generalized the theory to deal with more experience-based learning of the kind found in intelligent tutoring systems that use expert and student models, interactive simulations, expert demonstrations, and coaching.

An issue concerning the human–computer interface that we consider important but unexplored comes from recent developments in the theory of conversation. The communicative structure of human–computer interaction is generally considered in terms of either a student model in an instructional system or a user's model of a piece of technology, complete with "gulfs" between the user and the system (e.g., Hutchins, Hollan, & Norman, 1985). Analyses of communication in conversations by social scientists (e.g., Schegloff, 1972) and psycholinguists (e.g., Clark & Wilkes-Gibbs, 1986) present a more subtle and complex picture. Functions even as simple as reference to places, persons, and objects are achieved cooperatively, as part of a process of creating a shared pool of information, understanding, opinion, and belief. In the process, both partners know what is being said, and each one also knows that the other knows what is being said. An implication is that we should begin paying close attention to the student's understanding of the instructional system, in addition to the instructional system's understanding of the student's state of knowledge. A tutor should provide indications that what the student has said or done has been understood, and the student should have a model of the tutoring system that makes those indications comprehensible. Communication between human teachers and students depends on shared knowledge about each other's cognitive states, and teachers spend considerable effort teaching their students routines for classroom activities (Leinhardt, Weidman, & Hammond, 1984). Similar efforts to instruct students in how to use particular features of a computational instructional system seem warranted.

THEORY AND METHODOLOGY IN THE INSTRUCTIONAL-DESIGN PROBLEM-SPACE FRAMEWORK

We propose that instructional design be considered as a problem-solving task, and we have outlined a characterization of the problem space for instructional design that seems to us to make such a consideration feasible. We turn now to a discussion of some issues in the theory of instruction that we believe are clarified by taking the point of view of instructional design as problem solving.

Prescriptive and Descriptive Principles

One familiar distinction is that between descriptive and prescriptive theories (e.g., Landa, 1983). Descriptive, or natural, sciences are concerned with descriptions of how things are; with accumulating declarative statements that characterize our world. A descriptive science of instructional design is concerned with statements of the form "if constraints C hold and actions A are taken, then outcome G will occur." In contrast, prescriptive sciences are concerned with how artifacts ought to be in order to achieve certain goals. A prescriptive science of instructional design is concerned with imperative statements of the form "in order to achieve goal G under constraints C, then perform actions A" (Landa, 1983). One of the important outcomes of Simon's (1969) analysis of design science is to point out how the classical problem-solving framework reduces the imperative logic of design to the declarative, model-theoretic logic of natural science. This essentially means that the problem space approach allows us to analyze both prescriptive and descriptive theories in the same framework.

Considering instructional design as a form of problem solving enables the use of some general prescriptive principles of efficient problem solving as recommendations for instructional designers. These include heuristic principles that contribute to efficient search, such as identifying relatively decomposable components of the task and dealing with them as subproblems, considering more-constrained aspects of the task before considering less-constrained aspects, and delaying commitments to detailed implementations when higher level goals can interact. These considerations were discussed in the theory of planning, a well-developed field of research in artificial intelligence (e.g., Cohen & Feigenbaum, 1982).

The prescriptive view of instructional design suggested by the problem-solving perspective differs significantly from the sequential process that is often presented (e.g., Mager, 1962). Viewed as problem solving, the appropriate prescriptions are heuristics that can make the process more efficient and make a better solution more likely, rather than a sequence of steps that should be followed.

We expect that the problem-solving perspective also will favor productive descriptive studies of instructional design as a process. One promising approach would be to analyze the performance of designers to infer characteristics of their problem spaces, using and extending the methods of Newell and Simon (1972) and Kuipers and Kassirer (1984) in the use of protocol data for identifying the concepts, operators, and constraints that problem solvers use.

Principles of Instruction and Learning

It has often been pointed out (e.g., Landa, 1983; Reigeluth, 1983b) that theories of instruction are not theories of learning. The critical feature in this distinction lies in the description of means to achieve goals. Landa's (1983) version of the distinction is typical. Instructional theories are concerned with how actions taken by an instructor achieve instructional goals. In contrast, theories of learning are concerned with how actions taken by a learner achieve learning outcomes. Although we agree that this distinction is correct and useful, the distinction could be taken as a warrant for developing instructional theories that are independent of or only loosely related to learning theory (e.g., Landa, 1983; Merrill, 1983; Reigeluth, 1983b).

We prefer a view in which instructional and learning theories are linked closely, partly for the development of more effective instruction and partly because a close relation to instructional practice is beneficial for the progress of learning theory. One way to consider this relationship is by using learning theory as a source of constraints in the problem-solving task of instruction. In general, one can consider a subset of the constraints in the problem space of instruction to be natural laws that are relevant to the task. For example, there is an upper bound on the amount of information that can be perceived visually by a human looking at a display screen (Card, Moran, & Newell, 1983). Learning theory can be used as a specification of a subset of the natural laws that are relevant to the instructional task and consequently constrain the sorts of instructional methods that are used.

Another way to consider the relation of learning theory and instructional theory is to use principles of learning as theoretical resources that provide guidance and explanations for the selections of methods to achieve certain instructional goals. Cognitive science offers tools for modeling the states of student knowledge throughout the instructional process and the processes of transition between states. The problem for the instructional process is to move the student from some current state of knowledge to a goal state of knowledge. The transitions between these states, in principle, can be predicted by learning theory, given the student's experience and current knowledge state. In turn, we could, in principle, lay out the relations between instructional methods and student experiences.

It is apparent that different learning theories are explicitly or implicitly at the root of some differences among intelligent tutoring systems. For instance, PROUST (Johnson & Soloway, 1983), the BRIDGE Tutor (Bonar & Cunningham, chapter 16), and the LISP Tutor (Pirolli, 1986; Reiser, Anderson, & Farrell, 1985) are all targeted for instruction in introductory programming and use essentially the same representation of student knowledge.[1] PROUST and the BRIDGE Tutor use a goals-and-plans analysis of programming skill and misconceptions, whereas the LISP Tutor uses a production system scheme to represent such knowledge. Both of these representational schemes can be considered variants of the GOMS model of human information processing in computer-related tasks (Card, Moran, & Newell, 1983).

Despite these similarities, the instructional methods used in these systems are quite different. The LISP Tutor makes explicit use of a set of instructional principles (Anderson, Boyle, Farrell, & Reiser, 1984) grounded in the ACT* learning theory (Anderson, 1983). Some of the differences among these systems can be examined in light of these principles. For example, one principle followed by the LISP Tutor is to provide instruction and feedback in the context of problem solving. In contrast, PROUST takes syntactically correct programs that have already been written by a student and searches for semantic errors in the code and relates these errors to its catalogue of misconceptions. The BRIDGE Tutor is like the LISP Tutor in this respect. It provides feedback in the context of problem solving, but in contrast to the LISP Tutor it does not enforce a top-down refinement of programming goals. Rather, the BRIDGE Tutor proceeds by successively modifying a naive plan for an algorithm into an explicit program. The LISP Tutor is based on a principle of presenting the

---

[1]PROUST and the BRIDGE Tutor are used to teach introductory Pascal, whereas the LISP Tutor is used for introductory LISP.

goal structure of the task, whereas the BRIDGE Tutor appears to be based on the principle of illustrating how naive goals and plans can be transformed into programming goals and plans.

Another contrast can be made between Algebraland (Brown, 1983) and the LISP Tutor. Algebraland enables a student to reflect on the sequence of decisions that he or she made during an attempt to solve an algebra problem by providing a visual representation of the search space, and searching erroneous solution paths is allowed. Similar search information is displayed in the LISP Tutor, but students are kept on a correct solution path. The LISP Tutor uses an instructional principle of immediate feedback for errors (Anderson, Boyle, Farrell, & Reiser, 1984) that is grounded in skill acquisition research (Lewis & Anderson, 1985), whereas Algebraland seems to employ a principle stating that reflection on erroneous solution paths leads to learning about the search space.

Design Processes and Products

Our discussion, so far, has largely focused on characteristics of instructional products. That is, we have discussed various desirable goals and the instructional methods that can be used to achieve them. We can also view instructional design as a process. Viewing design as a process shifts concern from the study of effective and efficient pieces of instruction to the study of effective and efficient means for producing optimal instruction. In the world of instructional design science, a variety of prescriptive process models (e.g., Mager, 1962) have been proposed to organize and optimize the design process. These models are basically flowcharts of steps to follow—performing task analyses, constructing tests, and so on. In our informal discussions with instructional designers in industry who explicitly attempt to follow such models, we have found that the flowcharts act as a general and rough guideline; however, the actual process of search for a design solution is much richer and more complex than suggested by such design models.

Although we an distinguish between the processes and products of design, it is crucial to note that they are interrelated. Essentially, the relation is an extension of the notion that the representations used in problem solving have a substantial impact on style or form of problem solutions. For example, concepts and principles in instructional design science have led to Mager's (1962) prescriptive model of instructional design. On the other hand, concepts and principles from cognitive skill acquisition theory have led to a class of instruction called model tracing used in several intelligent tutoring systems (Anderson, Boyle, & Yost, 1985; Pirolli, 1986; and Reiser, Anderson, & Farrell, 1985).[2] As in other engineering disciplines, it is important to have design concepts that allow the designer to manage the complexity of his or her design problem through useful abstractions while leading ultimately to an efficient and effective design solution.

Integration of the processes and products of instructional design is a major motivating idea for the Instructional Design Environment, described by Russell, Moran, & Jordan, (chapter 7). IDE provides a notation and an electronic environment for construction of documents that includes instructional materials along with reasons and explanations for the decisions that a designer makes in the process of designing the instruction. Including the principles drawn from theoretical resources in a document with the instructional materials can provide a basis for reflective evaluation, criticism, revision, and comparative analysis of instructional materials.

Given the set of distinctions we have discussed, it is interesting to note a major gap in research on instructional design. There are descriptive and prescriptive theories of instructional design products, and there are prescriptive theories of the instructional design process (e.g., Mager, 1962), but there are few, if any, descriptive theories of what takes place in the instructional design process. We suggest that our understanding of prescriptive approaches to the process of instructional design can benefit from detailed studies of how instructional designers do in fact design instruction.

Relation to Other Frameworks

Our characterization of a problem space for instructional design makes many of the same distinctions that have been made in previous discussions of instructional design science. Comparison of our scheme with a recent discussion by Reigeluth (1983b) may be helpful. Figure 6.2 shows the diagram used by Reigeluth to present a framework of variables that are important in instructional design.

Our distinction between levels of decisions about sequences of lessons and activities and specific presentations and tasks is much the same as Reigeluth's distinction between macro- and microstrategies. Microstrategies are methods for organizing instruction about a single idea (e.g., Merrill, 1983). Macrostrategies are methods for organizing instruction about several ideas (e.g., Reigeluth & Stein, 1983).

On the other hand, there are several ways in which our problem-space view refocuses aspects of the design problem. First, we consider

---

[2]No prescriptive design model is associated with the model tracing approach.

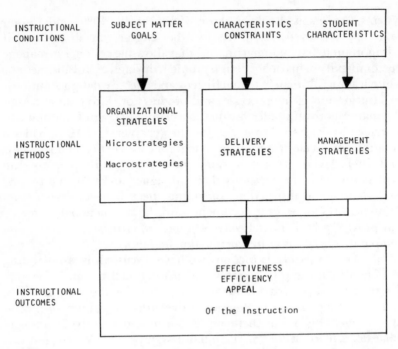

FIGURE 6.2 Reigeluth's instructional design framework. SOURCE: "Instructional Design: What Is It, and Why Is It?" by C. M. Reigeluth (1983). In C. M. Reigeluth (Ed.), *Instructional-Design Theories and Models: An Overview of Their Current Status*, p. 19. Hillsdale, NJ: Lawrence Erlbaum Associates. Copyright © 1983 by Lawrence Erlbaum Associates. Adapted by permission.

decisions about goals of instruction to be an integral part of the design process. Decisions about which topics to include and the general objectives of instruction seem to us to be issues that should be addressed in the context of instructional design, rather than considered as "givens" in the design environment.

We also understand management strategies to be integrally connected with the organization of subject matter. Decisions about management (e.g., how and when to individualize instruction) are included in the process of deciding on instructional environments, sequences of topics and activities, and detailed presentations of materials. Delivery strategies are similarly integrated into the process of deciding about goals and sequences of topics and transactions.

Methodological Role
of Intelligent Tutoring Systems

Instruction, learning, and instructional design are domains of extremely complex phenomena, and productive research in these domains requires matching complexity between theory and gathered data. Intelligent tutoring systems offer a technological resource that can be exploited to increase the complexity of theory and methodology.

Intelligent tutoring systems can drive theoretical development in at least two significant ways. First, by analogy to the role of computer simulations in developing models of performance, intelligent tutoring systems reify theories of instruction and learning, and facilitate the management of ever more-detailed and complex theoretical formulations. Second, intelligent tutoring systems act as sophisticated data-gathering tools that test the theories that they instantiate.

In our framework, a design process searches through the instructional design space selecting instructional means that achieve desired outcomes under certain constraints. In effect, the design process is making a prediction that a particular instructional product will achieve a certain possible world specified by the constraints and desired goals (cf. Simon, 1969). The standard validational logic of science thus applies: If the actual world differs from the predicted world, then something is wrong with the theory underlying the design.

To use a concrete example, the LISP Tutor was designed to optimize the efficiency and efficacy of instruction in introductory LISP programming. Descriptive models of instruction and learning based on the ACT* theory plus a set of instructional prescriptions were used to generate and select means for optimizing this instruction (e.g., Pirolli, 1986). The prediction is therefore that the LISP Tutor stands as the king of the mountain with respect to instruction in LISP. Observations gathered in studies of the LISP Tutor can be used to revise the underlying models of cognition, learning, and instruction used to produce the LISP Tutor. Similarly, experimental contrasts of the LISP Tutor with other systems such as PROUST or the BRIDGE Tutor might invalidate the king-of-the-mountain claim.

It is important to note, however, that we are likely to need a more sophisticated methodology than simple experimental contrasts of systems or instructional principles, given the richness of competing theories and data. For instance, the hardcore empiricist approach to determining the validity of the eight instructional principles outlined in Anderson, Boyle, Farrell, and Reiser (1984) would involve performing a factorial-designed experiment that contrasts all possible combinations of instantiating or not instantiating a principle in a piece of instruction. This would involve contrasts among 2^8 different pieces of instruction and would still ignore many other factors that are involved in the design of a system as complex as the Geometry Tutor or the LISP Tutor. It seems that more detailed and sophisticated methods of comparisons along the lines of competitive argumentation (VanLehn, Brown, & Greeno, 1984) will be needed.

Intelligent tutoring systems can thus be viewed as instructional products that embed models of cognition, learning, and instruction, and gather data concerning those models[3] Furthermore, developing such systems drives our theories about instructional design products to much greater sophistication and detail, because of the rigor required in producing a system that runs and attains desired outcomes. What about theories of the instructional design process? We suggest that intelligent tutoring systems research can drive theory in this area in much the same way. The example we have in mind is the IDE system discussed elsewhere in this book (Russell, Moran, & Jordan, chapter 7, this volume). IDE is a computer-based environment for the design, development, and delivery of computer-based instruction. As a design tool, the system allows an instructional designer to make decisions at a number of levels that can be mapped onto the levels we have proposed in our instructional-design problem space. IDE also provides designers with tools that allow them to rationalize the particular decisions they have made. These rationalizations are arguments for why a decision has to be "just so" based on other decisions and instructional principles that may be grounded in the research literature. In essence, these rationalizations fit with the competitive argumentation scheme discussed by VanLehn et al. (1984).

The IDE system is thus an attempt to reify the levels in the instructional-design problem space and, with further research, lay out the alternatives within that space. IDE, or analogous tools, can be used in similar ways in intelligent tutoring systems to collect data about the instructional-design processes—an area that we pointed out earlier has received no substantive attention. Further, systems such as IDE that encourage designers to provide theoretical rationale for their design decisions could prove to be important in a methodology of competitive argumentation among competing theories of learning, instruction, and instructional design.

ACKNOWLEDGMENTS

We would like to thank Andy diSessa, M. David Merrill, and John Mitterer for comments on earlier drafts of this chapter. This work was supported by grant MDA 903-83-C-0189 from the Army Research Institute. It was also supported by a National Academy of Education Spencer Fellowship to the first author.

---

[3]This may be more of a prescription rather than an accurate description of the current state of the art.

REFERENCES

Anderson, J. R. (1983). *The architecture of cognition.* Cambridge, MA: Harvard University Press.

Anderson, J. R., Boyle, C. F., Farrell, R., & Reiser, B. J. (1984). Cognitive principles in the design of computer tutors. In the *Proceedings of the Sixth Annual Conference of the Cognitive Science Society* (pp. 2–9). Boulder, CO: Institute of Cognitive Science, University of Colorado.

Anderson, J. R., Boyle, C. F., & Yost, G. (1985). The geometry tutor. In A. Joshi (Ed.), *Proceedings of the Ninth International Joint Conference on Artificial Intelligence* (pp. 1–7). Los Altos, CA: Morgan Kaufmann.

Belenky, M. F., Clinchy, B. M., Goldberger, N. R., & Tarule, J. M. (1986). *Women's ways of knowing: The development of self, voice, and mind.* New York: Basic Books.

Bork, A. (1981). *Learning with computers.* Bedford, MA: Digital Press.

Brown, J. S. (1983). Process versus product: A perspective on tools for communal and informal electronic learning. In *Report from the learning lab: Education in the electronic age.* Educational Broadcasting Corporation.

Brown, J. S., & Burton, R. R. (1978). Diagnostic models for procedural bugs in basic mathematical skills. *Cognitive Science, 2,* 155–192.

Burton, R. R., & Brown, J. S. (1982). An investigation of computer coaching for informal learning activities. In D. Sleeman & J. S. Brown (Eds.), *Intelligent tutoring systems* (pp. 79–98). New York: Academic Press.

Card, S. K., Moran, T. P., & Newell, A. (1983). *The psychology of human–computer interaction.* Hillsdale, NJ: Lawrence Erlbaum Associates.

Carey, S. (1985). *Conceptual change in childhood.* Cambridge, MA: Bradford/MIT Press.

Clark, H. H., & Wilkes-Gibbs, D. (1986) Referring as a collaborative process. *Cognition, 22,* 1–40.

Cohen, P. R., & Feigenbaum, E. A. (1982). *The handbook of artificial intelligence* (Vol. 3). Los Altos, CA: William Kaufmann.

deKleer, J., & Brown, J. S. (1984). A qualitative physics based on confluences. *Artificial Intelligence, 24,* 7–84.

diSessa, A. A. (1982). Unlearning Aristotelian physics: A study of knowledge-based learning. *Cognitive Science, 6,* 37--75.

diSessa, A. A. (1985, June). Knowledge in pieces. *Address to the Fifteenth Annual Symposium of the Jean Piaget Society.* Philadelphia.

Dugdale, S. (1982). Green globs: A microcomputer application for graphing of equations. *Mathematics Teacher, 75,* 208–214.

Fawcett, H. P. (1938). *The nature of proof.* The thirteenth yearbook of the National Council of Teachers of Mathematics. New York: Teachers College, Columbia University.

Forbus, K. (1984). Qualitative process theory. *Artificial Intelligence, 24,* 85–168.

Gagné R. M., & Briggs, L. J. (1979). *Principles of instructional design* (2d ed.). New York: Holt, Rinehart & Winston.

Greeno, J. G., Brown, J. S., Foss, C., Shalin, V., Bee, N. V., Lewis, M. W., & Vitolo, T. M. (1986). *Principles of problem solving and computer-assisted instruction.* Berkeley, CA: School of Education, University of California.

Gropper, G. L. (1983). A behavioral approach to instructional prescription. In C. M. Reigeluth (Ed.), *Instructional-design theories and models: An overview of their current status* (pp. 101–162). Hillsdale, NJ: Lawrence Erlbaum Associates.

Heines, J. M. (1984). *Screen design strategies for computer-assisted instruction.* Bedford, MA: Digital Press.

Hutchins, E. L., Hollan, J. D., & Norman, D. A. (1985). Direct manipulation interfaces. *Human–computer Interaction, 1,* 311–338.

Johnson, W. L., & Soloway, E. (1983). *PROUST: Knowledge-based program understanding* (Tech. Rep. No. 285). New Haven, CT: Computer Science Department, Yale University.

Kitcher, P. (1984). *The nature of mathematical knowledge.* New York: Oxford University Press.

Kuipers, B., & Kassirer, J. P. (1984). Causal reasoning in medicine: Analysis of a protocol. *Cognitive Science, 8,* 305–336.

Lampert, M. (in press). On knowing, doing, and learning multiplication. *Cognition and Instruction.*

Landa, L. N. (1983). The algo-heuristic theory of instruction. In C. M. Reigeluth (Ed.), *Instructional-design theories and models: An overview of their current status* (pp. 163–212). Hillsdale, NJ: Lawrence Erlbaum Associates.

Lave, J., Murtaugh, M., & de la Roch, O. (1984). The dialectic of arithmetic in grocery shopping. In B. Rogoff & J. Lave (Eds.), *Everyday cognition: Its development in social context* (pp. 67–94). Cambridge, MA: Harvard University Press.

Leinhardt, G., & Greeno, J. G. (1986). The cognitive skill of teaching. *Journal of Educational Psychology, 78,* 75–95.

Leinhardt, G., Weidman, C., & Hammond, K. M. (1984). *Introduction and integration of classroom routines by expert teachers.* Paper presented at the annual meeting of the American Educational Research Association, New Orleans.

Lewis, M. W., & Anderson, J. R. (1985). Discrimination of operator schemata in problem solving: Learning from examples. *Cognitive Psychology, 17,* 26–65.

Mager, R. (1962). *Preparing instructional objectives.* Palo Alto, CA: Fearon.

Merrill, M. D. (1983). Component display theory. In C. M. Reigeluth (Ed.), *Instructional-design theories and models: An overview of their current status* (pp. 279–334). Hillsdale, NJ: Lawrence Erlbaum Associates.

Merrill, M. D. (in press). Component display theory: Instructional design for courseware authoring. *Instructional Science.*

Newell, A., & Card, S. K. (1985). The prospects for psychological science in human–computer interaction. *Human–computer Interaction, 1,* 209–242.

Newell, A., & Simon, H. A. (1972). *Human problem solving.* Englewood Cliffs, NJ: Prentice-Hall.

Norman, D. A., & Draper, S. W. (1986). *User-centered system design.* Hillsdale, NJ: Lawrence Erlbaum Associates.

Palincsar, A. S., & Brown, A. L. (1984). Reciprocal teaching of comprehension-fostering and comprehension-monitoring activities. *Cognition and Instruction, 1,* 117–176.

Pirolli, P. L. (1986). A cognitive model and computer tutor for programming recursion. *Human–Computer Interaction, 12,* 319–355.

Posner, G. J., & Rudnitsky, A. N. (1986). *Course design: A guide to curriculum development for teachers.* New York: Longman.

Reigeluth, C. M. (Ed.). (1983a). *Instructional-design theories and models: An overview of their current status.* Hillsdale, NJ: Lawrence Erlbaum Associates.

Reigeluth, C. M. (1983b). Instructional design: What is it, and why is it? In C. M. Reigeluth (Ed.), *Instructional-design theories and models: An overview of their current status* (pp. 3–36). Hillsdale, NJ: Lawrence Erlbaum Associates.

Reigeluth, C. M., & Stein, F. S. (1983). The elaboration theory of instruction. In C. M. Reigeluth (Ed.), *Instructional-design theories and models: An overview of their current status* (pp. 335–382). Hillsdale, NJ: Lawrence Erlbaum Associates.

Reiser, B. J., Anderson, J. R., & Farrell, R. G. (1985). Dynamic student modeling in an intelligent tutor for LISP programming. In A. Joshi (Ed.), *Proceedings of the Ninth International Joint Conference on Artificial Intelligence* (pp. 8–14). Los Altos, CA: Morgan Kaufmann.

Scandura, J. M. (1983). Instructional strategies based on structural learning theory. In C. M. Reigeluth (Ed.), *Instructional-design theories and models: An overview of their current status* (pp. 213–246). Hillsdale, NJ: Lawrence Erlbaum Associates.

Schegloff, E. A. (1972). Notes on a conversational practice: formulating place. In D. Sudnow (Ed.), *Studies in social interaction* (pp. 75–119). New York: Free Press.

Schoenfeld, A. H. (1985). *Mathematical problem solving.* New York: Academic Press.

Simon, H. A. (1969). *The sciences of the artificial.* Cambridge, MA: MIT Press.

Suppes, P. (1981). *University-level computer-assisted instruction at Stanford: 1968–1980.* Stanford, CA: Institute for Mathematical Studies in the Social Sciences, Stanford University.

Uarushalmy, M., & Houde, R. A. (1986). The geometric supposer: Promoting thinking and learning. *Mathematics Teacher, 79,* 418–422.

VanLehn, K., Brown, J. S., & Greeno, J. G. (1984). Competitive argumentation in computational theories of cognition. In W. Kintsch, J. R. Miller, & P. G. Polson (Eds.), *Method and tactics in cognitive science* (pp. 235–262). Hillsdale, NJ: Lawrence Erlbaum Associates.

The Instructional-Design Environment

Daniel M. Russell
Thomas P. Moran
Daniel S. Jordan
Intelligent Systems Laboratory
Xerox Palo Alto Research Center

In this chapter, we describe the problems surrounding instruction design and development, describe IDE, and demonstrate how IDE helps to solve those problems.

THE PROBLEMS OF CREATING INSTRUCTION

In a typical instruction-creation setting, there are many interacting and competing goals to satisfy. Creating instruction is difficult: There is often a great deal of material to be covered, developers are under time and cost pressures, and they often lack expertise in the domain to be taught. In a typical technical training creation task, a small team of instructional designers (two to seven members) works to create a workbook-based course to train technicians in the diagnosis and repair of a new machine. Often only one of the team members will be expert in the field, and, almost certainly, none will have any specialized expertise in the course subject matter. Because creating training material is usually the final step of production, there are many pressures to produce the material rapidly.[1]

IDE is an interactive design and development system to help instructional designers deal with the complexity of creating instruction

---

[1]This is certainly the case within Xerox, as we have discovered after visiting most of the corporate training production centers. In discussion with colleagues from other corporations, this experience seems representative of other large producers of in-house training materials, as well.

materials, and to provide a system for the design and development of complex instruction. IDE can aid in creating the course design, structuring the course contents, and creating instructional sequences for standard or adaptive delivery.

Creating instruction that is firmly and coherently grounded in instructional principles is an important goal that is rarely achieved. Too often, a gap exists between understanding a set of instructional principles and consistently employing those principles. This problem is magnified when creating instruction for complex or large domains or designing instruction for complex delivery systems (e.g., VideoDisk or ICAI).

We see an opportunity to improve the quality of instruction. Because of the sheer volume of material, courses are often overburdened with redundant information, poor organization, or ineffective presentation of topics and concepts. These problems persist due to the lack of adequate tools for the designer and developers to manage and manipulate a large body of knowledge. Further, the time and resources required to develop instruction are costly. Computer-assisted development tools can decrease these requirements and simultaneously improve the quality of the instruction.

IDE

In light of the problems faced by instructional designers, there is enormous potential to improve instruction by providing a computational resource to (a) help manage the process of instruction creation, (b) assist in articulating and structuring the domain knowledge, and (c) assist in constructing the course.

IDE is a software environment that makes explicit the process of instruction design and development. It requires articulation of both the content of the instruction and the rationale of an instructional design. An IDE instructional design is a set of implementation and refinement decisions describing how a course is organized and is based on an initial statement of instructional goals. A rationale is an explanation structure describing why a decision was made. IDE guides the design of instruction by providing the means to record and structure a set of decisions from course goals and specifications. Thus, the rationale is a data structure that records the reasons underlying a particular design. An IDE rationale records decisions about course structure, course content, instructional approach, and anticipated student behaviors.

Creating the rationale for a course design is important for several reasons:

1. Changes in either instructional approach or course content can be made easily and accurately, because the rationale represents both the theory of instruction underlying the course design and the course content.
2. It is a useful tool for communication between colleagues or collaborators.
3. It communicates to the instructor how and why a course is organized.
4. Once created, it simplifies changes to the course material or course structure.

Building a complete rationale for a course is a formidable task. However, we believe the process of building the rationale with a knowledge management tool (IDE) can improve course design by reminding designers of options and opportunities available, as well as providing helpful analyses of partially completed designs. Requiring a rationale forces the designer to articulate the principles underlying the course construction. IDE requires the designer to think more carefully about why and how the course design accomplishes its original goals. Further, once created, a rationale structure makes explicit the design of a course, allowing collaboration between analysts, and makes feasible the repair and reuse of the course.

IDE DESCRIPTION

IDE is built on Notecards (Halasz, Moran, & Trigg, 1986), an idea-structuring hypertext system written in Xerox LISP. IDE runs on any of the Xerox LISP Machines (1108, 1109, 1132, 1185, 1186).

We view IDE as an entire course design/development/alteration system. During course development, IDE provides the designer with management support for building the detail structure of the course. At the same time, IDE helps keep the materials consistent with instructional principles. After the course has been created, a rationale simplifies rework or alteration of the course (due to content or structure changes, student population change, or shift in instructional principles).

IDE is especially advantageous when dealing with large or highly complex courses. In particular, it is useful when constructing material for adaptive course delivery, in which the behavior of the student influences presentation of the material. (e.g., see Russell, chapter 12, this volume).

Using IDE to Structure Knowledge

IDE is a knowledge-structuring system in which the knowledge is course content, structure, and instructional method. At an abstract level, IDE accepts knowledge describing course goals as input, and assists the designer in creating a course as output. Figure 7.1 illustrates the flow of knowledge through IDE and represents a schematic map of the IDE user's display. In this figure, work proceeds roughly from left to right, moving from course objectives toward course decisions. Information about the course design is entered in the upper half of the column labeled "Requirements and Principles." This region contains course objectives, externally imposed constraints (class size, delivery technology, student capabilities, etc.). In using IDE, a designer creates a course design, guided by these input requirements, working within the knowledge areas IDE defines. After refining the design, the designer makes decisions about the substance of the course in the areas of the rightmost column. Included in this output column are the "Knowledge Structure" (KS—a representation of domain knowledge), the "Model of Student" (MOS—a representation of the student), course control (strategy, pedagogy, and tactics), and "Instructional Units" (IUs—which constitute the course material). The "Instruction" column represents everything needed to teach the course specified by the Course Description. Note that both domain knowledge and instructional knowledge are included.

The atomic representation element in IDE is a Notecard with text describing what is represented by that card. There are a variety of card types (Principle, Decision, Knowledge Element, etc.). Usually, a card represents a decision about course content or structure. To design a course, a user creates a linked network of Decision cards in the "Decisions" column. A Decision card is "rationalized" by creating linkages between the Decision card and other cards that act as warrants or reasons supporting that decision. A *rationale link* records the reasoning underlying the decision. The collection of Decisions forms a basis for the creation of Course Specification knowledge, which is represented in the right-hand column. (Currently, IDE provides the superstructure for the designer to "fill in" the columns with decisions and structure of his or her devising, and little in the way of automatic structure checking.)

As Figure 7.1 shows, creating a course consists of evolving the representation of the course objectives (left column) into decisions about the course design (middle column) and generating a detailed representation of instruction (right column). This partitioning of areas separates differing sets of concerns within a course design.

Between each of the columns in Figure 7.1 are shaded zones

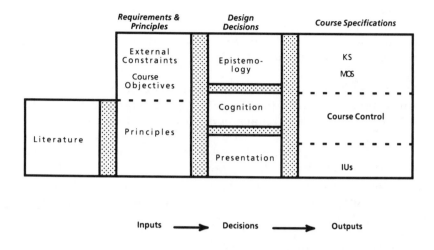

FIGURE 7.1 Knowledge areas of IDE.

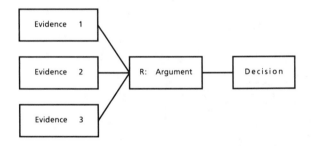

FIGURE 7.2 A rationale link "rationalizes" a decision in IDE by linking evidence that was the basis for making the decision to the decision record. The content of the rationale link is an argument specifying why the decision (on the right) follows from the evidence (on the left).

indicating places where a rationalization is constructed to explain the relationships between elements in each of the areas. Figure 7.2 illustrates a rationale (R) link—the basic element of a rationale structure—between a principle (in the Principles area) and a decision (in the Instructional Decisions area). For example, cards in the Principles area represent instructional principles used by the designer. A given principle is "rationalized" by a rationale structure showing how entries in the Literature argue for its validity.

IDE Areas on the Screen

IDE partitions screen space into a set of *columns* divided into *areas,* as in the schematic diagram of Figure 7.1. Each area contains a decision structure defined by the card types it contains and the way that the cards link to cards in other areas. The areas follow.

Literature. Literature contains references to primary sources for instructional principles. (See Figure 7.3.) Instructional and cognitive principles are rationalized in terms of the backing literature.

External constraints/course objectives. These represent course-specific information, such as course objectives, student abilities, available delivery media, amount of time available, and so on. This "input" area changes with each new course developed. (See Figure 7.4.)

Principles. Principles are references to theories of learning and instruction. They encode what an instructional designer must remember when creating a course design. Principles (usually) do not change from course to course, although different sets become relevant according to the style of the course being created. They are rationalized by elements in the Literature area. They, in turn, are used to rationalize decisions in the "Decisions" column. (See Figure 7.5.)

Epistemology. This contains decisions about the domain knowledge

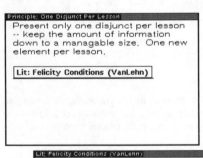

FIGURE 7.3 A Principle and a Literature Reference card. The rectangular icon in the Principle card is a typed pointer to the Literature card.

to be taught. Epistemological decisions are usually created by the subject matter expert, and are rationalized in terms of epistemological principles. (See Figure 7.6.)

Cognitive.   Cognitive decisions record how the student will learn the skill or knowledge to be presented. These decisions represent how to accomplish the course objectives within the posted constraints, guided by the epistemology decisions. Because they are so closely linked to the domain knowledge, cognitive decisions may be rationalized in terms of cognitive principles (from the principles area) or by decisions in the epistemology. (See Figure 7.7.)

Presentation.   Presentation decisions determine how the course is to be taught. They implement cognitive-level decisions and are rationalized in terms of instructional knowledge. Cards in this region form a course specification in terms of presentations and tests. (See Figure 7.8.)

KS (Knowledge Structure).   KS is a concept structure that represents the course content (i.e., the domain knowledge). It is a representation of the elements of domain knowledge to be taught (concepts and skills) and the relationships that exist between them. The final course design will teach some subset of this KS. (See Figure 7.9.)

MOS ("Model of Student" or student model).   The MOS records information about the student: concept understanding, typical bugs, common learning styles, instructional conditions, and so on. The MOS is a representation of the set of concepts and skills the student must acquire. At the same time, the MOS records information about the style in which the student learns. (See Figure 7.10.)

Course control.   This records the knowledge needed to guide the instruction of the course content. This knowledge is represented as rules and constraints describing how instruction proceeds. "Pedagogy" cards encode topic sequencing and topic inclusion information; "Strategy" cards encode the general instructional strategy; "Tactics" cards specify low-level information about how to implement instruction style and form. (See Figure 7.11.)

IUs (Instructional Units).   These are the units the student will interact with. If the course delivery system is a VideoDisk system, then the IU will be a single VideoDisk segment (e.g., a frame in a frame-based interactive videodisk course). IUs may also be quite complex; for example, an IU may be a simulation system, or an entire learning

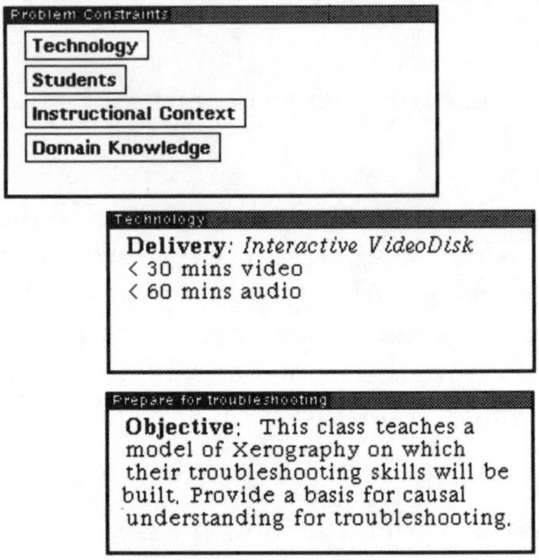

Problem Constraints
- Technology
- Students
- Instructional Context
- Domain Knowledge

Technology
Delivery: *Interactive VideoDisk*
< 30 mins video
< 60 mins audio

Prepare for troubleshooting
Objective: This class teaches a model of Xerography on which their troubleshooting skills will be built. Provide a basis for causal understanding for troubleshooting.

FIGURE 7.4 An External Constraint/Course Defs card represents goals and costraints that imposed on the course design and development process.

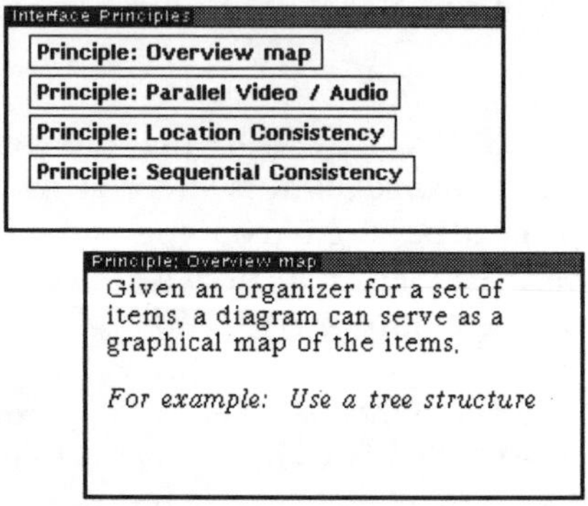

Interface Principles
- Principle: Overview map
- Principle: Parallel Video / Audio
- Principle: Location Consistency
- Principle: Sequential Consistency

Principle: Overview map
Given an organizer for a set of items, a diagram can serve as a graphical map of the items.

For example: Use a tree structure

FIGURE 7.5 A Principle card represents an instructional or learning principle that will be used to rationalize a decision in the Decisions column.

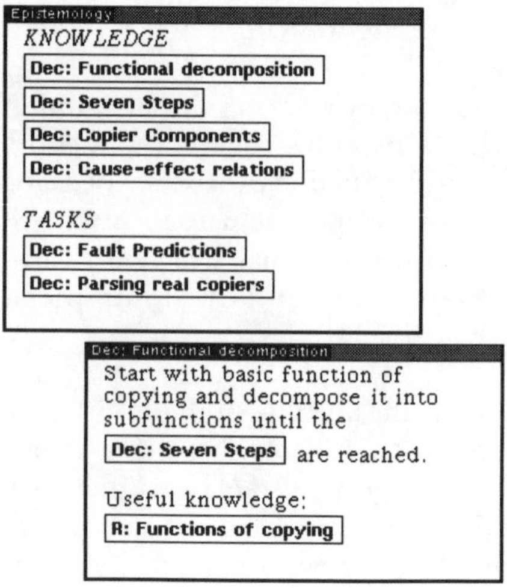

Epistemology
KNOWLEDGE
- Dec: Functional decomposition
- Dec: Seven Steps
- Dec: Copier Components
- Dec: Cause-effect relations

TASKS
- Dec: Fault Predictions
- Dec: Parsing real copiers

Dec: Functional decomposition
Start with basic function of copying and decompose it into subfunctions until the
Dec: Seven Steps are reached.

Useful knowledge:
R: Functions of copying

FIGURE 7.6 An Epistemological card contains a description of a chunk of domain knowledge. The "Epistemology" card records decisions about what domain knowledge must be taught, and how that knowledge is structured. The "Doc: Functional decomposition" card records a decision, illustrating how sub-decisions are used, and pointing to the rationale for this decision (the "R: Functions of copying" pointer).

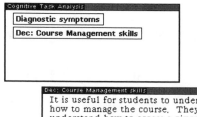

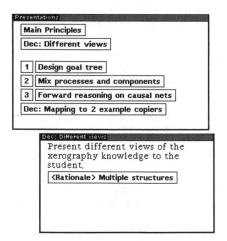

FIGURE 7.7 Cards in the Cognitive area record decisions about the task analysis of the course. Such cards record decisions about what cognitive tasks must be accomplished by the course. They are rationalized by principles and epistemology.

FIGURE 7.8 A decision in the Instructional area is specifies how the course will appear, how to present a concept or gives details on how a presentation should appear. These cards are created by the designer, forming the substance of the design. They are rationalized by cognitive decisions, instructional principles and course constraints. This figure shows a set of Cognitive level decisions, and the expansion of the first decision made, "Different views."

environment. From the designer's viewpoint, IUs communicate concepts (individually or in groups) from the KS. (See Figure 7.12.)

USING IDE

IDE for Making and Recording Decisions

With this framework, IDE provides a mechanism for the designer to record and rationalize course content decisions, as well as to structure and rationalize instructional knowledge. The IDE view of course

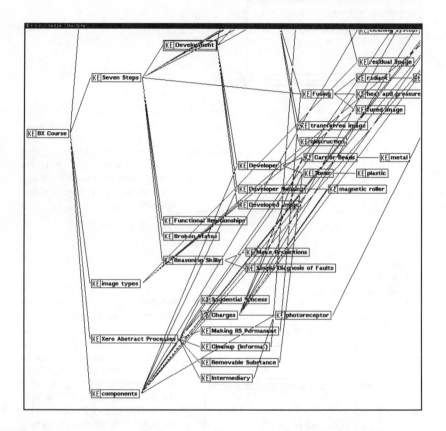

FIGURE 7.9 The Knowledge Structure (KS) is the conceptual structure of the course content. Nodes represent concepts or skills while links represent the relationships between them.

creation consists of deciding (a) course content (what gets included, what gets left out), (b) content structure (how the content is organized), (c) how the student will learn, (d) how the content is presented (instruction strategy), and (e) what the student must know (before, during, and after instruction). These decisions form the substance of the IDE course design. The IDE user has the task of making decisions (i.e., creating the decision/rationale structure) to implement the course objectives, creating an instructional strategy, and creating the IUs with which the student interacts during instruction.

Once developed, the decision structure can be used by the designer to understand how and why a choice was made in a course design. It is possible to work from entries in the KS or IUs back to the decisions and principles that give backing to those entries. Conversely, one can trace forward from a decision or principle to discover what the entailment of that choice is in the design.

IDE Analysis Tools

IDE is equipped with a pair of analysis tools: *tracers* for explaining why a decision was made and *checkers* for matching and mapping from one area into another. The *rationale tracer* tool displays the rationale associated with a particular decision. IDE accomplishes this by following links back from a single decision to each of its parents. In Figure 7.13, the graph displayed is a rationale trace of a decision made in the Epistemology area. Epistemology decisions are rationalized in terms of elements from the "Principles" column—that is, principles, and course specifications. Here, the decision to organize the domain knowledge along a "Functional Decomposition," is based on the three principles: "Forward reasoning," "Causality supports inference," "Diagnostic symptoms." When the rationale is displayed, each of the

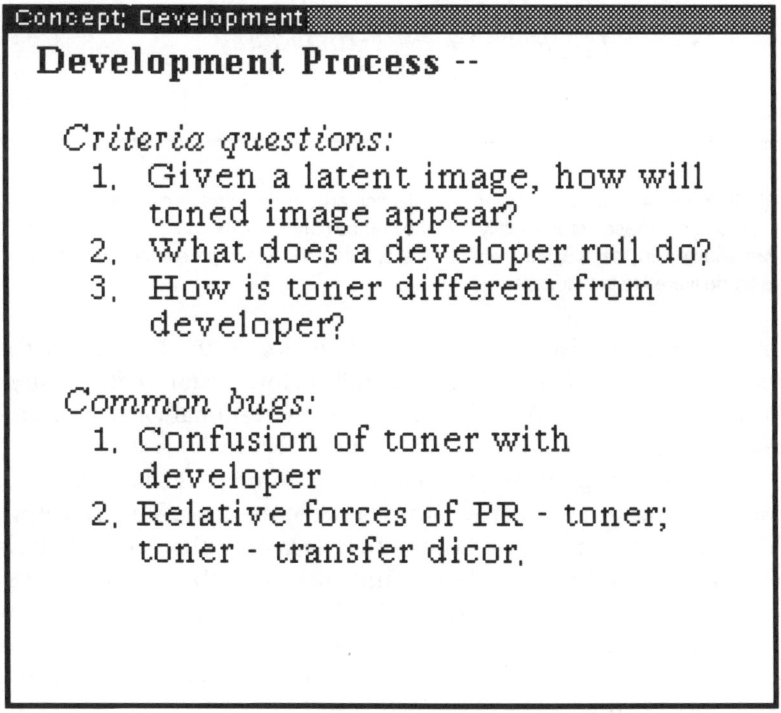

Concept: Development

Development Process --

Criteria questions:
  1. Given a latent image, how will toned image appear?
  2. What does a developer roll do?
  3. How is toner different from developer?

Common bugs:
  1. Confusion of toner with developer
  2. Relative forces of PR - toner; toner - transfer dicor.

FIGURE 7.10 An entry in the MOS is a card that represents either a student concept/ skill, or a card representing a student's learning behavior.

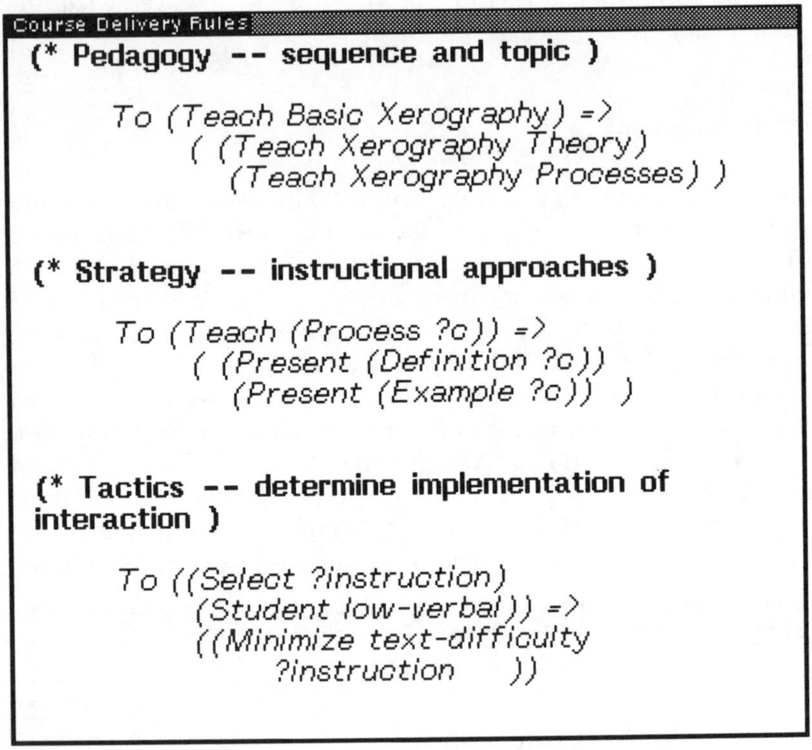

```
Course Delivery Rules

 (* Pedagogy -- sequence and topic )

     To (Teach Basic Xerography) =>
         ( (Teach Xerography Theory)
           (Teach Xerography Processes) )


 (* Strategy -- instructional approaches )

     To (Teach (Process ?c)) =>
         ( (Present (Definition ?c))
           (Present (Example ?c)) )


 (* Tactics -- determine implementation of
 interaction )

     To ((Select ?instruction)
          (Student low-verbal)) =>
         ((Minimize text-difficulty
             ?instruction    ))
```

FIGURE 7.11 Instructional strategy and tactics are represented in pedagogy, strategy or tactics rules. These cards specify how the course content—whose conceptual structure is represented in the KS, and whose presentation form is represented by the IUs— is to be delivered to the students.

parents for the decisions (i.e., the three nodes on the left side of the rationale trace) are displayed immediately below the rationale window (see the title of the window just below the rational browser), and the rationale argument (the contents of the "R" node) is shown.

A *checker* maps elements from one area onto elements in another area following specific relationships between the areas. Thus, creating a checker that maps from Course Defs area into the KS will show how many of the Course Defs are implemented in the KS. (This gives the designer a simple way to determine how many Course Definitions have been left unsatisfied.) Figure 7.14 shows a checker that maps from the instructional area into the IUs area. This display shows which of the Instructional objectives have been implemented by IUs. This checker yields information on topics that have been overlooked or omitted, and detects redundancies.

Using IDE: An Example

We have designed a course on Basic Xerography using IDE. Xerography is a representative domain because it combines many subdomains (electrical, mechanical, chemical) into a single course. The domain is complex enough to be challenging for course design, yet still tractable as a test case. We built several different versions of the course (a lecture-and-workbook version, a frame-oriented computer-delivered version, and an Interactive LaserDisk version) on this single design. In each version, the Epistemology and Cognitive area contents remained constant, and the linkages to the implementation varied from course to course.

Figure 7.15 shows a screen image of IDE in use during the design of the Basic Xerography course. Here, the Goals and Constraints are on the top of the screen (above the bar), the Principles are on the left side, and Decisions are grouped in the far right-hand column. (The "Instruction" column contents do not appear in this image.) Each card in this image (plus many not in this display) was created by the user and linked into the growing course design. The design

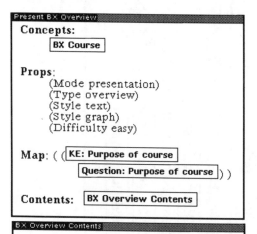

FIGURE 7.12 An Instructional Unit contains the presentation of course material to the student. The IU represents an instruction segment. The Concepts slot records what concepts in the KS this IU teaches; the Props slot is an attribute/value list representing properties of the instructional display; the Map slot points to questions that test understanding of some segment of this knowledge; and the Contents slot points to the actual substance of the display. In this figure, the "BX Overview Contents" card is what the student would actually see.

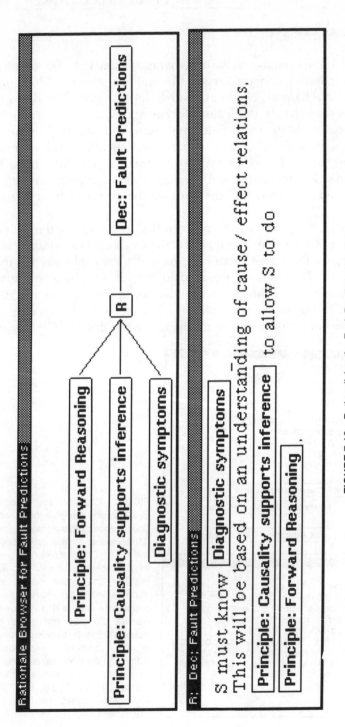

FIGURE 7.13 Rationalizing the Fault Prediction decision.

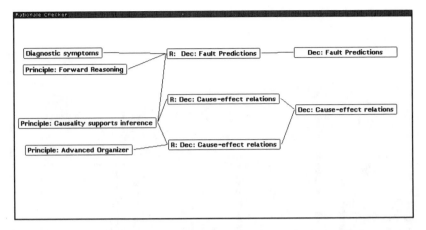

FIGURE 7.14 This checker shows the rationale links between Principles and Instruction. A checker browser shows how cards in one area map onto cards into another area via some specified path.

process is primarily top-down, guided by the designer's experience and knowledge of the domain. Generally, the process is to create the domain Epistemology, then perform the Cognitive analysis, and, finally, create the Instructional design. As in any design process, constraints and structure discovered during development can significantly affect the higher design levels. Thus, a designer may work in any column or area at any time, moving between design levels and areas as needed. IDE's ability to display rationale structure (the tree structure shown in Figure 7.15) makes modification of the complex design structure straightforward.

At this point in the design (Figure 7.15), the user is attempting to satisfy the objective "Prepare for Troubleshooting." This objective was set by the designer as part of the course specification and is represented as a card in the instructional context filebox in upper right. To satisfy this goal, the designer must make and record in IDE the decisions about how to achieve it. As stated, the goal is a declaration about a cognitive objective. The designer chooses to implement this objective by creating a decision stating that the student must be able to generate Fault Predictions. (The decision and the <Implements> link to the course objective are in the "Fault Predictions" card located mid-screen, on the right side.)

Normally, after the user creates a decision, the rationale in support of that decision is built. Figure 7.16 shows the rationale the designer constructed to support the "Fault Predictions" decision. The rationale card shown in the figure explains why the designer made this decision. In this instance, the explanation is straightforward; the cognitive

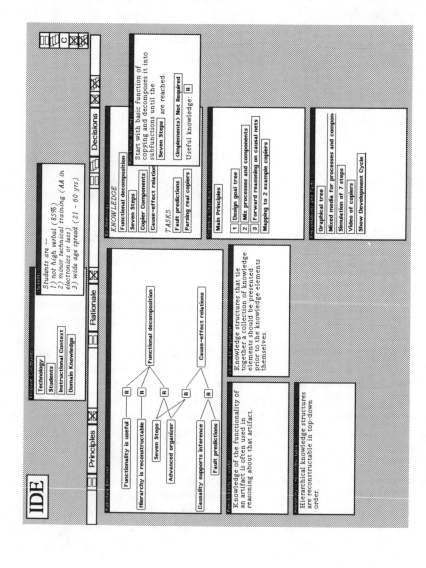

FIGURE 7.15 An IDE screen showing the development of the Basic Xerography Course.

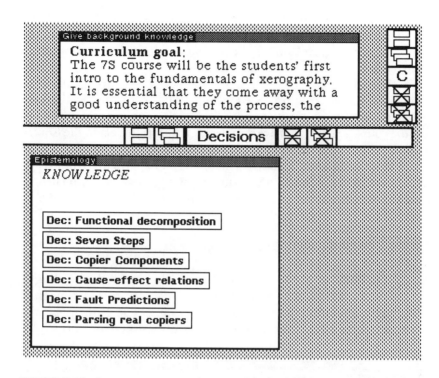

FIGURE 7.16 As a consequence of making Fault Prediction a cognitive task, the epistemology must be modified. The designer has introduced a decision in the Epistemology area to organize content along cause-effect relations.

decision to teach "Fault Predictions" is rationalized by arguing that in order to do the predictions, the student must be able to perform forward reasoning, based on his understanding of causality and diagnostic symptoms. In more obscure cases, the rationale card may contain more elaborate arguments discussing trade-offs and counterproposals. Note that the rationale states its argument in terms of Epistemology, Learning, and Cognitive Task Analysis principles.[2]

When building the rationale, the designer realizes that this decision affects the way the KS is built—that is, the Epistemology of the KS must be changed to support the Cognitive Objective decision. The designer then creates a new decision, "Cause–effect relations" (see Figure 7.17) recording the idea that the relationships between causes and effects are essential to doing "Fault Predictions."

---

[2]Notice that there are two parts to the rationale: the text which IDE stores in a card, and the links that organize a set of cards into an argument structure. IDE cannot process the contents of the cards, but is limited to working with the relationships that exist in the argument structure.

This new decision must be rationalized as well. (See Figure 7.18.) This time, the rationale supports the original course objective, the new decision to teach Fault Predictions, and the principle of supporting inference by teaching causal understanding.

With these two new decisions, the designer shifts attention to the "Instruction" column. (See Figure 7.19.) The designer has decided to make the instruction of cause–effect relations a distinct portion of the course. This Cognitive area decision has its impact in the Course Control area. The decision to teach cause–effect requires altering the rules describing how the course will be taught. In particular, the (Teach BX) rule in the "Teach BX" window of Figure 7.19 is updated to include this clarified view of the course material.

IDE as a Cognitive Aid to Course Design

IDE functions as a cognitive aid to the designer by providing a representation in which to work with course designs, and a set of reminders about potential problem solutions. The Principles area operates primarily as an on-line library of instructional principles

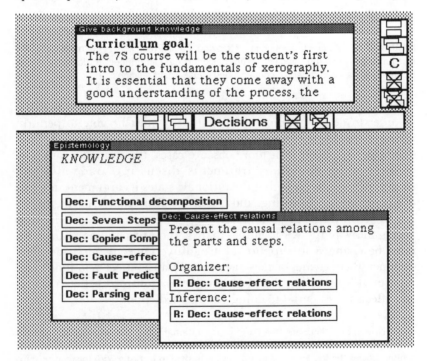

FIGURE 7.17   Adding a new decision to teach "Cause-effect" relations.

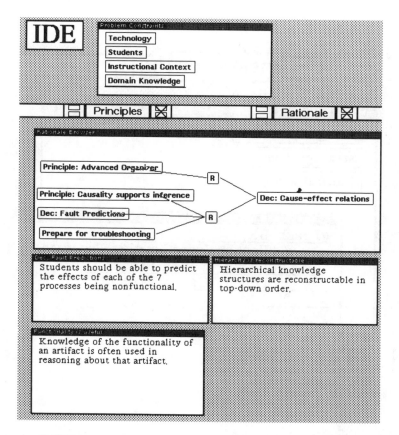

FIGURE 7.18 Rationalizing the Cause-effect Epistemology decision.

and techniques. Typically, elements in the Principles area are simply given to the designer, as part of IDE. However, this area may be tailored to the working requirements of a designer (as may all other areas). The user can add, delete, or rearrange elements as necessary.

In addition to these resources, pieces of previously successful course designs can be stored in the Principles section as an addition to the data base. These elements can be abstracted from designs created within IDE by the user. Hence, IDE can be used to create new course material or it can be used to analyze existing courses. The process of using IDE as a "reverse engineering" tool is similar, but instead of making new decisions based on Subject Matter Expert information and course objectives, decisions are inferred from the structure and content of course materials. The analysis results are then used to update the IDE Principles data base.

The implementation of IDE described here may be tailored to

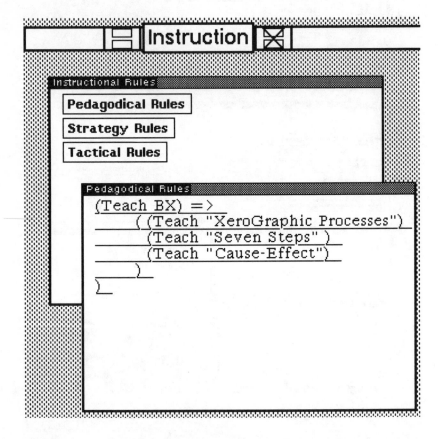

FIGURE 7.19 The decision now affects the way the course will be taught. This is recorded in the instruction column in the Pedagogy rules.

a variety of design/development methodologies. We envision the Principles and Literature areas as libraries in which the designer can explore, choosing and incorporating elements from these sources into the design under construction as desired. There are no restrictions on how the knowledge structures or course materials are created and developed. However, IDE could be operated more tightly, reducing the variety of options available to the designer. This enforces consistency of course design and delivery over a wide range of developers and courses. Tailoring a set of principles and their pattern of use to capture a style of instruction would be an effective means of standardizing course design across a set of IDE users.

Changing a Course Design

Course design modification is one of the most important uses of a design tool. IDE supports modifications during the initial creation of the design and material, or after the course has been developed and is in use. Computing the modifications necessary to design is simplified in both cases by having the rationale. Tracers and checkers can compute the consequences of a design change by following rationale links from objectives or design decisions to their entailments.

Maintaining a consistent design—especially over a large course, or during course redesign or repair—is usually a difficult task. Maintaining course consistency with IDE is simpler because the course design is explicitly represented (and inspectable) and because course presentation design is distinguished from course content.

Building a Conceptual Knowledge Structure
of Domain Knowledge

IDE requires construction of a KS representing the conceptual structure of the domain knowledge. We argue that requiring the instruction designers to articulate the knowledge to be taught (regardless of the final delivery structure or style) focuses attention on the problem of determining instructional content. But, once the designer captures the salient knowledge of a domain, that knowledge can be structured within the KS to reflect accurately the best way of teaching that knowledge (Pirolli & Greeno, chapter 6, this volume). IDE also provides a space for articulating this instructional strategy (the Course Control area) without carrying along the burden of all the course content. Of course, often the two cannot be cleanly divided, but will spill into both areas. The separation enforces an organization of material without confusion.

The KS is necessary for several reasons: (a) the KS (in conjunction with the Instructional Units) determines the course content exactly; (b) it reduces the number of tasks the designer must manage at any one time ("getting the knowledge right" is separated from the task of creating instruction delivery); (c) distinguishing instruction knowledge from domain knowledge allows the course to be described intentionally, and allows the possibility of automatic generation of course outlines; and (d) a Knowledge Structure opens the possibility of creating an adaptive course delivery system driven by the invariant knowledge in the KS. (See Russell, chapter 12, this volume.)

The Knowledge Structure is constructed by the Subject Matter

Expert with the course designer. The KS form is rationalized by decisions made within the Epistemology area.

Figure 7.9 shows a window onto the entire KS of the Basic Xerography course, whereas Figure 7.20 shows a portion of the KS in more detail. Each rectangle represents a concept or skill, and the links signify relationships between the concepts. In Figure 7.20, concepts are related (linked) by a variety of relations. The most common relationships in this diagram are *subconcept, subcomponent,* and *next-step*. Concepts and concept relationships represent the content the student should learn from the course. To the Subject Matter Expert and the course designer, the KS represents domain knowledge at a tractable level of instruction. Concepts in the KS map onto IUs; whereas concept–concept relationships in the KS guide the instructor in sequencing the delivery of IUs.

The KS browser is the designer's primary tool for creating and manipulating the KS. The browser is used to create the nodes, as well as the differing links (and link types). The global view browser is too complex, so the designer works with sub-browsers such as those seen in Figure 7.20. A sub-browser is created by the user by extracting a subgraph from the KS following only a subset of all the possible links types. Thus, the content of the KS maps directly onto the grain size of instructional content. Individual concepts are placed into the KS if they are dealt with individually in the course. This effectively defines the grain size the KS must represent.

Note that the structure of the KS as seen in these figures is simply a representation of the relational structure of the concepts of the domain, rather than a representation of the concepts themselves. The KS, as such, is a relatively large grain representation of knowledge.

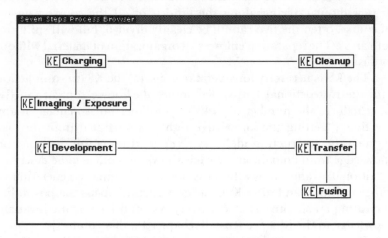

FIGURE 7.20   A sub-browser of the KS.

Each of the nodes in the KS represents a separable concept that must be taught. For the purpose of course design, this granularity is the desired resolution.

Representing Instruction and Presentation Methods

IDE supports articulation of the instructional strategy used to teach the course, in addition to representing course content. The skills required to teach a course are complex and occur at many levels of abstraction. IDE represents this knowledge as *rules* that create instructional goals, and as *constraints* on instructional performance. (Rules create instructional goals, whereas constraints restrict the way those goals are implemented). This knowledge is broken into three categories:

1. *Pedagogy* rules and constraints are course-specific, representing the sequencing of topics in the course.
2. *Strategy* rules represent general approaches to the presentation of information to the student. They encode instruction methods such as "drill and practice," "present three concepts, then test for understanding," or "monitor a student's solution of a problem, and intervene as soon as the student varies from the solution path." Strategy rules do more than provide recipes of instruction approaches; they are used to generate the major goals of the instructional plan.
3. *Tactical* rules and constraints govern how instructional goals are implemented, taking into account low-level concerns such as display format, potential IU characteristics, and so on. Tactical rules spell out how to implement an instructional goal in a particular instructional environment for a particular type of student.

The rules for the Basic Xerography course are shown in Figure 7.21.

Articulating the Course Control rules forces the designer to consider the subtleties of how course material will be taught. By distinguishing the way in which knowledge is taught from the representation of that knowledge, attention must be focused on the relationship of the teaching style to the mechanisms of learning. (This contrasts with standard instructional design practice, which confounds the issues. Instructional material is written with teaching style issues in mind, but teaching style and instructional practice are not separated.) Course Control rules capture the designer's understanding of the most effective instructional approach to the material, making that understanding explicitly available.

Pedagogy rules:

  To (Teach BX) = >
    Segment 1: Teach functions
    Segment 2: Teach steps sequenced by next-step
    Segment 3: Teach normal operations
    Segment 4: Teach broken-state

Strategy Rules:

  To (Teach functions) = >
    1: Present Function
    2: Teach linked processes
    3: Teach sub-functions
    4: Present summary

  To (Teach broken-state) = >
    1: Present broken-state
    2: Test broken-state

  When (Present ?X, Present ?Y, Present ?Z) = >
    Test ?X or Test ?Y or Test ?Z
    (* after presenting 3 concepts in a row, test for understanding of
    one of the concepts)

  When (Segment beginning) = >
    Test segment understanding

  When (Segment end) = >
    Test segment criterion

  When (Misunderstand ?X) = >
    Remediate ?X
    (* Remidiate immediately on detection of misunderstanding)

Tactic Rules:
  To (Select IU) = >
    Keep each display as visual as possible
  To (Select IU) = >
    Minimize amount of text to read
  To (Select IU) = >
    Don't use same IU twice to present same concept

FIGURE 7.21 The Course Content area represents the way the course should be taught. Rules and constraints represent the way an instructional plan should be formed.

Representing Instructional Units (IUs)

IUs are created by the designer in response to decisions made in the Instruction area, and are the final output of the IDE design process. An IU is a concrete piece of instruction that teaches a particular concept. It represents what the student will see and use. An IU may be a presentation of text on a concept, a segment of video, an exercise, a lecture segment, or a series of questions. In IDE, an IU is represented by a card that records (a) the presentation content (e.g., the text of a textual presentation), (b) what concepts the IU addresses, (c) an attribute/value list describing properties of the IU (e.g., presentation mode, level of detail, level of difficulty), and (d) the mapping of questions and answers onto concepts and misconcepts. (Figure 7.12 illustrates an IU as specified in IDE.)

PUTTING IT ALL TOGETHER

Creating a course design within IDE is essentially a process of creating design decisions and a rationale structure to completely specify each of the knowledge areas. Our design philosophy is very unrestrictive— the designer can work within any area at any time. (Other instruction design systems are very prescriptive according to Branson, 1975[3] This characteristic reflects our experience with IDE. Designing and developing a course from the initial course objectives down to a specific sequence of Instructional Units is largely a top-down refinement process. In practice, however, discoveries made as work progresses may have severe consequences on the overall design, often requiring many design iterations in a more structured design system. In IDE, the accessibility of each knowledge area permits changes to be made readily throughout the design.

After all IDE knowledge areas have been fully specified, the course must be transcribed into a delivery form. Each delivery mode (e.g., workbook & lecture, Interactive VideoDisk, Computer-Based Training, etc.) has its own special requirements, but the process can be generally described as transferring the "Course Specifications" column into the chosen medium. For instance, creating a workbook-based training course from an IDE design consists of transferring (and editing) the contents of the IUs into a textual representation following the sequence given by the Pedagogical rules (that is, converting the IU contents into a document). Creating an Interactive VideoDisk course requires that some of the Strategy and Tactical rules be converted into the program that will drive the videodisk (in addition to transcribing the IU contents into video segments). In each case, the final transformation is fairly straightforward and is driven by the set of IUs and the Course Control rules.

---

[3]There are many instructional design models. They focus on managing designer resources and giving designers a task profile to follow. Most of these models are very prescriptive, and none allows the generality of approach seen in IDE. See Andrews, 1980, for a summary of 40 models of instructional design. The Branson design model is also available from the National Technical Information Service, VA 22161.

SUMMARY

IDE is an on-line environment for dealing with the many decisions that must be made, recorded, structured, and accessed during the design and development of instruction. It is also a way to view instruction: Content is distinguished from delivery, both content and delivery are explicitly represented, and everything in the final instructional product exists for a specific, rationalized reason. With this representation for instruction, we can begin to explore what kinds of intelligent assistance can be supplied to designers and developers.

ACKNOWLEDGMENTS

This work was partially supported by a grant from the Army Research Institute: MDA 903-83-C-0189. Jim Greeno and John Seely Brown developed the original statement of what IDE could be; Peter Pirolli helped in developing significant portions of both the code and the ideas; Anne-Marie Jensen, Juliann Orr, and Richard Burton participated in many of the discussions that helped us develop these ideas; Joe Psotka made many helpful comments on paper and the ideas. To each, we give our thanks.

REFERENCES

Andrews, D. H., & Ludwika, G. (1980). A competitive analysis of models of instructional design. *Journal of Instructional Development, 3*(4).

Branson, R. K. (1975). *Interservice procedures for instructional systems development. Phase 1: Analyze* (Vols. 1–4). Center for Educational Technology, Florida State University.

Halasz, F. G., Moran, T. P., & Trigg, R. H. (1986). *Notecards in a nutshell.* Palo Alto, CA: Intelligent Systems Lab Publication.

8

Instructional Planners: Lessons Learned

Stuart A. Macmillan
Sun Microsystems
David Emme
Amdahl Corporation
Melissa Berkowitz
FMC Central Engineering Labs

INTRODUCTION

Every intelligent tutoring system (ITS) has a mechanism for deciding what to do next at each point during an instructional session. We refer to this function as *instructional planning*. Instructional planning by humans refers both to prelesson planning and to their dynamic decision making during a lesson. Instructional planning encompasses a wide range of instructional strategies including reactive environments, consulting, coaching, aiding, and tutoring. In this chapter we analyze research on instructional planning for ITSs. Based on this analysis and insights gained from our own research, we present the lessons we learned and propose a new architecture for dynamic instructional planning. The realization of this architecture is a Self-Improving Instructional Planner (SIIP) that dynamically creates instructional plans, executes these plans, replans, and improves its planning behavior based on students' responses to tutoring. Future instructional planners, we claim, will share many of the capabilities of SIIP. We are assuming that an instructional planner will be responsible for a broad range of instructional goals, and that students will vary in their entry-level knowledge and skills.

Only a small number of existing ITSs have nontrivial instructional planning capabilities, and there is little empirical evaluation of their instructional planning behavior. The majority of past ITS investigations focused on aspects other than instructional planning. Researchers wisely concentrated on ITS modules such as student modeling that are prerequisites to sophisticated instructional planners.

However, although ITS researchers may have been wise to take a somewhat simplistic view of instructional planning in the past, the field is now capable of producing more sophisticated and more extensive diagnostic hypotheses (see Anderson, 1985; Brown & Burton, 1978; London & Clancey, 1983; Sleeman, 1983; VanLehn, 1986), increased conceptual fidelity of expert models (Anderson, 1986; deKleer & Brown, 1983; Clancey, 1985), and more sophisticated machine planning behavior (Hayes-Roth, 1985).

The number and complexity of the activities of instructional planners indicates the need to treat the entire process as a planning problem (Leinhardt & Greeno, 1986; Ohlsson, 1986). Instructional planners are responsible for incrementally configuring plans that when executed are likely to facilitate students' achievement of specified instructional goals. Like human instructional planners, machine instructional planners must be capable of a wide range of instructional behaviors. Some of the common responsibilities of instructional planners are listed below.

1. *Select instructional objectives.* Dynamically create an individualized syllabus and determine the current instructional goals in the context of the overall instructional goals.
2. *Select instructional methods and materials.* Dynamically plan the instructional strategies and instructional actions to achieve the current instructional goals.
3. *Resolve ambiguities in the student model.* Plan instruction that aids the diagnosing of students' difficulties.
4. *Monitor instruction.* Make note of particular events in the delivery of instruction and student learning.
5. *Replan instruction.* Modify the current instructional plan when the student is not responding as anticipated to instruction.
6. *Diagnose and improve planning.* Improve the behavior of the instructional planner by noticing and acting on opportunities for correcting chronic planning deficiencies. Chronic planning deficiencies indicate the need to modify an instructional planner's existing machine theory of instruction.

These capabilities are being implemented in the SIIP, a research tool for developing, evaluating, and refining machine theories of instructional planning. In this chapter we identify lessons we have learned about the task of instructional planning and the capabilities required of machine instructional planners.

BACKGROUND

Before moving to a discussion of past and current research on instructional planning, we introduce a formalism that should help in our analysis of these systems. We will use this formalism to describe a new architecture to support instructional planning that addresses some of the deficiencies of prior planners.

Assume that two intelligent agents, A_t, a teacher, and A_s, a student, are interacting, and one or both have the goal to change the knowledge and subsequent behavior of A_s. Instructional planning is the process A_t uses to configure partial orderings of instructional operators that when executed are likely to result in A_s learning selected instructional goals. The goals for instruction may be set by A_t A_s, or both agents. The A_t develops plans in light of changing data, and controls the execution and dynamic refinement of these instructional plans. We begin our discussion by making the following assumptions about the agents.

Assumptions About the Teaching Agent

1. The teaching agent, A_t, cannot directly observe or manipulate the knowledge structures of the student agent, A_s; also, A_t cannot measure the state of A_s's knowledge without error. This applies to both knowledge about the domain and knowledge about how to learn. Thus A_t is never certain of A_s's state of knowledge and can only indirectly influence change of that knowledge structure.

2. A_t cannot predict with certainty A_s's response to an instructional action. A_t does not have a strong theory of how A_s learns, and, as noted above, A_t is not certain of A_s's knowledge state prior to instruction.

3. A_t and A_s do not share identical instructional goals. A_s learns best when her instructional goals are similar to those of A_t. This situation may require that A_t, A_s, or both agents modify their corresponding instructional goals.

4. A_t needs expectations about future opportunities and difficulties to plan effectively. Because these expectations are in part based on future plans, A_t needs to be capable of planning beyond the next instructional operation at each point in the instruction.

5. A_t must be capable of a wide range of instructional strategies if it is to be useful over many domains and A_ss. The instructional requirements of different domains and the demands of individualizing instruction call for an A_t with a rich set of instructional strategies

Assumptions About the Student Agent

1. The knowledge state of the student agent, A_s is affected by many factors including the execution of the A_t's instructional plan. A_t's execution of an instructional plan may have a positive effect, no effect, or a negative effect on A_s's learning with respect to an instructional goal. A_s may

exhibit apparent spontaneous learning when factors other than A_t's instruction alter A_s's knowledge state.

2. A_s's vary in their initial knowledge state prior to receiving instruction. This applies to both knowledge about the domain and knowledge about how to learn. A_s's variance in entry knowledge and learning skills indicates that A_t's instruction is best when it is individualized.

3. A_s's learning is not monotonically increasing. A_s forgets, becomes confused when previous learning interferes with current learning, and learns incorrect knowledge. On the other hand, A_s is capable of learning both from instruction and sources besides the given A_t.

4. A_s, when motivated, tries to integrate new knowledge with previous knowledge.

Limitations of Existing Instructional Planners

Instructional planning had a modest beginning in the first traditional computer-assisted instruction (CAI) systems developed in the 1960s (e.g., Suppes & Morningstar, 1969). Course authors specified a single conditional plan that determined all possible paths students could take through a lesson. Instructional planners using this approach were costly to build, inflexible, and depended heavily on the skill of the course designer. Cost here is measured in absolute terms and not relative to the development of other machine instructional planners. To their benefit these human-authored planners often resulted in well-organized and motivating instruction. Traditional planners were later augmented to keep an explicit model of a student's state of knowledge about the separate skills required for the tasks the student performed. One such planner, BIP (Wescourt, Beard, & Barr, 1980), used a planning algorithm to select a student's next task based on the system's estimate of the student's mastery of the skills required for these tasks. These systems modeled the student's knowledge state in terms of developing skills rather than tasks, yet retained the motivational and organizational strengths of human-authored instruction.

In parallel with research efforts on algorithmic planners were efforts on systems that encoded instructional knowledge as rules. Systems such as WUSOR (Goldstein, 1977) and WEST (Burton & Brown, 1982) encoded instructional strategies for coaching and used information about the current context and the student's previous learning to reason about when and what to advise a student. These means–ends planners and others, such as GUIDON (Clancey, 1979, 1984), O'Shea's quadratic tutor (1982), and SCHOLAR, (Carbonell, 1970) proved to be effective discourse managers for narrow domains and fixed instructional strategies. However there are at least three shortcomings of means–ends planners. First, if the domain is complex, an extensive specification of a large number of means–ends guidance rules is required. A second problem with using means–ends guidance rules for instructional planning is their insufficient flexibility in situations in which only uncertain diagnostic information is available about the student. In such cases, the tutoring system needs to experiment with a variety of alternative treatments that could be supported by these several diagnostic hypotheses. A third shortcoming of means–ends guidance rules is that they lack a global context for planning instruction. Means–ends planners do not take into consideration likely future instruction when determining the current instruction an A_s is to receive.

More recently, efforts by Woolf and McDonald (1985), Bonar (1985), Peachey and McCalla (1986), and Macmillan and Sleeman (1987) have proposed architectures that address some of the limitations of earlier instructional planners. Such limitations include the high cost to apply the planner to a new domain, lack of a global context for planning, inflexible control structures, and the inability to generate plans when there are multiple hypotheses about an A_s's state of learning. Following is a discussion of SIIP (Macmillan & Sleeman, 1987), a dynamic instructional planner, and the lessons learned from this research.

SIIP: A BLACKBOARD ARCHITECTURE FOR INSTRUCTIONAL PLANNING

SIIP is a generic architecture for building instructional planners for ITSs. The system builder extends SIIP by adding domain-specific instructional planning knowledge (e.g., skeletal plans and constraints) in the form of knowledge sources and domain-specific content area knowledge (e.g., syllabus, tasks, examples) in the form of graphs. SIIP provides a predefined blackboard structure, a set of control knowledge sources, a set of generic planning and replanning knowledge sources, a set of monitoring knowledge sources, a constrained graph search mechanism, and an execution module.

Figure 8.1 shows the relationship of the SIIP instructional planner to our overall BLACKBOARD-Instructor. Each module of this ITS architecture has been realized in many different ways by various research groups. SIIP research is concerned with these supporting modules to the extent that the various assumptions and capabilities of these modules impact the range of instructional planning behavior SIIP can realize.

The architecture for implementing the SIIP is an extension of the BLACKBOARD model, BB1 (Hayes-Roth, 1985). This model is

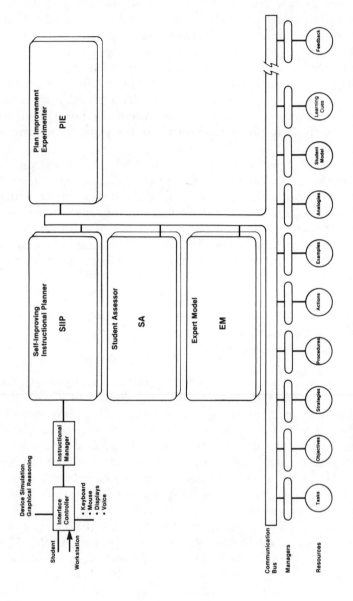

FIGURE 8.1 The BLACKBOARD-Instructor intelligent tutoring system.

a descendant of the HEARSAY II BLACKBOARD architecture that was developed for speech understanding. AGE, HEARSAY III, and BB1 represent subsequent system-building environments that extend the original HEARSAY II system. Problem domains that have been addressed using the BLACKBOARD architecture include scene interpretation (Hanson & Riseman, 1978), errand planning (Hayes-Roth, Hayes-Roth, Rosenschein, & Cammarata, 1979; Hayes-Roth, 1980), and cooperative distributed systems (Lesser & Corkill, 1981). The architecture supports planning as an opportunistic and incremental process that involves three basic assumptions.

1. All solution elements generated during problem solving are recorded in a structured, global database called the BLACKBOARD.
2. Solution elements are generated and recorded on the BLACKBOARD by independent processes called *knowledge sources.*
3. On each problem-solving cycle, a scheduling mechanism chooses a single knowledge source to execute (Hayes-Roth, 1985).

These three basic assumptions are elaborated in the context of SIIP in the following sections: BLACKBOARD design, knowledge sources, and control structure.

Plan BLACKBOARD Design

The BLACKBOARD database organizes elements of the instructional plan along two dimensions. (See Figure 8.2.) One dimension indicates levels of abstraction in the instructional plan, and the other dimension reflects the ordering of plan elements.

The plan blackboard for the SIIP is composed of four abstraction levels. Each successive level of the blackboard represents increasing detail of the instructional plan, as opposed to operators' abstraction levels (Sacerdoti, 1974). For example, the most abstract level, *Iobjective,* indicates the particular instructional objectives being pursued. The next level, *Istrategy,* specifies the pedagogical approach used to achieve the chosen objective(s). The next level, *Iprocedure,* outlines how to implement the chosen strategy. The most detailed level, *Iaction,* identifies the specific instructional actions proposed. Although an instructional plan includes all the nodes and links at each level of the plan blackboard, for purposes of execution, we refer to an instructional plan as the configuration of nodes at the level *Iaction.* It should be noted that because instructional planning is an incremental process the plan blackboard will contain plan elements that have been executed, elements that are actively being configured

SIIP Plan Blackboard

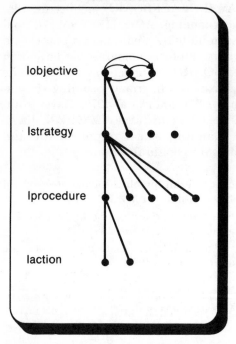

FIGURE 8.2 The SIIP plan blackboard records planning decisions.

for execution, and elements that represent contingency or future plans. A description of the type of data that is posted at each of the plan levels is shown in Figure 8.3.

The second dimension of the domain blackboard represents the temporal ordering of elements of the instructional plan. The solution elements for the instructional planner that appear to the right of other elements occur later in the instructional plan. If a partial ordering of the instructional sequence is required, the strict linear ordering can be altered by specifying temporal constraints among the various instructional actions (Sacerdoti, 1975). These constraints are used by the Instructional Manager at execution time to indicate plan sequences that can be executed in parallel. An extension of this idea, which we have also implemented, uses execution constraints to produce conditional plans that choose among plan options based on information available at execution time.

Knowledge Sources

Knowledge sources encode facts and heuristics that make independent contributions to the development of an instructional plan. Typically, knowledge sources are activated by events such as adding or modifying solution elements on the blackboard. Each blackboard event may activate one or more knowledge sources that become candidates for selection and execution. The execution of a knowledge source results in some action, often the production of new blackboard events. The sum of the individual contributions of the executed knowledge sources determines the instructional plan generated in response to the input instructional goal and student responses to instruction. Knowledge sources have no information about the expertise of other knowledge sources, so in this sense they are independent. Cooperation among knowledge sources is achieved by the indirect influence they exert on one another by working on a shared problem represented in a

Iobjective level

Each node posted at this level indicates an instructional objective under consideration by the SIIP. More than one objective node may be operative at a given time. Links between nodes record the plan development history. See figure. (e.g., student will master diagnostic skill A, B, and C.)

Istrategy level

Each node posted at this level represents a pedagogical strategy selected to help achieve the instructional objective (node at the Iobjective level).

The sequencing of strategies specifies the high-level plan to achieve the operative instructional objectives.

Strategies become operative/inoperative as they are completed or abandoned.

See figure 3. (e.g., use the sequence of instructional strategy to show a line of reasoning, have the student critique a line of reasoning, have the student extend a given line of reasoning, have the student generate the line of reasoning.)

Iprocedure level

Each node posted at this level represents an abstract specification of the procedure to implement an instructional strategy.

See figure 3. (e.g., use the sequence of instructional procedures; introduce example, focus student attention, preview example, show example, review example.)

Iaction level

Each node posted at this level represents an instructional action that implements a procedure and is executable by the IM.

See figure 3. (e.g., use the sequence of instructional actions; relate to prior learning, provide motivation.)

FIGURE 8.3 Design of the plan blackboard.

```
Name:                 Constrain-Objective-Prerequisite
Problem-domain:       (Instructional-Planning)
Description:          When determining the instructional
                      objectives for a session post con-
                      straints that prerequisites are taught
                      first.
Trigger:              New instructional goals are given or
                      current instructional goals are
                      inappropriate.
Invoker:              Instruction is at a breakpoint
Goal:                 constrain-objective
Rank:                 Medium
Action:               For each objective being considered
                      request that the actual objective
                      selected satisfies the constraint that
                      prerequisites are taught first.
```

FIGURE 8.4 Instructional planning knowledge source.

SIIP Control Blackboard

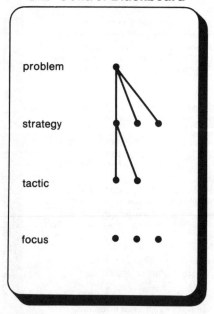

FIGURE 8.5 The SIIP control blackboard.

globally accessible data structure. For example, Figure 8.4 describes a knowledge source, "Constrain–Objective–Prerequisite."

Control Structure

The control structure for the SIIP blackboard architecture is explicitly defined by a control blackboard that records the system's decisions about desirable, feasible, and actual behavior, control knowledge sources that modify the system's problem-solving behavior, and an adaptive scheduling mechanism that manages the contribution of both domain and control knowledge sources. (See Figure 8.5.)

The abstraction levels for the control blackboard are specified by the SIIP system and are described in Figure 8.6. The blackboard data structure supports reasoning about controlling the problem-solving behavior of the system. Control knowledge sources implement problem-solving strategies by posting Strategies, Tactics, and Foci decisions on the control blackboard. The scheduling mechanism uses this information about operative Strategies, Tactics, and Foci to prioritize the list of knowledge sources that are invoked. The execution of control knowledge sources can dynamically alter SIIP's problem-solving behavior by controlling which Strategies, Tactics, and Foci are operative. Control can vary between very loose opportunities and detailed procedural requirements.

The adaptive scheduling mechanism is implemented by three basic control knowledge sources. The first control knowledge source updates the list of invoked and triggered sources. The second control knowledge source ranks the invoked knowledge sources based on Strategies, Tactics, and Foci information. The third control knowledge source executes the highest ranked invoked knowledge source.

SIIP Extensions to the BB1 Architecture

The SIIP architecture is an extension of several aspects of the BB1 architecture. First, the SIIP architecture supports dynamic planning. Plans are configured and executed incrementally with successive planning segments dynamically adjusting to new information. Second, generic instructional planning knowledge sources provide the capability to do both constraint-based (Stefik, 1980) and skeletal-based (Friedland, 1979) planning. Third, generic instructional planning knowledge sources provide the capability to monitor planning behavior and to replan or modify the current plan based on identified planning problems. Fourth, the flexible control capability of BB1 was extended to permit high-level procedural control for situations in which more control in the planning process is desired. Fifth, a mechanism for immediate execution of knowledge sources was implemented to support interprocess communication. Sixth, instantiation of plan nodes based on constraint lists was achieved by a constrained-graph search module. Seventh, the architecture was extended to interact with a Plan Improvement Experimenter, so SIIP can refine its planning behavior time. The last extension required is a garbage-collection routine that removes old plan elements from the plan blackboard and records a summary of the past planning in an instructional history file. SIIP is an attempt to integrate a diverse

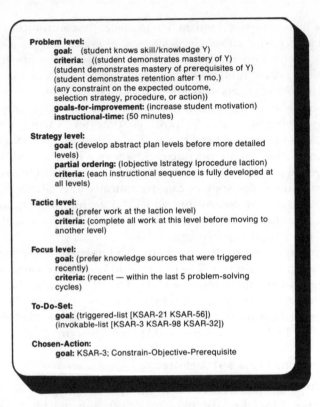

Problem level:
   goal: (student knows skill/knowledge Y)
   criteria: ((student demonstrates mastery of Y)
   (student demonstrates mastery of prerequisites of Y)
   (student demonstrates retention after 1 mo.)
   (any constraint on the expected outcome,
   selection strategy, procedure, or action))
   goals-for-improvement: (increase student motivation)
   instructional-time: (50 minutes)

Strategy level:
   goal: (develop abstract plan levels before more detailed
   levels)
   partial ordering: (Iobjective Istrategy Iprocedure Iaction)
   criteria: (each instructional sequence is fully developed at
   all levels)

Tactic level:
   goal: (prefer work at the Iaction level)
   criteria: (complete all work at this level before moving to
   another level)

Focus level:
   goal: (prefer knowledge sources that were triggered
   recently)
   criteria: (recent — within the last 5 problem-solving
   cycles)

To-Do-Set:
   goal: (triggered-list [KSAR-21 KSAR-56])
   (invokable-list [KSAR-3 KSAR-98 KSAR-32])

Chosen-Action:
   goal: KSAR-3; Constrain-Objective-Prerequisite

FIGURE 8.6   Design of the control blackboard.

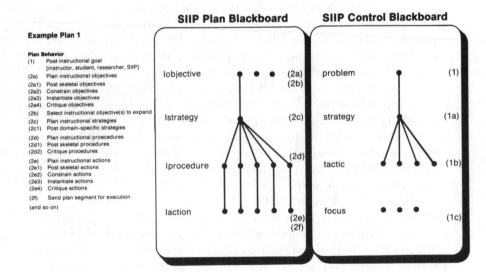

FIGURE 8.7   An example of SIIP planning behavior.

set of planning tactics within a single architecture (Sacerdoti, 1979). See Macmillan and Sleeman (1987) for a more detailed discussion of SIIP.

AN EXAMPLE OF SIIP PLANNING BEHAVIOR

Following is an example of the planning behavior of SIIP and a description of how this behavior is realized within the SIIP architecture. The particular example shown here typifies a rational and top-down planning style. The SIIP architecture, however, supports dynamic adjustment of its planning style to suit the requirements of its current planning context by modifying its control decisions on the control blackboard. Variations on the initial example are shown to illustrate flexible control of the SIIP's planning and replanning behavior.

As shown in Figure 8.7, this instructional planning session is initiated by posting an instructional goal at the *Problem* level of the control blackboard (1). Those knowledge sources whose triggering and involving conditions are satisfied due to this event become candidates for execution on the next planning cycle. In this example a series of knowledge sources posts an initial control strategy (1a, 1b, 1c) and then proposes that the next decisions should determine the specific objectives to cover in the session (2a). Competing decisions might recommend that the session objectives be derived from assessments of the student's interactions with an initial complex problem. A scheduling mechanism ranks the invoked knowledge sources based on operative Strategies, Tactics, and Foci decisions and selects a single knowledge source for execution. If a control knowledge source is selected, its execution will result in changed control behavior of the SIIP by modifying Strategies, Tactics, and Foci on the control blackboard (1a, 1b, 1c). If a domain knowledge source is selected, its execution results in modification of the developing instructional plan on the domain blackboard.

The SIIP planner next develops a complete plan at the *Iobjective* level of abstraction (2a1–2a4). First, a single knowledge source posts three skeletal objectives for the 50-minute session. Several knowledge sources then post constraints to reflect the desired attributes and relationships for the three objectives (e.g., prerequisite, postrequisite, corequisite). Other constraint information could be derived from the student model, the expert model, and the student history. After all invoked knowledge sources that post constraints have been executed, a knowledge source that instantiates the objectives is invoked and executed. Instantiation of the objective nodes involves a constrained-graph search of the Syllabus. When an instance cannot be found that satisfies all the constraints, the least important constraints are incrementally removed until an instance can be found. The SIIP is responsible for judging when an instance is acceptable and may initiate replanning when no acceptable instance can be found. Each resource contains instances of a class of instances such as tasks, examples, and objectives. Critic knowledge sources are now applied to check for specific violations of the group of instances that the constrained-graph search returned. If a critic notices a violation, it signals SIIP to initiate replanning.

Next, SIIP executes a knowledge source that marks one of the three objectives as selected (2b). This event initiates planning at the lower levels of abstraction. Planning behavior at the *Istrategy* level proceeds like that on the *Iobjective* level in the absence of domain-specific strategies for the selected objective(s). In this example, a domain-specific knowledge source exists and it is invoked and executed (2c1). In general, specific planning knowledge recorded in these domain-specific knowledge sources is given preference over generic planning knowledge.

The SIIP planner, still operating under the rational and top-down control structure, focuses its next planning activity at the *Iprocedure* level. The rational control structure reflects the planning behavior of a "rational" instructor who proceeds from the selection of an instructional goal to planning actions to achieve that goal. A knowledge source that knows of a skeletal plan for implementing the operative instructional strategy exists and is executed (2d1). As a result of executing this skeletal knowledge source, five plan nodes are added to the domain blackboard. These nodes indicate an ordering of abstract instructional actions. Finally, critic knowledge sources are invoked and executed (2d2).

In the absence of domain-specific facts and skeletal plans, the most detailed level of the developing instructional plan is generated in the same manner SIIP used at the *Iobjective* level (2e1–2e4). For each operative procedure node, associated action nodes are planned by posting constraint information and then instantiating each action node using the constrained-graph search mechanism. After these nodes are critiqued and found satisfactory, the resulting plan sequence is sent to the Instructional Manager for execution (2f), and planning continues.

As shown in Figure 8.8, the SIIP architecture supports a wide range of planning behaviors because of its flexible control structure. Incremental plan development may involve the opportunistic refocusing of planning activity as opposed to the top-down approach shown in the previous example. Typically instructional planning will

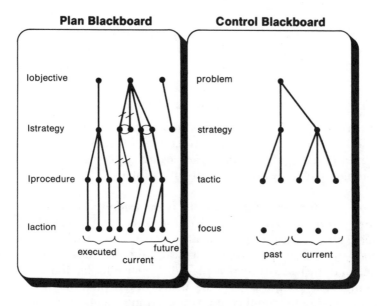

FIGURE 8.8 Possible SIIP planning behavior.

involve moving up and down the abstraction hierarchy to resolve contention between the desired *Iobjectives* and the *Iactions*. The control plan on the control blackboard may need to be altered in response to monitors identifying expectation violations in the planning process or resulting plans, to a request by an A_s to review and alter an instructional plan, and to process information from supporting modules such as the Student Assessor. Replanning, plan monitoring, plan execution, possible-worlds planning, and incremental plan extension each place additional demands on SIIP to support flexible control. SIIP's explicit and flexible control structure has made it easier to find solutions to each of these issues yet maintain a simple planning architecture. We are continuing to investigate the utility and practicality of SIIP's planning capabilities. (See Macmillan & Sleeman, 1987.) When required, we will extend SIIP's capabilities to meet the demand of the task of instructional planning.

LESSONS LEARNED

The process of instructional planning for ITSs is receiving increasing attention by researchers; however, we are still at an early stage in our understanding of this process and the requirements for machine instructional planners. Lessons we have learned should be considered tentative and subjected to further investigation. Following are lessons that are supported by our analysis of past instructional planners, the instructional planning task, and our current research on SIIP.

Associated with each lesson are a list of SIIP architecture requirements concerning planning capabilities. We are investigating the need for these capabilities and techniques for realizing these capabilities in our research on SIIP.

Lesson 1.0. Instructional Planning Is a Complex Process

Instructional planning is complex because of characteristics inherent in the instructional task. An instructional planner reasons in what is typically a large planning space using uncertain, unstable, and incomplete data to configure instructional plans.

Lesson 1.1. Instructional planning is an underspecified process in a large planning space. The planning space for A_t varies according to the nature of the domain of instruction and the set of instructional actions that can be performed. Typically the planning space is very large, and there exist many plausible plans to facilitate student learning. The complexity of the instructional planning process is proportional to the number of possible arrangements of instructional actions and instructional objectives. If A_t configures its plans in a hierarchy of abstraction spaces (Sacerdoti, 1974), the complexity increases proportionally to the possible arrangements at each abstraction level. The planning process becomes more complex when the instructional planner chooses to develop alternative plans in parallel or produce conditional plans for execution. A characteristic of this task of developing alternative plans that helps in coping with the complexity is that typically many possible plans are useful in realizing an instructional goal. A_t need only produce satisfying plans. Further, planning in a hierarchy of abstraction spaces has proven to be an effective means of focusing the planning activity, rather than adding to planning complexity.

The SIIP architecture requires hierarchy of abstractions and satisfying plans. The abstraction hierarchy for SIIP is the partitioning of the planning space into plan levels such that lower levels of the hierarchy contain more detailed plan information than do higher levels. For example, one level of an abstraction hierarchy may contain plan decisions about a sequence of instructional strategies, and a lower level of the abstraction hierarchy may contain plan decisions about specific instructional actions that realize these instructional strategies (see Hayes-Roth, 1980; Sacerdoti, 1974). Satisfying plans are plans that are sufficient but not necessarily optimal.

Lesson 1.2. Instructional planning requires reasoning with uncertain data. Instructional planning requires reasoning with uncertain data, because student assessment provides only hypotheses about A_s's state of knowledge, and theories of instruction do not prescribe optimal instruction even if the A_s's knowledge state is known. A_t has incomplete information about how A_s arrived at a result. A_t does not always have access to A_s's line of reasoning because it is not always practical or possible to elicit behavioral traces that reflect A_s's reasoning processes. This uncertainty adds to the complexity of the instructional planning process by increasing the number of possible interpretations of the available data and by increasing the number of plausible courses of action. A_t requires capabilities to cope with this complexity introduced by uncertainty.

The SIIP architecture requires a flexible and explicit control structure, replanning, plan monitoring, incremental and opportunistic planning, context planning, and conditional planning. A machine planner has explicit and flexible control when the knowledge about what the planner should do next is represented explicitly and the planner is capable of dynamically adapting its decision-making process based on the planning context. (See Hayes-Roth, 1985.) Replanning is the process of modifying an existing plan in response to a perceived deficiency with the plan or a request to modify the plan by the A_s. Plan monitoring is noticing and recording significant events in the planning process and the resulting plans. These evaluations are used to identify the need for replanning and plan improvement. Incremental planning refers to creation of a plan one step at a time. This is often required in situations in which the planner must wait for more information to continue its planning. Opportunistic planning is planning behavior that supports dynamic focusing of attention on different areas of a developing plan. (See Hayes-Roth, Hayes-Roth, Rosenschien, & Cammarata, 1979.) Context planning or possible-worlds planning is the parallel development of competing plans in which each plan is developed under different assumptions. Conditional plans are plans that contain decision rules to select among two or more plan options at execution time. The human-authored plans of traditional CAI systems are conditional plans. In the context of this work we refer to conditional planning as a machine planner's dynamic generation of conditional plans (Peachey & McCalla, 1986).

Lesson 1.3 Instructional planning is an unstable process. Instructional planning is an unstable process because A_s's knowledge state can change without any action by A_t. A_t is only one of several factors that affect A_s's learning. A_s is an intelligent agent that cognitively mediates instruction and is able to instruct himself. A_t's interpretation of this ability can be that the A_s has learned from instruction, forgotten, or learned without instruction. The fact that A_s's knowledge state does not necessarily improve monotonically and that his or her knowledge state can change without action from A_t requires A_t not only to achieve its instructional goal but also to maintain it.

The SIIP must incorporate incremental and opportunistic planning, flexible and explicit control, plan monitoring, context planning, conditional planning, and cooperative planning in response to this lesson learned. Cooperative planning is the capability of a machine planner to accept and act on input from a human planner.

Lesson 1.4 Instructional planners plan without complete information. A_t does not have complete information about what A_s knows and does not know. Further, instructional planners do not have complete information about how to realize an instructional goal through their instructional plans. Certain assumptions made at one point during planning may have to be retracted at a later time. The SIIP architecture thus requires replanning, plan monitoring, context planning, conditional planning, and cooperative planning.

Lesson 2.0 Instructional Planners Are Cooperative Planners

A_s must cooperate with A_t for learning to occur, because A_t does not operate directly on the knowledge structures of A_s. A_s cognitively mediates instruction by interpreting, modifying, and extending the cues given as a result of the execution of an instructional plan. The fact that A_t is a cooperative planner reduces the requirements for its plans to be complete, detailed, and without error. The A_s, when motivated, compensates for deficiencies in instruction.

Lesson 2.1 Plan generation and replanning are cooperative processes. Both A_t and A_s are responsible for planning and replanning. If the A_t's instructional strategy is direct instruction, for example, then the A_s influences the instruction by his or her responses. If the A_t's instructional strategy is student exploration, then A_s directs instruction and A_t reacts and offers advice. All instructional strategies, including direct instruction and student exploration, require A_t to plan incrementally in response to the dynamic needs of the instructional context. Instructional planning is also cooperative in the sense that A_s can offer advice to A_t about the planning and replanning process. The advice A_s gives must be represented in a language that A_t can process. The language of constraints and the skeletal plans support machine planning and knowledge acquisition.

The SIIP architecture requires cooperative planning, explicit and flexible control structure, and incremental and opportunistic planning, skeletal planning, constraint-based planning, and replanning to address this lesson. Constraint-based planning is a planning technique that configures plans by posting and reasoning about constraints that a plan must satisfy and then searching for plan elements that meet those constraints. (See Stefik, 1980.)

Lesson 2.2 Plan evaluation and monitoring are cooperative processes. Both A_t and A_s are responsible for evaluation and monitoring of instructional plans. The execution of an instructional operation does not guarantee that the expected results of the operation will be realized. Also, in the process of planning, past decisions may need to be reconsidered. A_t evaluates the instructional planning process, instructional plans, and A_s outcomes. When A_t identifies a planning problem, it may respond by changing its long-term planning behavior or replan to correct a specific difficulty. A_s evaluates the instruction received from A_t, possibly modifying it, and also evaluates A_t behavior over time. A_s's response to chronic difficulties with the instruction he or she receives may be to notify A_t of the problem. A_t may at times reveal its instructional plan as a means to explaining instructional planning behavior or to seek A_s's input on the plan.

This results in the SIIP architecture requirements for cooperative planning, flexible and explicit control structure, plan monitoring, plan improvement, and opportunistic and incremental planning. Plan improvement refers to a planner's ability to alter its planning knowledge in response to a chronic deficiency in its planning behavior. (See O'Shea, 1982.)

Lesson 2.3 Instructional plans are executed twice. Instructional plans are executed first by A_t and then by A_s. An instructional sequence is first executed by A_t, resulting in the presentation of an instructional sequence to A_s. The second execution happens when A_s processes the instructional sequence. Between A_t's execution of an instructional sequence and A_s's cognitive processing of the sequence, A_s reformulates the plan and possibly modifies it. A_t and A_s cooperate in forming instructional plans that are ultimately executed by A_s. This requires plan execution and cooperative planning as part of the SIIP architecture.

Lesson 2.4 The response time of instructional planners should be comparable to that of human instructional planners. The amount of time A_t has to plan and execute a response to A_s can only be estimated in advance. A_t's time to plan the next increment of instruction is equal to the time it takes A_s to respond to the last plan segment plus the time A_s expects a human would take to plan the next instructional sequence. These items are variable but can be estimated empirically.

The fact that A_t is interacting with A_s reduces the burden on A_t to produce the next plan increment by a fixed deadline. However, because A_t cannot precisely predict the time it will have to plan, A_t is burdened with having to adjust its planning behavior to accommodate variable time constraints. Hence the SIIP architecture requires flexible and explicit control, plan monitoring, and conditional planning.

Lesson 3.0 Instructional Planning Requires a Global Context

As long as the instructional planner operates within a global context, current planning can maintain continuity with previous planning. The planner can also develop expectations about future opportunities and anticipate difficulties.

Lesson 3.1 Current planning requires continuity with past planning. When A_t generates the next instructional sequence, it must take into consideration its prior plans and A_s's responses. If A_s's current learning is built upon his or her past learning, then there must be continuity between the goals and means of instruction from one interaction to the next.

The above indicates the SIIP architecture requirements for global planning and plan monitoring. A machine planner is a global planner to the extent that it has access to information about past, current, and likely future instruction and uses this information to make decisions that are believed to serve the planner's longer term goals. This is in contrast to planners who choose the next operator based on only the immediate needs of instruction.

Lesson 3.2 Current planning requires expectations about future opportunities and difficulties. When A_t generates the next instructional sequence, it should take into consideration likely future instructional events. Anticipation of future events enables the instructional planner to avert highly probable trouble spots and to delay actions to take advantage of later opportunities. It is important to be able to dynamically set the distance for how far into the future planning occurs, because the best planning horizon is different for different contexts. Here the SIIP architecture requires global planning, flexible and explicit control, and incremental and opportunistic planning.

Lesson 3.3 Instructional planning requires reasoning about plan options. The worth of a particular plan decision is usually not known immediately, and this results in the need to develop two or more plans in parallel that reflect the consequences of different plan decisions. This planning enables A_t to reason from different initial hypotheses and to select the plan that has higher value. A_t can produce conditional plans in cases in which it requires information at execution time to choose among several courses of action. These conditional plans include a decision rule for choosing the preferred action at execution time. As a result, SIIP architecture requires global planning, context planning, and conditional planning.

Lesson 4.0 Instructional Planners Require Both Domain-Dependent and Domain-Independent Knowledge About Instruction

Instructional planners benefit from both domain-dependent and domain-independent instructional planning knowledge. This lesson is different from the fact that instructional planning knowledge can be separate from domain knowledge about the subject matter. The proportion of domain-dependent to domain-independent knowledge required by instructional planners will vary over content areas. How much this proportion varies is an open question. If little instructional knowledge is domain-independent, then costs to develop planners for new domains may be prohibitive. Domain-independent planning knowledge can be knowledge that is general to all domains or general to a class of domains such as fault diagnosis. It may be more useful to consider the proportions of domain-independence to domain-dependence at various levels of plan abstraction. For example, decisions about the choice of a particular instructional strategy could be more domain-independent than decisions about particular instructional actions.

Lesson 4.1 Instructional planners require domain-dependent knowledge. Instructional planners require domain-dependent planning knowledge that captures instructional methods of expert teachers for a particular subject area. The compiled knowledge of expert teachers in a particular domain can be used when the domain-independent instructional planning knowledge is inadequate for generating good instruction. Domain-independent instructional planning knowledge is insufficient because it represents a general theory of instruction, and no theory of instruction has yet been proven to be adequate.

The related SIIP architecture requirements are constraint-based planning, skeletal planning, and independent knowledge sources. Knowledge sources are independent if they make contributions to planning. They do not need to know about the existence or the possible contribution of other knowledge sources (Hayes-Roth, 1985).

Lesson 4.2 Instructional planners require domain-independent knowledge. The requirement for domain-independent knowledge in instructional planners is pragmatic. If A_t's knowledge were largely domain-specific, the cost of developing planners for new domains would be prohibitive. There is evidence that instructional planners for particular classes of problems can be constructed to use primarily domain-independent knowledge (Clancey & Letsinger, 1981). SIIP architecture requires constraint-based planning, skeletal planning, and independent knowledge sources.

Lesson 4.3 Instructional planning knowledge can be at various levels of detail Instructional planners vary in the level of detail of their instructional plans. At a very high level of abstraction, the planner may assume responsibility only for deciding what to teach next, not how to teach it. In contrast, some instructional planners may generate the most detailed aspects of discourse. Planning can occur down to some level of detail between these two extremes after which compiled knowledge about instruction generates the instructional discourse. The SIIP architecture requires skeletal planning, hierarchical planning, and abstraction hierarchies.

Lesson 5.0. Instructional Planning Is Constrained by Capabilities of Supporting ITS Components

The behavior of an instructional planner is constrained by the capabilities of the Expert Model, Student Assessor, Instructional Manager, Plan-Improvement Experimenter, and the various Resource Managers. An instructional planner uses information from the supporting modules to resolve the tension between what is desirable and what is possible. Sophisticated instructional planners are incapable of producing higher quality plans when they lack the necessary information or resources.

Lesson 5.1 Instructional planning is constrained by capabilities of the Expert Model The Expert Model is responsible for modeling subject matter expertise. Two important roles for the Expert Model are to aid in the assessment of A_s's learning and to generate explanations. The expertise and reasoning behavior of the Expert Model should be comprehensible to A_ss to serve these two roles adequately. Multiple Expert Models that are tailored to various levels of A_s expertise may be required. Anderson (1986) has identified a continuum of expert models that are increasingly sophisticated and difficult to build. The continuum is Black-Box Models, Glass-Box Models, and Cognitive models. He recommends that instruction be based on a combination of issue-based instruction and model-tracing. Based on this lesson, the SIIP architecture requires an Expert Model with capabilities commensurate with the demands of the domain of instruction and the target set of instructional goals.

Lesson 5.2 Instructional planning is constrained by capabilities of the Student Assessor. The Student Assessor (SA) is responsible for generating hypotheses about A_s's state of learning and maintaining a record of this learning. The record of A_s's state of knowledge, referred to as the Student Model, may be in the form of a data structure or a runnable model that simulates the performance associated with a particular knowledge state. The quality and amount of information provided by the SA constrains the planning of A_t. VanLehn (1986) has proposed a three-dimensional classification scheme (bandwidth, knowledge type, and representation of student–expert differences) for student models. Decisions about the form of the student model and the capabilities of the SA constrain instructional planning. Here the SIIP architecture requires a Student Assessor with capabilities commensurate with the demands of the domain of instruction and the target set of instructional goals.

Lesson 5.3. Instructional planning is constrained by capabilities of the Instructional Manager. The Instructional Manager (IM) is responsible for executing the plans generated by the Instructional Planner and monitoring the execution of these plans. The manager can only execute plans for which it has the necessary resources. Instructional planning is similarly constrained to request only those instructional actions that can be realized by the manager. The SIIP architecture requires an Instructional Manager with capabilities commensurate with the demands of the domain of instruction and the target set of instructional goals.

Lesson 5.4 Instructional planning is constrained by capabilities of the Plan-Improvement Experimenter. The Plan-Improvement Experimenter (PIE) is responsible for improving the planning behavior of the Instructional Planner. Without such a capability, A_t's instructional planning behavior is constrained by its initial strengths and weaknesses. In addition, an instructional planner may lose its effectiveness over time due to changing goals of instructions, subject matter, and student population. The SIIP architecture now requires a Plan-Improvement Experimenter with capabilities commensurate with the demands of the domain of instruction and the target set of instructional goals.

Lesson 5.5. Instructional planning is constrained by the capabilities of the Resource Managers.   Resource Managers (RMs) are responsible for returning instances of resources, such as objectives and analogies, that satisfy specified constraints. For example, a Syllabus Manager returns an instance of an instructional objective. Resources such as objectives, examples, analogies, and instructional strategies define the limits of what is possible for the instructional planner. Here the SIIP architecture requires Resource Managers with capabilities commensurate with the demands of the domain of instruction and with the target set of instructional goals.

In this section we characterized instructional planning as a complex process involving cooperation between a teacher and a student. We claimed that instructional planning benefits from a global context and domain-dependent knowledge about instruction. Finally, we acknowledged that instructional planning is constrained by the capabilities of the supporting ITS modules. In response to these lessons we proposed capabilities for the SIIP architecture. These capabilities included flexible and explicit control, incremental and opportunistic planning, hierarchical planning, constraint-based planning, skeletal planning, variable-horizon planning, cooperative planning, replanning, and planning in a global context. Each of these capabilities is being investigated within the SIIP architecture.

UNRESOLVED ISSUES: LESSONS WE NEED TO LEARN

Clearly, instructional planning is complex and many-faceted. Lessons we appear to have learned may prove inadequate. If machine instructional planners are to model behaviors of effective human instructional planners, then we need to build our understanding of human and machine theories of instruction. In the area of human theories of instruction we need to better understand how teachers plan instruction and make decisions during instruction. To the extent that this planning and decision-making behavior can be generalized, we can use this knowledge in building machine instructional planners. Even if we had good human theories of instruction, the development of instructional planners would require a better understanding of the technical issues associated with representing instructional knowledge and planning or reasoning about this knowledge. Some of the important technical issues we face in our efforts to build instructional planners are featured in the discussion that follows.

Acquisition of instructional planning knowledge. The larger the scope of an instructional planner's knowledge, the less the need for domain-dependent, ITS-system dependent and learner-dependent knowledge about instruction. Machine instructional planners currently are narrow in their scope and remain costly to build. It is necessary to reduce the amount of application-specific knowledge. Tools are also needed to support the acquisition of this knowledge. Some initial questions in this area follow. What is the nature of application-specific instructional knowledge? What proportion of instructional planning knowledge is specific to particular classes of instruction? How is application-specific knowledge used by instructional planners? What are requirements for tools to support developers in acquiring application-specific instructional planning knowledge? What are requirements for tools that automatically tune or assist in tuning the instructional planner once it is fielded?

Representation of instructional planning knowledge. Given a well-formed human theory of instruction, decisions still need to be made about how to represent this knowledge to realize a machine theory of instruction. Existing instructional planners represent only a narrow range of instructional knowledge. Further, with the exception of an initial effort by Peachey and McCalla (1986), we know of no attempts to develop a representation formalism for instructional-planning knowledge. Following are some questions concerning representation. What knowledge is needed to plan instruction? How will this instructional-planning knowledge be used? What are candidate formal languages for instructional planning that can support knowledge acquisition, planning, and explanation? Are certain knowledge representations better suited to particular domain classes, instructional goals, and learners?

Planning and explanation based on instructional-planning knowledge. Issues in this category concern how encoded instructional planning knowledge is used to plan instruction and explain planning decisions. Most instructional planners were built as research efforts and were capable of only a narrow range of planning behavior. The limitations on the planning capabilities of an instructional planner constrain the range of instruction it can provide. We assume that a wide range of instructional strategies is required to individualize instruction. The following questions reflect the focus of our current SIIP. What are desirable capabilities of instructional planners? What are necessary and sufficient capabilities of instructional planners? What are known machine planning techniques that are likely to realize these desired capabilities? What are planning capabilities that require adapting known techniques or developing new planning techniques? What are the information requirements of ITS models that support instructional planning (i.e., Expert Model, Student Assessor)? How can a machine instructional planner explain its planning behavior to learners, system developers, and scientists engaged in theory building?

ACKNOWLEDGMENTS

We would like to express our appreciation to Derek Sleeman, Barbara Hayes-Roth, and Kathleen Gilbert-Macmillan, who have made several suggestions that resulted in an improved SIIP architecture.

REFERENCES

Anderson, J. R. (1985). *Skill acquisition: Compilation of weak-method problem solutions* (Tech. Rep.). Pittsburgh, PA: Carnegie-Mellon University.

Anderson, J. R. (1986). The expert module. *Minutes of the Air Force Human Resources Laboratory Research Planning Forum for Intelligent Tutoring Systems.* San Antonio, TX.

Bonar, J. (1985, June). Bite-sized intelligent tutoring. *Intelligent Tutoring Systems Group Newsletter, 85-3.*

Brown, J. S., & Burton, R. R. (1978). Diagnostic models for procedural bugs in basic mathematical skills. *Cognitive Science, 2,* 155–192.

Burton, R. R., & Brown, J. S. (1982). An investigation of computer coaching for informal learning activities. In D. Sleeman & J. Brown (Eds.), *Intelligent tutoring systems.* Orlando, FL: Academic Press.

Carbonell, J. (1970). AI in CAI: An artificial-intelligence approach to computer-aided instruction. *IEEE Transactions on Man-Machine Systems, MMS-11*(4).

Clancey, W. J. (1979). *Transfer of rule-based expertise through a tutorial dialogue.* Doctoral dissertation. Palo Alto, CA: Stanford University.

Clancey, W. J. (1984). Methodology for building an intelligent tutoring system. In W. Kintsch, J. R. Miller, & P. Polson (Eds.), *Methods and tactics in cognitive science* (pp. 51–83). Hillsdale, NJ: Lawrence Erlbaum Associates.

Clancey, W. J. (1985). *Acquiring, representing, and evaluating a competence model of diagnostic strategy* (Tech. Rep. No. KSL-84-2). Palo Alto, CA: Knowledge Systems Laboratory, Stanford University.

Clancey, W. J., & Letsinger, R. (1981). NEOMYCIN: Reconfiguring a rule-based expert system for application to teaching. *Proceedings of the 7th International Joint Conference on Artificial Intelligence.* Vancouver, BC.

deKleer, J., & Brown, J. S. (1983). Assumptions and ambiguities in mechanistic mental models. In D. Getner, & A. Stevens (Eds.), *Mental models*. Hillsdale, NJ: Lawrence Erlbaum Associates.

Friedland, P. (1979). *Knowledge-based hierarchical planning in molecular genetics*. Doctoral dissertation. Palo Alto, CA: Stanford University.

Goldstein, I. (1977). The computer as coach: An athletic paradigm for intellectual education. *Proceedings of the Association for Computing Machinery Conference* (pp. 227–233). Seattle, WA.

Hanson, A., & Riseman, E. (1978). VISIONS: A computer system for interpreting scenes. In A. Hanson & E. Riseman (Eds.), *Computer vision systems*. New York: Academic Press.

Hayes-Roth, B. (1985). A blackboard architecture for control. *Artificial Intelligence, 26*, 251–321.

Hayes-Roth, B. (1980). *Flexibility in executive processes* (Tech. Rep. N-1170-ONR). Santa Monica, CA: Rand Corporation.

Hayes-Roth, B., Hayes-Roth, F., Rosenschein, S., & Cammarata, S. (1979). Modeling planning as an incremental, opportunistic process. *Proceedings of the 6th International Joint Conference on Artificial Intelligence* (pp. 375–383). Tokyo, Japan.

Lesser, V., & Corkill, D. (1981). Functionally accurate cooperative distributed systems. *IEEE Transactions on Systems, Man, & Cybernetics*, 81–96.

Leinhardt, G., & Greeno, J. G. (1986). The cognitive skill of teaching. *Journal of Educational Psychology, 78*(2), 75–97.

London, B., & Clancey, W. J. (1983). *Plan-recognition strategies in student modeling: Prediction and description* (Tech. Rep. STAN-CS-82-909). Palo Alto, CA: Stanford University Computer Science Department.

Macmillan, S. A., & Sleeman, D. H. (1987). An architecture for a self-improving instructional planner for intelligent tutoring systems. *Computational Intelligence, 3*(1), 17–27.

Ohlsson, S. (1986). Some principles of intelligent tutoring. *Instructional Science, 14*, 293–326.

O'Shea, T. (1982). A self-improving quadratic tutor. In D. Sleeman & J. S. Brown (Eds.), *Intelligent tutoring systems*. Orlando, FL: Academic Press.

Peachey, D. R., & McCalla, G. I. (1986). Using planning techniques in intelligent tutoring systems. *International Journal of Man–Machine Studies, 24*, 77–98.

Sacerdoti, E. D. (1974). Planning in a hierarchical abstraction space. *Artificial Intelligence, 5*, 115–135.

Sacerdoti, E. D. (1975). The nonlinear nature of plans. *Proceedings of the International Joint Conference on Artificial Intelligence*. Tbilisi, Georgia, USSR.

Sacerdoti, E. D. (1979). Problem-solving tactics. *Proceedings of the International Joint Conference on Artificial Intelligence*. Tokyo, Japan.

Sleeman, D. H. (1983). A rule-directed modeling system. In R. Michalski, J. Carbonell, & T. M. Mitchell (Eds.), *Machine learning* (pp. 483–510). Palo Alto, CA: Tioga Press.

Suppes, P., & Morningstar, M. (1969). Computer-assisted instruction. *Science, 166*, 343–350.

Stefik, M. J. (1980). *Planning with constraints*. Doctoral dissertation. Palo Alto, CA: Stanford University.

VanLehn, K. (1986). Student modeling in intelligent teaching systems. *Minutes of the Air Force Human Resources Laboratory Research Planning Forum on Intelligent Tutoring Systems*. San Antonio, TX.

Wescourt, K. T., Beard, M., & Barr, A. (1980). Curriculum information networks for CAI: Research on testing and evaluation by simulation. In P. Suppes (Ed.), *University-level computer-assisted instruction at Stanford: 1968–1980*. Palo Alto, CA: Institute for Mathematical Studies in the Social Sciences, Stanford University.

Woolf, B., & McDonald, D. D. (1985). Building a computer tutor: Design issues. *AEDS Monitor, 23*(9–10), 10–18.

9

Using and Evaluating Differential Modeling in Intelligent Tutoring and Apprentice Learning Systems

David C. Wilkins
William J. Clancey
Bruce G. Buchanan
Stanford University

Artificial Intelligence (AI) has long been interested in methods to automatically refine and debug an intelligent agent. This is a central concern in machine learning and automatic programming, in which the agent to be improved is a program. It is also a central concern in intelligent tutoring, where the agent to be improved is a human problem solver. Many AI systems for improving an intelligent agent involve differential modeling of the agent against the observable problem-solving behavior of another agent. We focus on the situation in which one of the agents is a knowledge-based expert system and the knowledge structures to be improved encode factual information that is declaratively represented.[1]

This chapter describes the synthetic agent method, which allows calculation of a *performance upper bound* on improvement to an intelligent agent attainable by differential modeling of the agent against an expert system. A performance upper bound identifies missing or erroneous knowledge in an intelligent agent that a particular differential modeling system is inherently incapable of identifying. By contrast, most performance evaluation procedures aim to determine a performance lower bound; they experimentally demonstrate that a particular differential modeling system can successfully identify some missing or erroneous knowledge.

The *synthetic agent method* involves replacing the human

---

[1]As much domain-specific knowledge as possible is declaratively represented in a well-designed knowledge-intensive expert system. Domain-specific procedural knowledge is contained in an expert system shell for the generic problem class (Clancey, 1984).

problem solver in a differential modeling scenario with a synthetic agent that is another expert system. The knowledge in the synthetic agent expert system is systematically modified to be slightly different from the knowledge in the original expert system. The knowledge in the synthetic agent is modified to be slightly "better" in an apprenticeship learning scenario and slightly "worse" in an intelligent tutoring scenario.

This chapter is organized as follows: The first section describes the process of differential modeling; it surveys previous and current work on improving an intelligent agent via differential modeling. The second major section discusses performance evaluation issues, especially as they relate to evaluation of a differential modeler. The third major section presents and discusses the synthetic agent method. Finally, the last major section describes an application of the synthetic agent method that is currently underway. This chapter presents our framework for evaluating a differential modeling system. No experimental results are given. (A future work will describe the use of the framework to evaluate the ODYSSEUS modeling program, which is described in the last section of this chapter, in the context of intelligent tutoring and apprenticeship learning.)

THE PROCESS OF DIFFERENTIAL MODELING

Many AI systems that debug and refine an intelligent agent employ a method called *differential modeling;* this is the process of identifying differences between the observed behavior of a problem-solving agent and the behavior that would be expected in accordance with an explicit model of problem solving.

The differential modeling process is illustrated in Figure 9.1. The three major elements are a problem solver (PS), a differential modeler (DM), and a knowledge-based expert system (ES). The task of the DM is to identify differences between the knowledge structures of PS and ES in the course of watching PS solve a problem, for example, a medical diagnosis problem. In the figure, the problem-solving actions consist of all the observable behaviors of the problem solvers. The DM can be quite complex and can easily exceed the complexity of the ES.

Two major tasks that confront a DM are global and local credit assignment, which are performed by a global and local learning critic, respectively. The global critic determines when the observable behavior of PS suggests a difference between the knowledge structures of ES and PS. In such a situation, the local critic is summoned to identify

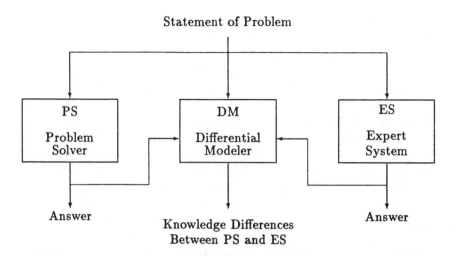

Statement of Problem

PS — Problem Solver → DM — Differential Modeler ← ES — Expert System

Answer — Knowledge Differences Between PS and ES — Answer

FIGURE 9.1 A general model of the differential modeling process. PS solves a problem, and DM finds differences between knowledge structures of PS and ES. In this chapter, equal attention is given to the situation of apprenticeship learning where PS is a human expert and the goal is to improve ES and the situation of intelligent tutoring where PS is a student and the goal is to improve PS.

possible knowledge differences between ES and PS that are suggested by the actions of PS. A complete learning system consists of a global critic, local critic, and a repair component (Dietterich & Buchanan, 1981); discussion of the repair stage is beyond the scope of this chapter.

Previous Work in Differential Modeling

AI systems that employ a differential modeling approach to debugging and refining a problem-solving agent are found in the areas of machine learning, automatic programming, and intelligent tutoring. We first describe systems that do not employ a knowledge-based expert system as the explicit model of problem solving and then describe systems that do.

The earliest such systems were in the area of machine learning, notably, Samuel's checker player and Waterman's poker player (Samuel, 1963; Waterman, 1970). The PS used by Samuel's DM program was a book of championship checker games. The DM global critic task was accomplished by comparing the move of PS to the move that Samuel's program made in the same situation. The local critic task is accomplished by adjusting the coefficients of a polynomial evaluation function for selecting moves so that the action of the program equalled the action of PS. A recent example of machine learning research that uses a differential modeling approach is the PRE system for theory-directed data interpretation (Dietterich, 1984). PRE learns programs for Unix commands from examples of the use of the commands. The DM employs constraint propagation to identify differences between the PS and the programs for commands.

In automatic programming, the synthesis of LISP and PROLOG functions from example traces falls under the rubric of debugging via differential modeling (Biermann, 1978; Shapiro, 1983). The PS consists of the input–output behavior of a correct program. The DM modifies the program being synthesized whenever it does not give the same output as PS when given the same input.

In intelligent tutoring the goal is to "debug" a human problem solver. Many intelligent tutoring systems contain an expert system and use a differential modeling technique, including the WEST program in the domain of games (Burton & Brown, 1982), SOPHIE III, and GUIDON in the domain of diagnosis (Brown, Burton, & deKleer, 1982; Clancey, 1979), and the MACSYMA-ADVISOR in the domain of symbolic integration (Genesereth, 1982). SOPHIE III uses an expert system for circuit diagnosis as an aid in isolating hypothesis errors in the behavior of students who are performing electronic troubleshooting. GUIDON is built over the MYCIN expert system for medical diagnosis (Buchanan & Shortliffe, 1984); student hypothesis errors are discovered in the process of conducting a Socratic dialogue.

Recent research within machine learning also uses an expert system as the explicit model of problem solving, especially within the subarea of apprenticeship learning. Apprenticeship learning is defined as a form of learning that occurs in the context of normal problem solving and uses underlying theories of the problem solving domain to accomplish learning. Examples of apprenticeship learning systems are LEAP and ODYSSEUS. The LEAP program refines knowledge bases for the VEXED expert system for VLSI circuit design (Mitchell, Mahadevan, & Steinberg, 1985). PS is a circuit designer who is using the VEXED circuit design aid, and the underlying theory used by the DM is circuit theory. ODYSSEUS refines and debugs knowledge bases for the HERACLES expert system shell, which solves problems using the heuristic classification method (Wilkins, 1986). When the ODYSSEUS problem domain is medical diagnosis, PS is a physician diagnosing a patient. The DM uses two underlying theories, the principal one being a strategy theory of the problem-solving method. ODYSSEUS is also applicable to intelligent tutoring; it functions as a student modeling program for the GUIDON2 intelligent tutoring system (Clancey, 1986).

Assumptions and Issues in Differential Modeling

Much of the power of an expert system derives from the quantity and quality of its domain-specific knowledge. For the purposes of this chapter, the principal function of the differential modeler is to find factual domain knowledge differences between the problem solver and the expert system. Our work assumes that the expert system represents domain knowledge declaratively, including domain-specific control knowledge. Further, as much as possible, the knowledge is represented independently of how it will be used by problem-solving programs. This practice facilitates use of the same domain knowledge for different purposes, such as problem solving, explanation, tutoring, and learning.

The framework provided by this chapter for understanding the limits of debugging via differential modeling has been fashioned with the following assumptions in mind. First we assume that an agent is differentially modeled against a knowledge-based expert system that is capable of solving the problems presented to the human PS. Second, we assume that the observed actions of the agent consist of normal problem-solving behavior in a domain. And third, we assume that the goal of the differential modeling system is to discover factual domain knowledge differences between the agent and the expert system's knowledge base, as opposed to the discovery of procedural control knowledge differences; procedural knowledge involves sequencing constructs such as looping and recursion.

There are many open questions regarding debugging via differential modeling against an expert system. For instance, what are the types of knowledge in the PS that can and cannot be debugged using a differential modeling approach? What characteristics and organization of an ES facilitate differential modeling? What characteristics and organization impose inherent limitations? How can the strengths and weaknesses of a particular DM be best described? The evaluation methodology proposed in this chapter, called the "synthetic agent method," provides a framework for the exploration of these questions.

PERFORMANCE EVALUATION ISSUES

DM performance evaluation is intimately related to ES performance evaluation. The function of a DM is to improve the performance of an ES and so DM performance evaluation requires ES performance evaluation. Although ES evaluation is a difficult and time-consuming task, there is agreement on the general approach that should be taken when ES is an expert system program. Examples of performance evaluation studies based on a sound methodology are the evaluations of the MYCIN, INTERNIST and RL expert systems (Fu & Buchanan, 1985; Miller, Pople, & Myers, 1984; Yu, Fagan, Wraith, & Clancey, 1979).

Two major functions of a DM are global and local credit assignment.[2] The general problem of assessing the limits of a DM consists of finding performance upper bounds on a DM's global and local critics. The difficulty of these functions is very domain dependent. In the domain used to develop repair theory, the global critic merely has to determine whether a student's answer to a subtraction problem is correct (Brown & VanLehn, 1980). Sometimes a DM has a person perform the global credit assignment, for example, in LEAP and MACSYMA-ADVISOR. In very difficult domains a DM might have a person perform both global and local credit assignment; TEIRESIAS takes this approach when debugging MYCIN (Davis, 1982). TEIRESIAS can be viewed as an intelligent editor that allows an expert to perform global and local credit assignment while watching MYCIN solve problems.

In domains where expertise involves heuristic problem solving, having a program perform global credit assignment is often very difficult. In a medical apprenticeship, a student may recognize that his or her knowledge is deficient when he or she can no longer make sense of the sequence of questions that the physician asks the patient. Because a weakly plausible explanation for any sequence of questions often exists, this can be very difficult to implement in a computer program. A similar situation exists in complex games such as chess or checkers. There is usually no way to know that a given move is necessarily bad; it depends on what follows. Samuel's checker player solved the global critic problem by declaring a discrepancy to exist whenever the expert (e.g., the book's move) and the checker program recommended different moves at a particular board configuration.

There are often many different changes the local critic can make to effect an improvement in the performance element. The selection process is usually based on which modification leads to the best improvement in the performance element. Selection is very much affected by how 'improvement' is defined. This is further discussed in the section on "Knowledge-Oriented versus Performance-Oriented Validation."

---

[2]Recall from the description of differential modeling that the global critic notices that something is wrong and the local critic determines which part of the knowledge base is responsible for the error. A learning program consists of a global and local critic and a repair component.

Performance Evaluation
and the Synthetic Agent Method

The synthetic agent method proposed in this chapter is considerably different from standard performance evaluation methods in two fundamental ways. The purpose of the remainder of this section on performance evaluation issues is to explain and justify these aspects of the synthetic agent method. The next section "Knowledge-Oriented versus Performance-Oriented Validation," argues that a fruitful evaluation criterion for a knowledge-based system should be quality of the individual knowledge elements, not the quality of the problem-solving performance of a particular problem-solving program. These metrics only partially overlap and certainly conflict in the short term. The following section, "Capability-Oriented versus Limitations-Oriented Validation," describes how the focus of the proposed synthetic agent method is to delineate a performance upper bound. A *performance upper bound* describes where and under what conditions a debugging system for a problem solver must fail. By contrast, a standard evaluation approach aims at showing the extent to which a debugging system can succeed. Further, instead of characterizing the limits of debugging in terms of a percentage of problems that cannot be solved, the synthetic agent method characterizes the performance upper bound in terms of the knowledge representation language and the inference constructs used in the expert system.

Knowledge-Oriented versus
Performance-Oriented Validation

The ultimate goal of a DM is to improve the performance of a PS or ES. The architecture of knowledge-based systems requires a shift in our concept of improved performance. We refer to the type of validation technique we advocate as *knowledge-oriented* validation and distinguish it from the traditional practice of *performance-oriented* validation.

Performance-oriented validation requires that modifications to a particular problem-solving program improve problem-solving performance. Because this type of validation has traditionally focused on improved performance with respect to a single problem-solving program, the veracity of the underlying knowledge has not been of overriding concern. A system designed exclusively to maximize problem-solving performance of a particular problem-solving program may use a method of knowledge representation in which the semantics of the domain knowledge cannot be represented easily, if at all. A polynomial evaluation function for rating checker positions, for example, captures none of the meaning of its terms.

Knowledge-oriented validation might be defined as performance-oriented validation that prohibits lessening the truth of individual knowledge elements solely for the sake of problem-solving performance. The advent of large declarative knowledge bases used by multiple problem-solving programs makes this perspective important. Examples of multiple problem-solving programs that might use the same medical knowledge base are programs to accomplish medical diagnosis, knowledge acquisition, intelligent tutoring, and explanation. When multiple programs use the same declaratively specified factual knowledge base, it is helpful to specify knowledge in a manner that is independent, so far as possible, of its use. Knowledge-based validation accomplishes this by requiring that changes to the knowledge base be semantically meaningful.

Suppose we wish to be faithful to the traditional performance-oriented validation paradigm when using multiple-purpose knowledge bases. This requires that every time a learning program finds a change to the knowledge base that will improve one problem-solving program, before that change can be recorded, the validation method must insure that the aggregate performance of all programs is improved. This policy will be expensive and computationally overwhelming. Further, programs for all the intended uses of a knowledge base are not necessarily in existence at the time learning is taking place.

Another rationale for knowledge-oriented validation is our belief that performance in the long term will be more correct and robust if the knowledge structures are carefully developed. Moreover, when PS is a person, it is unrealistic, probably even unwise, to attempt to replace semantically rich knowledge structures with others that deviate radically from them merely to improve short-term performance.

It should be noted that to some extent all programs for improving an intelligent agent aim at both good performance and good knowledge; nevertheless, almost all past research in machine learning, intelligent tutoring, and automatic programming has adopted a pure performance-oriented validation approach. This is especially true in automatic programming, where any mutation to the program to be debugged is judged to be acceptable if it causes the program to produce the correct output when given a correct input–output training instance (Shapiro, 1983).

In machine learning, one of the best systems for refining an expert system knowledge base is the SEEK2 program for the EXPERT expert system shell (Ginsberg, Weiss, & Politakis, 1985). This learning system takes a performance-oriented validation approach. One possible input to SEEK2 is a representative set of past solved cases and an initial knowledge base of rules. Given this input, SEEK2 attempts to modify elements of the knowledge base so as to maximize the problem-solving performance of the EXPERT expert system on the given representative set of solved problem cases. In EXPERT, the strengths of inexact rules in the knowledge base are represented using certainty factors (CFs). Examples of modification operators used by SEEK2 to improve performance are LOWER-CF and RAISE-CF (Ginsberg, 1986). When a representative set of past cases is present, the strengths of inexact rules are determined, because certainty factors can be given a strict probabilistic interpretation (Heckerman, 1986). We strongly believe that an arbitrary change to the strength of a rule just to improve performance is unjustifiable and unnecessary (Wilkins & Buchanan, 1986). The cost of this improved performance is a knowledge base that may contain incorrect knowledge. The SEEK2 refinement approach is not an instance of knowledge-oriented learning; it does not use knowledge-oriented validation.

A good example of knowledge-oriented learning is repair theory in the domain of subtraction problems (Brown & VanLehn, 1980). Repair theory is concerned with detecting underlying bugs, given the observable problem-solving behavior of students. Repair theory has a procedural model of problem solving that claims to be a plausible model of the associated human skill; bugs of students are correlated with possible bugs in the problem-solving procedure for subtraction. Repair theory is similar in spirit to the synthetic agent method we propose for assessing a differential modeling system. Repair theory generates most of the significant possible bugs by deleting parts of the procedural knowledge; likewise we expect our approach to generate most of the significant possible types of bugs in the declarative domain knowledge base, mainly by deleting parts of the knowledge base, as we describe in the section on the synthetic agent method. The main difference is that in the repair-theory model of subtraction the PS and ES knowledge is almost completely procedural, whereas the relevant knowledge in our domain is factual knowledge that is declaratively represented.

Capability-Oriented versus Limitation-Oriented Validation

A typical way of validating that a DM improves an ES involves using a disjoint set of validation and training problem sets. The ES solves the validation problem set and its performance is recorded. Then the DM improves the ES while watching a human expert PS solve a training problem set. Finally, ES solves the validation problems again;

the amount of improvement in performance provides a measure of the quality of DM.

This scenario establishes a lower bound on the quality of a DM. By increasing the size of the training problem set, DM might improve ES even more. We refer to validation methods that establish a lower bound on the quality of a DM as capability-oriented. For a given set of training and validation problems, capability-oriented validation shows that the DM is responsible for a more capable ES.

Another method of validating a DM is to have the DM watch a student solve a training problem set. Let us assume that the student exhibits a representative set of the types of domain knowledge errors that could be made in the problem domain. A domain expert can manually identify the domain knowledge errors connected with each training problem. This manual analysis provides a performance upper bound with respect to this training set for the DM, and the DM modeling program is measured against this standard. The goals of this type of manual analysis and our proposed automated analysis using the synthetic agent method are identical, in the case where the student and the problem set both have been constructed so as to allow all possible types of domain knowledge errors to be made.

We desire to know those types of differences in an expert system knowledge base that cannot be detected or corrected via differential modeling. In contrast to the capability-oriented approach, our validation approach aims at determining when the differential modeler must fail—we are limitation-oriented. For example, a limit of a program for inducing LISP functions from examples might be that the program cannot induce cases that require certain types of loop constructs. In our work, we have focused on showing certain conditions that force the differential modeling approach to fail under the most favorable of conditions, the single fault assumption. The multiple fault assumption would allow determination of a broader performance upper bound.

SYNTHETIC AGENT METHOD OF VALIDATION

The apprenticeship learning and tutoring scenarios shown in Figures 9.2 and 9.3 involve two agents: a person and an expert system. The person serves as an expert and student, in the context of apprenticeship learning and intelligent tutoring, respectively. The synthetic-agent method consists of replacing the person with a synthetic agent, which is another expert system, in order to experiment with and validate the differential modeling system objectively. The knowledge in the synthetic agent expert system is modified to be slightly different from the knowledge in the original expert system. The knowledge is modified to be slightly "better" in an apprenticeship learning scenario and slightly 'worse' in an intelligent tutoring scenario.

An advantage of the synthetic agent method is control over interpersonal variables involved in differential modeling. An example of an interpersonal variable is the problem-solving style of a PS, as exemplified by the set of strategic diagnostic operators used by the PS. Diagnostic operators specify the permissible task procedures that can be applied to a problem as well as the allowable methods for achieving the task procedures. Examples of problem-solving operators in the domain of diagnosis include: ask general questions, ask clarifying questions, refine hypotheses, differentiate between hypotheses, and test hypotheses. Another interpersonal variable is the quantity of domain-specific knowledge that the PS possesses.

Whereas control of interpersonal variables almost always leads to an incorrect DM performance lower bound, conclusions reached concerning a performance upper bound are sound when interpersonal variables are controlled. If a system is inherently limited under the most optimal assumptions possible for differential modeling, it will still be inherently limited in those settings that involve a less-optimal differential modeling setting.

In the learning and tutoring scenarios, the synthetic agent method treats the original expert system knowledge base as a "gold standard." The apprentice ES and the student PS always have a deficiency with

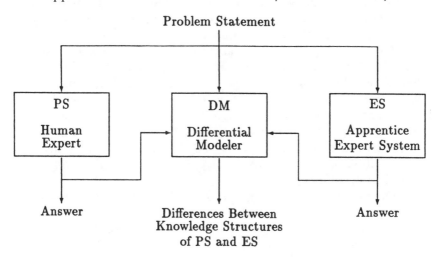

FIGURE 9.2 Apprentice learning scenario: Apprentice expert system watches human expert through the differential modeling program, with the goal of improving the apprentice program's knowledge.

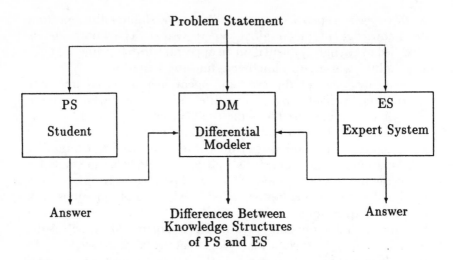

FIGURE 9.3 Intelligent tutoring scenario: Expert system watches student through the differential modeling program, with the goal of improving the student's knowledge.

respect to this gold standard. In this chapter we restrict our analysis to the situation in which the apprentice's knowledge differs from the gold standard by a single element of knowledge; hence, we have a single-fault assumption. Two types of knowledge-base discrepancies are possible: missing knowledge and erroneous knowledge. The synthetic agent method procedure described in the next section shows how deletion of knowledge can represent the space of missing and erroneous knowledge. Other methods for creating erroneous knowledge are described in a following section on categories of errors.

For a given problem statement, a distinction is made between referenced, observable, and essential knowledge in the ES's knowledge base. The relation between these categories is illustrated in Figure 9.4 *Referenced knowledge* is simply knowledge that is accessed during a problem solving case. *Observable knowledge* is knowledge whose removal leads to different external observable behavior of a PS, either in the sequence of actions that the PS exhibits or the final answer. *Essential knowledge* is knowledge whose removal leads to a significantly different final answer.

Of most concern is the apprentice's ability to acquire the *essential knowledge elements* connected with a problem statement. These are the relations most important for solving a given case. For plausible reasoning systems, what comprises a significantly different answer needs to be specified. For instance, if there are multiple diagnoses, the significance of the order in which the hypotheses are ranked needs to be determined. Acquisition of elements that are observable but not

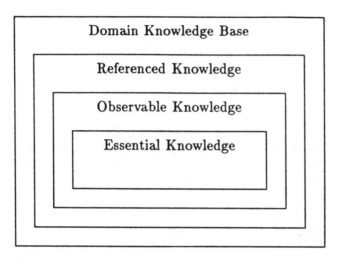

FIGURE 9.4 The relation between different categories of knowledge, with respect to a particular problem case.

essential are also of interest, because they can be essential elements with respect to another problem statement.

The procedure for calculating a performance upper bound on a differential modeling system is now presented.

The Synthetic Agent Method

Step 1: *Create synthetic agent.* Replace PS with a synthetic agent— a copy of ES with initially the same domain knowledge.

Step 2: *Solve problem case.* Solve a problem using PS and save the solution trace (the observable actions of PS and the final answer).

Step 3: *Identify observable knowledge.* For a particular problem case, collect all elements in the knowledge base that were referenced by PS during problem solving. Identify the observable knowledge—the subset of the referenced knowledge whose removal would lead to a different solution trace or a different final answer.

Step 4: For each observable knowledge element:

Step 4a: *Remove the element from ES.* In an apprenticeship learning scenario this creates an apprentice expert ES with missing knowledge. In an intelligent tutoring scenario the element removed from the ES is declared to be erroneous[3] Because the element is still present in PS, the synthetic student PS has erroneous knowledge.

Step 4b: *Detect and localize knowledge discrepancy.* Have the PS

---

[3]N.B. This element of knowledge is treated as erroneous for purposes of validation. In reality, the element is true knowledge.

solve the problem case. See if DM can detect (the global critic problem) and localize (the local critic problem) the knowledge difference.

Step 5: For each observable knowledge element:

Remove the element from PS. In an intelligent tutoring scenario this creates a synthetic student PS with missing knowledge. In an apprenticeship learning scenario the element removed from the PS is declared to be erroneous (see footnote 3). Because the element is still present in ES, the apprentice expert ES has erroneous knowledge.

Detect and localize knowledge discrepancy. Have the PS solve the problem case. See if DM can detect (the global critic problem) and localize (the local critic problem) the knowledge difference.

Discussion of Synthetic Agent Method

An expert system's explanation facility can be helpful in locating the observable knowledge with respect to a given problem case. One of the hallmarks of a good expert system is its ability to explain its own reasoning. So it is not too much to ask for those pieces of knowledge used on a problem case, and a good explanation system might even be able to identify the essential knowledge. At worst, given the pieces of knowledge that were used to solve a particular problem, the essential pieces of knowledge can be determined by experimentation. Usually, only a small amount of an expert system's domain knowledge is observable with respect to a given problem, and our experiences in the medical diagnosis domain have shown us that only a small amount of the observable knowledge is essential knowledge.

Some knowledge that is referenced by the expert system may not have observable consequences, even if it is used by the problem solver, because the removal of knowledge does not always affect the external behavior of a problem solver. For instance, in MYCIN and NEOMYCIN, terms that represent medical symptoms and measurements, such as patient weight, have an ASKFIRST property. The expert system uses the value of this property to decide whether the value of a variable is first determined by asking the user or first determined by derivation by some other method, such as from first principles. However, if the system does not possess techniques for deriving the information from other principles, then the external behavior of the system is the same regardless of the value of the ASKFIRST property.

When testing the global critic in Steps 4a and 4b of the synthetic agent method, part of the assessment must relate to whether the apprentice detects knowledge base differences close to the point in the problem-solving session where the different knowledge was used.

This temporal proximity is important, since the problem-solving context at this point in the problem-solving session strongly focuses the search for missing or erroneous knowledge.

Categories of Errors

The knowledge organization that we focus upon specifies all factual domain knowledge in a declarative fashion. In such a knowledge base, there are two main categories of errors: missing and erroneous knowledge. Missing knowledge is absent from the knowledge base, and erroneous knowledge is factually incorrect knowledge that is present in the knowledge base.

The space of missing knowledge is easy to generate, especially with the single fault assumption. Recall that the original expert system serves as our gold standard and the domain knowledge in the expert system is declaratively represented. Hence, the number of single faults from missing knowledge is equal to the number of elements in the declarative knowledge base.

The space of erroneous knowledge is much more difficult to describe. The synthetic agent method takes a novel approach to the problem in Steps 5a and 6a. An erroneous element is created by declaring a correct knowledge element to be erroneous for purposes of validation. We are also considering other approaches. Much of the knowledge is represented declaratively and typed. Therefore, erroneous knowledge can be generated by substituting different values for the knowledge in the range of the type, as long as the assumption can be made that the erroneous knowledge is at least correctly typed by the problem solver. The space of possible variations of declarative association-rule knowledge is significantly reduced by the practice used in the HERACLES expert system shell of factoring different types of knowledge from the domain knowledge, such as causal, definitional, and control knowledge (Clancey, in press).

APPLICATION OF SYNTHETIC
EXPERT METHOD

Our investigations of a performance upper bound for a differential modeler are being performed in the context of the HERACLES and ODYSSEUS systems. HERACLES is an expert system shell that solves classification-type problems using the heuristic classification method (Clancey, 1985). The ODYSSEUS program differentially models a PS

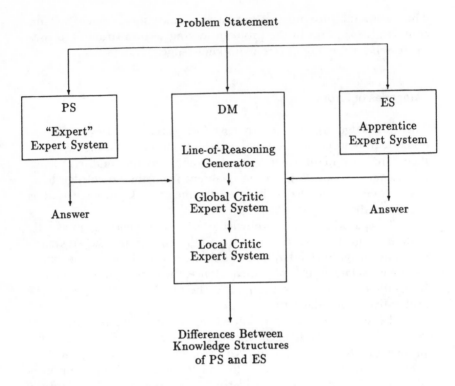

FIGURE 9.5 Synthetic agent validation situation for apprenticeship learning in which the role of the PS has been filled by a synthetic expert system. In apprenticeship learning, the DM watches PS to improve ES's knowledge structures.

against any ES implemented using the HERACLES expert system shell (Wilkins, 1986). When PS is a human expert, ODYSSEUS functions as a knowledge acquisition program for the HERACLES expert system shell. When PS is a student, ODYSSEUS functions as a student modeling program for the GUIDON2 intelligent tutoring system, which is built over HERACLES.

In HERACLES domain knowledge is encoded using a relational language and MYCIN-type rules (Clancey, 1986a). The knowledge relations of the relational language are predicate calculus representations of the domain knowledge, written using the logic programming language MRS. For example, an instantiation of the proposition (SUGGESTS $PARM $HYP) represents the fact that if a particular parameter is true then this suggests that a particular hypothesis is true. An instantiation of the template (ASKFIRST $FINDING $FLAG-VALUE) specifies whether the system should first ask the user for the value of a finding, or derive the information from existing information. The major domain knowledge base for HERACLES at this time is the NEOMYCIN knowledge base for diagnosing meningitis and neurological problems (Clancey, 1984). A second effort in the sand-casting domain is called CASTER (Thompson & Clancey, 1986).

Three aspects of the HERACLES expert system shell facilitate the task of differential modeling faced by ODYSSEUS. First, distinctions are made between the different types of knowledge in HERACLES' knowledge base, such as heuristic, definitional, causal, and control knowledge. Second, the method of reasoning, called 'hypothesis-directed reasoning,' approximates that used by human experts (Clancey, 1984). Hence, HERACLES can be viewed as a simulation of an expert's process of diagnosis. Third, the control knowledge is explicitly represented as a procedural network of subroutines and metarules that are both free of domain knowledge; the subroutines and metarules use variables rather than specific domain terms (Clancey, in press). By contrast, the heuristic rules in MYCIN have a great deal of control knowledge imbedded in the premises of the rules (Buchanan & Shortliffe, 1984; Clancey, 1983).

Figure 9.5 shows the place of the ODYSSEUS DM in the context of debugging an apprentice expert system. The DM tracks the problem-solving actions of the PS step by step. For each observable step of the problem solver, ODYSSEUS generates and scores the alternative lines of reasoning that can explain the reasoning step. If the global critic does not find any plausible reasoning path, or all found paths have a low plausibility, ODYSSEUS assumes that there is a difference in knowledge between the human problem solver and the expert system. The local critic attempts to locate the knowledge difference either automatically or by asking the expert specific questions. ODYSSEUS' analysis of problem-solving steps uses two underlying domain theories: a strategy theory of the problem-solving method called "hypothesis-directed reasoning" using the heuristic classification method, and an inductive predictive theory for heuristic rules that uses a library of previously solved problem cases.

The ODYSSEUS global and local critics are themselves being implemented as two HERACLES-based expert systems. There are three reasons why we choose to implement the critics as expert systems. First, the task that confronts the learning critics is a knowledge-intensive task (Dietterich & Buchanan, 1981), and expert-system techniques are useful for representing large amounts of knowledge. Second, with an expert-system architecture, the reasoning method used by the critics can be made explicit and easily evaluated, because the domain knowledge is declaratively encoded using HERACLES' knowledge relations and simple heuristic rules. Third, because ODYSSEUS is designed to improve any HERACLES-based expert system, it can theoretically improve itself in an apprenticeship learning setting.

Approximately 60 different knowledge relations in HERACLES specify the declarative domain knowledge. It would be useful to know how successful the global and local critics are at detecting discrepancies in the different knowledge relations of the knowledge-representation language. Are there certain types of knowledge relations whose absence is always noticeable? Are there particular types of knowledge whose absence is very hard to recognize? For example, HERACLES represents final diagnoses in a hierarchial tree structure; discovering that a problem is caused by a missing link in this structure may be very difficult for the apprentice. By contrast, it may be very easy to discover whether a trigger property of a rule is missing. A trigger property causes the conclusion of a rule to be treated as an active hypothesis if particular clauses of the rule premise are satisfied. Clearly global and local credit assignment are greatly affected by the complexity of the procedural control knowledge used in the expert system shell.

SUMMARY

With the proliferation of expert systems, methods of intelligent tutoring and apprenticeship learning that are based on differential modeling of the normal problem-solving behavior of a student or expert against a knowledge-intensive expert system should become increasingly common. The synthetic agent method is proposed as an objective means of assessing the limits of a particular differential modeling program in the context of intelligent tutoring and apprenticeship learning. The power of a differential modeler is crucially dependent upon the expert system's method of knowledge representation and control. The synthetic agent method provides a means of expressing the limitations of a differential modeler in terms of the knowledge representation and control vocabulary.

The synthetic agent method involves a systematic perturbation of a program that takes the place of the student or expert. Traditionally, methods of evaluating a differential modeler have focused on a performance lower bound. The described synthetic agent method focuses on establishing a performance upper bound. It provides a means of exploring the extent that a differential modeling system is able to detect and isolate an arbitrary difference between a knowledge base of an expert system and the problem-solving knowledge of a student or expert. Our work to date confirms our belief that the task of differential modeling is easier the more an expert system represents factual domain knowledge in a declarative fashion.

The validation framework described in this chapter is being used to assess the limits of the ODYSSEUS modeling program in the context of intelligent tutoring and apprenticeship learning. Students and experts are being differentially modeled against knowledge bases for the HERACLES expert-system shell. This should lead to a better understanding of the synthetic agent method, the ODYSSEUS modeling program, and the extent to which HERACLES' method of knowledge representation and control facilitates differential modeling.

ACKNOWLEDGMENTS

We are grateful for very substantive critiques of draft versions of this paper by Marianne Winslett, Haym Hirsh, and Devika Subramanian.

This work was supported in part by NSF grant MCS-83-12148, ONR/ARI contract N00014-79C-0302, Advanced Research Project Agency (Contract DARPA N00039-83-C-0136), the National Institute of Health (Grant NIH RR-00785-11), National Aeronautics and Space Administration (Grant NAG-5-261), and Boeing (Grant W266875). We are grateful for the computer time provided by SUMEX-AIM and the Intelligent Systems Lab of Xerox PARC.

REFERENCES

Biermann,A. W. (1978). The inference of regular LISP programs from examples. *IEEE Transactions on Systems, Man, and Cybernetics*, SMC-8(8); 585–600.

Brown, J. S., Burton, R. & deKleer, J. (1982). Pedagogical and knowledge engineering techniques in SOPHIE I, II and III. In D. Sleeman & J. S. Brown (Eds.), *Intelligent tutoring systems* (pp. 227–282). London: Academic Press.

Brown, J. S. & VanLehn, K. (1980). Repair theory: A generative theory of bugs in procedural skills. *Cognitive Science, 4,* 479–426.

Buchanan, B. G., & Shortliffe, E. H. (1984). *Rule-based expert systems: The MYCIN experiments of the stanford heuristic programming project.* Reading, MA: Addison-Wesley.

Burton, R., & Brown, J. S. (1982). An investigation of computer coaching for informal learning activities. In D. H. Sleeman & J. S. Brown (Eds.), *Intelligent tutoring systems,* (pp. 79–282). London: Academic Press.

Clancey, W. J. (1979). *Transfer of Rule-Based Expertise Through a Tutorial Dialogue.* PhD thesis, Stanford University, Stanford Technical Report (STAN-CS-79-769).

Clancey, W. J. (1983). The epistemology of a rule-based system: A framework for explanation. *Artificial Intelligence, 20,* 215–251.

Clancey, W. J. (1984). NEOMYCIN: Reconfiguring a rule-based system with application to teaching. In W. J. Clancey & E. H. Shortliffe (Eds.), *Readings in medical artificial intelligence,* (pp. 361–381). Reading, MA: Addison-Wesley.

Clancey, W. J. (1985). Heuristic classification. *Artificial Intelligence, 27,* 289–350.

Clancey, W. J. (in press). Representing control knowledge as abstract tasks and metarules. In M. Coombs & L. Bolc (Eds.), *Computer expert systems.* New York: Springer Verlag.

Clancey, W. J. (1986). From GUIDON to NEOMYCIN to HERACLES in twenty short lessons. *AI Magazine, 7,* 40–60.

Davis, R. (1982). Application of meta level knowledge in the construction, maintenance and use of large knowledge bases. In R. Davis & D. B. Lenat (Eds.), *Knowledge-based systems in artificial intelligence,* (pp. 289–485). New York: McGraw-Hill.

Dietterich, T. G. (1984). *Constraint propogation techniques for theory-driven data interpretations* (Tech. Rep. STAN-CS-79-XXX). Unpublished doctoral thesis, Stanford University.

Dietterich, T. G., & Buchanan, B. G. (1981). *The role of the critic in learning systems* (Report HPP-81-19). Stanford University.

Fu, L. & Buchanan, B. G. (1985). *Inductive knowledge acquisition for rule based expert systems* (Tech. Rep. KSL 85-42). Stanford University, Computer Science Dept.

Genesereth, M. R. (1982). Diagnosis using hierarchical design models. *Proceedings of the Second National Conference on Artificial Intelligence* (pp. 278–283). Pittsburgh: American Association for Artificial Intelligence.

Ginsberg, A. (1986). A metalinguistic approach to the construction of knowledge base refinement systems. *Proceedings of the 1986 National Conference on Artificial Intelligence* (pp. 436–441). Philadelphia.

Ginsberg, A., Weiss, S., & Politakis, P. (1985). SEEK2: A generalized approach to automatic knowledge base refinement. *Proceedings of the 1985 IJCAI* (pp. 367–374). Los Angeles.

Heckerman, D. (1986). Probabilistic interpretations for Mycin's certainty factors. In L. Kanal & J. Lemmar (Eds.), *Uncertainty in artificial intelligence* (pp. 167–196). New York: North Holland.

Miller, R. A., Pople, H. E., & Myers, J. D. (1984). INTERNIST-1: An experimental computer-based diagnostic consultant for general internal medicine. In W. J. Clancey & E. H. Shortliffe (Eds.), *Readings in medical artificial intelligence* (pp. 361–381). Reading, MA: Addison-Wesley.

Mitchell, T. M., Mahadevan, S., & Steinberg, L. I. (1985). LEAP: A learning apprentice for VLSI design. *Proceedings of the 1985 IJCAI* (pp. 573–580). Los Angeles.

Samuel, A. L. (1963). Some studies in machine learning using the game of checkers. In E. Feigenbaum & D. Feldman (Eds.), *Computers and Thought.* New York: McGraw-Hill.

Shapiro, E. H. (1983). *Algorithmic Program Understanding.* Cambridge: MIT Press.

Thompson, T., & Clancey, W. J. (1986). A qualitative modeling shell for process diagnosis. *IEEE Software, 3*(2), 6–15.

Waterman, D. (1970). Generalization learning techniques for automating the learning of heuristics. *Artificial Intelligence, 1,* 121–170.

Wilkins, D. C. (1986). Knowledge base debugging using apprenticeship learning techniques. In *Knowledge Acquisition for Knowledge-Based Systems Workshop* (pp. 40.0–40.14). Banff, Canada.

Wilkins, D. C. & Buchanan, B. G. (1986). On debugging rule sets when reasoning under uncertainty. *Proceedings of the 1986 National Conference on Artificial Intelligence* (pp. 448–454). Philadelphia.

Yu, V. L., Fagan, L. M., Wraith, S. M., & Clancey, W. J. (1979). Evaluating the performance of a computer-based consultant. *Journal of the American Medical Association, 242*(12), 1279–1282.

Knowledge Representation

Joseph Psotka
Army Research Institute
L. Dan Massey
BBN Laboratories
Sharon A. Mutter
Catholic University

Tools for Knowledge Representation

Because of the complexity of ITS and the heavy computational burden they place on computers, it is particularly important to create knowledge representations that are compact and run efficiently. The last few years have seen an incredible explosion in techniques available, primarily in object-oriented systems that capture hierarchical information in compact form, using inheritance to take advantage of redundancies in the system. These kinds of object-oriented encapsulations (built into systems like LOOPS, KREME, FLAVORS, and many others) are only beginning to be used in ITS, for example, MACH-III (de Bruin, Massey & Roberts, chapter 14).

Although these basic tools and environments are appearing and beginning to be refined, there is very little experience in using these tools for large-scale knowledge organizations needed for most realistic ITS. As a result, many investigators are replicating each other's work, often arriving at dissimilar structures that cannot easily be shared. The fundamental problem is organizing knowledge into a clear hierarchy to take best advantage of the redundancies in any particular domain. Without extensive experience doing this, we are largely ignorant of the kind of links and predicates to use. We are still far from cataloging the kinds of links needed for these semantic hierarchies. The basic predicates that might describe these knowledge structures simply, beyond ISA and PARTOF hierarchies, still need to be defined.

Too little work has been aimed at developing new representations for information and relationships. For much of the work on ITS for training technical skills there are several important categories, representing justifications, consequences, and causal mechanisms. Within these object-oriented frameworks, a representation is a structure of objects, relationships, and operations together with a mapping that places this structure in some explicit relation with other representations. Of most obvious importance is the development of structures that encode and make explicit causal connections and decompose systems into simpler causal structures where functional relationships are more apparent.

Graphic browsers are the best developed of these representation systems and have indeed an enormous utility (see Russell, Moran, & Jordan, chapter 7). Similar structures are also used by IMTS (Towne & Munro, chapter 18) and Govindaraj (chapter 11) to provide overviews of the system architecture. The most important task in developing useful ITS is often one of finding ways to connect trainees to the knowledge-representation system with dynamic interfaces.

Interfaces to Knowledge Structures

Beyond the development of tools to assist creating abstract semantic structures, there is a real need to provide dynamic, interactive interfaces to these complex object-oriented structures. Qualitative models, viewed generically, address the possibilities most directly. The graphics packages used in MACH-III (developed out of the STEAMER projects) make inspections of the causal relationships among components much more direct than any physical device can allow. The graduated models of QUEST (Frederiksen, White, Collins & Eggan, chapter 13) and the direct views of simulated radar screens (Ritter & Feurzeig, chapter 10) make it possible to manipulate complexity of representation and provide extensive, repetitive drill and practice on the most difficult procedures to learn. By having integrated and graduated perspectives on a domain, the more familiar structures and relationships can be used as a scaffolding to support and hang on more complex, abstract, and hidden structures and functions.

The story constructed here in these chapters is very much concerned with a view elaborated by Carey (1986): knowledge restructuring. This view focuses on alternative mental models of the world, and the development of consistent causal stories. However, both alternative models and consistent causality are easy to implement with well-understood knowledge domains (e.g., science and mathematics) but not nearly as easy for everyday, heuristic knowledge. Formal concepts can in fact be organized into a fairly consistent description of reality, but the unstructured growth of concepts that is characteristic of situated learning requires the mediating influence of experts. Creating such situated learning environments within an ITS calls for the development of principles that govern interaction.

Control Strategies

The issues of using knowledge structures in a dynamic environment call for special techniques that prevent the elaborate knowledge structures from overwhelming the interactivity of the system. Using special rule systems that become active only when needed, and keeping these rules to a minimum, has been suggested as one solution (Ritter & Feurzeig, chapter 10).

When the knowledge structures are text, rather than more complicated objects, simpler control rules can be used to implement strategies and overarching principles for instruction (Russell, chapter 12). These rules can operate independently of the actual text itself, as long as the structures in which the text is imbedded follow coherent semantic rules. In this lies the real power of hypertext systems: they can be used to create knowledge structures that follow a clean semantics in an exploratory fashion, from many perspectives. The most efficient of these structures can then be used for actual instruction.

All too often reactive learning environments are interpreted in terms of a formal theory of learning associated with the instruction of laws, equations, and well-formed powerful concepts. The alternative, instruction of a haphazard collection, a "bag of tricks," or superficial rules linked in a shallow network or chain, may be more consistent with empirical learning by doing. This is the focus of many of the ITS for military applications where the instruction tries to capture expertise that has accumulated slowly and pragmatically. Yet, it would seem to be very difficult to derive a complex, coordinated theory to cover many disparate findings in a reactive environment without a clear and explicit instruction in such a theory. This kind of explicit instruction would seem to demand explicit declarative representations of these theories, in a form perhaps quite consistent with the framework of open semantic networks like those provided in hypertext systems such as IDE.

Text Versus Rules

VanLehn (in press) has proposed a useful hierarchy that organizes the complexity of knowledge structures into three distinct levels.

Beginning with simple linear strings of procedures, it advances to hierarchically ordered procedures, and then to the third level of declarative structures. This classification is nicely paralleled by knowledge representation techniques in the form of rules, hierarchical rule sets, and declarative hypertext. Much of the current work in ITS attempts to incorporate knowledge representations of increasing complexity into their design. One outstanding technique for creating a migration path to ever more complex knowledge structures is that of graduated qualitative models.

Evolutionary sequences of qualitative models may lead to more principled growth of knowledge in trainees (Frederiksen, White, Collins, & Eggan, chapter 13). In practical ITS, they lead to a better intuitive understanding of the role of each component in any real instrument than does the usual sort of straightforward functional description found in Technical Manuals. However, these evolutionary systems still rely heavily on workbook materials and explanations (some of which are clearly declarative and descriptive). Because explanation is clearly such an important function, it seems that more emphasis should be given to the kinds of (presumably) hierarchical structures composed for explanatory purposes.

The knowledge base needs to be modular so that different components can be swapped or altered independently. The semantics of each module must be apparent so that changes can be made without complex interpretation (Swartout, 1983). The knowledge should be in a form the expert can understand to modify it most conveniently. However, in declarative textual structures, unlike in rule systems, the logic of predicate calculus cannot be used to verify or check the contents in a deductive way. The onus for consistency of the knowledge base is directly placed on the creator.

Some constraints on the structure of the knowledge base are as follows.

Grain size. Often knowledge is too specific to a particular problem and not general enough to handle complexities in the domain. A particular piece of knowledge may be used only to match one particular rule, and not be involved in any other problems. This makes it very hard to understand why that knowledge was encoded. A more general representation in which that knowledge is made part of a hierarchy may force the assertion of more general predicates and extended the power of the system.

IDE's representation (Russell, Moran, & Jordan, chapter 7) is at a larger grain than knowledge intended for explicit hierarchies, but it is motivated by a similar concern: to unify the knowledge base and make it consistent; to remove redundancies and eliminate extraneous and misleading material; and to leverage as much as possible the overlapping semantic relations of the content by ordering information into as small a network as possible.

Separation of control, strategic, terminological, and functional knowledge. Many expert systems confound the structure of knowledge in their systems by combining many different knowledge components into any one rule (Larkin, Reif, Carbonell, & Gugliotta, 1985). This makes it difficult not only to update and modify, but also difficult to get direct access to the information for explanatory or control purposes (Clancey, 1986).

Make hierarchies explicit. Many rule systems are really flat semantic structures. Often when the rules are coherently ordered and systematically constructed for a particular problem space, there is an implicit hierarchical semantic structure. Usually, however, this implicit structure is not fleshed out and certainly not used for explanation purposes. There are very few attempts to map out the hierarchical structure of a problem domain, although one of the earliest attempts at constructing ITS made use of semantic networks just for this purpose (Carbonell, 1970; Collins & Quillian, 1969).

Codify the problem space. Laird and Newell (1983) describe the various operators and steps in a problem solution as a *problem space.* A rule-based description of the problem space defines its terms on the basis of how rules interact with each other. There is no independent description of the concepts and terms of one rule in relation to any other rule. A hierarchical system with inheritance provides an effective way to describe such interrelationships explicitly. Such a system is being developed by Lenat, Prakash, and Shepard (1986). Using these structural and semantic interrelationships, the meaning of rules can be described explicitly, actions can be explained, and special control structures evolved to affect the rules. In IDE, the explicit structure of the domain is combined with strategic and pedagogical rules to control the presentation of materials and to elaborate a student model.

Combine structural and functional descriptions. The intertwining of structural and functional descriptions provides a synergy of explanation and firing that far exceeds the potential of each form of knowledge representation. This synergy is particularly appropriate for ITS. Not only does the ITS have to function in a reasonable way according to the logical intuitions of expert instructors, but it must also be able to explain itself coherently to novices.

Novice and expert perspectives. The peculiar difficulties of needing to satisfy both novices (students) and experts (trainers) requires that ITS have multiple levels of representation for both structural and functional components. Part of the enormous load of individualizing instruction and of developing elaborate student models can be supported by varying viewpoints on the knowledge representation schemes and by varying the level of abstraction and the grain of this knowledge representation. Thus an expert may want only a top-level overview of the system for some purposes and a very detailed, elaborate view of components for other purposes. A novice might well be overwhelmed by too much detail in the beginning and needs a graduated system of perspectives to lead into the complexities.

Qualitative representations. Qualitative simulations provide convenient vehicles for creating systems with both meaningful structural and functional components. Instead of a textual description of terminology and its interrelationships, the structure is described visually. Functional relations can also be described by using animation, color, arrows, and textual descriptions. However, visual descriptions of both structure and function are notoriously concrete: It is difficult to obtain the right level of abstraction without the use of conceptual descriptions in a textual and hierarchical form. Furthermore, it is difficult to create visual descriptions at different levels of abstractions in a truly hierarchical format. Functional and structural relations must be compressed or eliminated in arbitrary ways that defy accurate concrete representations. So, it is only when conceptual (textual) and concrete (visual) representations complement each other that adequately faithful models can be created.

Teaching Real-Time Tactical Thinking

Frank Ritter[1]
Wallace Feurzeig
BBN Laboratories

TEACHING THINKING IN REAL-TIME

Virtually all AI system development to date has concerned tasks that do not involve real-time decisions in time-critical situations. Medical diagnosis, electronic troubleshooting, geological exploration, and computer systems configuration are representative of the kinds of task domains addressed in AI applications. In these kinds of tasks, the world within which the task is carried out (the task environment) does not significantly change while the user contemplates his next action. The user has essentially unlimited time between successive "moves." The AI system also benefits by having a great deal of time to process the user's inputs and make informed responses.

It is not surprising that considerably less AI development has been done in domains where interactions are complicated by the intrinsic need for real-time processing and response on the part of the system and its users. There is an important class of military tasks, those involving strategic or tactical decision-making in rapidly changing environments, in which real-time operations are essential, for example, air traffic control or radar intercept operations. AI systems for real-time operational tasks, for example, the pilot's associate, are only beginning to be developed. The AI methods and the instructional principles relevant to the design of the related Intelligent Computer

---

[1]This work was performed while the author was at BBN Laboratories. He is currently with the Department of Psychology, Carnegie Mellon.

Aided Instruction (ICAI) systems for real-time training are beginning to emerge from current work in progress.

The problems of instructional design for ICAI applications to real-time tactical decision-making tasks are significantly different from those involved in complex systems maintenance and troubleshooting tasks. The knowledge acquisition problem is more complicated for real-time tasks. Expert performers tend to "compile" their knowledge to enable efficient and rapid execution. They cannot explicitly or precisely describe how they do what they do. The development of indirect knowledge acquisition methods to characterize expert performance is essential here.

Similarly, the problem of diagnosing student errors and performance behaviors is severely exacerbated by real-time constraints. Diagnostic methods like those used in QUEST (Feurzeig & Ritter, chapter 15, this volume), where the student is queried for his or her reasons and hypotheses, can be very useful. However, in a real-time task, it is not possible to stop the world and interrupt the student to elicit the reasons for his or her actions in the way shown in QUEST.

The diagnosis of real-time performance, particularly in rapidly changing tactical decision-making tasks, has to be carried out after task completion. Even if the student's performance can be analyzed in real-time, it is not usually possible to engage the student until his or her problem-solving session is over. The system can then replay the student's recorded run in a debriefing session, critiquing his or her task performance along the way. Real-time tasks call for distinctly different methods, such as those being investigated currently in a system called TRIO, described in the subsection that follows.

AN OVERVIEW OF TRIO

TRIO (Trainer for Radar Intercept Officers) is an expert instructional system for training F-14 interceptor pilots and radar officers in dynamic spatial reasoning and the basic tactics of high-speed air intercepts (Feurzeig, Ash, & Ricard, 1984). As of the fall of 1987, it is in place at Pensecola N.A.S., and is undergoing advanced test. The TRIO task environment supports simulations of airborne radars, interceptor and target aircraft operations, and weapons models. It provides dynamic displays of heading, bearing and displacement vectors, radar screens, flight instruments, intercept parameters, radar and missile envelopes, and interceptor and target aircraft ground tracks. It incorporates real-time speech recognition and synthesis subsystems including advanced capabilities for recognition of naturally articulated utterances from an extensive lexicon. TRIO supports three instructional modes: (a) demonstrations by the TRIO expert program, (b) student practice with optional guidance, and (c) performance analysis and student debriefing following student practice.

The Radar Intercept Task

The F-14's primary mission is air defense of the carrier. This is carried out by intercepting approaching hostile aircraft (bogeys) as directed by the carrier. Because the speeds are so great and the missile envelopes so small, there is little margin for error. The intercept has to be right the first time.

The RIO (Radar Intercept Officer) interprets the radar displays and other flight instruments from the back seat of the F-14. He verbally directs the pilot based on his electronic (radar) view of the world until the pilot has visual contact with the bogey. Only after visual contact has been established does the pilot take command.

TRIO trains proficiency in a standard intercept tactic called a *gouge*. In the typical gouge, the RIO attempts to get off three coordinated missile shots: a long- and a medium-range forward-quarter missile shot, and a rear-quarter missile shot, ending up behind the nonmaneuvering bogey. To maximize performance, the student takes all three shots as if none of them were successful. Even though the bogey may not deviate from its straight flight path, the situation geometry is constantly changing. Each position requires a different set of maneuvers for successful positioning, culminating in a series of very precise turns to maneuver into a position behind the bogey.

The conceptual intercept space, shown in Figure 10.1, classifies each airplane position in three dimensions: (a) Lateral Separation: the distance between the fighter's and the bogey's flight path—along with the F-14's turning radius, this determines whether the fighter has room to turn in behind the bogey; (b) Range: the distance between the two planes—each missile has an optimum firing range; and (c) Target Aspect: this angle between the fighter bearing and the bogey's heading—in the gouge, this angle is optimized to provide the least radar cross-section to the bogey, while enabling the interceptor to stay in front of the bogey and to get a good radar picture of it. The RIO must also adjust his airspeed and altitude to gain the maximum advantage in intercept performance over the bogey. Finally, the RIO must maneuver the plane to achieve optimal missile shot parameters.

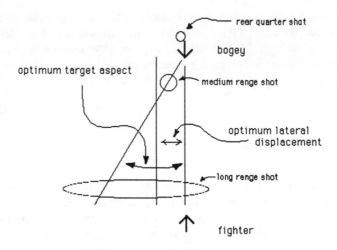

FIGURE 10.1 The intercept solution space.

As Figure 10.1 indicates, the missile envelopes and maneuvering space decrease as the intercept unfolds and the plane approaches the bogey.

Student RIOs tend to have difficulty with the central aspect of intercept work, that is, spatial mapping from a two-dimensional radar screen to the three-dimensional world. The radar screen shows the motion of the bogey and other objects relative to the interceptor symbol, not the more familiar bird's-eye view. The coordinate mapping requires students to use dimensions on the radar screens that are orthogonal to their real-world axis, or to use translations that compare different units. (For example, up and down, the Z dimension on both radars, is range in the X–Y plane. The lateral, or X dimension, on the DDD (Detailed Data Display) is not a measurement of displacement, but of angular offset in degrees.) To gain a real understanding of the radar screens requires the development of dynamic spatial reasoning skills as well as considerable practice. The acquisition and assimilation of these skills is further complicated by the need to employ them while under stress in the rapidly changing air battle environment.

TRIO Radar Displays and Flight Instruments

Figure 10.2 shows the instruments on TRIO's control panel. In the top left is an altitude readout in feet—in our example, 20,000. Next to that is an airspeed indicator reading .6 mach. Beneath both of them is the compass.

The window in the top center position is the DDD. It is an image

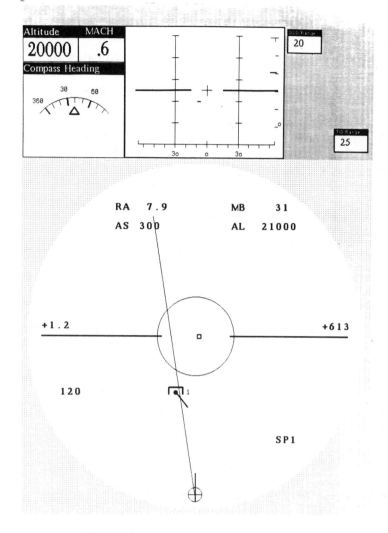

FIGURE 10.2 The student's situation displays.

of the raw analog radar data. The more easily read Tactical Information Display (TID) is the large round window taking up the bottom two-thirds of the display, beneath the DDD.

The TID displays the bogey's position relative to the fighter, and several flight constants in digital form. The fighter's position is represented by the circle on the bottom with a line pointing straight up it. This line represents the fighter's velocity vector. Because the fighter is always moving forward with respect to itself, this vector always points in the same direction. The thin dashed line from the fighter to the upside-down box is the antenna train angle (ATA) between the fighter and the bogey. Each dash is 20 miles—this makes range estimation easy.

The bogey is represented by the open-box symbol with a vector pointing in the direction of the bogey's flight. In Figure 10.2 the bogey is headed across the fighter's flight path. The closing velocity is 613 knots, which is displayed on the right side midway down the TID. The closure velocity can also be estimated from the vector lengths. The heavy horizontal bar is the artificial horizon. A circle appears when a missile is selected, indicating the allowable firing parameters for that type of missile. The missile steering dot, visible in the circle, indicates the current firing parameters. When the dot is inside the circle, the missile is correctly positioned for firing. In addition to the circle, the two-letter abbreviation for the missile and the number of those missiles on board are displayed on the lower right side; our example screen shows that a Sparrow missile is selected, with one remaining.

The two-letter combinations on the top of the TID are abbreviated names for the flight parameters displayed to their right. RA is range in nautical miles. MB is magnetic bearing from the fighter to the bogey. AS, bogey airspeed in knots, and MH, magnetic heading of the bogey, alternate being displayed every 2 seconds. AL is the bogey's altitude in feet.

The vertical angle between the fighter and the bogey is printed below and to the left of the block of bogey flight parameters, and above the artificial horizon. Below this is a timer that serves as an indicator that the TID is functioning correctly. On the top left there are two windows for displaying the radar range scales selected.

REAL-TIME INSTRUCTIONAL METHODS IN TRIO

Students learning a complex real-time procedural task generally need to be instructed before, during, and after practicing the task. Before attempting the task, the student needs instruction on how to do it. A dynamic explanation, such as an actual demonstration, is a great deal more desirable than a static description. While performing the task the student may need help to focus his attention on critical features at appropriate times, or to guide him through difficult situations. An instructor looking over the student's shoulder can provide enlightening and productive practice sessions. Instructors like to coach students learning procedural skills in the dynamic environment as they are learning. This enables students to be taught the features that experts use to understand the situation while in the context of the ongoing task. Such coaching also allows exercises to continue that would otherwise have been lost due to early, correctable errors. The student will not have time for discussions of alternative strategies, or for detailed fault analysis while performing the task. Postpractice debriefing is a natural place for these discussions. We have implemented and integrated in TRIO instructional facilities for all three aspects of real-time training—demonstrations, guided practice, and critical debriefings.

The TRIO Articulate Expert

On current training simulators, instructors of tactical tasks must spend time executing sample runs for the students to observe, emulate, and learn from. Automating this capability with an expert system is highly attractive to instructors and students. It can provide more viewing time for the students. When the expert performs at an appropriate level of performance accessible to a student, it provides a standard for the students to measure themselves against, while teaching them to use a common terminology. Instructors like an expert facility because it standardizes the initial training steps and frees them to spend more time teaching advanced topics.

Designing and building expert systems to explain what experts are doing while performing a procedural task is difficult; human experts often have trouble explaining while doing. One would like the explanations not just to inform, but also to gradually educate the student to think like an expert. Human experts think in terms of goals; and goal-driven actions; so should an expert program. The expert must also run quickly and efficiently because it sits on top of a simulation.

The TRIO expert program is capable of performing the same intercept tasks that it trains. TRIO provides an articulate goal-directed flying expert (FEXPERT) as an exemplar for student RIOs. The TRIO expert is articulate—as it performs air-intercept engagements it explains its performance along the way. Each time it takes an action (e.g., calls for a change in heading, altitude, or airspeed, selects or fires a weapon, or changes the radar display presentation) it can state the reason for the action, not only in terms of what the action is intended to accomplish, but also why this is desirable in terms of the RIO's goals.

The goal structures of the tactics employed in performing intercepts are explicitly represented in the rules that drive the FEXPERT. The use of a goal-based rule hierarchy enables rapid evaluation and execution of the rules and facilitates real-time intercept performance in rapidly changing air battle situations. It also aids in the generation and presentation of tactically based explanations of the expert's actions to better motivate the sense and purpose of the strategic thinking and spatial reasoning involved.

When each goal is seen as desirable or necessary to achieve, it is introduced. Each action taken to achieve this goal then has a context to which it can refer. The use of a goal-based expert system by providing rule structure also provides the means to keep the number of active rules low. This significantly speeds up the expert system. If the expert can think quickly, it can be checked more often, which implies a higher level of expertise and of control over the exposition.

The expert's actions and explanations are given as spoken utterances, from a real-time speech-synthesis device. The use of speech as the output mode is necessary because the RIO trainee has to attend closely to the radar scope and tactical information displays generated during the rapidly changing air battle. This poses a heavy visual workload. The use of another modality that does not distract the trainee's monitoring of the displays or otherwise hamper his visual performance is essential.

TRIO also supports speech-recognition capabilities to simulate the RIO's voice communications with the F–14 pilot. The student RIO directs the intercept through commands to a simulated pilot provided in TRIO. The TRIO speech-recognition facility is capable of real-time recognition of naturally spoken English messages from a specified lexicon of allowable RIO utterances, consisting of flight directives such as "Come starboard hard as possible to a heading of two four zero degrees." The TRIO "pilot" interacts with the flight simulation to carry out the flight directives spoken by the RIO.

The articulate expert capability is central to TRIO's capability for instructional demonstrations. In this mode of instruction the expert performs an intercept in very much the same way the trainee is expected to perform it. The intercept problem is usually assigned by an instructor or generated by TRIO, but problems may also be posed to the expert by the trainee. The expert explains its actions and the underlying reasons for them in terms of its current goal structure. The knowledge is represented using a special type of production rule system— continuous running, interrupt-driven, goal-directed rules—to operate the articulate expert program. The expert performs intercepts in real-time and explains its actions and reasoning along the way. It uses the identical information that the student sees and drives the simulation through the same interface. The intent is to provide the trainee with concrete models that prepare him for his own attempt to do similar intercepts.

The expert system has to be efficient to work in this environment.

The simulation generates and displays considerable information to provide real-time response from the radar and aircraft models. Maintaining current information at the rates imposed by the high closing speeds of the two aircraft requires rapid processing. The student is polled continuously for new intercept control instructions. (The expert's performance must be attainable by the student, so the expert is only polled every few seconds.) The correct and rapid performance of the expert is achieved through the shaping of the rules into a goal tree and the use of a clean control structure.

The goal hierarchy that is taught to the student also guides the expert in running an intercept. The expert's task is represented in the rules as a series of high-level goals together with associated subgoals or actions for fulfilling each goal under any contingency. The top-level rules expand to access the rule sets that are appropriate for the current situation. Each rule has several components, including a test to check if this rule is to be fired now, an action to be taken (none for goals), a rule set to access next (none for actions), rules to remove from current consideration, and a rationale for why the current goal was established or the current action taken that becomes part of the explanation given to the student.

To illustrate the way rules interact, consider the following. When running an intercept, one would like to have a slight (.1 mach) speed advantage on the bogey. One of the first goals is to achieve this. Its test is set to be always true, because it is always desirable to achieve a speed advantage. When it fires it tells the student "Get co-speed plus." (Explanations must be terse because additional actions and explanations will quickly follow.) The co-speed goal then brings in three action rules to achieve itself. One of them will match the current situation of being either too fast, too slow, or at the desired speed. When one of them fires, it removes the others which cannot apply. It also gives a command to the simulated pilot instructing how to set the throttle. (All commands to the pilot are printed out on the screen or spoken for the student.)

The expert is called periodically by the simulation. If a rule has recently fired, the expert may suspend action for an appropriate time set by that rule. (The designated time represents the time between successive actions that a good student would require.) Without this delay, FEXPERT could run much faster during certain periods of the intercept, but it would fail as an exemplar because a student would not be able to achieve its speed.

Figure 10.3 shows the display of the expert's command to the pilot (on the top screen labeled FEXPERT's Commands), with the rationale that is normally spoken to the student printed below it.

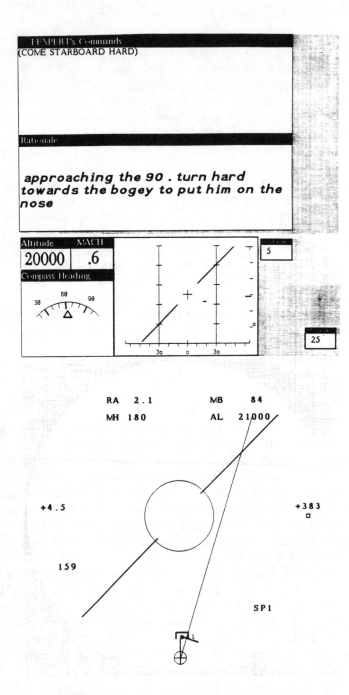

FIGURE 10.3 Example of FEXPERT output.

Student Practice and TRIO Daemons

After a trainee has seen the articulate expert fly an intercept to demonstrate a new tactical procedure or the application of a familiar tactical procedure to a new situation, he typically tries to do it on his own using TRIO's guided practice facility. The trainee's performance is monitored and recorded for subsequent analysis. The trainee may choose to attempt the intercept without help. Otherwise, TRIO is available throughout the run to provide specific guidance to aid his understanding, and to help the trainee notice and avert major errors that threaten the success of the intercept. This is accomplished in TRIO by the use of daemons.

A daemon is a continuously active, rapidly executing program that monitors the state of task-critical parameters to detect a specific event, such as the imminent loss of radar contact (also called radar lock) or missile threshold. Daemons are used in TRIO primarily to detect and report imminent errors in time for correction by the trainee. For example, the missile envelope daemon's test checks to see if the current range is less than the maximum firing range. If its event occurs, a daemon takes two actions. It records the event on the history list for use in the post–flight-performance analysis debriefing narrative. It also alerts the trainee so that he can try to take corrective action. The alert is communicated as a short message in a daemon display window, possibly accompanied by flashing, speech, or alerting sounds generated by the speech-output device. This warning may just be a static warning like the missile daemon's warning to "Load the phoenix missile" (if the student has failed to do so), but it may also be customized to the current situation. For example, another daemon warns the student when he asks the simulated pilot to go above the maximum ceiling by computing the current maximum ceiling and reminding the student what it is. After the warning is generated, an action may also be taken by the daemon to correct the error. For example, some daemons reset a student-specified parameter, such as the plane's speed, to be within the safe range.

The daemons in TRIO are invoked either individually or in toto by the instructor, the student, or by other programs in TRIO. Their use is particularly valuable during the early phases of training when it is instructionally useful to develop a trainee's awareness of critical events that need attention and must be acted on.

Rapidly changing tactical situations such as those occurring in air battle engagements impose intense attentional demands. For real-time tasks with high cognitive loads, guidance must be presented in a way that allows a trainee to maintain his attention on the tactical situation while noticing and assimilating instructional communications. Interrupting real-time problem solving in an intrusive way can actually impair training (Munro, Towne, Cody, & Abromowski, 1982). So the guidance offered by TRIO, which may come when the trainee is absorbed in the intercept, is communicated in a clear and nonintrusive manner without stopping or slowing the action or breaking the trainee's concentration. This is accomplished by the use of terse spoken warnings about correctable inflight errors. Their use does not further task the visual workload of the student, and it provides all the desired guidance.

The Daemon System (DaemonS) provides this capability in TRIO. It checks all the daemons on a frequent periodic basis for applicability to the current situation. If one of them applies, its warning is given to the student through the speech-generation device. Only one daemon is allowed to fire at a time—this ensures that the student is not overwhelmed with advice.

Figure 10.4 shows a student about to lose radar contact with the bogey because the student has allowed the bogey to drift too far to the right. The system warns the student, who may be attending to other instruments, of this imminent event. The daemon's warning that is spoken to the student is displayed here below the radar screens. If the student does not heed the warning by taking corrective action, he will lose radar contact, as shown in Figure 10.5. It is very difficult for novices to complete an intercept after losing radar contact. This warning may enable the student to complete the intercept and continue to learn.

Daemons help make the instruction in TRIO flexible. The student can select with the main menu which groups of daemons he would like available when running in guided practice mode. Daemons allow the student to control the amount of advice that he receives, and the areas that the daemons cover, such as safety-of-flight rules, or the use of radar-range scales. The debriefer is also able to activate daemons. This opens up a rich world of possibilities. For example, when the student makes an error, the debriefer can specify daemons to help the student on the next guided-practice flight. If the debriefer-selected daemon fires again, the debriefer can point out and emphasize this chronic error to the student.

Daemons do have limitations. Because they are being used in a real-time simulation that has its own computational requirements, there is a limit to the resources that are available. This limits the number that can be active, and imposes the restriction that the test be simple. The student's ability to process a limited number of corrections also limits the number that one would want active. The faults and the daemon's explanations must be easily understood by the student. Complicated faults must wait for the more leisurely pace

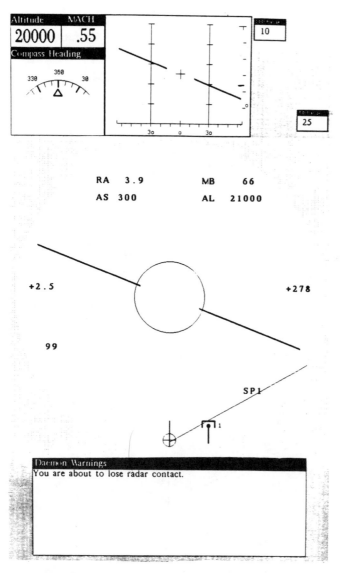

FIGURE 10.4 Display at radar lock daemon warning.

and clarity of expression provided by the debriefer. The debriefer, which has more time and resources, should also deal with faults that cannot be corrected in flight.

Performance Analysis and Student Debriefing

Following the practice run, TRIO analyzes and debriefs the trainee's performance. The trainee's intercept control actions are mapped into the solution space defined by tactical doctrine. The analysis of the

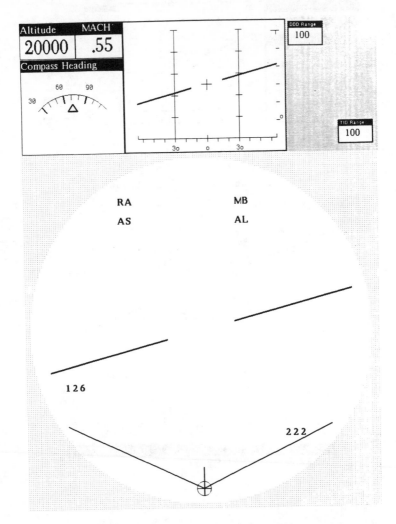

FIGURE 10.5 Display after radar lock lost.

trainee's performance is based on the use of pattern matching methods that translate and then compare the trainee's actions in a solution space to allowable performance behaviors. The solution space represents alternative solution paths during each phase of the intercept as permitted by the prescribed engagement rules and procedures. These paths allow considerable variation in the kind, number, and timing of trainee actions over those demonstrated by the expert program in its execution of an intercept.

The trainee's actions are examined by the performance analysis program. The solution space analysis identifies faulty action sequences. This is, those that could not be effective in realizing the

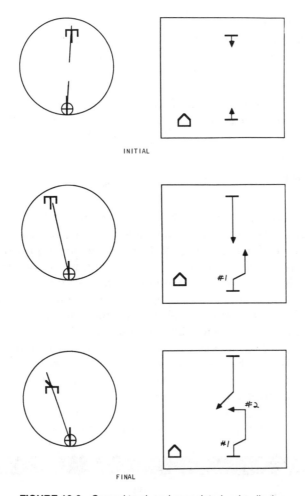

INITIAL

FINAL

FIGURE 10.6 Ground track and associated radar displays.

appropriate subgoals in the intercept solution space, and determines very specific reasons for their unaccaptability in terms of their adverse effects on the intercept. The analysis enables TRIO to generate explanations of what the trainee did wrong, where it happened, why it was wrong, and what he should have done. The explanations are given in terms of the top-level goal structure.

A debriefing program generates the corresponding narrative. The narrative is driven by two major sources of performance-history data —the solution space analysis and the procedural errors detected by daemons during the run. During the trainee debriefing, TRIO replays the relevant segments of the intercept together with the accompanying narrative. The trainee's actions and omissions, and relevant related events in the intercept situation, are identified during the presentation through the use of ground tracks of the interceptor and bogey, the associated radar displays, and related displays showing the state of the flight instruments and key intercept parameters.

Figure 10.6 shows the series of ground tracks and radar displays that the student saw while he was flying and which are redisplayed by the debriefer. The debriefer's output is shown in Figure 10.7.

CONCLUSION

The methods used in TRIO—goal-directed rules for expert presentations, daemons for guided practice, and analysis based on solution spaces for critiquing student performance—provide a rich autonomous learning environment for real-time procedural tasks. Providing an autonomous learning environment frees instructors to spend more time on advanced topics. This training paradigm has potential relevance for other real-time training applications in a variety of operational environments. Examples include ship navigation, GCI (ground controlled intercept), and flight-controller training. The methods generated by TRIO are now being employed as the central framework of an intelligent instructional system under development for training Patriot air defense operators.

More complex real-time training (involving coordinated intercept operations, for example) will require more sophisticated methods than

---

Critic's Output

At #1 on the ground track display you turned right (probably to increase your lateral displacement). You increased it to the proper amount. However, you should have turned left to protect the carrier.

You updated the TID range scale to 25 miles too late (when the range was under 15 miles).

At #2 you noticed that the bogey jinked, and you responded quickly and correctly. But it was too late because you had started out of position.

FIGURE 10.7 Critic's output.

those currently used in TRIO. We are beginning to explore extensions of TRIO methods toward these ends.

ACKNOWLEDGMENTS

This work is being supported by the Human Factors Laboratory, Naval Training Systems Center, Orlando, Florida, under contract N61339-82-C-0143. We would like to acknowledge the invaluable technical guidance provided by our project consultant, Mr. Edward P. Harvey. Mr. Harvey was a Senior Instructor in the F–14A Fleet Replacement Squadron at Naval Air Station Oceana, responsible for training pilots and RIOs in tactical employment of the F–14A Tomcat.

REFERENCES

Feurzeig, W., Ash, W. L., & Ricard, G. L. (1984, October). TRIO, an expert system for air intercept training. *Proceedings, Interservice/Industry Training Equipment Conference and Exhibition.* ITEC.

Munro, A., Towne, D. M., Cody, J. A., & Abromowski, H. (1982, October). *ONR final report: Techniques for computer-based training of air-intercept decision-making skills* (Tech. Rep. No. 101). Redondo Beach, CA: Behavioral Technologies Laboratories, University of Southern California.

Intelligent Computer Aids for Fault Diagnosis Training of Expert Operators of Large Dynamic Systems

T. Govindaraj
Georgia Institute of Technology

INTRODUCTION

Fault diagnosis of complex dynamic systems depends on the human operator's use of system knowledge at multiple levels of abstraction and detail (Rasmussen, 1985). Expert operators possess domain knowledge about the system including basic physical principles that govern the system's functions and behaviors. They are familiar with the structural topographic relationships between components and subsystems. In most cases, the operators also have experience in operating the systems under normal, and some abnormal, conditions. As a result of their operational experience, the operators develop a repertoire of basic symptom–cause patterns common to events that occur often. Their experience also leads to the formation of mental models of varying levels of sophistication and completeness about the system. Often these mental models are simplified functional and/ or behavioral representations of the actual dynamic systems, where certain components are represented with high accuracy.

The natural hierarchies inherent in complex dynamic systems are helpful for forming good mental models. In the actual systems, as well as in adequate mental models, lower-level modules or subsystems represent specific functions. For instance, in an oil-fired marine power plant, the boiler subsystem that transforms water to steam is composed of the economizer, tubes and drum, regulators, and components, such as the furnace, needed for combustion. Subsystems interact with one another through components common to more than a single subsystem. Functions of different subsystems are generally governed by different physical principles. An understanding of the different principles involved, along with their interactions within components common to multiple subsystems, is essential for fault diagnosis in complex dynamic systems.

Knowledge of basic principles alone is not sufficient, however, for problem solving and troubleshooting. Simple failures, where the interaction among subsystems is minimal, are relatively easy to diagnose using direct reasoning from first principles. Failures that tend to occur often, as well as simple failures that follow directly from first principles, help the operators form symptom–cause patterns that are readily accessible when symptoms are observed. However, failure of a single component sometimes leads to changes in system state that propagate to other components and subsystems, resulting in new symptoms as time progresses. The level of difficulty of troubleshooting increases with the occurrence of new, and possibly ambiguous, symptoms.

During troubleshooting one starts by considering higher level system functions, using patterns established during prior experience and training. Simple pattern matching, when possible, is the fastest means of troubleshooting (Rasmussen, 1981). However, such an approach, based on shallow or surface knowledge concerning causes of failures and symptoms, is not helpful for difficult problems. Recourse to detailed, "deep"-level knowledge of basic principles is necessary, at least during parts of the troubleshooting process, when any portion of the symptoms cannot be explained in terms of simple pattern matches alone. Judicious choice of lower level modules for reasoning and detailed investigation may be necessary for an efficient fault diagnosis and problem-solving process.

Efficient investigation based on selective analysis of subsystems and components depends on the degree to which one can form associations between patterns in the symptoms, system behaviors, and suspected failures. The difficulties experienced during fault diagnosis arise primarily from the operators' inability to combine symptom information with their mental resources concerning system knowledge. Efficiency of troubleshooting depends on timely compilation, integration, and organization of appropriate pieces of operational information about components on the basis of observed symptoms. Ineffectiveness of control or problems with the metacognitive aspects of the operators' fault diagnosis and problem-solving behaviors adversely affect the performance. A training program that helps remedy the inadequacies of control by developing the operators' metacognitive skills and organizing relevant system knowledge to facilitate problem solving is extremely valuable. Such a training program is described in this chapter where simulation of a marine power plant based on approximate, qualitative representation of system dynamics together with a high-resolution graphical interface is used. The training program emphasizes the development of skills necessary to retrieve relevant information and the structuring of knowledge to improve an operator's performance.

An intelligent tutoring system based on the blackboard architecture is under development to achieve the goals of the training program. The tutoring system will be used in conjunction with the simulator of the marine power plant. A brief description of the qualitative approximation methodology and the marine power plant simulator is given in the next section, and the section that follows feature the architecture of the tutoring system. Finally, the chapter concludes with a discussion of plans for experimental evaluation of the training methods used.

SIMULATION VIA QUALITATIVE APPROXIMATION

The qualitative approximation methodology discussed in this section provides a tool for the development of a simulator that results in cognitive compatibility with the operator. In simulators using qualitative approximation, the system states are represented by qualitative measures such as "pressure low" and "temperature slightly high." Exact numerical values are not used. The qualitative state representation aids the human operator by eliminating the need to compare observed state values to nominal values. Also, large systems can be simulated with a moderate amount of computational power due to reduced computational requirements. Basic principles of the design methodology and details of a simulator implementation are described in this section.

Hierarchies Within a Dynamic System

The simulator design using qualitative approximation methodology is based on a hierarchical description of the system. System components are grouped into a number of subsystems based on their function. For instance, an oil-fired steam power plant on a ship comprises the following primary subsystems: fuel oil, feedwater, steam, lube oil, and control air (Anonymous, 1978). Some components belong to more than one subsystem. For example, the condenser is part of the feedwater subsystem as well as the steam subsystem. Components are classified into a number of generic types, which are then broken down into a small number of primitives. A condenser as well as an economizer, therefore, can be classified as a heat exchanger. This is a rather simple arrangement or design of the hierarchy based on the functions of the components that form the system.

Subsystems form functionally related loops or circuits. Interactions between different loops occur within certain components. Figure 11.1 provides an example in which three interacting loops for water, steam, and seawater are shown. The condensate and feedwater subsystem shown in the figure is a typical example of a subsystem. It is made up of a number of components, three of which are shown in Figure 11.2.

The primitives form the basic, generic units in the qualitative approximation methodology. The primitives are the simplest form of components performing a single operation or a function, for example, providing a path for some fluid in the case of a conduit. Primitives defined in this methodology include: conduit, source, sink, heat exchanger, and transducer.

Each of the primitives has a structure and a set of parameter values. Structures of the primitives are based on approximate

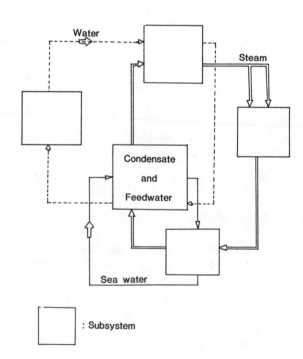

FIGURE 11.1 Water, Steam, and sea water loops.

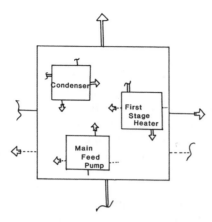

FIGURE 11.2 Condensate and feedwater sybsystem.

functional equations of system dynamics. The structure, characterized by simplified differential and algebraic equations, is the same for a primitive regardless of the component to which it belongs. The parameter values depend on the component of which a particular primitive is a part. Parameters associated with the primitives of a component are determined so as to maintain temporal fidelity of state evolution.

System States and Their Evolution

The most significant part of the modeling process in simulator design is the qualitative description of the state space. The states are represented as deviations or "perturbations" from their nominal values. In the simulator design methodology, the perturbed states evolve using approximate functional representations rather than exact representations of the primitives. Under normal operation with no failures, the (perturbed) state values are zero. When an event occurs, thus disturbing the equilibrium, state variables take on nonzero values.

At each time point, system state is updated in a two-step process: during the first step, the states of individual components are updated; during the second step, the updated states are propagated to successor components. Numerical values corresponding to deviations from nominal values are used to represent the states in the simulation. Because these numerical state values are derived from functionally approximate system equations, they represent system states only qualitatively. The state values are transformed into qualitative descriptions, for example, "pressure low and level high," before presenting them to the operator.

The perturbed states decay exponentially to reach the steady state in a short time. When the system is functioning normally, the exponential reduction can bring the states to the equilibrium value of zero. When events occur, the stabilizing effects of the exponentials are not sufficient to bring the states to zero, resulting in symptoms of the failure. The exponential decay is simulated by reducing the state value by a certain amount each time a state is propagated.

A system event could be an intentional change in operating conditions or a failure within a component. When the system is made to change states by some intentional action, the simulation must also show changes in states that would normally appear to the operator before being reset to zero. The states are reset to zero, under normal operating conditions, only when the new steady state has been reached. When a failure occurs, the resulting state changes are deviations from nominal, and hence not set to zero until corrective actions are taken.

An approximate, qualitative representation of system states enables the simulator to maintain cognitive compatibility with trainees. The simulator is said to be cognitively compatible with its human operator when the qualitative states are similar to state descriptions used by the human. Humans often use qualitative descriptions of system states, for example, "pressure is low, and temperature is fluctuating," rather than specific values, for example, "pressure is 1150 psi." The simulator uses similar states; in training, there is no need for an extremely precise numerical state description. Although the simulation evolves qualitatively, temporal fidelity is maintained, because the sequence of state changes that occurs as a result of an event is the same as it would be in a real system.

Simulator Implementation and the Control-Display Interface

The qualitative approximation methodology has been used to design a marine power plant simulator (Govindaraj, 1987). This simulator, called Q-Steam1, runs on a Xerox 1100 series LISP machine. The control/display interface to the simulator reflects the spirit of the qualitative approximation. The interface provides access to any portion of the system that an operator of an actual system could access. The interface has been designed so that a user can obtain the status of a component using a mouse and appropriate icons that are logically arranged. To eliminate problems because of the wrong choice of mouse buttons, the mouse is programmed to respond to the left button only. Details of how this is accomplished follow.

A training session starts with a list of failures to be invoked in that session. Each failure constitutes a single problem. At the beginning of each session, a set of icons is drawn with which the user can call up a specific subsystem, review the symptoms page, or indicate the failed component to the computer. An introductory page provides brief background information about the simulator. After a predefined amount of time, 30 seconds in the simulation, this page is replaced by the symptoms page showing the initial conditions and any symptoms that are present when a failure occurs (Figure 11.3). The user is provided prompting information on a black background in the prompt window. The prompt information includes component status, subsystem to be displayed, and so on. Other windows and pages appear as requested.

To obtain additional information and change display pages, the user selects a subsystem icon from the main menu after viewing the initial symptoms. Selecting a subsystem icon darkens (i.e., video-inverts, interchanging dark and light shades) the corresponding icon, and replaces the current window (symptom schematic window in the beginning) with the subsystem schematic chosen. A video-inverted icon from the main menu also appears on the schematic as an aid to quick confirmation that the chosen icon is indeed being displayed. The user is now free to investigate the status of any displayed component by moving the cursor to that component using the mouse and pressing the left button. The component video-inverts to a dark shade. If the component does not have a gauge in the actual system represented by the simulator, a message to that effect is displayed in the prompt window. Otherwise, a menu is displayed showing all the gauges grouped according to whether the gauges are in the input side or the output side. Icons are used to indicate whether they provide information about pressure, temperature, flow/level, or smoke. The user can then pick the menu item desired. Figure 11.4 provides an example of how a component is investigated.

When a particular gauge is picked from the gauge-menu, the qualitative state value corresponding to that gauge is displayed in a pop-up icon of a gauge. This gauge shows whether the state is "low," "slightly low," "normal," "slightly high," or "high" using a pointer on a circular gauge. The corresponding value is also shown in the prompt window verbally, for example, "Forced Draft Blower to Air Heater Pressure Low." The gauge icon and the gauge-menu disappear when another component or subsystem schematic is chosen. The user can continue the investigation by looking at more components from any subsystem or review the symptoms investigated by selecting the "Symptom" icon from the main menu.

Diagnosis is indicated by selecting the "Diagnose" icon from the main menu. When this icon is chosen, the user is prompted to "Pick the failed component." The user can then identify the component suspected to have failed, from the subsystem currently being displayed.

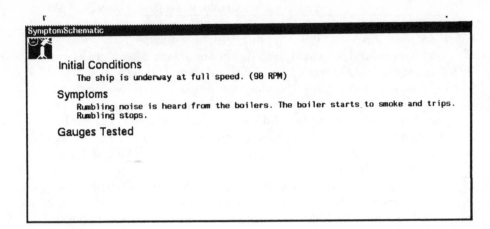

Initial Conditions
The ship is underway at full speed. (90 RPM)

Symptoms
Rumbling noise is heard from the boilers. The boiler starts to smoke and trips. Rumbling stops.

Gauges Tested

FIGURE 11.3 Initial symptoms, window image.

If the component is contained in a schematic other than the one currently displayed, the appropriate schematic must be first displayed using the main menu. The failed component is indicated by locating the cursor on the component and pressing the left button. If the component indicated by the user is indeed the failed component, the simulator congratulates the user and reveals the exact nature of the failure, for example, "Air Damper is stuck open." Otherwise, the user is told that the chosen component has not failed; the user must continue with the same problem. The simulation proceeds until all the problems in a session have been attempted. The simulation is fun to use because all the components are arranged with a remarkably high degree of realism into appropriate subsystems and any component can be easily investigated.

The simulator is used in training programs for experienced marine engineers and Naval ROTC cadets. Failures used in the problems are taken from a detailed list of failures that has been compiled from information provided by expert marine engineers at Marine Safety International, New York. An intelligent tutoring aid to be used along with the simulator is being developed. Requirements for the aid and design features of a particular implementation are described in Fath, Govindaraj, and Mitchell (1986), and Fath (1987). More complete details of the simulator and the qualitative approximation methodology are described in Govindaraj (1987). Details of the research on intelligent tutoring systems appear in the next section.

TUTOR ARCHITECTURE AND DIAGNOSTIC PROBLEM SOLVING

Even though the qualitative state values produced by the marine power plant simulator result in a reduced information-processing load, the

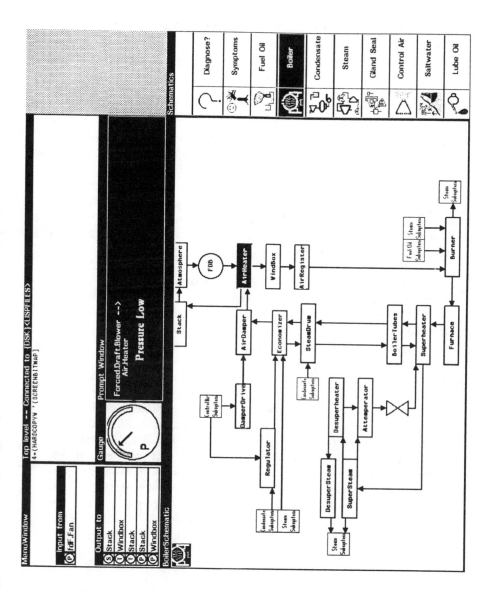

FIGURE 11.4 Boiler subsystems schematic display, window image.

human operator must still combine the state information with his or her mental model of the system so that he or she can identify problems promptly and take corrective action. Intelligent tutoring aids can help an operator form accurate mental models or internal representations of complex dynamic systems and develop general problem-solving skills. This section addresses the design of intelligent computer aids for training that make use of the qualitative representation of the dynamic system.

An intelligent aid for improving performance in a dynamic environment must meet several requirements. Depending on the system state and operator work load, the aid is either active or passive. Ideally, the aid must be adaptive, monitoring the human's work load as well as the type of operations that need to be performed. As an operator's associate, it must also be able to exercise control over specific aspects of system operation. Because such an aid must have good models of system dynamics and operational guidelines and procedures, it assumes the dual roles of associate and aid.

This section starts with a description of an aid that adapts to the student and also functions as both a tutor and an associate to share responsibilities. Such an aid must be able to organize information about the system hierarchy and to represent the system at different levels of abstraction. The blackboard architecture provides a possible means of organizing the structural information about the system, because it enables different levels of the hierarchy to communicate as the need arises. Following discussion of implementation details of the blackboard architecture, certain strategic issues in knowledge representation and organization are described. These strategic issues deal with how concepts from machine learning and intelligent tutoring can be adapted for the design of the tutor-associate. Possible problems in adapting these techniques appear in the context of complex dynamic systems, such as a marine power plant. Previous research suggests that a tutor should incorporate diagnostic knowledge based on past experience with system knowledge derived from physical principles (Su, 1985; Su & Govindaraj, 1986; Govindaraj & Su, 1987). The hypothesis frame described at the end of this section provides a possible means of structuring this knowledge. Table 11.1 overviews the specific modeling methods discussed in this section.

Adaptive Aid as a Tutor-Associate

The computer aid must be dynamic, functioning at different levels of description. These levels correspond to different levels of abstraction such as physical form, physical functions, generalized functions, and

TABLE 11.1
Overview of Models and Methods

Adaptive Aid as a Tutor-Associate

    Operation at different levels of abstraction (Rasmussen, 1985)

    Examples of different levels of abstraction

    Use of product and process measures to infer the level of abstraction

    Candidate methodologies for module design (Bonar, 1985; Bobrow, 1984; Mitchell, 1987; Mitchell & Miller, 1986; Mitchell, Rubin, & Govindaraj, 1986)

Blackboard Architecture and Levels of Abstraction

    Blackboard architecture (Erman et al., 1983; B. Hayes-Roth, 1985; Nii, 1986)

    Hierarchical descriptions (Rasmussen, 1985)

    Example methodologies for knowledge sources and modules

Strategic Issues in Knowledge Representation

    Combining and integrating modules: genetic graphs (Goldstein, 1982), planning models (Genesereth, 1982), WEST (Burton & Brown, 1982), case-based reasoning (Kolodner, 1985)

    Levels of expertise and levels of abstraction

Characteristics of Training in Complex Engineering Systems

    System dynamics integrated with simulator interface (Hollan, Hutchins, & Weitzman, 1984)

    Need for top-down approach

Structuring Diagnostic Information via Hypothesis Frames

    Hypothesis frames (Su, 1985; Govindaraj & Su, 1987)

    Finite state automata (Miller, 1985; Mitchell & Miller, 1986; Fath, Govindaraj, & Mitchell, 1986) to organize frames

abstract function (Rasmussen, 1985). Intelligent aids for problem solving that are capable of functioning at multiple levels of abstraction in a marine power plant environment might operate as follows: The highest level of abstraction, the abstract function, would deal with mass, energy, and information flows. A typical inference made at this level is that increased demand (information) for power would require burning more fuel (mass) to produce the required power (energy). The physical function level would deal with electrical, mechanical, fluid, and thermodynamic processes. At a lower abstraction level, physical form, where device details and interconnections, become important. For instance a dirty air heater results in cooler air entering the burner, which leads to a reduction in thermal efficiency. The aid must be able to identify, by observing the operator's actions, the appropriate level of abstraction within the hierarchy.

In order to shift among these levels of description, therefore, the aid must be adaptive. It must infer the current level of a trainee's expertise and provide an appropriate level of explanation and help.

The aid will use various "product measures," such as the number of actions and time taken to diagnose a failure, and "process measures" that analyze problem-solving strategies by matching patterns to infer the level of trainee expertise. Rule-based models augmented by frames that hold specific information and operational details are being developed for this purpose. These will provide operational advice and take appropriate control action based on current system state and knowledge of normal operation. As the trainee acquires expertise, the aid will modify the type and amount of information and/or advice presented. At its simplest, the aid will provide suggestions to the human operator about possible causes of a failure based on shallow reasoning. These suggestions will be in the form of a list of components that the operator should investigate for the failure symptoms noticed. At its most sophisticated, the aid will provide detailed procedures and explanations for various alternative actions and/or hypotheses using deep-level system knowledge.

The computer aid will also be designed to function as the human operator's associate by incorporating relevant systems engineering descriptions of human operator functions along with appropriate cognitive science methodologies that are discussed below. A computer aid merely provides suggestions and explanations about possible actions, whereas an associate performs some operations when the human's work load becomes high. The computer associate can complement the human operator's capabilities and limitations so that the controlled system is maintained at some desired level of operation even when certain components fail or degrade. This computer aid, which also functions as an associate and a tutor, is referred to as a *tutor-associate* in the following discussion.

Design principles for student modeling and instruction in relatively constrained problem-solving domains such as solving algebra problems must be adapted and modified to design a tutor-associate for the power plant simulator. Need for this adaptation arises from inherent differences among various domains. Complex engineering systems are characterized by the interdependence of a large number of functionally diverse subsystems where the system state vector evolves continuously in real time. In contrast, the number of states in simpler domains is rather small, states do not necessarily change often, and complex interactions are usually absent. Therefore, efforts are being made to extend relevant design principles from simpler, less-constrained domains to complex engineering systems. Further details are given later in this section.

Choice of a particular methodology for design of a specific component or module of the tutor-associate depends on its functions, the relationship of that component with other components, and how the structure of those other components is represented. Hence, suitable adaptation and refinement of tutoring methodologies are necessary throughout the process of design and system integration. Candidate methodologies for the design of the tutor-associate include bite-sized tutoring architecture (Bonar, 1985), various qualitative reasoning models (Bobrow, 1984), operator function models (Mitchell, 1986; Mitchell & Miller, 1986; Mitchell, Rubin & Govindaraj, 1986), as well as the qualitative approximation methodology discussed in the previous section, in a blackboardlike architecture.

Blackboard Architecture and Levels of Abstraction

Blackboard architectures (Erman, F. Hayes-Roth, Lesser, & Reddy, 1983; B. Hayes-Roth, 1985; Nii, 1986), with suitable adaptations, are being developed for information sharing between human operator(s) and the computer. A "blackboard" is a global data base for the integration of knowledge sources. Blackboard architectures provide a convenient means of incorporating and representing knowledge sources at different levels of abstraction. Such a framework can reduce the amount of explicit communication between human and computer that may slow down or otherwise interfere with the diagnostic process. Intelligent training aids based on an understanding of expert problem-solving strategies can be adapted to the experience and expertise levels of trainees by appropriate choice and structuring of knowledge sources.

Basic blackboard architecture is being adapted and modified to problem solving in a dynamic system domain via hierarchical descriptions suggested by Rasmussen (1985). The blackboard provides a formal structure for organizing the hierarchy and for communication between various levels. A combination of qualitative models and exact methods using symbolic and algebraic descriptions will be used to represent system knowledge at different levels in the simulator. The lower-level system knowledge deals with the detailed state evolution and conceptual descriptions of physical processes. The upper levels of the hierarchy describe various functional aspects and knowledge of how the elemental individual processes are integrated.

A hierarchical arrangement of modules and knowledge sources in a blackboardlike architecture with the refinements suggested above is appropriate for the design of a computer aid that plays the role of a tutor as well as an associate. Different design principles, including qualitative approximation methodology, are being adapted for representing knowledge about the individual modules. The modules include instructional units designed to teach basic physical principles for lower-level components, such as a heat exchanger. Qualitative approximation, bite-sized tutoring architectures (Bonar, 1985), qualitative process theory (Forbus, 1984), commonsense reasoning (Kuipers, 1984), and operator function models (Mitchell, 1987; Mitchell & Miller, 1986) may be useful for designing the modules. These modules concern the lower level, tactical issues in problem solving and fault diagnosis.

Strategic Issues in Knowledge Representation

In contrast to the qualitative reasoning models however, design of intelligent tutors for complex dynamic systems requires a top-down approach that takes into account the overall system functions. System functions that constitute higher level, strategic issues in problem solving can be modeled using appropriate structures such as genetic graphs (Goldstein, 1982) for rule-based knowledge, and planning models (Genesereth, 1982) when solution "paths" can be identified. Finite-state automata with nodes defined by individual modules and arcs representing their interactions can be used to organize knowledge in order to produce a structure analogous to those used in WEST (Burton & Brown, 1982). A major part of modeling for the teacher (and student) will be concerned with how the modules representing specific functions are connected. Case-based reasoning (Kolodner, 1985) and its associated memory organization may be useful to organize information for rare events and difficult problems as well as to provide a structure for developing new cases from experimental data. Qualitative approximation is especially appropriate for modules that affect temporal fidelity or require a simplified state representation. Hierarchical knowledge representation schemes may also be useful for integrating various modules.

Characteristics of Training in Complex Engineering Systems

In the past, research in intelligent tutoring has been concerned with the teaching of basic skills in algebra, arithmetic, electricity, physics, and programming (e.g., Sleeman & Brown, 1982). In contrast, the research discussed here deals with complex engineering systems. Training systems in these domains have concentrated on the development of simulators and interfaces that facilitate the learning of basic concepts of system operation.

With the possible exception of Steamer (Hollan, Hutchins, & Weitzman, 1984), where the graphical interface was integrated with system dynamics to provide an exploratory environment for the student so that he or she can observe results of his or her actions, training systems were either expensive simulators or provided inflexible, preprogrammed explanations. In the operation of complex systems, a certain level of expertise related to physical principles, system knowledge, and operational details is necessary before a student can solve realistic problems. Therefore, the tutor must incorporate knowledge of the system dynamics. A top-down approach, where the tutoring system starts with detailed knowledge of the simulator and the overall system functions, is most appropriate for the design of the tutor. Such an approach is also natural for our system, because the basic structures are already available in the form of primitives that approximate functions of components and component interconnections.

Structuring Diagnostic Information
via Hypothesis Frames

Hypothesis frames (Govindaraj & Su, 1987; Su, 1985), where subsystem knowledge, failure symptoms, and plausible consequences are organized ("compiled") in frames, are used to combine system knowledge with symptoms. Such a representation was postulated based on our previous experimental evidence that included protocols. Hypothesis frames must be augmented to take into account the functions required of the "associate."

Individual rules and frames representing various possibilities for failure, based on symptoms observed, can be arranged at the nodes. These nodes are joined by common functional relationships. A particular realization of a tutoring system based on an operator function model represented as a network of finite state automata (Miller, 1985; Mitchell & Miller, 1986) has been developed (Fath, 1987; Fath, Govindaraj, & Mitchell, 1986). Finite state automata and network representations can capture formal relations concerning dynamics as well as interactions between different subsystems. When actions for a given condition are clearly defined, or when symptoms can be related to one of a finite number of causes, this representation provides a natural means of encoding problem-solving and symptom-specific knowledge. Future nodes can be added whenever new hypothesis frames are formed. Growing levels of expertise and the depth of knowledge can easily be represented.

In power plant troubleshooting, or in problem solving in a complex dynamic system in general, the ultimate objective is to identify the failed component from the symptoms observed. The intermediate goals include the maintenance of specified levels of system operation and/or the compensation for the symptoms (i.e., providing symptomatic relief) to avoid major problems from developing caused by a combination of operator actions and the failure. Hence, a number of plausible plans are appropriate. Because of the dynamic nature of the problem and because the system state changes continuously, it is almost impossible to develop plans off-line. Plans must be developed dynamically depending on the system state and current symptoms. A suitable "metaplanner" must be developed. Because there is no precedent in terms of suitable models and methodologies for developing such a metaplanner, new methodologies and modeling techniques may need to be developed.

This section described the general framework for the design of intelligent tutoring systems. Details of an experiment to evaluate the tutoring systems and the simulator are described in the next section.

EXPERIMENTAL EVALUATION
AND EVOLUTION OF THE TUTOR

Evaluation of the intelligent tutor-associate will be performed by means of experiments at Marine Safety International (MSI), where experienced marine engineers participate in a training program to improve their problem-solving skills. This training program provides an environment where diagnostic problem solving on dynamic systems can be observed in a real-life situation. Two types of data will be gathered in these experiments. Subject actions will be recorded and protocols will be taken while the subjects solve specific fault-diagnosis problems. Performance measures include the number of problems solved, steps taken during diagnosis, and relevance of subject actions to the actual failure. The results will be used to refine the models of human diagnostic problem solving used by the tutor-associate.

In addition to expert trainees at MSI, Naval ROTC cadets will be used as subjects in a series of experiments. These experiments will be conducted on the simulator with and without the intelligent aid, before the cadets have had any shipboard experience, and after they have had some power plant experience at sea. Performance differences with and without aiding, and before and after shipboard experience will help us understand the effectiveness of the simulator and the aid. The performance data will help identify features of the simulator and aid that are especially helpful for problem solving by novice trainees.

The two subject populations have very different backgrounds. The MSI trainees are generally more experienced, some with more than 15 years on large ships and hence with a high level of expertise, whereas the Naval ROTC cadets operate at relatively low levels of expertise, having had minimal or no shipboard experience. Data from the MSI experiments should provide valuable insights into the strategic aspects of problem solving and information concerning the way in which lower level subsystems and components are aggregated, integrated, and used for efficient operation and problem solving. Data from the Naval ROTC cadets, on the other hand, should help us understand the tactical aspects of how low-level details are organized and understood. This should be useful for gaining an understanding of concept formation and development of basic skills.

The data will also be used for further refinement, development, and validation of the hypothesis-frame approach. Experimental data and the modeling process using these data will provide valuable insights concerning knowledge organization and structuring of system knowledge for problem solving and troubleshooting. The modeling results can be used to develop explanation-generation systems and adaptive decision aids tailored toward specific problem-solving styles. These aids will be incorporated into an enhanced intelligent tutor-associate for the system.

SUMMARY

In this chapter we discuss certain important characteristics of the fault diagnosis and problem-solving process when operators attempt to troubleshoot for failures in complex dynamic systems. Success and efficiency of problem solving depend on the operators' knowledge of the systems at different levels of abstraction, including their ability to combine aspects of the system knowledge related to behavior and function. A training program designed to develop the problem-solving skills of operators is described. The training program uses a simulator designed with qualitative-approximation methodology. An intelligent tutoring system based on the blackboard architecture is to be used along with the simulator to impart the necessary skills. The chapter outlines the tutoring system and an experimental program to test, validate, and improve the tutor.

ACKNOWLEDGMENTS

I wish to express my gratitude for the support and encouragement provided by Henry Halff, Marshall Farr, Susan Chipman, and Michael Shafto. This work was started while Drs. Halff and Farr were still with the Office of Naval Research, and I thank them for initial support and encouragement, which was so essential during the early stages of an academic career. Drs. Chipman and Shafto believed that there was a need to continue this work, managed to find the Xerox D-machines that were sorely needed, and provided useful comments, constructive criticism, and encouragement. Finally, I wish to acknowledge the help and support provided by the Intelligent Tutoring Systems Group at the Learning Research and Development Center, University of Pittsburgh, whenever I had problems with the D-machines or Interlisp-D. This work was supported in major part by the Office of Naval Research under Contract N0014-82-K-0487 (Work Unit NR 154-491).

REFERENCES

Anon. (1978). *Steam: Its generation and use.* New York: Babcock & Wilcox.

Bobrow, D. G. (Ed.). (1984). *Qualitative reasoning about physical systems.* Cambridge, MA: MIT Press.

Bonar, J. (1985, June 27). *Bite-sized intelligent tutoring.* Newsletter 85-3, Intelligent Tutoring Systems Group, Learning Research and Development Center, University of Pittsburgh.

Burton, R. R., & Brown, J. S. (1982). An investigation of computer coaching for informal learning activities. In D. Sleeman & J. S. Brown (Eds.), *Intelligent tutoring systems.* (pp. 157–183). New York: Academic Press.

Erman, L. D., Hayes-Roth, F., Lesser, V. R., & Reddy, D. R. (1983). The HEARSAY-II speech-understanding system: Integrating knowledge to resolve uncertainty. *Computing Surveys, 12,* 213–253.

Fath, J. L. (1987). *An architecture for adaptive computer-assisted instruction programs for complex dynamic systems.* Unpublished doctoral dissertation. Georgia Institute of Technology, Atlanta, GA.

Fath, J. L., Govindaraj, T., & Mitchell, C. M. (1986, October 14–18). A methodology for development of a computer-aided instruction program in complex, dynamic systems. *Proceedings of the 1986 International Conference on Systems, Man, and Cybernetics.* Atlanta, GA. 1216–1221.

Forbus, K. D. (1984). Qualitative process theory. *Artificial Intelligence, 24*(1–3) 85–168.

Genesereth, M. R. (1982). The role of plans in intelligent teaching systems. In D. Sleeman & J. S. Brown (Eds.), *Intelligent tutoring systems.* (pp. 371–155), New York: Academic Press.

Goldstein, I. P. (1982). The genetic graph: A representation for the evolution of procedural knowledge. In D. Sleeman & J. S. Brown (Eds.), *Intelligent tutoring systems* (pp. 51–77), New York: Academic Press.

Govindaraj, T. (1987, November/December). Qualitative approximation methodology for modeling and simulation of large dynamic systems: application to a marine steam power plant. *IEEE Transactions on Systems, Man, and Cybernetics* (Vol. SMC-17, pp. 937–955).

Govindaraj, T., & Su, Y. L. (1987). *A model of expert fault diagnosis performance.* Submitted for publication.

Haye-Roth, B. (1985). A blackboard architecture for control. *Artificial Intelligence, 26*(3), 251–321.

Hollan, J. D., Hutchins, E. L., & Weitzman, L. (1984, Summer). STEAMER: An interactive inspectable simulation-based training system, *The AI Magazine* pp. 15–27.

Kolodner, J. L. (1985, October). Experiential processes in natural problem solving. GIT-ICS-85/23, Georgia Institute of Technology.

Kuipers, B. (1984). Commonsense reasoning about causality; Deriving behavior from structure. *Artificial Intelligence, 24*(1-3), 169-203.

Miller, R. A. (1985). A systems approach to modeling discrete control performance. In W. B. Rouse, (Ed.), *Advances in man-machine systems research* (Vol. II). Greenwich, CT: JAI Press.

Mitchell, C. M. (1987, July/August). GT-MSOCC: A research domain for modeling human-computer interaction and aiding decision making in supervisory control systems. *IEEE Transactions on Systems, Man, and Cybernetics,* Vol. SMC-17(4), pp. 553-572.

Mitchell, C. M., & Miller, R. A. (1986, May/June). A discrete control model of operator function: A methodology for information display design. *IEEE Transactions on Systems, Man, and Cybernetics,* Vol. SMC-16(3), 343-357.

Mitchell, C. M., Rubin, K. S., & Govindaraj, T. (1986, October 14-18). OFMspert: An operator function model expert system. *Proceedings of the 1986 International Conference on Systems, Man, and Cybernetics.* Atlanta, GA.: 282-285.

Nii, H. P. (1986, Summer). Blackboard systems: The blackboard model of problem solving and the evolution of blackboard architectures. *The AI Magazine, 7*(2), pp. 38-53.

Rasmussen, J. (1981). Models of mental strategies in process plant diagnosis. In J. Rasmussen & W. B. Rouse, (Eds.), *Human detection and diagnosis of system failures* (pp. 241-258). New York: Plenum Press.

Rasmussen, J. (1985, March/April). The role of hierarchical knowledge representation in decision making and system management. *IEEE Transactions on Systems, Man, and Cybernetics,* Vol. SMC-15(2), pp. 234-243.

Sleeman, D., & Brown, J. S. (Eds.). (1982). *Intelligent tutoring systems.* New York: Academic Press.

Su, Y. L. (1985). *Modeling fault diagnosis performance on a marine power plant simulator.* Unpublished doctoral dissertation, Georgia Institute of Technology.

Su, Y. L., & Govindaraj, T. (1986, January/February). Fault diagnosis in a large dynamic system: Experiments on a training simulator. *IEEE Transactions on Systems, Man, and Cybernetics,* Vol. SMC-16(1), pp. 129-141.

IDE: The Interpreter

Daniel M. Russell
Xerox PARC

The IDE design system helps instructional designers create principled and sound instruction. Because the output of IDE represents both instructional knowledge and domain knowledge, this knowledge can guide construction of new course material.

The IDE-Interpreter uses the IDE design structures as knowledge sources to guide the automatic synthesis of instruction. Enough information is represented in the design structure to allow a planner-based interpreter to create sequences of instructional modules that will satisfy course objectives. The interpreter builds a plan of instruction based on a description of the instruction method (as specified in the Course Control rules), creating a sequence of Instructional Units that will satisfy the stated instructional goals.

Instruction delivered by the IDE-Interpreter depends on the interaction between the instructional strategy, domain knowledge bases, and the student model. Instructional strategies and tactics are represented explicitly, and student behavior is modeled to provide information on student understanding to the planner.

The Interpreter generates instruction guided by an explicit instructional theory represented as rules. This permits the Interpreter to be used as a testbed for theories of instruction and learning. In addition, the IDE-Interpreter architecture is sufficiently general to act as a "meta-ITS." That is, other ITS systems may be translated into the IDE-Interpreter's design without loss of functionality. The Interpreter's approach of separating domain-specific tools and instruction from instructional content is sufficiently broad to model much of the work in ICAI within a single paradigm, leading us to propose that the abstractions of planning, student modeling, instructional units, and explicit instructional strategy are powerful generalizations of the field.

THE IDE-INTERPRETER:
A PLANNER-BASED ADAPTIVE INSTRUCTION SYSTEM

It is generally believed that individual tutoring is an extremely effective teaching method (Bloom, 1984). However, it is difficult to specify exactly what constitutes effective tutoring. The IDE-Interpreter is a planner-based adaptive tutoring system that allows explicit statement of a tutoring strategy, and shows the consequences of that strategy by synthesizing and delivering instruction accordingly. It is a first step toward creating an articulate and computable representation of effective tutoring. The goal is, ultimately, to represent and reason about instruction. The IDE-Interpreter is a system that allows us to represent and test the entailments of instructional theories.

The IDE-Interpreter (Figure 12.1) uses knowledge structures produced in IDE as knowledge sources to guide the automatic creation of instruction—in effect, interpreting them to create instruction. The Interpreter synthesizes an instructional plan based on the description of the instruction method (in the Course Control rules), and then follows that plan to create a sequence of presentations and tests to satisfy the stated instructional goals. The IDE-Interpreter adapts its instructional sequence by continuously replanning to achieve the stated instructional objectives.

Description of the IDE-Interpreter

The IDE-Interpreter creates an instructional plan to satisfy a set of instructional goals. The plan is then implemented by primitives termed *Instructional Units* (IUs), which present instructional materials, pose questions, and interact with the student. The student's interaction with the IUs is recorded and analyzed to update a student model. The planner uses the updated student model to modify the instructional plan, constantly updating its plan to achieve the instructional goals.

The IDE-Interpreter cycles through four modules to create, execute, and monitor an instructional plan (Figure 12.2). Each cycle corresponds to planning and implementing a single instructional goal at the grain size of a single instructional interaction—a presentation

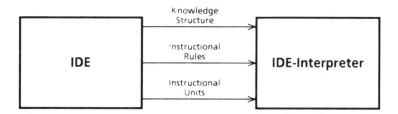

FIGURE 12.1 IDE is a instructional design system that can be used to design instruction for the IDE Interpreter.

of a page or two of material, asking the student a few questions, or presenting an open workstudy environment. The four modules are:

Instructional Problem Solver (IPS). The IPS creates the plan representing goals that must be satisfied to accomplish the given instructional objectives. The IPS uses two rule sets to guide plan creation and modification. *Strategy* and *Pedagogy* rules generate new goals, create the plan structure, and modify it when replanning is needed. Pedagogy rules specify topic selection and topic sequencing, whereas Strategy rules determine overall instructional approach and style. The IPS planner uses the rules to forward-chain from goals to final plan structure. The Strategy rules are applied first, creating an instructional plan at an abstract level. The Pedagogy rules are then applied to refine the strategic plan.

Instructional Unit Selector. The IPS creates an Instructional Goal to satisfy during the current cycle. This goal is satisfied by selecting an Instructional Unit (IU) from the set of available IUs. (IUs are canned fragments of instruction.) A third rule set, the Tactical rules, select an IU that best implements the primitive instructional goal.

Instructional Unit Applier. When the Selector has chosen an IU, the Applier delivers the IU to the student, recording all student/IU interactions in the History List data base. (The History List is simply a record of student/IU interactions: how questions are answered, how a simulation is used, etc.)

MOS Update. The MOS (Model of Student) represents the student's current understanding of the subject domain. Each concept and skill the student must understand is represented by an entry in the MOS. Also represented are a set of parameters describing what conditions this student finds most productive for learning (e.g., style of information presentation, level of abstraction, rate of concept acquisition, etc.). The MOS analyzes the History List to update its model of the student. The MOS then informs the IPS of changes in student understanding, and returns control to the IPS.

These four modules create and modify an instructional plan. The plan is used to sequence IUs into a single, coherent instruction stream

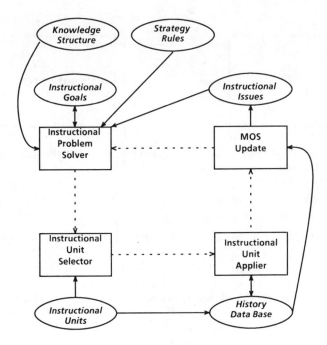

FIGURE 12.2 The structure of the IDE Interpreter. Ovals are knowledge bases, with solid lines showing the flow of data. Rectangles are program modules, with dashed lines showing the flow of control.

for the student. While interacting with the IUs, student behavior is monitored, and the MOS is updated to reflect inferences about student understanding. The IPS uses the MOS and its rule base to modify the current instructional plan, and the cycle repeats.

Linking each of these modules is a set of "languages."[1] Here, a language is a convention for representing information that must be exchanged between the modules (for example, between the IU Applier and the MOS Update modules). Through the creation of these languages, we begin to understand what is salient about the tutorial knowledge expressed within each module.

Knowledge Bases

The IDE-Interpreter uses several knowledge bases to accomplish its task. These include the Knowledge Structure (KS, which represents

---

[1]The "languages" of the IDE-Interpreter are not very complex; it is just attributes and values. However, there are many of them, and they all interlock. Taken together, the "languages" can be complex and expressive.

the domain knowledge to be taught), the instructional plan, the MOS, and the History List. This section describes these knowledge bases in detail, following the flow of control through each of the four modules, and describing the languages linking the knowledge bases.

Knowledge Structure (KS) — Representing Domain Concepts and Bugs

Domain-specific knowledge is represented in the Knowledge Structure (KS), and is the major resource for the IPS in creating instruction. Developing a multidomain knowledge representation is an ambitious goal; hence, the KS instead represents domain knowledge using a simple epistemology. Basic KS node types are "concepts," "skills," "concept-bugs," and "skill-bugs," whereas the basic KS relations between nodes are "subconcept," "subskill," "prerequisite," and "bug." Concepts are pieces of knowledge the student must command (part names, part locations, or component behaviors). Skills are performance behaviors the student must command (e.g., "place red and black leads into circuit with correct polarity"). Bugs represent commonly mistaken concepts or common errors in skills (for example, color/polarity reversal). As such, bugs do not represent domain knowledge, but domain-specific instructional knowledge.

In the KS, concepts[2] are defined by their relationships to other concepts and to the IUs that can teach these concepts. That is, no attempt is made to represent domain knowledge per se as in KL-ONE (Brachman, 1978). Rather, concept meaning in the KS is specified by:

1. a concept's relationship with other concepts in the KS,
2. the IUs attached to the concept,
3. a list of attribute/value pairs describing the concept in instructional terms.

A concept's meaning in the KS is a consequence of how that concept is used to create instruction. The IPS uses the KS to determine what should be taught, how it should be taught, and what the presentation sequence should be. IPS rules create and modify plans depending on the structure and contents of the KS. Typically, the IPS uses the concept/subconcept structure and the state of the MOS to determine what concepts should be taught (and, correspondingly,

---

[2]I use the word "concept" throughout as a collective noun to refer to concepts, skills, concept-bugs and skill-bugs together. It should be clear from context when concept means *just* concept.

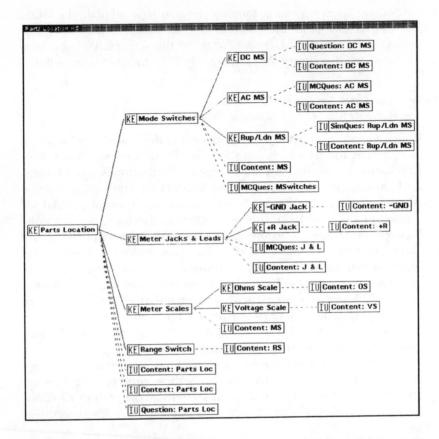

FIGURE 12.3 A Knowledge Structure (KS) in IDE is a concept hierarchy with Instructional Units (IU) linked to concepts they are able to teach.

what concepts to be avoided) to achieve an instructional goal.

Figure 12.3 is a fragment of KS for the entire Analog Multimeter course. All nodes labeled *KE* are concepts (*KE* for Knowledge Element) linked by subconcept relations. Nodes labeled *IU* are Instructional Units attached to concepts for which they provide instruction.

KS concepts also contain information encoded as an attribute/value list representing instructional features of that concept. The attributes and permissible values for describing a concept, along with the link types used to connect concepts in the KS form the "Concept Description Language," and represent those characteristics the IPS uses to make concept selection during planning. For example, the language used to describe the concepts in Figure 12.3 is given by the following table of attributes and values:

Attributes	Possible Values
Difficulty	1, 2, ..., 10
Criticality	1, 2, ..., 10

In addition to a concept's position within the KS, its attributes are used by the IPS to discriminate between alternate concepts to teach. Thus, the concepts represent facts and skills deemed significant by the instructional theory.

Bugs in the KS embody anticipated student problems. Like other KS concepts, bugs (both concept-bugs and skill-bugs) have associated IUs, which are used to give instruction about that bug. This also illustrates the way in which the Concept Description Language represents theoretical understandings about the salience of instructional features. An IU can teach a variety of lessons, even on an individual concept. "Bug concepts" in the KS have IUs attached that "deliver instruction" about those concepts. But what kinds of instruction do they deliver? There are a wide variety of alternatives (e.g., point out the bug to the student; suggest ways to avoid the bug, etc.) with respect to teaching about a bug. If these distinctions are important, then the Concept Description Language must represent those distinctions so the IPS can select between the alternatives.

Bugs are represented in the KS because the KS also forms the base upon which the student model (MOS) is constructed. Each concept (skill, concept-bug, skill-bug) maps onto a single Instructional Issue (II) within the MOS. The KS hierarchy (inherited into the structure of the MOS) is used by the MOS to infer student understanding.

Instructional Units

An Instructional Unit (IU) is an isolable fragment of instruction. IUs are the elements composed to synthesize an instructional sequence.

An IU, in simple systems, corresponds to a "frame" in other tutoring environments. That is, an IU encapsulates information to be presented, or questions to be asked. A typical IU encompasses a page or two of text, perhaps with accompanying graphics, presenting a (small) set of concepts. However, an IU can also include complex questions, simulations, interactive game settings, and exploratory environments. Any display or interaction with a pedagodical goal, implementable within the computational environment and described in terms of the KS, can form an IU. An IU can be a generator for a class of instructional interactions. For example, an IU that poses algebra problems may be implemented by a problem generator (see

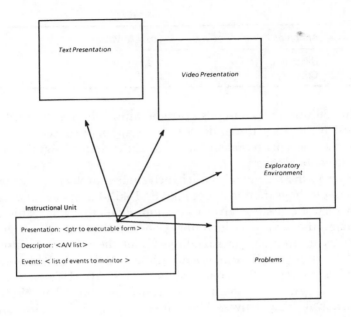

FIGURE 12.4 An Instructional Unit presents instructional material to the student.

as an example, McArthur, Stasz, Hotta, Peter, & Burdorf, 1987). This way, one IU could be used repeatedly, each time creating a new interaction for the student. Ideally, all IUs should be generated by the system in response to the instructional goals created. Our use of "canned IUs" is a computational (and manpower) compromise. In this approach there is a certain amount of course consistency as it is delivered to different students (see Figure 12.4). With a sufficiently rich set of IUs, course delivery is very adaptable to individual learning behaviors (all students need not be taught the same material in the same sequence) and individual leaning styles (all students need not be taught in the same way).

Describing IU Behavior

Like concepts in the KS, each IU has a description specifying what it does (e.g., present information, ask questions, etc.), what properties its presentation has, and links from the IU to the KS concepts it can teach. The IU descriptor is represented as an attribute list of items.

This simple description language (the IU description language) embodies a particular view of pedagogy (i.e., that presentations and questions are the only major types of student interactions). The description language is used by the planner to select IUs from the data base. In the Interpreter, the IU description language is determined by what features the IPS expects to see in the IU descriptor and what attributes its goals may have. That is, the IPS creates goals describing features of presentations it expects will satisfy an instructional objective. This goal is then used by the IU Selector to choose an IU to run.

Example. An IU that displays a picture of a multimeter, and discusses the location of components on that illustration would be described by the following attribute list:

```
( (IU Task Present)
  (PresentationStyle Textual)
  (PresentationStyle Graphical)
  (Present Content)
  (Concept 'Location-of-range-Switch)
  (Concept 'Location-of-Meter) )
```

The quoted atoms represent pointers to concepts in the KS. Since this IU is linked to two concepts in the KS, it presents instruction on two concepts simultaneously.

Selecting an IU

A goal, created by the IPS, specifies a concept to teach or test the student. Because IUs are linked to the concepts they teach, finding a set of IUs that may teach a concept is not difficult. The IU Selector has a set of rules—the Tactical rules—that encode knowledge about how to select an IU from a set of candidates. Once a set of IU candidates is formed, the Tactical rules are run. These rules modify entries in a vector of selection variables. A variable in the vector represents one of the IU properties (PresentationStyle, IU Task, etc.). Each Tactical rule examines an entry in the Student Model and modifies entries in the selection vector to minimize or maximize the importance of IU features. Each IU in the set is then measured with respect to the selection vector, and the IU with the largest value is selected.

Running an IU and Recording Student Behavior

An IU runs when it is selected and given control by the IU Selector. It executes, presenting material to the student, or otherwise implementing its instructional goal.

An important part of the IU's task is to record the student's actions for interpretation by the MOS. As the IU executes, it creates an entry on the History List as specific events occur (for instance, timeouts, student interacting with a simulation, or answering a test question). Events are processes that monitor world states. As each event occurs, an entry is written onto the HL using the History Language (see Appendix D). In this way, a transcript of student behavior is created, each student action associated with the particular IU and instructional goal that prompted it. After a termination event occurs (e.g., the student clicks on the "Done" button), the IU stops recording events on the History List, and control is then passed to the next module in the Interpreter—the MOS. The History List is then interpreted by the MOS to update its model of student understanding.

Plans and the Instructional Problem Solver (IPS)

How goals and plans are represented. The Interpreter's teaching behavior is determined by the instructional plan created by the IPS to satisfy a set of instructional goals. The initial instructional goals are specified by the user (e.g., "Teach Skill: How to use an analog multi-meter") and then refined by the IPS into the instructional plan. The plan is represented by a hierarchical plan tree composed of individual instructional goals (see Figure 12.5).

The plan tree is an AND/OR tree, with sequencing information to order the execution of sibling AND nodes. (In these figures, only the current AND subtree is shown for simplicity.)

A goal comprises two parts: a world state expressed in the Goal Description language, and a current status (Figure 12.6). A goal represents some world state to be achieved, taking concepts from the KS as arguments. For example, in the course shown here, the Goal Language has three predicates: PRESENT, QUESTION, or TEACH. (See Appendix D for details on predicate semantics.) Note that a goal is not necessarily satisfied simply by running an IU: a TEACH goal may be satisfied by running many IUs of many different kinds. The

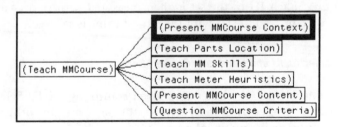

FIGURE 12.5 The plan structure browser.

interaction of the IPS rules and the contents of the KS determine goal implementation.

A goal's current status represents its state as an element of the plan. Since each goal implements a single concept, the goal state reflects the student's current understanding of that concept. A goal may be:

1. EXPANDED. The goal has just been created (initial value); no information on student understanding.
2. SATISFIED. The goal has passed criterion in the MOS.
3. UNSATISFIABLE. There is no IU associated with this goal; it can never be satisfied.
4. PRESENTED. The concept associated with the goal has been presented to the student; no information on student understanding.
5. FAILED. When all possible plans to satisfy this goal have been attempted, the goal has failed.

A typical goal is (TEACH 'Meter-Leads) where the symbol 'Meter-Leads is the name of a concept node in the KS. A goal is either primitive (i.e., implementable by running a single IU), or nonterminal, requiring subgoals to be implemented. Nonterminals represent abstract instructional goals that must be implemented by some sequence of more primitive instructional actions. Nonterminals are refined into terminals by the IPS planner.

Creating the plan. The IPS module creates the instructional plan by forward-chaining from the current goal to a set of primitive instructional actions. Unlike many planning domains, creating an instructional plan is relatively straightforward largely because the effects of primitive actions are difficult to predict precisely[3] and rarely have interactions with other plan steps that would require replanning. Because of these properties, a very simple planner suffices. The IDE-Interpreter does forward-chaining with backtracking as needed. Backing up and replanning occurs only when a nonterminal cannot be implemented. When this occurs, the planner backtracks to the previous choice point and searches the "instruction space." These failures occur when an instructional action is planned, but no IU can be found to implement that task. Other kinds of failures, such

---

[3]It is difficult to model the "cognitive world" of the student precisely because we don't have a good predictive model of knowledge acquisition. Thus, it is nearly impossible to predict what the consequence of an instructional action might be. If a more predictive model could be created, then instructional planning would begin to have all of the classical problems of other problem-solving domains (e.g., interference of actions). But see (Peachy & McCalla, 1986) for a different view.

```
┌─────────────────────────────────────────────┐
│        World State: (Teach 'Meter-Leads)     │
│        Current Status: Expanded              │
└─────────────────────────────────────────────┘
```

FIGURE 12.6 A goal consists of two parts, a world state to achieve, and a current status.

as when a student fails a test or an IU times out, are best handled by explicit error handling rules that can take the overall instructional strategy into account.[4]

On each cycle, the IPS first updates the status of all goals, depending on the information given it by the MOS. To keep up-to-date with the MOS (and avoid teaching something the student already understands), the IPS monitors all goal states. Thus, if the MOS infers a concept is understood, the status of all goals to teach that concept is changed to SATISFIED.

In addition to creation by forward chaining from the initial instructional goals, goals can also originate from external sources. Student control may be implemented by having buttons that create new instructional goals. For example, buttons such as "Why Learn This?" "Speed Up," "Slow Down," and "More Detail" may be implemented by creating new goals (attached to the current goal) within the plan. On the next cycle, appropriate Strategy rules in the IPS will create instruction for those goals in the same manner as ordinary goals. (An example: the "Why Learn This?" button might generate a (PRESENT 'Context ?X) goal, where ?X is the concept of the current goal, adding it with a priority higher than the current goal.)

Instructional rule mechanics. A rule application rewrites the plan tree. That is, an individual goal may be expanded, retracted, or modified, and goal hierarchies may be created and removed in a single rule application. For instance, if the initial goal is (TEACH 'MultiMeterCourse), under the rules shown in Appendix B, applying the Pedagogy rules would apply rule P1 to the current goal creating the plan tree of Figure 12.5. The current goal would now be the

---

[4]Automatically backtracking on all failure types is appealing. However, in our experience we've found that while it produces robust tutoring behavior (because you can prove that all topics will be covered regardless of failures), it is difficult for a user to understand the tutoring that results. It's also difficult to create tutorial strategies that make sense, since the backtracker is seemingly always "taking control" away from the strategy rules whenever an error takes place.

(PRESENT 'Context 'MultiMeterCourse) goal, because it is the highest level unexpanded goal.

Strategy rule S1 then applies, creating Figure 12.7. (note that the application of the Strategy rule did not duplicate subgoals—redundant subgoals are not generated.) After the application of S1, the current goal is still (PRESENT 'Context 'MultiMeterCourse), because no goal was introduced with a higher priority.

The current rule language and its interpretation is described in detail in Appendix C.

Tutoring Rules in IPS — Representing Instructional Knowledge to the Interpreter

The three rule sets in the IDE-Interpreter (Strategy and Pedagogy rules in the IPS; Tactical rules in the IU Selector) each represent an aspect of tutorial knowledge. Strategy rules represent the tutorial approach from a domain-independent, instructional view. Issues such as shifting instructional strategy, merging similar goals into one, when and how to remediate, and so forth, are handled by these rules.[5] Pedagogy rules, by contrast, represent domain-specific tutorial information, such as topic presentation sequence and concept presentation styles.

The instructional rule language is intended to allow instructional knowledge to be represented easily. The rules provide the main mechanism for guiding the action of the interpreter while tutoring, mapping from instructional theories to goal structures and behavior. The entities and operations on goal structures the rule language enables delimits the kinds of theories that may be represented. The language presented here (in Appendix C) allows the IPS to set up alternative instructional strategies that take control of planning behavior conditionally, allowing resetting of plans, and so on.

Each rule set is created by the course author to guide the interpreter in delivering effective tutoring. Strategy rules form rule sets associated with a particular instructional approach (e.g., didactic, learning-by-doing, etc.) remaining fairly constant from course to course. Pedagogy rules, because they are tied to the course domain structure, are built anew for each course. Tactical rules, like strategy rules, tend to remain constant, reflecting particular theories of material presentation.

The author building a course for implementation in the IDE-Interpreter chooses strategy and tactical rules to best teach the domain

---

[5]"Opportunism" is grouping goals together that would have otherwise been handled separately. Example: while teaching how to replace the battery in the multimeter, the tutor also teaches about a built-in meter repair tool, because the tool is stored next to the battery.

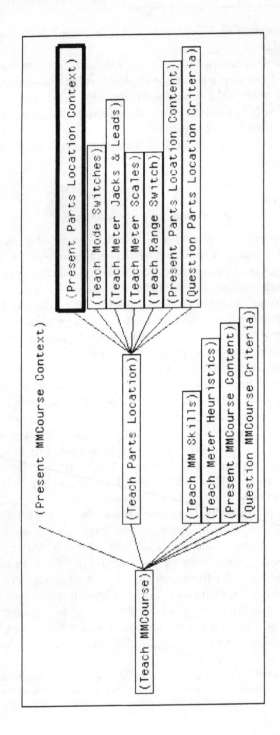

FIGURE 12.7   The plan structure browser after strategy rule S1 is applied to Figure 12.5.

knowledge and constructs the pedagogical rules to modify the way the instructional strategy is realized.

Plan complexity depends on student learning behavior (how much the student understands will affect the course content), student asking behavior (causes goals to be spliced into the plan), MOS inference ability, and the sophistication of the instruction knowledge.

Modeling Student Behavior (MOS)

The Interpreter must have some measure of student understanding. The MOS—Model Of Student—tracks student understanding of concepts, ability to perform skills, and predicted conceptual bugs. The Interpreter's KS forms the basis on which the MOS is constructed. Each concept in the KS is used to create an "Instructional Issue" (hereafter "II") to monitor student's performance, inferring student concept understanding from an analysis of the History List. (An II is very much like the Instructional Issues of Burton & Brown, 1982.)

An II comprises a set of rules, and a set of variables used to maintain II state information. The II's representation of student concept understanding is encoded within the local variables. Typically, a single variable represents a confidence measure, with tolerances for acceptable understanding or misunderstanding. (As with much of the Interpreter, this representation is based on a set of local agreements—the MOS language—which assigns semantics to II variables.)

On each cycle of the Interpreter, each II in the MOS applies its rules to the latest History List addition, using this information to update its local variables. If an II generates an inference indicating that the student now understands (or doesn't understand) a concept, the inference is temporarily saved by the MOS. After all IIs have been run and all inferences about the latest interaction made, the cached inferences about changes in student knowledge (i.e., changes in student concept understanding) are communicated to the IPS for use during the next cycle of instructional planning. The MOS examines the most recent entry on the History List. Each relevant II examines the History List and evaluates its rule set. II rules encode how to modify local instance variables based on evidence from the HL entry. In their simplest form, IIs track evidence for and against the student's understanding of a concept. However, IIs may also examine the state of other IIs. For example, an IU presents a set of test questions to the student about that concept to test concept understanding. The student interacts with the IU, making menu selections to answer questions. When the IU completes, the History List element for this cycle will have the entire interaction recorded. For test IUs, the events placed on the History List are lists of the form:

((Concept-Tested 'Volt-Scale-Location)(Answer-Given 'b)(Correct-Answer 'c)(Time-Taken 8))

The II rules are written by the author in the MOS rule language. Because concepts of the same type tend to be evaluated in the same way, the MOS is organized into a class hierarchy (as in Smalltalk, LOOPS or other object-oriented language). (See Figure 12.8.) IIs of different types are instances of different MOS classes. This means that the author need create II rules only for each class, and for IIs that specialize the inherited class-defined rule structure.

The set of IIs is created initially from the knowledge structure by mapping each concept in the KS onto an II of corresponding type. (A bug in the KS maps onto a bug II in the MOS, and so forth.) Note that if a KS concept has no IUs, it will still create an II entry in the MOS. This implies that the KS need not be fully executable (in IU terms), but rather, that the KS represents domain knowledge even if that knowledge may not be taught explicitly.[6].

In addition to the concept, bug and skill II types, there is another II type to monitor student characteristics that are not explicitly represented within the KS. These "student parameters" reflect individual student learning styles (such as visual/textual preference, learning rate, expected repetition rate, level of preferred abstraction, etc.). IIs of this type are run during each cycle, and analyze the History List in terms of response time, required reading time, and error rates.

USING THE IDE INTERPRETER:
THE INTERPRETER AS TUTORING SYSTEM

The Interpreter creates an instructional plan based on the initial instructional goals, the KS, the MOS and the Strategy rules. It synthesizes a sequence of IUs, but also replans on each cycle depending

---

[6]Why would anyone want to create a concept in the KS that has no IUs? Because the "empty" concept could function as a place-holder, signifying a critical concept to monitor, but that is difficult to teach explicitly. For instance, in the domain of foreign language instruction, we might want to teach a particular pronunciation style. However, our pedagogical theory might claim that this topic cannot be taught explicitly. When the KS is mapped to produce the MOS, the empty KS concept will create an II to monitor the student's pronunciation skills. If that II should indicate that the student's pronunciation needs work, the planner might elect to give all subsequent examples in audio, rather than by using written texts.

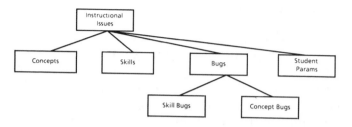

FIGURE 12.8 MOS class hierarchy.

on the state of the MOS. The Interpreter delivers the IUs with which the student works. At each step, the student's interactions are examined, and the MOS updates its Instructional Issues as required. The instructional plan is then reexamined and repaired or updated as needed based on new information. This cycle continues until the Interpreter has determined that the instructional objectives have been satisfied, or that the initial instructional goals cannot be met.

This describes one-on-one tutoring as implemented by the IDE Interpreter. In practice, the course author must create a large amount of material to make the Interpreter operate. A KS must exist to provide fundamental information about a domain; IUs must be associated with key concepts in the KS. The IPS requires Strategy and Pedagogical rules. The MOS must then be compiled from the KS, with student parameter IIs and other IIs modified as necessary.

We are using the Interpreter to create courses. The Analog Multi-Meter course is a simple example. From the student's perspective, a course taught by the Interpreter "looks and feels" like almost any other ICAI or CBI course as he or she is led through a sequence of presentations, frames, and questions. The power of the Interpreter isn't apparent until multiple student interactions are observed and compared. One can then appreciate how different the individual sessions can be, all guided by the same tutorial mechanism.

The Interpreter as Instructional Theory Articulation Medium

The IDE-Interpreter can also be viewed as a way of articulating a theory of instruction, in addition to being a general-purpose, adaptive ITS. The Interpreter is a medium for expressing important features of an instructional strategy. An instructional strategy must be "computationally precise" for the Interpreter to function, a powerful requirement on the development and expression of an instructional theory.[7]

Considerable effort is required to make the Interpreter function. However, this work can be illuminating. Creating the languages that tie the Interpreter modules together is an iterative process. An instructional theory is rarely so well understood that all of the terms and relations used in the different languages are self-evident. The process of implementing an instructional strategy within the infrastructure of the IDE-Interpreter forces the author to confront many issues that might otherwise be ignored. By centralizing requirements in the Interpreter—from material selection to student modeling—the articulation process spans the complete instructional process, focusing on the workings of the entire instructional theory as a coherent whole.

OTHER SYSTEMS

O'Shea's "self-improving quadratic tutor" is the first system to attempt to use rules as a method for controlling instructional plans to generate instruction (O'Shea, 1982). Two other seminal systems using planners in Intelligent Tutoring Systems are Meno-Tutor (Woolf, 1984) and the proposed ITS of McCalla, Reid, and Schneider, 1982. Meno-Tutor is especially interesting for its three-way division of tutoring knowledge much like IDE-Interpreter's.

The IDE-Interpreter is similar in structure to both the SIIP system (MacMillan, chap. 8) and to SMITH (Osin, 1976). SMITH is an early system that provided a fixed language for categorizing concept types and then used a simple algorithm to traverse a data base of Instructional Units. SMITH is very much like IDE in outline, but lacks all of the instructional knowledge captured in the rule bases. By contrast, SIIP centers on using a blackboard architecture as the basis for building a sophisticated instructional planner, representing the instructional plan at multiple levels of abstraction.

EUROHelp, a system under development at the University of Amsterdam, is also a planner-centered system that attempts to infer user plans from behavior, interrupting them as appropriate (Breuker, Winkels, & Sandberg, 1987). The planner in EUROHelp does successive refinement of skeletal plans from a plan library, also using a History List to allow references to past events and avoid repetition.

---

[7]The instruction demonstrated as an example in this paper is *not* held up as an example of a good instructional theory. It is a simple strategy intended to illuminate the operation of the Interpreter.

At RAND, (McArthur, et al., 1987) have been creating an ITS to deliver skill-oriented algebra tutoring. Their analysis of the domain into skill sets, and manipulation of student models allows them to determine a plausible next set of skills to teach. Partly because of the domain, they are able to synthesize much of the instructional sequence from goal descriptions of what must be taught. (For example, "Create a problem that uses distribution, and doesn't require variable isolation.")

FUTURE DIRECTIONS

An early goal was to integrate the IDE-Interpreter with IDE as an instruction design aid. With the addition of the Interpreter's synthesis capability to IDE, the designer's job would become one of specifying an instructional approach to the delivery of knowledge. The course designer would set course objectives, determine an instructional style, and create atomic pieces of instruction. The IDE Interpreter would then combine these knowledge sources to create the actual instruction as a whole, coherent piece. In *thumbnail mode* the Interpreter would create a sequence of IU *descriptions* to form an outline of the course material (i.e., it generates a thumbnail sketch of the course). These descriptions are concept names plus a list of properties that this piece of instruction must have. This kind of outline creator would be driven by an instructional strategy that could be carefully tuned to the requirements of a class of instruction. The resulting outline could then be turned over to instructional analysts for the detail work of actually creating the materials. With such a system, it would be a simple matter to create alternative versions of a single course by varying the instructional strategies.

A further possibility would be to consider allowing the IDE-Interpreter to gain access to the course rationale created when using IDE. With the rationale as an additional knowledge source, it might be possible to create instruction that has the ability to rationalize its design as it is being delivered to the student. A possibility that would permit the student to constantly ask "Why am I learning this?" and receive an instructionally useful answer.

SUMMARY

The Interpreter generates instruction guided by an explicit instructional theory. This rule-based representation makes the Interpreter useful for testing theories of instruction and learning. Rather than being a single rigid architecture for intelligent tutoring, the IDE-Interpreter is a more flexible system for expressing instructional theories explicitly and empirically. Using the language conventions between modules and providing a rule-based mechanism for computing, the Interpreter allows a wide variety of tutoring mechanisms within a single system.

The Interpreter also becomes a mechanism for articulating theories of instruction. Representations, rules, and terms must be precise and consistent to be computable. This requires that the course author make explicit the important concepts, which form the essence of instruction. In this way, the IDE-Interpreter not only builds on IDE, but adds a new dimension.

ACKNOWLEDGMENTS

The ideas in the IDE-Interpreter belong to many people. Special credit must go to Jim Greeno, John Seely Brown, Tom Moran, Richard Burton, and Tim O'Shea for helping to inspire and articulate the Interpreter's vision. Daniel Jordan, Peter Pirolli and I constructed the system, with Dave Davis supplying the analog multi-meter simulation. Special credit must also go to Joe Psotka and Merryanna Swartz of the Army Research Institute for their forebearance.

Research on the IDE-Interpreter was partially supported by a grant from the Army Research Institute, Contract MDA-903-83-C-0189.

REFERENCES

Bloom, B. S. (1984). The 2-sigma problem: The search for methods of group instruction as effective as one-to-one tutoring. *Educational Researcher, 13*, 3–16.

Brachman, R. J. (1978). A structural paradigm for representing knowledge (Rep. No. 3605). Cambridge, MA: Bolt, Beranek, & Newman.

Breuker, J., Winkels, R., Sandberg, J. (1987). Coaching strategies for help systems: EUROHELP. In *Proceedings of the Third International Conference on Artificial Intelligence and Education*. Pittsburgh, PA: University of Pittsburgh.

Burton, R. R., & Brown, J. S. (1982). An investigation of computer coaching for informal learning activities. In D. Sleeman & J. S. Brown (Eds.), *Intelligent Tutoring Systems* (pp. 79–98). New York: Academic Press.

McArthur, D., Stasz, C., Hotta, J. Y., Peter, O., & Burdorf, C. (1987). *Skill-oriented lesson control in an intelligent tutor for basic algebra*. The RAND Corporation. Submitted for publication.

McCalla, G. I., Reid, L., & Schneider, P. G. (1982). An architecture for the design of large scale intelligent Teaching systems. In *Proceedings of the Fourth CSCCI/ SCEIO Biennial Conference*, 85–91.

O'Shea, T. (1984). Tools for creating intelligent computer tutors. In A. Elithorn & R. Banerji (Ed.), *Artificial and Human Intelligence*. Elsevier Science: NATO.

Osin, L. (1976). SMITH: How to produce CAI courses without programming. *International Journal of Man–Machine, 8*, 207–241.

Woolf, B. P. (1984). Context dependent planning in a machine tutor. (COINS Tech. Rep. 84-21). Amherst, MA: University of Massachusetts.

APPENDIX A: IDE-INTERPRETER LANGUAGES

THE INSTRUCTIONAL RULE LANGUAGE

Basics

The instructional rules are used by the interpreter to guide the instructional plan creation process. The algorithm for using these rules to create and modify plans is discussed in the text.

An IPS rule comprises two portions: a Left Hand Side (LHS) and a Right Hand Side (RHS). To execute a rule, the LHS is evaluated. If it evals to T, then the RHS is executed.

Both the LHS and RHS of a rule are composed of functions and patterns.

Functions are marked with a $ prefix. Functions execute outside of the scope of the plan tree (all non$-prefix lists are elements that are matched to or added to the plan tree). On the LHS, a $ function must evaluate to T for the rule to execute and must have no side-effects on the plan tree. On the RHS, a $ function must either (a) return a value that will be used to compute a new addition to the plan tree, (b) modify the plan tree (e.g., reduce it or change focus), or (c) have a side-effect that modifies subsequent planning (e.g., change a strategy).

Patterns on the LHS must match with the current goal in the plan tree. Patterns on the RHS are added as goals in the plan. That is, patterns become goals, and must therefore be consistent with the World Description Language (see the following appendix).

APPENDIX B: SAMPLE INSTRUCTIONAL STRATEGY RULES

Here is a set of rules for a simple instructional strategy for teaching the Analog Multi-Meter.

STRATEGY RULES

S1: (* The normal way of teaching a concept is to say why you want to teach it (context),
then test to see if the student already knows the concept,

then teach the subconcepts,
then the prerequisites,
then present the concept body (Content),
and finally, question the student to see if at criteria)

($Strategy 'Instructional 'Exposition)
(Teach ?X) = >
    (Present 'Context ?X)
    (Question 'Criteria ?X)
    $Expand 'Teach ($Subconcepts ?X))
    ($Expand 'Teach ($Prerequisites?X))
    (Present 'Content ?X)
    (Question 'Criteria ?X)

S2: (* If remediation fails, change the pedagogical stragegy and try again.)

(Teach ?X)
($Already Taught ?X)
($Unknown ?X) = >
    ($ChangePedStrategy 'CaseStudy)
    ($ResetPlan)
    (Teach'BasicXerography)

S3: (* If 3 concepts have been presented in a row, check that the student is following you. Ask a question.)

($Type ($HL 1) 'Present)
($Type ($HL 2) 'Present)
($Type ($HL 3) 'Present) = >
    (Question 'Understanding ($Select ($Concept ($HL 1))
                                     ($Concept ($HL 2))
                                     ($Concept ($HL 3))))

S4: (* Remediate immediately)

    ($KnownToUnknown) = >
        ($Expand 'Remediate ($KnownToUnknown))

(Remediate ?X) = >
    (Present 'Content ?X)
    (Question 'Criteria ?X)

PEDAGOGY RULES

P1: (*The default teaching strategy for the Analog MM is Defs, then Skills)

($Strategy 'Pedagogical 'Normal)
(Teach 'AnalogMultiMeter) = >
    (Teach 'Definitions)
    (Teach 'Skills)

P2: (* To teach Defs, first define the Processes, then the components)

(Teach 'Definitions) = >
    (Teach 'ProcessTerms)
    (Teach 'ComponentTerms)

TACTICS RULES

T1: (* Select an IU type that is appropriate to the student profile.)

($StudentModel 'StudentParams 'ReadingSkills 'LowVerbal) = >
    ($SelectionParam 'PresentationStyle 'Verbal 'Minimize)

($StudentModel 'StudentParams 'ReadingSkills 'HighVerbal) = >
    ($SelectionParam 'PresentationStyle 'Graphic)

T2: (* Choose an IU that hasn't been used before. Put the A/V pair (Status Unpresented) on.)

(Present ?type ?concept) = >
    ($Prop ?concept 'Status 'Unpresented)

APPENDIX C: INSTRUCTIONAL LANGUAGE FUNCTIONS

This list describes the functions available for use in the instructional rules. This is a preliminary set of rules, under revision and extension as we continue to expand the abilities of the Interpreter.

$AlreadyTaught [?concept]　returns T if ?concept has already been taught during the current session

$ChangeStrategy [?strategyClass ?strategyName]　sets the strategy class (Instructional or Pedagogical) to the new value.

$HL [?n]　returns the ?n-th element of the history list (the most recent entry is 1).

$KnownToUnknown [ ]　returns a list of the concepts that have changed status from known to unknown during the last cycle.

$Prop [?concept, ?attribute ?value]　puts an attribute value pair on an instructional goal. Used to constrain how a goal will be instantiated.

$ResetPlan [ ]　flushes the entire plan tree.

$Select [?concepts]   returns one from the ?concepts list (randomly).

$SelectionParam [?selectionParameter ?dimension ?new Value]   sets a selection parameter (one of PresentationStyle, PresentationSpeed, AbstractionLevel) to determine how an instructional unit is selected.

$Strategy [?strategyClass ?strategyName]   returns T if the strategy class (Instructional or Pedagogical) is equal to the strategy name.

$StudentModel [?issue ?attribute ?value]   returns the T if ?issue's ?attribute value is equal to ?value in the student model.

$Type [?HLentry ?type]   returns T if the ?HLentry was of type ?type (e.g., Presentation or Question).

$Unknown [?concept]   returns T if ?concept is not known by the student [i.e., (GREATERP ($StudentModel (IssueFromConcept ?concept) 'Understanding) 5)]

APPENDIX D: IDE-INTERPRETER LANGUAGES

WORLD DESCRIPTION LANGUAGE

The World Description Language is a set of predicates that describe world states to be achieved as a result of instructional planning. Predicates in the World Description Language takes KS concepts as arguments. For the AMM course, there are 3 predicates: TEACH, PRESENT, and QUESTION.

Attributes	Possible Values
PRESENT	<concept>
QUESTION	<concept>
TEACH	<concept>

Represents: goals in the instructional plan

Used by: IPS to describe world states for plans

Implies represents instructional goal types

Semantics:

(TEACH ?X)   holds when ?X is understood by the student; that is, when the MOS II for ?X has a value of "Understand."

(PRESENT ?X)   holds when the concept ?X has been presented to the student by running an IU that is attached to concept ?X in the KS.

(QUESTION ?X)   holds when the student has been asked a question that probes the student's understanding of ?X.

CONCEPT DESCRIPTION LANGUAGE

Concepts are described by their relationships in the KS and by a set of attributes. They are used to discriminate between concepts when the IPS selects a topic to teach.

Attributes	Possible Values
Difficulty	1, 2, . . . , 10
Criticality	1, 2, . . . , 10

Represents: concepts in KS

Used by: IPS to select between concepts

Implies: terms of distinction between concepts

Semantics:

> **Difficulty**   represents the difficulty of learning this concept; 1 is easy, 10 is difficult for most students

> **Criticality**   how critical is this concept to understanding the overall course; 1 is "not critical," 10 is "absolutely critical"

IU DESCRIPTION LANGUAGE

IUs are described by a set of attributes used by the IPS Tactical rules to do IU selection from a primitive instructional goal.

Attributes	Possible Values
IU Task	Present | Question
PresentationStyle	Textual | Graphical | Animation | Simulation
Type	Content | Context
Concept	<link to concept in KS>

Represents: IU characteristics

Used by: IPS to select an IU that best implements a goal

Implies: secondary instructional categories used by IPS to select an IU given a goal

Semantics:

> **IU Task**   this IU either Presents information or asks a Question

PresentationStyle the presentation (or question) is in one of these styles

Type the kind of information in the presentation focuses on content (i.e., what this concept is) or on context (i.e., why the student needs to understand this concept)

Concept a pointer to the concept inthe KS

HISTORY LANGUAGE

Attributes	Possible Values
Action	Presented | Questioned
TimeDuration	\<integer\>
QuestionType	MultipleChoice | Simulation
StudentResponse	\<symbol\>
MeterState	\<list of A/V pairs describing meter state\>
CorrectAnswer	\<symbol\> | \<list of A/V pairs describing meter state\>

Represents: interaction of student with IU; as one of these event types occur, an entry is placed onto the History List.

Used by: MOS to infer state of student knowledge about IIs.

Implies: secondary instructional categories used by IPS to select an IU given a goal.

Semantics:

Action Presented text or Questioned student on concept

TimeDuration time in seconds from start of IU until student advances to next IU

QuestionType if (Action Questioned) then the question was either a MultipleChoice or a Simulation test environment

StudentResponse if (QuestionType MultipleChoice) then \<symbol\> was the student's selection for an answer

MeterState the state of the analog multimeter simulation is encoded as a set of attribute value pairs

CorrectAnswer if (QuestionType MultipleChoice) then \<symbol\> was the correct answer; if (QuestionType MultipleChoice) then \<list\> is the correct meter state after the simulation has been run by the student

MOS INSTRUCTIONAL ISSUE LANGUAGE

Attributes	Possible Values
Type	Skill | Concept | Skill-bug | Concept-bug | Parameter
Status	Presented | Unpresented
Understanding	1, 2, . . . , 10
Concept	<pointer to KS concept> | NIL

Represents: student's understanding of individual and collective concepts; also represents individual student learning parameters

Used by: MOS inference rules

Implies: a theory about how to model student knowledge

Semantics:

Type   an II in the MOS is one of these types (see text above); the type determines what rules are used to make inferences about student understanding

Status   for concepts and skills, have either been Presented to the student, or are currently Unpresented

Understanding   for concepts and skills, a value indicating how well the student seems to understand this concept as measured by questions answered (or MOS inferences drawn; for bugs, a value indicating if the student has this bug; 1 is low, 10 is high

Concept   pointer to the KS concept, skill or bug; if NIL, then this II monitors a learning parameter

Intelligent Tutoring Systems for Electronic Troubleshooting

John R. Frederiksen
Barbara Y. White
Allan Collins
BBN Laboratories, Inc.

Gary Eggan
University of Pitsburgh

INTRODUCTION

The Air Force has invested heavily in developing complex electronic units for its aircraft. Consequently, it has developed equally complex test equipment systems to test and repair these aircraft units. Modern-day work environments have been influenced by these technological advances that resulted in more complex human–machine interactions. Among the most complex test equipment systems in the Air Force are the test stations used for repairing units on the F-15, F-16, and F-111 aircraft. Although these test stations are efficient at diagnosing and isolating faults in the aircraft units, the stations themselves often fail, so the Air Force inevitably needs air personnel with the skills to troubleshoot these complex electronic testing systems. Research initiated by the Air Force has examined the job skills of expert Air Force personnel in a number of technical domains. Bolt, Beranek, and Newman is currently using the products of these research efforts to develop computer-based instruction to help personnel acquire the needed complex skills.

To prepare air personnel to become repair technicians, the Air Force sends them to technical school to learn electronics and how to operate the test stations. The trainees do not actually learn troubleshooting in the school, for several reasons: (a) they are given inadequate time working on actual test stations in order to familiarize themselves with test station operation; (b) they are given inadequate training on the functional relationships between the subcomponents of the test stations; (c) they receive no training in troubleshooting strategies; and (d) they receive no practice in actually repairing the test stations. What they do learn is abstract knowledge, such as quantitative circuit analysis and digital logic, but this knowledge is not grounded in the kinds of tasks their jobs will encompass.

When the trainees are assigned to work in a test station shop their real learning and problems begin. They work in teams with an experienced troubleshooter, who is there to teach and advise them when they encounter problems. Unfortunately, test stations do not fail in any systematic order to foster learning by the trainees. Trainees quickly find themselves observing the more experienced technicians solve the problem; they often do not know the real nature of the failure or why the skilled technicians are doing what they are doing in their troubleshooting. The novice trainees end up learning only the basic operation of the test station and how to repair faults identified by the test station in units under test (UUTs) from the plane. They do not learn to troubleshoot the test station itself, except for very common problems, such as a loose connection in the interface between the test station and the UUTs from the plane.

INTELLIGENT TUTORING SYSTEMS CAN IMPROVE TRAINING

We think there is a better way to teach troubleshooting to the trainees. The experts who train them have sophisticated mental models of what the different drawers (subcomponents of the test station) and circuit cards within them do, of how to analyze the computer code that runs the station to determine where a failure may have occurred, of how to manually program the control panel to help them track down where the fault is occurring, of how to trace through the huge array of schematics to pinpoint where to make tests, and so forth. Moreover, they have a general knowledge of how devices within a system interact functionally in its operation. They have a general knowledge of troubleshooting strategies for deducing possible faults from system behavior and for isolating faults given the space of possibilities. And finally, they have general problem-solving skills for planning, for subdividing the search space, for monitoring their ongoing troubleshooting performance, and for checking products of problem-solving operations.

We think that novices can learn all these skills if they are given problems to work in a systematic order that builds from basic electronics knowledge toward strategies for using the history of test station behavior at the time of the fault, along with the manual control panel and schematic tracing. By actively solving problems, they can begin to build up the knowledge and skills necessary to troubleshoot the test station itself. The keystone of this training is for personnel to build a qualitative model of how the test station operates as it carries out the coded instructions it is executing. This model should enable air personnel to reason about possible locations of faults and to carry out tests to further isolate the failure. Given such a model, they can then learn to apply general problem-solving strategies and troubleshooting techniques to the fault isolation task. We believe that such training can have a major impact on the skill levels that air personnel attain, on the time required to achieve those levels, and on the generalizability of trained skills to the troubleshooting of systems that are less familiar than the one that is explicitly the focus of training.

In order to give trainees the kind of practice they require, we are building a series of intelligent tutoring systems to tutor different aspects of the automatic test stations used in the Air Force. The tutoring systems will be based on qualitative simulations (White & Frederiksen, 1987; in press) of the functioning of the test station, which includes "device models" for the most critical drawers in the automatic test stations and their subcomponents, and principles for propagating the effects of changes in one device on the operation of other devices within the test station. The tutoring systems will pose problems to the students, model qualitative reasoning about the system, model expert troubleshooting strategies, and provide help to students as they try to solve problems on their own. There will be manuals provided with the tutoring systems, containing the information provided in the technical orders for the actual test station (tables, schematics, and computer code) for the simulated test station. The tutoring system will be located near the test stations themselves, so that trainees can work problems with the simulator at the same time they are working as an apprentice on the test station itself.

An Overview of the Research Plan

Our objective is to design intelligent tutoring systems to train air personnel working on the Automatic Test Stations (ATSs) for the F-15, F-16, and F-111. Based on our analysis of expert performance, and on cognitive task analyses by Glaser et al. (1985) and by the HUMRRO group, we are constructing three intelligent tutoring systems. These three are ordered in the degree of complexity of the underlying simulation models for ATS functioning, both for development purposes and also for training purposes.

The first system to be built is a simplified, "signal flow"

simulation of the test station. The test station consists of subcomponents called *drawers* that have specialized functions. The first system will model the behavior of these drawers with respect to their signal flow, that is, signals flowing from stimulus drawers through the switching complex to a unit under test and from the UUT back through the switching complex to measurement drawers (see Figure 13.1). It also includes a computer code interpreter so that the coordination of ATS behavior with program statements can be modeled. The device models for drawers will in general be black box models, that is, there will in most cases be no subcomponents of drawers, and the drawer rules will specify outputs that occur when given inputs are received.

The second system to be built will be a full F–15 ATS simulation. This system will incorporate additional device models to cover the control logic of the ATS (data flow). In other words, mechanisms will be added to model how the ATS decodes the parallel data generated by the computer in running its language code called FAPA, and uses it to control the functioning of drawers that were modeled in the initial, signal flow simulation.

Finally, the F–15 simulation will be extended to cover (in a generic sense) the F–16 and F–111 ATSs as well. We plan to create two modifications to the F–15 system, one for the F–16 and the other for the F–111. In the former, for example, FAPA code will be replaced with ATLAS code interpretation. In the latter, machine code interpretation will be incorporated.

Instructional Principles

Our approach is to decompose the knowledge needed to support troubleshooting of the ATS into subdomains of expertise. Based upon this decomposition, we will create a community of computer-based experts who can articulate their knowledge as air personnel attempt to solve problems. Further, this decomposition will enable us to define classes of problems that require (a) single components of expertise for their solution, and (b) combinations of these knowledge components. These problems can then be used to help trainees focus, respectively, on (a) acquiring the components of expertise, and (b) integrating the use of multiple components of expertise when troubleshooting.

To illustrate the types of expertise that we will model, the following represent alternative approaches to troubleshooting, which can all be utilized if needed, when troubleshooting the ATS.

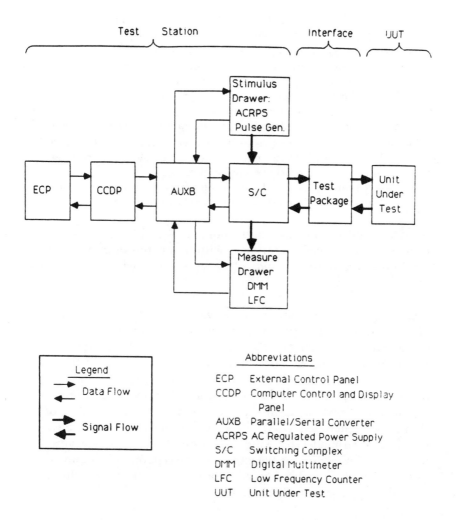

FIGURE 13.1   Data and signal flow in automatic test station.

1. *Strategies based upon FAPA code interpretation.* By analyzing the FAPA code executed by the ATS before and at the time of failure, the troubleshooter can gain knowledge of the possible locations of the fault. To do this, the troubleshooter must understand the concept of a procedure, the language for representing procedures, and what parts of the station are active as it carries out procedural steps.

2. *Strategies based upon behavioral analysis.* Given the symptoms at the time the fault occurs, the troubleshooter can reason about possible test station faults that are consistent with those particular symptoms. Such reasoning depends on having a domain model for simulating the behavior of the station. These models are qualitative causal models that

allow one to derive test-station behavior from a knowledge of the operation of the drawers and how they are interconnected.

3. *Strategies based upon schematic tracing/backtracking.* At times, troubleshooters must analyze schematics for a drawer and derive an understanding of the components within that drawer that are possibly faulty. This analysis depends upon the application of general knowledge of how components interact within an electrical circuit, rather than on a previously learned model for the operation of the particular drawer.

4. *General troubleshooting heuristics.* General circuit analysis principles such as forward reasoning, dependency-directed backtracking, or dividing the circuit, may be employed in the course of troubleshooting for determining possible locations of a fault and for choosing tests to perform that will be most informative at any given stage.

Given a decomposition of the domain, we will incorporate three primary instructional techniques within the tutoring systems for developing the different kinds of expertise required and the ability to integrate them.

Teaching by problem solving and induction. A given component of expertise is formally modeled within the tutorial system. The formal specification of expertise enables us to determine problems that require particular aspects of expertise within a knowledge component. In the process of gaining expertise, students develop a series of partial models for the domain that are then transformed (elaborated) into more sophisticated models. As in the QUEST system we have developed (White & Frederiksen, 1987; in press), students are motivated to transform their models by being given carefully chosen problems that require for their solutions the particular concept or model refinement to be accomplished. Thus, graded problems in the ATS tutor will be used to motivate model transformations.

Teaching by tutorial assistance and feedback. This instructional technique is based upon an evaluation of student performance. The tutoring system compares its solution with that of the student as indicated by the student's troubleshooting actions. Based upon this comparison, the system can provide the student with feedback about his or her performance and, if desired, can give the student tutorial assistance.

Teaching by example and explanation. Because each component of expertise is formally modeled, it is possible to generate demonstrations and explanations of expert performance by having the computer-based expert solve a problem for the student.

Demonstrations and explanations can be used in a number of ways:

1. *Full demonstration.* In this mode, the system describes and illustrates the concepts and reasoning in their entirety by solving the problem for the student. In giving explanations in the course of problem solving, the system employs several principles for focusing explanations. For example, explanations can focus on the new principle that is involved (summarizing explanations for portions of the problem-solving sequence that are already familiar), or it can emphasize a common principle being applied in two novel problem situations.

2. *Partial demonstration as a means of focus.* One can use demonstrations to lead a student to a particular subdomain of troubleshooting. Using this technique the trainee can focus on one aspect of troubleshooting while the tutoring system handles the rest of the troubleshooting for the student.

3. *Partial demonstration as a means of reducing load.* Another instructional use of a partial demonstration is to start a problem for the trainee to complete. As the trainees gain competence, the system can let them tackle a greater proportion of the problem.

In designing the tutoring systems, we will enable them to employ all of these instructional techniques by modeling the components of troubleshooting expertise that we want trainees to acquire, and using these models to select problems, monitor student performance, and generate tutorial explanations.

Skills to Be Developed

In the course of training, a large number of job-related skills are to be trained. In general, skills will be developed in the course of solving problems, and the instruction is not organized at the individual skill level. However, it is useful to compile a list of basic skills for troubleshooting the automatic test station that are to be developed in subjects as they work with the tutor. A partial list of such skills is contained in Table 13.1.

Instructional Plan

The instructional plan addresses five general areas: (a) understanding test-station behavior, (b) the FAPA/ATLAS control language, (c) ATS control logic, (d) troubleshooting strategies based on symptoms and computer code, and (e) troubleshooting strategies based on manipulating the behavior of the ATS by using the ECP (external or manual control panel) and measurements of card outputs. Each of these areas is briefly described in this section.

TABLE 13.1
Skills Students Need to Learn for Automatic Test Station

Basic Skills

FAPA, ATLAS, or Machine Code

1. Identify drawer and mode or operational area referred to in code (chunking of cards, components into operation areas).
2. Be able to trace where the program goes when it calls subroutines.
3. Identify what type of signal (DC, AC), continuity, or waveform is being measured.
4. Know whether dealing with static, waveform, or voltage (AC or DC) stimuli.
5. Know what voltage, waveform, or ohm reading to expect when checking pins.
6. Know what test equipment to use.
7. Group tests to determine reasons for tests.

Device Models

1. Know what each drawer does functionally.
2. Understand how it achieves that.
3. Understand how the drawers interact.

Manual Control Panel

1. Convert hexadecimal to octal, hexadecimal to binary, and octal to binary.
2. Specify which device 12 bit address refers to (Part ——> bit pattern).
3. Convert codes used in the technical orders.
4. Know how to send a bit pattern to a drawer and how to read a bit pattern from a drawer.
5. Figure out what bits are lost.
6. Use bit data to aid in fault determination.
7. Know what the bits do operationally.
8. Identify what bit pattern may be (by analyzing fault) vs. what the pattern should be (first 6 bits ——> drawer, last 6 bits ——> OCWD or subaddress).

Circuit Schematics

1. Know which pins to check.
2. Trace a bit entering a card and through the card.
3. Trace a bit from the computer out to a drawer and back.
4. Apply dependency logic to determine output of chip with several inputs.
5. Understand analog circuit tracing.
6. Understand chunking analog and logic circuits into operational areas.
7. Locate the optimal points to test (input, output pins, and resistors vs. transistors).

Making Measurements

1. Know how to attach a meter or oscilloscope to a pin and to ground or return.
2. Know how to interpret a bad reading as a fault somewhere upstream.
3. Understand proper use of test equipment: mode, ranging, and so on.

(Continued)

TABLE 13.1

(Continued)

Integrated Skills

ECP and Circuit Schematics
1. Be able to identify where a bit enters a drawer on the schematic.
2. Convert serial to parallel and vice versa.
3. Use ECP for loop program.

Circuit Schematics and Making Measurements
1. Be able to go from a point on the schematic to the point in the drawer where a test should be made.

Strategic Skills
1. Follow diagnostic tests and purpose of tests after original fail, gaining insights from *all* available data.
2. Use hypothetical reasoning fault analysis: "If x were bad, would I encounter indications similar to the present ones?"
3. Know how to predict what a meter should read in a working circuit.

Understanding the Behavior of the Test Station

Tutoring will begin by presenting problems involving the behavior of the test station in troubleshooting units under test. From these problems trainees learn the elements of test-station behavior as it operates in troubleshooting. They learn that the UUT is interfaced to the test equipment by means of a test package, which is connected to a set of switches in the switching complex (S/C). They learn that the station is composed of "stimulus" devices for sending the UUT power or other signals used in troubleshooting and "measurement" devices for measuring the outputs from the UUT. They learn that these devices are connected to the proper ports of the UUT by means of switches in the S/C. They also learn the elements of a test procedure: (a) setting up the appropriate test conditions, (b) measuring appropriate outputs, and (c) comparing those outputs with the values that should be generated by the UUT if it is operating correctly. Finally, they learn how to go about executing an appropriate series of tests on a UUT when given a procedure to follow.

At this stage in learning, the trainees will manually control the operation of the station, using menus that allow them to select operations for setting up tests, delivering stimuli, measuring responses, and comparing outcomes with those specified in the technical order for the particular UUT. The menu labels will correspond to FAPA commands. While a trainee is controlling the test station and following a troubleshooting procedure, he or she will be developing a model of how such a procedure is properly carried out, a model that the trainee can later transfer to his or her own troubleshooting of the test station. It would also be possible here to introduce some knowledge of device models and of troubleshooting logic, if that seems appropriate.

Introducing the FAPA/ATLAS Control Language

Trainees would next learn a language for describing the sequence of operations they have been carrying out as they manually control the test station. The commands of the language will be similar to the labels they have been using in selecting from menus as they manually control the simulated test station. Thus, the new things to learn will be the syntax of the language, the idea of a program as a way of representing a whole series of operations, and a formal way of representing the logic involved in comparing measurements with expected results and branching on the results of such tests. The problems given at this point will be similar to those they have been solving, except that students will have to understand FAPA-like statements that initiate the operations to be performed. Some examples of the types of knowledge air personnel need to learn about FAPA are given in Table 13.2.

In the case of the F-111, students will need to learn the machine-language program used to control the ATS. They will need to learn how to locate and read machine language statements, and how to interpret them.

Introducing Models of ATS Functioning as it Carries Out FAPA Instructions

At this point, trainees would begin to learn the structures (computer control, serial to parallel conversion, and other control logic) included within the test station that enable it to carry out operations encoded in the FAPA language. The station is represented by a simulation model containing "articulate" devices corresponding to these station elements. The operation of the station in carrying out a line of FAPA code (i.e., an operation) is explained by the simulation as it operates. The trainee must learn to predict the operation of the station in response to particular FAPA instructions. Trainees will also be introduced to the notions of faults within the test-station control logic by hearing explanations of station operation when it has faults introduced. They also will be given predictive problems involving the effects of faults on station operation as it executes a series of operations coded as FAPA instructions.

TABLE 13.2
Types of Knowledge Airmen Need to Learn About FAPA Code

The basic strategy in reading FAPA is first to find the step where the program stopped. Then one works back from that step to all the steps that have been executed since the last set-up statement. The goal is to identify all the drawers (and the routing in and out of these drawers) that are addressed in this part of the program where the fault might have occurred.

The Statement that Appears[1]	The Meaning of the Statement
1. Connect	Switches are being set in the *stimulus* routing part of the switching complex.
2. Route TPX (xx)	Switches are being set in the *measurement* routing part of the switching complex. Routing enters the switching complex at pin labeled TPX (xx)on the schematic of the switching complex.
3. Route Reference to TPX Term (xx)	
4. Perform [XXXX] TAGS$	Subroutine *XXXX* is called, which is listed elsewhere in the program. All of the statements in it must be checked out to see what drawers are called.

[1]*X* is a letter variable and *x* is a number variable.

By carefully varying types of FAPA instructions being executed in a predictive problem as well as the types of test-station faults introduced, the level of a student's knowledge of test-station operation can be increased in an incremental fashion. Factors that will come into play as problems increase in difficulty include: flow of control, the serial bus (parallel to serial conversion in the AuxB, serial to parallel conversion in the A1 cards), addresses and subaddresses, hexadecimal and octal to binary conversion, card logic for decoding addresses within a drawer, and hierarchical schematic diagrams down to the card level.

As trainees attempt new problems, when they encounter problems that they cannot solve they can enlist the aid of the system, which will explain how to solve the new problem. The system will use new concepts and strategies when appropriate for solving the problem. For example, when the problem requires it, the explanations will make reference to new subjects (such as HEX to binary conversion), and the trainee will be motivated to seek additional knowledge of these subtopics. Separate tutorial systems will be available for developing these additional subdomains of knowledge. Thus, the trainee can make his or her own choices as to when to go off and explore these topics, at points where the topics become important to problem solving.

Troubleshooting Strategies Based
on Symptoms and FAPA Code

Troubleshooting problems will be chosen to involve faults that can be localized down to the drawer or card level solely by analyzing the instructions that were being attempted by the simulated test station when the fault occurred, along with a consideration of the other instructions that were successfully executed and the error codes that appear on the console. Knowledge of the way in which the simulated test station implements the instructions allows inferences about the probable locus of the fault.

Troubleshooting Strategies Using the ECP
and Manual Measurement of Card Outputs

For some faults (e.g., inability to program a drawer in some modes), information contained in the error code and in the computer code that was being executed at the time of the fault allows one to infer that the fault is localized within a particular drawer, and within some subset of the cards within the drawer. For example, the ability to power up the drawer and to program it in some modes suggests that the A1 card (used in serial to parallel decoding) is likely to be good, and the problem may be in further address decoding or in the control logic used in interpreting the bits directed to particular cards within the drawer and carrying out the action the bits have encoded.

Troubleshooting strategies used in localizing faults within a drawer include the following:

1. Interpret octal address codes and look them up in a technical order to find what part of drawer is involved.
2. Use the external control panel to send specified bit patterns to that part of the drawer.
3. Discern the logical basis for choosing bit patterns to send.
4. Use drawer and card schematics to find where to make manual measurements to check if the bits are reaching their destination, and if they are being properly processed by the card.
5. Understand card-level models to determine what bit patterns should be produced by a particular card when given a particular set of input bits.
6. Know procedures for extending cards.
7. Know strategies for tracing faults in a drawer composed of multiple cards (such as space splitting and dependency-directed backtracking).
8. Know digital logic in general.

THE TRAINING SYSTEMS

Characteristics of these training systems will be described in the following subsections.

A Simplified Signal Flow Simulation

The simplified signal flow system models signal flow within a simplified test station containing a Signal Generator, Programmable Power Supply, Switching Complex, Digital Multimeter, Frequency Counter, and an Oscilloscope (not programmable). In addition, a Test Package and a UUT will be modeled. The simplified signal flow simulation, though driven by the FAPA/ATLAS control language, does not include any explicit representation of parallel or serial bit patterns associated with the FAPA commands to the test station, and does not include any of the control devices within drawers that decode the functions encoded in those bit patterns.

The simplified signal flow simulation permits students to learn a number of important features of the test-station behavior as it carries out tests.

The anatomy of test procedures carried out. Test procedures have a predictable form. First, the power supplies, signal generators, and instruments are set to the proper values and operating ranges, the outputs of such devices are connected to the proper terminals of the UUT, power and signals are then supplied to the UUT, outputs of the UUT are routed to measurement drawers, and measurements are made of voltages or signals appearing at the terminals of the UUT. Decisions are then made as to whether or not the measurement is the correct one by comparing it with an expected value. If it is bad, the UUT is found to be at fault. Otherwise, another test is performed. A the tutor describes how the test station executes a test, the student will begin to learn the functional interrelatedness of the test-station drawers and how measurement results are interpreted.

Knowledge of the FAPA/ATLAS control language. Although the simplified signal flow system does not contain any mechanism for interpreting FAPA statements, it does allow each statement to be implemented behaviorally by the system. Thus, students can learn the basic commands and syntax of the control language, and the mapping of those statements to actual test-station behavior (see Table 13.2 for examples of FAPA knowledge to be taught).

Device models. Students using the simplified signal flow model will learn what each drawer does functionally and how the drawers interact in carrying out tests. They will be introduced in general to the concept of a device model as a way of understanding how a complex system's operation can be broken down into the interactions among a number of smaller devices having predictable functions and behavior.

System structure. Students will become acquainted with the concept of block and schematic diagrams of the system, particularly with respect to the signal flow organization of the test station. They will learn how to read and interpret schematics in relation to the set of interacting device models.

Signal flow troubleshooting. Finally, students will become acquainted with the set of faults that occur with respect to signal flow and will learn troubleshooting strategies for locating those faults. Measurements used in troubleshooting will be restricted to a hand-held digital multimeter (DMM) or oscilloscope. Students will learn how to make measurements using these devices. Troubleshooting techniques will include (a) use of FAPA code to isolate drawers that may be faulty from those that can be presumed to be good, (b) using device models, schematics, and a model of device interactions to infer what the proper values should be at designated test points, and (c) strategies (such as space splitting, or dependency-directed backtracking) to establish possible faulty drawers, connections, and so on.

The simplified simulation will contain no Computer Control (CCDP) or Data Transfer Drawer (AuxB), and the drawer simulations will have no A1 cards or other device-control logic contained within them. Drawers will directly carry out FAPA/ATLAS instructions. Though there will be an interpretation of FAPA statements, there will be no parallel to serial or serial-to-parallel-data conversion, and no control logic within drawers. Nor will there be data flow simulated, either in the computer sending addresses, clock pulses, or data to drawers, or in its receiving data back from drawers.

A Full F-15 ATS Simulation

We plan next to extend the training system to incorporate the data flow aspects of ATS operation. Devices added to the simulation model will include the following drawers: a Computer Control (CCDP), a Data Transfer Drawer (AuxB), and a Manual Control Panel (ECP). These will all be modeled as black boxes. In addition, the stimulus drawers, measurement drawers, and switching complex models will be modified to incorporate subdevices (cards) to carry out interpretation of the addresses and data that are sent to them from the computer control. Cards to be incorporated within these drawers include an A1 (serial-to-parallel-converter) card and additional cards to carry out decoding of the subaddress and data received and implementation of the instructions. The cards will be modeled as black boxes.

The addition of these device models to the ATS simulation permits a large number of additional skills to be addressed in instruction. These include:

1. *Knowledge of device models for device controller cards.* The student's knowledge of device models will be extended to encompass cards needed for device control. These include parallel-to-serial encoders/decoders, address decoders, logic circuits, and so forth.

2. *Tracing flow of control within the ATS.* The student will learn how the flow of control operates within the test station. The Control Computer issues parallel instructions having a specified form, as well as timing pulses. (The generation of these parallel codes will not be modeled.) The functions of the AuxB in transferring these instructions to a particular drawer and the A1 card within that drawer in converting the serial bit code will be modeled for the student, as well as the means by which information is sent back to the control computer for verification.

3. *Data coding and decoding.* Students will learn hex to decimal and decimal to hex conversions, conversions to binary code, conversions of parallel binary to serial codes, and the components of the coded information (addresses, subaddresses, data, and timing signals).

4. *Card logic within drawers.* Students will learn how cards interact within drawers to interpret a parallel bit code output from the A1 card and carry out the proper drawer function.

5. *Data flow troubleshooting.* Students will learn skills and strategies involved in data flow troubleshooting. These include digital circuit tracing, knowledge of fault types, modeling the effects of faults on circuit operation, and strategies for reasoning about what components could be faulty given that certain bit patterns are input and certain output bits are bad.

6. *Use of ECP and card measurements in troubleshooting.* Students will learn to use the External Control Panel to transmit bit patterns to a particular part of a drawer, and to extend cards within a drawer so as to measure the output bits produced by a card when the specified bit pattern is transmitted to it.

A more complete list of skills addressed is contained in Table 13.1. The full F-15 trainer will, of course, also be able to support signal flow troubleshooting, as in the signal flow simulation.

The Job Family Trainer (F-15, F-16, F-111)

When completed, the intelligent tutoring system for the F-15 test station will be extended to tutor airmen who work on automatic test stations for the F-16 and F-111. The simulated test-station design we have developed represents components that are common to all three test stations. The major differences between the test stations are that (a) the F-15 runs FAPA code, the F-16 runs ATLAS codes, and the F-111 runs machine code, and (b) the inputs and outputs for manual control are somewhat different in the three stations. Therefore, our modifications to the F-15 trainer will be in the Computer Control and Manual Control devices to accommodate these differences.

Our current plan is to build different interfaces for students in the three different specialities. The computer code running the simulated test station will be FAPA in all three cases, but the computer code listings the students will have to search to find information will be in the language they will be working with (i.e., FAPA, ATLAS, or machine code). To accomplish this, we will have to translate the FAPA code that runs the station into its equivalent code in ATLAS and machine code. The error messages will also need to be changed to reference the different computer code listings. We anticipate that all the computer listings for the three test stations will appear in manuals to accompany the use of the station. Finding the correct computer code in these manuals will be like finding the correct code in a technical order. These manuals, therefore, will be tailored to the particular test station (F-15, F-16, or F-111) the air personnel are being trained to troubleshoot.

Changing the inputs and outputs for the manual control panel will be a simpler job. The air personnel will have mostly the same options for controlling the test station through the manual control panel. But we will change the black box model of the panel to conform with the way manual control is handled in each of the three stations.

Other minor adjustments will no doubt be necessary in extending the system developed for the F-15 to the F-16 and F-111 test stations. But these two examples illustrate our design philosophy, that is, to make modifications to the interfaces between the system and the air personnel, in order to make the system look as much as possible like the actual system they are working with. This will facilitate transfer from the lessons they learn with the trainer to troubleshooting in their job.

EXTENDING THE TUTOR
TO OTHER JOBS IN THE AIR FORCE

Most electronic specialties in the Air Force involve working with a similar set of components: pulse generators, power supplies, digital multimeters, oscilloscopes, routing drawers, control panels, and so on. The tasks to be carried out with these pieces of equipment, and the way the different components are configured, will be different for different electronic specialties, but the basic components, the basic set of faults, and the basic strategies for troubleshooting these faults will be very similar. We intend to exploit these commonalities in building tutors to cover 12 to 14 electronic specialties in the Air Force.

Our plan is to identify from the task analyses what are the critical components and how they are configured, and what are the problems faced and strategies that experts use in troubleshooting the system for each of the new specialities. Then we will take our simulation models developed for the automatic test stations and configure a system (or systems) that reflects the structure of the system(s) the trainees will be troubleshooting on the job. To do this we will undoubtedly have to develop qualitative models for new components specific to each specialty. But we hope to be able to carry over a large part of the curriculum we have developed for the automatic test stations, including black box models of components with their associated faults, the kinds of problems that the trainees will tackle in a graduated sequence, and the kinds of troubleshooting strategies we will teach them.

Finally, in our evaluations of tutor effectiveness, we hope to demonstrate that trainees not only can acquire models of system operation and strategies for troubleshooting the test station itself, but can also develop a more general knowledge of system functioning as well as generic problem-solving skills that they can apply to systems other than the one that is the focus of training. Such generalizable skills, if they can be successfully developed using a job family tutor such as the one we are building, will enable trained personnel to adjust more readily to changing job requirements that are brought about by changes in the technology of the systems for which they are responsible.

ACKNOWLEDGMENTS

This research was supported by the Air Force under contract number F33615-84-C-0058 to the Human Research Resources Organization (HUMRRO). We thank Eric Cooper who is helping to design and is the chief implementer of the tutoring system, and Sherrie Gott, Alan Lesgold, Suzanne Lajoie, Barbara Means, Chris Roth, and Bob Pokorny, who have helped to design the project.

REFERENCES

Glaser, R., Lesgold, A., Lajoie, S., Eastman, R., Greenberg, L., Logan, D., Magone, M., Weiner, A., Wolf, R., & Yengo, L. (1985). *Cognitive task analysis to enhance technical skills training and assessment.* (Final Report, Air Force Human Resources Laboratory, Contract No. F41689-83-C0029). Pittsburgh, PA: Learning Research and Development Center, University of Pittsburgh.

White, B. Y., & Frederiksen, J. R. (1987). *Qualitative models and intelligent learning environments.* In R. Lawler & M. Yazdani (Eds.), *AI and Education.* Norwood, NJ: Ablex.

White, B. Y., & Frederiksen, J. R. (in press). Causal model progressions as a foundation for intelligent learning environments. *Artificial Intelligence.*

A Training System
for System Maintenance

L. Dan Massey
Jos de Bruin
Bruce Roberts
BBN Laboratories Inc.

INTRODUCTION

The MACH-III system is intended to be a training device in which state-of-the-art techniques in artificial intelligence and cognitive science are applied to support the training of novices in troubleshooting complex electronic devices at the organizational maintenance level. Organizational maintenance encompasses those maintenance and repair activities that are performed on equipment in the field, that is, at the tactical site to which it is deployed, to render it operational as quickly as possible. Organizational maintenance generally involves routine adjustment of equipment and replacement of defective major components.

For the purposes of the present development and demonstration project, the AN/MPQ-57 High-Powered Illuminating Radar (HIPIR) component of the HAWK air defense missile system has been selected as the complex electronic device for which MACH-III is to provide organizational maintenance training. The USAADASCH training program for HAWK Firing Section Mechanics (MOS 24C) has been selected as the program of instruction within which the usefulness of the MACH-III system will be demonstrated and assessed.

This chapter presents an introduction to the project and a review of our approach to the design and implementation of this demonstration training system. We give an overview of the radar and discuss what is involved in repairing it and how this is currently trained. This introduction to the domain is followed by a brief overview of related work and our basic position in relation to those other approaches. The chapter finishes with an outline of our design. Information about the analytical and experimental studies undertaken by this project to support the cognitive and instructional validity of our approach can be found in two companion chapters in this volume (Kurland & Tenney, Tenney & Kurland, chapters 5 and 3). These companion papers also present our plans for the instructional design.

THE HAWK RADAR SYSTEM

The AN/MPQ-57 HIPIR is a mobile, continuous-wave, frequency-modulated, steerable dish antenna radar system that serves as the target engagement component of the HAWK air defense system. The HIPIR is able to accept remotely specified target designation information, perform a target acquisition scan, establish tracking lock on the target, compute and provide optimum launch data to the HAWK missile launcher, illuminate the tracked target while the missile flies to the point of interception, and verify target destruction.

Although the original design of the HIPIR is more than 30 years old, several major Product Improvement Program cycles have upgraded parts of the basic design to incorporate modern fabrication techniques (e.g., the use of solid-state integrated circuit technology), to reduce system cost, to improve maintainability, and to improve system performance in anticipated battle environments. As a result of these many retrofits and in-production modifications, the overall electronic design of the current generation HIPIR displays an almost archaeological layering of technologies. The earliest parts of the radar are fairly simple but use technologies unrelated to modern design practice. The most recently upgraded parts of the radar make full use of complex and/or high-speed digital logic, presenting a formidable challenge to detailed functional comprehension.

As information within the radar flows between these layers, it must repeatedly pass through interfacing subsystems, where, for example, shaft position is translated to or from analog voltage, or analog voltage is converted to or from digital data. Because the HAWK system, including the HIPIR, will remain in service beyond the year 2000, and because additional improvement cycles are already being developed, it is likely that the heterogeneity of the system will continue to increase. As a result of this, the total body of general background knowledge of electronics required for thorough understanding of the HIPIR at the various maintenance levels encompasses elements of radar system design practice spanning more than 30 years.

The HIPIR is the size of a small truck. Its five major subsystems are the transmitter, the receiver, the digital signal processor, the antenna positioning system, and the target intercept computer. The transmitter generates the signal that illuminates the target. The receiver amplifies the reflected signal and compares it to the transmitted signal to detect the target. The signal processor computes the range and velocity of the target, which enables the antenna positioning system to track the target in azimuth and elevation and the target intercept computer to compute the correct launch parameters.

Except for the target intercept computer, organizational maintenance of these subsystems is supported by automatic built-in test equipment (BITE). The HIPIR BITE subsystem is able to isolate critical sections of circuits, inject standardized test signals, measure outputs at test points, and report exceptions to the operator. There are four major BITE functions available to the operator. These consist of a preprogrammed sequence of tests that is initiated by pressing the appropriate test button. Such tests are available for the radar system as a whole and for the antenna positioning system, the transmitter, and the combination of receiver and signal processor. Within a few minutes, the BITE subsystem indicates whether the subsystem tests "good" and, if this is not the case, what the nature of the fault is.

The BITE systems do not actually report the specific measurement found to be out of tolerance. Rather, hundreds of possible BITE faults are grouped into fewer than 50 distinct fault indications. Although the BITE fault indications bear directive labels, such as "replace module A6" or "perform receiver noise procedure," these actions typically correct fewer than half of the component-level faults that produce these BITE indications. The many interfaces between modules within a subsystem provide paths for the propagation of failures, which causes the BITE to give erroneous indications of fault location. Its coverage is also incomplete. The BITE conducts a series of automated tests of circuit sections and signals a fault at the first location in the sequence at which the test result is out of tolerance. Subsequent tests in the BITE sequence that might yield additional diagnostic information about complex faults are not performed. Because the BITE itself can also fail, and because the way in which the BITE works is basically unknown to the operator, interpreting BITE indications can be very difficult.

The BITE does not directly test the power distribution subsystem of the radar; it is assumed that any failure in power distribution will affect one of the directly tested functions. As a result, basic maintenance doctrine for the HIPIR requires that, whenever a BITE fault is reported, the power distributions system must be checked before any attempt is made to correct the Fault. More primitive, nonautomatic test devices, such as fuses and meters, are built into the radar to support troubleshooting the power distribution system and parts of the transmitter.

ORGANIZATIONAL MAINTENANCE OF THE HAWK RADAR SYSTEM

Organizational maintenance is based on a combination of general domain knowledge, practical skills, experience, and the use of written sources of information. The required domain knowledge ranges from the names and locations of relevant parts to the general design of the radar and its underlying technologies. Skills needed range from the operation of the radar to running the various BITE tests, making adjustments, using multimeters, and disconnecting and replacing parts. Experience is not only needed to guarantee efficiency in those skills, but also to acquire the kind of empirical knowledge that tells experts which problems are the most likely ones for a given system in a given situation. The use of written materials, finally, does not only presuppose at least some domain knowledge, but also requires skills and knowledge of its own, such as verbal ability and knowledge of the symbols and conventions used in the schematics.

Technologies Confronting the Radar Technician

The technology of radar-directed fire control engineering is a product of some of the major developments in mathematics, science, and engineering since the eighteenth century. The design and development of an effectively operating guided missile system draws on virtually every type of electrical and electronic technology developed since then. Although the physical science that supports these technologies constitutes a more-or-less integrated body of consistent principles, the same cannot be said of the knowledge of engineering and maintaining these technologies. Within electrical engineering there exist many nearly disjoint specializations. Power distribution, antennas, digital circuits, electronic imaging, radio transmission, audio reproduction, and data communications, though based on the same fundamental physical principles, have little in common in actual application. An even greater divergence of knowledge can be found in the community of electrical and electronic technicians. They are highly specialized and tend to receive little education in the unifying scientific and/or engineering principles underlying the products with which they work.

Reviewing the development of electrical science, it is possible to see how the emergence of new theoretical understanding gave rise to related fields of engineering. As each new technology attained practical use, one or more trades or crafts arose to support it. Radar system mechanics are special in that they have to be reasonably skilled in most of these crafts in order to be able to maintain a device as complex as the HIPIR. To appreciate the diversity of knowledge involved, the following is a list of some of the major theoretical breakthroughs underlying this system, and the specialized trades occasioned by them.

- *Direct current circuits* opened the door to the most basic applications of electricity, such as illumination and resistance heating, creating the need for trade electricians.
- *Alternating current circuits* made practical long-distance power transmission and efficient conversion of electric power to mechanical work, including both power equipment and telephony, creating the need for electromechanical technicians.
- *Electromagnetic radiation* led directly to the development of radio broadcasting, creating the need for a wide range of basic electronic technicians.
- *Feedback control systems* permitted the creating of devices with adaptive behavior, able to respond to environmental influence and correct for deficiencies of design. Ubiquitous in modern technology, they have become a specialty for engineers, but are studied by technicians on an ad hoc basis.
- *Information theory* led to optimized applications of all prior technologies to the storage, recreation, and transmission of information, with particular impact on communications and electronic sensing. An engineering specialty, information theory is viewed as more important for design than for maintenance of products.
- *Electronic data representation* made possible electronic digital computing, with its many specialties. Although a class of nonprofessional programmers has slowly begun to emerge, most other technicians in this area specialize in digital logic and work with exclusively digital systems.

Unfortunately for the radar system mechanic, the device to be maintained involves all these varied technologies in important ways, yet is intended to be maintained by a single individual, often with rather limited education, training, and experience.

Reference Sources

The primary reference for information about the structure of the HIPIR is a series of Government-published technical manuals. Four of these are relevant to some aspect of subject matter development:

1. The *operations manual* presents the overall layout of the components of the HIPIR, including control panels. This manual provides detailed directions for the operation, routine checkout, and adjustment of the radar.
2. The *functional diagrams* explain the theory of operation of the HIPIR at the level that is taught to the 24C, and present a functional decomposition of the radar at three different levels of detail.
3. The *fault isolation procedures* (FIPs) contain the detailed instructions for repairing the HIPIR. FIPs are indexed by BITE indications.
4. The *wiring schematics* depict the actual physical interconnections and cabling arrangements within the HIPIR.

In order to gain an understanding of the way these documents are being used in actual organizational maintenance, we watched and interviewed mechanics with varying degrees of experience. The way in which their approaches varied with experience is described in detail by Tenney and Kurland (chapter 3, this volume). Here we focus on the general characteristics of the troubleshooting task and on the ideal approach that we were able to abstract from these studies.

Although documents such as those listed above are never written with the general public in mind, and will always require a certain amount of background knowledge to be used correctly, the documents to be used by the HAWK mechanic do seem to be harder to use than strictly necessary. The functional diagrams and the wiring schematics are mainly hard to use because they are not aimed specifically at troubleshooting at the level of organizational maintenance. Instead of just describing the components that (conceptually) play a role in the troubleshooting, they describe the radar in great detail, providing a complete blueprint of the radar.[1]

The FIPs are hard to use because of their "compiled-out" character. The procedures, chosen on the basis of the BITE indications, instruct the mechanic to make tests and, depending on the results, to continue with the next step, to skip a number of steps, or to insert a number of steps taken from another procedure. Jumping around through the procedures, the mechanic is often asked to make redundant tests, because the procedures do not always reflect the various paths the

---

[1]As is inevitable with a changing system in a bureaucratic environment, the schematics and diagrams contain a certain number of errors. Mechanics maintain a carefully updated personal copy to work around this.

mechanic may have taken in reaching a particular step.[2] The FIPs do not really discuss the hypotheses being considered at various steps, and contain no explanation at all of the relation between those hypotheses and the actual tests being made. This lack of structure makes it very hard to gain an understanding of the purposes of the tests and therefore makes it dangerous to skip apparently redundant tests.

Apart from a lack of information on troubleshooting goals and diagnostic strategies, the FIPs are in general poorly written, requiring a high level of verbal ability and a great deal of additional background information. They cannot incorporate more empirical troubleshooting knowledge specific to particular radars and sites (e.g., problems caused by operating in extremely hot or wet climates). They reflect the probabilities associated with various possible faults only indirectly by the priority they assign to specific tests. They also contain no guidance on effective actions to take when the prescribed procedures are without effect.

A Guide to Troubleshooting

From our discussions with expert mechanics and our study of the various documents we abstracted a practical troubleshooting doctrine that we believe to adequately reflect the structure of the HIPIR, the capabilities of the BITE, the overall plan of organizational maintenance, and the cognitive capabilities of the current trainees. This doctrine is intended as a task analysis that can guide us in structuring the more detailed troubleshooting expertise to be captured in MACH-III. We believe it will be possible to justify the various actions of the practical doctrine in mnemonically and cognitively helpful ways.

The principal steps of this practical troubleshooting doctrine can be summarized as follows:

1. Most individual radars, operated in specific environments (e.g. Ft. Bliss, West Germany) develop consistent and commonly recurring faults, which can be anticipated when the maintenance call first comes from the TAC site. To the extent the problem is immediately identified as falling in this category (e.g., condensation in the transmitter waveguides), take the appropriate corrective measures without further detailed analysis.

---

[2]FIPs are like compiled computer programs, written in a very specific, detailed language, lacking visible modularity and internal documentation.

Frequent faults will occur in the waveguides (chronic arcing), the high voltage power supplies, high voltage connectors, and the low voltage power distribution circuits (especially 28 volts, which is routed throughout the HIPIR). Understand and correct these faults before attempting any of the BITE and FIP procedures outlined following.

2. In general, the person calling for 24C assistance will not have a symptomatic description of radar malfunction sufficiently detailed to support fault diagnosis, so the first step is to begin the daily checks to obtain evidence of the fault. Usually, this will disclose a malfunction through the operation of the BITE, the low-voltage test circuits, the fuses, and so on. If this fails to disclose a correctable fault, continue with the weekly checks. The weekly checks will yield a fault indication, which is the basis for the following remedial actions.

For each indicated fault, perform the first procedure indicated by the FIP, either an alignment, adjustment, or a module replacement (except for power faults, which have their own checkout logic). Usually, this will correct the problem. Return to and continue with the routine checks.

a. If the identical fault recurs, and a module was replaced, put the original module back in the HIPIR before proceeding. Continue the trial replacement procedure using data in FIPs, as modified by experience. Normally, next make a trial replacement of the subsystem BITE card, followed by appropriate other cards. If all this fails, proceed to trial exchange of related modules and to test of relevant connectors and cables, using either the procedures in the FIPs, or following the wiring diagrams, or (in some cases) being guided by experience to establish the sequence of checks.

b. If an identical fault recurs, and an adjustment was made, consult the FIPs for a menu of appropriate checks, or derive ideas from the schematics, or proceed with tests derived from experience if relevant.

3. If no amount of individual module replacement (with appropriate adjustments and cable testing) will make the HIPIR check out properly, a decision must be made about overall troubleshooting strategy. Normally, replace single, larger functional assemblies until the BITE tests "GOOD." Replace one or several modules at a time. If a given replacement fails to correct the problem, leave the changed modules in place while additional replacements are made. The source of replacements can be spares or parts from a radar known to be good; however, parts from another radar should be used only with the approval of the responsible officer. Be certain to keep a record of all replacement actions in the order in which they are performed.

If this procedure is not practical, for example, due to lack of adequate spares or manpower to perform major part substitutions return to the basic checkout procedure and carefully establish the closest possible tolerances for each testable subsystem and signal, replacing (unconditionally) any component that cannot be brought within specification.

4. If the identical fault does not recur, proceed with the routine checks,

treating additional faults in the same manner. At the conclusion of this process, all faults detectable by the BITE and related systems will have been isolated and corrected, and the HIPIR will usually operate correctly.

5. If the HIPIR tests good, but will not perform a combat-critical function correctly (if the impaired function is not combat-critical the HIPIR is normally returned to service at this point), the symptoms of the malfunction must be characterized by careful observation, usually performed by a team (one person in the BCC and one or more at the HIPIR, communicating by phone).

6. Once the malfunction is understood, identify the possible contributing subsystems and perform standard tests and adjustments to bring each component within spec at all measurable points. Replace any component that cannot be adjusted to spec. If the malfunction persists, replace in-spec components until the symptoms are eliminated.

7. The HIPIR is tested after every replacement action. When the HIPIR tests good, the last component replaced will be one of the faulty ones. With a full understanding of the risks involved, swap back in all the other replaced modules one at a time, beginning with the in-spec ones and working backward until a fault reoccurs, at which point the last module swapped back is presumably also defective. Because some multiple faults induce other faults, this is a very risky operation. Do not attempt this refinement unless combat readiness is not critical at this time, a large number of apparently good modules have been replaced, and a knowledgeable (and confident) senior warrant officer is supervising the activity.

This doctrine effectively addresses most of the difficulties faced by a mechanic who tries to repair a HIPIR using the Technical Manuals described at the beginning of this section:

- It recognizes the role played by knowledge specific to particular radars and radar sites.

- It draws on highly verbal materials, such as the FIPs, only when absolutely required to document specific complex actions.

- It organizes actions into intuitively appealing groupings that are relatively easy to understand and motivate, and are relatively efficient in their use of intellectual and physical effort.

- It provides guidance about effective action in essentially all circumstances that will be encountered in organizational maintenance of the HIPIR.

- Once mastered, it can be performed without reference to large and complex documents, except when access to a specific, detailed diagnostic procedure is required.

- It provides goals that direct troubleshooting behavior which, though not always ideal or correct from a technical viewpoint, have significant mnemonic value.

The doctrine provides an overall strategy to organizational maintenance. It does not address the knowledge needed to adequately use the FIPs, neither does it indicate how to derive ideas concerning the right modules to replace or test, whether from experience or from the schematics.

TRAINING A RADAR MECHANIC

The Army draws the majority of individuals who will eventually become equipment support technicians from the population of young people who have completed secondary school and do not expect immediately to continue to college. The only possible source of technical training for the majority of these enlistees is the Army's own technical schools, such as USAADASCH. Although trainees at USAADASCH are selected for overall mental ability and for demonstrated interest in elementary electrical concepts, they are faced with a formidable educational challenge.

Civilian trainee technicians in their age group will typically spend 2 years at a junior college level acquiring a general education in electronic technology before beginning specialized training on the job. Only a few of these students will ever be required to maintain a system of the conceptual complexity of an air defense radar system. Although formally educated in principles underlying the organization of modern electronic technology, most will spend their lives working on elementary electronic maintenance tasks.

The military trainee, by comparison, typically receives 9 months of general and specialized training, which is sharply focused on a specific occupation. Half the training is general, in that it addresses job skills that would be useful in any electronic maintenance specialty. Half is specific, in that it focuses on the actions the trainee must be able to perform as a part of basic qualifications for a specific maintenance specialty, that is, to maintain one or more specific pieces of equipment. The fledgling radar mechanic will be expected, immediately upon graduation from this program, to maintain a device of fundamentally greater complexity and engineering sophistication than his or her civilian compatriots will encounter in a lifetime.

Much civilian vocational training in electronics may be criticized as excessively theoretical and academic. On the other hand, much military vocational training, because of its brief time span, is so focused on job-related manipulative skills that the trainee fails to obtain an adequate understanding of the task domain. Such an understanding of the basic principles at work in a domain is needed to support effective application of these skills to new problems. Our observations of the problem-solving behavior of recent graduates of one USAADASCH training program, and comparison to expert technicians, show that recent school graduates are particularly deficient in the knowledge needed to organize the many separate facts learned. Such organizing concepts are mainly acquired through experience, and are therefore exhibited only by the more experienced radar mechanics (see Tenney & Kurland, chapter 3, this volume).

The Current Program of Instruction

The USAADASCH program of instruction for MOS 24C occupies a total training interval of 39 weeks. Twenty weeks, or approximately one-half of this period, is devoted to training specific to the HAWK air defense system. Major elements of the HAWK system covered include the radar, the launcher, and the loader. Eight weeks are devoted to detailed study of the HIPIR. The content of the radar course is organized to cover overall system operation as well as the operation of each subsystem.

Instruction of 24C trainees at USAADASCH in HIPIR organizational maintenance is supported by four classes of nonadministrative personnel: technical writers, conference instructors, platform instructors, and equipment maintenance staff. It is not uncommon for individuals to work in several of these groups during a tour of duty at USAADASCH; however, the platform instructors and equipment maintenance staff are military personnel, and the majority of the conference instructors are civilian employees of the Army.

The technical writers are responsible for creation and maintenance of the lesson plans and associated materials supporting the 24C program of instruction. The conference instructors conduct lectures about radar, circuit, and maintenance theory for groups of about sixteen 24C trainees. The platform instructors work with the actual radar equipment to demonstrate correct troubleshooting procedures and to assist students in hands-on troubleshooting. Groups of eight 24C trainees work on a single unit. The equipment maintenance staff are responsible for repair of the radars used by the platform instructors. They constantly test the equipment to assure that it contains no faults other than ones that the platform instructors deliberately introduce for training purposes. At times they are called in to discover and correct a fault inserted for training purposes that was improperly documented or unsuccessfully removed.

The instruction presented in conference is essentially a walk-through of the entire HIPIR documentation set. This walk-through not only includes basic nomenclature, radar organization, radar operation, and routine maintenance checks, but also extends to a full presentation of all standard troubleshooting procedures and a detailed discussion of the operation of all circuits of the HIPIR.

Because the theory presented in many of these lectures is very detailed and presumes a good grasp of radar system function, much of it is not well understood by the majority of the 24C trainees. Job performance may not be seriously affected by this lack of comprehension, because the 24C trainee is not authorized or qualified to repair the HIPIR at the component level dealt with in the most detailed part of these lectures. However, the absence of any need to understand the radar at the level of detail presented in many of the lectures may be demotivating to some 24C trainees.

The instruction presented in the platform exercises affords the 24C trainee an opportunity to attempt fault diagnosis and correction on an actual radar. Within each instructional unit, a number of possible system faults have been identified that can be easily induced in the HIPIR. The platform instructor inserts one of these faults into a radar and then guides the 24C trainee through its detection, isolation, and correction. Because the faults are necessarily limited to defects that will not seriously damage the radar, and that can be easily inserted and removed, the 24C training experience is somewhat unrealistic. Further, groups of eight trainees work on the radar at one time, and the individual opportunity to learn by doing is very limited.

Goals of the Instruction

The current training program has four important goals, each of which is thought essential to future job performance of the 24C.

Nomenclature. The program of instruction familiarizes the 24C trainee with the nomenclature, terminology, and physical layout of the radar. He or she learns to identify the major functional parts of the radar in terms of their correct names and positions within the HIPIR. The trainee also learns the decomposition of the functional parts into replaceable components.

Documentation. The 24C trainee learns the organization and use of the various technical manuals that support HIPIR operation and maintenance. He or she learns the representation of the functional parts and replaceable components of the radar in the documentation and becomes familiar with the applicability of the various elements of the documentation to different phases of the operation, maintenance, and troubleshooting process. He or she is instructed in the use of the documentation to identify a faulted component or connection or to determine the need for adjustment of a subsystem.

Procedures. The 24C trainee learns how to operate the HIPIR for the purpose of performing routine checks and adjustments. He or she learns to power up the radar through various standby states, and power it down. He or she learns to observe indications of proper radar operation, and to take appropriate corrective action. The trainee learns to perform system and subsystem tests using the automatic BITE and related equipment and to replace failed components as indicated.

Conceptual framework. The 24C trainee acquires more than just a general familiarity with the HIPIR layout and its operation and maintenance. Ideally, he or she also gains some understanding of the way the equipment achieves its purpose, that is, how the design of the radar explains its functionality. Such an understanding (or mental model) of the way the radar works can be used to organize and interpret future experiences. The completeness, consistency, and accuracy of this mental model, together with the 24C trainee's ability to expand and correct it as needed, will strongly affect his or her ability to learn from experience on the job and to progress to expert status as a radar mechanic.

Implications for MACH-III Design

The emphasis in the current program of instruction is on the first three goals. Given this emphasis, the most obvious problem confronting the current program is a lack of opportunity for hands-on experience. As pointed out earlier, a given 24C trainee will spend only a limited time actually trying to fix a radar, whereas the set of problems he or she may get to solve is a relatively small, and not necessarily representative, sample of the problems faced in the field. Allowing the 24C trainee more opportunity to gain experience in practical problem solving is therefore an important goal of the MACH-III project.

A more fundamental problem faced by the 24C trainee is the lack of a clear model to tie his or her experience and knowledge together. Although the students are given an overview of the main functional components of the radar, there is no systematic and unified story presented to organize all the diverse facts, principles, heuristics, and skills that are being taught. Developing such a story is generally difficult, and especially so for the HAWK HIPIR. It should strike a balance between listing specifics, without given any underlying principles, and presenting principles without specifying how they apply in a particular case. Such a story is also hard to devise because of the large choice of perspectives from which it may be told.

In the case of the HIPIR, at least two very different, although not unrelated, perspectives have been derived by careful analysis: an informational one, from which the radar is presented as a kind of computer, processing (target) information, and an electrical one, from which the radar is presented as a complex electronic device processing electromagnetic signals. Whereas the first perspective is useful to present the various functions of the radar and give a general idea of the constraints on the actual hardware, the second perspective is needed to make sense of the actual troubleshooting procedures to be learned. Although in the design phase a faulty device might have to be analyzed for functional faults, that is, for faults in the design, the only faults relevant in maintenance of existing equipment are faults in the various components implementing this design.

The choice of correct perspective and level of detail is guided by the ultimate purpose of the story one is trying to tell. The purpose of training the 24Cs is to prepare them to keep the radar working correctly. This means that they should be able to identify incorrectly working radars, to diagnose the problem and to take the right corrective action. Large parts of this task have been automated, or at least codified. There are explicitly spelled-out check routines, there is built-in test equipment to indicate the general problem area and corrective action, and there are explicitly spelled-out procedures to find the precise action to take, given the BITE's general indications. If these various job aids were complete and correct, one might argue that the 24C trainee just needs to know how to perform these procedures, that is, to identify the various items mentioned in them, and to actually perform the prescribed actions. Because the job aids are not complete, and not always correct, the 24C trainee does need more knowledge to enable him or her to devise his or her own troubleshooting procedure when left stranded by the ones available.

Given this need, MACH-III should concentrate on reconstructing the fundamental functional organization of the HAWK radar and the rationale underlying the various troubleshooting procedures. This concentration will guide the construction of an environment in which the student can explore and troubleshoot the radar "in principle," that is, in which he or she can learn to decide when and why to apply a particular test or replacement. How to apply these procedures, in terms of the actual adjustments and manipulations involved, will receive much less emphasis.

BACKGROUND

The MACH-III prototype development effort is intended to produce a prototype training device of demonstrable value to the 24C training program. This value will ultimately be reflected in improved job performance by new 24C graduates. We believe this objective can best be achieved by designing the MACH-III to provide augmented hands-on experience in reasoning about troubleshooting in a setting that will emphasize development of the fourth area of course content described above, the development of a sound conceptual framework to use in classifying and interpreting future experience. We firmly believe that, in order to acquire such a framework, the student needs to be able to interact with a system that provides more than merely the correct symptoms and measurements. In addition to a simulation of the radar, we need an articulate expert, that is, a simulation of the way an expert would reason about the radar, both to explain its working and predict its behavior, and to show how to troubleshoot the radar.

Computers can be used in several ways to support the two goals of more practical training and better understanding of how the radar works. One approach would be to focus on providing the student with a realistic environment in which to experiment with trouble-shooting representative problems. This is basically the approach followed by most of the current simulation and training systems in use by the Army. These systems provide the student with a (realistic) mock-up of a cockpit, or a (less realistic) layout of the piece of equipment to be repaired, and use a numerical simulation to give realistic feedback to the actions (operations, measurements) taken by the student. Many would agree that such a training system should be primary, and that the goal of acquiring a better understanding should be secondary: With a good training system, students will be able to learn by doing, using whatever information they have available (in the form of manuals, diagrams, and instruction materials) to organize their experiences into an understanding of the domain. In this form of training instructors provide some background and try to coach the students when they are working on problems.

In Intelligent CAI, the computer is also used to directly assist in instruction and coaching. The most straightforward way of doing this is to structure the knowledge to be transmitted into small chunks (concepts, knowledge units) and use associated tests to schedule their presentation dynamically. However, this works only for cases where the knowledge to be taught is static and declarative and the problems used to test whether the student has acquired a given piece of this knowledge are fairly simple and factual. When the goal is to teach procedural knowledge, for example, medical diagnosis or electrical troubleshooting, the system itself should be capable of solving the problems and, in addition, of showing how it solves them and why it does it in that way.

The first condition is, by definition, satisfied by all successful expert systems that have been developed for diagnosis and trouble-shooting. However, the other two conditions are much harder to satisfy. Most troubleshooting systems developed within AI have emphasized relatively shallow reasoning strategies. Typically, they directly encode the associational or empirical rules that permit an expert to proceed directly from observing symptoms to hypothesizing faults. This shallowness is intentional. A motivating idea behind the development of expert systems is that one should not try to reason from first principles, but instead use the many inferential leaps that experts have found to be useful after many years of practice.

Although highly successful in specific applications, this pragmatic approach is not very useful when the system is meant to do more than just solve a well-circumscribed set of problems. When the system is expected to explain its reasoning, a deeper knowledge is required. For instance, the MACH-III system should be able to explain why, in a particular troubleshooting situation, it checks for the presence or absence of certain symptoms. The answer to this question should contain both the rationale behind the particular symptoms-to-fault rule it is considering and the reason for considering that rule at this point during troubleshooting. The explanation of the rule will have to refer to the way the particular device works. The explanation for the use of a rule at a given point requires reference to the troubleshooting strategy being followed.

Good explanation is needed mainly for education (and perhaps for convincing reluctant users of the correctness of the system's reasoning). Another reason to look beyond the mere correlation of symptoms and faults and to try to capture the underlying mechanisms explaining these correlations, is the need to make troubleshooting systems more robust, that is, capable of dealing with situations that have not been foreseen by the experts generating the rules. In research dealing with this need for a richer knowledge representation, two different approaches can be distinguished. The first can be characterized as an attempt to elaborate the classification model, to enrich the representation of the diagnostic rules by distinguishing the various types of knowledge they reflect (definitional, strategic, causal, etc.) and by organizing them in networks that make explicit the relations between the rules, the general faults, the specific symptoms, and the causes. The second approach tries to develop runnable models of the particular devices to be diagnosed, to build simulations. Diagnosis is just one possible use of these general device models.

Classification Models

Troubleshooting radar equipment can be seen as an example of classification. A set of symptoms has to be classified as a particular fault, that is, as belonging to the set of symptoms associated with that fault. If all symptoms for each fault were known in advance, and if the description of the system to be diagnosed were complete, this would be a straightforward, although possibly time-consuming, pattern-matching task. However, neither condition is fulfilled in most real-life cases of diagnosis. Not all possible faults (not all of their symptoms) are known in advance, and, even more important, the initial description (set of symptoms) is almost always incomplete. Therefore, reasoning is needed to extend both the problem description and the fault models in such a way as to focus in on the solution as quickly as possible. This reasoning can follow different directions. The initial set of symptoms might indicate a general fault, which restricts the set of more specific faults to look at. The initial set of symptoms may allow the deduction of additional symptoms. A candidate fault will point to additional symptoms to look for. A set of candidate faults can be used to derive a differential test.

Research on classification models (e.g., Clancey, 1983, 1985) aims to clarify the different types of knowledge used in this reasoning, and thereby create diagnostic systems that are easier to build, maintain, explain and teach. Models are built that distinguish the different types (symptoms, faults, causes, general strategies, specific heuristics) and their relations (definitional, causal, etc.). This should allow a diagnostic system to distinguish, for instance, the general principle of a differential diagnosis from its specific instantiations in a particular session or domain. How the systems to be diagnosed work (when working correctly or when broken) is generally not made explicit, at least not in the sense of being able to describe the actual process and predict the consequences of different inputs or settings of parameters. The causal relations in such models are mostly of an implicational nature: "X being broken causes Y to be broken" most often means "if X is broken, then Y will also be broken," not that "X breaks before Y breaks." There are often good reasons for this lack of attention to how the device works: In natural systems (e.g. the human body), diagnostic knowledge exceeds our knowledge of how they work. In man-made systems, much of the knowledge of how the thing "really" works is irrelevant for effective troubleshooting.

However, when it is possible to formalize the mechanisms embodied in a given device, the product of general troubleshooting strategies applied to such general formalizations could lead to much more powerful (and even "cleaner") diagnostic systems. This is the model-based approach discussed in the next subsection.

Model-Based, Qualitative Reasoning

A large body of work on reasoning about devices is beginning to emerge (e.g., Bobrow, 1985, Chandrasekaran & Milne, 1985). The fundamental question in this research is how the behavior of a (faulted) device is related to and arises from its structure. Answering this question in a machine-reproducible form requires the formalization of the causal accounts given by engineers, that is, the development of a qualitative or common-sense physics. The noncausal framework of mathematical physics, in which system behavior is described by the values of its variables at each time instant, is rejected because it does not provide insight in how a system works. It leaves implicit the concepts used by people to explain the workings of a system (e.g., cause, feedback, oscillation), which make it very hard to generate explanations that are grounded in the commonsense physics encountered in our daily lives. It also makes it impossible to reach reasonable conclusions when certain parameters are missing. Reasoning with incomplete knowledge is crucial for troubleshooting.

To overcome these problems, this research attempts to formalize a style of rational exposition termed *qualitative reasoning*. This term is applied because such reasoning is not based on quantitative (numerical) relationships, but on constraints between qualitative changes in the state of the components. (e.g., "If the voltage across a resistor increases, the current is also increased"; "If the temperature of a gas in a closed vessel increases, its pressure will rise.") This kind of reasoning not only captures the intuitiveness needed for explanations of how things work, but also works with little and even incomplete information, (Forbus, 1984).

Several systems have been built that can generate qualitative accounts of the behavior of a system on the basis of device models (general descriptions of the components and their behavior) and their connectivity. As deKleer and Brown (1984) point out, devices show two different behaviors: intrastate and interstate. Within a state, each of a composite device's components remains in the same state and all its variables keep changing in the same way. Between states one or more components change state, and the state variables may change in different directions. Interstate behavior can be modeled in a state diagram, but intrastate behavior requires the introduction of some order to the way a new equilibrium is calculated. To this end they introduce the notion of mythical time and a set of heuristics for propagating the calculation in a way that captures (mythical) causation.

This capability to generate a causal account is fundamental to explanation and prediction, both of correct and faulty devices. Other uses are simulation and diagnosis. Simulation places stricter demands on the way the causal account is constructed. It is desirable for the reasoning process itself to simulate the behavior of the device. This requires the reasoning to take place as if it were in the device itself, instead of being handled by some external reasoner. The components, in such a view become special-purpose information processors with only local access to their direct neighbors, instantiating local constraints specifying component behavior.

In troubleshooting or diagnosis, the problem is to infer structural changes from erroneous behavior. Sometimes symptoms will be specific enough to point directly to particular faults. These are the cases handled accurately by current expert systems for troubleshooting. Only a few systems are able to handle the more complicated case in which the initial symptoms allow a set of very general fault hypotheses among which the system must distinguish by a process of differential diagnosis. An example of a medical diagnosis system capable of such diagnosis is CASNET (Weiss, Kulikowski, Amarel, & Safir, 1978). This system uses causal relations between symptoms and hypotheses to find the most discriminating tests; however, these causal links are part of its knowledge and not derived from more fundamental principles of anatomy and physiology.

Unless the system disposes of complete, precompiled knowledge of the tests for each of the possible hypotheses (in which case the discriminating test might be derived by comparing those tests), the system will have to engage in backward reasoning to find the structural changes that could have accounted for the observed faulty behavior. By using qualitative reasoning to predict other faulty behavior given these changes, discriminating tests can be derived. This is the approach followed by Davis (1984) and Genesereth (1984). The work of Davis and associates is particularly interesting in that it tries to combine heuristics and general approaches to troubleshooting in a principled way. An algorithmic solution to finding faulty components (in their case an iteration of simulation, dependency-directed backtracking, and consistency checking via constraint suspension) is dependent on a number of underlying assumptions: localized failure, single failure, consistent failure, correct schematics, and so on. Davis and Genesereth see these assumptions as restricting the number of possible pathways of causation and suggest an ordering of these assumptions that allows the troubleshooter to relax these restrictions systematically and in an empirically defensible way.

It is unlikely that this or similar approaches can be used without modification in the MACH-III system. One difficulty arises from the much greater complexity and diversity of the HIPIR. In digital devices the "stuff" flowing between components can always be treated as numbers at all levels of analysis. In the HIPIR, the "stuff" is essentially multidimensional, simultaneously including such attributes as signal level, signal bandwidth, carrier frequency, level and class of noise, and phase relationship to a reference standard. A system such as SOPHIE, which follows a more pragmatic approach, is probably a better example of what will be achievable within this project.

SOPHIE (Brown, Burton, & deKleer, 1982) combines local propagation of ranges of numerical values with qualitative rules that infer possible modes of behavior for the various components on the basis of their device models. This general knowledge is augmented with circuit-specific knowledge that captures the causal relations needed for troubleshooting. This knowledge is represented in two forms. It is represented first as behavior trees that relate the modes of behavior of components to that of modules (aggregates of components or "lower" modules). Second, it is represented in the form of state-to-state rules that relate behavior modes of modules to neighboring modules. The latter relation is causal in the interactive sense, whereas the former relation is akin to implication (e.g., "If this module is faulty, this will be because one of its components is behaving in a faulty way.")

In MACH-III the qualitative simulation will drive the animation. Such a direct coupling of simulation and animation with the causal reasoning is different from the approach followed in Steamer (Williams, Hollan, & Stevens, 1981; Hollan, Hutchins, & Weitzman, 1984) in which separate numerical simulation is used to drive the animation. In the latter approach one needs to rephrase the numerical model in qualitative terms in order to generate explanations. In such an architecture it is very difficult to keep a close coupling between the qualitative reasoning and the quantitative simulation, especially when introducing faults. We can use the qualitative simulation to drive an animation, because the animation is not primarily intended as a realistic mimicry of the radar, but as a graphical illustration of an interpretation (a mental model) of what is happening in the radar. Obviously the student will have to learn to relate this interpretation to actual physical aspects of the radar, that is, to lights, meters, switches, and so on. Control panels will therefore be simulated as accurately as possible. However, the precise indications of panel devices such as volt meters will be based somewhat arbitrarily[3] on the qualitative signal values used by the simulation.

OVERVIEW OF MACH-III DESIGN

The MACH-III system will be an intelligent tutoring system centering on instruction in the diagnosis and correction of faults in the AN/MPQ-57 HIPIR radar of the HAWK air defense system. The approach to instruction will emphasize the development within the 24C trainee of a useful mental model of the organization, function, and operation of the radar and its various components, through guided practice in simulated troubleshooting activities. Development emphasis lies primarily in the areas of system simulation, explanation generation, and representation of expert troubleshooting knowledge.

MACH-III will be a stand-alone tabletop training device, suitable for use in individual or classroom settings. Because MACH-III will offer the 24C trainee virtually unlimited access to HIPIR simulations in normal and faulted modes, without the need to use actual radar equipment, it can be applied in the existing program of instruction to increase the quantity of quality of "near-hands-on" experience available to the 24C trainee.

MACH-III will function as a two-dimensional training device, providing diagrammatic representations of HIPIR controls, indicators, components, interconnections, and organization. As such, the primary focus of MACH-III training will be on the cognitive processes that support effective troubleshooting, and not as much on the physical actions associated with actual equipment repair. For example, a student will be able to give instructions to the trainer such as "Disconnect plug P1" or "Replace card A4 with a good unit," without having to perform the physical task described or to describe its method of performance in detail.

The user/student will interact directly with diagrams. The kind of interactions supported will depend on the mode. There will be three global modes: an exploratory mode, in which the student can inspect all the knowledge available to the simulation and in which the diagrams will directly reflect the signal flow; a show mode, in which the MACH-III troubleshooting expert will solve selected faults; and a troubleshooting mode, in which the student will have to repair faults inserted by the instructor and for which the student will have

---

[3]Most qualitative values will correspond to some range or type of indications (e.g., "peak in the blue zone").

to repair faults inserted by the instructor and for which the student will only have access to the types of information available in real life.

Results of cognitive studies that inform the design of MACH-III are presented in the report of Tenney and Kurland, (chapter 3, this volume). Interpretation of these studies, analyses of the instructional problem, and plans for instructional design of the MACH-III interactive experience are reported in Kurland and Tenney, (chapter 5, this volume). These companion chapters should be consulted for a full exposition of these parts of the MACH-III design, which are treated briefly in the following overview.

Cognitive Background. Research in cognitive science indicates that an expert's knowledge of complex systems differs significantly from that of a novice. Specifically, experts have relatively accurate and complete mental models of system operation, function, and interconnection, which support their knowledge and application of troubleshooting procedures. In addition, experts display an understanding of the functioning of a system at different levels of aggregation, ranging from the broad functional level to the level of specificity actually required on the job. The results of experiments we have conducted at USAADASCH indicate that 24C trainees do not acquire substantially effective mental models during their brief period of training on the HIPIR, although some 24Cs eventually succeed in acquiring such models with increasing periods of experience on the job. In a series of interviews about how the radar works, we have found that novice 24Cs focus on physical aspects of the radar and emphasize the distribution of power through the system. Experts, on the other hand, talk about functional aspects of the radar and emphasize the flow of information. The expert's model facilitates the job of interpreting symptoms and narrowing down possible fault locations. The limited conceptual understanding of the radar demonstrated by students appears to arise from the limited time available for hands-on work diagnosing faulty radar operation during the platform exercises and the focus of these exercises on the physical organization and assembly of the radar. MACH-III will attempt to remediate this deficiency by affording 24C trainees the opportunity to practice troubleshooting skills on a HIPIR simulation that is organized to emphasize the functional structure of the radar system. When the MACH-III trainer is integrated into the 24C Program of Instruction (POI) it will become the principal vehicle for practical development of cognitive skills required for troubleshooting. The program of platform exercises can then be more aptly focused on transference of these skills to the physical equipment and training in equipment assembly, alignment, and disassembly.

Instructional Design. MACH-III is conceived as a supplementary training device that supports, but does not fully attempt to substitute for, other parts of the 24C POI. 24C trainees will receive a brief orientation to MACH-III early in their course of instruction and will perform exercises on MACH-III in conjunction with each instructional segment of the POI. MACH-III will support the POI by providing an inspectable symbolic simulation of HIPIR operation at various levels of component aggregation. The simulation will reproduce patterns of faulty HIPIR operation associated with specific faults defined at the level of Battery Replaceable Units (BRUs), and smoothly reflect the effects of these faults on major functions and subsystems of the radar. Inspection of the simulation will be controlled by an articulate expert. It will demonstrate, guide, and monitor the student's progress in the various activities that support effective troubleshooting, such as observation, correlation, diagnosis, and corrective action. Troubleshooting expertise embodied in this system will be based on practical maintenance doctrine derived from consultations with experienced 24Cs, standard procedures documented in HIPIR technical manuals, and formal inferencing procedures generally applicable to the systems.

Many important issues relating to the instructional design of MACH-III lie in the area of the man–machine interface. The experience of the trainee will necessarily be very different with MACH-III than in the platform exercises. The MACH-III human interface will not require the trainee to master unusual skills that will impede transference of the training to operational equipment. In general, the MACH-III visual presentations will be diagrammatic and symbolic. Because the 24C trainee will ultimately have to work with existing HIPIR documentation, no systems of designation or description will be used that conflict with this material. On the other hand, it is desirable to extend the presentation style of the technical manuals to achieve worthwhile instructional goals, as long as care is taken to avoid creating a permanent reliance on these extensions. MACH-III presentations will utilize color graphics extensively to augment the two-dimensional presentation of the system. We are currently working with Symbolics 36 40 workstations equipped with a 9 bit plane color system with approximately 1000x1000 pixel resolution.

Complex System Simulation

A simulation model of the HIPIR is central to the MACH-III tutoring system. This simulation is intended to serve two purposes. First, it provides a picture of the radar and its operation as they appear to the 24C radar mechanic. Second, it presents this information in a way that reflects the functional perspective on radar organization and operation that we wish the 24C trainee to acquire (see Kurland and Tenney, chapter 5, this volume). In systems such as Steamer, the first goal is achieved by means of a numerical simulation, whereas the second goal is achieved by having a separate symbolic representation of the device, which is used by an articulate expert module to reason about the device and generate explanations. In our approach, one underlying representation is used to support both functions. In addition to simulation of the correctly functioning HIPIR, this representation should support simulations of the various fault modes. We have discussed research that attempts to deal with this by designing reasoning mechanisms for deducing behavior from structure (and, conversely, predicting structure from behavior) in a very general way. This effort has only begun, and it seems too early to try to apply these ideas to a system as diverse and complex as the radar. Therefore, we have begun to pursue a more pragmatic approach, taking advantage of the fact that we are dealing with one particular device, about which there exists a great deal of specific knowledge concerning typical faults and effective procedures for fault isolation.

Devices

The basic element of the simulation is the *device*. A device is a functional part of the radar and is characterized by its type, its inputs, its outputs, and its state. The types are characterized by rules specifying the output(s) of devices of that type for each of their possible states and inputs. Two different states are maintained for each device: its *repair state*, that is, whether it is in working order or in one of a predefined set of faulty states, and its *internal state*, to indicate the functional state of the device, for example, whether a switch is open or closed. Device types are used to capture what is common in the behavior of different devices. An example of a device type is an *adjuster*, a device that changes some aspect of its main input under the control of its secondary input.

Some devices are complex; they have parts that are themselves (possible complex) devices. Although all devices ultimately consist of one or more physical components, only some devices correspond directly to replaceable modules, that is, to physical parts of the radar that the mechanic needs to be able to identify and replace. Some devices are subcomponents of replaceable modules, whereas others are composites of (parts of) several replaceable modules. The introduction of devices is solely governed by the need for an adequate and coherent decomposition of the radar in terms that can be used for a reasonable justification of the troubleshooting procedures.

The receiver provides a good example of the discrepancies between the obvious physical decomposition and the actually needed functional decomposition. The physical layout of the receiver is shown schematically in Figure 5.4 of Kurland and Tenney (chapter 5, this volume). The physical components can, of course, each be given a functional role within the receiver. However, these roles would be extremely complex to specify and would hide the much more natural functional breakdown shown in Figure 5.3 of Kurland and Tenney. The basic function of the radar receiver is the development of an accurate video image of the target containing range, radial velocity, azimuth, and elevation information. To this end, the received target reflection has to be amplified and compared with the transmitted signal, while removing unwanted noise caused by reflections off other objects (buildings, mountains). To remove unwanted reflections *(feedthrough)*, these two signals are amplified in what we have called *cancellation loops,* feedback devices that remove certain properties (in this case feedthrough) by canceling them. To do this, such a device needs a carrier with similar properties that can be inverted (in this case by a 180 degrees phase shift), a way of determining how much of the unwanted property is present in the output signal, and, using that, a way of controlling the amount of canceling signal to be mixed with its input. In the receiver, this type is instantiated twice, in the Side Feedthrough Nulling Loop and in the Main Feedthrough Nulling Loop. Both use the transmitter reference signal as the canceling signal, and both use a low-pass filter on their output signal to determine the amount of feedthrough present. The elements of these feedback loops are distributed over two boxes, the Receiver IF and the Frequency Converter. In other words, these loops are not implemented by a unique and separate physical component of their own.

Behaviors

As indicated by the above description of cancellation loops, the simulation consists of two different hierarchies: a type hierarchy capturing the (behavioral) similarities and differences between the various types of devices, and a part–whole hierarchy representing the way complex devices consist of more basic devices. The type hierarchy allows devices of a given type to inherit the behaviors of its more general ancestors. For example, wires and waveguides are both a kind of *connector* and, as such, simply propagate their input signals when in correct working order. However, they differ in their behavior when faulty. Whereas wires can be open, shorted, or noisy, waveguides can be "dirty" (e.g., because of condensation) and thereby cause arcing.

For each combination of repair and internal state, a device can have many rules. These rules are either exclusive (i.e., only one is applicable in each state) or inclusive (any number may be applicable in a given state). MACH-III allows these rules to be specified in a straightforward format. It knows how to combine the various behaviors inherited by a more specific type, and how to present the resulting combined behavior to the student in quasi-natural language, keeping track of which device type contributed which parts of the final behavior. The left-hand side of a rule consists of the repair state, the internal state, and signals present at the various input terminals; the right-hand side specifies the signals to be put on the outputs. Right-hand sides can also be used to specify the beginning or end of an action to be performed when the device is simulated. Examples of such actions are running a BITE test or performing an adjustment. An action always changes the internal state of a device (and in addition may put some signals on specific terminals), after which the simulation is restarted and used to propagate any changes this may have caused. So the actual action is specified in the rules. By keeping actions thus restricted, it remains possible to use general methods to present these actions in understandable terms to the students.

Complete behaviors are currently only specified for the lowest level devices, that is, those devices that do not contain parts. Although this is enough to be able to run the simulation, it does not allow concise explanations of the system behavior in terms of the behavior of more complex devices. The behavior of loops could, for instance, be specified by rules directly relating the inputs and outputs of the loop as a whole. This could be used to provide high-level process overviews before explaining the detailed steps.[4]

Terminals and Connections

The topology of a complex device is specified by the connections between the output and input terminals of its parts. In MACH-III these connections are represented by a shared terminal: If the Output

---

[4]Having these global behaviors available would also provide an alternative way of handling loops at the more detailed level: whenever a loop is entered, the loop as a whole is simulated to find its outputs, which are then available to stop the otherwise looping backpropagation.

of X is connected to Input 1 of Y, X and Y would both store the same terminal (i.e., the same datastructure representing that terminal) under their respective terminal names. This same terminal object can also be pointed to by other devices connected to the output of X, including any more complex devices of which Y is a part. For instance, in Figure 5.3 of Kurland and Tenney (chapter 5, this volume), the output of the Main Feedthrough Nulling Loop is also one of the outputs of the Splitter of that loop (and of course also the input to the Main Band Pass Filter).

Terminals hold the signals and know the devices of which they are a terminal. Whenever their signal changes, they indicate this to the devices for which they act as input terminal, thereby causing these devices to consider simulating themselves (which in turn may lead their output terminals to receive new signals, and so on). Terminals normally stand for some piece of wire or waveguide connecting two devices, but they can also stand for direct connections, or for more complex connecting devices that are ignored for purposes of clarity and simplicity.[5] In all cases terminals are graphically represented by pipes (in the sense of Steamer), and their signals by flow in those pipes.[6]

Signals

The radar is a signal processing device. The signals processed by the radar can be described in terms of the meaning of their informational content, that content itself, or in terms of their physical characteristics. Just as the devices in our simulation stand for physical parts with a certain function, signals simultaneously stand for the carrier, the code, and the message. Signals are represented as bundles of properties. As an example, the signal received by the antenna might be described as an RF signal containing range information, noise, jamming, and transmitter feedthrough. Devices add or remove properties, as specified in the various behavior rules.

---

[5]Until now, we have not run into the need to expand such terminals into their constituent parts. When required, to provide adequate fidelity or to support troubleshooting operations, this capability will be added.

[6]The one exception is the jack-plus-plug, which is a particular kind of direct terminal, that can be disconnected by the mechanic. In this case the attached wire(s) are represented as pipes, whereas the connectors themselves are represented by a specialized icon which consists of one box (to represent the connected state) or two boxes (to represent the disconnected state).

Running the Simulation

Running the simulation means deducing the (properties of) the signals at each of the terminals. There are two situations in which this has to be done: when starting up the radar in a given state, or when changing the state of some device in a running radar. The same propagation mechanism is used in both cases. Devices that need to be simulated are put on a stack and simulated when they are the first device on that queue at the start of a new cycle. The stack initially contains just the device that changed state, or, in the case of a re-initialization, those devices that do not require inputs (so-called producers). When all inputs to the first device on the queue are known, it is removed from the queue and simulated, that is, the appropriate behavior rules are run. When running these rules causes a terminal to receive a new signal, (that is, a signal different from its current one) this terminal adds to the queue all devices for which it is an input terminal.[7] When not all inputs are known, the devices that could provide the unknown inputs are added to the front of the queue and simulated first.

The backpropagation scheme would run into problems when dealing with loops. To handle these, the simulator checks whether the device under consideration and any of the devices to which it intends to backpropagate belong to the same loop (remember that all loops are explicitly represented as complex devices). If so, the simulator assumes that the loop is working correctly and continues with an assumed value for the terminal between the two devices belonging to the same loop. The simulator will eventually get back to this terminal, and if the assumed value turns out to be incorrect, will redo the loop once more. The simulation currently involves only the lowest level, basic devices. There is no reason why the complex devices, such as loops, could not be simulated directly, at least in the nonfaulty mode. First simulating the loop as a whole before simulating its parts would provide a slightly different way to handle loops.

Explanations

How loops are dealt with is important, because the simulation not only is used to derive the signals at the various terminals—which can then be inspected by the student and form the basis for

---

[7]These devices are added to the front of the queue if the device being simulated is in focus, and to the end if it is not. See the subsection on generating explanations.

troubleshooting—but also is used to generate a causal explanation of why signals are what they are at the various terminals. The order in which the signals are derived should therefore correspond to a plausible causal story. In general, there are multiple ways to tell such a story, and finding a good one will be a matter of trial and error. Nevertheless, a number of general characteristics can safely be postulated: The reasoning will have to be forward, generally following the signal flow; depth-first, that is, focused on the main process, with additional inputs derived when needed; and hierarchical, sketching the process in broad outline before filling in the detailed steps. Some of these restrictions on the order in which the steps of a process can be reported are a direct reflection of the sequentiality of verbal communication. In MACH-III we will rely heavily on animated diagrams. One of the advantages of these is their ability to mimic the parallel flow of signal propagation. Although this is useful (and will be used) to present the complete picture, explanation will require the simulation to single-step through the process in some sensible order.

Order of derivation is only one aspect of the explanation of a device. One needs to be able to report which rule was applied at each step and why this rule does indeed characterize the behavior of this particular device. More general questions to be answered concern the purpose of the device, how its behavior achieves that purpose, its function within some larger part, and, in the case of complex devices, how the behavior of its parts and the way they are structured combine to form a mechanism that shows the required overall behavior. Although we do expect our system to be capable of answering some of these questions in a principled way, much of this knowledge will have to be stored in a predetermined form. Behavior of complex devices will be derivable from the behavior of their parts, but purpose and function of devices, and explanations of the way basic devices achieve their purpose, will have to be stored explicitly.

One way to explain how something works is to reconstruct the design process used in creating the device. Beginning with the purpose to be fulfilled by the device, state the basic idea or principle to be used to achieve this purpose. Then, identify the subgoals established by this principle and elaborate the method for achieving each of them, where this is not obvious. By repeatedly applying this process of progressive refinement, and by testing the quality of the resulting explanation against the perceptions of a suitable target audience, it is possible to converge toward an acceptable presentation. For example, to explain *feedthrough,* one could start by describing the problem (reflections off nearby objects and direct spillover) and pointing out that what we have here is a problem of wanting to get rid of something.

One way of getting rid of something is by *cancellation,* that is, by adding its inverse (adding sugar to compensate for sourness, adding minus 3 to subtract 3, etc.). Because the amount to add will vary over time, this calls for a kind of cancellation loop—a feedback loop that tunes the amount added to the amount needed. Having thus reduced the goal of feedthrough nulling to the cancellation loop function, the next step is to instantiate this function: What is the appropriate "inverted" stuff to add to the "dirty" signal, and how can the amount be controlled? Because the problem is caused by unwanted transmitter signal, we can take a sample of that signal as our source of stuff to mix in. To get cancellation of the feedthrough component in the dirty signal, we shift the phase of the sample 180 degrees in relation to the feedthrough, while making the amplitude equal to that of the feedthrough. The feedthrough is determined after amplification and detection.[8]

An important goal of this project is the development of representations that support easy specification of the various types of knowledge needed, and that free the instructor/system builder of the need to literally specify the way in which these questions should be answered by incorporating general methods for generating presentations based on these representations. Current interface technology allows these presentations to be much more than mere pieces of text. Bidirectional pointers can be maintained between words (or larger pieces of text) and their corresponding icons in the graphical displays or between different pieces of information, allowing the user/ student very flexible ways of accessing and searching for information.

Troubleshooting

There is no single, correct approach to troubleshooting the HIPIR. Practical troubleshooting involves a number of different strategies. As pointed out in our practical troubleshooting doctrine, a number of problems are very specific to the radar and its particular site. Checking for these specific problems seems to be a matter of the straightforward application of symptom-fault rules. Such rules might

---

[8]Obviously this explanation can be expanded almost indefinitely: The determination is done using a (pair of) low-pass filters, so one could continue to explain why low-pass filters are used, why two, and so on. This would be needed if one wants to justify the two cables that are used to implement the control branch of the cancellation loop. Alternatively one could stop before that when one decided that adding this further detail would not really add anything to the student's capability to troubleshoot. In this case the student would just have to accept that this particular branch of the loop is using two cables instead of one.

be augmented by an explanation for their applicability. For example, certain climates cause severe condensation, and this water can enter the transmitter waveguide to cause predictable malfunctions.

A second skill required for effective troubleshooting is the application of routine (daily and weekly) check procedures and recognition of the various indications these can yield. Finding the right procedure to perform in case of a particular indication is straightforward, because it is indicated in the check procedure, and involves either an adjustment or a module replacement. Adjustment involves the coordination of manipulative and observational skills that are better taught by performing the task on the actual equipment. Before that experience, however, it will be useful to let the student assess the need for such an adjustment on a simulation of relevant aspects of the radar. This simulation should know about the interdependencies that have to be taken into account when making certain adjustments.

Problems with the power supplies involve the kind of trouble-shooting taught in QUEST (White & Frederiksen, 1984, 1985). These include the use of schematics to trace paths of power/current, use of strategies such as split-half, augmented with device-specific heuristics that take into account the likelihood of a particular component being faulty, and recognition of the cost of actually checking certain modules or paths. Problems with circuitry contained within individual BRUs, such as circuit cards, call for systematic methods for board substitution.

The major problem however, is to learn to make full use of the large amount of troubleshooting knowledge written down in the FIPs, without getting lost. FIPs are, in a sense, a full specification of a troubleshooting expert, presented as a huge flowchart containing many paths with redundant steps, leaving it to the troubleshooter to decide whether a particular test has already been done and whether the results of that step are still valid. MACH-III will reconstruct and make explicit the principles and systematic reasoning underlying the FIPs. In general, a given FIP is called for when the BITE measures an incorrect value at some particular point in the radar. Except for power supply problems, this incorrect value can be caused by any upstream device. The FIP takes the mechanic through a list of candidates, without specifying the reasons particular ones are chosen in the order given. MACH-III should be able to generate those candidates and the tests needed to rule them out, both with and without taking into account constraints such as the cost of particular tests or replacements (in particular terms of time) and the probability of that particular component breaking. The FIPs are silent on this point, but are thought to be insensitive to such empirical constraints. The representation of the radar will allow the troubleshooting component of MACH-III to generate the list of potential candidates, but the best order in which to test those, and the tests to use for this purpose, will have to be specified by the instructors. We will develop a language for specifying FIPs and specify the general strategies and tests to be instantiated for each particular fault. An example of general strategy is a general approach to troubleshooting a feedback loop. An example of a general type of test is checking a wire for shorts and opens.

CONCLUSION AND STATUS REPORT

In the foregoing presentation we have explained the factors influencing our design plan for the MACH-III Intelligent Tutoring System for radar mechanics. Central to this effort has been the decision to develop a fault model of the radar based on a functional decomposition into units which correspond closely to mental models held by expert troubleshooters. The diagnosis and repair strategies applied to this model have been developed from published maintenance documents and the insights of experienced mechanics. At the same time, the fault model has been embellished by adding capabilities for generating explanations of normal and faulted system operation directly from the model. The model structure is also used to provide an organizing structure for prepared explanations of component function and purpose.

In the months that have passed since preparation and presentation of this design description we have reduced many of these concepts to practice and begun a program of formative evaluation at USAADASCH. The initial reception of the simulation, exposition, and demonstration capabilities of the system has been most favorable among the instructors at Ft. Bliss.

At the present time we are working to plan an effective point to introduce MACH-III into the POI. The potential of the system to provide a bridge between classroom instruction and hands-on work with actual equipment and to serve as a remedial tutor for selected trainees was immediately recognized by instructors. We believe a fuller appreciation of the function of MACH-III as a developer of cognitive skills of troubleshooting will appear as we complete implementation of the troubleshooting expert component.

Although we have limited consideration of applications of these concepts to specific major subsystems of the HAWK HIPIR, the principles employed in development and implementation of this system should readily extend to apply to organizational maintenance training for similar complex systems. A very large number of self-acting systems employed in the military and in industry are organized and maintained according to similar general principles.

Though MACH-III is designed as an entry-level trainer for new radar mechanics, we believe it will also be useful as a job aid for more experienced users. Our early studies reported in chapter 3 indicate that the organizing models we have employed are extant in the minds of only the most experienced mechanics. Thus, MACH-III offers the opportunity to develop a diagnostic consultant for use by the relatively large number of radar mechanics who have not acquired the ideal mental models or have acquired incorrect ones. We speculate that continued utilization of an appropriately configured MACH-III job aid not only will improve current job performance but also will hasten the development of desirable mental models.

ACKNOWLEDGMENTS

The research, design, and development activities of the HAWK MACH-III demonstration project are being performed by BBN Laboratories Inc., a wholly owned subsidiary of Bolt Beranek and Newman, Inc., under contract to the U. S. Army Research Institute for the Behavioral and Social Sciences (ARI). Significant assistance in this project is being provided by the U. S. Army Air Defense Artillery School (USAA-DASCH), Fort Bliss, Texas.

REFERENCES

Bobrow, D. G. (Ed.). (1985). *Qualitative reasoning about physical systems*. Cambridge, MA: MIT Press.

Brown, J. S., Burton, R. R., & deKleer, J. (1982). Pedagogical, natural language and knowledge-engineering techniques in SOPHIE I, II, and III. In D. Sleeman & J. S. Brown (Eds.), *Intelligent tutoring systems* (pp. 227–282). New York: Academic Press.

Chandrasekaran, G., & Milne, R. (1985, July). Reasoning about structure, behavior, and function. *ACM SIGART Newsletter, 93*, pp. 4–7.

Clancey, W. J. (1983). The epistemology of a rule-based expert system. *Artificial Intelligence, 20*(3), 215–251.

Clancey, W. J. (1985). *Heuristic classification*. Working paper, KSL 85-5. Stanford, CA: Stanford University.

Davis, R. (1984). Diagnostic reasoning based on structure and behavior. *Artificial Intelligence, 24*, 347–410.

deKleer, J., & Brown, J. S. (1984). A qualitative physics based on confluences. *Artificial Intelligence, 24*, 7–84.

Forbus, K. D. (1984). Qualitative process theory. *Artificial Intelligence, 24*, 85–168.

Genesereth, M. R. (1984). The use of design descriptions in automated diagnosis. *Artificial Intelligence, 24*, 411–436.

Weiss, S. M., Kulikowski, C. A., Amarel, S., & Safir, A. (1985, July). A model-based method for computer-aided medical decision making. *Artificial Intelligence, 11*, 145–172.

White, B. Y., & Frederiksen, J. R. (1984). Modeling expertise in reasoning and troubleshooting about simple electrical circuits. *Proceedings of the Sixth Annual Conference of the Cognitive Science Society*. Boulder, CO.

Williams, M., Hollan, J., & Stevens, A. (1981). An overview of STEAMER: An advanced computer assisted instructional system for propulsion engineering. *Behavior Research Methods and Instrumentation, 13*(2), 85–90.

Intelligent Tutoring Architectures

Joseph Psotka
Army Research Institute
L. Dan Massey
B. B. N. Laboratories
Sharon A. Mutter
Catholic University

The previous sections have offered a tantalizing view of the diversity and variety of components that may need to be integrated into a working ITS. Implementing such an architecture is an exquisite exercise in compromise. The potential constraints are manifold: speed, power, resilience, and portability of the computational environment; skill, patience, time pressures, and expertise of the learner; diversity of the user population; size of the knowledge domain and problem sets; need for updating and maintaining the ITS; skill levels to be trained; degree of overlearning required; usefulness of adjunct media, video, sound, or even physical mockups and simulators. The list can easily be extended and is extraordinarily long. It should be quite clear that prescriptive statements about combining these components are really quite premature. Until a greater number of working ITS exist and are cleanly described and assessed, judgments about how to form the architecture of ITS will be varied.

Tutoring Control Strategies

The most complex challenge to developing an ITS arises with the creation of a component that models the student in order to control the presentation of instruction. Some of the difficulties attendant on the enterprise have been examined by Wilkins, Clancey, and Buchanan (chapter 9). The fundamental problem is that the action of mediating experts must be guided by a thorough understanding of the knowledge domain, particularly the trainee's version of that domain. Given the computational complexity of maintaining even modest knowledge bases, the additional burden of indexing this knowledge with the peculiar misconceptions and bugs of a large group of novices is often unwieldy. In the place of such computational burdens, effective shortcuts must often be taken. One set of techniques available is judicious use of direct questions and menu systems that indirectly offer information about a student's plans, expectations, and bugs. This is yet another example of the enormous computational burden that can be relieved by a well-designed human interface. It is the essential ingredient of the approach adopted by Bonar and Cunningham (chapter 16) and Feurzeig and Ritter (chapter 15).

It is clear that understanding human–computer interaction and interface issues is critical to the development of good working ITS, and it is also clear that we have a long way to go before this is a scientifically advanced field (Frye, Littman, & Soloway, chapter 17). Even simple interfaces are not well understood, and the more complex interfaces provided in this section lie at the apex of our computational and engineering capabilities. In order to provide access to very complex domains, the interface design of an ITS must be integrated throughout the system, and in some sense can be seen as virtually the entire ITS by itself. The dynamically interactive graphics system created by Towne and Munro (chapter 18) should be viewed from this perspective.

It is instructive that none of these ITS have used natural-language processing as a mechanism for creating a simple human interface. Although this technique has enormous potential, it is computationally overwhelming, and it appears that menu systems (akin in spirit to the natural language menus popularized for database retrieval (Tennant, Ross, Saenz, Thompson, & Miller, 1983) can provide much of the functionality more efficiently. The integration of natural-language processing capabilities with ITS can clearly improve on these techniques but will proceed slowly because of the high communication bandwidth of visual displays and menus, and because of the large developmental effort and cost of implementing these systems for each ITS. At the moment, the only efficient systems are semantic grammars that are intimately connected to a particular application and are not easily transferable to other tutors in different domains (Brown, Burton, & deKleer, 1982).

Theoretical Alternatives

In spite of the many difficulties remaining to resist the development of useful ITS, many lessons have been learned. The list of constraints is becoming clearer. In particular, any implementation needs to decide on the issues that affect learning itself, and working ITS are shedding increasing light on the proper alternatives that need to be selected. The alternative structures that affect learning and instruction include the following:

1. Didactic presentation of information, versus crafted microworlds that situate the learner in a reactive environment
2. Immediate feedback and error correction, versus controlled floundering and supported exploration
3. Depth-first versus breadth-first access to knowledge
4. Multiple mental models, graduated for the learner, or a single guiding model for all learners
5. Relatively abstract perspectives on the knowledge, versus concrete instantiations that can be manipulated directly
6. Knowledge structured in simple trees, versus complex networks
7. Composition of media: the information loading of graphics, audio, and text

These and other dimensions to the structure of ITS are beginning to find definition in the complex ITS that are under construction. In many other cases, basic research is addressing the importance of these dimensions. The question is not whether to use one particular alternative or the other, but how to select the most appropriate form for a particular function in a particular situation. We are still far from a scientific classification of the criteria, but the directions for research are quite clear.

Pragmatic Alternatives: One Particular Case

At the meeting of the VITA conference that formed the basis for this book, Mark Miller spoke eloquently of his experiences over five years of developing an ITS for teaching Ada, the copyrighted computer language developed by the Department of Defense. The conclusions he presented are so striking that we will discuss them here as an introduction to this section.

Miller's project created the prototype of an Ada tutor. Over the five years of this continuing project's life, several spin-off products were produced: an Ada editor, standard CBI software for teaching Ada, an expert system shell, and several other software tools. The ITS itself contains many lessons that teach essential Ada concepts. It has a semantic network of concepts it wants to teach and a database that relates a student's previous programming skills to these concepts. The ITS uses this student model to select menu items in a frame-based, template-driven exercise generator that is designed to teach specific algorithms. The system makes frequent and detailed use of graphics for demonstrations to assist program understanding. It uses both dynamic and static analyses of student programs as the basis for explanations, debugging, and general advice. As a rough estimate, the project has created 150,000 lines of source code on five dedicated LISP machines in 20 person-years of effort costing about $2.5 million. In other words, this project has been extensive enough to learn many lessons, and Mark Miller was quite willing to share the insights he has derived from this experience.

General Lessons

Some of the conclusions Miller drew are necessarily specific to the development of a tutor for Ada. How much his other conclusions are affected by particular factors that are peculiar to this project is a matter of debate. Other conclusions need to be interpreted in the light of each requirement or special situation. But, given all these caveats, the conclusions stand by themselves with the conviction of an extraordinary wealth of experience behind them.

1. Building a friendly environment is just as much work as building the tutor (and about as beneficial). Create environments for learning and capitalize on the learner's strengths.
2. Use strong, domain-dependent analogies for predictive student modeling. Use dynamic analyses of student performance (such as interactive menus).
3. Use special-purpose rules, handcrafted to address particular issues, rather than fully executable expert systems to provide explanations, answers, and examples.
4. Use readily available technologies, such as expert system shells, rather than reduplicating their efforts throughout the ITS.
5. Conventional software engineering rather than AI, is at least 50% of the effort.
6. Conventional CAI and CBI must play a role. Carefully analyze the relative costs and benefits of each and use them accordingly. There is a real possibility in many instances that a CBI system that costs 20% of an ITS could provide 80% of the benefit.
7. The biggest bottleneck to creating ITS effectively is in the authoring tools. Create them first or use any generally available tools. Otherwise you may wind up reduplicating code throughout the ITS with only minor and uninteresting differences each time the code appears.

8. Ad hoc approaches are best.

9. Natural language interfaces are a diversion.

10. Prepare to deliver the tutor on PCs. With large, one-MIP machines becoming available, the ITS should be structured to use them.

11. The ITS must interface with the real-world environments: mainframes, line editors, absence of graphics, compilers, job performance aids, and so on.

12. Experience with toy systems or academic prototypes does not necessarily scale up easily into economically viable tutors.

13. Developing the exercises is still the biggest part of the work.

14. The technology base of computers and software is changing so rapidly at the leading edge of these efforts, that as much effort may be expended in keeping up with these changes as in developing the ITS. However, if the changes are not maintained, the ITS can suffer from "extreme bitrot" and will not function on any viable computer. This is as true for academic prototypes as it is for commercial products.

Obviously, some of these general lessons are contradictory if they are taken too broadly. For instance, authoring tools are simply and largely not available for creating ITS. It certainly would be terrific to have them, but it is unlikely that they will appear on smaller, PC machines in the near future, so this is advice that is not readily helpful. As a whole, these lessons learned function as useful guideposts for the construction of ITS. Some of these lessons are implicit in the approaches adopted in the chapters in this section. Others will undoubtedly be relearned in the years to come.

Conclusion

Musen, Fagan, Combs, and Shortliffe (1986) draw a set of conclusions that are entirely appropriate for this volume. They make a potent argument with a graphical demonstration from their own experience with medical expert systems that expert systems of all kinds (presumably including ITS) in the long run will disappear into the environment. Implicit in this argument is a widening of the role these systems will play in everyday interactions.

Instead of just training novices, ITS may well become part of devices and appliances in the world, offering critiques when asked for help, suggesting new alternatives with explanations of the reasoning and overview of the relevant knowledge base, and even controlling the invocation of other help systems. These imbedded systems will not only provide help and dynamic instruction on issues of immediate concern, they will undoubtedly be silent servants and assistants, taking care of routine housekeeping chores and maintaining other components in proper functioning order, asking only for help when they require it. When ITS become an integrated part of the environment, their effectiveness will be strengthened in two dramatic ways. They will be able to deliver instruction when it is needed, so that the learner is fully motivated to understand it. The situated instruction can take full advantage of the local conditions of invocation to explain the reasons and conditions for all prescribed actions. In other words, an ITS embedded in the world can take on many of the strengths of a master craftsman tutoring an apprentice.

For now, this is still a vision, since most current systems are still so limited it is often easier to carry out actions manually than it is to rely on them, but as the technology becomes cheaper and more powerful the silication of more and more human instructional functions is bound to continue.

Bridge: Tutoring the Programming Process

Jeffrey G. Bonar
Robert Cunningham
Learning Research and Development Center
University of Pittsburgh

I cannot really imagine any other law of thought than that our pictures should be clearly and unambiguously imaginable.

—L. Boltzmann, 1897

INTRODUCTION

Our goal is a complete development and tutorial environment for novice programmers. Not only should the tutor find and report student conceptual errors, but it should also understand student designs and partially complete programs. The tutor should provide and teach a language, or languages, that allow a student to talk about his or her designs and partial work. In addition, the tutor should take into account what we know about the cognitive processes of novice programmers. This includes errors stemming from confusion with step-by-step natural language procedures (Bonar & Soloway, 1985), incorrectly merged goals and plans (Spohrer, Soloway, & Pope, 1985), and losses in student working memory (Anderson & Jeffries, 1985).

Current programming tutors fall short as such a complete tutorial environment. The PROUST system (Johnson, 1986) acts as a consultant for the novice programmer, examining potentially buggy novice code and reconstructing the reasoning that might have led to the novice's errors. The PROUST system performs a sophisticated diagnosis of student errors but is limited in that it cannot have a rich interaction with the student. The LISP tutor developed by

Anderson's group (Reiser, Anderson, & Farrell, 1985) is highly directive, forcing a student to proceed in a more or less top-down manner. Although the LISP tutor has been demonstrated to be useful, there is no provision for informal ideas and intermediate components not directly contained in the top-down goal decomposition.

In this paper we introduce *Bridge,* a prototype tutorial environment for novice programmers. The name comes from our intended "bridge" between novice and expert conceptions of programming. The key starting point for the thinking that led to Bridge was our attention to the relative opacity of the syntax and semantics of programming languages like PASCAL to the purpose and goals of the code. To illustrate how the programmer's goals may be obscured rather than highlighted by PASCAL, consider the goal of "keeping a count" as implemented in PASCAL:

1. *Above the loop.* A programmer must declare the variable and initialize it to zero using an assignment statement.
2. *Inside the loop.* The counter must be incremented, again using an assignment statement with the peculiar construction Count := Count + 1. This is only likely to make sense to an experienced programmer who has a clear model of how this is implemented in terms of extracting a value from a memory cell, incrementing the value, and storing the result back in the same cell.
3. *Below the loop.* A student needs to actually use the value of the counter.

In summary, the simple goal of "keeping a count" has been spread throughout the program and buried in general purpose constructs. These constructs are more closely related to the architecture of a register-based machine than to any problem actually being solved in the code.

In fact, languages like PASCAL are rooted in a register-transfer tradition of constructs and programming models. Recent research into how novices learn programming reveals that the semantics of register-transfer programming models are not at the root of novice understanding of programming. Instead, success with programming seems to be tied to a novice's ability to recognize general goals in the description of a task, and to translate those goals into actual program code (see, for example, Eisenstadt, Laubsch & Kahney, 1981; Mayer, 1979; or Soloway & Ehrlich, 1984). In Bridge, we are building a programming environment that supports a novice in working with goals. In particular, novices are supported in initial statement, subsequent refinement, and ultimate implementation of goals from a programming task. Ultimately, Bridge requires the student to translate into a standard programming language. Bridge requires this final set because we do not want to leave the student disconnected from the real-world concerns (i.e., outside of the Bridge environment) for efficiency and compatibility with standard languages. In a later section of this chapter we argue that this might not be the best approach.

Bridge allows the student to work explicitly on stating an informal initial solution, refining it, and finally translating it into the syntax of a programming language in three phases:

1. *An informal statement and refinement of the goals for the code.* The language we provide to the student is based on simple natural language phrases typically used when people write step-by-step instructions from other people.

2. *Refinement of the phase description into a series of semiformal programming plans.* Plans are schema-like structures that describe how goals are transformed into actual programming code (see Soloway & Ehrlich, 1984, for a complete description of plans). Plans typically have various roles that interrelate with the roles of other plans. So, for example, the counter plan has initialize, increment, and use roles that interact with parts of a loop. The interaction of roles is reflected in the final code for the counter being distributed throughout the program. In this phase of Bridge, students focus on relating various plan roles, but without the syntactic complexity required when relating a code representation of those roles.

3. *Translation of the plan-based description of phase 2 into actual PASCAL code.* Students are provided with a PASCAL structure editor (much like that of Chandhok, Garlan, Goldenson, Miller, & Tucker, 1985), and an interpreter with a stepping mode.

In the next section we discuss the principles upon which Bridge is built. Then we overview the current Bridge implementation, outline our experience with students using Bridge, and discuss future possibilities for Bridge.

DESIGN ISSUES FOR AN INTELLIGENT PROGRAMMING TUTOR

We begin with a discussion of the design principles used in Bridge. Although these principles do not constitute a theory of teaching programming, they are a step in that direction. We make a point of explicating these principles because they often contrast with the approach used in most programming textbooks.

Start with Informal (Natural) Specifications

A programming tutor should allow novice programmers to initially formulate their programming ideas informally, using English phrases.

The tutor should be able to understand these informal specifications and provide initial tutorial advice based on them. Our proposal for these informal specifications is based on the preprogramming experience of novice programmers and the errors that arise from this experience.

Beginning programming students have extensive experience with *step-by-step* informal (*natural*) *language* *procedures* (SSNLP). These are simple written procedures for accomplishing day-to-day procedural tasks such as getting to a friend's house, lighting an oil furnace, or assembling lawn furniture. Studies suggest that there are many regularities in the way nonprogrammers write SSNLP (Miller, 1981; Biermann, Ballard, & Sigmon, 1983; Bonar, 1986). For example, different nonprogrammers will use the same phrases to indicate looping structures and other standard programming tasks.

SSNLP has been shown to play a key role in novice programmer errors (Bonar & Soloway, 1985). Students confuse phrases in SSNLP with the English keywords of a language like PASCAL, writing the PASCAL as if it had the semantics of the corresponding SSNLP. So, for example, students write a PASCAL "while" loop expecting the demonlike semantics of "while" in English (e.g., "while the road is two lanes, keep heading north").

As the most relevant knowledge a novice brings into programming, we feel that SSNLP can be an important bridge between a novice's ideas and a final PASCAL program. Also, because many novice errors are rooted in their experience with SSNLP, allowing a student to use SSNLP gives an intelligent tutor more direct access to the misconceptions and naive models in use by the novice.

Teach About Programming Plans

Most programming texts teach students almost nothing about standard programming practice above the statement level. That there are standard concepts and techniques for implementing common tasks like running totals and array traversals is usually only covered implicitly through examples. (See Bonar, Weil, & Jones, 1986, for a collection of such concepts and techniques for introductory PASCAL programmers.) We call these "standard concepts and techniques" *programming plans*. Studies of novice programmers have shown an understanding of plans to be crucial for their success (Soloway & Ehrlich, 1984). We propose to include programming plans as the second building block for our programming tutor.

Programming texts introduce a programming language by discussing the syntax and semantics of each statement type.

Unfortunately, this approach exacerbates a common novice tendency to adopt a syntactic matching strategy to problem solving. For example, physics students will often attempt to solve elementary mechanics problems by matching knowns and unknowns against standard formulae (Chi, Feltovich & Glaser, 1981). Their problem solving degenerates into a syntax-directed search with no understanding of the quantities being manipulated. Experts, in contrast, analyze a problem in terms of standard intermediate concepts and techniques from past experience. In physics, for example, these concepts and techniques include "component vectors," free body diagrams, and conservation of energy.

Programming novices exhibit syntactic strategies similar to those of the physics novices. In our video protocols of novice programmers (Bonar, 1985) we see novices working linearly through a program, choosing each statement based on syntactic features of the problem text or program code. Programming plans are exactly the concepts students need to step above the syntactic approach. Students can work on programming problems using standard approaches as encoded in plans.

A tutor that allows students to use programming plans has other advantages. Because the plans are high level, they allow the student to address issues of plan merging. Plan merging is necessary because programming plans typically have several facets that end up as dispersed lines of code. We saw this earlier with the counter example. When the counter increment must be placed inside a loop body after the loop test, we are merging a facet of the counter plan with a facet of the loop plan. Errors in this plan-merging process are a critical area of novice difficulty (see Spohrer, Soloway, & Pope, 1985). With an explicit plan representation, students can work directly with plans and plan interactions without confusion about exactly how the merged plans will be turned into code.

Students Can Request Feedback
as Programming Proceeds

A programming tutor should allow students to request feedback as they work. One of the main features of intelligent tutoring is the possibility of supervising student work when a human teacher is not available. A programming tutor like PROUST only runs on a nearly finished program. No matter how sophisticated its diagnostic capability, it can only provide assistance when a student's program is relatively complete.

Coaching Should Be Provided
as Problems Arise

Without intermediate feedback from a tutor, programming students can get very far off track. A tutor must be able to recognize common error patterns and address them before a student's solution has become hopelessly muddled. On the other hand, the feedback must not be so quick that a student never has an opportunity to discover his or her own solution (a problem in the LISP tutor, described in Reiser, Anderson, & Farrell, 1985).

In Bridge, students are interrupted based on a series of novice models of programming operations. A student is only interrupted if there is an error relative to the model the tutor decides the student is using. Students with an error that is unimportant at their current level of understanding will not be interrupted. The mechanism for this approach is explained in the following subsection.

Students Can Approach
a Solution by Successive Approximation

The "final answer" to a programming problem is very rich: There are many correct answers and many answers that are close to correct but still contain several errors. A programming tutor should recognize a solution that is close to correct. Also, it should recognize the correct components in a program that is only partially complete. Most work in Bridge involves translating from one representation to a more formal representation. Bridge knows what the student is working on because the student is translating a component from one representation into the equivalent component in another representation. This makes it relatively easy for Bridge to understand student partial solutions.

Students Should Be Able
to See a Problem-Solving Trace

It is useful for a programming tutor to support a student with effective visual representations of the problem solving. There are two advantages to such an approach. First, there is less load on a student's working memory, because more of the solution steps are available on the screen explicitly. Anderson and Jeffries (1985) have documented the relationship between working-memory failures and novice programming errors. The second advantage to a visual representation is that it provides students a visual model for the abstract operations and relationships represented in the text.

We discuss our use of visual representations in Bridge in the following overview.

AN OVERVIEW OF THE BRIDGE SYSTEM

In Bridge, the student user is given a problem of a complexity that could be presented in the first 10 weeks of an introductory programming course. The student passes through three phases while solving the problem.

In the first phase, the student constructs a set of step-by-step instructions using English phrases. In the next phase, the student matches these instructions to programming plans and builds a program using a representation of these plans. In the final phase, the student matches the plans to programming language constructs and uses these to build a programming language solution to the original problem. Currently, the only language implemented in Bridge is PASCAL, although many other programming languages could be used with the same approach.

We will use an example problem to demonstrate the three phases of Bridge. This problem is the ending value averaging problem (EVAP). The problem is: Write a program that repeatedly reads in integers until it reads in the integer 99999. After seeing 99999, it should print out the CORRECT AVERAGE without counting the final 99999.

In the following description, several things should be kept in mind. First, Bridge is highly interactive. The figures will only give some sense of the display in action. Most of the objects of concern to the student are created, manipulated, and edited by the moving of objects on the screen with a mouse.

Bridge has been designed for students who have some familiarity with programming plans. Because these plans are not covered in most texts, we have developed a programming plan workbook for our students (Bonar, Weil, & Jones, 1986). We assume that users of Bridge are familiar with the plans in the workbook, including the exercise they are attempting. Of course, students do not need skill in using the plans, only familiarity with the idea and basic purpose of plans.

Finally, the terminology and complex screen display of Bridge may seem overwhelming. The EVAP is approximately two-thirds of the way through the programming curriculum we have designed. The problems students will see initially are much simpler than EVAP, initially involving only one or two plans at a time.

Phase 1: Building the Natural Language "Program"

Figure 15.1 shows the screen from Phase 1 with EVAP as the current problem. The problem specification is in the lower left corner of the screen.

The user is to build his or her English language solution to the problem by making choices from the "Natural Language Selections" menu. The menu selections are the beginnings of phrases. Some of these selections are redundant: "Print . . ." and "Output . . ." This is because people use different phrases to refer to the same task.

After the student chooses the beginning of a phrase, a smaller menu appears to the right of the selection. This menu contains choices to complete the phrase (see Figure 15.2). This second choice may or may not affect the meaning of the phrase. The student is to construct the phrase which most precisely states his or her intentions.

Once a phrase is completed, it appears in the "Natural Language Plans" window (see Figure 15.3). The student then moves the phrase to where he or she wants it. The student builds the "natural language program" by combining these phrases in an order that correctly specifies a solution to the problem. At any time during Phase 1 the student may reposition or delete phrases from the program.

Solving the problem. If the student needs help or thinks that the program is correct, he or she can select "HINTS" from the main menu. The program responds to the student in the guise of Gworky, the friendly troll, who lives under the Bridge (see Figure 15.3). When "HINTS" is selected, Gworky checks the programs and coaches the student if there are any errors. To do this checking, the tutor builds a formal representation of the natural language program where each English phrase corresponds to a Programming Language Plan. The tutor notes the order and detailed contents of each plan. The student's natural language program is compared with requirements for a correct solution to the problem. The first requirement that the student has failed to satisfy becomes the subject of Gworky's remarks. (Details of the language used for specifying a solution's requirements used for diagnosis and coaching follow.) The requirements are supplied by the instructors as part of a problem description.

Based on our empirical work with SSNLP, we have found that a novice's natural language solutions reflect one of four overall strategies for specifying looping in natural language (Bonar & Weil, 1985). Figure 15.4 shows the student model with which the tutor diagnoses the student's solution. The four levels are indicated by the four columns in the model. Each level shows the plans that must

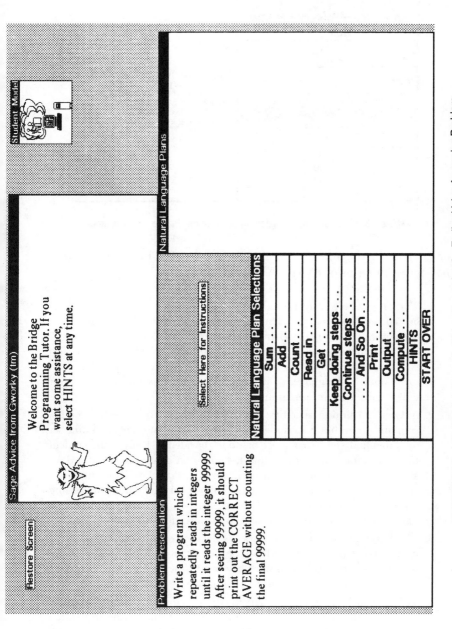

Student Model

Sage Advice from Gworky (tm)

Restore Screen

Welcome to the Bridge
Programming Tutor. If you
want some assistance,
select HINTS at any time.

Problem Presentation

Write a program which
repeatedly reads in integers
until it reads the integer 99999.
After seeing 99999, it should
print out the CORRECT
AVERAGE without counting
the final 99999.

Natural Language Plans

Select Here for Instructions

Natural Language Plan Selections

Sum . . . .
Add . . . .
Count . . . .
Read in . . . .
Get . . . .
Keep doing steps . . . .
Continue steps . . . .
. . And So On . . . .
Print . . . .
Output . . . .
Compute . . . .
HINTS
START OVER

FIGURE 15.1 Initial Bridge screen for Phase 1, running the Ending Value Averaging Problem.

417

Natural Language Plan Selections	
Sum . . .	
Add . . .	
Count . . .	
Read in . . .	Until what happens?
Get . . .	99999 is seen
Keep doing steps . . .	all the numbers have been read
Continue steps . . .	the sum exceeds 99999
. . . And So On . . .	the count exceeds 99999
Print . . .	the average is computed
Output . . .	
Compute . . .	
HINTS	
START OVER	

FIGURE 15.2 Selection of English phrases for the Phase 1 specification.

be present in the solution to satisfy that level. The levels are best illustrated in terms of EVAP:

1. The only requirement for Level 1 is that the Result Value Plan must be part of the program. The phrase that starts out "Compute . . ." corresponds to this plan. So, in a sense, the phrase "Compute the average" is a natural language solution to the problem. Clearly, this solution is not specific enough to use as a guide to solving the problem in a programming language, so if the student uses this solution the tutor will ask for more information.

2. A Level-2 solution specifies that it is necessary to keep track of the sum and count but does not explicitly mention that there are a number of individual steps that must be done repeatedly. Rather, the student may use phrases that imply that the sum and count are calculated all at once. An example of such a phrase is "Add . . . all the integers." A Level-3 solution mentions getting individual data values in keeping track of the sum and count. It also explicitly uses some phrase that indicates a looping construct, such as "Continue until 99999 is seen."

3. The Level-3 solution need not specify detailed coordination among the individual steps within the loop. So, for example, a student need not specify that the "read" step must be done before the test, which is done before the update of the running total or increment of the counter.

4. To complete Phase 1 it is necessary to satisfy all four levels of the problem. To satisfy the fourth level, the student must mention the individual steps of getting an integer, adding the integer to the running total, and updating the count. The student must also use the loop construct effectively, indicating both the beginning and end of the loop. Finally, the user must explicitly use a phrase that prints the average.

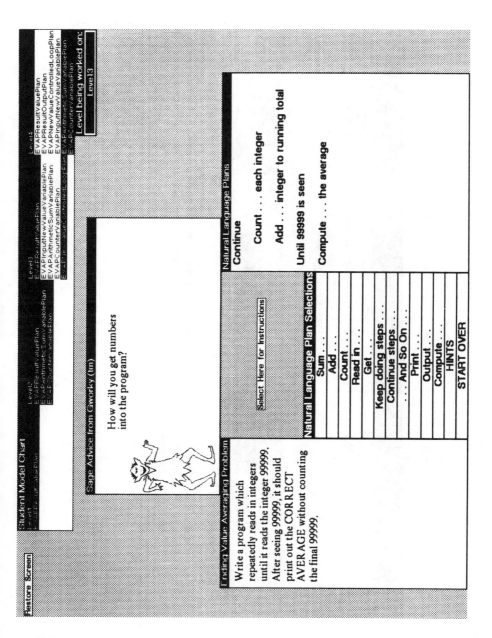

FIGURE 15.3 Building a Phase 1 informal program by combining and ordering English phrases.

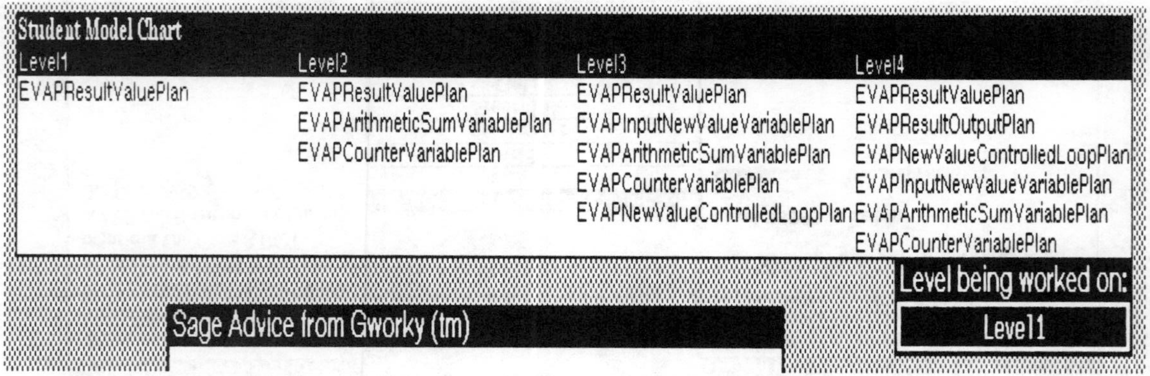

Student Model Chart

Level1	Level2	Level3	Level4
EVAPResultValuePlan	EVAPResultValuePlan	EVAPResultValuePlan	EVAPResultValuePlan
	EVAPArithmeticSumVariablePlan	EVAPInputNewValueVariablePlan	EVAPResultOutputPlan
	EVAPCounterVariablePlan	EVAPArithmeticSumVariablePlan	EVAPNewValueControlledLoopPlan
		EVAPCounterVariablePlan	EVAPInputNewValueVariablePlan
		EVAPNewValueControlledLoopPlan	EVAPArithmeticSumVariablePlan
			EVAPCounterVariablePlan

Level being worked on:

Level1

Sage Advice from Gworky (tm)

FIGURE 15.4 The student model used to diagnose the student's Phase 1 informal program. Each level represents a more sophisticated implementation of the program and a correspondingly more detailed set of requirements for a correct solution.

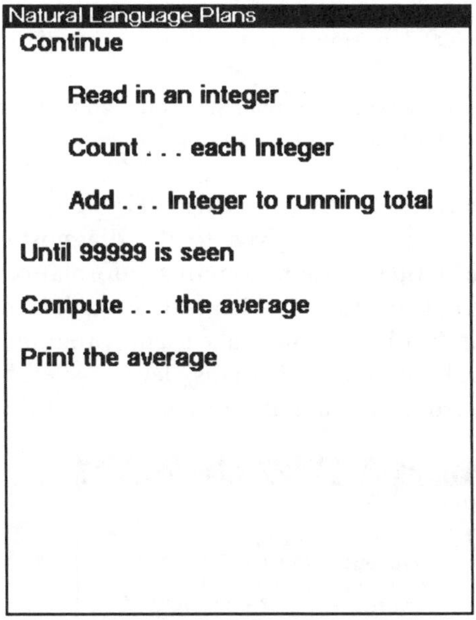

```
┌─────────────────────────────────────────┐
│ Natural Language Plans                    │
│ Continue                                  │
│                                           │
│     Read in an integer                    │
│                                           │
│     Count . . . each Integer              │
│                                           │
│     Add . . . Integer to running total    │
│                                           │
│ Until 99999 is seen                       │
│                                           │
│ Compute . . . the average                 │
│                                           │
│ Print the average                         │
│                                           │
│                                           │
│                                           │
│                                           │
│                                           │
└─────────────────────────────────────────┘
```

FIGURE 15.5 A correct Phase 1 solution to the Ending Value Averaging Problem.

A Level-4 solution to the problem is shown in the natural language plans window of Figure 15.5.

Representation of requirements. The requirements for a correct solution to the problem are associated with a problem-specific part of each plan specification. These requirements include information about what phrases should appear in the program and the correct order of those phrases. We have defined a special language to specify the requirements. This language defines a group of operators that specify plan components, order information for those components, and determine the relationship among various components. Some of the operators we have found useful are:

1. *Sequence* This describes the order in which the plans should appear in the program. Figure 15.6 shows three such sequence requirements. The " . . ." that separates some plans indicates that zero or more plans can come between them in the student's solution.

2. *Exists?* This indicates that the plan mentioned must appear in the program. In Figure 15.6, the Counter Variable Plan is required to be in the program.

3. *Any Of* This is the equivalent of an "OR" operator. It is satisfied if any of its arguments are satisfied.

4. *All* This is the equivalent of an "AND" operator. It is satisfied only if all of its arguments are not satisfied.

5. *Not* This is the usual "NOT" operator. It is satisfied only if its argument is not satisfied.

6. *PushToHighest* This manages several requirements at once and selects a hint dealing with the first unsatisfied plan.

When the student requests help by selecting "HINTS," a representation of the student's solution is given to the diagnostic component of the tutor. This representation contains information about what phrases are present in the problem, their order of appearance, and the wording of the phrases that make up the program. The tutor then iterates through the required plans, level by level, and matches the requirements from the plan at that level against the

```
DEdit of expression
(PushToHighest (EVAPCounterVariablePlan
               Exists?
               (Hints (In order to compute the
                           average, you will need to
                           divide the sum of the
                           integers by the number of
                           integers read in. Include a
                           plan to read in the number
                           of integers.)
                      (To compute the average, you
                           must divide the sum of all
                           the integers read in by the
                           count of the number of
                           integers. Include the
                           %"Count ... %" plan now.)))
               (EVAPCounterVariablePlan Sequence ...
                   EVAPInputNewValueVariablePlan ...
                   EVAPCounterVariablePlan ...
                   (Hints (You have to acquire the numbers
                               BEFORE you can count them.)
                          (Put the step you use to acquire
                               the numbers above the step
                               you use to count them.)
                          (Put %"Count ...%" plan below the
                               %"Read in ...%"
                               or %"Get ....%" plan.)))
               (AnyOf (EVAPCounterVariablePlan Sequence ...
                          EVAPCounterVariablePlan ...
                          EVAPResultOutputPlan ...)
                      (EVAPCounterVariablePlan Sequence ...
                          EVAPCounterVariablePlan ...
                          EVAPResultValuePlan ...)
                      (Hints (You must count the numbers BEFORE
                                  you can compute the average.)
                             (Put the statement you use to
                                  count the numbers higher than
                                  the one you use to compute
                                  the average.))))
```

FIGURE 15.6 A small section of the requirements for a correct solution in Phase 1. This specification describes the Counter variable in the Ending Value Averaging Problem.

representation of the student solution. When a requirement is unsatisfied, the tutor uses the first hint that is associated with that requirement. If the student selects "HINTS" a second time, he or she receives a second, more detailed, hint. Requirements usually have three hints: the first hint is fairly vague, the second, more specific, and the third usually gives the answer away.

Phase 2: Building a "Plan Program"

A student begins this phase by matching his or her English phrases from Phase 1 with a menu selection of programming plan names. The plan names are intended as a more formal description of the program steps described with English in Phase 1. The student is checked for the correct match after each match is made. After the matching is complete, the student begins building the Programming Language Plans ("PL Plans") version of his or her program. Figure 15.7 shows the screen during Phase 2. The natural language version of the program constructed in Phase 1 is now shown in the lower left corner of the screen.

Matching. The first thing that the student must do is match each English phrase with a selection from the "Plans" menu that describes the purpose of the phrase. For instance, the phrase "Add integer to running total" matches the "Plan to: Keep a Running Total." Once the correct match is made, the box that will represent this plan in Phase 2 appears on the screen. The student must match all of the phrases to the appropriate plans before proceeding to build the PL Plans program. As he or she continues to match the phrases, the PL Plans representations are constructed and stacked in the middle of the screen.

Boxes and tiles. In Phase 2, we use boxes and tiles to represent the PL Plans. Each plan has its own box and many of the plans have tiles as well. The tiles represent the different roles of the plan. In Figure 15.7 we see the representations of the "Plan to: Input a New Value from the User," "Plan to: Count the Numbers," and "Plan to: Sum the Numbers." The last plan, for example, contains three tiles that represent the "initialize," "update," and "value" roles.

There are two kinds of boxes: those that supply tiles to the program and those that have empty slots into which tiles are placed. An example of the second type is the "Plan to: Control Loop with Sentinel." If an action is to be performed inside the loop, its tile should be placed in the bottom-most slots inside this box.

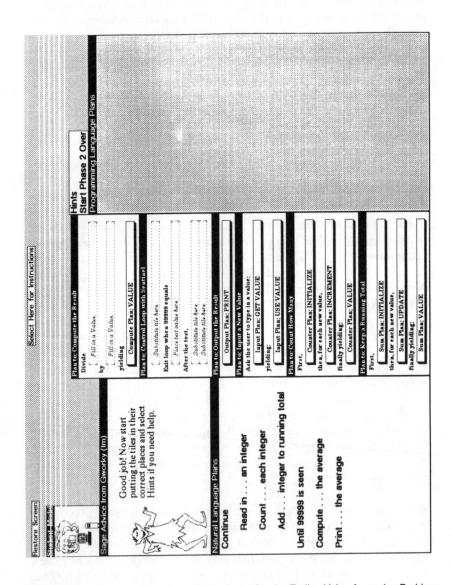

FIGURE 15.7 Bridge screen during Phase 2, running the Ending Value Averaging Problem. The student has selected formal programming plans, represented visually with boxes and titles, to correspond to the informal plans of Phase 1.

Building the PL Plans program. After the matching is complete, the "Plans" menu disappears and a new menu appears at the top of the "Programming Language Plans" window. This menu has two selections, "HINTS" and "Starting Phase 2 Over." At this point the student can begin to build the program. The student must select a box or tile from the center of the screen and place it in the "Programming Language Plans" window. The student continues placing the boxes and tiles in the window until he or she arrives at a correct solution to the problem. The correct solution to EVAP is shown in Figure 15.8.

Hints in Phase 2. Hints in Phase 2 are very similar to hints in Phase 1. Students select "HINTS" whenever they need help or think they have a correct solution to the problem. The diagnosis is performed similar to Phase 1, comparing students' solutions to the requirements. In this phase, however, there is only one level at which the problem can be solved.

Phase 3: Building the PASCAL Program

In Phase 3 the student builds a programming language solution to the original problem. Currently, this solution must be in PASCAL. Bridge, however, could easily be adapted to work with a wide range of similar languages.

Matching and building the PASCAL program. Figure 15.9 shows the screen at Phase 3. The PL Plans program from Phase 2 is now in the lower left corner of the screen. The student will use this to match each box or tile to the appropriate programming language construct. Once constructs are selected, they are inserted and manipulated with a PASCAL structure editor provided in the "PASCAL Edit Window" on the right side of the screen.

The student works by selecting a plan or role, indicated by a box or tile from the PL Plans program, and then selecting the programming language construct that would best implement that plan or role. This usually means selecting a statement type from the "PASCAL Statement Types" menu in the middle of the screen. If the student makes the correct choice, he will then be asked to indicate the position for the statement in the "PASCAL Edit Window." Occasionally, boxes or tiles will match something other than an entire statement. For example, the "Input Plan: USE VALUE" tile inside the loop box matches the <Expression> nonterminal node in a "while" loop. Such a counterintuitive match is an illustration of the nontrivial

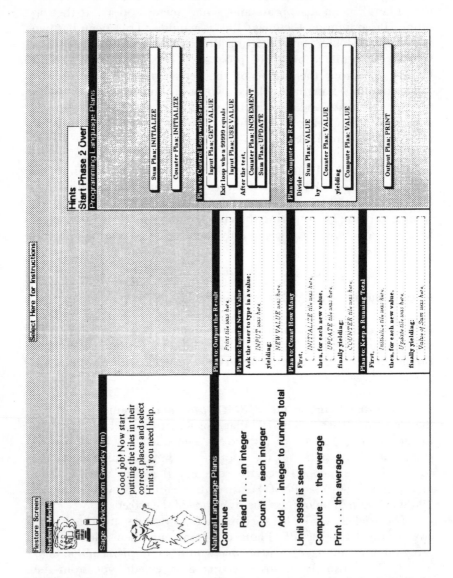

FIGURE 15.8 Bridge screen at end of Phase 2, showing a correct solution to the Ending Value Averaging Problem.

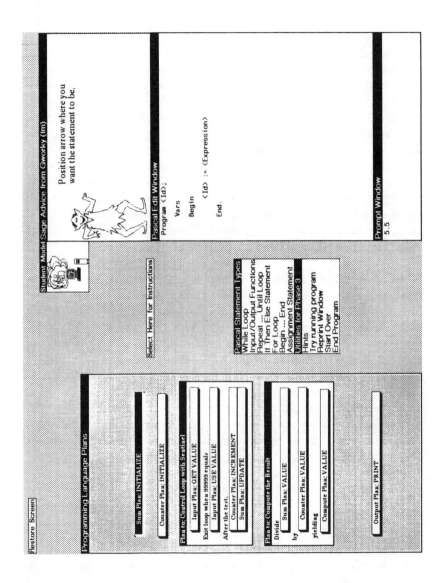

FIGURE 15.9 Bridge screen during Phase 3. The student is translating the formal programming plans into a Pascal code solution for the Ending Value Averaging Problem.

match between PASCAL constructs and the fundamental plans of programming. Not only is it a difficulty for students working with raw PASCAL, it also is a human-interface problem for Bridge. We are currently working on a smoother way of associating plans with programming language constructs.

Bridge isolates the student from syntax errors through a structure editor provided in Phase 3. This editor implements a subset of PASCAL that does not include procedure and function definitions. The editor does not allow the student to build a syntactically incorrect program. We decided to use such a structure editor to minimize the syntactic concerns of the novice programmer, thus allowing him or her to concentrate on semantic and pragmatic aspects of the program (see Garlan & Miller, 1984, for a detailed discussion of structure editors). In addition to managing syntactic concerns, the editor also manages variable declarations. Figure 15.9 shows an assignment statement before its nonterminal nodes are expanded. Figure 15.10 shows a finished PASCAL program.

Editing the PASCAL program.   Once a statement is added to the PASCAL program, there are several things that the student can do with it. First, any nonterminal nodes must be expanded before the program can be run. There are two kinds of nonterminal nodes: expressions and identifiers. To expand them, the student selects the node he or she wants to expand and then types the identifier or expression that is to appear at that location. The tutor currently checks the type-in to verify that it is correct for the statement.

There are three things that the student can do with entire statements once they are part of the program. He or she can move them to another location in the program, delete them from the program, or show the role or plan that the statement represents.

Phase 3 utilities.   Several utilities are at the student's disposal in Phase 3:

1. *Hints* This is very similar to Phases 1 and 2. The student selects "Hints" whenever he or she needs help or thinks he or she has a correct program. The diagnosis is done the same way as Phase 2. There is only one level at which the problem can be solved.

2. *Try Running Program* This selection will attempt to execute the program. As it runs through the program, it will highlight each statement as it is encountered. If some error is discovered during the run, a type mismatch, for example, the program will halt and indicate where the error occurred by flashing the offending line of code. The tutor will also give a message that explains the error.

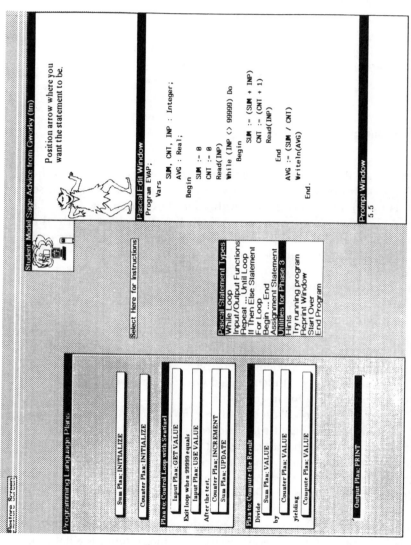

FIGURE 15.10 Bridge screen at end of Phase 3, showing a correct solution to the Ending Value Averaging Problem.

3. *Reprint Window*   This reprints the PASCAL program. Sometimes part of the program may not look like it is indented properly. This is corrected by selecting this option.

4. *Start Over*   This starts Phase 3 over, setting both boxes and tiles and the PASCAL program to their initial states.

5. *End Program*   This ends Bridge. When this is selected, everything in Phase 3 is destroyed and BRIDGE is exited.

USING BRIDGE WITH STUDENTS

We have run Bridge with approximately 10 students, about one-third of the way through an introductory PASCAL programming course. This is by no means a complete evaluation, but does allow an initial report about student reactions. A significant problem with this evaluation is that students could work on only two problems: one involving reading two numbers and reporting their sum, and the second EVAP. A fairer test of the tutor would use students having taken the plans curriculum and worked through a 10 to 15 problem sequence on Bridge. Despite these problems, our early experience with Bridge is interesting and worthy of report.

Phase 1 was quite successful with the students. They were usually able to work through the phase with little or no intervention from our human monitor. Students were pleased to be able to represent their ideas informally. Students liked Gworky and were usually able to successfully follow his instructions.

Initial versions of Phase 1 had several interesting strengths and errors. Students have very little patience or interest for the monolithic written instructions that documented features of the program. For example, the instructions consisted of page-length blocks of text. Because there was an experimenter available to the subjects, they had little real need for the written material. In fact, though, they used the experimenter very rarely in Phase 1. The phrases in the natural language menu seemed to adequately capture the concepts the students wanted to express and the overall approach seemed more or less natural. When the text could not provide a quick and simple answer, they went back and tried to figure it out by looking at the screen. Our second version of Phase 1 provided help in a series of short paragraphs tied to leading phrases like "Help in learning how to use the mouse . . ." or "What to do when your program is complete . . ."

One of the most interesting problems with the early versions of Phase 1 was difficulty students had in understanding that Bridge needed both the bottom and the top of the loop delimited. Typical SSNLP instructions do not specify the top of the loop—it is usually obvious from context. Originally Bridge would give students two phrases for the loop: "Repeat" and "Until 99999 is seen," for example. We expected students to use these to delimit the top and bottom of the loop, respectively. Instead, the students would, in almost every case, place the phrases next to each other at the bottom of the loop. Students would have no idea what Bridge meant when it asked them to use one of these phrases at the top of the loop. No amount of specificity in Gworky's instructions seemed to help. Ultimately, we allowed them to specify the loop this way through Level 3. In Level 4 the student must use a special "Top of Loop" token to indicate the top of the loop. Students had little difficulty with this operation. We are struck by how this trivial change of interface made such a striking difference in performance.

Phase 2 was not as successful as Phase 1. Students found the display too complex. In particular, they lost track of the relationship between a plan and its associated tiles. Also, the textual material in the plans was not always clear. We are currently improving the comprehensibility of Phase 2 by using shading to make connections between selected plan components and by simplifying the texts that label the plans and tiles. Our next round of tests with Bridge will have students work many more problems before attempting EVAP.

Phase 3 was moderately difficult for our students. They liked the structured editor and had little trouble using it. Matching between the Phase 2 output and PASCAL code was difficult for the students, however. Because there is not always a simple match between a plan component and PASCAL code, students will often make a reasonable selection that Bridge does not accept. For example, a single PASCAL statement might represent parts of two plans. Unless the student explicitly matches the statement with both plans, Bridge will complain. Students do not always think to make the match twice. We are currently working on a smoother interface that still maintains all the correct matches.

FUTURE PLANS

Bridge now has 25 problems designed to cover the first third of a college level introductory programming course. Bridge has been informally tested with approximately 25 students. A larger scale evaluation will take place in the fall of 1987 with a group of Air Force recruits. We have developed a set of indices and protocol analysis tools to assist in characterizing a student's performance with Bridge.

On a longer time scale we see two directions for Bridge. In one direction, we want to make Bridge a more effective tutor for traditional programming languages like PASCAL (including, for example, Ada and LISP.) To make Bridge more effective in teaching these languages, we need to more directly support the model underlying those languages. We also need to provide a learning trajectory that moves students away from dependence on Phases 1 and 2. We plan to do this by relaxing some of the rigidities of Bridge. In particular, we would like students to begin in Phase 3 after they become experienced with Phases 1 and 2.

In this intermediate mode, the tutor would ask the students to work in Phase 1 or 2 only if the student's actions in Phase 3 cannot be understood by the tutor. This would greatly simplify the use of Bridge for a good student without making large changes for weaker students. Although this would require a more sophisticated diagnostic capability in Phase 3 than is currently implemented, it would not require the power of full PROUST (Johnson, 1986). In this proposed approach, we could recognize correct code and very simple errors with match routines roughly corresponding to the power of Micro-PROUST (Johnson & Soloway, 1985.) If the student produces a program that is not understandable with this relatively simple paradigm, the student would need to work through Phases 1 and 2. In a sense, the deep diagnostic power lies in Bridge's ability to have a conversation with the student about design.

Bridge invites a more radical possibility than more effective tutoring of traditional programming languages. Once we realize that the plan program is runnable, we ask the question raised by Bridge: "Why force the student to deal with PASCAL at all?" Except for syntactic and idiosyncratic semantics details, the program is fully specified at the end of Phase 2. Why should the student, or the typical programmer, be forced to learn and use those details? Although a detailed discussion of this question is beyond the scope of this article, we have been actively investigating the notion of an intention-based programming language with constructs at the level of plans.

Finally, we are interested in developing principles for use of intermediate representations, like those in Phase 1 and 2, for domains other than programming. What if, for example, students could use similar structures to reason about mechanics problems, geometry proofs, algebra word problems, or even arguments in an essay? The possibility is intriguing for two reasons. Planlike structures have played a central role in a cognitive understanding of learning and thinking (see, e.g., Resnick, 1983). A seemingly important gap in research with these structures exists, because they have not been used directly for instruction. A Bridgelike framework allows us to explore this possibility.

ACKNOWLEDGMENTS

An earlier version of the Bridge system was developed by Mary Ann Quayle. John Corbett, Jamie Schultz, and William Weil contributed substantially to the development of Bridge. We are grateful to the Intelligent Tutoring Systems group for their suggestions and encouragement in this project. In particular, we wish to thank Alan Lesgold for his support and leadership.

This work was supported by the Air Force Human Resources Laboratory under contract number F41689-84-D-0002, Order 0004 and by the Office of Naval Research under contract numbers N00014-83-6-0148 and N00014-83-K0655. Any opinions, findings, conclusions, or recommendations expressed in this report are those of the authors, and do not necessarily reflect the views of the U. S. Government.

REFERENCES

Anderson, J., & Jeffries, R. (1985). Novice LISP errors: Undetected losses of information from working memory. *Human–Computer Interaction, 1,* 107–131.

Biermann, A. W., Ballard, B. W., & Sigmon, A. H. (1983). An experimental study of natural language programming. *International Journal of Man–Machine Studies, 18,* 71–87.

Boltzmann, L. (1974). *Ludwig Boltzmann: Theoretical physics and philosophical problems* (pp. 16–22). B. McGuiness (Ed.) and P. Foulkes (Tans.). Boston: Reidel Press. (Original work published 1897).

Bonar, J. (1985). *Understanding the bugs of novice programmers.* Unpublished doctoral dissertation. Amherst: University of Massachusetts.

Bonar, J. (1986). *Mental models of programming loops.* Unpublished Technical Report, Pittsburgh: Learning Research and Development Center, University of Pittsburgh.

Bonar, J., & Soloway, E. (1985). Preprogramming knowledge: A major source of misconceptions in novice programmers. *Human–Computer Interaction, 1,* 133–161.

Bonar, J., & Weil, W. (1985). An informal programming language. In *Proceedings of the Expert Systems Government Conference,* October 23–25. Washington, DC.

Bonar, J., Weil, W., & Jones, R. (1986). *The programming plans workbook.* Unpublished Technical Report. Pittsburgh: Learning Research and Development Center, University of Pittsburgh.

Chandhok, R., Garlan, D., Goldenson, D., Miller, P., & Tucker, M. A. (1985). Programming environment based on structured editing: The GNOME approach. Appears. In *Proceedings of the 1985 National Computer Conference* (pp. 241–256).

Chi, M., Feltovich, P., & Glaser, R. (1981). Categorization and representation of physics problems by experts and novices. *Cognitive Science, 5,* 121–152.

Eisenstadt, M., Laubsch, J., & Kahney, H. (1981). Creating pleasant programming environments for cognitive science students. In *Proceedings of the Third Annual Cognitive Science Society Conference.* Berkeley, CA: Cognitive Science Society.

Garlan, D. B., & Miller, P. L. (1984, April). GNOME: An introductory programming environment based on a family of structure editors. In *Proceedings of the Software Engineering Symposium on Practical Software/Development Environments.*

Johnson, W. L. (1986). Intention-based diagnosis of errors in novice programs. Palo Alto, CA: Morgan Kaufman.

Johnson, W. L., & Soloway, E. (1985) Micro-PROUST. Yale University Computer Science Department Research Report No. 402. New Haven, CT: Yale University.

Mayer, R. E. (1979). A psychology of learning BASIC. *Communications of the Association for Computing Machinery, 22*(11), 589–598.

Miller, L. A. (1981). Natural language programming: Styles, strategies, and contrasts. *IBM Systems Journal, 20,* 184–215.

Reiser, B., Anderson, J., & Farrell, R. (1985). Dynamic student modeling in an intelligent tutor for LISP programming. *Proceedings of the Ninth International Joint Conference on Artificial Intelligence,* 8–14.

Resnick, L. (1983). A new conception of mathematics and science learning. *Science, 220,* 477–478.

Spohrer, J., Soloway, E., & Pope E. (1985). A goal/plan analysis of buggy PASCAL programs. *Human–Computer Interaction, 1,* 163–207.

Soloway, E., & Ehrlich, K. (1984). Empirical studies of programming knowledge. *IEEE Transactions of Software Engineering, SE-10,* 595–609.

16

Understanding Reflective Problem Solving

Wallace Feurzeig
Frank Ritter
BBN Laboratories

STUDENT MODELING AND THE DIAGNOSIS PROBLEM

How can an ICAI system make plausible hypotheses concerning a student's knowledge state about a problem domain? The task of the diagnostic module of the system is to make intelligent inferences about the student's knowledge, knowledge gaps, surface bugs, and, if possible, the associated underlying misconceptions. The essential starting point for such deep inferences is the observations of the student's task performance — the sequence of actions taken by the student as he or she works on a problem. This constitutes the initial knowledge base of the student diagnostic module. This surface performance information is necessary for diagnosing and characterizing faulty behaviors, but it is not sufficient even for diagnosing student difficulties in relatively simple intellectual tasks such as the performance of simple arithmetic computations using prescribed algorithmic procedures.

The diagnosis problem has been addressed by a number of ICAI systems, including WEST, DEBUGGY, SOPHIE, and QUEST. The concept of a differential student model was developed in WEST (Burton & Brown, 1982), a computer board game designed to teach computational skills through computation-based game-playing strategy. The approach to diagnosis in WEST is to model the problem performance of an expert player and to contrast that with the observed performance of the student working on the same problem. This kind of performance analysis can identify weaknesses in the student's play, but not the underlying difficulties responsible for them. For example, a poor move might be due to the student's failure to consider an alternative move or to an incorrect computation of a move, two distinctly different kinds of difficulties calling for qualitatively different instructional treatments.

DEBUGGY (Burton, 1982) is the instructional form of the well-known BUGGY system for modeling the procedural bugs accounting for most student subtraction errors. In DEBUGGY, the diagnosis of a student's procedural bugs is done using a pattern-matching scheme. DEBUGGY incorporates a substantial data base of subtraction problem bugs—faulty subtraction procedures obtained from empirical studies of subtraction problem work across large student populations. If a student's performance across a set of representative problems is identical to that of a buggy procedure in the data base, the system identifies the buggy procedure as the student's bug. This approach is severely limited to those relatively simple types of problems for which there is a small enough set of distinct types of bugs to permit their explicit enumeration. It is not a feasible diagnostic methodology for the problems of typical interest and complexity such as tactical military tasks.

SOPHIE (Brown, Burton, & Bell, 1974), a pioneering ICAI system for electronics troubleshooting training, used a general circuit simulation program as a dynamic knowledge base for evaluating the behavior of the circuit under working or faulted conditions. A substantial part of the understanding capabilities in the SOPHIE ICAI system was based on its use of this mathematical simulation model, a general purpose circuit simulation called SPICE (Nagel, 1975), together with a LISP-based functional simulator incorporating circuit dependent knowledge. These facilities were essential for inferring complex circuit interaction sequences such as fault propagation chains. SOPHIE's capabilities for modeling and understanding causal chains of events formed the basis for its powerful explanation and question-answering facilities.

SOPHIE used the simulator to make powerful deductive inferences about hypothetical, as well as real, circuit behavior. For example, it determined whether the behavior of the circuit was consistent with the assumption of specified faults and whether a student's troubleshooting inferences were warranted, that is, whether the student had acquired information of the voltage and current states of relevant circuit components sufficient to unambiguously isolate the fault.

SOPHIE could infer what the student should have been able to conclude from his or her observations at any point. For example, it determined the currently plausible hypotheses and those that were untenable. However, because SOPHIE did not determine the reasons for the student's tests and measurements, the hypotheses the student was actually considering, it could not tell whether his or her conclusions were based on logically complete and consistent reasoning. It was unable to diagnose the student's specific misconceptions or difficulties in understanding circuit behavior or in troubleshooting faults. Despite these deficiencies, SOPHIE was one of the first ICAI systems capable of supporting compelling and educationally effective instructional interactions.

There is a straightforward approach to improving a system's knowledge of a student's thinking during a problem-solving interaction. Instead of basing the system's inferences solely on the external actions taken by the student (for example, voltage measurements or continuity tests in electrical troubleshooting), the system can also attempt to elicit associated information concerning the student's hypotheses, goals, and plans. This approach has been developed in the context of the QUEST instructional system.

AN OVERVIEW OF QUEST

QUEST (Qualitative Understanding of Electrical System Trouble-shooting) is a current ICAI system for teaching electrical system troubleshooting (White & Frederiksen, 1986; 1987). QUEST uses qualitative simulation methods (White & Frederiksen, 1985; Ritter, 1986) to teach knowledge-based reasoning about circuit behavior and troubleshooting. Humans think about the behavior of phenomena and systems in a qualitatively different way from that used to describe such behavior in mathematical simulation models. Experts in a domain (not only beginning students) use qualitative modes of thought and qualitative models to reason about system behavior. Thus, though it is necessary to employ mathematical simulations to obtain precise detailed descriptions of system behaviors, we also want to teach conceptually sound qualitative reasoning. The use of qualitative simulation models is valuable for producing understandable explanations and for generating animated displays to show dynamic behavior in a clear manner. This facilitates learning by fostering the student's development of effective mental models for understanding and reasoning about system behavior.

QUEST employs a qualitative simulation model for reasoning about the behavior of simple electrical circuits composed of batteries, wires, resistors, coils, condensers, lamps, switches, and testlights. An example of a QUEST circuit is shown in Figure 16.1. The qualitative simulation includes a description of the circuit topology, a runnable function model for each device in the circuit, rules for evaluating

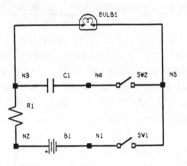

FIGURE 16.1 A typical QUEST circuit.

device states at each time increment, and circuit-tracing procedures to aid in evaluating conditions for device states. It is designed to support a dynamic presentation environment by generating graphical representations of circuit operation. An expert troubleshooting program is provided to demonstrate troubleshooting concepts and strategy within that environment. The expert troubleshooter can be called upon to solve problems and to explain its reasoning along the way. QUEST also provides an instructional mode that allows students to practice troubleshooting (Feurzeig, 1985). In this mode the instructional system provides students with a problem-solving environment within which circuits can be built, tested, and modified. When requested, the program generates qualitative explanations of circuit operation in both working and faulted states. Circuit problems given to students include predicting circuit behavior and troubleshooting faults within circuits.

When solving problems, students can call upon the qualitative simulation and expert troubleshooter programs to explain reasoning about circuit operation or troubleshooting logic. Each tutorial program utilizes a model that articulates reasoning at a level of explanation that is appropriate for the particular stage of instruction. The circuit simulation program can explain to students the operation of circuits in either faulted or working condition. Explanation of troubleshooting logic are produced by the troubleshooting expert and are coordinated in level of complexity with the explanations of circuit behavior offered by the circuit simulation.

KNOWLEDGE ACQUISITION
FOR STUDENT MODELING IN QUEST

The distinctive diagnostic feature of QUEST that sets it apart from the other ICAI systems is its facility for eliciting explicit information from the student about the intended purpose of his or her actions before they are performed and about his conclusions afterward. This interaction is carried out throughout the detailed course of the troubleshooting activity. An example of the use of the QUEST instructional monitor is shown in Figure 16.2. The scenario shows a student troubleshooting a simple circuit consisting of a battery, two resistors, a wire, and a bulb to illustrate the interaction (QUEST is also capable of modeling the dynamic behavior of capacitors and inductors in relatively complex circuits.)

This scenario represents just a few minutes of interaction during the problem-directed explanation mode of QUEST. The querying of the student proceeds effortlessly. The student is asked before each action (for example flipping a switch or inserting a test light) what he or she hopes to learn through taking this action. After his or her response, the action is carried out by the system. The student may also take other actions at this point, call the simulation to be run, and see the effects of these actions. After this, the student is asked what he has learned. Following his response, the entire process resumes with the student's next troubleshooting action. In addition to gathering data, this procedure helps shape a student's thinking and approach to circuit problems by providing an explicit model and an analytic framework.

The interface is easy to use. The student answers a question by choosing from an appropriate range of responses on a display window, clicking the mouse when it points to the response selected. Some answers require more than one response; for example, when the student wants to add a new fault, he must also select the component of the subcircuit suspected of being faulty and designate the fault. The instructor can set up the system to require that the student answer all the questions posed. At the opposite extreme, the system can be set up so that it is possible for the student to bypass the entire monitoring process.

The Quest Instructional Monitor (QUIMON) is invoked each time the student takes an action. This elicitation procedure is designed to be non-intrusive and unforced. The student is not required or even requested to be deliberative about every single action taken along the way. A more sophisticated procedure, incorporating knowledge of the circuit and utilizing the information elicited from the student about his current plans, could be designed. This kind of procedure would need to be invoked less frequently, at points corresponding to completion of a global operation sequence or to a shift in the student's current focus of attention.

The session produces a substantial knowledge base of the student's plans and goals with minimal interference to his troubleshooting activity. We believe that such finegrained information about the student's intentions, expectations, and conclusions can be uniquely

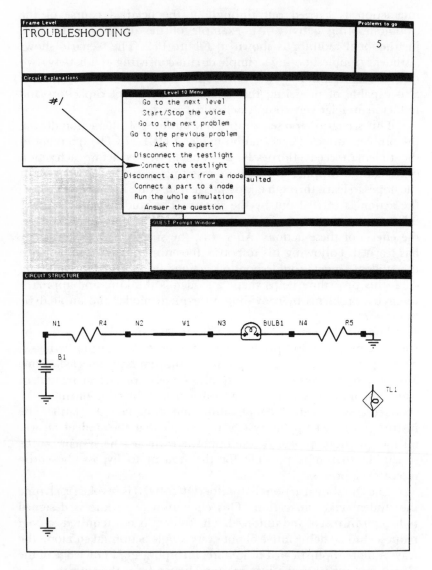

FIGURE 16.2a A student interaction with Quest Instructional Monitor.

valuable for understanding his performance and making plausible diagnoses of his misconceptions and difficulties. Moreover, such information can only be elicited from the student—it is, at the very least, extremely difficult for an ICAI system based on present AI methods to infer the student's mental states from his surface behaviors. Thus we believe that QUIMON work provides an effective starting point for development of more competent student diagnostic models.

A sample operation of QUIMON follows.

QUEST has created a circuit for the student to troubleshoot. The student has a menu from which to choose several possible actions. In Figure 16.2a, the student points an arrow (1) to "Connect the test light."

In order to model the student's behavior, a menu pops up to ask the student why he wants to insert a test light. The student is allowed to answer simply "Don't know." In Figure 16.2b, however, the student clicks where arrow 2 is pointing, "To explore general circuit behavior," indicating a lack of specificity to his actions. A student who would like to be more specific can go as far as specifying that he is testing the feed to a device. In that case, the system would prompt him for the specific device.

The system responds by entering the test light, pointed out by arrow 3, (see Figure 16.2c) into the circuit at the place where the student indicates (not shown here), and brings the student back to the action menu. The student then clicks where arrow 4 is pointing, to run the simulation of the current circuit.

The tail end of the written explanation of the qualitative simulation in QUEST, detailing the state changes of parts, and explanations of why the parts changed state, is visible in the Trace Output Window, arrow 5 (see Figure 16.2d). The spoken output is not shown, nor is the system's use of flashing in inverse video to show the paths that the simulation used in computing voltage drops. The student is asked if he wishes to continue the simulation for another clock cycle. He does not (see Figure 16.2d) arrow 6, and clicks on "Stop."

After the simulation has run, the student is asked what he or she has learned—for example, what new possible faults he has discovered. Arrow 7 in Figure 16.2e points to the list of faults identified by the student. The list of possible faults ruled out by the student is also displayed. The student can indicate that he has not drawn any conclusions from the current action, and can proceed directly back to the action menu. In this scenario, the student clicked at arrow 8 (Figure 16.2e) indicating that he or she suspects a new fault in the circuit.

The student now is asked to indicate the exact part that he or she thinks is faulted by clicking on it with the mouse. The student does so by clicking on "BULB1" (arrow 9, Figure 16.2f). The system knows the set of faults each part can have, and now pops up the menu for bulb faults. The student picks "Open" (arrow 10, Figure 16.2f).

The new fault is now displayed in the window containing possible faults (arrow 11, Figure 16.2g). The student also believes he learned

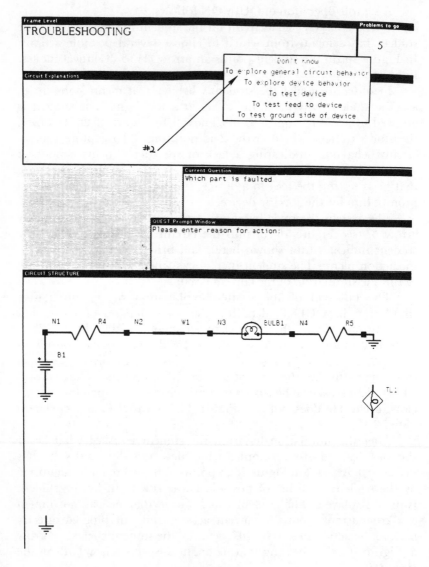

TROUBLESHOOTING

Don't know
To explore general circuit behavior
To explore device behavior
To test device
To test feed to device
To test ground side of device

Circuit Explanations

#2

Current Question
Which part is faulted

QUEST Prompt Window
Please enter reason for action:

CIRCUIT STRUCTURE

N1   R4   N2   W1   N3   BULB1   N4   R5

B1

TL1

FIGURE 16.2b

that another part is unfaulted and indicates this by clicking (where arrow 12 points): "Rule out possible fault."

The student is then prompted for the part that is to be marked as not faulted. He clicks on the wire "W1," pointed to by arrow 13 in Figure 16.2g.

The choice of W1 as an unfaulted part is shown in the appropriate window. The student is returned to the menu that allows him to specify additional information, for example other faulted or unfaulted parts. The student declines to do so, by clicking where arrow 14 indicates (see Figure 16.2h), and is returned to the action menu to continue troubleshooting.

The final figure shows the end of the session and displays the fault. The student was correct in choosing BULB1 being open as the fault (arrow 15, Figure 16.2i).

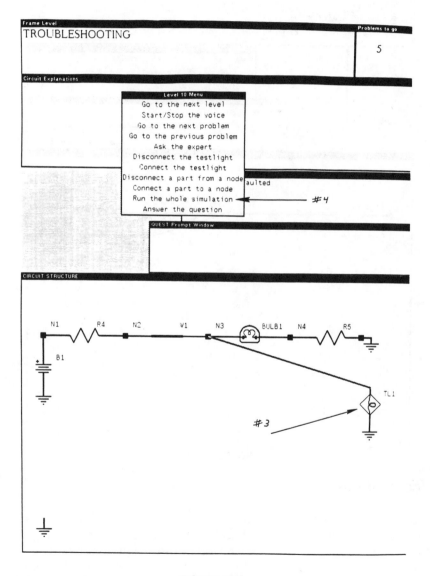

FIGURE 16.2c

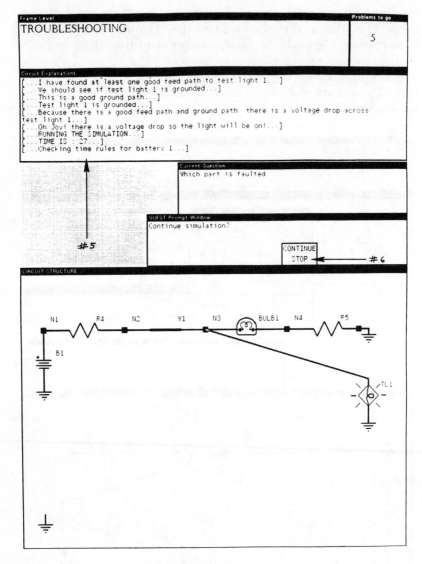

FIGURE 16.2d

CONCLUSIONS

The addition of information about the student's intentions, expectations, and plans, as well as his observed actions is, we believe, essential to making informed and insightful diagnostic hypotheses. This approach to diagnosis integrates commonsense principles from cognitive science with powerful AI inferencing methods. It substantially enhances the power and reliability of ICAI inferencing capabilities, and it has importance for a wide range of applications to complex systems maintenance and troubleshooting training.

This approach does have limitations. In common with other approaches, it is ineffective with noncooperative students. Also, it assumes the principle of rationality, that problem-solving behavior, whether correct or not, is always rational behavior even when based

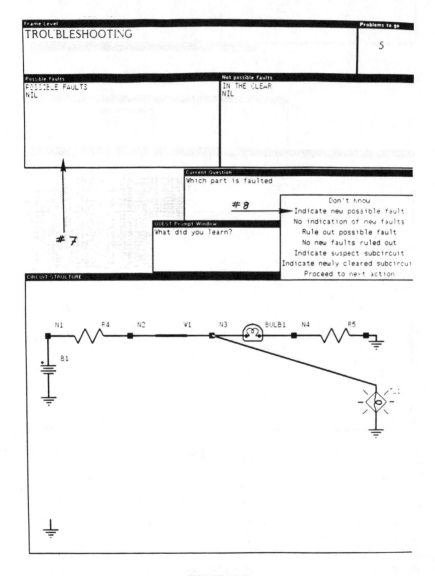

FIGURE 16.2e

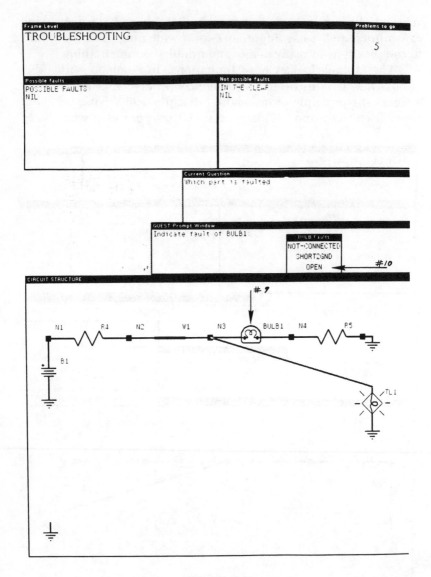

FIGURE 16.2f

on incorrect knowledge. Further, the elicitation procedure that is central to it will not be applicable in problem-solving situations where students lack either the knowledge or an appropriate vocabulary or language for talking about their problem-solving plans and goals. For example, beginning students of mathematics may be ill-equipped to discuss their strategy, or even their step-by-step actions, in performing tasks such as solving equations. This problem can be mitigated in QUIMON by placing items the student should be considering on the menu to prompt his or her thinking. Finally, in certain real-time situations, where tasks have to be performed on the fly, there is little time or attention available for the kind of interventions required to discuss actions, much less their antecedents and consequences. Other kinds of intelligent instructional methods must be developed to deal with such real-time interactions.

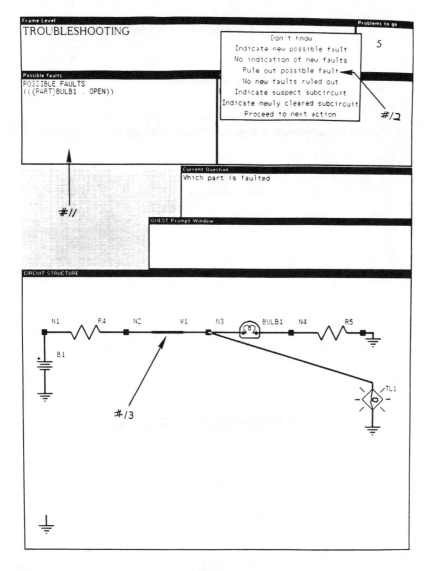

FIGURE 16.2g

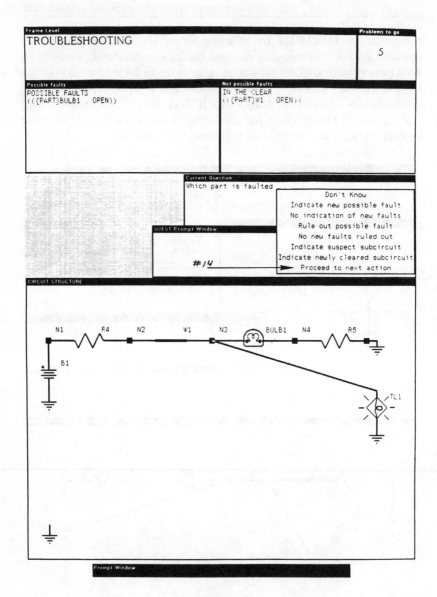

FIGURE 16.2h

Characterizing a student's problem-solving knowledge solely or primarily by observations of his overt actions has unnecessarily limited the power of student models. Soliciting the student's assistance in the attempt to determine the intentions and the reasoning, correct and faulty, that underlie his actions, is not at variance with the purpose or spirit of the intelligent instructional enterprise. Inviting students to rationalize their actions and to identify their hypotheses and goals can enormously enrich a program's knowledge of the student. The use of a mouse, menu, and window-based interactions on current machines enables rapid and nonintrusive elicitation during problem solving in intelligent tutoring systems that acquire and use this new rich source of data.

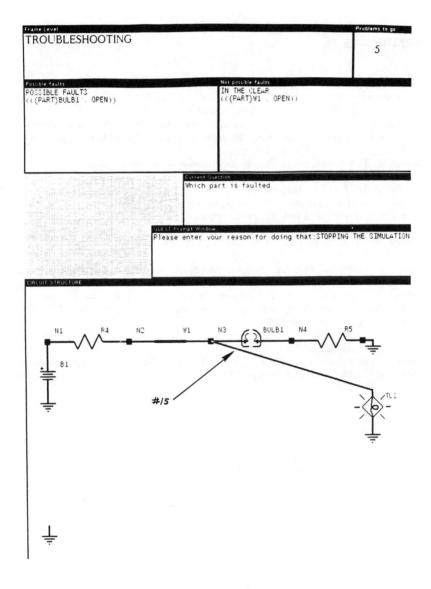

FIGURE 16.2i

ACKNOWLEDGMENT

This research was supported by the U. S. Office of Naval Research and the U. S. Army Research Institute under Contract N0014-82-C-0580.

REFERENCES

Brown,J. S., Burton, R. R., & Bell, A. G. (1974). *SOPHIE: A sophisticated instructional environment for teaching electronic troubleshooting (an example of AI in CAI) Final Report* (Tech. Rep. 2790). Bolt, Beranek & Newman.

Burton, R. R. (1982). Diagnosing bugs in a simple procedural skill. In D. Sleeman & J. S. Brown (Eds.), *Intelligent Tutoring systems* (pp. 157–199). London: Academic Press.

Burton, R. R., & Brown, J. S. (1982). An investigation of computer coaching for informal learning activities. In D. Sleeman & J. S. Brown (Eds.), *Intelligent tutoring systems* (PP. 79–98). London: Academic Press.

Feurzeig, W. (1985, January). *Student modeling in QUEST*. Presentation at ONR program review on AI and education. Georgia Institute of Technology.

Nagel, L. W. (1975, May). SPICE2. *A computer program to simulate semiconductor circuits* (Tech. Rep. ERL Memo No. ERL-M520). Berkeley, CA: University of California.

Ritter, F. (1986). OREO. Orienting electrical circuits for qualitative reasoning. Unpublished manuscript.

White, B. Y., & Frederiksen, J. R. (1986). *Progressions of qualitative models as a foundation for intelligent learning environments* (Technical Report 6277). BBN Laboratories, Cambridge, MA.

White, B. Y., & Frederiksen, J. R. (in press). Qualitative models and intelligent learning environments. *AI and Education.*

White, B. Y., & Frederiksen, J. R. (1985). QUEST: Qualitative understanding of electrical system troubleshooting. *ACM Sigart Newsletter, 93,* 34–37.

17

The Next Wave
of Problems in ITS:
Confronting the "User Issues"
of Interface Design
and System Evaluation

Douglas Frye
David C. Littman
Elliot Soloway
Yale University

MOTIVATION AND GOALS

The standard architecture of an Intelligent Tutoring System (ITS) is depicted in Figure 17.1. By and large, the majority of research effort goes into developing the student modeling module, the expert module, and the tutorial module, just as almost all effort is put into building these modules, since they do form the core of the ITS. However, we have found that developing an effective interface and developing an effective evaluation may require as many resources as did the development of the three core modules. We are not alone in this experience. Yet, there are few guidelines for how to build an effective interface for educational software, and how to design an effective evaluation for intelligent tutoring systems. Even though human–computer interaction is a topic of growing interest, that field has not focused on the special properties of educational software. Similarly, even though educational evaluation is an established field, methodologies have not been developed for evaluating educational systems that attempt to teach students to "understand"—rather than simply to get the right answer.

In this chapter, we present two case studies, one dealing with our efforts to understand the special properties of interfaces for educational software, and one dealing with our efforts to evaluate an intelligent tutoring system. Our intent is more to spotlight the problems than to present a coherent, well-worked-out theoretical framework in which these issues can be viewed and resolved. The bottom line is this: As ITS become usable entities, and not merely

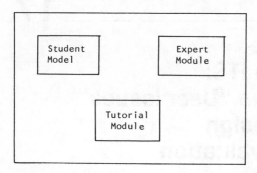

FIGURE 17.1 The three components of an ITS.

research curiosities, significant effort will need to be directed toward looking at user issues—interface design and evaluation—if we really want these ITS to be effective instructional devices.

In the next section, we present some of our experiences in studying young children as they attempted to use several popular programs for teaching arithmetic. We particularly focus on some of the misconceptions about the programs' interfaces that made it hard for children to use them effectively. Then, we show how our efforts to evaluate ITS have led us to conceptualize evaluation in a way somewhat different from the view of traditional educational evaluation, and we describe how we evaluated the educational effectiveness of PROUST, one component of our tutor for novice programming. Finally, we draw some preliminary conclusions about our research on interfaces and evaluation.

THE INTERFACE PROBLEM IN EDUCATIONAL SOFTWARE

Interface design for educational software, including that for Intelligent Tutoring Systems, seems to be one of those things that everyone does but few talk about. It is understandable that interface issues are not given primary importance; educational software and especially ITS are recent developments themselves. Yet there are good reasons not to ignore interface issues. The most obvious, of course, is that the best piece of educational software can be entirely ruined by a bad interface. Students cannot learn from a program they cannot use. There are two other particular points about educational software that elevate the importance of the interface: With educational software, the interface must provide an entry to the content domain rather than vice versa. In other types of software, the user typically knows what application a program is meant to have and can use that knowledge to decipher the interface. The first-time user of a word processor may expect to find certain commands because he or she knows the program is meant to manipulate text. Virtually by definition, users of educational software will not have a similar advantage. They will not have a good understanding of the domain being taught and so will not have that entry to the interface.

A further requirement for an interface to a piece of educational software is that it must be sensitive to the student's general knowledge and/or developmental level. Given that the interface must introduce the user to the domain, and not the reverse, the interface will need to provide for variations in the skills of different users. This is especially important for educational software designed for children, where skill and developmental differences form the rule rather than the exception. If an interface cannot span some of these difficulties, then it will be of very limited utility in education. Further, different educational domains can require different interfaces. John Anderson and his group's tutors for LISP (Farrell, Anderson & Reiser, 1984) and geometry (Anderson, Boyle, & Yost, 1985) are derived from the same theory of human cognition, yet the interfaces the two use are very different.

We have chosen to begin our research examining the importance of the interface in educational software by studying very simple computer-assisted instruction (CAI) software available in the schools now, specifically, testing software that provides instruction in arithmetic. We find that the interface to this software, an interface that is not unusual, caused the students a large number of problems. These include some simple, but very persistent problems such as difficulties using the return key. There were also instances of deep misunderstandings, in which the students did not recognize the point of a major component of a program or of the program itself. These difficulties clearly limited the instructional effectiveness of the software we tested.

Our overall aim in this research is to develop an approach to interface design that can be employed with all types of educational software. Because of the special demands on the interface in educational software, we believe that the approach will clearly need to consider the content domain being taught and the general skill and developmental level of the student. Thus, the approach requires that researchers know as much as possible about how students learn in a particular subject domain and derive implications from that knowledge for the design of the interface. With arithmetic software, as will be discussed later, we believe that there is a prima facie case that "direct manipulation"-style interfaces (Shneiderman, 1983) will be best suited to this domain.

HIGHLIGHTS OF OUR STUDIES

We highlight some of the observations we have made in studying children using several pieces of educational software designed to teach arithmetic skills. These studies have been directed toward discovering exactly how children interact with the types of educational software now available to the schools. Our general strategy has been to conduct our studies in a way that allows the children to use the software much as they would normally.

Description of the Software Tested

The arithmetic software we have been testing is a part of a series of commerically available programs. The particular software we used in our studies was produced by Compu-Teach, Inc. However, although this software has some unique features (e.g., excellent color graphics), it nontheless closely resembles that of the popular "Sticky Bear" series of software produced by Xerox, and most other programs designed to teach counting, adding, and subtracting. Thus, we believe that our results have importance beyond the particular make of software we tested. (As an interesting aside, the programs we tested have won awards from various parents and software magazines. Needless to say, adults awarded the prizes—not the children who had to use the software!) There were separate programs for counting, addition, and subtraction. A detailed description of the responses necessary to operate the addition program and a picture of the initial screen are given in Figs.17.2 and 17.3. Essentially, the program is designed to present a simple addition problem on the screen, along with two sets of objects equal to the numbers in the problem. The user has to give the answer to the problem by pressing number keys from the normal keyboard. It is necessary to press the return key to enter the final (possibly multidigit) answer. If a problem is answered incorrectly three times in a row, the program enters a remedial sequence that illustrates the correct answer. After every problem, it is again necessary to use the return key to operate a small menu that allows the choice between a new problem, the repetition of the previous problem, or exit from the program. The counting and subtraction programs follow very similar design principles.

The programs were tested by giving them to 20 five- and 20 seven-year olds to operate. We first demonstrated the programs. The children were then allowed to work through them freely. Their responses over an hour-long session were recorded on videotape.

The Addition Program

Initial display. The program begins with the presentation of an addition problem in large characters across the top of the screen. Problems are restricted to single-digit numbers and are always shown in the form of "x + y." Next, a square box is drawn beneath each number. Each box is filled with as many instances of an object as the number above the box. The question "How many?" is then written in normal text at the bottom of the screen.

Correct response. The child responds to the program by entering a 1- or 2-digit number using the keyboard. The number entered is displayed next to the "How many?" question. The return key must then be struck. If the child has given the correct answer, then the problem is replaced by the correct sum, the boxes are dissolved, and all of the objects are grouped together. They then move off the screen one by one while the sum decrements to zero.

Incorrect response. If the child's answer is incorrect, it disappears from the screen and two more chances are given. On the third attempt, an incorrect response causes the computer to beep. The program then draws crossed lines through each of the objects in turn in the two boxes. A number is shown incrementing as each object is marked. The final number, of course, represents the correct sum.

Final display. No matter whether the correct or error sequence was followed, the final frame for the problem always shows a number on top representing the correct sum with that many instances of the object below it. There is also a line across the lower third of the screen. Beneath that line is a picture of the object used in the problem, a picture of another object and a stop sign. Pressing the space bar on the keyboard moves an arrow so that it points to these pictures one after another. Pressing the return key when the arrow is in the proper position results in the same addition problem being presented again, a new problem, or exit from the program.

FIGURE 17.2 Operations necessary to use addition program.

Survey of the Results

The study found, rather surprisingly, that the children experienced many difficulties operating these apparently simple programs. Some of the children's errors were quite obvious. Others constituted what seemed to be very subtle misunderstandings between the children and the programs. The problems were often severe enough to make it hard to imagine children mastering the operation of the programs without the assistance of an adult. Besides making them hard to use, the difficulties clearly interfered with the program's instructional value; in fact, the children who were able to operate the programs were also the ones who already tended to have competence in the subjects the

FIGURE 17.3 A picture of the initial screen for addition program.

programs were designed to teach. In line with this finding, younger children clearly had more difficulty operating the programs; however, certain features of the interface were disruptive to the older children, but not to the younger ones.

Some Specific Misconceptions

Three examples of children's difficulties with the programs follow. They have been selected to illustrate the range of problems the children encountered.

The return key.   Difficulties with the return key very clearly exemplify problems having to do with the operation of the program. Virtually all of the children had trouble using the return key both in entering their answers to problems, and to a lesser extent, in making the selection for the next problem. The difficulty usually took the form of the subjects typing in their answers, but then omitting to press the return key. In this event, they would often simply sit waiting for the computer to respond. Typically, the error could not easily be overcome. In spite of the experimenter repeatedly reminding the child to press return, almost half of the 5-year-olds did not press the return without help in the entire session, even though the majority were able to key in their actual answers on their own (see Table 1 in Figure 17.4).

Operating the return key may have been difficult because it served two functions: entering answers and selecting the next problem. However, mistakes similar to ones we observed have been found for adults who had to use the return key to give commands to a text editor (Norman, 1982). Probes of our subjects indicated that they did not understand why it was necessary to press the return key. They assumed that the computer "had gotten" their answer because their numbers had appeared on the screen or the menu arrow had been moved. Pressing the return made no immediate change on the screen, although it eventually, of course, produced an action on the part of the program.

Instructional sequences. The parts of the programs meant to instruct generated some problems that went beyond the simple operation of the software. The clearest example involves the remedial sequence presented after incorrect answers. Specifically, only 4 of the 20 five-year-olds and 7 of the 20 seven-year-olds realized that this sequence was depicting the correct answer to the problem (see Table 2 in Figure 17.4).

One possible explanation of this problem is that it has proven a poor design choice to use crossed lines to mark objects as they were being counted—because x's are usually associated with mistakes—but the children did not comment to this effect. They just seemed not to associate this part of the program with a remediation routine.

Miscommunications. A further class of difficulties arose that can only be seen as misunderstandings between the child and the intent of a particular program. A striking instance of this sort occurred with several of the younger children and the addition program. These children were able to count through all of the objects in both boxes on the screen during an addition problem. They were also able to key in the total, so if they had counted correctly, they arrived at the correct answer to the problem. Our probing showed, however, that 17 out of the 20 five-year-olds could not read the addition problem that had originally been set on the screen (see Table 3 in Figure 17.4). They had an especially difficult time recognizing the plus sign.

It appears that when a number of identical small objects are drawn on the screen, young children will count them. In this case, the program seems to be giving practice on addition, but actually these younger children were not even aware that they were answering an addition problem; they just counted. This effect first became apparent with the subtraction program. In this program, the young children were even less likely to be able to read the minus sign. Except here, of

TABLE 1
Numbers of Children (out of 20) at Each Age
Needing Help on One Trial and on the Majority of Fifteen Trials

	5-year-olds	7-year-olds
Needed help on at least one trial:		
Keying in answer:	17 (85%)	0
Using return to enter answer:	18 (90%)	6 (30%)
Using return for next problem:	17 (85%)	6 (30%)
Needed help on majority of trials:		
Keying in answer:	3 (15%)	0
Using return to enter answer:	9 (45%)	0
Using return for next problem:	8 (40%)	0

TABLE 2
Numbers of Children (out of 20) at Each Age
Recognizing What the Wrong Sequence Signified

	5-year-olds	7-year-olds
Knew what wrong sequence signified:	4 (20%)	7 (35%)

TABLE 3
Numbers of Children (out of 20) at Each
Age Unable to Read Relevant Parts of the Screen

	5-year-olds	7-year-olds
Were unable to read on the screen:		
The numbers in the problem:	17 (85%)	0
The plus sign in the problem:	18 (90%)	6 (30%)
The "How many?" prompt:	17 (85%)	6 (30%)

FIGURE 17.4 Tables showing effects of misconceptions.

course, simply counting the objects on the screen always led to an incorrect answer.

The Interface and the Programs' Instructional Effectiveness

Difficulties with the interface clearly interfered with the instructional effectiveness of the software. Nearly half of the 5-year-olds (Table 17.1 in Figure 17.4) needed help throughout the session just to operate the programs. Obviously, without that help, these children would never have come in contact with the instructional content of the programs. Similarly, some of the other 5- and 7-year-olds who needed help only at the beginning of the session would probably not have mastered the operation of the programs if help had not been available at the outset.

The results also revealed that the children who were best at arithmetic were the ones who had the fewest difficulties with the operation of the program. So, for example, it was found that the children's scores on the arithmetic subscale of the Wechsler were negatively correlated ($rs = -.50s$, $ps < .05$) with the number of prompts they had to be given. It might be that these children knew how to operate the programs, so their arithmetic improved compared to the others, but no such improvement in performance during the session was found. The pattern of results is consistent with the possibility that the children who were good at arithmetic had one less thing to worry about when they were trying to learn to use the programs.

Finally, there was some evidence that the programs at times directly interfered with some children's understanding of arithmetic. For 6 of the 20 five-year olds, there were occasions when they spontaneously showed (by speaking aloud or pointing) that they knew the answer to a problem and yet were unable to convey that answer to the program. When the program did not respond correctly, they, more often than not, changed their answer because they concluded it was wrong.

Interaction with General Skill and/or Development Level

There were obviously very large age differences in the children's responses to the interface to the programs. The 5-year-olds required many more instances of direct prompting ($ts > 3.59$, $ps < .05$) to overcome difficulties, and they were still less successful than the 7-year-olds in operating the programs. Yet, we discovered a few aspects of the interface that were more detrimental to the 7-year-olds than the 5-year-olds. For example, a probe question showed that the 7-year-olds consistently found the pace of the programs to be boring, whereas the 5-year-olds did not ($t = 2.49$, $p < .05$). As a consequence, it was not unusual for the 7-year-olds to stop attending to the program when they had to wait for it to respond. The age differences must be interpreted in light of the fact that the children in the study differed in age by only two years and that the software was intended for children of these ages. With larger age differences, of course, the problem would increase, and an interface that did not provide better for developmental level would generate an even greater number of difficulties.

IMPLICATIONS OF THE RESEARCH
FOR INTERFACE DESIGN

The Cognitive Perspective
on Interface Design

The interface, we argue, is especially important in educational software because it must lead students into the domain, and not vice versa, and it must accommodate different students' general skill and/or developmental levels. To design an interface that can meet these needs, we think it important to use what is known about how students typically learn in the domain in which they are being instructed. Information from recent studies in cognitive science is accumulating on precisely this point—how students learn in various domains. This information may help to inform interface design and to improve instructional software. We have selected arithmetic as a promising domain to explore this approach to interface design.

Arithmetic and Direct Manipulation Interfaces (DMI)

Arithmetic is attractive as a domain because there is extensive research (see review by Fuson & Hall, 1983) on how children acquire arithmetic skills. Research shows, as might be expected, that counting is the first skill children acquire. Algorithms for addition and subtraction are built from that base. The algorithms follow a standard progression. With addition, for example, the child will first count through both numbers in an addition problem to reach the total. Later the child will take one number as a starting point and only count through the second. Eventually counting will become unnecessary.

A consistent finding in this domain is that having objects present aids the child. Being able to try out operations on objects, for instance, initially helps the child to count (Shannon, 1978) and acquire the various addition algorithms (Secada, Fuson, & Hall, 1983). This characteristic of how addition is learned is in line with what is known in general from developmental psychology about children of this age. From Piaget onward it has been accepted that young children's thought is less abstract and more closely tied to action and situation than is that of adults.

What is known about how children typically learn arithmetic would seem to suggest that a "direct manipulation" style of interface (Shneiderman, 1983) would be the interface of choice for software in this domain. For this age group, a direct manipulation interface could be built around a touchscreen and voice synthesizer. The interface would then allow "objects" to be moved around the screen under the child's and/or the computer's control. It would permit the child to carry out arithmetic operations: combining sets of objects for addition and taking objects out of a set for subtraction. The computer would be able to manipulate the symbols—numbers—associated with the operations. It would be able to speak the numbers and print them on the screen. The computer also could instantiate the progression of algorithms children use for addition and subtraction. Practice on these could lead the child through the progression. Thus, this type of interface has the capability of giving the child the type of experience that research has shown to be important for acquiring competence in this domain. Furthermore, this interface, compared to the old one, gives a better "match" with the general nature of the child's thought, because it encourages the child to act, and it is not purely abstract.

How a DMI Might Reduce the Specific Errors Shown

It is useful to consider if a direct manipulation interface could also correct the specific sorts of interface difficulties we observed in the programs we initially tested. With the touchscreen interface, for instance, the problems we observed children having with the return key could be corrected by allowing the child to choose the next problem by pointing to that item. During a problem, answers could be entered in the usual way, but the child would have to move them (by pointing) down into a special box on the screen to send them to the program. The error sequences, and problems themselves, perhaps, could be made more meaningful and made to follow the child's pace by having the child touch or move objects on the screen, instead of having the program draw crossed lines through the objects or move them on its own. The interface could not eliminate all miscommunication with the child, but it should certainly make the possibility more remote.

SUMMARY REMARKS

The results of our studies show very clearly that the interface to a program—how it presents itself to a young user - is an essential consideration in the design of educational software. The design decisions made in the programs we tested were not unreasonable and were surely well intentioned. However, at critical places they violated the criteria we have identified for educational interfaces:

1. *The interface must provide an entry to the content domain, rather than vice versa.* In other types of software, the user typically knows what application a program is meant to do and can use that knowledge to decipher the interface. Users of educational software will not have a similar advantage. They will not have a good understanding of the domain being taught and so will not have that entry to the interface. In our studies of software to teach addition, for example, our subjects appeared to need to know how to add already in order to be able to master the operation of the program.
2. *The interface must be sensitive to the child's developmental level.* The importance of this point became apparent several times in our studies. For example, we found that our younger students had more difficulty than the older ones in using the return key to enter their arithmetic answers and operate the program, and the older subjects objected more to the slow pace of the software. Given that the children differed in age only by two years, it is obvious that the interface must make some allowance for development if it is to be effective.

We believe that studying users of educational software, and how people learn in particular domains is necessary to inform interface design. Arithmetic is a promising domain in this regard—a great deal is known about how children begin to learn this subject. Some of these findings indicate that a direct manipulation interface might be particularly well suited to teaching arithmetic. More important, this work illustrates a general approach to guide interface design for educational software.

EVALUATION OF ITSs

Evaluating Intelligent Tutoring Systems is costly, frustrating, and time consuming. For example, in our own efforts to build PROUST, one of the components of an ITS for novice programming students, we have spent nearly as many resources to evaluate PROUST as to construct it; in fact, for us, evaluation has become an intrinsic part of the process of building PROUST. Evaluation is extremely costly; why do developers bother to evaluate ITS at all? Wouldn't it be better just to finish one ITS and then build the next one? The answer is no. Our experience with PROUST has taught us that, far from being a burden, evaluation can pay off by helping us answer the Evaluation Question about ITSs that is at the center of Cognitive Science, Artificial Intelligence, and Education: "What is the educational impact of an ITS on students?"

Focusing attention on the evaluation question applied to

PROUST has been very beneficial to our understanding both of PROUST and of how PROUST affects students' learning: By doing evaluations we have discovered a great deal about how novices learn to program, how to teach programming, and how to build ITSs to actually teach programming, understanding that we might not have obtained if we had not maintained a strong commitment to evaluation. As we have gained experience in constructing evaluations of PROUST, we have found that addressing the evaluation question leads to a perspective on evaluation that is somewhat different from that of traditional educational evaluation. Traditional educational evaluation consists of two main categories, formative and summative evaluation. *Formative evaluation* attempts to assist designers of educational technology to define and refine their goals and methods during the design process. *Summative evaluation* tries to determine whether a finished educational product is effective after it has been built. Because building ITSs is still somewhat of an art and there are few ITSs that we would be prepared to say are "finished," designers of ITS are naturally more concerned with usefully guiding the development of their ITS than with determining whether they are effective educational end products. At least for the time being, then, the idea of formative evaluation seems more appropriate for designers of ITS than does the idea of summative evaluation. Hence, we interpret the evaluation question to be much more focused on the development of ITS than on determining whether they are effective educational end products.

Unfortunately, because the field of ITS is still young, there is no standard set of evaluation methods appropriate to address the evaluation question. However, as a result of our ongoing attempts to develop evaluation strategies that we can use to guide our work on PROUST, we have begun to define a class of evaluation methods that seem potentially useful in addressing the evaluation question. We have found that methods based on recent progress in student modeling (cf. VanLehn, 1986) provide a useful point of departure for assessing the educational impact of an ITS. Student modeling methods may enable us to assess the educational impact of ITSs directly in terms of changes in students' knowledge and problem-solving skills. We call the perspective on evaluation based on student modeling methods the "Cognitive Perspective" because evaluation from the Cognitive Perspective looks at educational effectiveness explicitly in terms of the impact of an ITS on students' cognitive processes.

In the next section of the chapter we explore some of the specifics of how to do assessment from the Cognitive Perspective as well as some of the useful results we have derived from this kind of evaluation. In particular, we show how applying these methods to evaluating PROUST has made it possible for us to begin to isolate specific aspects of PROUST that have particular effects on students' learning. Even though we have found the Cognitive Perspective on evaluation to be productive, we are aware that we tread new, and potentially controversial, ground. We are equally aware that, at this time, we cannot present a fully formed theory of evaluation from the Cognitive Perspective. Nonetheless, we feel that the potential usefulness of the directions and techniques for evaluation that we identify in this chapter warrant presenting them to the ITS community.

THE COGNITIVE PERSPECTIVE ON EVALUATION

We suggest that progress in student modeling methods might provide a useful basis for evaluating the impact of ITS on students, because recent developments in student modeling methods provide the field of computer-based instruction with new, powerful methods for representing, in ITS, knowledge and skills of students that were not available to designers of CAI. In fact, this emphasis of ITS on the cognitive processes of students has led directly to a difference in the goals of evaluating effectiveness of CAI and ITS. The goal of evaluating CAI has been primarily to determine whether students who use it can respond correctly to questions, and the goal of evaluating an ITS should be to discover how well it teaches students knowledge and skills that support the processes of solving problems. Thus, the lack of powerful methods for student modeling led designers and evaluators of CAI to make the reasonable, pragmatic assumption that answers to test questions were a good reflection of the student's internal processes.

Our goal for evaluating ITSs can be much more ambitious, however. We propose that the goal of evaluating an ITS should be to discover how well it teaches students specific knowledge and skills that support their processes of solving problems. With the advent of sophisticated tools for modeling students' problem-solving processes, we now have the opportunity to take the next step toward such precise evaluations from the Cognitive Perspective. In this section, therefore, we first define what we mean by student models and discuss the role that student models could play in evaluation. Then we present an extended account of how we have begun to conduct an evaluation of PROUST, our program for finding bugs in novices' PASCAL programs, from the Cognitive Perspective.

Student Models and Their Use in Evaluation

As an ITS interacts with a student, it builds up an understanding of the student's knowledge and skills, which it uses to interpret the student's behavior and to guide, in part, its own actions. The common name for the ITS's understanding of the student is *student model.* In order for an ITS to build a student model, its designers have to give it methods for reasoning about students' problem solving in the ITS's domain of instruction; these methods are called *student modeling methods.* There are many kinds of student modeling methods. In this section, however, we wish to focus on the distinction between student modeling techniques that are based on process models of problem solving, which embody a designer's theory of how people actually solve problems in the domain of instruction, and student models that are not based on process models. Thus, student modeling techniques based on process models solve problems in a way that is supposed to be like a human's. For example, the student modeling component in Anderson's LISP tutor is based on a process model of how students write simple LISP programs; the process model is embodied in the LISP tutor's GRAPES simulator (Anderson, Farrell, & Sauers, 1984). The LISP tutor uses the GRAPES simulator to simulate the problem solving performed by novice LISP programmers when they write simple LISP programs and, thus, represents and reasons about specific cognitive processes the student engages in while solving a problem.

Student modeling techniques that are not based on comprehensive process models do not construct their student models by solving problems in the way that humans do. For example, WUSOR, the tutor for the dungeons-and-dragons–like discovery game WUMPUS, built by Carr and Goldstein (Goldstein, 1982), has a checklist of skills required to play WUMPUS. WUSOR's student model simply consists of the skills the student has for playing WUMPUS that are "checked off" in WUSOR's representation of the skills. WUSOR does not try to "play" WUMPUS as a student would in order to build its student model and, hence, does not use process models in its student modeling. In fact, student models can be very useful in performing evaluations of ITS from the Cognitive Perspective.

An evaluation of an ITS from the Cognitive Perspective should assess how well the ITS teaches students skills and knowledge for solving problems that are similar to problems encountered during learning. Because student models identify knowledge and skills that are used in solving problems, whether or not they actually have process models that simulate students' behavior, they can be used to guide the construction of the problems posed to students in the evaluation of the ITS. Because student modeling techniques capture how students solve problems, and not just the fact that students can solve the problems, they can be used to identify problems that students should be able to solve and problems students should not be able to solve, as well as to predict what knowledge and skills the student will use in solving them (in the case of non–process-based student modeling techniques) or the actual process the student will go through to solve the problems (in the case of process-based student modeling techniques.) Thus the evaluation of ITS can be substantially different from the evaluation of CAI, because evaluation of CAI focuses primarily on correct and incorrect problems and evaluation of ITSs assesses the reasons that students make correct and incorrect answers.

In the foregoing discussion, we have purposely glossed over an important issue: the degree of completeness, or comprehensiveness, of the process model underlying the ITS. For example, Repair Theory (Brown & VanLehn, 1980) is a relatively comprehensive process model of how people carry out subtraction. In contrast, the process model underlying PROUST, our system that diagnoses students' buggy programs, is considerably less comprehensive. Though it would be nice to have more comprehensive process models for ITS, this is not always possible, and it is not even necessary in order to perform evaluation. In fact, an overlay model, for example, the checklist of skills used in WUMPUS and WEST, can still provide leverage into the microstructure of the skills and concepts that students use when they solve problems. The point is that in an evaluation of an ITS from the Cognitive Perspective, we do not look to see how many answers the student got correct, but rather, we use the student model to try to look at the underlying, fine-grained skills that are learned. Thus it is important to be able to perform evaluations of ITS with student models that are not comprehensive. In the next subsection, we address the problem of evaluation from the Cognitive Perspective with incomplete process models by showing how we were able to evaluate the impact of PROUST on a circumscribed aspect of students' programming.

An Example of Evaluation
from the Cognitive Perspective: PROUST

In this subsection, we discuss our initial attempts to perform an evaluation of PROUST from the Cognitive Perspective. First, we describe PROUST and how it works; then we discuss how we approached the problem of evaluation from the Cognitive Perspective. Our evaluation of PROUST was based on a process model of novice PASCAL programming. We reasoned about the process model to identify skills we thought PROUST should help students learn. Of course, we do not have a complete process model of novice programming; thus, one implication of the success of our evaluation of PROUST is that it is not necessary to have a complete process model in order to perform an evaluation from the Cognitive Perspective. This is encouraging because we have proposed to intertwine the development and evaluation of ITS. Evaluations in the face of incomplete process models will be the reality we all will have to face in our evaluation efforts.

A Description of PROUST

PROUST is a large LISP program written by Lewis Johnson (Johnson, 1985) that finds the nonsyntactic bugs in student's PASCAL programs. PROUST is especially expert at finding bugs in programs that students write for the Rainfall Assignment, shown in Figure 17.5. The assignment, which is usually given during the fifth week of class, calls for an enhanced "averaging program" that requires the student to take in an input stream of rainfall values, calculating the average, the maximum rainfall on any day in the period, the number of rainy days, and so forth. Finally, the program writes out several summary values.

A correct solution to the Rainfall Assignment is shown in Figure 17.6, whereas a fragment of a buggy solution is shown in Figure 17.7; the fragment shown in the latter contains three extremely common bugs. Figure 17.8 shows what a student sees as a result of asking PROUST to identify the bugs in the program in Figure 17.7. Notice especially that the output of PROUST is essentially an identification of the student's bugs, possibly accompanied by a brief statement of how the bug violates the specifications of the assignment. In addition, PROUST makes an effort to tell the student which bugs it thinks are important for various parts of the program (e.g., the "OUTPUT part"). Thus, the first bug that PROUST reports is a very common bug; students often neglect to consider the case in which the user does not enter any valid data. If no data are entered, a run-time "division-by-zero" error occurs and can cause the program to discontinue its run.

To analyze a student's program, PROUST attempts to see how a student's program has tried to meet the specifications of a problem statement. PROUST understands problem specifications in terms of goals that must be solved and uses a knowledge base of plans that students know about to achieve those goals. PROUST's main analytic task is to locate in the student's code the plans for each of the goals in the problem specification. For example, in the Rainfall Assignment,

The Noah Problem: Noah needs to keep track of the rainfall in the New Haven area to determine when to launch his ark. Write a program so he can do this. Your program should read the rainfall for each day, stopping when Noah types "99999", which is not a data value, but a sentinel indicating the end of input. If the user types in a negative value the program should reject it, since negative rainfall is not possible. Your program should print out the number of valid days typed in, the number of rainy days, the average rainfall per day over the period, and the maximum amount of rainfall that fell on any one day.

FIGURE 17.5   The rainfall assignment.

the main goal is to calculate the average of a series of rainfall values entered by the user. PROUST recognizes that to achieve the averaging goal an iterative looping plan is required to achieve the main goal's subgoals: The loop must (a) collect the rainfall values, (b) sum the values to calculate the running total, and (c) count the number of days. After the running total and counter have been calculated, the running total must be divided by the counter to obtain the average. PROUST thus sets up an agenda of goals and subgoals and attempts to match each to the student's code. By using techniques for finding buggy implementations of plans, PROUST matches the student's code to goals on its agenda. When all the goals on the agenda have been successfully matched to the student's code, possibly invoking the techniques for finding buggy plans, PROUST has "understood" the student's program, because PROUST knows how the student solved, or failed to solve, each of the goals in the specification. Each of the failures is understood by PROUST as a bug.

Evaluation of PROUST from the Cognitive Perspective

The focus of our current evaluation efforts with PROUST is on whether a program that simply identifies nonsyntactic bugs for novice programmers and provides only minimal, noninteractive, tutorial advice can have a positive impact on their programming skills. Because evaluations of PROUST's ability to find bugs have been reported in several places (e.g., Johnson, 1985, whose analyses showed that PROUST is able to understand between 70% and 80% of all programs written by novices trying to solve the Rainfall Assignment) we do not address that issue here. Our evaluation of the effects of PROUST's identification of bugs for students stems from our process model of programming. Though, as we have noted, our process model of novice programming is incomplete and somewhat idealized, it does nonetheless make some interesting statements about bugs which novices should find very hard to discover and correct.

One kind of bug we have focused on is the *boundary condition* bug. In a boundary condition bug, the student neglects to guard some aspect of the program (e.g., an arithmetic calculation) against an unexpected value. For example, the boundary condition bugs shown in Figure 17.9 all illustrate this class of bugs. In BUG 1, the student has overlooked the boundary condition in which the user does not enter any valid data and the calculation of the average results in a division by zero, which causes the program to crash. The remainder of the bugs arise in the same boundary condition; here the result is not a crashed program but the illegal output of a value that never was calculated by the program. For example, BUG 2 permits the average

```
Program Rainfall(input,output);
  Var DailyRainfall,TotalRainfall,MaxRainfall,Average : Real;
    RainyDays,TotalDays : Integer;
  Begin
    RainyDays:= 0; TotalDays:= 0; MaxRainfall:= 0; TotalRainfall:= 0;
    Writeln ('Please Enter Amount of Rainfall');
    Readln(DailyRainfall);
    While (DailyRainfall <> 99999) Do
      Begin
        If DailyRainfall >= 0 Then
          Begin
            If DailyRainfall > 0 Then RainyDays := RainyDays + 1;
            TotalRainfall := TotalRainfall + DailyRainfall;
            If DailyRainfall > MaxRainfall
              Then MaxRainfall := DailyRainfall;
            TotalDays := TotalDays + 1
          End;
        Else Writeln ('Rainfall Must Be Greater Than 0');
        Read(DailyRainfall)
      End;
    If TotalDaysCounter > 0 Then Begin
      Average := TotalRainfall/TotalDays;
      Writeln('Average is: ', Average: 0:2);
      Writeln('Maximum is: ', MaxRainfall: 0:2);
      Writeln('Total Number of Days is: ', TotalDays);
      Writeln('Total Number of Rainy Days is: ', RainyDays)
    End;
    Else Writeln('No Valid Days Entered.');
  End.
```

FIGURE 17.6 Sample correct rainfall program.

```
01 Program Rainfall(input,output);
02 Var DailyRainfall,TotalRainfall,MaxRainfall,Average : Real;
03    RainyDays,TotalDays : Integer;
04 Begin
05    RainyDays:= 0; TotalDays:= 0; MaxRainfall:= 0; TotalRainfall:= 0;
06    While (DailyRainfall <> 99999) Do
07      Begin
            .
            .
            .
33      End;

     Bug 1: Missing Divide-By-Zero Guard
34      Average := TotalRainfall/TotalDays;
     Bug 2: Missing Output Guard On Average
35      Writeln('Average is: ', Average: 0:2);
     Bug 3: Missing Output Guard On Maximum
36      Writeln('Maximum is: ', MaxRainfall: 0:2);
            .
            .
            .
End.
```

FIGURE 17.7 Sample incorrect rainfall program.

to be written out even if it was never calculated.

Boundary condition bugs are predicted by our process model to be easy to make but hard to find, and, therefore, they are prime candidates for PROUST's assistance bug identification strategy. In contrast, the failure to include an update for the counter that serves as the divisor in an averaging program would be easy to make and easy to find, because its effects would be apparent as soon as an attempt was made to calculate an average. The prediction that bugs are easy or hard to make, and easy or hard to find, derives from our process model of the programming process.

Very generally, our process model of program generation posits that a programmer reads a problem statement, identifies goals to solve in the problem statement, and then selects and implements plans to achieve the goals. The process model predicts that boundary condition bugs are easy to make but hard to find because to handle them requires using plans that solve goals not directly identified in problem statements. Because goals for handling boundary conditions do not

Starting Bug Analysis, please wait ... NOW BEGINNING BUG REPORT:

Now Reporting CRITICAL Bugs in the OUTPUT part of your program:

Bug 1: You need a test to check that at least one valid data point has been input before line 34 is executed. The Average will bomb when there is no input.

Now Reporting MINOR Bugs in the OUTPUT part of your program:

Bug 2: The average is undefined if there is no input. But line 35 outputs it anyway. You should output the average only when there is something to compute the average of.

Bug 3: The maximum is undefined if there is no input. But line 36 outputs it anyway. You should output the maximum only when there is something to compute the maximum of.

BUG REPORT NOW COMPLETE.

FIGURE 17.8 PROUST output for program in Figure 17.7.

typically arise directly from the statement of a problem, a programmer needs to use specialized programming knowledge about (for example) what to do about users who do not enter any valid data, to infer that boundary conditions must be handled by the program. Thus, the programmer must realize that there are boundary conditions and then use a plan to insure that legal values have been entered. But, according to our process model, novices are deficient in generalized programming knowledge and, therefore, do not identify goals such as guarding for boundary conditions; moreover, novices typically do not know plans for achieving the boundary condition goal even if they can identify it. Thus, they frequently make boundary condition bugs.

Boundary condition bugs are hard to find because they show up only under very specific input conditions. If students are deficient in generating test data for their programs, then they will rarely find their boundary condition bugs. Because effective testing of programs requires extensive generalized programming knowledge, most novices are poor program testers; boundary condition bugs are therefore hard

```
Program Rainfall(input,output);
  Var DailyRainfall,TotalRainfall,MaxRainfall,Average : Real;
    RainyDays,TotalDays : Integer;
  Begin
    RainyDays:= 0; TotalDays:= 0; MaxRainfall:= 0; TotalRainfall:= 0;
    Writeln ('Please Enter Amount of Rainfall');
    Readln(DailyRainfall);
    While (DailyRainfall <> 99999) Do
      Begin
        If (DailyRainfall > 0) Then
          .
          .
          .
      Read(DailyRainfall)
    End;
  BUG 1: "Divide by zero guard" missing
    Average := TotalRainfall/TotalDays;
  BUG 2: no guard for undefined average
    Writeln('Average is: ', Average: 0:2);
  BUG 3: no guard for undefined maximum
    Writeln('Maximum is: ', MaxRainfall: 0:2);
    Writeln('Total Number of Days is: ', TotalDays);
  BUG 4: no guard for undefined rainydays
    Writeln('Total Number of Rainy Days is: ', RainyDays)
  End.
```

FIGURE 17.9 Some boundary-condition bugs.

for them to find.[1] Thus, because boundary condition bugs are common, they can be accounted for in our process model and because they possess the attribute that PROUST is very good at finding them, our initial assessments of PROUST's educational effectiveness attempted to assess how well PROUST could help students manage boundary condition bugs.

In addition, though we do not discuss these results here, we assessed PROUST's impact on student's ability to manage other types of bugs.

How We Evaluated PROUST

In addition, though we do not discuss these results here, we assess

---

[1] On the basis of empirical data about students' buggy programs, J. Spohrer (1986) has elaborated the process model in a way that more fully accounts for the prevalence of boundary condition bugs.

PROUST's impact on student's ability to manage other types of bug. In order to determine the effect of PROUST's identification of bugs for students, we defined two performance tests that reflect our process model of programming and allow us to make inferences from students' performance on the tests to the underlying problem-solving processes they used to solve the problems on the performance tests.

1. *The pattern of boundary condition bugs in the student's versions of the Rainfall Assignment.* When students complete the Rainfall Assignment they typically generate 15 versions on the path to producing a final version that they feel they can submit for grading. We reasoned from our process model that students would have difficulty with boundary conditions, which are easy to make and hard to find. Further, if PROUST identified boundary condition bugs for students, the students would be less likely either to make as many of the boundary bugs in the first place or leave the bugs in their final versions.

2. *The student's score on the midterm examination.* We reasoned that, because PROUST could help students isolate the class of boundary condition bugs, they would be better able to find such bugs in programs written by other programmers. Therefore, the student's task on the midterm examination was to identify, describe, and fix bugs that had been seeded in programs that were similar to the ones the students had been writing in their assignments. Boundary condition bugs, as well as other types (such as performing the wrong arithmetic calculation) were seeded in the programs on the midterm examination.

Thus, even though both measurements of improvements in students' bug-identification performance are essentially "numbers of answers correct" measures, we arrived at the measures by reasoning about our process model and we used the measures to make inferences about the effect of PROUST on students' knowledge and skills.

In carrying out the evaluation of the impact of bug identification on students' performance, we have followed a five-step process that has evolved as we have gained experience with evaluation.

1. We identified classes of bugs which, according to our process model of novice programming, all have the same cause; here we chose the boundary condition bugs.

2. We inferred that because the student may have neglected to consider the case in which the user failed to enter any valid rainfall values, perhaps if PROUST simply pointed this out it would be sufficient to help the student repair the bug and avoid making it in the future. Thus, we focused on the educational effectiveness of PROUST's bug-identification tutorial strategy.

3. We identified two aspects of students' program-generation behavior that

should be affected by PROUST's ability to identify boundary condition bugs, namely (a) the pattern of bugs in the sequence of versions of the Rainfall Assignment and (b) the identification and repair of bugs on the midterm.

4. We generated a test of the impact of the PROUST on students' ability to manage boundary condition bugs. The test consisted of two parts, as noted above. First, we looked at the number of versions of programs students had to write to generate bug-free solutions to the Rainfall Assignment. Second, we constructed a midterm examination to test students' ability to find and correct bugs. Some, but not all, of the bugs seeded in the midterm were boundary condition bugs.

5. We evaluated students' performance on these two tasks. In fact, we compared the performance of groups of students who had access to PROUST with groups of students who did not have access to PROUST. In addition, to control for PROUST's ability to identify bugs, we assessed the effect of the accuracy of PROUST's identification of bugs for students.

Briefly, the findings support the claims that (a) PROUST is helpful to students when they are writing their sequences of versions of programs to solve the Rainfall Assignment, in that it helps them repair and avoid boundary problems and (b) access to PROUST appears to facilitate students' ability by approximately 16% to identify seeded boundary condition bugs in programs they did not write.[2]

In summary, our evaluation of the educational effectiveness of one aspect of PROUST's performance was based on the Cognitive Perspective in that it began with our process model of buggy novice student programming. From the model, we identified an area of program generation that students typically find troublesome, namely managing boundary cases. Then, we attempted to determine how PROUST's bug-identification strategy should affect students' ability to handle boundary cases. The finding that PROUST is only somewhat helpful gives us valuable information about how effective we can expect the simple bug-identification strategy to be. Because we considered the results of the evaluations of the impact of PROUST's assistance in terms of the process model of students' debugging activities, we have some understanding of why bug identification is not enough to lead students to handle boundary conditions once and for all. Because bug identification is not enough, the next version of PROUST will have to include stronger tutorial capabilities to help students learn debugging skills that they can use when they find bugs or have bugs pointed out to them. As a result of evaluation, we have noted aspects of the process model that must be changed. We had predicted that

---

[2]See Sack et al. (1986) for a full report of these evaluation results.

if a student knew about a certain kind of bug, for example, boundary condition bugs, they would not make them. Because we did not find that merely identifying bugs led to the elimination of that class of bugs, it seems apparent that a more complex mechanism is required in our process model to account for this failure of "one-trial learning" for managing boundary condition bugs. The mechanism that will be needed to account for this phenomenon is still somewhat unclear, but evidently we will have to understand the conditions under which students are able to achieve goals that are not explicitly called for in the problem assignment and, therefore, called for specialized programming knowledge.

Possible Objections to the Cognitive Perspective

The foregoing picture of evaluation may seem too clean, and several objections can be raised against both the practicality and the justification for performing such evaluations. We now identify, and briefly respond to, three major criticisms of the Cognitive Science approach.

1. *It is too hard.* The detailed evaluations of students' cognitive processes we recommend are simply too hard.

   The development of effective, cognitively based, evaluation strategies should proceed hand in hand with our growing expertise as a discipline. Thus, whereas full blown, cognitively based, evaluations are too hard to do now, we should hold them out both as a goal to achieve and as a measure of our own progress toward truly intelligent tutoring systems.

2. *We might use the wrong student models in our evaluations.* In assessing any particular student, we might use the wrong model and conclude that the ITS was not performing effectively because the evaluation suggests that the student failed to acquire the skills we intended the ITS to teach.

   We must be sensitive to different ways of representing knowledge and skills. A single model of student knowledge may not be sufficient for evaluation. We should investigate alternative ways that students can adaptively represent knowledge and skills, and build our evaluation methodology to accommodate different student models.

3. *We should not be concerned with students' internal representations.* The microworlds approach to Intelligent Tutoring suggests that we should not teach so much as we should provide tools that make it possible for students to learn. One of the potential implications of this view is that student models, and hence process models, are superfluous, if not overtly counterproductive.

> We believe that educational philosophy should be divorced from the philosophy of assessment. That is, no matter what one might believe about the advisability of directive tutoring in education, evaluating the effectiveness of Intelligent Tools for facilitating learning requires having process models of students' problem solving.

Thus, though there are several objections to the Cognitive Perspective on evaluation, several of the most interesting can be seen as practical objections rather than fundamental objections. Indeed, it appears possible that by working on the problems of cognitively based evaluations of ITS, we may make significant contributions to the theory of ITS itself.

Summary Remarks on Evaluation Issues

All in all, we feel that this initial evaluation of PROUST from the Cognitive Perspective taught us three important lessons. First, we discovered some positive educational effects of PROUST. Second, we learned some important principles of how to formulate and execute evaluations of ITS. Third, and perhaps most important, we were successful in evaluating PROUST with an incomplete process model and using the evaluation to identify insufficiencies in that model. Thus, it appears from our experience with PROUST that it is quite reasonable to expect that the process of developing an ITS can be integrated with assessing its educational effectiveness. This suggests that, by performing evaluations based on student models during development, we can facilitate the development of ITS.

CONCLUSION

In order to build the three core modules of an intelligent tutoring system, the science underlying them has had to move significantly beyond the old behavioral theories of education: The emphasis in ITS is on teaching for understanding, on providing individual users with instruction tailored to each individual's specific cognitive state. Similarly, in developing interfaces and evaluation, we need to break out of the surface models that typically underlie these areas: Both the interface and the evaluation must be seriously designed with a cognitive theory in mind.

In this chapter we have given examples of how one might go about designing interfaces and evaluating ITS using this cognitive perspective. We were forced to confront "user" issues of interface design and system evaluation because we wanted real people to use, and benefit from, our system. Developers of ITS and supports of those developments need to keep clearly in mind the types of issues we raised here—if they want to build usable, effective ITSs.

ACKNOWLEDGMENTS

The research reported in this chapter was cosponsored by the Personnel and Training Division Research Groups, Psychological Sciences Division, Office of Naval Research, and the Army Research Institute for the Behavioral and Social Sciences, under Contract No. N00014-82-k0714, Contract Authority Identification No. 154-492.

REFERENCES

Anderson, J., Boyle, C. & Yost, G. (1985). The geometry tutor. In *Proceedings of the Ninth International Joint Conference on Artificial Intelligence*, Vol. 1. Los Angeles, CA.

Anderson, J., Farrell, R., & Sauers, R. (1984). Learning to program in LISP. *Cognitive Science, 8*, 87-129.

Brown, J. S. & VanLehn, K. (1980). Repair theory: A generative theory of bugs in procedural skills. *Cognitive Science, 4*, 379-426.

Farrell, R., Anderson, J. & Reiser, B. (1984). Interactive student modeling in a computer-based LISP tutor. In *Proceedings of the Sixth Annual Conference of the Cognitive Sciences*. Boulder, CO.

Fuson, K. & Hall, J. (1983). The acquisition of early number word meanings: A conceptual analysis and review. In H. Ginsburg, (Ed.), *The development of mathematical thinking*, New York: Academic Press.

Goldstein, I. (1982). The genetic graph. In D. Sleeman & J. S. Brown (Eds.), *Intelligent tutoring systems* (pp. 51-75). Academic Press, London, England.

Johnson, L. (1985). *Intentions-based diagnosis of errors in novice programs*. Doctoral Dissertation. New Haven, CT. Department of Computer Science, Yale University.

Norman, D. (1982). Learning and memory. San Francisco: Freeman.

Sack, W., Littman, D., Spohrer, J., Liles, A., Fertig, S., Hughes, L., Johnson, L., & Soloway, E. (1986) Empirical evaluation of the educational effectiveness of PROUST. Working paper. New Haven, CT. Department of Computer Science, Yale University.

Secada, W., Fuson, K., & Hall, J. (1983). The transition from counting-all to counting-on in addition. *Journal of Research in Mathematics Education, 4*, 47-57.

Shannon, L. (1978). Spatial strategies in the counting of young children. *Child Development 49*, 1212-1213.

Shneiderman, B. (1983). Direct manipulation: A step beyond programming languages. *IEEE Computer 16*, 57-69.

Spohrer, J. A generative theory of novice programming errors. Doctoral dissertation in preparation. New Haven, CT: Department of Computer Science, Yale University.

VanLehn, K. (1986). Student modeling in intelligent tutoring systems. Paper presented at AFHRL Workshop on Intelligent Tutoring Systems, San Antonio, TX.

The Intelligent Maintenance Training System

Douglas M. Towne
Allen Munro
University of Southern California

INTRODUCTION

Background

This chapter describes the Intelligent Maintenance Training System (IMTS), under development at Behavioral Technology Laboratories, University of Southern California, since early 1985. Our first report on this work (Towne, Munro, Pizzini, & Surmon, 1985) set out the underlying instructional principles fundamental to the design of an intelligent maintenance training system, the training characteristics sought for IMTS, the desired environment for constructing domain-specific simulation and training scenarios, and generalizable techniques for assessing and supporting human diagnostic performance. For completeness, this chapter will reiterate some of the research findings that motivated major aspects of the system design. However, the primary objectives of the chapter are (a) to provide a relatively comprehensive interim report of progress and problems, and (b) to provide more timely and detailed information about the instructional processes being developed.

Objectives of the Work

One premise of the development project is that there have been numerous research projects in the area of intelligent training and in maintenance training that have yielded useful results, principles, and techniques in relatively restricted or isolated environments, (and often in rather abstract environments), and that the time has arrived to begin trying to interpret and apply those findings in a functioning system.

One major objective of the IMTS project is to attempt to construct a cohesive maintenance training system largely of these concepts and techniques. This process has identified the areas of instruction that are well supported by research and those that are not. In areas where there has been a substantial amount of research, applying the findings in a direct manner can be a very difficult matter, either because it is difficult to interpret the work in an operational way, or because findings and principles from different sources seem to be in partial or complete conflict. It has been our experience, however, that most of the apparent conflict can be resolved by carefully considering the setting in which the research was conducted and some of the unstated assumptions or objectives.

The second major objective is to produce an operational maintenance training system that can be used by instructors to meet a wide range of pressing training needs. To meet this objective the IMTS must (a) be sufficiently flexible that it can be set up to simulate the function of many types of devices, (b) be sufficiently robust that a wide range of student behaviors and training requirements can be appropriately addressed, and (c) be easily embedded within a suitable range of curricula and training environments to assist the instructor in meeting the student's needs. The first application of the IMTS will be in training corrective maintenance of the SH-3H helicopter's bladefolding subsystem. In this setting the IMTS will be interfaced to the Generalized Maintenance Trainer—Simulator (GMTS), a simulator of the Bladefold system using videodisk display with graphic overlays. The role of the IMTS in this environment will be to assess student performance on the GMTS, to intervene when necessary, and to provide supporting guidance in performing the diagnostic activities.

The nature of fault diagnosis allows some relatively specialized consideration of the ways computer-generated intelligence can contribute to training effectiveness. Much of the IMTS design attempts to take advantage of the character of fault diagnosis. Readers should understand that approaches followed in the IMTS may not be entirely applicable in domains outside of maintenance training.

Organization of the Chapter

The next section of this chapter summarizes the research findings and principles that were considered in the design of the IMTS. The section following that describes the instructional techniques and processes of the IMTS. Then we present the techniques used to create new training scenarios for systems, and describe the techniques employed to model individual student proficiency and knowledge states in terms of demonstrated abilities and problems. That section includes details on the problem-selection process as well as the processes employed to track student learning. The next section describes Profile, the subsystem within the IMTS that models an expert troubleshooter. It is this process that allows the IMTS to demonstrate expert diagnostic strategies, to evaluate student performance, and to assist learners in completing practice problems.

Because the IMTS relies so heavily upon simulation of the real system, simulation issues are critical to the effectiveness of training and to understanding the range of application of the IMTS. We describe the simulation techniques employed in the IMTS and some of the particularly difficult simulation requirements that were confronted.

The IMTS is under development at the time of writing this chapter, and a number of features and training features remain to be implemented. We cover some of these features, which are to be implemented in the coming year. The chapter concludes with a brief list of some of the conclusions based upon IMTS work to date.

PRINCIPLES UNDERLYING
THE DESIGN OF THE TRAINING SYSTEM

In this section we summarize the principles employed in the design of the IMTS, the research findings that influenced the character of the system, and other factors that influenced the design, such as hardware cost, hardware limitations, and practical realities of the military training environment.

Premises

A number of characteristics of the IMTS were determined by practical issues having little to do with instructional theory. First, the IMTS was envisioned from the start as a system that would operate on off-the-shelf hardware manufactured in quantity and sold and maintained commercially. Even though minor hardware modifications might have been considered to meet some critical interfacing requirement, none have been required. This also implied that general-purpose media would be used for student-computer interactions—no special hardware would be constructed to emulate characteristics of particular equipments being taught.

From the beginning the IMTS was planned to be simulation based and responsive to student actions. The IMTS would emulate the behavior of the real equipment as students carried out diagnostic functions upon the simulation. This objective was based on many years' experience in developing and evaluating computer-based maintenance training systems. The approach addresses a critical need in the services to provide individual students an opportunity to practice diagnosing faults.

Another decision made early in the planning phase was to place some operating characteristics of the IMTS under the control of the instructor. This decision was based upon three realities. First, instructors often know of time constraints, problems with training in prerequisite areas, and entering-class characteristics. The instructor should be able to adjust the characteristics of the training system to meet local needs, rather than subjecting students to inappropriate training while the instructional system is adapting to the environment. Second, because the IMTS is not designed to automatically adjust its processes based on experience with previous students, the instructor is a vital mechanism in the control loop.

Finally, as a practical matter, instructors are more receptive to a training device in their classroom if they can have some control over its behavior. Because excessive or persisting requirements for instructor input can produce other types of resistance, the instructor control actions are set up to be simple and entirely optional.

Like all the previous computer-based training systems we have developed, the IMTS is not intended to eliminate the human instructor. Instead, it is viewed as a potentially powerful and intelligent aid to the instructor, which can take over a massive workload in dealing with individual students as they work exercises, thereby freeing the human instructor for preparation and presentation of other instructional material, and for dealing with unusual problems. As a research goal it is challenging to attempt to automate as many of the instructor's functions as possible. It is clear, however, that there remain a number of critical instructional functions that are currently performed effectively only by a skilled human instructor.

The IMTS is reactive. It responds to students' diagnostic performances, first to resolve immediate problems, and more globally to update its conception of the individual student. These conceptions in turn affect the kinds of exercises the IMTS schedules for the individual student, and the way the IMTS deals with each student in the future. The instructor, on the other hand, may be able to anticipate individual needs by reviewing previous education, job experience, and equipment training. The instructor may employ knowledge of training problems being reported from the field to shape the instruction provided. And the instructor may recognize characteristics of the equipment to be trained that will require particular emphasis in certain areas. These abilities can be applied to influence the type of instruction provided prior to hands-on practice phases. When the instructor has the time and the skill to consider these factors, he or she might be able to configure the training in a manner that will prevent many student difficulties before they occur. Although such functions may someday be within the domain of artificial instructional intelligence, the IMTS does not attempt to take on these responsibilities.

Instructional Issues and Principles

The design of the IMTS addresses five fundamental instructional issues:

1. When to intervene to provide instruction
2. What to say to the learner in various conditions
3. How to interact to accommodate user limitations
4. How to interact to promote deep understanding
5. How to maintain learner affect.

To the extent possible, previous research findings were interpreted and applied in dealing with these issues. Table 18.1 lists some of the key instructional principles that were extracted from the research literature and directly considered during design of the IMTS. Some of these principles are pertinent to problem selection, others to design of the interface between student and trainer, including the types of dialogues between them, and others to the ways in which the student is evaluated and remediated. An earlier report (Towne, Munro, Pizzini, & Surmon, 1985) provides a more detailed account of particular ways in which these principles were interpreted and applied in the development of the IMTS.

The design of the IMTS is also based upon an intensive analysis of corrective maintenance performance and diagnostic expertise, involving detailed observation and analysis of nearly 600 diagnosis and repair sequences for 87 different technicians (Towne, Johnson, & Corwin, 1982, 1983). This research played an important role in forming basic concepts of the IMTS design, and it provided the data upon which to construct a model of expert diagnostic performance,

TABLE 18.1
Instructional Principles Underlying the IMTS System Design

---

1. Instruction should be relevant to the problem-solving context (Tulving, 1983; Tulving & Thompson, 1973).

2. Provide immediate feedback on errors (Bilodeau, 1969; Skinner, 1958).

3. Where possible, attempt to sustain diagnostic exercises by postponing instructional content that would reveal the solution to the exercise until after the exercise is completed.

4. An intelligent training system should respond quickly to student's actions and requests for assistance.

5. A good tutor should explicitly identify the goal structure of the problem domain (Anderson, Boyle, Farrell, & Reiser, 1984).

6. Minimize working memory load for students (McKendree, Reiser, & Anderson, 1984).

7. Prevent superstitious behavior (protect students from chance positive outcomes).

8. Students should approach target skills by successive approximations (Anderson, 1983; Anderson, Farrel, & Sauers, 1984).

9. Protect students from building extended chains of misconceptions.

10. Protect students from chance negative consequences from appropriate actions.

11. Be opportunistic in providing instruction as context permits.

12. Maintain the credibility of the intelligent trainer.

13. Before giving advice, be sure the issue used is one in which the student is weak. (Principles 13-21 are from Burton & Brown, 1982.)

14. When illustrating an issue, use only an example (an alternative move) in which the result or outcome of that move is dramatically superior to the move made by the student.

15. After giving the student advice, permit him or her to incorporate the issue immediately by allowing the turn to be repeated.

16. If a student is about to fail, interrupt and coach only with moves that will keep him or her from failing.

17. Do not tutor on two consecutive moves, no matter what.

18. Do not tutor before the student has a chance to discover the game for himself or herself.

19. Do not provide only criticism when the coach breaks in! If the student makes an exceptional move, identify why it is good and congratulate him or her.

20. Always have the computer expert play an optimal game.

21. If the student asks for help, provide several levels of hints.

Of principles explicitly considered during system development, not all were rigorously followed. For example, principle 2 (providing immediate feedback of errors) is in partial conflict with principles 3, 17, and 18.

called *Profile*. The Profile model forms the central resource for evaluation and remediating student performance.

The following briefly summarizes major aspects of diagnostic performance that influenced design of the IMTS.

Computability of Optimal Performance

Instruction in fault diagnosis of physical systems can rely heavily upon the fact that optimal testing procedures can be computed. Unlike a domain such as chess, for which the optimum decisions cannot be feasibly computed, system diagnosis allows computation of a testing sequence that will minimize the expected time or cost to isolate the fault. This is not to say that deviations from optimal strategies should always be corrected. The important point is that the ability to compute an optimal testing strategy for a particular equipment provides a baseline upon which to judge individual performance, and it serves as the model that can be demonstrated to a student when expert coaching is required.

Additionally, it is fortunate that it is possible to compute the optimal next step (test), given a sequence of tests already performed by the learner. Thus it is possible to track nonoptimal performance by a learner, yet compute what the expert would do next, regardless of the quality of the student's completed work. This is not always possible in other training domains. In instructing computer programming, for example, the student's work might have to be substantially corrected before an expert could complete the programming task started by the student.

Ability and Necessity to Perform Optimally

Even though optimal diagnostic performance is computable, and useful in an instructional system, it is not reasonable to expect students (or even experts) to perform optimally. Our studies of expert troubleshooters clearly show that optimal performance is rare and exceedingly difficult to attain. In an early study (Rigney, Cremer, Towne, & Mason, 1968), technicians maintained perfect suspicions about possible faults only 1.3% of the time. Some might argue that the individuals studied needed more training, but experience shows that even the designers of a system cannot accurately predict all the system interactions without the aid of computer analysis (thus the important emergence of computer-aided design software).

Instructional implications of this error-prone environment are crucial. Should an automated coach react immediately upon noting that a learner is performing a seemingly poor test? The best answer probably relates to the cost of performing the test. If it is time consuming in the real world, then the coach should probably step in and find out why the student is doing the test, that is, it should determine if the student has misinterpreted previous tests or has misunderstood the implications of the current test.

In general, however, we believe the coach must give the learner some room to explore, thereby gaining the experience of monitoring his own performance. Furthermore, we wish to avoid destroying the problem by revealing so much that the fault becomes obvious to the learner. The net result of these concerns is that the IMTS coach steps in for error correction only when the error indicates a serious misunderstanding or when much student time can be saved by intervention.

Maintenance training should also be realistic about the need to perform optimally. Analyses of alternative diagnostic strategies (Towne, Fehling, & Bond, 1981) showed that substantial departures from optimality were quite tolerable, in terms of time to isolate the failure, as long as certain catastrophic errors could be avoided, or detected and corrected. The most serious errors are (a) the erroneous interpretation of test results such that the actual malfunction is eliminated from suspicion, and (b) performing lengthy tests that are not logically appropriate. The seriousness of continuing to suspect an element that could be eliminated from suspicion, based upon available test results, depends upon the subsequent troubleshooting workload required to ultimately dismiss the suspicion. Again, it is fortunate that quantification of excess workload is possible in the fault-isolation domain.

These findings motivate the use of continuous measures in the IMTS that reflect the degrees to which a student's performance departs from optimal. The IMTS intervenes when the deviation exceeds some specified amount, rather than interrupting each time the student makes an imperfect decision. This approach also has the advantage that the amount of the deviation can be adjusted depending upon the student's demonstrated ability, the difficulty of the problem, and the preferences of instructors and students.

A low effectiveness value (high deviation from optimal) for an ongoing problem is one indication that the student is having difficulties that should be attended to within the problem, especially if the current effectiveness is significantly below the student's cumulative effectiveness rating. Low effectiveness for a student over a series of problems is taken as an indication that some (automated) tutoring is in order, either directed toward a better understanding of the particular system behaviors or toward improving more generic troubleshooting skills.

Individual Differences

Another concern in the design of IMTS is that instruction should allow for individual differences in cognitive style, which are exhibited in differences in diagnostic approach. Pask (1975) offers the principle that students be enabled to learn in an environment that does not conflict with their own style of learning. The spirit of this principle could be extended to apply to the subject matter as well. We also argue that there must be some allowed variability in the troubleshooting strategies recommended by a training system, and used as the basis for evaluating student performance. In field studies we have encountered students and experts who are relatively adept in employing the most powerful available tests during fault isolation (splitting the possible malfunction space into the largest number of equally likely sets). Such individuals may be found to expend more time thinking about the options and the significance of results than students who employ less powerful tests.

Other individuals, including experts, were found to achieve very acceptable diagnostic results pursuing a strategy that reduces cognitive workload (and associated error). More specifically, some troubleshooters find that they can best keep track of what they are discovering during a troubleshooting problem if they systematically perform tests in a sequence closely aligned with the structure of the system. For example, such a troubleshooter might make a series of tests along the path of a signal until an abnormal reading is obtained, rather than starting in the middle and then jumping to the side which appears faulty from the first test result. Even highly skilled troubleshooters have been observed following such a strategy when signal forms are highly complex, for this technique allows them to monitor the build-up of the signal in a series of small, easy steps.

The point here is that the student should be allowed considerable leeway in forming a diagnostic strategy, as long as progress is being made. The range of allowable learner behaviors may be reduced as research produces more sensitive measures of cognitive workload. Until that time, however, it is important that training systems tolerate a relatively wide range of approaches to fault isolation, and recognize that individuals may be employing a superior approach in light of the exposure to, and consequences of, error.

All of the above argue for multiple measures of student performance that are chosen to collectively sense an individual's level of progress and achievement. Thus, for example, if an individual's strategy is not highly efficient, he could still progress satisfactorily through the IMTS instruction if his average time per problem is acceptable. Conversely, an individual who solves problems very quickly will still be provided some remediation and guidance if he makes an excessive number of incorrect replacements. The measures of student performance are used within IMTS to determine when and how it should intervene in ongoing student performance.

The three measures most appropriate for measuring student proficiency are (a) relative efficiency compared to the Profile model, (b) time spent on the problem, and (c) number of incorrect replacements. Values are specified for these three variables, both individually and in combination, at which the IMTS coach steps in and interacts with the learner. The criterion values are a function of problem difficulty, a subjective measure associated with each malfunction. Initially, these difficulty values will be obtained from experienced subject matter experts. Instructors may override the default difficulty values to reflect their knowledge of the class progress and their past experience with each problem. An obvious option is to maintain historical data within IMTS that would allow it to adjust difficulty levels based upon students' performances. This is not planned for the near future.

The three-variable measure of student proficiency just described is only one of the grounds for invoking coaching with the student. Other actuators include requests by the student, authored "triggers" that sense domain-specific errors worthy of treatment, and a number of well-defined generic errors that are described later.

Authoring Principles

An overriding goal in the IMTS project has been the development of tools that permit the creation of high-quality simulation training. One approach to providing consistently high-quality training is to provide simulation-training authors with tools that help to ensure accurate interactive simulations without requiring unusual skills (such as LISP programming) or sophisticated pedagogical expertise. Much of our efforts has been devoted to providing extensive tools for extracting device-specific knowledge from authors who are neither computer programmers nor training specialists. To the largest extent possible, instructional interactions are automatically guided by the reliable, factual data base so extracted. The same underlying data base is used to drive several different types of instructional presentations and interactive environments, thereby increasing the payoff for the simulation-authoring time expended by the device expert.

The simulation data structures are derived from the author's use of an editor that incorporates a direct manipulation interface described later. Using this system, authoring a simulation is something like using Apple Corporation's MacDraw coupled to an object-oriented data-entry system, rather than like computer programming. The behavior of a complete simulation is determined by the behavior rules of the individual objects and the topology of the system, and does not require the authoring of underlying simulation rules for the whole system. Device experts can put their authoring effort into specifying behavior of object types, rather than into accounting for behaviors of the simulated system. The behavior of the system is derived from the behaviors of the objects plus the topology of the system. Like Steamer (Hollan, 1983; Hollan, Hutchins, & Weitzman, 1984), the IMTS provides powerful tools for describing the appearances of objects in response to values generated inside simulations. Like SimKit, the IMTS permits new simulations to be created by positioning objects in the display, without a separate step of simulation coding.

The expert troubleshooting sequences are generated by Profile by referring to the simulation data. The only additional authoring step required to automatically produce these sequences is the identification of important system configurations or modes for conducting tests.

Although the majority of our efforts have been directed to the development of generic tools for authoring and presenting simulations and to providing instruction based on the same data as used in the simulation, simple authoring tools have also been created for adding more customized instructional materials. These tools make it possible to (a) present digitized images of system objects, (b) present instructional or admonitory texts, and (c) perform and explain procedures on the IMTS simulation that can be played back with student interactions. The quality of the products created with these tools depends more on the skills of the author (in writing or videotaping, for example) than do the simulation-building tools, and a greater variation in the quality of the instructional materials built with these tools can be expected.

THE INSTRUCTIONAL ENVIRONMENT

The instructional process performed by the IMTS involves the following major steps: (a) it selects malfunctions within the target system that will most effectively exercise the individual students at their current stage of understanding and proficiency, (b) it inserts the malfunctions into the simulations of the target system and allows the students to manipulate the simulation much as they would manipulate the real system, (c) it simulates the response of the system to student actions, providing an opportunity to practice diagnostic tasks, (d) it provides "within-problem" support, as necessary, to ensure that students proceed to problem completion in a productive manner while exercising their problem-solving skills as much as possible, and (e) it provides "between-problem" support, as necessary, to resolve more general deficiencies. Thus the IMTS plays the role of the actual equipment and of the instructor.

Figure 18.1 presents a view of the IMTS screen during a diagnostic exercise. There are four major sections of the display:

1. *The fixed view of the system organization.* (Shown at the top left.) This window provides the student with a means for selecting close-up views of system subsections, for those simulations that are too large to display in one section. The Bladefold application, for example, requires 12 screens to display the entire system. Selecting one of the rectangles brings a detailed diagram into the largest window at the lower right of the screen area. The selected box remains highlighted in the upper window.

2. *The text area.* Verbal messages from the IMTS are presented in this window. These may be words generated by IMTS in response to student actions, or they may be messages created by an expert as part of a guided simulation.

3. *The main simulation display area.* (The largest window, at the bottom right.) In this window is shown a detailed diagram of one portion of the system. All of the objects that change appearance are displayed in their current state, according to the positions of switches and possible malfunction state. The student operates the simulated system by setting switches in this window and by observing indicators and test equipments displayed here.

4. *The convenience viewing area.* (Along the lower left side of the screen.) This window is used to display copies of some of the system elements that appear in the detailed diagrams. The copies change exactly as their originals do, in response to actions by the student, but are always available for easy view or manipulation.

The IMTS is always in an operate mode, that is, the student may change switch settings and attach simulated test equipment at any time during a problem. In addition, the student may request additional information about any of the objects in the simulation area. Upon selecting an object on the screen the student observes a pop-up menu next to the selected object and indicates whether he or she wishes to (a) see a "photograph" of the object (actually a bit-

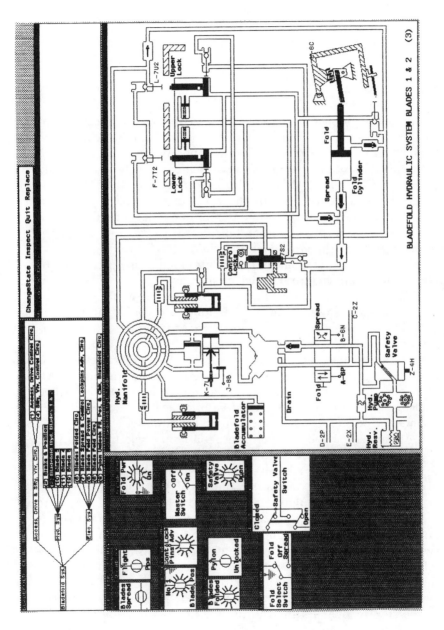

FIGURE 18.1 IMTS screen.

491

mapped representation of a photograph), (b) read a textual explanation of the object's operation or purpose, or (c) operate the object out of the context of the simulation. The third capability is not yet operational.

Practice Problems

Each practice problem consists of a malfunction, an initial equipment configuration (mode), and an operator's complaint (which may be "none"). A particular malfunction may be involved in a multitude of problems that can differ greatly in difficulty and diagnostic activity required as a result of differing initial conditions. The IMTS first selects a problem that best fits the needs of the student (described later), inserts the malfunction into the simulation data for the system, initializes the control settings, and displays the operator's complaint (sometimes called the *squawk*) in the text display area.

The complaint presents the type of information an operator might offer to the maintenance technician, such as "The override light is coming on in standby mode." In more difficult problems the complaint might not offer any starting information, or it could purposely be authored to present incorrect or inconsistent information. Problems can also involve no malfunction (because this is a common type of diagnostic situation actually encountered in the field), either with or without associated errors in the initial setup of the equipment. All of these real-world possibilities offer useful experience to more skilled students, although students should be informed if the ground rules include the possibility of incorrect initial conditions.

All student actions are performed via mouse selections (moving the mouse until the screen cursor is at the desired location, then pressing the mouse button). The student performs tests by selecting the portions of the system diagrams containing controls, indicators, and test points of interest, and manipulating the displayed elements as if they were the real equipment. Switches are set by positioning the screen cursor on the switch of interest, and clicking the mouse button when the switch is shown in the desired setting. Test points are measured by selecting one of the displayed test equipments and "attaching" it to the test point by clicking on the point of interest.

In most cases the states of all indicators on the screen are displayed as the student operates the equipment. In this situation the IMTS cannot know exactly what the student is observing because the screen display may contain many indicators. In some cases the IMTS may require the student to identify each indicator checked before displaying its reading, in order to track the student's actions precisely.

Evaluating Student Performance

In general, the quality of the student's work is partially known to the IMTS at all times during a practice problem. The IMTS maintains data on how long the student has been working on the problem and which incorrect replacements have been made. It also keeps track of which tests have been performed, and what conclusions could be made from the results of those tests. If the global measures of time, tests, and replacements become excessive, the IMTS intervenes. Also, if the student is seen to be performing unproductive tests, given the symptoms already obtained, the IMTS may intervene. In some cases the student will be performing tests that have no value in further discriminating from the failures indicated by the results already obtained. In other cases, the completed tests are sufficient to identify the failure, yet the student continues performing tests. In either case, the IMTS detects that tests are being performed that yield no information, had the completed tests been correctly interpreted.

Unfortunately, there are two limitations on the precision of the knowledge IMTS can have about the student. First, there is no direct and reliable way to know what the student has concluded from each test result, because continual inquiries would be unreasonably distracting (although they can be tolerated during periods of close interaction). Thus at the point of intervention the IMTS must inquire about the student's current suspicions in order to determine where and in what manner the student has gone astray.

Second, the student may have performed some tests that are not recognized by the IMTS. This occurs because the IMTS must preanalyze the diagnostic implications of the tests prior to instruction, as a result of the heavy computation workload involved. Because there might be a very large number of possible tests for some system, analysis of all possible modes may be infeasible. Thus there may be occasions in which the student performs a test whose diagnostic value is unknown. The solution to this problem has been to limit the student's testing to the preanalyzed modes.

Within-Problem Support Functions

Upon intervening, the IMTS attempts to (a) identify more precisely the cause of the student's difficulty, (b) instruct the student about the misconceptions or misconclusions made, and (c) assist in forming new plans. This type of support is termed *within-problem support,* or *coaching.* Upon stepping in to provide coaching, the IMTS first directs the student to identify those portions of the system that he or she suspects, based upon the tests completed.

If the given suspicion set does contain the component that the IMTS introduced as a problem, the IMTS assists the student in continuing to reduce the set in an effective manner (the IMTS also attempts to detect whether the student has fortuitously eliminated more components from suspicion than the test readings would warrant). The support provided assists the student in (a) selecting a good next test or action (including a replacement or adjustment), (b) assessing the normality of a test result, considering the current switch settings, and (c) forming conclusions about the significance of test results in terms of possible failures. These coaching functions are generated by applying the Profile model to the suspicion set.

If the student is not suspecting the actual fault, then the IMTS knows that he or she has committed one or more serious errors in interpreting the symptoms. The IMTS cannot directly inquire why the student is not suspecting the actual fault, or suggest that he or she reconsider that fault possibility, as this would immediately end the usefulness of the exercise. Instead, the IMTS begins to interact with the student about the tests already completed. The goal of the IMTS is to identify and correct student errors in interpreting test results without revealing the fault.

By calling Profile, the IMTS is able to select and convey to the student the next recommended testing action, considering the previous tests that have been performed. The IMTS (through Profile) is also able to generate and present a relatively detailed rationale for the recommended test. The rationale will appear something like the following:

> Checking the <some indicator or test point> in the current configuration is a good test because:
>
> a. If a normal result is received, the following currently suspected areas of the system are then known to be functioning correctly:
>> <a list of system elements>
>
> b. If an abnormal result is received, the following areas of the system may be suspected highly:
>> <a list of system elements>

Between-Problem Support Functions

Some types of support are most appropriately provided outside the context of a practice diagnostic problem. One type of between-problem support is the expert demonstration, during which the IMTS demonstrates an expert's approach to resolving the problem just completed. The demonstration is offered following each problem completion; however, those students who received high support on the problem would find it to be largely redundant and have the option of forgoing it. A second type of between-problem support is the debriefing, during which the IMTS critiques each of the student's earlier testing actions. The critique evaluates the power of the tests and the inferences that could be drawn from the symptoms received.

The IMTS also provides students the opportunity to explore fault effects of the same malfunction—or a different one—before continuing on to the next system-selected problem. The student may request that the IMTS reintroduce the original fault, so that further examinations of its effects may be made. Or, if the student suspected the wrong fault for much of the practice problem, he or she may request the introduction of that fault, so that its effects may be observed under a number of modes of interest.

Many other types of exercises could be developed that would involve close interaction between training system and student and would be intended to resolve difficulties perceived during diagnostic practice. These could include mode drills, involving the setting of controls to attain particular system states, further symptom-interpretation drills generated to resolve possible confusion concerning abnormal and normal test results, and fault-effect drills designed to resolve confusion about similar failures. Drills such as these are currently not implemented but will be developed in the future. These types of drills can be generated by the IMTS at no further authoring expense—all interactions would be produced from the existing data base for the particular device.

In a later section we describe another instructional mode that does require additional authoring, called *guided simulation*. In this mode, students are required to perform a sequence of actions on the simulation, following text instructions and explanations that appear on the screen. This mode permits instructors and other authors to prepare special examples that demonstrate certain procedures or that provide more detailed explanations of aspects of a system than are automatically generated by the generic expert.

Surrogate Instructor Functions

Managing each individual student's instruction are functions that serve as a private instructor. These functions select problems for the student according to demonstrated progress and difficulties (as described later), they effect simulated replacements when requested by the student, and they call in the expert (Profile) when appropriate. Surrogate instructional functions are also responsible for routing the student to special between-problem instructional modes, including drills and preauthored guided simulations.

Operational Implications

To introduce a malfunction into a simulation, the IMTS instructor program simply replaces one of the normal object specifications with an abnormal description. When the simulator calls upon (executes) that failed component, it receives the correct information for how that failed component behaves. Some attractive implications of this are:

1. Students may request the introduction of failed components, to explore their effects.
2. A wide range of failure modes may be specified for a component, allowing very selective simulation of abnormalities.
3. Multiple failures may be introduced with virtually no complication in the simulator or in the authoring process.
4. The student, or the surrogate instructor program, may ask for the simulation of virtually any type of short circuit or open circuit without requiring that the simulation author anticipate the possible requests.
5. "Cascading" failure effects, in which a failure in one component causes a failure in a second component, and so on, are simulated correctly, without anticipation by the simulation author (as long as the object definitions specify the conditions under which the object will fail).

Coordinating Training with GMTS

IMTS is designed to provide training and tutorial interactions in two environments—stand-alone, and physically coupled to a Generalized Maintenance Trainer–simulator. GMTS is a static-scene simulation system based on a simulation construction system developed at Behavioral Technology Laboratories in the late 1970s, and now distributed by Cubic Corporation, a defense contractor. GMTS simulates the behavior of systems through the presentation of static videodisk images in response to student touch inputs. A medium resolution graphics overlay system is used to provide textual annotation and simple simulation graphics.

There are many important differences in philosophy and in implementation between the IMTS and GMTS trainers. The most important consequences of these differences are in the intelligent generation of training and in the ease and naturalness of authoring simulations. Because GMTS is inherently a surface simulation system, there is little underlying representation of cause and effect in the behavior of the complete system. In an IMTS simulation, on the other hand, surface (or system-level) behavior is automatically derived from what is known about the behavior of elements and how they are connected. This permits the automatic generation of more insightful and intelligent instruction than is possible in a purely surface simulation. Authoring is more straightforward in a deep simulation system such as IMTS, because the author does not have to independently consider all the possible combinations of control settings and their effects on indicators in the system. Because all global behavior is derived from local effects, a more modular approach to simulation authoring is possible, with attendant benefits in building, documenting, and maintaining a simulation.

The hardware in the IMTS *stand-alone* configuration consists of a Xerox 1108 or 1186 computer alone. The student uses the mouse to directly manipulate simulated objects and to select menu commands and other options that provide specific items of instruction or information.

In the *coupled* trainer configuration, the same Xerox 1108 or 1186 hardware is used together with equipment that makes up the GMTS delivery system. This hardware includes an Intel 8086 microcomputer development system equipped with a special-purpose video graphics overlay interface, a videodisk player, and a large-screen RGB color monitor. The Intel development system is driven by GMTS software programmed in PASCAL. This software includes a generic simulation driver that accesses a database of Bladefold-specific surface behavior information to determine which videodisk still image should be shown on the display and which (if any) overlayed graphics should be displayed on that image.

In the coupled configuration, the two training systems' computers are connected through their RS232C interfaces. During training the GMTS system provides IMTS with information about student interactions with the GMTS surface simulation. IMTS selects training problems for GMTS to present to students, and coordinates the flow of coaching, tutorial, and instructional activities in the two systems. In addition, IMTS provides a window for the presentation of GMTS menus and other textual interactions. (In a stand-alone GMTS, a separate Visual 55 alphanumeric terminal with touchscreen is required for the presentation of GMTS text interactions. In stand-alone IMTS, the window that emulates the GMTS Visual 55 is not present.)

Most of the instructional features of IMTS are available in both the stand-alone and the GMTS-coupled environments. GMTS provides a more surface-oriented approach to the Bladefold simulation than does IMTS, but the IMTS system could equally well be used to author a set of scenes of front panels and other surface indicators and controls. At present the IMTS system in stand-alone mode cannot provide color images, as the GMTS system does.

REPRESENTING DEVICES FOR INTELLIGENT INSTRUCTION

Configuring the IMTS for new training applications consists almost entirely of describing the architecture of the system (to IMTS). From this specification the IMTS infers the system's behaviors under whatever conditions the student produces by manipulating the switches and controls, determines how each malfunction will affect the system indicators and test points, and computes diagnostic sequences that it can demonstrate to the student or employ when the student needs assistance.

The system used to create the graphics and fault information required for training is shown in Figure 18.2. The system includes (a) an *object construction editor* for defining generic objects (both their graphic appearance and their functions), (b) a *system construction editor* for combining the generic objects into specific system diagrams, and (c) a *simulator* capable of determining the symptoms produced by each fault mode of each part. (The IMTS approach to fault simulation is well suited to handle any malfunction that can be attributed to faults within one or more simulated primitive objects, including open wires. Future versions will also provide the capability to simulate failures that alter the system topology, such as short circuits.)

The approach used in the IMTS for relating the graphical appearance of an object to its role and state within a particular system was heavily influenced and inspired by work on Steamer (Hollan, 1983; Hollan, Hutchins, & Weitzman, 1984). Steamer allows experts to construct interfaces between existing simulations of particular systems to graphical "objects" that display their response to system conditions. When attached to a particular system by a content expert, the objects determine how they react to their inputs and how they appear under any condition. As a student alters the system configuration by setting switches, the intelligent objects respond by changing their appearances appropriately. IMTS extends the Steamer model of simulation construction by automatically constructing the underlying simulation based on graphical data and object-behavior data alone, avoiding the need for a separate simulation programming step.

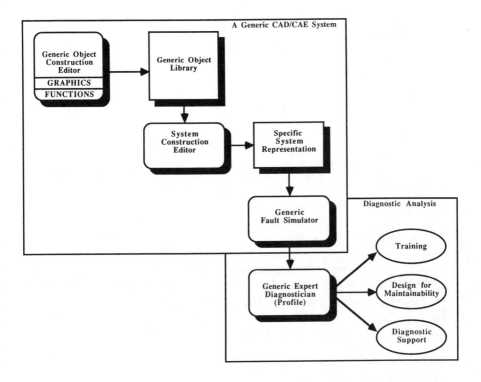

FIGURE 18.2 Components of the IMTS system. *Source:* Behavioral Technology Laboratories U.S.C.

Our objectives have been (a) to produce an object editor and a system editor that can be used by nonprogrammers to create new objects and systems, (b) to develop a system simulator that will respond correctly as a learner alters switches and attaches test equipment, and (c) to embed Profile into this simulation environment to interact intelligently with a learner about his or her diagnostic approach.

Creating a New Graphical Object

If the simulation author determines that the existing library of generic objects lacks a required object, he or she constructs it using a graphical object editor. This involves constructing on the screen that part of the object which does not change, called the *static part,* then entering those graphics that change according to the state of the object. Frequently the graphics for one state of an object can be created by simply copying and moving the graphics for another state. Figure 18.3 shows an object in its two states.

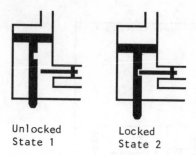

| Unlocked | Locked | **FIGURE 18.3** An object in its two |
| State 1 | State 2 | states. |

The generic library currently contains all the components necessary to simulate and train the first application of the IMTS. This system, Bladefold, is a moderately complex, electrically controlled hydraulic system that, after landing, causes the blades of the SH-3 helicopter to brake to a stop, rotate to a designated orientation, and then fold into a compact stowed position. The examples that follow all relate to this particular application of the IMTS.

Although we have defined only those objects required to simulate the Bladefold system, such as wires, switches, indicator lights, meters, valves, relays, and pipes, these objects would take authors a long way toward simulating many new systems.

Getting Objects to Behave

Once a new object is defined graphically it must be provided its rules of behavior. This is done within a special generic-object behavior editor, as shown in Figure 18.4. This editor provides four windows as follows:

1. The *Defined Objects* window. (Upper right-hand part of the screen.) This lists the names of all objects whose graphics have already been created; the user scrolls through this window and selects the name of the object previously created in the graphics editor.
2. The *Object Display window*. This displays whatever object has been selected; as the user steps through each object state, the display cycles to the proper state.
3. The *Constant Object Specification window*. (On the left of the screen.) This prompts the user for information about the object that is not state dependent. Via menus that come and go as required, the user identifies the types of inputs and outputs the object processes, such as hydraulic vs. Electrical or mechanical (the alphabetic labels shown in Figure 18.4 are seen only by the object creator). Here the user also enters information about the object that is important to the Profile troubleshooting model (replacement time, spares cost, and mean-time-between-failures).

4. The *State Definition window*. (At the lower center of the screen.) This prompts the user for information about each state of the object. Here are entered the rules governing what processes the object performs upon its inputs, and what causes the object to enter each state.

The object shown in Figure 18.4, called a *Bladelock Cylinder*, has only two graphical states, but it has four different behavior states: The first two states, "Locked" and "Unlocked," are normal states. The other possible states are failure conditions: "Stuck-locked" and "Stuck-unlocked."

Virtually all the components of the Bladefold system are elements that exist in a few discrete states, such as extended/retracted, locked/unlocked, or on/off. Although these happen to be common in the Bladefold system, the IMTS is not limited to simulating discrete-state elements. The pressure meter, for example, is an object that performs the simple function of sensing the pressure in a pipe and reflecting that reading via a needle. One could just as easily define an amplifier whose function is to output the square of its input.

There may be objects in systems whose current state depends in part upon their previous state (like a flip-flop, e.g.). The generic-object editor offers the object definer the means for including an object's previous state into its definition of current state.

The Library of Generic Objects

When an object has been defined both graphically and behaviorally, it passes into a general library that can be used as a resource by any simulation author. A portion of the generic library is shown in Figure 18.5.

Constructing New Simulations for Training

The content expert constructs a specific system simulation (and all associated training interactions) by simply selecting appropriate objects from the library and positioning them on the screen, using a special graphics editor. Fortunately, perhaps, this is the easiest authoring function. Though the author must be certain that each object selected actually operates as intended, the job of constructing the simulation is primarily one of subdividing a big system into separate screens, or drawings, and then producing each individual diagram in the editor provided with the IMTS. Normally, existing technical diagrams serve as an excellent starting point for creating

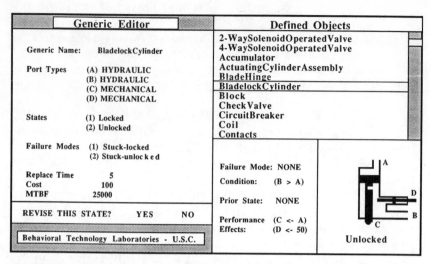

FIGURE 18.4 The object behavior editor. *Source:* Behavioral Technology Laboratories, University of Southern California.

the diagrams. It is also common, however, that drawings from technical references are wrong and not created for ease of understanding. Typically, the simulation author will massage the drawings considerably before being satisfied with the clarity of the displays.

As the objects are positioned, the editor detects the connections between elements and retains the connectivity data in a file. Though the connectivity data are necessary for computing how a system will behave under a current condition, these data are a small part of the intelligence used to simulate the system behaviors. The IMTS uses the connectivity information plus the behavior rules of each object involved to determine the nature of the signal conversions, and hence the particular appearance of system indicators and associated test equipment.

Once all the individual diagrams have been created, and outputs from one diagram have been linked to inputs to others, the representation is completed. Next the IMTS simulation routine is run in a batch mode, successively substituting in each possible malfunction to observe its effects on the system. After this step, IMTS can be used for training. It can select and insert practice malfunctions for each student, it can accept and display the results of student testing actions, it can monitor each learner, providing individualized assistance, and it can demonstrate expert diagnostic strategies as required.

MODELING THE STUDENT

For each student, a *student model* is maintained to serve as a basis for problem selection and other student-specific decisions about

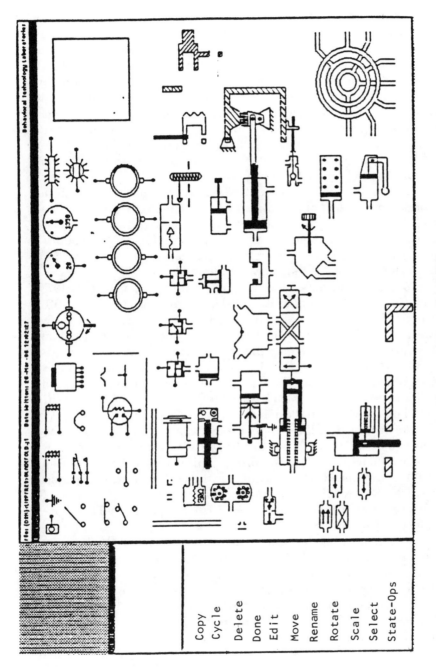

FIGURE 18.5 The generic object library.

instruction. IMTS maintains and modifies three kinds of data to represent the student. One type is a moderately detailed representation of the student's conceptual model of the equipment system being taught. The second type of student data includes simple global measures of student competence and learning preferences (difficulty levels, amounts of intrusion and support, etc.). The third kind of data is a detailed breakdown of tests performed for the current problem, together with the successive malfunction suspicion sets that should have been entertained as a result of those tests. All three kinds of student model data are updated based on student performance on troubleshooting problems.

The first type of data relies on a normative approach to representing student knowledge and skills. The second type of data— global measures of competence and learning preferences—is preauthored for each student based on instructor judgments of ability. Actual performance on practice problems can quickly overcome any instructor bias, establishing appropriate values for these measures.

Wescourt and his colleagues (Wescourt, Beard, & Gould, 1977; Wescourt, Beard, Gould, & Barr, 1977; Wescourt & Hemphill, 1978) developed an approach toward the representation of student knowledge based on a componential analysis of the content of a curriculum. The curriculum content was represented as a set of elementary concepts and skills. Each instructional exercise or problem was considered diagnostic for a particular subset of these concepts and skills. Student performance on the problems was used to modify a student-specific model of knowledge in the domain.

We have modified this approach by requiring that the knowledge elements of the training domain be organized in a strict hierarchy. This facilitates an initial authoring step, in which the top portion of the entire knowledge structure for the domain can be generated from the Scenes Hierarchy window, and much of the lower levels can be generated from the scene membership of objects and the modes of their object types.

A normative model of an expert's understanding of the target equipment is developed using a special knowledge-network editor. The model has the form of a tree, in which each node represents the knowledge about some aspect of the equipment. The highest nodes in the tree represent the most abstract knowledge about the global functions of the equipment. The nodes immediately below them represent top-level knowledge about the major subsystems. Lower nodes represent more specific skills and knowledge about modules and components. The terminal nodes in the knowledge tree represent knowledge about specific component modes, including different possible types of component failures.

The normative model is linked closely to the structure of the equipment system being simulated. This has the advantage of making the creation of such models fairly straightforward and offers the potential for making the normative modeling process automatic. A disadvantage is that some more generic kinds of knowledge, such as Ohm's law, are not easily represented in such an equipment-specific knowledge model.

For each node in the knowledge tree, the author of the model makes an estimate of the extent to which the average student will already understand this aspect of the system, and this estimate is stored as the default mastery for that concept or skill. Whenever a new student begins to work with an IMTS simulation, a copy of this set of default mastery levels is made to represent the IMTS estimate of the student's knowledge.

A model for an individual student consists primarily of an updated set of mastery levels for the knowledge/skill elements in the structure. These values are changed to reflect troubleshooting problem performance as the student progresses through the problem curriculum.

The Knowledge Network Editor

The Intelligent Trainer's Knowledge Network Editor is the configuration editor used to build the domain-specific framework that serves as the basis of individual student models of knowledge and skill in a device domain. A *device domain* is an area of knowledge dealing with the structure and behavior of a particular device. In the IMTS, those aspects of device knowledge that are particularly relevant to troubleshooting and maintenance are of special concern.

The current implementation of the Knowledge Network Editor makes very few assumptions about the structure of knowledge in device domains. (Enhancing the editor to capitalize on domain-specific features is a likely topic for future research and development efforts.) At present, providing structure is the task of the knowledge network author. One assumption of this Editor is that device knowledge can be represented in a simple tree structure. Less specific, more global information is represented by nodes near the top or root of the tree. Detailed information, such as the failure modes of particular elements in the device, are represented by nodes at the bottom of the tree.

Figure 18.6 shows the Knowledge Network Editor in use. The top window of the editor presents the organization of the knowledge elements. Higher elements represent abstract knowledge about the system that is not tied to any particular subsystems or components.

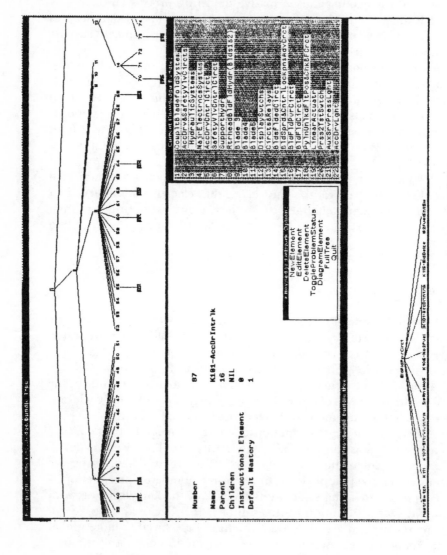

FIGURE 18.6   The knowledge network editor.

Such a knowledge element might represent a broad understanding of the function or purpose of the complete equipment system. Lower elements in the hierarchy represent more detailed knowledge elements. The terminal nodes shown in black boxes represent specific knowledge about a given failure state of a particular component. These knowledge nodes can correspond to particular troubleshooting problems. Other windows of the knowledge editor provide a scrollable list of knowledge element names, a "local area" graph of the knowledge structure, and a knowledge node editing window.

Assessing Student Progress
and Updating the Student Model

After a student has finished a troubleshooting problem, several gross measures are used to evaluate performance on that problem. At present, the measures used to derive a simple score for the problem are time to solution and number of replacements. These measures, adjusted for comparison to either average performance or to criteria for time and replacements, are combined to produce a numerical score on the problem. The range of values for the problem score is the same range used to represent mastery for knowledge nodes in the student model.

For each problem, there is a corresponding node in the knowledge representation—the node that represents knowledge about a particular failure mode for a certain component. When a student finishes a problem, the default mastery score for the corresponding terminal node is replaced with the score on the problem. The node that represents failure-specific knowledge is not the only one that must be updated when a student finishes a problem. A student who does very well on a number of problems in one subsystem could reasonably be assumed to understand that subsystem better than a student who had done very poorly on the same set of problems. Changes in mastery values for the knowledge elements are propagated upward through the knowledge tree. These changes combine with old values, rather than replace them, because non-terminal nodes represent knowledge complexes. A change in mastery value for a problem knowledge node affects the ancestor nodes to a lesser extent when the node is higher up in the tree than when it is closer, and to a lesser extent when the number of sibling nodes is greater than when it is small. In other words, the propagated effect of a change in represented mastery depends on the remoteness of the affected node and on the number of corresponding nodes that contribute to the affected node.

Problem Selection

The IMTS is responsible for determining when the student should work in the free-play troubleshooting mode and when a different instructional mode should be selected. In addition, whenever the student is in the free-play troubleshooting mode, IMTS must decide which problem should be presented next. Problem selection is made on an individual basis, using what is known about how well the student has done on previous troubleshooting problems, as encoded in the student model, and based on the global measures of student ability and cognitive style.

The problem-selection process relies on two measures taken from the knowledge structure: conceptual distance and conceptual difficulty. *Conceptual distance* is a simple measure of how related two problems are in terms of the domain representation. The conceptual distance between two problem nodes is the number of node links that must be traversed in the knowledge element hierarchy to find one node from another, weighted by the student's current mastery levels for the intervening nodes. *Conceptual difficulty* is the value of the "Problem Difficulty" field created by the instructor.

When it is time to select a new problem, the remaining troubleshooting exercises are evaluated for their conceptual distances from the last problem and their difficulty. An ideal conceptual step size and an ideal difficulty for the next problem are then computed for the student. The desired conceptual step size is a function of the student's estimated learning speed (which is based on prior performance and an instructor estimate), a student-controlled value that expresses how large a conceptual jump the student likes to make, and the student's performance on the last problem.

- If the student has a high learning speed, conceptual distance can be larger.
- If the student prefers larger conceptual steps, the conceptual distance can be larger.
- If the student did well on the last problem, the conceptual distance can be larger. (If the student did poorly on the last problem, a related one is called for.)
- The ideal difficulty level for the student is a function of the student's learning speed.

It is rare that the ideal conceptual distance metric and the ideal difficulty metric select the same problems. A weighting scheme combines these factors.

Modeling the Student's Suspicion Set

At the end of the simulation-construction process, a one-time analysis is done to compute the results of a large group of good tests for every malfunction state. This large group of tests includes all the tests that are likely to be recommended in formal instruction, plus many others that may be useful in special circumstances. Whenever a student performs one of these tests during a problem, a record is made of the fact. Using the results of a sequence of such tests, we can determine what the student's current suspicion set—the set of elements that is suspected to be the cause of the abnormal symptoms—should be. The sequence of suspicion-set changes during troubleshooting provides a set of useful data to discuss with a student who is having difficulties during a problem.

GENERATING EXPERT DIAGNOSTIC BEHAVIORS

A key course of earlier research at Behavioral Technology Laboratories has been the development of a generic (device-independent) model of troubleshooting behavior that can be applied to a wide range of specific equipments (Towne, 1984, 1987). The model, Profile, generates a detailed sequence of testing actions required to isolate any fault of interest.

When provided complete data about the internal design of a system, Profile's troubleshooting sequences are near optimal, and appear very much like those of expert maintenance technicians. Studies (Towne, Johnson, & Corwin, 1982) comparing Profile performance to that of actual technicians have yielded insights into the ways in which poorer maintainers differ from experts. The studies showed that varying the precision of fault-effect knowledge in the model produced variations in diagnostic performance very much like those observed in human technician samples, whereas varying the effectiveness of the troubleshooting strategy did not.

Operation

Profile is a form of expert system whose rules have been generalized and built into the model, rather than expressed as domain-specific data. The primary advantages of following the generic approach are (a) the cost and effort of capturing the necessary system-specific data are kept modest; (b) the quality of diagnostic prescriptions generated by Profile are not dependent upon an individual expert's skill, attention to detail, and recall abilities; and (c) the process can be used for training and for the generation of diagnostic approaches.

Currently, Profile requires that a subject matter expert enumerate a modest-sized set of potentially useful modes, or combinations of switch settings. Profile employs this set as its repertoire of testing modes as it computes testing sequences. The number of possible tests considered by Profile is normally a large multiple of the number of modes provided, for all indicators and test points offer potential information in each mode. In the first IMTS application, for example, each specified mode offers approximately 125 testing points. Thus, the human content expert is not burdened with providing an immense selection of testing modes. If Profile is unable to resolve certain groups of malfunctions with the modes provided, it lists the faults that are confounded, allowing the subject matter expert to add further modes that can discriminate them. Automated identification of these modes could be implemented some time in the future, although the process that would efficiently generate useful modes could be a formidable research venture.

The Model's World View

The general structure of the Profile model is a hierarchy of rules, expressed in Interlisp-D. The model performs three primary functions for each step of a corrective maintenance problem: (a) action selection, (b) symptom evaluation, and (c) replacement consideration. This cycle is repeated until the true failure is identified and resolved. The organization of the data and processes is shown in Figure 18.7 The Test Selector considers the time to perform alternative actions and potential (expected) information available at each test to determine the best course of action. The Test Performer simply looks up the symptom information that the selected test yields (and adds on the test time to the expert's solution time). The Test Interpreter judges the normality of the test result and determines what failures could have produced (or permitted) such a symptom. Further, this function adjusts the suspicion levels of all the possible failures to reflect the new information gained.

When Profile starts a fault-isolation process, the initial suspicion level of each failure possibility is set according to its relative generic reliability. The inherent failure likelihoods of components tend to influence Profile's test selections, because it prefers tests that discriminate among the more highly suspected areas of the system. Generally, the reliability information is simply that related to each

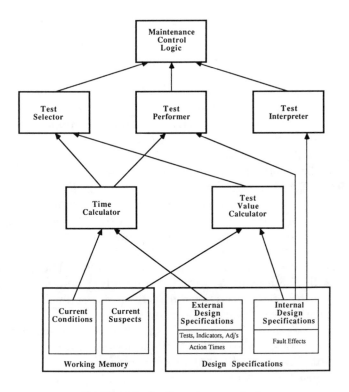

FIGURE 18.7 Profile system organization.

generic component in the system, as entered in the Generic Object library. If component reliabilities change drastically in a particular system configuration, however, they may be revised to reflect the impacts.

Test Selection

The Test Selector evaluates each test in terms of the information value it offers (in relation to the current suspicion set), the time required to perform it, and the estimated time to complete fault isolation following performance of the test. This requires that the time required to complete fault isolation following each test under consideration be estimated (although a rigorous dynamic-programming solution was developed, the compute-time requirements were enormous, and the resulting testing sequences were only slightly faster than the heuristically determined solutions). Profile estimates the time to complete fault isolation following each test by determining the fault sets resulting from each possible symptom of the test and estimating the remaining fault isolation workload in terms of the replacement times of those components. This causes Profile to favor tests that discriminate effectively among components with high replacement times, and to favor shorter tests.

Undoubtedly, other concerns can affect a technician's approach to a maintenance problem. Avoidance of danger, discomfort, excessive cognitive effort, or catastrophic error are almost certain to play major roles in maintenance of military systems. Such issues as these are often explicitly addressed in conventional expert-system approaches to capturing diagnostic strategies. Though such factors have not yet been included in Profile's rules for diagnostic decisions, the consideration of danger or discomfort would not be a difficult enhancement to incorporate. It would require a subjective evaluation of the negative characteristics of each of the major testing operations.

Profile includes a parameter that reflects the environment in which a particular maintenance task is to be analyzed. The parameter expresses the relationship between restoration time and cost of spares. A high setting of the parameter reflects an environment in which restoration time is paramount; consumption of spares is secondary to restoring the system as quickly as possible. A low setting reflects a depot environment in which additional testing is usually preferred to replacing expensive units that are not certain to be faulty. By varying this parameter one can explore the maintenance workloads under varying conditions.

Replacements and adjustments are regarded as tests in Profile, because these maintenance actions also have the property of providing new information. These actions, followed by a confirming test that previously produced an abnormal symptom, offer a small amount of new information (about one possible fault). As a result, Profile rarely selects these types of actions until it has exhausted more informative choices. Replacements are further penalized with the cost of the spare part being replaced, so that replacements are not often performed until there is high certainty that the failure has been identified. This rule is weakened, however, when time pressure is extreme. In this case, expensive components and subassemblies may be replaced by Profile in its effort to minimize restoration time. In all cases, more expensive spares are less likely to be replaced than cheaper ones, all other factors being equal.

The simple expression for minimizing expected fault-isolation time yields surprisingly diverse diagnostic behaviors under differing situations. As just mentioned, it drives the diagnostic model toward efficient performance, with which an expert would agree. In addition to avoiding costly replacements, as discussed above, Profile exhibits these characteristics:

1. It generally performs front-panel checks before calling for test equipment usage, because first use of test equipment involves a considerable set-up time cost. Once a particular test equipment has been used, Profile prefers its use to other equipments, because further testing is economical.
2. If "known-good" spares are available for short-term substitution, it will use these if the time to swap them in and out is low, because the cost of using these spares is considered to be negligible.
3. It can profit from past field experience, if component reliabilities are maintained to reflect their true values. All other factors being equal, Profile will pursue the testing of the more failure-prone areas of a system.

Because there is uncertainty about what symptom will actually be obtained when a test is performed, the model will at times select tests that turn out to provide almost no new information (even though they had the potential of providing much new information), and it may at times replace units that are not the actual faulty unit. When this is done, however, it can be shown that the test or replacement selected was the most productive course of action to take, considering the time cost of alternative actions.

Test Interpretation

Whereas the Test Selector is concerned with considering all possible symptoms of each possible test under consideration, the Test Interpreter function in Profile is concerned with drawing inferences from the symptom information actually obtained from the selected test (as provided by the Test Performer).

The Test Interpreter maintains a cumulative score for each failure possibility, reflecting the extent to which the pattern of received symptoms matches the possible symptoms the failure might produce. A high distance score for a failure indicates high mismatch between the symptoms received and those that would be produced by the failure, that is, there is little likelihood that the failure in question has produced the symptoms received. These scores are initially set according to the component failure rates (for simplicity, all failure modes for a component are assigned an equal share of the component's failure rate). This initialization affects the likelihood of replacing each component, by the Profile model, and it causes early test selection to focus on tests that relate to more failure-prone areas of the system.

The current version of Profile does not recognize that some tests are more error-prone than others, and are therefore less attractive than tests performed with higher certainty. Future versions of Profile may weight the symptom information according to the probability that the test can be performed and interpreted correctly. In this fashion the results of error-prone tests would be less significant than those for more easily performed tests.

Replacement Consideration

A replacement is selected by the Test Selector as the next action under two possible conditions: (a) a replacement, followed by a confirming check, offers the greatest information value per unit time, compared to all the other possible actions; and (b) the received symptoms strongly implicate a particular fault.

Under all but the most urgent conditions, a replacement decision by Profile will first trigger the performance of a special test, called the *most direct* test. The most direct test, for each component, is that test which most clearly monitors the correct operation of the suspected component, and no others. Even though this is a very poor test to perform early in a diagnostic sequence, its performance previous to a replacement will minimize the chance of replacing a component that is not actually faulty.

SIMULATION ISSUES

This section is concerned with the portions of IMTS related to simulating the behavior of a target system. At present the IMTS simulator deals with systems whose responses reach a steady state in a short period of time following actions upon them. The Bladefold application is such a system. All Bladefold system responses stabilize within a maximum of 30 seconds of technician actions, and most system responses occur within a few seconds. The simulation is not restricted to discrete-state effects, although the graphical-object editor does not currently provide for continuous variations in graphical appearances. To implement a continuous-change type of object, the object creator would currently have to build a number of similar states and then relate each to a range of actual values.

In general, the behavior of a time-invariant, real-world system is a function of the malfunction state, of settings of controls, and of previous states, as described in the following subsection.

Malfunction State

The simulation process is basically the same when IMTS simulates a normal, fail-free system and when it simulates a system that contains a malfunction. When the problem-selection routine identifies the malfunction that will provide the best practice to the student, it simply replaces the part in the target system with a version of that part that contains the fault of interest. Because the failed version of the part contains rules of behavior in exactly the same form as normal parts, the simulator does not need to distinguish between simulating a normal system and a failed system, although other routines in the IMTS do note whether symptoms seen by the student are normal or abnormal. When the student calls for replacing the part that is failed, the IMTS replaces the failed-part definitions with normal ones.

Settings of Control

Changing the setting of a single control can drastically alter the set of elements of a system that is involved in system operation and the way in which they are interconnected. In the Bladefold application, a single switch change can trigger mechanical movements that actuate other microswitches, which in turn trigger other mechanical, hydraulic, or electrical functions. For these reasons the simulator functions in the IMTS are extremely compute-bound and are far more complicated than originally expected.

Special Simulation Problems

A number of researchers have documented the difficulties of automatically evaluating and explaining complex system behaviors. This subsection will describe the kinds of problems that were confronted in constructing a general-purpose simulator that could deal with the types of behaviors found in the Bladefold system. Although it is too early to judge the general range of application of the IMTS simulation system, it is encouraging that the IMTS simulator is successful in accurately computing the responses of the system to student actions and to malfunctions.

The major problem which persists is that the time to respond to a student action is longer than we would wish, for the Bladefold application, because the simulator must update the state of the Bladefold system following each student action. Though compute time has been reduced by more than a factor of 10 since the simulator routine was originally made operational, this speed increase was achieved almost exclusively by replacing high-level LISP functions on lists with more intricately coded two-level operations on fixed arrays and direct memory addressing. This has progressed to a point where there is now almost no "garbage-collection," or recovery of temporarily used memory, being done by the system software. The one area where LISP functions have been crucial is in the object-behavior editor, wherein user entries describing object behaviors are converted into LISP code.

Efforts to speed simulation by preanalyzing the topology of the target system have been generally unsuccessful. One such approach attempted to selectively avoid recomputation of some object states, depending upon the nature of the student action. Unfortunately, the distributed architecture of the Bladefold system works to defeat this approach, as it minimizes the extent to which effects can be localized to system modules. Further, Bladefold, like many other real systems, contains objects that will change state even when they become stranded from the main body of the system. Thus a simulator cannot limit evaluation to just those components encountered in a trace of connectivity.

A second major difficulty encountered during development of the simulation logic was in determining the order in which object states should be evaluated. Suppose, for example, that a pipe is connected to a tee, and that the two branches of the tee lead to subsystems that ultimately come together. The question arises as to which of the branches should be evaluated first. Often the order of evaluation is of no consequence. But in some cases the actions of one branch have some impact upon what happens in the other branch. If the evaluation is performed in the wrong order, the system behavior can be erroneously determined. A related problem has to do with objects that perform multiple functions. Some of the objects in the Bladefold system alter both hydraulic and electrical ports. We have found that, in the systems we have simulated, propagating electrical effects before propagating hydraulic effects results in correct simulations.

Another problem that complicated the simulator is the fact that an object's normal behavior rules are sometimes overruled by other objects. For example, one simple object has the rule that it extends when the pressure at port A exceeds the pressure at port B, otherwise it retracts. In some situations, however, the part cannot extend because an adjacent part is obstructing it. The cause of this may be far from the part that would normally extend. The effects may chain backward through many parts, each of which is being prevented from following its rules because of the offending part. This type of complication is very apparent for mechanical parts, but it is just as serious a concern for electrical and hydraulic effects. The major implication of this effect is that object definitions must account for a wider range of situations than is initially apparent.

The final type of issue to be detailed here is related to recognizing the spatial orientation of mechanical parts and determining the effects of movements in those parts. Because mechanical objects are described in the IMTS editors out of context, one cannot specify how the movement of one part will affect surrounding parts. A simple lever, for example, may move to its left when pressed by an adjacent part, but move to its right when it is rotated 180°. Because orientation is determined at the time generic objects are brought together to form specific systems, the simulator must infer these mechanical relationships from the specific orientations rather than from specifications provided in the generic-object-behavior rules.

SCHEDULED FUTURE DEVELOPMENTS AND APPLICATIONS

To test the generality of IMTS, a second equipment system will be simulated. This system, the WSC-3 Satellite Communications System, is far more complex than Bladefold, but will be simulated only to the level of detail of block diagrams, such as automatic generation of complex waveform displays.

Providing Practice in Diagnosing Multiple Failures and Cascading Failures

In a deep simulation system such as IMTS, simulation builders should be able to simulate multiple failures and cascading failures with virtually no additional authoring cost. No additional simulation-behavior data need be entered in order to simulate multiple faults. A failed object is simulated when IMTS replaces the normal behavior rules of the object with special failure-mode-behavior rules. It can simulate the failure of multiple elements by loading the failure-mode rules for all the failed objects in place of the normal behavior rules.

To implement cascading failures, the object author will specify the triggering conditions that cause the object to fail. For example, pressure of greater than a threshold amount may cause a reducing valve to blow out and to begin behaving like a pipe. In an actual simulation, the introduction of a certain failure in a hydraulic component connected to a reducing valve may cause the pressure to exceed that valve's threshold and thereby induce the blow-out failure. Adding the failure-triggering conditions to an object's behavior description ensures that the object will exhibit appropriate cascading-failure behavior.

Simulating Student-Selected Failures

The IMTS system encourages simulation builders to describe the failure modes of each object type at the time that the object's behaviors are described. This makes it possible to easily simulate any of the possible failures of any object in a particular equipment simulation. In a surface simulation system, the consequences of each failure for all the behaviors of the whole simulated system must be analyzed and described. In a deep simulation system such as IMTS, the symptoms of a particular failure are determined at run time, using the failure rules of the failed object type, the normal behavior rules of the other objects, and the topology of the simulated equipment.

The ability to simulate any failure makes it feasible to offer troubleshooting exercises for any failure, rather than restricting these exercises to a fixed preauthored curriculum. We plan to develop a simple student option for inserting new malfunction conditions into the system. This will permit an exploratory style of learning. If a student wonders what would be the effects of a blockage in the safety valve, he or she can experimentally insert such a failure into the simulation and then examine the behavior of the entire equipment system. If computation-speed issues can be satisfactorily dealt with, the same pedagogical features that are provided for curriculum troubleshooting exercises can also be made available for student-generated exercises.

Guided Simulation

A new instructional mode, called *guided simulation,* will allow experts to perform operations on the simulation and to enter explanations of their procedures and the system's responses. Students can then observe replays of the process at their own pace, and they can participate in the decision making that produced the process. This mode will be useful for providing procedure drills and for giving interactive demonstrations of troubleshooting approaches. In guided simulation, a student reads a series of brief instructions in a small text window on the screen and carries out those instructions by manipulating simulated controls, by using simulated test equipment, and by replacing components in the IMTS scene window.

Specific guided simulations can be easily created by an instructor who is familiar with the proper procedures for the actual target equipment. The instructor creates the student prompt texts using a simple editing window. To specify the student actions required after each such prompt, the instructor merely performs the action in the scene window. Guided simulation authoring is a very straightforward way to generate non-free-play simulation lessons. Once a simulation has been constructed for general IMTS use, guided simulation lessons can be developed unusually quickly—perhaps with as little as two or three hours of development time for each hour of instruction.

Pedagogical Views for Instructional Purposes

The simulation scenes constructed for IMTS must be complete, because they are executed almost as if they were physical constructs. As such, the simulation scenes may become complex, and they may be poor representations for novice students, who would benefit from the initial presentation of simplified drawings. Other students might benefit from being able to simultaneously view several active objects from different scenes, so that they could see how the behavior of one affects the other. Thus there is a strong need for the ability to display portions of the system in ways designed to ease understanding as opposed to driving the simulation. We call such simplified presentations *pedagogical views.*

In order to support the pedagogical-view approach, we have developed the capability to make "active snapshots" of portions of scenes. A rectangular portion of any scene can be copied from its scene into other views, such as the convenience view area described above. The objects in these snapshots retain all the characteristics of objects in the full scene window. They change in response to simulation events, and control objects can be directly manipulated with the mouse.

A composition tool must now be developed for the use of instructors and course designers to extend this concept. This tool will permit a course developer to build special scenes consisting primarily of snapshots of portions of existing scenes and to create images of subsystems that are physically realistic rather than schematically accurate. It will also be possible to add background graphical elements and text to these scenes. Different explanatory sequences can be authored with different pedagogical views, so that each instructional interaction can make use of the most appropriate visual presentation. Pedagogical views will improve the presentation of simulation and instruction to students with different levels of understanding.

CONCLUSIONS

The IMTS project is an attempt to build a useful tool for simulation-based maintenance training, undertaken despite the many obvious and serious gaps in our knowledge about the nature of human learning and human instruction expertise. It could be argued that it would be better to wait until a more complete understanding of these difficult issues is at hand. We believe that although more research is needed to explore basic issues about human understanding, the IMTS project demonstrates that important strides can also be made by attempting to produce a functioning system now, relying largely on techniques we and our colleagues have developed in recent research efforts.

The IMTS is not a conventional experimental test of a single, well-controlled instructional variable, and it is difficult to attribute each IMTS feature to a particular psychological theory or finding. A significant portion of the IMTS is necessarily concerned with matters that have very little to do with instructional strategy, and therefore do not have psychological principles at their root. For example, the functions that support the simulation of the target system (in response to student actions and to malfunction conditions) and the functions that compute expert diagnostic actions have virtually nothing to do with instructional issues, yet they constitute a major portion of the IMTS software. Certainly the form of the simulation is a critical instructional issue, but the IMTS imposes almost no constraints on the form of the graphic simulation. The IMTS does not rely upon research in visual imagery, and few constraints on the form of visual imagery are imposed by the system. We see the IMTS as an environment for studying the learning effectiveness of alternate graphic forms and other issues in simulation-training research. We invite our research colleagues to consider using IMTS as a tool in their research.

Lessons Learned

Many of the lessons emerging from this work are specific to the peculiarities of simulation authoring and of programming in LISP. Nonetheless, there are some lessons that may prove of benefit to others working in the area of computer-based simulation training, and we discuss them now.

Powerful simulation software requires powerful computers. This research project has been guided by two not necessarily compatible goals—to advance the state of the art in simulation-training systems and to provide practical computer-based training, first for a helicopter bladefold system. To achieve the first goal, we made a fundamental departure from earlier approaches we had taken to simulation-composition systems (Towne & Munro, 1981; 1984; Towne, Munro,

Johnson, & Lahey, 1983; Towne, 1987). With those earlier, surface-oriented systems, simulation authors had to manually precompute all the possible states of a system. In the new deep-simulation approach, this intellectual work is automated. This not only makes life easier for authors, but also increases the power and range of the simulations delivered to students. In addition, it makes it possible to automatically generate some instruction that would have had to be authored by hand in a surface-simulation system.

The down side of these advances is that the computation load for on-the-fly generated simulations is very much greater than for look-up-the-stored-effects simulations. For the Xerox 1108/1186 class of machines, and the Bladefold application, the response time to update the simulation is now averaging approximately 15 seconds. For simpler applications, involving fewer than five or six screens of graphics, the response time is under 5 seconds. These times hold for a version of IMTS in which many conventional LISP constructs have been replaced by direct access and manipulation of data in memory. These methods have resulted in a tenfold speedup from a version that used conventional list-building techniques.

Even using good tools, describing object behaviors is not simple. One of the goals of this project was to make it possible for nonprogrammer device experts to build more powerful simulations with less effort. We believe that this goal has been attained, but some of our expectations for ease of authoring have been tempered by experience. The object-behavior editor lets the author describe the behavior of an object in terms of the relationships among its ports—the electrical, mechanical, and hydraulic connections that it can have with other objects. For many authors, it is sometimes difficult to analyze the behavior of an object in isolation. When put together in a system, objects sometimes cause effects based on their behavior descriptions that were not expected by the author. As a consequence, there is more cyclic describe/debug activity than we expected.

Although the task of object-behavior analysis in isolation has proven to be more involved than we expected, several new authoring tools make the describe/debug cycle easier. The IMTS system editor contains a "breadboard" mode that makes it possible to connect several objects experimentally and observe their interactive behaviors. This makes it easy to build a temporary local context for a new object in order to test its behavior in a more comprehensible environment than a complete simulation like Bladefold.

The results of our experiences in behavior editing suggest that some aspects of this task may be inherently complex. A cyclic design/debug process may be inevitable when implementing these aspects.

As with other complex intellectual activities, experience at the task of describing object behavior improves performance significantly.

In the long run, three factors should limit the problems of authoring object behaviors. First, authors can now experiment with behavior effects during the authoring process, making it easier to arrive at correct behavior descriptions and to learn how to avoid possible problems. Second, as more systems are simulated, the library of reusable object definitions will grow. Eventually, many simulations could be created simply by putting together new scenes composed of existing object types. At this point, simulation composition—and authoring intelligent instruction based on simulation—would consist simply of drawing the new system using existing pieces. Third, it may be possible to extract object behavior definitions for new objects from existing sources, such as CAD/CAM libraries. This feature would integrate the equipment-design-and-training process.

We have not yet isolated ideal "locality of effect."   In a simulation system with local effects, behaviors are specified at the component level. Effects must be propagated from one object to the next, following the equipment connectivity data and the behavior rules of the objects. In a simulation with global effects, the behavior of one object may be determined by the state of an arbitrarily remote object.

In earlier simulation-authoring systems created in our lab—the ancestors of GMTS and Lockheed's Equipment Simulation Authoring System (Towne & Munro, 1984)—simulation effects were authored as though all were entirely global. If turning a switch to "standby" in one module could, under certain circumstances, cause a "ready" light to light up in a remote module, this effect would be authored directly, without referring to the propagation of effect from the switch through the relevant circuits to the light. If there were intervening objects that changed state when the switch was thrown, then their behavior would also have to be globally specified. This approach had the advantage that simple remote effects could be directly authored. At simulation time, such effects were quickly computed. It had the disadvantages that it was extremely difficult to build accurate simulations for complex devices and that such simulations were even more difficult to maintain. Furthermore, there was no potential for reusing portions of such simulations, because effects were all intertwined at a global level.

In IMTS, simulation effects are authored as though they are entirely local. Remote effects are derived at run-time through a sequence of behavior computations and value propagations. This has the advantage that authors can take a modular approach to simulation construction, describing each element in isolation. Once the correct component behaviors have been authored, simulations can be easily maintained and modified. Even more important, from an instructional viewpoint, the local-effects approach offers the opportunity to generate intelligent instructional interactions using the model of the equipment embodied in the simulation data. The disadvantages of this approach are that it places significant burdens on the generic simulation-management software, it is likely to result in slower simulations than is a global approach, and it enforces a less natural approach to authoring when the builder of a simulation has a surface understanding rather than a deep understanding of the system.

In IMTS, the simulation propagation software does a great deal of work when delivering an interactive simulation. In many cases, the entire topology of connections among objects may be traversed several times in response to a single control-setting change. Where two objects directly affect a third object, the first may be computed to put the third into a new state, but when the effect of the second object is computed, that state change for the third object may be blocked. Certain effects must be treated as provisional by the simulator until other propagations have taken place. This prevents displaying the changes-of-object changes in the correct order. We intend to explore the possibility of providing for judicious authoring of nonlocal effects and the consequences of such an approach on simplifying and speeding up the simulation process.

We have encountered some cases in which simulation authoring would clearly be simpler if locality of effect could extend beyond the object level. Ohm's law, for example, provides a simple nonlocal model for the propagation of effect. The voltage in an object in a given circuit depends not just on the resistances of the immediately adjacent objects, but on the resistances of all the objects in the circuit. Although local models to account for these effects can be created, they are likely to be less inherently appealing to authors and less computationally efficient than a nonlocal model based on Ohm's law.

The solution to this conflict is almost certainly not to abandon the local-effects approach entirely, but rather to modify it by providing for limited or constrained global effects. One direction for this work would be to incorporate into the IMTS model a provision for authoring composite objects. These would be modules made up of more primitive objects grouped in a particular topology. Certain of the value computations for the primitive objects in such a composite would be specified not at the component-behavior level, but rather at the composite-behavior level. Many substantive issues in design and implementation must be resolved before the feasibility of this approach can be evaluated.

Future Directions

One goal for future work is to reduce the dependence of simulation training on the skill of simulation/tutorial authors. Ultimately, we would like to see authors simply draw a correct representation of a complex equipment system, and let an intelligent training system generate simulations and instructional materials from those drawings. This goal is not as remote as one might expect, if it is understood that the drawing primitives are previously defined objects with complex behaviors and other attributes that can be referred to in simulation and training. This goal can be approached in a modular fashion, and we have identified a number of enhancements to be explored. We describe them here.

Test repertoire generation. At present, an author must identify the tests that may be of interest for troubleshooting before running the Profile generic troubleshooting expert to generate symptom-malfunction data using the simulation. If an intelligent process could deduce which tests are likely to be fruitful, this step could be automated. The process would have to use its understanding of the propagation of effects in a simulated system to determine where the effects of a malfunction could appear. If the process is extremely accurate, it could be used to reduce the volume of data that must be computed and stored, directing the simulation to compute test results for those cases in which they are likely to depart from normals.

Problem difficulty assessment. In IMTS, an author must use the knowledge editor to tell the system how difficult each troubleshooting problem is. These difficulty ratings are used, together with information about the student, to select appropriate problems. Ideally, these difficulty assessments would be made by an IMTS function. Such an assessment would depend on a technical decomposition of the system. Subtle judgments, such as identifying remote or mediated malfunction effects, noting symptom-set similarities, and determining behavioral complexity, would play a role in assessing problem difficulty.

Generation of the normative model. To a large extent, the normative model for the structure of knowledge about the Bladefold system reflects the organization of the simulation into scenes. The scenes correspond to functional elements of the equipment, and such a functional organization provides a reasonable organizing schema for knowledge about the equipment. The entire normative model could conceivably be generated based on the organization of scenes, component groupings, component typology, and malfunctions. Such a model would be far less sophisticated than one that might be generated by a trained knowledge engineer working for a long period with a number of experts and students. However, it would be a great deal less expensive to produce, and would probably be just as useful for guiding decisions about problem selection and curriculum management.

Pedagogical scene composition. The scenes that authors compose using IMTS are views that accurately reflect the topology of the target equipment, and that, in the author's judgment, display a pedagogically useful organization. Unfortunately, these scenes may not be equally appropriate for all students. An unsophisticated novice might do better if presented with a set of simpler scenes, emphasizing input and output devices. When a student's understanding of the basic functioning of the system is established, he or she could be introduced to progressively more complex and more accurate renderings that expose the mediating devices.

A crude approach to this need for different pedagogical views could be achieved using the present IMTS authoring system. For each desired pedagogical "level," a different simulation could be authored. This approach would be exhausting and prone to error. It would be difficult to maintain the different simulations together, in that topology changes made in one would have to somehow be reflected, through hand editing, in the others.

One approach to pedagogical scene composition would be to provide authors with tools for building simplified views of the simulation scenes. The behavior of these views would depend on the actual simulation scenes themselves, thus assuring both the surface accuracy of the pedagogical views and their maintainability. (Changes to the simulation would automatically be reflected in the views.) An even more ambitious approach to pedagogical scenes would be to have the training system compose scenes on an individual basis in response to assessed student needs. New scenes would be built up based on student needs, as represented in the student model, and on the functional relatedness of objects.

Additional presentation modes and features. A number of technologically unchallenging enhancements would improve the instructional appeal of IMTS. Although they do not present significant research hurdles, these improvements could be expected to have significant training benefits. Graphically simulated motion, such as hydraulic flow in pipes, would improve understanding of simulated effects, especially for novice students. This is not a viable option using the present IMTS delivery system, due to the computational limitations of the Xerox AI machines. Videodisk presentations under IMTS control would enhance the viability of IMTS as a stand-alone training system in real-world training environments. Improved "view" options could be delivered with videodisk, and motion sequences could be presented to demonstrate difficult maintenance procedures. Voice output technology could be used to supplement the (already-minimal) reading requirements that the system imposes on students.

Summary

Despite a number of problems related to computational limitations, the feasibility of direct manipulation authoring of simulations and the object-oriented approach to specifying behavior has been amply demonstrated in IMTS. Moreover, the IMTS demonstrates that intelligent maintenance training interactions can be generated automatically by executing functions that operate upon a specific system representation in a generic manner. The IMTS is intended to address immediate training requirements and to offer an attractive environment for continuing research in learning and instruction. A number of challenges remain, and there is a great potential for further exploiting the intelligence embodied in this training system.

ACKNOWLEDGMENTS

Development of the IMTS is being supported by the Personnel and Training Research Program of the Office of Naval Research and by the Navy Personnel Research and Development Center. The original development of Profile, the generic diagnostic expert, was supported by the Engineering Psychology Program of the Office of Naval Research.

Quentin A. Pizzini and David S. Surmon, of our organization, were the primary designers and implementors of the object creation and simulation capabilities. William B. Johnson, of Search Technology, Inc. and Ronald Renfro of ManTech Mathetics Corporation provided subject matter expertise for the first IMTS application, the SH-3H helicopter Bladefolding system. We thank Richard Burton for comments on an earlier version of this chapter.

REFERENCES

Anderson, J. R. (1983). *The architecture of cognition.* Cambridge, MA: Harvard University Press.

Anderson, J. R., Boyle, C. F., Farrell, R., & Reiser, B. (1984). Cognitive principles in the design of computer tutors. *Proceedings of the Sixth Annual Conference of the Cognitive Science Society*. Boulder, CO: Institute of Cognitive Science.

Anderson, J. R., Farrell, R., & Sauers, R. (1984). Learning to program in LISP. *Cognitive Science, 8*, 87–130.

Bilodeau, I. McD. (1969). Information feedback. In E. A. Bilodeau (Ed.), *Principles of skill acquisition*. New York: Academic Press.

Burton, R. R., & Brown, J. S. (1982). An investigation of computer coaching for informal learning activities. In D. Sleeman, & J. S. Brown (Eds.), *Intelligent tutoring systems* (pp. 79–98). London: Academic Press.

Hollan, J. D. (1983). *Steamer: An overview with implications for AI applications in other domains*. Presented at the Joint Services Workshop on Artificial Intelligence in Maintenance, Institute of Cognitive Science, Boulder, CO.

Hollan, J. D., Hutchins, E. L., & Weitzman, L. (1984). STEAMER: An Interactive Inspectable Simulation-based Training System, *The AI Magazine, 2*, p.2.

McKendree, J., Reiser, B. J., & Anderson, J. R. (1984). Tutorial goals and strategies in the instruction of programming skills. *Proceedings of the Sixth Annual Conference of the Cognitive Science Society*. Boulder, CO: Institute for Cognitive Science.

Pask, G. (1975). *Conversation, cognition, and learning: A cybernetic theory and methodology*. New York: Elsevier.

Rigney, J. W., Cremer, R. H., Towne, D. M., & Mason, A. K. (1968). *An analysis of structure and errors in corrective maintenance work*. Report No. TR-55. Los Angeles: Behavioral Technology Laboratories, University of Southern California.

Skinner, B. F. (1958). *The technology of teaching*. New York: Appleton-Century-Crofts.

Towne, D. M. (1984). A generalized model of fault-isolation performance. *Proceedings, Artificial Intelligence in Maintenance: Joint Services Workshop*.

Towne, D. M. (1987). The generalized maintenance trainer: Evolution and revolution. In W. B. Rouse (Ed.), *Advances in man-machine systems research* (Vol. 3, pp. 1–63). Greenwich, CT: JAI Press.

Towne, D. M. (1987). A generic expert diagnostician. In *Proceedings of the Air Force Workshop on Artificial Intelligence Applications for Integrated Diagnostics*.

Towne, D. M., Fehling, M. R., & Bond, N. A. (1981). *Design for the maintainer: Projecting maintenance performance from design characteristics*. Report No. TR-95. Los Angeles: Behavioral Technology Laboratories, University of Southern California.

Towne, D. M., Johnson, M. C., & Corwin, W. H. (1982). *A technique for projecting maintenance performance from design characteristics*. Report No. TR-100. Los Angeles: Behavioral Technology Laboratories, University of Southern California.

Towne, D. M., Johnson, M. C., & Corwin, W. H. (1983). *A performance-based technique for assessing equipment maintainability*. Report No. TR-102. Los Angeles: Behavioral Technology Laboratories, University of Southern California.

Towne, D. M., & Munro, A. (1981). *Generalized maintenance trainer simulator: Development of hardware and software*. Technical Report No. 81-9. San Diego: Navy Personnel Research and Development Center.

Towne, D. M., & Munro, A. (1984). *Preliminary design of the advanced ESAS System* (Tech. Rep. No. 105). Los Angeles: Behavioral Technology Laboratories, University of Southern California.

Towne, D. M., Munro, A., Johnson, M. C., & Lahey, G. F. (1983). *Generalized maintenance trainer simulator: Test and evaluation in the laboratory environment* (NPRDC TR 83-28). San Diego: Navy Personnel Research and Development Center.

Towne, D. M., Munro, A., Pizzini, Q. A., & Surmon, D. S. (1985). *Development of intelligent maintenance training technology: Design study* (Tech. Rep. No. 106). Los Angeles: Behavioral Technology Laboratories, University of Southern California.

Tulving, E. (1983). *Elements of episodic memory*. London: Oxford University Press.

Tulving, E., & Thompson, D. M. (1973). Encoding specificity and retrieval processes in episodic memory. *Psychological Review, 80*, 352-373.

Wescourt, K. T., Beard, M., & Gould, L. (1977). Knowledge-based adaptive curriculum sequencing for CAI: Application of a network representation. *Proceedings of the Association for Computing Machinery*, 234-340.

Wescourt, K. T., Beard, M., Gould, L., & Barr, A. (1977). *Knowledge-based CAI: CINS for individualized curriculum sequencing*. Technical Report 290. Stanford, CA: Institute for Mathematical Studies in the Social Sciences, Stanford University.

Wescourt, K. T., & Hemphill, L. (1978). *Representing and teaching knowledge for troubleshooting/debugging*. Technical Report 292. Stanford, CA: Institute for Mathematical Studies in the Social Sciences, Stanford University.

EDITORS' REFERENCES

Amsler, R. A. (1980). *The structure of the Merriam-Webster pocket dictionary*. Technical Report No. TR-164. Austin, TX: University of Texas.

Anderson, J. R. (1983). *The architecture of cognition*. Cambridge, MA: Harvard University Press.

Anderson, J. R., Boyle, C. F., & Reiser, B. J. (1985). Intelligent tutoring systems. *Science, 228*, 456-462.

Barr, A., & Feigenbaum, E. A. (Eds.) (1982). *The handbook of artificial intelligence: Vol. II*. Los Altos, CA: William Kaufmann, Inc.

Barsalou, L. W. (in press). Intra-concept similarity and its implications for inter-concept similarity. In S. Vosniadou & A. Ortony (Eds.), *Similarity and analogy*. Hillsdale, NJ: Lawrence Erlbaum Associates.

Bloom, B. S. (1984). The 2 sigma problem: The search for methods of group instruction as effective as one-to-one tutoring. *Educational Researcher, 13*(6), 4-16.

Bork, A. (1981). *Learning with computers*. Bedford, MA: Digital Press.

Bransford, J. D. (1987). *Enhancing thinking and learning*. New York: W. H. Freeman.

Brown, J. S., & Burton, R. R. (1986). Reactive learning environments for teaching electronic troubleshooting. In W. B. Rouse (Ed.), *Advances in Man-Machine Systems Research* (Vol. 3). Greenwich, CT: JAI Press.

Brown, J. S., Burton, R. R., & deKleer, J. (1982). Pedagogical, natural language, and knowledge engineering techniques in SOPHIE I, II, and III. In D. H. Sleeman & J. S. Brown (Eds.), *Intelligent tutoring systems* (pp. 227-282). London: Academic Press.

Brown, J. S., Moran, T., & Williams, M. (1982). *The semantics of procedures*. Xerox Proposal No. 4393-105.

Carbonell, J. R. (1970). AI in CAI: An Artificial Intelligence approach to computer-assisted instruction. *IEEE Transactions on Man-Machine Systems, 11*.

Carey, S. (1986). Cognitive science and science education. *American Psychologist, 41*, 1123-1130.

Clancey, W. J. (1986). Qualitative student models. *Annual Review of Computer Science, 1*, 381-450.

Collins, A., Brown, J. S., & Newman, S. E. (1987). *Cognitive apprenticeship: Teaching the craft of reading, writing, and mathematics.* BBN Report No. 6459. Cambridge, MA: BBN Laboratories.

Collins, A., & Quillian, M. R. (1969). Retrieval time from semantic memory. *Journal of Verbal Learning and Verbal Behavior, 6,* 240–247.

Collins, A., & Stevens, A. L. (1981). Goals and strategies of effective teachers. In R. Glaser (Ed.), *Advances in instructional technology* (Vol. 2). Hillsdale, NJ: Lawrence Erlbaum Associates.

DiSessa, A. A. (1982). Unlearning aristotelian physics: A study of knowledge-based learning. *Cognitive Science, 6,* 37–75.

Farr, M. (1986). *The long-term retention of knowledge and skills: A cognitive and instructional perspective.* Report M-205. Alexandria, VA: Institute for Defense Analyses.

Fletcher, D., & Psotka, J. (1986, June). Intelligent training systems for maintenance. *Signal,* 89–95.

Forbus, K. D., & Gentner, D. (1986). *Learning physical domains: Toward a theoretical framework.* Report No. UIUCDCS-R-86-1247. Urbana, IL: University of Illinois.

Glaser, R., Lesgold, A., Lajoie, S., Eastman, R., Greenberg, L., Logan, D., Magone, W., Weiner, A., Wolf, R., & Yengo, L. (1985). *Cognitive task analysis to enhance technical skills training and assessment.* Final report of project on Feasibility of Cognitive Information Processing Models for Basic Skills Assessment and Enhancement, prepared for the Air Force Human Resources Laboratory, Learning Research and Development Center, University of Pittsburgh.

Haertel, H. (1987). *A qualitative approach to electricity.* Working Paper. Palo Alto, CA: Institute for Research on Learning.

Hagman, J. D., & Rose, A. M. (1983). Retention of military tasks: A review. *Human Factors, 25,* 199–213.

Halff, H. M., Hollan, J. D., & Hutchins, E. L. (1986). Cognitive science and military training. *American Psychologist, 41,* 1131–1139.

Laird, J., & Newell, A. (1983). *A universal weak method.* Technical Report CMU-CS-83-141, Pittsburgh, PA: Carnegie-Mellon University.

Landauer, T. K. (1986). How much do people remember? some estimates of the quantity of learned information in long-term memory. *Cognitive Science, 10,* 477–493.

Larkin, J. H., Reif, F., Carbonell, J., & Gugliotta, A. (1985). *FERMI: A flexible expert reasoner with multi-domain inferencing.* Final report on Project ARI/ONR No. N-000114-82-0767.

Lave, J., Murtaugh, M., & de la Rocha, O. (1984). The dialectic of arithmetic in grocery shopping. In B. Rogoff & J. Lave (Eds.), *Everyday cognition: Its development in social context* (pp. 67–94). Cambridge, MA: Harvard University Press.

Lawler, R. W., & Yazdani, M. (Eds.). (1987). *Artificial Intelligence and education: Learning environments and intelligent tutoring systems.* Norwood, NJ: ABLEX Press.

Lenat, D., Prakash, M., & Shepherd, M. (1986, Winter). CYC: Using commonsense knowledge to overcome brittleness and knowledge-acquisition bottlenecks. *The AI Magazine,* 65–85.

Malone, T. (1981). Toward a theory of intrinsically motivating instruction. *Cognitive Science, 4,* 333–369.

Massey, L. D., Tenney, Y. J., Kurland, L., deBruin, J., & Roberts, B. (1987). *The HAWK MACH-III design document.* ARI technical Report. Alexandria, VA: Army Research Institute.

Merrill, M. D. (1987). Prescriptions for an authoring system. *Journal of Computer-Based Instruction, 14,* 1–10.

Musen, M. A., Fagan, L. M., Combs, D. M., & Shortliffe, E. H. (1986). *Using a domain model to drive an interactive knowledge editing tool.* Knowledge Systems Lab memo KSL-86-24. Stanford, CA: Stanford University.

Nickerson, R. S., Perkins, D., & Smith, E. E. (1985). *The teaching of thinking.* Hillsdale, NJ: Lawrence Erlbaum Associates.

Orr, J. (1986). *Talking about machines: Social aspects of expertise.* Xerox PARC ISL working paper. Palo Alto, CA. Also in the Proceedings of the Conference on Computer Supported Cooperative Work: Austin, TX.

Palincsar, A. S., & Brown, A. L. (1984). Reciprocal teaching of comprehension fostering and monitoring activities. *Cognition and Instruction, 1,* 117–175.

Pliske, D. B., & Psotka, J. (1986). Exploratory programming environments for designing ICAI. *Journal of Computer-Based Instruction, 13,* 52–57.

Reitman, J. S., & Rueter, H. H. (1980). Organization revealed by recall orders and confirmed by pauses. *Cognitive Psychology, 12,* 554–581.

Richardson, J. J., & Polson, M. (in press). *Intelligent training systems.* Hillsdale, NJ: Lawrence Erlbaum Associates.

Schvaneveldt, R. W., Durso, F. T., & Dearholt, D. W. (1985). *Pathfinder: Scaling with network structures.* MCSS # 85-9. Las Cruces, NM: New Mexico State University.

Scribner, S. (1984). Cognitive studies of work. *The Quarterly Newsletter of the Laboratory of Comparative Human Cognition, 6.*

Sleeman, D., & Brown, J. S. (1982). Introduction: Intelligent tutoring systems. In D. Sleeman & J. S. Brown (Eds.), *Intelligent tutoring systems* (pp. 1–11). New York: Academic Press.

Swartout, W. (1983). XPLAIN: A system for creating and explaining expert consulting systems. *Artificial Intelligence, 21,* 285–325.

Tennant, H. R., Ross, K. M., Saenz, R. M., Thompson, C. W., & Miller, J. R. (1983). Menu-based natural language understanding. In *Proceedings of the 21st Annual Meeting of the ACM* (pp. 151–158). New York: Association for Computing Machinery.

Uttal, W. R. (1962). On conversational interaction. In J. E. Coulson (Ed.), *Programmed learning and computer-based instruction* (pp. 1–11). New York: Wiley.

VanLehn, K. (in press). Student modeling in Intelligent Tutoring Systems. In J. J. Richardson & M. Polson (Eds.), *Intelligent Training Systems.* Hillsdale, NJ: Lawrence Erlbaum Associates.

Wenger, E. (1987). *Artificial Intelligence and Tutoring Systems.* Los Altos, CA: Morgan Kaufmann.

White, B. Y., & Frederiksen, J. R. (1987). Qualitative models and intelligent learning environments. In R. Lawler & M. Yazdani (Eds.), *AI and education.* Norwood, NJ: Ablex Publishing, Inc.

Woolf, B., Blegen, D., Jansen, J. H., & Verloop, A. (1986). *Teaching a complex industrial process.* COINS Technical Report 86-24. Amherst: University of Massachusetts.

Glossary

Apprenticeship Teaching System. A situated learning environment in which a novice is given the opportunity of learning by doing with an expert providing feedback and motivation.

Artificial Intelligence (AI). The study of techniques and principles for applying computers to issues normally reserved for human intelligence. AI systems typically exhibit some characteristics of human intelligence (including silly errors) when learning, reasoning, simulating, or understanding natural language.

Backward Chaining. A pattern matching technique that tries to prove the condition part of rules whose actions match the conditions of proven rules. (See Forward Chaining.)

Bug Catalog. A set of well-analyzed and carefully collected patterns of typical errors.

Case-Based Reasoning. Problem solving based on a collection of individual experiences rather than general rules.

Causal Stories. Causal stories, in troubleshooting contexts, are elaborate knowledge structures (and narratives drawn from those structures) that relate observable evidence and symptoms to causes of faults through various models and knowledge about the device in question.

Coach. A form of student modelling in which the ITS intervenes only when it is fairly sure the student is doing something wrong. The intervention is with graduated hints and examples.

Computer Based Instruction (CBI). The use of computers for instruction and training. Generally this refers to instruction in which no expert system or production rules are used to order the sequence of information presented. It often results in linear sequences, or chains, of presented material. (However, see Microworlds.)

Concept Hierarchy. A graph of more and less general topics or ideas.

Daemons. Rules that actively wait for their conditions to become true and fire in dynamic systems.

Declarative Knowledge. A form of knowledge representation distinct from Procedural knowledge (although the distinction is not always useful) in which the knowledge is portrayed as static and structural; e.g., data structures, frames, productions, and semantic nets.

Direct Manipulation. An interface approach that provides simulations (usually visual) that can be altered (visually) to produce corresponding changes in the underlying symbolic representation.

Dynamic Systems. Complex mechanisms that require swift and effective interaction, so that instruction and tutoring must be terse and to the point, and more lengthy instruction delayed to a later debriefing.

Explanation Based Simulations. Simulations or models whose design are predominantly driven by the need to provide explanations to students about device functions. Veridicality is subordinated to simplicity of explanations.

Fault Diagnosis. A problem-solving technique used to uncover the source of system malfunction.

Forward Chaining. A pattern matching technique that tries to prove the condition part of rules whose actions are then used to prove other rules. (See Backward Chaining.)

Graduated Models. Qualitative models whose power and extension grow in some sort of correspondence with the capabilities of students using them.

Heuristics. Rules of thumb that are practical and often work, but are not based on a principled, theoretical understanding and therefore are not guaranteed to work.

Hypertext. A text-based system that goes beyond text to include graphics, video, and sound (hypermedia) as well as links, crossreferences, and hierarchical structures. It is interactive so that one word can be expanded on command into other media (hypermedia). The term was coined by Ted Nelson.

Instructional Amplifier. A computer used to enlarge the scope and powers of teachers for instruction, that lets teachers personalize instruction more than they now can.

Instructional Design. A process of organizing knowledge and selecting frameworks for effective instruction.

Instructional Strategy. A general approach toward teaching or training, including objectives, plans, and teaching style.

Intelligent Tutoring Systems (ITS). An advanced form of ICAI and CBI that tries to individualize instruction by creating a computer-based learning environment that acts as a good teacher, correcting mistakes, offering advice, suggesting new topics, and sharing curriculum control. It should have the ability to analyze student responses, develop a history of the learner's preferences and skills, and tailor the materials to suit the trainee. Some important subtopics for ITS are knowledge representation, simulation, natural language, expert systems, and induction.

ITS Architectures. A systematic approach to structuring the many components that comprise an effective, working ITS. Usually these consist of a student model, an organized domain of knowledge, instructional principles, and a tutorial interface.

Knowledge Base. Codified knowledge (usually represented on a computer) of a domain or subject matter.

Knowledge Acquisition. The fundamental bottleneck in instructional design for informal systems: How does one acquire and organize the subject matter or knowledge base?

Knowledge Representation. Computer-based techniques for storing and retrieving knowledge organized according to specific principles. Prominent techniques include frames, semantic networks, and object oriented techniques.

Link. An arc that joins nodes in a graph.

Mental Model. A popular theoretical construct for a knowledge representation form that supposes that people simulate their environments with models of the world that they are able to run in their minds. These runnable mental models can be used to predict the outcomes of thought experiments using novel conditions. Mental models can also be used to trace the causal connections of events and devices in the world.

Microworlds. Computer-based learning environments in which trainees are free to explore and discover the limits of their own understanding. The computer provides little direction or guidance, but it does narrow and constrain the topics for search to those that are valid within the current world. The environments can also raise sharply focused contrasts between alternative hypotheses about the world to facilitate insight and discovery.

Node. An entry in a graph that is usually labelled and boxed. Often it is a concept or a relation of some sort.

Novices. Students or trainees learning a knowledge domain.

Overlay Models. Student modelling technique in which trainee performance is measured against the standard of an expert's model.

Predicate. A relation defined for a set of concepts; e.g., If an apple is red, an appropriate predicate that links "apple" and "red" could be called "color."

Procedural Knowledge. A form of knowledge representation distinct from Declarative knowledge (although the distinction is not always useful) in which the knowledge is portrayed as active and functional; e.g., functions, objects, demons, and algorithms. Sometimes production systems are viewed as a procedural form of knowledge to distinguish them from the organized declarative structures of semantic networks.

Qualitative Approximation. *Qualitative approximation* is a term designated by T. Govindaraj to refer to the use of difference equation modelling techniques and other good engineering practices to create efficient working models of devices as simulation components of Intelligent Training Systems.

Qualitative Models. A computer-based simulation composed of ordinal or even nominal metrics, such as "good" and "better," rather than higher-order mathematical models.

Reify. To make concrete and experiential. Within the context of ITS, to make something inspectable and interactive.

Semantic Networks. A graph structure that links concepts with conventional links such as "part-of," "isa," "instance," "super," "class," etc. Often seen as a Declarative form of knowledge. See Concept Hierarchy.

Situated Learning. The context or situation of much expert activity directly supports (learning) the skills the expert has. These skills are otherwise rarely invoked. The result is that learning by doing is cued and accelerated by the environment. (See Lave, 1986 and Orr, 1987.)

Student Model. The component of an ITS that is used to make inferences about a trainee's state of knowledge. Various student modelling systems have been proposed: bug catalogs, overlay models, issue oriented models, coaching systems, and psychometric systems.

Subject Matter Experts (SMEs). Subject Matter Experts are knowledgeable in a domain and possess a fragmented, self-imposed organization of things that has considerable pragmatic value in dealing with everyday problems.

Technical Manuals (TMs). Written descriptions of complex systems, outlining system operation and troubleshooting.

Temporal Fidelity. The degree of verdicality with which the propagation of effects of a change (including failures) in a simulation over time approximates the temporal sequence of changes in the real system.

Author Index

Subject Index